THE BAPTISMAL REGENERATION / BELIEVER'S BAPTISM DEBATE

A Theological and Historical Overview
Of The Most Contested Subject
Of The Church Age.

By J. O. Hosler

Copyright © 1999 by J. O. Hosler

All rights reserved. No part of this book shall be reproduced or transmitted in any form or by any means, electronic, mechanical, magnetic, photographic including photocopying, recording or by any information storage and retrieval system, without prior written permission of the publisher. No patent liability is assumed with respect to the use of the information contained herein. Although every precaution has been taken in the preparation of this book, the publisher and author assume no responsibility for errors or omissions. Neither is any liability assumed for damages resulting from the use of the information contained herein.

Unless otherwise noted, all Scripture references are from the King James Version of the Bible.

ISBN 0-7414-0590-3

Published by:

Infinity Publishing.com
519 West Lancaster Avenue
Haverford, PA 19041-1413
Info@buybooksontheweb.com
www.buybooksontheweb.com
Toll-free (877) BUY BOOK
Local Phone (610) 520-2500
Fax (610) 519-0261

Printed in the United States of America

Printed on Recycled Paper

Published March-2001

Acknowledgments

To my beloved wife, Susan, who challenged me to begin this work on her birthday in February of 1998 and finish it on her birthday in 1999. Next to the glory of God and the evangelism of souls, her pride in my work has been my greatest reward this side of heaven.

ABOUT THE AUTHOR

Dr. Hosler approaches this crucial subject from a rich background in education, pastoral ministry, with historical and biblical research skills. He has earned two undergraduate degrees in Bible and Pastoral Studies, a B.S. in History, an M.A. in History / Political Science from Butler University, and a Ph.D. in Philosophy of History. He also holds an M. Div. and Th.D. from Trinity Theological Seminary. In addition to having served as a Sr. pastor and adjunct college instructor for three decades, Dr. Hosler also serves as a Chaplain, Lt Colonel in the U.S.A.F. Auxiliary Civil Air Patrol. His primary passion in life is to promote the clarity of the Bible's teaching regarding the good news of eternal redemption purchased by the supreme sacrifice of Christ the Savior. He holds to and defends the *Sole Authority of Scripture* for faith and doctrine, believing that the canon of Scripture contains a closed system of doctrine to which no new doctrines can be added through ecclesiastical tradition. Though the ordinances of baptism and the Lord's Table are sacred to his religious experience, he defends the position that, in order to be scriptural, both are contingent upon a prior conversion to Christ through the good news of God's plan of salvation. Dr. Hosler's research is within the intellectual grasp of the average Christian yet will provide valuable supplemental reading for all theology students on both the undergraduate and graduate levels. Travel with him through the following chapters as he takes large and complex concepts and breaks them down into small understandable bites.

Table Of Contents

PREFACE i

1. The *Ritual-Equals-Reality* Controversy
   In The Apostolic Church 1

2. Where Does *Law* Factor Into Christianity? 31

3. One Plan Of Salvation For All Ages 59

4. The Gospel And Baptism Of John
   The Baptist: Was It Christian? 105

5. Does Baptism Replace Circumcision? 149

6. Infant Baptism And Believer's Baptism 209

7. Historical Overview Of The Baptismal
   Regeneration Tradition 261

8. The Subjective And Extra-Biblical
   Arguments For Baptismal Regeneration 339

9. Scriptural Arguments For Baptismal
   Regeneration Examined 397

10. Attaching Personal Righteousness To The
    Back-Side Of The Gospel's Requirements 439

11. Does The Baptism Debate Needlessly
    Divide The Body Of Christ? 483

BIBLIOGRAPHY 505
INDEX OF SCRIPTURE REFERENCES 518
INDEX OF SUBJECTS 519

Show me your authority.... If you are an ordinary Christian [not an apostle], believe what has been handed down to us.... That which had been handed down was true. For truth must necessarily precede the forgery, since it proceeds directly from those from whom it has been handed down.

Tertullian 3.522

And the things that thou hast heard of me among many witnesses, the same commit thou to faithful men, who shall be able to teach others also. Thou therefore endure hardness, as a good soldier of Jesus Christ.

II Timothy 2:2-3

AUTHOR'S PREFACE

Custom without truth is simply the antiquity of error

Cyprian, 5.389

Most published materials on the subject of the place of baptism in the process of regeneration and redemption are mere affirmations of beliefs rather than scholastic defenses of the various positions. Here is a definitive work that will expose the reader to the defensive positions of both the sacramental and non-sacramental views of baptism. The research seeks to take a large complex subject and break it down into small understandable bites. To accommodate the average Christian who does not have access to extensive research materials, complete Scripture verses and quotations from ancient authors have been compiled and not merely footnoted. This may seem unnecessary to the experienced theologian or church historian who may wish to merely look at the footnotes for verification of the sources which will qualify the points being documented.

On the lighter side, someone has suggested that the present work be titled *Everything You Always Wanted To Know About Baptism But Were Afraid To Ask*, or perhaps *Baptism For Dummies*. It is good to keep a sense of humor without compromising the seriousness of one's convictions. Still others will be offended at the very idea of *debate* on the subject of religion. However, when eternal destiny is at issue the Bible itself makes repeated use of the concept and process of debate. Here is a work that will record both sides of the controversy without any attempt to use pejorative language or fallacies of applied logic.

When speaking of OT ordinances and holidays, Paul used the image of a body casting a shadow. The body was Christ Himself and His shadow was the OT offerings and special days. When I contemplate

Christendom today I think of millions of sincere people falling to the ground upon the shadow thus making the shadow, and not the body, the object of their faith—

> Let no man therefore judge you in meat, or in drink, or in respect of an holyday, or of the new moon, or of the sabbath *days*: Which are a shadow of things to come; but the body is of Christ (Col. 2:16, 17).

For decades of ministry I have felt a compelling need to address and challenge the prominent belief in Christendom that the saving grace of Christ is imparted to the sinner through outward ritual and/or works of personal righteousness. I recommend the forthcoming material to be employed as valuable reading in evangelical Bible colleges and seminaries. I have never tired of dealing with the subject of the purity of the gospel in my preaching ministry and in training church members for personal evangelism. Therefore, though my true pulpit passion lies in evangelism and exposititory preaching, I also feel that the Christian in the pew has a need to touch base with the historical roots of what is traditionally believed today regarding the terms of personal salvation. Such a Christian is in the middle of a career and family and must at great cost pursue the cause of Christ through his local church. Attending seminary is out of the question for him and reading five shelves of books on church history is not going to present an opportunity. There is, therefore, a need for a non-technical book that will do most of this work for him in one reading, using original source material. This material should prove valuable to peers and colleagues in the academic world as well, providing a quick overview of the historical roots of this most crucial debate.

Christians have already been saturated with the arguments contending that the debate over the nature of the gospel is a non-issue. Therefore, we will document from Scripture the great contest in the New Testament over the essentiality of ritual in the impartation of salvation. This documentation will graphically display the fundamental importance of this controversy down to our present time in history.

It will be important to demonstrate why the Mosiac Law (or any law of works) cannot make one righteous before God. Nevertheless, we will also survey the divine purposes of God in giving the Law to mankind as a source of wisdom and divine judgment. Without immersing ourselves in the debate over dispensationalism versus covenant theology, it will be affirmed that there has been only one plan of salvation from before the foundation of the world until now, and to the end of the age.

There is a need for a fresh discussion of John's baptism in order to determine if it was, or was not, Christian baptism. The reader will observe that John the Baptist was neither practicing a Jewish proselyte baptism nor an Essene Baptism. Although his ministry had many unique factors pertaining to Christ's offer of the Kingdom to Israel, his gospel of personal salvation and subsequent *believer's baptism* was the same as that presented in the remainder of the New Testament.

Most Christians in the pew have never read a response to the traditional argument that ritual baptism replaced ritual circumcision and that it therefore imparts the saving grace of Christ in the same way that circumcision supposedly did in the days of old. The observation will be made that neither ordinance ever imparted eternal life to its recipients. This will be logically followed by a presentation of the strongest historical arguments in favor of salvation by infant baptism with a scriptural response to each argument.

Giving sacramentalism the benefit of the doubt, this work will proceed to document the fact that the baptismal regenerationist position of the gospel has been the mainstream established view of salvation throughout Christian history. While conceding to this historical fact, we will respond again from the Scriptures in defense of the gospel of grace prior to and apart from outward ritual.

In chapter eight, this work will admittedly digress from the historical and scriptural debate and give the reader an overview of the fallacies used to put forth the subjective, mystical arguments in favor of baptismal regeneration and other gospel errors. This chapter is necessitated by the rise of mysticism and charismatic claims of direct revelation from God in this century.

Returning to the objective Scriptures, there will be response to each of the New Testament texts that has been used to argue baptismal regeneration from the Bible alone. It will also be necessary to address the very difficult subject of whether or not to back-load the gospel with works of personal righteousness in order to have assurance of salvation. This is a very confusing issue for our day. While many will readily admit that one cannot earn salvation by acts of personal righteousness, they will argue that the born again experience must be followed by an all-consuming personal righteousness in order to be a saving experience. This may turn out to be one of the most important sections of the entire work.

The final chapter will be a response to the charge that insisting on a clear definition of the gospel is causing needless division within the Body of Christ. We will present the argument that the local/visible church is the only institution on earth which has been authorized by God to carry out the Great Commission of Jesus Christ. Accomplishing such a mission would be an impossible task for a *universal/invisible* entity of all NT saints by virtue of the fact that most of them are dead and have no function on earth at this time. If such an entity exists, it cannot be organized into a ministry on this planet.

Though this work is designed for the world of academia, I wish to encourage the Christian in the pew in just a few areas. First, do not fear material that is new to you as if it is over your head. It is not. Many historical names will be new and new words will be defined in English. *New* does not mean *technically incomprehensible*. Secondly, this will be a long reading objective and an easy task from which to walk away. Read a little at a time and check out each footnote. When you are finished, you will have touched base with materials which you could have overviewed otherwise only after reading an entire wall of books that may very well have been too technical for you to comprehend. Thirdly, remember that someone's personal salvation may be hanging contingently upon your ability to communicate the truths presented in these pages. My prayer is that the God of grace will touch your heart with a passion for the gospel as He has touched my own.

This is a day in which churches seek to grow by addressing only the felt needs of saints this side of the grave. Whether or not a person has eternal life and the assurance of it is the greatest personal need of anyone, and yet it is seldom a felt need. Satan and the flesh keep people so busy and concerned with daily problems that they have little time to realize the contingency of their own mortality. Therefore, the carnal reasons for not reading this work will be overwhelming, while the eternal and spiritual dividends for reading this material will be eternal.

The gifts granted through a faithful servant are not equal to those bestowed by the true Son. If, then, the Law of Moses had been sufficient to confer eternal life, it was to no purpose for the Savior Himself to come and suffer for us.

Clement of Alexandria 2.593

I do not frustrate the grace of God: for if righteousness come by the law, then Christ is dead in vain.

Galatians 2:21

We do not now deal with the Law any further than [to remark] that the apostle here teaches clearly how it has been abolished—by passing from shadow to substance. That is, it has passed from figurative types to the reality, which is Christ.

Tertullian 3.471

All of these persons, therefore, were highly honored, and were made great. This was not for their own sake, or for their own works, or for the righteousness which they wrought, but through the operation of His will. And we, too, being called by His will in Christ Jesus, are not justified by our own wisdom, understanding, godliness, or works that we have done in holiness of heart. Rather, we are justified by that faith through which, from the beginning, Almighty God has justified all men.
Clement of Rome 1.13

Chapter One

The *Ritual-Equals-Reality* Controversy In The Apostolic Church

The connection between the idea that Old Testament ritual creates or imparts eternal salvation and the idea that New Testament ritual (sacramentalism) does the same is not immediately obvious. A background study of this misconception in the NT regarding OT ritual is essential in approaching the apostolic controversy with comprehension.

Those who were in error regarding circumcision and other Jewish customs would persecute from without while others would come into the New Testament church and insist that standard orthodoxy should require the equivocation of ritual and reality. Jesus told the disciples that they would come; the Apostle Paul told the Ephesian elders that they would come; they came claiming apostolic authority; the Ephesian church put them on trial and found them to be liars (cf. Rev. 2:2). Also:

> (Matt. 10:16-18) Behold, I send you forth as sheep in the midst of wolves: be ye therefore wise as serpents, and harmless as doves. But beware of men: for they will deliver you up to the councils, and they will scourge you in their synagogues; And ye shall be brought before governors and kings for my sake, for a testimony against them and the Gentiles.[1]

> (Luke 10:3) Go your ways: behold, I send you forth as lambs among wolves.

> (John 10:12) But he that is an hireling, and not the shepherd, whose own the sheep are not, seeth the wolf coming, and leaveth the sheep, and fleeth: and the wolf catcheth them, and scattereth the sheep.

---

[1] Unless otherwise noted, all Scripture quotations are from The Holy Bible King James Version.

(Matthew 7:15) Beware of false prophets, which come to you in sheep's clothing, but inwardly they are ravening wolves.

(Philippians 3:2) Beware of dogs, beware of evil workers, beware of the concision.

(Acts 20:29) For I know this, that after my departing shall grievous wolves enter in among you, not sparing the flock.

The seventh chapter of Matthew's Gospel is Christ's conclusion to the Sermon on the Mount. The section begins with an admonition to *Judge not that ye be not judged*" (Matt.. 7:1). The Pharisees were judging Christ Himself for not establishing the political kingdom they expected and for not promoting the kind of ceremonial righteousness that they were professing. [2]

Without listing all of the errors of the Pharisees, we should note two of the most devastating in terms of understanding entrance into everlasting life. The first error was in their interpretation of the Old Testament. They were not distinguishing between ritual and reality in Jewish ceremonialism, as Paul noted:

> Thou that makest thy boast of the law, through breaking the law dishonourest thou God? For the name of God is blasphemed among the Gentiles through you, as it is written. For circumcision verily profiteth, if thou keep the law: but if thou be a breaker of the law, thy circumcision is made

---

[2] One of the earliest objectives of the scribes was to catalog the contents of the written Torah (tora se-biktab). They itemized 613 commandments, 248 positive, 365 negative. Their next task was to supplement these with traditions that would prevent the violation of the commandments by accident or by ignorance. One example is the thirty-nine principal species of prohibited acts on the Sabbath. The commandments were further applied by analogy to situations not directly covered by the Torah. All these developments together with thirty-one customs of "immemorial usage" formed the "oral law" (tora se-be-al peh). This was the *tradition of the elders* mentioned in Christ's day. The Pharisees would argue that the 'tradition of the elders' (Mk. 7:3) came from Moses on Sinai.

uncircumcision. Therefore if the uncircumcision keep the righteousness of the law, shall not his uncircumcision be counted for circumcision? And shall not uncircumcision which is by nature, if it fulfil the law, judge thee, who by the letter and circumcision dost transgress the law? For he is not a Jew, which is one outwardly; neither *is that* circumcision, which is outward in the flesh: But he *is* a Jew, which is one inwardly; and circumcision *is that* of the heart, in the spirit, *and* not in the letter; whose praise *is* not of men, but of God (Rom. 2:24-29).

The only circumcision that could save us, according to the Apostle Paul, was the crucifixion of Christ as he noted:

> For "the circumcision of Christ" see Col. 2:10, 11... And ye are complete in him, which is the head of all principality and power: In whom also ye are circumcised with the circumcision made without hands, in putting off the body of the sins of the flesh by the circumcision of Christ.

> For neither they themselves who are circumcised keep the law; but desire to have you circumcised, that they may glory in your flesh. But God forbid that I should glory, save in the cross of our Lord Jesus Christ, by whom the world is crucified unto me, and I unto the world. For in Christ Jesus neither circumcision availeth any thing, nor uncircumcision, but a new creature (Gal. 6:13-15).

The signs, which were designed by God to point to the coming Messiah as the only true object of faith, were made the objects of faith themselves, thus pointing away from the Messiah, As Paul wrote:

> (Gal. 5:1, 2) Stand fast therefore in the liberty wherewith Christ hath made us free, and be not entangled again with the yoke of bondage. Behold, I Paul say unto you, that if ye be circumcised, Christ shall profit you nothing.

The second deadly error was that of developing extra-biblical traditions; proclaiming them to be revelational mandates from God and calling them contingencies for obtaining eternal life. Jesus would tell them that this is the academic equivalent of disbelief in the Word of God altogether and that, even though they were reciting pious words of praise, their worship would be in vain:

> Why do ye also transgress the commandment of God by your tradition?... Thus have ye made the commandment of God of none effect by your tradition... But in vain they do worship me, teaching *for* doctrines the commandments of men (Matt. 15:3b, 6b, 9).

They were leading naive victims to believe that they were drawing nigh to God by participating in great worship services when in reality their hearts were far from Him. True worship begins with possessing eternal life on Christ's terms of grace and mercy: as Scripture states:

> (Phil. 3:1-3) "Finally, my brethren, rejoice in the Lord. To write the same things to you, to me indeed is not grievous, but for you it is safe. Beware of dogs, beware of evil workers, beware of the concision. For we are the circumcision, which worship God in the Spirit, and rejoice in Christ Jesus, and have no confidence in the flesh."

> (Heb. 12:28) "Wherefore we receiving a kingdom which cannot be moved, let us have grace, whereby we may serve God acceptably with reverence and godly fear."

The premise upon which the Pharisees judged others to be void of eternal life is the same that they will deceptively use to judge themselves as worthy when they someday stand before God. They will plead that they had spoken forth what they believed was the "word of God", and they will think that they had exorcised demons and had performed a life of good works. Not only will Jesus proclaim their worship to have been in vain and their belief in the "word of God" to have been of none effect, He will affirm that they will not enter into eternal life because He never knew them in the first place:

> Not every one that saith unto me, Lord, Lord, shall enter into the kingdom of heaven; but he that doeth the will of my Father which is in heaven. Many will say to me in that day, Lord, Lord, have we not prophesied in thy name? and in thy name have cast out devils? and in thy name done many wonderful works? And then will I profess unto them, I never knew you: depart from me, ye that work iniquity"(Matt. 7:21-23)[3]

Jesus wanted us to know that even acts of worship, enmity against demons and "good" works are works of iniquity if one is not in possession of eternal life on God's terms.[4]

Jesus is telling His listeners to judge not nor to consider themselves qualified to make distinctions using themselves as the measurement standard—

---

[3] Note: "The will of My Father" does not refer to righteous deeds but to understanding and accepting God's terms of eternal life…(vss. 7, 8) "Ask, and it shall be given you; seek, and ye shall find; knock, and it shall be opened unto you: for every one that asketh receiveth; and he that seeketh findeth; and to him that knocketh it shall be opened." That which is to be received and opened in this discussion is eternal life. And again: (vss. 13, 14) "Enter ye in at the strait gate: for wide is the gate, and broad is the way, that leadeth to destruction, and many there be which go in thereat: Because strait is the gate, and narrow is the way, which leadeth unto life, and few there be that find it."

[4] Satan is always pleased to profess enmity against his own forces if by so doing he can point people away from the saving knowledge of Christ— (II Cor. 11:13-15) "For such are false apostles, deceitful workers, transforming themselves into the apostles of Christ. And no marvel; for Satan himself is transformed into an angel of light. Therefore it is no great thing if his ministers also be transformed as the ministers of righteousness; whose end shall be according to their works." Satan is also willing to give Christ credit for satanic miracles if it will blind people to the knowledge of salvation— (II Thess. 2:9-12) "*Even him*, whose coming is after the working of Satan with all power and signs and lying wonders, And with all deceivableness of unrighteousness in them that perish; because they received not the love of the truth, that they might be saved. And for this cause God shall send them a strong delusion, that they should believe a lie: That they all might be damned who believed not the truth, but had pleasure in unrighteousness."

> Thou hypocrite, first cast out the beam out of thine own eye; and then shalt thou see clearly to cast out the mote out of thy brother's eye. Give not that which is holy unto the dogs, neither cast ye your pearls before swine, lest they trample them under their feet, and turn again and rend you (Matt. 7:5, 6).

It is important to observe that after admonishing the Pharisees to refrain from judging, Jesus then exhorts the true believer to judge, or to distinguish, true messengers from those who attribute reality to mere ritual. Why is the *judge not* verse almost always used in commanding Christians to be undiscerning regarding false gospels? Discernment necessitates godly judgment because the false teachers are to be openly identified, as Christ said: *Beware of false prophets, which come to you in sheep's clothing, but inwardly they are ravening wolves* (Matt. 7:15).

The unregenerate sinner cannot deduce a saving knowledge of Christ from a false gospel. Jesus taught that the disciple could identify a wolf in sheep's clothing by his bad fruit, which is a false gospel:

> Ye shall know them by their fruits. Do men gather grapes of thorns, or figs of thistles? Even so every good tree bringeth forth good fruit; but a corrupt tree bringeth forth evil fruit. A good tree cannot bring forth evil fruit, neither can a corrupt tree bring forth good fruit. Every tree that bringeth not forth good fruit is hewn down and cast into the fire. Wherefore by their fruits ye shall know them (Matt. 7:16-20).

This is the precise kind of judgment that Christ commended the Ephesian church for exercising when He said:

> I know thy works, and thy labour, and thy patience, and how thou canst not bear them which are evil: and thou hast tried them which say they are apostles, and are not, and hast found them liars (Rev. 2:2).

This is the same judgment that Paul was trying to teach the Corinthians when he wrote:

> For such are false apostles, deceitful workers, transforming themselves into the apostles of Christ.

And no marvel; for Satan himself is transformed into an angel of light. Therefore it is no great thing if his ministers also be transformed as the ministers of righteousness... (II Cor. 11: 13-15).[5]

Having entered the visible church, these "Judaizers" immediately went to work becoming a powerful and intimidating force within. They even practiced bigotry against other Jews who held to different cultural preferences. In the early days of the Jerusalem church the membership was primarily Jewish and no doubt many Jewish proselytes. The Grecian Jews were probably of the Diaspora who had moved to Israel from the provinces.[6] They had been Hellenized in many of their cultural preferences. Some of them might have been Gentile proselytes to Judaism who later became Christians as well. Most of the Grecians could not speak Aramaic, which was the native tongue of the Jews living in Israel. They were bilingual, speaking their native tongues as well as Greek (cf. Acts 2:5-11). The native Hebraic Jews could speak both Aramaic and Greek The Jewish community outside the walls of the church considered the Grecian Jews to be a lower class of citizen.

There may also have been a "Bible version" debate in that the Grecians preferred the Greek Septuagint translation of the Old Testament while the Palestinian Jews used the Hebrew translation. Christ and the apostles quoted both translations as the "Word of God."[7] This urban social and political problem spilled over into the church as the Hebraic Jewish converts gained executive control over the administration of the benevolent fund for widows. It was decided that funds would be withheld from the Christian widows of Hellenistic Jews and allocated only to the Christian widows of Palestinian Jews. This created tension in the church necessitating the election of the first board of deacons in Church history. Luke wrote:

---

[5] This is not an ungodly form of judgment but rather a true mark of spirituality— (I Cor. 2:15) "But he that is spiritual judgeth all things." (cf. Heb. 5:14).

[6] The term *diaspora* means *dispersion* and denotes either Jews scattered in the non-Jewish world (as in Jn. 7:35; 1 Pet. 1:1) or the places in which they reside (as in Jas. 1:1; Judith 5:19). This would also include proselyte Jews.

[7] Obviously the Apostles did not consider variation between text types to be a corruption as long as doctrine and historical record remained unaltered.

> And in those days, when the number of the disciples was multiplied, there arose a murmuring of the Grecians against the Hebrews, because their widows were neglected in the daily ministration. Then the twelve called the multitude of the disciples *unto them*, and said, It is not reason that we should leave the word of God, and serve tables. Wherefore, brethren, look ye out among you seven men of honest report, full of the Holy Ghost and wisdom, whom we may appoint over this business (Acts 6:1-3).

Even though the Judaizers made circumcision and the Law of Moses essentials in the plan of salvation, they had to be doctrinally orthodox in several areas in order to become baptized members of the local church at Jerusalem. They had to have professed Christ to be the Messiah and to have expressed belief in the death, burial and resurrection. Again, Luke wrote:

> Then they that gladly received his word were baptized: and the same day there were added *unto them* about three thousand souls. And they continued stedfastly in the apostles' doctrine and fellowship, and in breaking of bread, and in prayers (Acts 2:41, 42).[8]

It was an eternal life and death question and one of great consequence. Is faith in the death of Christ on the cross for salvation, plus circumcision, plus works, a saving Gospel? Is faith in Christ only the beginning (or only a down payment) of our salvation? Or, are we to look to Jesus as the "author and finisher of our faith" (Heb. 12:2)?[9]

---

[8] Note the doctrinal content of Peter's message on the Day of Pentecost. To become numbered with the 3000 baptized that day one had to profess a change of mind about the things of which Peter spoke.

[9] Trypho asked Justin Martyr if keeping the Mosaic Law after conversion to Christianity will contribute to salvation: " 'But if some, even now, wish to live in the observance of the institutions given by Moses, and yet believe in this Jesus who was crucified, recognizing Him to be the Christ of God, and that it is given to him to be absolute Judge of all, and that His is the everlasting kingdom, can they also be saved?' he inquired of me. And I replied, 'Let us consider that also together, whether one may now observe all the Mosaic institutions.' And He answered, 'No. For we know that, as you said, it is not
(Continued on next page)

In many modern ecumenical mass crusades, all who can profess what "they of the circumcision" professed are considered Christian brothers even though they believe that eternal life is not a personal possession until baptism, communion, church membership, or endurance in personal holiness transpires. Understanding the "circumcision" doctrine will enable one to know whether Christ plus anything else can be a saving object of faith. The writer of Hebrews said:

> Looking unto Jesus the author and finisher of our faith; who for the joy that was set before him endured the cross, despising the shame, and is set down at the right hand of the throne of God (Heb. 12:2).

Can we come to Christ and say: *Lord, I only need you to start it and I will finish it,* and then walk away truly born again? Make no mistake, Christians have races to run, battles to fight, and courses to finish, but their personal eternal salvation is not one of them.[10] Paul had to challenge his own converts, who later became harnessed to a gospel that cannot save, when he asked the question:

> This only would I learn of you, Received ye the Spirit by the works of the law, or by the hearing of faith? Are ye so foolish? having begun in the Spirit, are ye now made perfect by the flesh? (Gal. 3:2, 3).

---

possible either anywhere to sacrifice the lamb of the Passover, or to offer the goats ordered for the fast; or, in short, [to present] all the other offerings.'" *Ante-Nicene Fathers*, Rev. Alexander Roberts, D. D. And James Donaldson, LL.D., Editors (Grand Rapidss, Michigan: Wm. B. Eerdmanss Publishing Company, 1977), Vol. 1, p 217.

[10] The Apostle Paul said: "I have fought a good fight, I have finished *my* course, I have kept the faith" (II Tim. 4:7) but his salvation was kept by the finished work of Christ— (I Pet. 1:3-5) "Blessed *be* the God and Father of our Lord Jesus Christ, which according to his abundant mercy hath begotten us again unto a lively hope by the resurrection of Jesus Christ from the dead, To an inheritance incorruptible, and undefiled, and that fadeth not away, reserved in heaven for you, Who are kept by the power of God through faith unto salvation ready to be revealed in the last time." And Again: (John 17:11) "...Holy Father, keep through thine own name those whom thou hast given me, that they may be one, as we *are*."

Thus, we find in the earliest church a corrupting element insisting that obedience to law and ritual are essentials of salvation. The Apostle Peter had to deal with "they of the circumcision" after converting the Gentile house of Cornelius. God had to show Peter that they were saved independently of any ritual when He baptized them in the Holy Ghost before ritual water baptism was ever mentioned. This is how Peter could say:

> To him give all the prophets witness, that through his name whosoever believeth in him shall receive remission of sins. While Peter yet spake these words, the Holy Ghost fell on all them which heard the word (Acts 10:43, 44).

When he reported this incident to the Jerusalem church, the Apostle Peter described the conversion of Cornelius' household as the baptism of the Spirit prophesied by Christ Himself:

> And as I began to speak, the Holy Ghost fell on them, as on us at the beginning. Then remembered I the word of the Lord, how that he said, John indeed baptized with water; but ye shall be baptized with the Holy Ghost (Acts 11: 15, 16).

This was supposed to have convinced *they of the circumcision* that uncircumcised Gentiles could be saved by belief in Christ alone, as Luke wrote:

> And they of the circumcision which believed were astonished, as many as came with Peter, because that on the Gentiles also was poured out the gift of the Holy Ghost (Acts 10:45).

> When they heard these things, they held their peace, and glorified God, saying, Then hath God also to the Gentiles granted repentance unto life (Acts 11:18).

Only after the clear baptism of the Holy Spirit did Peter even mention ritual as he asked the question: *Can any man forbid water, that these should not be baptized, which have received the Holy Ghost as well as we?* (Acts 10:46b-47). It became incumbent upon Peter to defend the fact that this was not a separate Gospel but that Jews and Gentiles were to be saved through faith alone apart from ritual:

> Forasmuch then as God gave them the like gift as *he did* unto us, who believed on the Lord Jesus Christ; what was I, that I could withstand God? (Acts 11:17).

Just when it would seem that the point was made and accepted in the tenth and eleventh chapters of Acts we find that the Judaizers were only licking their wounds and innovating in order to contend another day. That day came when Paul and Barnabas returned to the church of Antioch from their first missionary journey and began to report the conversion of uncircumcised Gentiles—

> And when they were come, and had gathered the church together, they rehearsed all that God had done with them, and how he had opened the door of faith unto the Gentiles (Acts 14:27).

Then suddenly there arose the self-appointed committee of Judaizers from the Jerusalem church to contend that none of the aforesaid converts were really saved unless they became circumcized. Luke records:

> And certain men which came down from Judaea taught the brethren, and said, Except ye be circumcised after the manner of Moses, ye cannot be saved (Acts 15:1).

Paul and Barnabas immediately recoiled, springing forth into a great dispute with these men over the true nature of the Gospel. It was then decided that an open debate on the subject should transpire on the Judaizers' home turf at Jerusalem in a plenary session of the apostles and elders. Again Luke records:

> When therefore Paul and Barnabas had no small dissension and disputation with them, they determined that Paul and Barnabas, and certain other of them, should go up to Jerusalem unto the apostles and elders about this question (Acts 15:2).

Immediately upon arrival, the Jerusalem assembly did indeed call the first historic church council. Paul delivered the same report that he had given in Antioch: that the uncircumcised Gentiles had been converted to Christianity:

> And when they were come to Jerusalem, they were received of the church, and of the apostles and elders, and they declared all things that God had done with them (Acts 15:4).

Again, the Judaizers, who were "believing Pharisees", interrupted with the argument that circumcision was necessary. However, this time they innovated by adding the point that the Mosaic Law was part of the plan of salvation as well.

> But there rose up certain of the sect of the Pharisees which believed, saying, That it was needful to circumcise them, and to command them to keep the law of Moses (Acts 15:5).

The first remonstrance speech of the council was given by Peter who was no doubt wondering why the issue had not been settled in the eleventh chapter of Acts when he reported the conversion of the household of Cornelius as follows:

> And when there had been much disputing, Peter rose up, and said unto them, Men and brethren, ye know how that a good while ago God made choice among us, that the Gentiles by my mouth should hear the word of the gospel, and believe (Acts 15:7).

Peter again rehearsed how that the Gentiles had received the Gospel from him and believed, no doubt remembering his own words at the house of Cornelius: *To him give all the prophets witness, that through his name whosoever believeth in him shall receive remission of sins* (Acts 10:43). This was his second rehearsal of this event, the first taking place in the same church when Peter said:

> And when Peter was come up to Jerusalem, they that were of the circumcision contended with him, Saying, Thou wentest in to men uncircumcised, and didst eat with them. But Peter rehearsed the matter from the

beginning, and expounded it by order unto them...
(Acts 11:2-4).

God Himself had verified this by giving them the same baptism of the Holy Spirit that the disciples received on the Day of Pentecost.[11] Peter explained, therefore, that whether one is a circumcised Jew or an uncircumcised Gentile his heart can only be purified by faith in Christ apart from ritual— *And put no difference between us and them, purifying their hearts by faith* (Acts 15:9).

Peter knew that no one had ever kept the Law of Moses, especially those who were making the argument that day. He therefore wanted to know why the Judaizers were asking the Gentile disciples to do something that neither themselves nor the Old Testament fathers were able to do.

> Now therefore why tempt ye God, to put a yoke upon the neck of the disciples, which neither our fathers nor we were able to bear? (Acts 15:10).

Peter then concluded his argument by saying in effect: "not only do the Gentiles not have to get saved your way but you Jews have to get saved their way if you wish to live forever"—*But we believe that through the grace of the Lord Jesus Christ we shall be saved, even as they* (Acts 15:11). The Apostle Paul confirmed this same affirmation when he wrote to the Romans:

> Therefore we conclude that a man is justified by faith without the deeds of the law. Is he the God of the Jews only? is he not also of the Gentiles? Yes, of the Gentiles also: Seeing it is one God, which shall justify the circumcision by faith, and uncircumcision through faith (Rom. 3:28-30).

Their Jewish hearts must be purified by faith apart from the Mosaic Law and circumcision or else remain unpurified altogether. Peter would later take the position that these Judaizers were false prophets. Although they professed Christ to be the Messiah who died on the cross, they

---

[11] Compare 15:8 with 11:16.

were denying Him by their gospel of circumcision and law, as Peter stated:

> But there were false prophets also among the people, even as there shall be false teachers among you, who privily shall bring in damnable heresies, even denying the Lord that bought them, and bring upon themselves swift destruction. And many shall follow their pernicious ways; by reason of whom the way of truth shall be evil spoken of (II Pet. 2:1, 2).

Peter's words silenced the multitude at the Jerusalem Council so that Paul and Barnabas could be called upon to give their report. The two missionaries gave a resume of miracles and wonders that God had granted to confirm the conversion of the Gentiles apart from circumcision:

> Then all the multitude kept silence, and gave audience to Barnabas and Paul, declaring what miracles and wonders God had wrought among the Gentiles by them (Acts 15:12).

Apostolic miracles were the final and ultimate confirmation in the First Century, even as the writer of Hebrews admitted when he said:

> How shall we escape, if we neglect so great salvation; which at the first began to be spoken by the Lord, and was confirmed unto us by them that heard him God also bearing them witness, both with signs and wonders, and with divers miracles, and gifts of the Holy Ghost, according to his own will? (Heb. 2:3, 4).

Finally, the Apostle James stepped up to bat for the remonstrators. He reminded them for the third time how that Peter had preached the gospel to the Gentiles from the Old Testament prophets (Acts 10:43)[12] and then proceeded to defend Peter's testimony from an Old Testament passage.

---

[12] Note the words of Jesus: "Then he said unto them, O fools, and slow of heart to believe all that the prophets have spoken: Ought not Christ to have suffered these things, and to enter into his glory? And beginning at Moses *(Continued on next page)*

The next few statements from James could cause the average Christian to toss his hands in confusion until he reminds himself to consider the audience being addressed. It was a Jewish audience and James was able to assume a prior knowledge on the part of his listeners that the typical Christian of today would not normally have, as Luke stated:

> And after they had held their peace, James answered, saying, Men *and* brethren, hearken unto me: Simeon hath declared how God at the first did visit the Gentiles, to take out of them a people for his name. And to this agree the words of the prophets; as it is written, After this I will return, and will build again the tabernacle of David, which is fallen down; and I will build again the ruins thereof, and I will set it up: That the residue of men might seek after the Lord, and all the Gentiles, upon whom my name is called, saith the Lord, who doeth all these things. Known unto God are all his works from the beginning of the world (Acts 15:13-18).

James' objective is to prove that God intended Gentiles to be saved without circumcision and this he does by quoting Amos 9:11, 12. He is not saying that the New Testament church is the fulfillment of this prophecy.[13] But he is saying unequivocally that God has made it clear

---

and all the prophets, he expounded unto them in all the scriptures the things concerning himself" (Lk. 24:25-27).

[13] The New Testament church was a mystery in that it was a New Testament truth not revealed in the Old Testament, as Paul noted: (Rom. 16:25, 26) "Now to him that is of power to stablish you according to my gospel, and the preaching of Jesus Christ, according to the revelation of the mystery, which was kept secret since the world began, But now is made manifest, and by the scriptures of the prophets, according to the commandment of the everlasting God, made known to all nations for the obedience of faith." Also (Eph. 3:5, 6) "Which in other ages was not made known unto the sons of men, as it is now revealed unto his holy apostles and prophets by the Spirit; That the Gentiles should be fellow heirs, and of the same body, and partakers of his promise in Christ by the gospel." Also (Col. 1:24-27) "Who now rejoice in my sufferings for you, and fill up that which is behind of the afflictions of Christ in my flesh for his body's sake, which is the church: Whereof I am made a minister, *(Continued on next page)*

in the Old Testament that He has a love for Gentiles and desires to save them apart from circumcision. The word "prophets" is plural telling us that James is using his interpretation of the passage in Amos as representative of all the prophets just as Peter stated in Acts 10:43.

James' quotation of the Amos passage does not match the Greek Septuagint nor the Hebrew text. He is therefore quoting from a different text type or else paraphrasing under Divine inspiration. He may have done this to avoid being sidetracked into a Bible version debate between the Hellenists and the Hebraic Jews.

Regardless of James' reason for his variable translation, there were now four building blocks upon which to demonstrate that uncircumcised Gentiles could be saved and join the church: First, the testimonies of Paul and Barnabas; second, the testimony of Simon Peter; third, the testimony of signs and miracles; and fourth, the testimony of all the Old Testament prophets. Next, the Apostle James offered his personal judgment (*krino*) on the whole matter: "let us not annoy (*parenochlein*) the Gentile converts"— *Wherefore my sentence is, that we trouble not them, which from among the Gentiles are turned to God* (Acts 15:9).

Additionally, James recommended the drafting of a letter to Gentiles telling them to honor three commandments of Mosaic ceremonial law by abstaining from: food polluted by idols (cf. Acts 21:25 and I Cor. 8-10), sexual immorality (Lev. 18:6-20), and the meat of strangled animals and blood (Lev. 17:10-14). Since we know that the New Testament Church is in no way under the Mosaic ceremonial law, we might conclude that these are moral instructions and not ceremonial commandments to the Gentiles.[14] The point is that God expects

---

according to the dispensation of God which is given to me for you, to fulfil the word of God; *Even* the mystery which hath been hid from ages and from generations, but now is made manifest to his saints: To whom God would make known what *is* the riches of the glory of this mystery among the Gentiles; which is Christ in you, the hope of glory"

[14] If these were commandments rather than moral suggestions they would be a serious violation of the Mosaic Law itself— (Rom. 2:25) "For circumcision verily profiteth, if thou keep the law: but if thou be a breaker of the law, thy circumcision is made uncircumcision." (Gal. 5:3) "For I testify again to every man that is circumcised, that he is a debtor to do the whole law." (Jam. *(Continued on next page)*

converted Gentiles to be gospel witnesses to unconverted Jews and observing these prohibitions will create such opportunities, as James stated: *For Moses of old time hath in every city them that preach him, being read in the synagogues every sabbath day* (Acts 15:21). Obeying these three prohibitions would be an act of love and mercy upon the Gentile converts, even as Paul exhorted the Romans, saying:

> For as ye in times past have not believed God, yet have now obtained mercy through their unbelief: Even so have these also now not believed, that through your mercy they also may obtain mercy (Rom. 11:30, 31).

There is a great difference between a Judaizer attempting to compel a Gentile to be circumcised and a Gentile Christian being circumcised as an act of love in overcoming a barrier against witnessing to Jews. When Paul returned to Jerusalem with Barnabas and Titus the Judaizers attempted to compel Titus to be circumcised.[15] Paul stated that he would not compromise with them even for an hour for he knew that no less than the truth of the gospel was at stake: *To whom we gave place by subjection, no, not for an hour; that the truth of the Gospel might continue with you"* (Gal. 2:5). Paul explained this to the Galatians when he said:

> As many as desire to make a fair shew in the flesh, they constrain you to be circumcised; only lest they should suffer persecution for the cross of Christ. For neither they themselves who are circumcised keep the law; but desire to have you circumcised, that they may glory in your flesh. But God forbid that I should glory, save in the cross of our Lord Jesus Christ, by whom the world is crucified unto me, and I unto the world. For in Christ Jesus neither circumcision availeth any thing, nor uncircumcision, but a new creature (Galatians 6:12-16).

2:10) "For whosoever shall keep the whole law, and yet offend in one *point*, he is guilty of all."

[15] Of the five reported visits of Paul to Jerusalem, this is probably the famine visit of Acts 21:15-23, 35.

However, because Timothy had a Jewish mother and a Greek father, Paul circumcised him in love to avoid an unnecessary offence while preaching to Jews (cf. Acts 16:3). In the case with Titus the issue was the gospel itself while Timothy's was a question of not giving offence. Paul distinguished between avoiding offence and submitting to compulsion when he said:

> For though I be free from all *men*, yet have I made myself servant unto all, that I might gain the more. And unto the Jews I became as a Jew, that I might gain the Jews; to them that are under the law, as under the law, that I might gain them that are under the law; To them that are without law, as without law, (being not without law to God, but under the law to Christ,) that I might gain them that are without law. To the weak became I as weak, that I might gain the weak: I am made all things to all *men*, that I might by all means save some. And this I do for the gospel's sake, that I might be partaker thereof with *you*. (I Cor. 9:19-23).

The judgment of James was in agreement with the Apostles, elders, and the whole church and they sent letters to Antioch, Syria, and Cilicia addressed to the Gentile brethren and carried by specially chosen men. The letters greeted the Gentiles as brethren and then made it perfectly clear that those who visited Antioch from the church at Jerusalem were not authorized in any way to impose circumcision and the Mosaic law upon them—

> Forasmuch as we have heard, that certain which went out from us have troubled you with words, subverting your souls, saying, *Ye must* be circumcised, and keep the law: to whom we gave no *such* commandment (Acts 15:24).

The letters go on to give an endorsement of Paul and Barnabas by the Apostles, elders and the church and attest to the fact that the appointed carriers of the letters will say the same thing:

> It seemed good unto us, being assembled with one accord, to send chosen men unto you with our beloved Barnabas and Paul, Men that have hazarded their lives for the name of our Lord Jesus Christ. We have sent

therefore Judas and Silas, who shall also tell you the same things by mouth (Acts 15:25-27).

In verse 29 the letters of communication spell out the three prohibitions but care is taken not to make these essential to salvation. They stated that if the Gentiles did these things they would "do well" with no indication that they would be saving themselves by doing so.

After what appeared to be a unanimous agreement in the Jerusalem church one would naturally surmise that this problem was resolved for all time. However, everyone seemed to underestimate how intent, perseverant, and intimidating these Judaizers were. They knew they had lost the day and were even willing to break one of the ten commandments by participating in the unanimous vote to send out these letters. But they would never go away, as the Apostle Paul would come to realize in his battle with them that continued to the end of his life— *For I am now ready to be offered, and the time of my departure is at hand, I have fought a good fight...* (II Tim. 4:6,7a).

The Apostle Paul knew them well. They had already corrupted many of the churches that he had founded. He knew that they claimed to be ministers of Christ—*Are They ministers of Christ? (I speak as a fool) I am more...*(II Cor. 11:23a). They claimed apostolic authority— *For such are false apostles, deceitful workers, transforming themselves into apostles of Christ* (II Cor. 11:13). They were Pharisees who professed belief in Jesus Christ and had become baptized members of the visible church—*And they of the circumcision which believed were astonished, as many as came with Peter, because that on the Gentiles also was poured out the gift of the Holy Ghost* (Acts 10:45). They believed that the salvation of Jesus Christ was bestowed or imparted through the ritual of circumcision— *But there rose up certain of the sect of the Pharisees which believed, saying, That it was needful to circumcise them, and command them to keep the law of Moses* (Acts 15:5).

Consider the occasion in which the Apostle Paul gave his last farewell to the Ephesian elders, just prior to making his final journey toward Jerusalem. As elders they were the first among equals in the church of Ephesus whose task it was to oversee and feed the flock and to stand as guardians of the Gospel truth. Paul had told the Corinthians that they were "stewards of the mysteries of God"—

> And now, behold, I know that ye all, among whom I have gone preaching the kingdom of God, shall see my face no more. Wherefore I take you to record this day, that I am pure from the blood of all men. For I have not shunned to declare unto you all the council of God. Take heed therefore unto yourselves, and to all the flock, over the which the Holy Ghost hath made you overseers, to feed the church of God, which he hath purchased with his own blood (Acts 20:25-28).

The Ephesians were to be sacred guardians of the purity of the Gospel, as indeed they became when John wrote: *...and thou hast tried them which say they are apostles, and are not, and hast found them to be liars* (Rev. 2:2). When Paul commissioned Titus to ordain elders in every city of Crete, one of the chief qualities he was to seek out in such men was the ability to stop the mouths of "they of the circumcision"—

> For this cause left I thee in Crete, that thou shouldest set in order the things that are wanting, and ordain elders in every city, as I had appointed thee...Holding fast the faithful word as he hath been taught, that he may be able by sound doctrine both to exhort and to convince the gainsayers. For there are many unruly and vain talkers and deceivers, specially they of the circumcision: Whose mouths must be stopped, who subvert whole houses, teaching things which they ought not, for filthy lucre's sake (Titus 1:5, 9-11).

Paul was more able to contend with these enemies of the Cross than probably any other defender of the gospel in his day. Yet, even the Apostle knew that they would never go away and, although he covered many subjects in his preaching and teaching, he never dared to drop this one challenge:

> For I know this, that after my departing shall grievous wolves enter in among you, not sparing the flock. Also of your own selves shall men arise, speaking perverse things, to draw away disciples after them. Therefore watch, and remember, that by the space of three years I ceased not to warn every one night and day with tears (Acts 20:29-31).

When Judaizers came to Antioch they were so intimidating that they temporarily harnessed Peter to their apostate gospel necessitating an open rebuke from the Apostle Paul—

> But when Peter was come to Antioch, I withstood him to the face, because he was to be blamed. For before that certain came from James, he did eat with the Gentiles: but when they were come, he withdrew and separated himself, fearing them which were of the circumcision (Gal. 2:11, 12).

This maneuver on Peter's part caused other converted Jews, as well as Barnabas, to separate from the uncircumcised Gentile converts as if they were not really brethren. One cannot do this and still be a representative of the true gospel and Paul knew it full well when he said:

> And the other Jews dissembled likewise with him; insomuch that Barnabas also was carried away with their dissimulation. But when I saw that they walked not uprightly according to the truth of the gospel, I said unto Peter before them all… (Gal. 2:13, 14a).

Paul accused Peter of living like the Gentiles while teaching them by example that they could not be saved unless they lived like the Jews—

> …if thou, being a Jew, livest after the manner of Gentiles, and not as do the Jews, why compellest thou the Gentiles to live as do the Jews? We who are Jews by nature, and not sinners of the Gentiles, Knowing that a man is not justified by the works of the law, but by the faith of Jesus Christ, even we have believed in Jesus Christ, that we might be justified by the faith of Christ, and not by the works of the law: for by the works of the law shall no flesh be justified (Gal. 2:14b-16).

They of the Circumcision were not factoring Christ and the cross out of the gospel, they were just trying to factor circumcision and the law into the equation. The Apostle Paul affirmed that if the righteousness that saves is through obedience to the Law rather than the imputed righteousness of Christ then the crucifixion was merely an act of suicide— *I do not frustrate the grace of God: for if righteousness come by the law, then Christ is dead in vain* (Gal. 2:21).[16] Why would Christ die to save people who could have saved themselves?

Salvation is not by faith plus works but by faith without works—*And by him all that believe are justified from all things, from which ye could not be justified by the law of Moses* (Acts 13:39). Note Romans 3:28—*Therefore we conclude that a man is justified by faith without the deeds of the law.* Note also Paul's words when he exclaims:

> But to him that worketh not, but believeth on him that justifieth the ungodly, his faith is counted for righteousness. Even as David also describeth the blessedness of the man, unto whom God imputeth righteousness without works, *saying*, Blessed *are* they whose iniquities are forgiven, and whose sins are covered. Blessed *is* the man to whom the Lord will not impute sin. (Rom. 4:5-8).

There is a strong argument that Paul is not speaking of faith without works but only faith without the works of the Law of Moses. In answer to this argument it should be noted that Paul is including Abraham (who was 430 years before the Mosaic Law) into his equation of faith without works—

> *Cometh* this blessedness then upon the circumcision *only*, or upon the uncircumcision also? for we say that faith was reckoned to Abraham for righteousness. How was it then reckoned? when he was in circumcision, or in uncircumcision? Not in circumcision, but in uncircumcision. And he received the sign of circumcision, a seal of the righteousness of the faith which *he had yet* being uncircumcised: that

---

[16] Contrast personal righteousness with the imputed righteousness of Christ... Isa. 64:6 "But we are all as an unclean *thing*, and all our righteousnesses *are* as filthy rags; and we all do fade as a leaf; and our iniquities, like the wind, have taken us away." Compare II Cor. 5:21, "For he hath made him *to be* sin for us, who knew no sin; that we might be made the righteousness of God in him."

he might be the father of all them that believe, though they be not circumcised; that righteousness might be imputed unto them also: And the father of circumcision to them who are not of the circumcision only, but who also walk in the steps of that faith of our father Abraham, which *he had* being *yet* uncircumcised. For the promise, that he should be the heir of the world, *was* not to Abraham, or to his seed, through the law, but through the righteousness of faith (Rom. 4:9-13).

The Judaizers came into the churches of Galatia and converted Paul's converts to an apostate gospel. It is imperative to point out that there are two categories of *they of the circumcision*: those who are saved and those who never were saved. Both categories profess the same apostate gospel. The difference is that the first group is made up of those who were truly saved by grace and then converted to another gospel. This is exactly what happened temporarily to Peter and Barnabas in (Gal. 2:13,14). In the first chapter of Galatians, Paul contrasts both categories of apostates when he said:

> I marvel that ye are so soon removed from him that called you into the grace of Christ unto another gospel: Which is not another; but there be some that trouble you, and would pervert the gospel of Christ (Gal. 1:6-7).

The Apostle Paul had won them to Christ and now they were removed, not from salvation, but from Paul and unto an apostate Gospel. To demonstrate the seriousness of this removal the Apostle pronounces a curse upon himself, any angel, or any man who would preach this other gospel:

> But though we, or an angel from heaven, preach any other gospel unto you than that which we have preached unto you, let him be accursed, As we said before, so say I now again, If any man preach any other gospel unto you than that ye have received, let him be accursed (Gal. 1:8, 9).

This curse (*anathema*), at least in the case of saved Judaizers, did not mean God's condemnation in Hell. It meant physical condemnation this side of the grave or perhaps even physical death.[17] Paul was speaking to fellow Christians when warning them of the danger of physical damnation if they misused the ordinance of the Lord's Table:

> For he that eateth and drinketh unworthily, eateth and drinketh damnation to himself, not discerning the Lord's body, for this cause many are weak and sickly among you, and many sleep (I Cor. 11:29, 30).

The writer of Hebrews was not speaking of sinners escaping Hell but of Christians failing to escape God's judgment if they neglect the plan of salvation. Notice the word "we" as he writes:

> Therefore we ought to give the more earnest heed to the things which we have heard, lest at any time we should let them slip. For if the word spoken by angels was stedfast, and every transgression and disobedience received a just recompence of reward; How shall we escape, if we neglect so great salvation (Heb. 2:1-3a).

In addition to possible physical judgment from God, the true believer who becomes harnessed to a false gospel will forfeit rewards upon entering eternal life, even as Paul warned the Colossians when he said:

> Let no man therefore judge you in meat, or in drink, or in respect of an holyday, or of the new moon, or of the sabbath days: Which are a shadow of things to come; but the body is of Christ. Let no man beguile you of your reward in a voluntary humility and worshipping of angels, intruding into those things which he hath not seen, vainly puffed up by his fleshly mind (Col. 2: 16-18).

---

[17] Note the difference between the salvation of a lost sinner from hell and the salvation of a brother in Christ from physical death— "Brethren, if any of you do err from the truth, and one convert him; Let him know, that he which converteth the sinner from the error of his way shall save a soul from death, and shall hide a multitude of sins" (Jas. 5:19-20).

Paul expressed his frustration with those who muddied the gospel by saying sarcastically that he wished that they would be "cut off" (Gal. 6:12). He was wishing that they would go all the way and castrate themselves in imitation of the pagan priests of Cybele in Asia Minor. The resulting physical impotence would illustrate Paul's desire that they also be spiritually impotent as well and therefore unable to produce new converts to their apostate gospel.

Regarding the saved who converted to the circumcision gospel, Paul does not tell them that they have lost their salvation. However, they have lost the effectiveness of Christ in their lives and they have separated themselves from the Gospel of Grace—

> Behold, I Paul say unto you, that if ye be circumcised, Christ shall profit you nothing. For I testify again to every man that is circumcised, that he is a debtor to do the whole law. Christ is become of no effect unto you, whosoever of you are justified by the law; ye are fallen from grace. For we through the Spirit wait for the hope of righteousness by faith. For in Jesus Christ neither circumcision availeth any thing, nor uncircumcision; but faith which worketh by love. Ye did run well; who did hinder you that ye should not obey the truth? This persuasion *cometh* not of him that calleth you. (Gal. 5:2-8).[18]

---

[18] John F. Walvoord and Roy B. Zuck, editors: *The Bible Knowledge commentary: New Testament Edition* (Victor Books, 1983)...Section on Galations by Donald K. Cammpbell, p. 605. "Turning to the Law and accepting circumcision as a meritorious work has further dire implications which the Galatians were called on to consider. Anyone seeking justification by Law has been alienated (katergathete) from Christ, that is, such a person would not be living in a sphere where Christ was operative. The KJV has a helpful rendering, 'Christ is become of no effect unto you.' In addition, said Paul, they would have fallen away from grace. The issue here is not the possible loss of salvation, for 'grace' is referred to not as salvation itself but as a method of salvation (cf. 2:21 where 'a Law' route is mentioned as an unworkable way to come to Christ). If the Galatians accepted circumcision as necessary for salvation, they would be leaving the grace system for the Mosaic Law system. The same error is repeated today when a believer leaves a church that emphasizes salvation by grace through faith and joins one which teaches that salvation depends on repentance, confession, faith, baptism, and church membership."

When the Apostle Paul made his final visit to Jerusalem with the money collected for their benefit, he and his party were received "gladly" by the brethren. The following day Paul and his companions met with James and the elders of the Jerusalem church. The first item on the agenda of this meeting was a rehearsal of God's blessings on their ministry to the Gentiles (Acts 21:19). James and the elders responded by glorifying God and then immediately drawing the attention of the missionaries to the fact that many "thousands" of Jews believed in Christ but were still zealous for the Law of Moses. They were baptized members of the church and dedicated constituents of the Temple as well.

These "thousands" of converted Jews had received a negative report that Paul was teaching Jews not to circumcise their sons. Paul was careful to remind the Jews that the Law could not save, but he never said that its moral requirements were inconsequential to Christian living.[19] He did teach the Gentiles that Jewish customs and circumcision were inconsequential to them.[20] Yet Paul was so emphatic to point out how level the ground is at the foot of the cross that it would have been natural for anyone to conclude that he meant to say that Jewish custom and circumcision was just as inconsequential to the salvation of Jewish families as they were to the conversion of Gentiles, which is precisely what he was saying—

> There is neither Jew nor Greek, there is neither bond nor free, there is neither male nor female: for ye are all one in Christ Jesus. And if ye *be* Christ's, then are ye

---

[19] Remember that the Epistle to the Hebrews was written to Jewish believers who were doubting their Christianity and were tempted to go back to their old Jewish faith. The author affirms the superiority and all-sufficiency of Christ over all (1:1-4; 9:11-14). His sacrifice is enough to take away our sin.

[20] "Is any man called being circumcised? let him not become uncircumcised. Is any called in uncircumcision? let him not be circumcised" (I Cor. 7:18). Paul was not only telling the Gentiles to remain uncircumcised, he was telling Jews to not become uncircumcised as was done in I Maccabees 1:13-15: "Then certain of the people were so forward herein, that they went to the king, who gave them licence to do after the ordinances of the heathen: Whereupon they built a place of exercise at Jerusalem according to the customs of the heathen: And made themselves uncircumcised, and forsook the holy covenant, and joined themselves to the heathen, and were sold to do mischief."

Abraham's seed, and heirs according to the promise (Gal. 3:28. 29).

Therefore by the deeds of the law there shall no flesh be justified in his sight: for by the law *is* the knowledge of sin. But now the righteousness of God without the law is manifested, being witnessed by the law and the prophets; Even the righteousness of God *which is* by faith of Jesus Christ unto all and upon all them that believe: for there is no difference (Rom. 3:20-22).

For there is no difference between the Jew and the Greek: for the same Lord over all is rich unto all that call upon him. For whosoever shall call upon the name of the Lord shall be saved (Rom. 10:12, 13).

Where there is neither Greek nor Jew, circumcision nor uncircumcision, Barbarian, Scythian, bond *nor* free: but Christ *is* all, and in all. (Col. 3:11).[21]

Just as Peter and Barnabas had once temporarily succumbed to the circumcisers in Gal. 2:11-16, James and the elders asked Paul to help prove to these "thousands" of Jewish believers that there was indeed a difference. By so doing, the rumor could be dispelled once-for-all. Paul responded to their request by agreeing to take four members of the Jerusalem church, who had made Nazarite vows at the temple, and officiate over their ceremonial release from the vows. It would require the shaving of their heads and the blood sacrifice of a lamb without spot or blemish for their cleansing (Acts 21:21-23).[22] This would serve to prove to the "thousands" of Jewish believers that Paul still considered himself under the Law and customs of Moses, making them different from Gentile converts. Luke records their words as follows:

---

[21] Remember the words of Peter (Acts 15:8, 9)... "And God, which knoweth the hearts, bare them witness, giving them the Holy Ghost, even as *he did* unto us; and put no difference between us and them, purifying their hearts by faith."

[22] At the end of his vow the Nazirite had to offer various prescribed sacrifices, and thereafter cut his hair and burn it on the altar. After certain ritual acts by the priest, the Nazirite was freed from his vow. See Num. 6:13-21.

> Them take, and purify thyself with them, and be at charges with them, that they may shave *their* heads: and all may know that those things, whereof they were informed concerning thee, are nothing; but *that* thou thyself also walkest orderly, and keepest the law. As touching the Gentiles which believe, we have written *and* concluded that they observe no such thing, save only that they keep themselves from *things* offered to idols, and from blood, and from strangled, and from fornication (Acts 21:24,25).

Paul did as he promised and waited for a blood offering to be made for his own purification (Acts 21:26). We can only speculate as to why Paul agreed to this. He was no doubt fatigued from his missionary labor and from the anxiety over the threats against his life. He was there to deliver money and be of help to the church. But he, of all people, knew that blood sacrifices were totally irrelevant to a Christian's faith in Christ. Paul would later speak of Christ—

> Who gave himself for us, that he might redeem us from all iniquity, and purify unto himself a peculiar people, zealous of good works. These things speak, and exhort, and rebuke with all authority. Let no man despise thee. (Titus 2:14,15).[23]

The same is confirmed by the writer of Hebrews when he states:

> The Holy Ghost this signifying, that the way into the holiest of all was not yet made manifest, while as the first tabernacle was yet standing: Which *was* a figure for the time then present, in which were offered both gifts and sacrifices, that could not make him that did the service perfect, as pertaining to the conscience; *Which stood* only in meats and drinks, and divers washings, and carnal ordinances, imposed *on them* until the time of reformation. But Christ being come an high priest of good things to come, by a greater and

---

[23] For "purification" or (cleansing) note (Acts 15:9) "And put no difference between us and them, purifying their hearts by faith."

> more perfect tabernacle, not made with hands, that is to say, not of this building; Neither by the blood of goats and calves, but by his own blood he entered in once into the holy place, having obtained eternal redemption *for us*. For if the blood of bulls and of goats, and the ashes of an heifer sprinkling the unclean, sanctifieth to the purifying of the flesh: How much more shall the blood of Christ, who through the eternal Spirit offered himself without spot to God, purge your conscience from dead works to serve the living God? (Heb. 9:8-14).
>
> By the which will we are sanctified through the offering of the body of Jesus Christ once *for all*. And every priest standeth daily ministering and offering oftentimes the same sacrifices, which can never take away sins: But this man, after he had offered one sacrifice for sins for ever, sat down on the right hand of God; From henceforth expecting till his enemies be made his footstool. For by one offering he hath perfected for ever them that are sanctified (Heb. 10:10-14).

We already know that it is possible for even an Apostle to be intimidated into succumbing to these powerful advocates of the Mosaic system. Although Paul openly judged Peter for this at Antioch, we will not judge any Apostle here. Though it might be said that Paul committed error by participating in animal sacrifice at this point in his career, his motive may have been that of opening a door of witness to the Jews. Paul himself had previously taken a Nazirite vow in Acts 1:18 and admitted it to Felix in 24:17, 18. So, one could also interpret this act as Paul's attempt to become like one under the Law in order to win those under it, as he stated:

> For though I be free from all men, yet have I made myself servant unto all, that I might gain the more. And unto the Jews I became as a Jew, that I might gain the Jews; to them that are under the law, as under the law, that I might gain them that are under the law (I Cor. 9:19, 20).

One thing we know for certain is that this act not only did not appease the Jews, it caused a riot resulting in Paul's arrest and ultimate execution (cf. Acts 21:27-36). We have no record of James nor the "thousands" of Jewish believers coming forward to clear up the misunderstanding for Paul after being accused of polluting the temple by bringing Greeks into it. In fact, the accusation against him at the riot was similar to the rumor that was creating a problem in the church, as Luke recorded:

> The Jews which were of Asia, when they saw him in the temple, stirred up all the people, and laid hands on him, Crying out, Men of Israel, help: This is the man, that teacheth all men every where against the people, and the law, and this place (Act 21: 27b, 28a).

So, Christ said these wolves would come; Paul said they would come; Peter said they would come, and they came. They were with Christ as Pharisees and lawyers. They were with Paul as *Pharisees which believed*. They were with all the churches which Paul had founded and they were tried by the Ephesians and found to be liars (Rev. 2:2). Thus, we see that perhaps the greatest challenge to New Testament Christianity was the belief that ritual, rather than pointing to reality, was itself a reality which could regenerate and save the soul of the conforming sinner.

Chapter Two

Where Does *Law* Factor Into Christianity?

> 𝕴 contend that, before the
> Law of Moses was
> written on stone tablets,
> there was an unwritten,
> natural law that was
> habitually understood
> and that the fathers
> habitually kept.
>
> *(Tertullian 9c. 197, W), 3.152*

Observation has been made, and will be expanded upon in the next chapter, to the fact that forgiveness of sin and eternal life were in all ages bestowed by the imputed righteousness of Christ when God's grace was received by faith. Thus, there never was a time when the Mosaic Law, or any other law obeyed by man, could give life or take away sin. Paul was not just speaking of a change in the terms of salvation when he spoke the words:

> And by him all that believe are justified from all things, from which ye could not be justified by the law of Moses (Acts 13:39).

He was speaking of the way salvation had always been. To prove his argument he pointed to the fact that the Mosaic Law could not have justified in the time of David:

> And as concerning that he raised him up from the dead, now no more to return to corruption, he said on this wise, I will give you the sure mercies of David (Acts 13:34).

Moving backwards, the Law could not justify from the days of Paul to the time of David, nor from David past Moses through the time of Abraham. Paul connects David with Abraham in his argument against work for salvation when he says:

> For if Abraham were justified by works, he hath whereof to glory; but not before God (Rom. 4:2)

Then Paul applies the same precept to David when he wrote:

> Even as David also describeth the blessedness of the man, unto whom God imputeth righteousness without works, Saying, Blessed are they whose iniquities are forgiven, and whose sins are covered. Blessed is the man to whom the Lord will not impute sin (Rom. 4:6-8).

David was describing a salvation stemming, not from the righteousness of the law, but from the imputed righteousness of Christ. The writer of Hebrews traces the gospel of imputed righteousness all the way back to Abel (Heb. 11:4).

The Judaizers would love to enter the argument at this point and contest that, of course the law alone could not save, but faith plus law would. This is when they would need to see Paul's point unmistakably as he affirms:

> But to him that worketh not, but believeth on him that justifieth the ungodly, his faith is counted for righteousness (Rom. 4:5).

The Apostle wanted all to know that if salvation could be even partially earned by man then it was a debt God owed him and not a gift of grace—

> Now to him that worketh is the reward not reckoned of grace, but of debt (Rom. 4:4).

What is meant by the term *law*? The Bible often takes one term and uses it in a number of totally divergent applications. If one combines them all into one usage and application he can lose his focus

Where Does *Law* Factor Into Christianity?

on the whole Word of God. A prime example is the word *law*. This term can refer to the *Tora*—the first five books of Moses (Luke 24:44; John 1:41; 8:5). *The Law* sometimes refers to all the books of the Old Testament. John 10:34; 12:43; 15:25 quote the book of Psalms, but calls it *the law*. Sometimes the term refers to the general doctrines of the Scriptures (Psalms 19:7). It may refer to the Gospel itself in reference to the Messiah (Isaiah 2:3; 42:4). The doctrine of the imputed righteousness of Christ is called the *law of faith* (Rom. 3:27).[1] Sometimes it refers to the whole body of Mosaic Law as distinct from the gospel, as John wrote: *For the law was given by Moses, but grace and truth came by Jesus Christ* (Jn. 1:17).

The Mosaic Law had three divisions: the ceremonial, the judicial-civil, and the moral law. The ceremonial law concerned priests, sacrifices, feasts, fasts, washings, distinguishing clean from unclean creatures, and circumcision. It was the ceremonial law that veiled the gospel in types and figures. Priests foreshadowed Christ and heavenly things—

> And they truly were many priests, because they were not suffered to continue by reason of death: But this man, because he continueth ever, hath an unchangeable priesthood. Wherefore he is able also to save them to the uttermost that come unto God by him, seeing he ever liveth to make intercession for them (Heb. 7:23-25).

Sacrifices foreshadowed the crucifixion of the Savior—

> For such an high priest became us, who is holy, harmless, undefiled, separate from sinners, and made higher than the heavens; Who needeth not daily, as

---

[1] "Where *is* boasting then? It is excluded. By what law? of works? Nay: but by the law of faith" (Rom 3:27). Paul demonstrates a play on words where he uses *law* as the standard by which God excludes human works of any kind. Therefore, *faith* can be called God's standard but faith is not a meritorious work. God's standard is *faith* (Jn. 6:29). In 6:29 Jesus refers to *belief* as a work (singular). The term *work* in this case means *requirement* and faith in Christ is what God requires of man. But, this faith is not a meritorious work of righteousness, cf. Rom. 4:5.

those high priests, to offer up sacrifice, first for his own sins, and then for the people's: for this he did once, when he offered up himself (Heb. 7:26, 27).

The burnt, meal, and peace offerings were to maintain fellowship with God (Lev. 1-3). The sin and trespass offerings were to restore fellowship to God (Lev. 4-5), but they never did give life.

The holy feasts spoke of God's work of redemption. The Feast of Passover spoke of Calvary; Feast of First Fruits spoke of the resurrection; Feast of Pentecost ultimately became the occasion of the coming of the Holy Spirit; Feast of Trumpets spoke of the second coming; Feast of Atonement spoke of the tribulation; and Feast of Tabernacle spoke of the Millennium (Lev. 23, 25).

The Tabernacle was a preview of Christ. The Brazen altar (Ex. 27:1-8; 38:1-7) pictured the slain Lamb of God (John 1:29). The Brazen Laver (Ex. 30:18; 38:8) spoke of the water of life (Jn. 4:14). The table of shewbread (Ex. 25:23-30; 37:10-16) pointed to the bread of life (Jn. 6:35). The lampstand (Ex. 25:31-40; 37:17-24) introduced one to Christ as the light of the world (Jn. 9:5). The altar of incense (Ex. 30:1-10; 37:25-28) represents the great prayer of Christ (Jn. 17). Finally, the mercy seat (Ex. 25:10-22; 37:1-9) speaks of the witness of Christ our mercy seat (I Jn. 2:2). The washings foreshadowed cleansing by the blood of Christ (Rev. 1:5; 7:14).

The whole served as a schoolmaster to the Jews until Jesus came. But when the object of their faith came they were no longer under the schoolmaster. It was disannulled (fired as the schoolmaster) because of its weakness and unprofitableness, having its fulfillment and accomplishment in Christ. It was not disannulled as a giver of life because it never was such. It was not done away as a giver of righteousness unto salvation because it never was such. It was fired as God's ordained means to illustrate the finished work of Christ and educate us about salvation, as Paul wrote:

> Wherefore the law was our schoolmaster to bring us unto Christ, that we might be justified by faith. But after that faith is come, we are no longer under a schoolmaster (Gal. 3:24, 25).

Where Does *Law* Factor Into Christianity?

We still learn this by reading the Law, but God does not require us to obey it in order to learn the object of its foreshadowings.[2]

The judicial law concerns civil government in Israel and consists of statutes and judgments upon which political rulers in Israel governed the Jews and passed sentence upon lawbreakers (Deut. 17:8-11). Its categories related to injuries to person or property, and to punishment of violations. The judicial law describes a theocracy—a government ruled by God's law. Even when there were kings and judges, they were to enforce only God's laws. God alone was the author of these laws and they were for Israel and no other nation.[3]

The weekly, seven-year, and fifty-year Sabbaths not only spoke of God's great work of creation (Rev. 4:11), but also of Christ's rest from the finished work of salvation as well as the saint's rest from the idea of salvation by works, As the writer of Hebrews states: *For he that is entered into his rest, he also hath ceased from his own works, as God did from his* (Heb. 4:10).[4] And again:

> Let us therefore fear, lest, a promise being left *us* of entering into his rest, any of you should seem to come

---

[2] In a Roman home the *schoolmaster* was the *paidagogos* (Child leader). He was a slave or a servant who had charge of the children in the house. It was his job to feed, dress, bathe, blow the noses, spank, lead by the hand to school. The Law took us by the hand and led us to Christ and turns us over to Him so that we are no longer under the old *paidagogos*— (Gal. 4:1-5) "Now I say, *That* the heir, as long as he is a child, differeth nothing from a servant, though he be lord of all; But is under tutors and governors until the time appointed of the father. Even so we, when we were children, were in bondage under the elements of the world: But when the fulness of the time was come, God sent forth his Son, made of a woman, made under the law, To redeem them that were under the law, that we might receive the adoption of sons (Gal. 4:1-5).

[3] Christians, on the other hand, are under human government and are to submit to manmade ordinances for the sake of the Lord and their consciences (Rom. 13:1-7; Titus 3:1; I Pet. 2:13,14).

[4] The only qualification for entering eternal rest is belief and the only disqualification is disbelief— "Seeing therefore it remaineth that some must enter therein, and they to whom it was first preached entered not in because of unbelief" (Heb. 4:6). Furthermore, unbelief can prevent a redeemed person from experiencing the peace of God in this life as when redeemed Israelites were not allowed to enter the earthly Promised Land (see argument #3 in chap. 10 of this present work).

short of it. For unto us was the gospel preached, as well as unto them: but the word preached did not profit them, not being mixed with faith in them that heard *it*. For we which have believed do enter into rest, as he said, As I have sworn in my wrath, if they shall enter into my rest: although the works were finished from the foundation of the world. For he spake in a certain place of the seventh *day* on this wise, And God did rest the seventh day from all his works (Heb. 4:1-4).[5]

The moral law is mostly in the Decalogue—or Ten Commandments (Exodus 20:3-17). Christ reduced both the judicial and moral tables of law into two capital ones—to love God whole-heartedly and to love neighbor as self (Matt. 22:36-40). The Apostle went further and reduced these two into *love* (Rom. 13:8), which would fulfill the whole law. If anyone ever loved that much he would be in perfect obedience to the Law of Moses— a point which no man but Christ has ever achieved. Even the Law of Love condemns the best of mankind. God was the author and giver of the moral law and wrote it with His finger on tables of stone. Moses administered it from God; it was spoken by angels (Psa. 68:17; Acts 7:53; Heb. 2:2); and ordained by angels as it was mediated in the hands of Moses when he stood between God and the people (Gal. 3:19).[6]

Next, it must be understood that the Mosaic Law was a covenant with the Jewish state and with no other political entity. It pertained to their continuance in the land of Canaan until the Messiah would come—

---

[5] Not only was the Sabbath a picture of resting from works for salvation but was also a picture of entrance into the Promised Land— "And in this *place* again, If they shall enter into my rest. Seeing therefore it remaineth that some must enter therein, and they to whom it was first preached entered not in because of unbelief: Again, he limiteth a certain day, saying in David, To day, after so long a time; as it is said, To day if ye will hear his voice, harden not your hearts. For if Jesus had given them rest, then would he not afterward have spoken of another day. There remaineth therefore a rest to the people of God" (Heb. 4:5-9).

[6] Dr. Harold Willmington lists 613 commandments in the Mosaic Law. Dr. H. L. Willmington, *Wilmington's Guide to the Bible,* (Wheaton, Illinois: Tyndale House Publishers, Inc., 1984), p. 940.

> The sceptre shall not depart from Judah, nor a lawgiver from between his feet, until Shiloh come; and unto him shall the gathering of the people be (Gen. 49:10).

The law of inheritances would cease, alienation of inheritance by marriage would cease, restoration of inheritance at the year of jubilee would cease, marrying a brother's wife when he died without issue would cease – the design of which was to keep the tribes distinct until the Messiah came, so that it might be clearly known from what tribe He came forth. There was a cessation of laws regarding release from debts; letting the land rest every seventh year; of laws regarding lending on usury; of leaving a corner of the field for the poor, and the forgotten sheaf; of laws concerning divorces, and the trial of a suspected wife; and of the cities of refuge to flee from the avenger of blood. These would cease when Jewish polity ceased but they were never binding on other nations.

A primary example of the Jewishness of the Mosaic Law is the Sabbath day. It was given uniquely to the Jewish people (Ex. 16:29, 30). The whole decalogue was a covenant with the Israelites only, made with them when they were in the wilderness, giving them preference over all other nations and even their fathers before them (Deut. 5:2-21; 4:6-8). This is also confirmed by the Psalmist when he said:

> He sheweth his word unto Jacob, his statutes and his judgments unto Israel. He hath not dealt so with any nation: and as for his judgments, they have not known them. Praise ye the LORD (Psa. 147:19-20).

Paul also supports the same conclusion as he writes:

> ...my brethren, my kinsmen according to the flesh: Who are Israelites; to whom pertaineth the adoption, and the glory, and the covenants, and the giving of the law, and the service of God, and the promises (Rom. 9:3b, 4).

The fourth commandment is for Israel only—

> And the LORD spake unto Moses, saying, Speak thou also unto the children of Israel, saying, Verily my sabbaths ye shall keep: for it is a sign between me and you throughout your generations; that ye may know that I am the LORD that doth sanctify you (Ex. 31:12, 13).[7]

Nehemiah spoke of the Sabbath as God's covenant with Israel, which had not been made known to them before the wilderness. He mentions this along with other precepts, statutes and commandments:

> And madest known unto them thy holy sabbath, and commandedst them precepts, statutes, and laws, by the hand of Moses thy servant (Neh. 9:14).

God spoke through Ezekiel saying:

> Moreover also I gave them my sabbaths, to be a sign between me and them, that they might know that I am the LORD that sanctify them. But the house of Israel rebelled against me in the wilderness (Ezek. 20:12,13a).

The Bible never charges anyone but Jews for breach of the Sabbath (Ezek. 20:20-24). In Nehemiah's time the Tyrians sold fish to the Jews on the Sabbath and were threatened, shut out of the city and prohibited from entering with their goods. But it was the Jews who brought them into the city on the Sabbath in the first place and it was the Jews who were charged with the profaning of the Sabbath (Neh. 13:15-20).

This brings us to the fundamental question regarding law and order for Gentiles. If the Mosaic Law is for the earthly nation of Israel, then how can law and order exist in Gentile nations? Gentile nations are ruled by natural law, which has the same God as its author. It is inscribed on the heart of every human by the Creator. Herein God reveals His nature and the nature of moral good and evil—

---

[7] The same is repeated in vss. 16, 17.

> For the wrath of God is revealed from heaven against all ungodliness and unrighteousness of men, who hold the truth in unrighteousness; Because that which may be known of God is manifest in them; for God hath shewed *it* unto them. For the invisible things of him from the creation of the world are clearly seen, being understood by the things that are made, *even* his eternal power and Godhead; so that they are without excuse (Rom. 1:18-20).

The natural law of God is also perfect but, because of the fallen nature of man, Adam's posterity can only discern it imperfectly. Yet, by God's common grace, natural man discerns it enough to create law and order in a godless society—

> For when the Gentiles, which have not the law, do by nature the things contained in the law, these, having not the law, are a law unto themselves: Which shew the work of the law written in their hearts, their conscience also bearing witness, and *their* thoughts the mean while accusing or else excusing one another (Rom. 2:14,15).

Now, the moral laws of Moses are the same in substance as divine-natural moral law. This is why the heathen can have law, order and decency without the establishment of a theocracy and a particular religion. Paul describes the unregenerate as *holding the truth in unrighteousness* and as knowing God but glorifying *Him not as God* (Rom. 1:18,19, 21). Paul is not giving unregenerate man meritorious credit for his intellect but attributes understanding of natural law to God's sovereign, yet common, grace upon all flesh. We see traces of divine-natural law in the code of Ur-Nammu of ancient Sumer (c.2113-2006 B.C.) where the king was concerned that orphans did not fall prey to the wealthy and that the man of one shekel did not fall prey to the man of sixty shekels.[8] Natural law can be observed, though imperfectly, in the code of Hammurabi of ancient Babylon (c. 1792-1750 B.C.), whose purpose was: *to cause justice to prevail in the land, to destroy the wicked and the evil, to prevent the strong from oppressing*

---

[8] S. N. Kramer, *From the Tablets of Sumer* (Indian Hills, Colorado.: The Falcon's Wing Press, 1956), p. 50.

the weak...and to further the welfare of the people.[9] The Ancient Hittite empire (after 1450 B.C.) had a similar code, but differed in prescribing more humane punishments. Instead of retaliation (*an eye for an eye*), the Hittite code made greater use of restitution and compensation. In 450 B.C. Roman law was inscribed on twelve tablets of bronze (called The Law of the Twelve Tables) and set up publicly in the Forum. When Justinian commissioned scholars to compile the mass of Roman laws into a unified Justinian Code, it became formally titled *Corpus Juris Civilis.* It was replete with traces of natural laws of right and wrong, virtue and vice, and justice and wrath. The Napoleonic code was completed in 1804. It was a great Civil Code written with precision and clarity. It guaranteed many of the achievements of the French Revolution, such as religious toleration and the abolition of elite privilege. It had a marked influence upon the laws of many other countries. It would be too tedious here to speak of ancient African laws; Aztec laws, Chinese laws; Germanic folk law; Japanese laws, and Russian laws. Suffice it to say that, without the Mosaic system or established Christianity, pagans have always held the truth of God in unrighteousness and understood His righteousness and wrath from their collective conscience (Rom 1:18-19).

Gentiles do not know in their hearts to keep the Sabbath because its law is not of a moral nature. Otherwise it could not have been dispensed with in that God does not dispense with natural law. But the Sabbath has been abolished (Matt. 12:1-12), so that the Apostle Paul could say to the Colossians:

> Let no man therefore judge you in meat, or in drink, or in respect of an holyday, or of the new moon, or of the sabbath *days*: Which are a shadow of things to come; but the body *is* of Christ (Col. 2:16, 17).

When considering Natural Law it is essential to remember it also cannot bestow life on the one who would follow its precepts—

> Is the law then against the promises of God? God forbid: for if there had been a law given which could have given life, verily righteousness should have been

---

[9] R. F. Harper, T*he Code of Hammurabi* (Chicago: University of Chicago Press, 1904), p. 3.

by the law. But the scripture hath concluded all under sin, that the promise by faith of Jesus Christ might be given to them that believe (Gal. 3:21, 22).

Both Mosaic and Natural laws serve to restrain, forbid, and punish men for offences. But primarily, they serve to make the offence abound so that men may see themselves as exceedingly sinful and worthy of God's condemnation—*Moreover the law entered, that the offence might abound. But where sin abounded, grace did much more abound* (Rom. 5:20). And again:

> Wherefore the law *is* holy, and the commandment holy, and just, and good. Was then that which is good made death unto me? God forbid. But sin, that it might appear sin, working death in me by that which is good; that sin by the commandment might become exceeding sinful (Rom. 7:12, 13).

So, the severity of the Law convinces man that he is lost and leads him to the grace of Christ—*Wherefore the law was our schoolmaster to bring us unto Christ, that we might be justified by faith* (Gal. 3:24). When a bearded man looks into a mirror it will show him that he needs a shave, but it will not shave him. And when an unregenerate man looks into the Law it will show him his need to be saved, but it will not save him.

The Mosaic Covenant was not a pure covenant of works. However, many self-righteous Jews turned it into one, and sought for life and righteousness by it. Thus, it became bondage and a killing letter. Though not the plan of salvation, it was partially a covenant of grace in that it was given as a distinguishing favor to the nation of Israel—

> But ye that did cleave unto the LORD your God *are* alive every one of you this day. Behold, I have taught you statutes and judgments, even as the LORD my God commanded me, that ye should do so in the land whither ye go to possess it. Keep therefore and do *them*; for this *is* your wisdom and your understanding in the sight of the nations, which shall hear all these statutes, and say, Surely this great nation *is* a wise and

> understanding people. For what nation *is there so* great, who *hath* God *so* nigh unto them, as the LORD our God *is* in all *things that* we call upon him *for*? And what nation *is there so* great, that hath statutes and judgments *so* righteous as all this law, which I set before you this day? (Deut. 4:4-8).

> He sheweth his word unto Jacob, his statutes and his judgments unto Israel. He hath not dealt so with any nation: and *as for his* judgments, they have not known them. Praise ye the LORD (Psa. 147:19, 20).

> Who are Israelites; to whom *pertaineth* the adoption, and the glory, and the covenants, and the giving of the law, and the service *of God*, and the promises (Rom. 9:4).

There is much mercy and kindness to be observed within the Law of Moses. The moral law begins with a declaration of Jehovah being the God of Israel, Who had, in His great goodness, delivered them out of the land of Egypt (Ex. 20:2, 6, 12). The Mosaic system pointed to Christ Who was made under the Law and became the surety of His people—

> But when the fulness of the time was come, God sent forth his Son, made of a woman, made under the law, To redeem them that were under the law, that we might receive the adoption of sons (Gal. 4:4, 5).

Christ became the fulfillment of the righteousness of the Law (and all righteousness)—

> And Jesus answering said unto him, Suffer it to be so now: for thus it becometh us to fulfil all righteousness (Matt. 3:15).

> And again: Think not that I am come to destroy the law, or the prophets: I am not come to destroy, but to fulfil (5:17).

He became the end of the law or the object at which it aimed—

> *For Christ is the end of the law for righteousness to every one that believeth* (Rom. 10:4).

The Mosaic law was *perfect* (Psa. 19:7)[10], spiritual (Rom. 7:14)[11], holy (Rom. 7:12); just (Romans 7:12; Deut. 4:8; Psa. 19:9), and good (Rom. 7:21, 22). And, though it did not give life, it would give great reward for those who at least sought to live by its commandments for the right reason. One such reward being peace of conscience (Psa. 19:11; 119:165). Thus, the law was good *if a man use it lawfully* (I Tim. 1:8). The Law is used unlawfully when a man seeks to obtain life and righteousness before God by it—

> For I bear them record that they have a zeal of God, but not according to knowledge. For they being ignorant of God's righteousness, and going about to establish their own righteousness, have not submitted themselves unto the righteousness of God. For Christ is the end of the law for righteousness to every one that believeth. For Moses describeth the righteousness which is of the law, That the man which doeth those things shall live by them (Rom. 10:2-5).

But the Law is used lawfully when one attempts to obey its moral precepts faithfully, from a motive of love, with a view of eternal reward and inheritance; but most of all, to glorify God.

Even though the Law is no longer the schoolmaster and is helpless to give life, it is not altogether useless. The Law convinces us of sin (Rom. 3:20; Jn. 16:8), condemns and punishes sin (I Tim. 1:9, 10)[12], and restrains from sin (Rom. 13:3).[13]

---

[10] When Paul looked into the mirror of the law he saw himself *carnal, and sold under sin* (Rom. 7:14).

[11] This refers to the moral law in that the ceremonial law was a *carnal commandment* which stood in *carnal ordinances* (Heb. 7:16; 9:10).

[12] The law accuses of sin, charges with it, brings evidence of it, stops the sinner's mouth from pleading his own cause, pronounces guilty before God, curses, it is the ministration of condemnation and death, and its sentence takes place where the righteousness of Christ is not imputed.

[13] This is accomplished by the laws of men making civil magistrates the terrors to evildoers (Rom. 13:3).

The moral law of God, though it does not give life, becomes a rule of life to the believer in Christ and is therefore of great use to him also. It points out the Christian's duty to God and man and what is to be avoided (Psa. 119:105; Rom. 12:1, 2). Therefore, though believers are freed from the Law, yet we are *not without law to God, but under the law to Christ* (I Cor. 9:21). Christians approach the Law not at Sinai but in Christ. It is a mirror by which the saint constantly reminds himself of his own imperfection when compared to the imputed righteousness of Christ. The Psalmist said:

> I have seen an end of all perfection: but thy commandment is exceeding broad (Psa. 119:96).[14]

The Law is not only a glass to magnify our sin, but the righteousness of Christ is a glass to magnify the Law and make it honorable. Therefore, the saint's desire is to be found in Christ, as Paul proclaimed:

> And be found in him, not having mine own righteousness, which is of the law, but that which is through the faith of Christ, the righteousness which is of God by faith (Phil. 3:9).

In the sense we have just described, the Law continues today. It is in this sense that Christ did not come to destroy the Law or to loosen our obligations to its moral demands. These obligations have not been nullified but neither do they give life. What has been nullified is the Law's power to condemn the believer when he sins. In that sense it has been *done away*, and saints are *delivered* from it – *that being dead wherein* they *were held*, as in a prison; they *become dead to it by the body of Christ*, that is, by His obedient suffering under it—

> Wherefore, my brethren, ye also are become dead to the law by the body of Christ; that ye should be married to another, *even* to him who is raised from the dead, that we should bring forth fruit unto God. For when we were in the flesh, the motions of sins, which were by the law, did work in our members to bring forth fruit unto death. But now we are delivered from

---

[14] The commandment is broad, to which the imperfect works of the saint are not commensurate.

the law, that being dead wherein we were held; that we should serve in newness of spirit, and not *in* the oldness of the letter (Rom. 7:4-6).

The Law does not continue as a covenant of works for salvation because it never was such, though it was a covenant of works for Israel's possession of the Promised Land. The Jews turned it into a covenant of works for salvation and sought righteousness and life by it. But God has never made a covenant of works for salvation since the fall of man because it never was in the power of man to meet such conditions.

So, in what sense is the Mosaic Law abrogated and the New Covenant inaugurated? First, the old administration was only intended to continue for a time, until a period called *The time of reformation* (Heb. 9:10), when there would be a reform from burdensome rites and ceremonies. The ceremonial law was the schoolmaster until Christ came, which was when—*the fullness of time was come, God sent forth his Son, made of a woman, made under the law* (Gal. 4:4). This was agreed upon by the council of the Trinity before the foundation of the world, so that Jews would no longer need their ceremonial schoolmaster (Galatians 3:24, 25).

Secondly, the Mosaic Law, in its course of time, was limited to Jewish People in the Promised Land, worshipping at a specified place, and sacrificing on the same altar (Psa. 147:19, 20; Rom. 3:1, 2; 9:4). All their males were obligated to appear at Jerusalem three times a year and worship together. Their offerings and sacrifices were to be presented on the altar there, and no where else (Deut. 12:11, 14; 16:16). The people of all nations could never have been convened into one country, and worshiped at one place, and have sacrificed on one altar.

Thirdly, it was foretold that Mosaic sacrifices would cease, and be no more acceptable to God.[15] These offerings never were in as high esteem with God as the true condition of the heart—

---

[15] If you are a millennarian you will see that there is a ceremonial/sacrificial system there but its details are definitely not Mosaic. There will be a temple (Ez. 40:39, 40). There will be a priesthood and an altar at this temple (Ez. 43:18-27; Jer. 33:16-18). There will be offerings for the Sabbath (Ez 46:1-5; Isa. 66:23). There will be offerings for the New Moon (Ez. *(Continued on next page)*

> Hath the LORD as great delight in burnt offerings and sacrifices, as in obeying the voice of the LORD? Behold, to obey is better than sacrifice, and to hearken than the fat of rams (I Sam. 15:22).
>
> I will praise the name of God with a song, and will magnify him with thanksgiving. This also shall please the LORD better than an ox or bullock that hath horns and hoofs (Psa. 69:30, 31).
>
> For I desired mercy, and not sacrifice; and the knowledge of God more than burnt offerings (Hosea 6:6).

Jer. 31:31, 32 prophesied that the Old Covenant would be replaced by the New and is reiterated in Heb. 8:13:

> In that he saith, A new covenant, he hath made the first old. Now that which decayeth and waxeth old is ready to vanish away.

David said it when he proclaimed:

> Sacrifice and offering thou didst not desire; mine ears hast thou opened: burnt offering and sin offering hast thou not required. Then said I, Lo, I come: in the volume of the book it is written of me (Psa. 40:6, 7).

The writer of Hebrews affirmed the same words (Heb. 10:5-7).[16]

The Scriptures give several reasons why the Mosaic system must cease. First, it was a covenant of types for a people who were a

---

46:6-8). There will be Millennial sacrifices (Isa. 56:7). There will be Levites with new job descriptions (Mal. 3:2-4). There will be Gentile worship (Zech. 14:16). And there will be funerals (Isa. 65:20). But all of this is not the Mosaic system that was abrogated. These rituals will serve the Millennial saints as Baptism and Communion serve Church Age saints. They are the testimonies of believers pointing retrospectively back to the Cross of Christ as the object of faith.

[16] The Prophet Jeremiah prophesied the same thing in 3:16.

type of the true spiritual people of God, both Jews and Gentiles. The works, duties, and services required of them with so much strictness, rigor, and severity, were typical of the obedience of Christ. The blessings of the Mosaic system were typical shadows of good and spiritual blessings that were to come by Christ (Hebrews 9:11; 10:1). The land of Canaan was a type of their eternal inheritance on the same land.[17] The city of Jerusalem was a type of the New Jerusalem which, *hath foundations, whose builder and maker is God* (Heb. 11:10).[18] The sacrifices, the priests who offered them, the garments they wore, were only examples and shadows of heavenly things (Heb. 8:4, 5; 9:23). Moses, the mediator of the old covenant, was typical of Christ, the mediator of the New Covenant. The blood of the Mosaic sacrifices was typical of the blood of Christ—called: *the blood of the everlasting covenant* (Heb. 9:18; 13:20). When the Antitype of all these came, the types ceased—*Which are a shadow of things to come; but the body is of Christ* (Col. 2:17).

The Mosaic system must pass away because it was faulty—

> For if that first covenant had been faultless, then should no place have been sought for the second. For finding fault with them, he saith, Behold, the days come, saith the Lord, when I will make a new covenant with the house of Israel and with the house of Judah (Heb. 8:7, 8).

It did not exhibit Christ in Person but only in figure, promise and prophecy. It pointed to salvation in Christ but did not offer salvation in itself. It could not make propitiation, reconciliation, or satisfaction for

---

[17] Though the Promised Land was a land of milk and honey, the curse was still there; weeds were still there; poisonous snakes were still there and carnivorous predators were still there. It was good but it was only a type of the prophetic Promised Land with the curse lifted (Isa. 11). And this is a type of the Christian who is delivered from bondage and condemnation and now possesses eternal life. This is better than being lost and condemned but he is still in a physical body that is under a curse. He is quickened but he waits for the quickening of his body (Rom. 8:11). He is redeemed but he groans with all creation and waits for the redemption of his body (Rom. 8:22, 23).

[18] The Old Jerusalem waiting for the New Jerusalem illustrates the redeemed saint in a corruptible body waiting to put on incorruption; a mortal body waiting to put on immortality (I Cor. 15:51-58).

sin, nor redemption from it (Rom. 3:25; Heb. 9:15). The sacrifices were imperfect, and, for some sins, there were no sacrifices appointed, such as for sabbath-breaking, murder, and adultery. The sacrifices that were appointed could not take sins away. They sanctified only *to the purifying of the flesh* but could not clear the conscience to purge it from dead works. Only the blood of Christ could do that (Heb. 9:13, 14).

The old system was faulty in its being a state of darkness and obscurity. But, in reality, most Israelites *could not stedfastly look to the end of that which is abolished*, (i.e. the ceremonial law, II Cor. 3:13:b). Most Jews could not see the end and design of the ceremonies, rituals and ordinances. Though there were promises of grace, they were covered with the veil of ceremonies of which the veil on the glory of Moses' face was only a type (II Cor. 3:7, 13).

The old system was faulty because it was a state of bondage, as signified by Hagar the bondwoman (Gal. 4:30, 31), and by Mount Sinai, which tended to bondage and answered to Jerusalem (Gal. 4:3, 24, 25). They, through fear of physical death, were all their lives subject to bondage (Heb. 2:15).

The Apostle Paul calls the old rites and ceremonies *weak and beggarly elements* (Gal. 4:9) and therefore they were disannulled because of their weakness and unprofitableness—

> For there is verily a disannulling of the commandment going before for the weakness and unprofitableness thereof. For the law made nothing perfect, but the bringing in of a better hope did; by the which we draw nigh unto God   (Heb. 7:18,19).

They could not take sin from the conscience nor from the sight of God, so that there would be no more remembrance of them. Notwithstanding the morning and evening sacrifices, in addition to all others, there was an annual remembrance made of sin again on the Day of Atonement (Heb. 9:9; 10:1-4).

The abrogation of the old system was signified by the rending of the veil between the holy place and the holy of holies at the death of Christ, because Christ is now our way into the holiest. And now, with boldness and freedom, we enter in to the holiest of all by the blood of

Jesus, a new and living way, consecrated through the veil of His flesh, of which the former veil was a type—

> Having therefore, brethren, boldness to enter into the holiest by the blood of Jesus, By a new and living way, which he hath consecrated for us, through the veil, that is to say, his flesh (Heb. 10:19-20).

The ceremonial law enclosed the court of the Israelites in the temple, over which the Gentiles might not pass.[19] The abrogation of the old system broke down *the middle wall of partition* which stood between Jews and Gentiles (Eph. 2:14-16). This is also called *a bloting out the hand-writing of ordinances that was against us*, in which Christ nailed it to His cross, where the wrath of God was poured out and where the justice and holiness of God were satisfied (Colossians 2:14).[20]

Now, it must be observed that the abrogation of the old system and the inauguration of the new were both accomplished in Christ, but implemented gradually and in stages. A misunderstanding of this could lead to great confusion. The writer of Hebrews suggests as much when he says:

> In that he saith, A new covenant, he hath made the first old. Now that which decayeth and waxeth old is ready to vanish away (Heb. 8:13).

The old system began to decay at the Babylonian captivity and under the second temple. The old temple was burnt, temple worship and service ceased, and the vessels of it were carried to Babylon. During the return when the temple was rebuilt and worship restored, the ark and

---

[19] Paul was falsely accused of taking Greeks into the court of the Israelites and thus defiling the temple (Acts 21:28, 29). But what if he had? For Paul knew that such had been abolished— "For he is our peace, who hath made both one, and hath broken down the middle wall of partition *between us*; Having abolished in his flesh the enmity, *even* the law of commandments *contained* in ordinances; for to make in himself of twain one new man, *so* making peace; And that he might reconcile both unto God in one body by the cross, having slain the enmity thereby" (Eph. 2:14-16)

[20] This is signified by the fleeing away and disappearance of *shadows*. When the Sun of Righteousness arose, these shadows fled. Cf. Canticles 2:17; 4:6.

many other things were not there. The sect of the Pharisees arose and set up their own traditions on a level with the written word, if not above it, and there was great confusion when the priesthood and civil government became blended together. The priesthood was often obtained by corruption and bribery. Then came John the Baptist saying: *Behold the Lamb of God, which taketh away the sin of the world* (Jn. 1:29)— which the Mosaic sacrifices could not do. Yet the Law continued during John's ministry. Jesus himself was circumcised on the eighth day, at twelve years of age He went up to Jerusalem with His parents to keep the Passover, and, upon entering His public ministry, He attended synagogue and temple worship. When He healed the leper, He sent him to the priest to offer his gift. He kept the Passover with His disciples. But at His death, all Mosaic ceremonies ceased, as Luke expressed it:

> For I say unto you, that this that is written must yet be accomplished in me, And he was reckoned among the transgressors: for the things concerning me have an end (Lk. 22:37).
>
> For Christ is the end of the law for righteousness to every one that believeth (Rom. 10:4).

Yet *they of the circumcision* had such strong influence over weak minds that it was thought advisable to continue the ceremonies into the new dispensation even after it was known by Peter and others that they were no longer in force. Because of the many "thousands" of Jewish converts, who were still zealous for Mosaic ceremony, it was judged proper that compliances should be made (Acts 21:23-29). But the saints were exhorted to stand fast in the liberty wherewith Christ had made them free, and not to be entangled again with the yoke of bondage (Gal. 5:1). Indeed, the Jews continued these sacrifices and ceremonies until the destruction of Jerusalem [70 A.D.], which put an historical end to them, for the law specified that sacrifices could only be offered upon the altar at Jerusalem. The Epistle to the Hebrews was written just shortly before Jerusalem's destruction. This is why there is such an emphasis on the decay of the old covenant as waxen old and *ready to vanish away* (Heb. 8:13).

It is also important to notice that the New Covenant is gradually introduced. Did it begin at the birth of Christ, the ministry of

Where Does *Law* Factor Into Christianity?

John the Baptist, the death of Christ, His resurrection, His ascension, the baptism of the Holy Spirit on the day of Pentecost, or during the Millennium as Jeremiah prophesied?[21] At the birth of Christ *the fullness of time* was come for the redemption of His people from the law and from their enemies. It was on that day that the Gospel was preached by the angels to the shepherds, but later even more clearly by John the Baptist, then by Christ and finally by His apostles. Mark notes the beginning of the gospel of Jesus Christ the Son of God to be with the ministry of John the Baptist (Mk. 1:1-3), which agrees with what Christ said:

> The law and the prophets were until John: since that time the kingdom of God is preached, and every man presseth into it (Lk. 16:16).

And yet grace and truth came by Jesus Christ more clearly and fully than ever before (Jn. 1:17). He not only preached that the kingdom of heaven was at hand, as John did, but that it had already come (Lk 17:20-21), though not with the pomp and victory that will be displayed at His second coming and during the millennium. By His death and shed blood, the New Covenant was sealed, ratified, and confirmed by Himself as its Testator. Therefore, His blood is called: *the blood of the New Testament,* and *the blood of the everlasting Covenant* (Matt. 26:28; Heb 13:20). But the new covenant appeared even more clearly at the ascension and at the baptism of the Holy Spirit, for Christ ordered them to not yet begin carrying out the great commission (Matt. 28:18-20), but instead, to tarry at Jerusalem until they were endued with the power of the Holy Spirit. Yet again, Jer. 31:31-34 speaks of aspects of the New Covenant that will be fulfilled only during the Millennium.[22] The plan

---

[21] The New Covenant is everlasting (Isa. 55:3), of peace (Ez. 34:25), of life (Mal. 2:5), God is its author (Eph. 2:4), God's love is its cause (John 3:16), Christ is its Mediator (I Tim. 2:5), it originated in eternity past (Rom. 8:29,30), it was introduced when man fell (Gen. 3:15), it was realized at Christ's death (Eph. 2:13-22), the apostles were ministers of it to both Jews and Gentiles (II Cor. 3:6), it has promises just to the Jews (Heb. 8:8), it replaces the Old Covenant (Heb. 8:13), it will be consummated in the millennium and into eternity future (Eph. 2:7).

[22] The O.T. saints, and even angels, only understood the ancient prophecies of the coming New Covenant to anticipate one advent of the Messiah. This is why the wise men, the shepherds, and even the angels thought that the birth of Christ was the beginning of the millennium. The Angels sang:
(Continued on next page)

of salvation is complete in Christ and is integral to the New Covenant, but the New Covenant is more than just the plan of Salvation, in that it contains millennial promises as well.[23]

In the New Covenant, Christ is the author and finisher of our eternal salvation (Heb. 12:2; I Tim. 1:15; 3:16). This gospel was first spoken by Christ in the clearest and fullest manner; and then by His apostles, confirmed by signs and miracles (Mk. 16:19; Heb. 2:3, 4). And the New Covenant with its plan of eternal salvation is seen in ordinances more spiritual than the old ordinances, the latter of which are called *carnal*. Baptism and the Lord's Supper do not teach us about the gospel but are our testimony of what we already know. They are not our schoolmasters but our testimonies of what we are already assured that Christ has accomplished in order to save us eternally.

Some of the reasons why Old Testament Jews stumbled over Christ, the *Stumbling Stone*, were: their inability to distinguish fleshly seed of Abraham from the spiritual seed of Abraham, ritual circumcision from spiritual circumcision, present Palestine from eternal Palestine, and corporate Israel from spiritual Israel. Many Jews believed that they were saved eternally by the heredity of Abraham's physical seed. John the Baptist confronted them regarding this when he said:

> And think not to say within yourselves, We have Abraham to our father: for I say unto you, that God is able of these stones to raise up children unto Abraham (Matt. 3:9).[24]

"Glory to God in the highest, and on earth peace, good will toward men" (Lk. 2:14), but Christ said: "Think not that I am come to send peace on earth: I came not to send peace, but a sword" (Matt. 10:34). The New Covenant for Israel in the Millennium will make teachers obsolete in that the earth shall be full of the knowledge of the Lord. This is not true of the Church Age (Jer. 31:31-34).

[23] In the plan of salvation (which is integral to the New Covenant) there is neither Jew nor Greek (Gal. 3:28). And yet the New Covenant contains promises that pertain only to Judah and Israel being recombined as one in a day when no one will need to be taught and when the grace of God will cause saved Jews to obey and follow God's statutes (Jer 31:31-34; Isa. 11:9; Hab. 2:14). The New Covenant promises the preservation of the nation of Israel as a key element (Jer 31:35-37).

[24] See (Ez. 33:24, 25; Jn. 8:39-44, 53; Rom. 9:7, 8).

Where Does *Law* Factor Into Christianity?

They did not think they had a need for salvation if they were Abraham's seed—

> And ye shall know the truth, and the truth shall make you free. They answered him, We be Abraham's seed, and were never in bondage to any man: how sayest thou, Ye shall be made free? (Jn. 8:32,33).

The Apostle Paul tried to show the Jews the difference when he said:

> Men and brethren, children of the stock of Abraham, and whosoever among you feareth God, to you is the word of this salvation sent (Acts 13:26).

Paul knew that they relied on being of the stock of Abraham to save their souls. If any Jew is going to inherit the Promised Land forever by simply being Abraham's stock then the Abrahamic promises are cancelled—

> For if they which are of the law be heirs, faith is made void, and the promise made of none effect (Rom. 4:14).

There are two kinds of Jews and only one of the two inherit forever—

> That is, They which are the children of the flesh, these are not the children of God: but the children of the promise are counted for the seed (Rom. 9:8).

In fact, there will come a day when uncircumcised believers will stand in judgment of lost circumcised Jews—

> And shall not uncircumcision which is by nature, if it fulfil the law, judge thee, who by the letter and circumcision dost transgress the law? For he is not a Jew, which is one outwardly; neither is that circumcision, which is outward in the flesh: But he is a Jew, which is one inwardly; and circumcision is that of the heart, in the spirit, and not in the letter; whose praise is not of men, but of God (Rom. 2:27-29).

Many Jews were certain that ritual-fleshly circumcision and spiritual circumcision were one and the same and therefore on that premise they claimed the eternal promises made to Abraham. Moses taught them differently than this from the very beginning when he wrote: *Circumcise therefore the foreskin of your heart, and be no more stiffnecked.* (Deut. 10:16). Only when the Jewish heart becomes circumcised can he claim the eternal promise in the Abrahamic covenant—

> ...if then their uncircumcised hearts be humbled, and they then accept of the punishment of their iniquity: Then will I remember my covenant with Jacob, and also my covenant with Isaac, and also my covenant with Abraham will I remember; and I will remember the land (Lev. 26:41b,42). Cf. Deut. 30:6.

Jeremiah warned the Jews that failure to learn this truth would provoke God to take their Promised Land from them—

> Circumcise yourselves to the LORD, and take away the foreskins of your heart, ye men of Judah and inhabitants of Jerusalem: lest my fury come forth like fire, and burn that none can quench it, because of the evil of your doings (Jer. 4:4).

Jeremiah taught circumcised Jews that if they did not experience heart circumcision they would experience the same judgment of God reserved for uncircumcised pagans—

> But let him that glorieth glory in this, that he understandeth and knoweth me, that I *am* the LORD which exercise lovingkindness, judgment, and righteousness, in the earth: for in these *things* I delight, saith the LORD. Behold, the days come, saith the LORD, that I will punish all *them which are* circumcised with the uncircumcised; Egypt, and Judah, and Edom, and the children of Ammon, and Moab, and all *that are* in the utmost corners, that dwell in the wilderness: for all *these* nations *are*

uncircumcised, and all the house of Israel *are* uncircumcised in the heart (Jer. 9:24-26).[25]

Many Jews of Ezekiel's day thought that fleshly circumcision was all that qualified them to commune with God in His sanctuary but the prophet taught them differently:

> In that ye have brought *into my sanctuary* strangers, uncircumcised in heart, and uncircumcised in flesh, to be in my sanctuary, to pollute it, *even* my house, when ye offer my bread, the fat and the blood, and they have broken my covenant because of all your abominations. And ye have not kept the charge of mine holy things: but ye have set keepers of my charge in my sanctuary for yourselves. Thus saith the Lord GOD; No stranger, uncircumcised in heart, nor uncircumcised in flesh, shall enter into my sanctuary, of any stranger that *is* among the children of Israel (Ezek. 44:7-9).

Even though Christ was ritually circumcised and ritually baptized, His crucifixion is also called His circumcision and His baptism. It is this latter circumcision and baptism that saves us for eternity—

> In whom also ye are circumcised with the circumcision made without hands, in putting off the body of the sins of the flesh by the circumcision of Christ: Buried with him in baptism, wherein also ye are risen with *him* through the faith of the operation of God, who hath raised him from the dead. And you, being dead in your sins and the uncircumcision of your flesh, hath he quickened together with him, having forgiven you all trespasses; Blotting out the handwriting of ordinances that was against us, which was contrary to us, and took it out of the way, nailing it to his cross (Col. 2:11-14).[26]

---

[25] Jeremiah describes the unreceptive, haughty and proud as having an uncircumcised ear (Jer. 6:10).

[26] "Buried with him in baptism" does not mean that we were baptized to get with Him, but that we were already with Him when we were buried in *(Continued on next page)*

> But I have a baptism to be baptized with; and how am I straitened till it be accomplished (Lk. 12:50)
>
> But Jesus said unto them, Ye know not what ye ask: can ye drink of the cup that I drink of? and be baptized with the baptism that I am baptized with? (Mk. 10:38)

Physical circumcision has nothing to do with becoming a new creature in Christ Jesus—*For in Christ Jesus neither circumcision availeth any thing, nor uncircumcision, but a new creature* (Gal. 6:15). Those who understand this rule are the true spiritual seed of Abraham—

> And as many as walk according to this rule, peace be on them, and mercy, and upon the Israel of God (Gal. 6:16).[27]

There is only one plan of salvation for circumcised Jews and uncircumcised Gentiles—

> Seeing it is one God, which shall justify the circumcision by faith, and uncircumcision through faith (Rom. 3:30).

Gentiles are made partakers of the eternal salvation of the Abrahamic covenant, not by ritual, but by the blood of Christ—

> Wherefore remember, that ye *being* in time past Gentiles in the flesh, who are called Uncircumcision by that which is called the Circumcision in the flesh made by hands; That at that time ye were without Christ, being aliens from the commonwealth of Israel, and strangers from the covenants of promise, having no hope, and without God in the world: But now in Christ Jesus ye who sometimes were far off are made nigh by the blood of Christ (Eph. 2:11-13).

---

water. This concept will be discussed with more detail in chapter nine of this present work.

[27] See (I Cor. 7:18, 19; Gal. 5:2-4).

Where Does *Law* Factor Into Christianity?

The only way a Jew or a Gentile can lay hold of eternal life and promise is through the same faith that Abraham possessed before he was ever circumcised—

> *Cometh* this blessedness then upon the circumcision *only*, or upon the uncircumcision also? for we say that faith was reckoned to Abraham for righteousness. How was it then reckoned? when he was in circumcision, or in uncircumcision? Not in circumcision, but in uncircumcision. And he received the sign of circumcision, a seal of the righteousness of the faith which *he had yet* being uncircumcised: that he might be the father of all them that believe, though they be not circumcised; that righteousness might be imputed unto them also: And the father of circumcision to them who are not of the circumcision only, but who also walk in the steps of that faith of our father Abraham, which *he had* being *yet* uncircumcised. For the promise, that he should be the heir of the world, *was* not to Abraham, or to his seed, through the law, but through the righteousness of faith (Rom. 4:9-13).

We know that the same faith, prior to and distinct from outward ritual, is the only assurance of our own salvation—

> Now it was not written for his sake alone, that it was imputed to him; But for us also, to whom it shall be imputed, if we believe on him that raised up Jesus our Lord from the dead; Who was delivered for our offences, and was raised again for our justification (Rom. 4:23-25).

This chapter may have been difficult for some Christians to read. It might seem to have been an exercise in beating a dead horse because no one in Christendom has argued for circumcision in the plan of salvation for over fifteen hundred years. But, when "Christendom" proclaimed that baptism replaced circumcision, all of the arguments for circumcision became arguments for baptismal regeneration. Particularly was this true in the baptism of infants. Thus, to this very day, millions of professed Christians believe that regeneration, illumination, salvation, and entrance into the spiritual body of Christ are created by, or at least imparted by or through, the ritual of water baptism.[28] The same is believed regarding the Lord's Supper. Both are considered a means of saving grace. It will be the ultimate purpose of this present study to demonstrate that this idea is the old circumcision error with a different name.

So, how does one receive the eternal promise of salvation? First, the sin of Adam is imputed to all mankind. Second, mankind also commits sins. Third, man's sin is imputed to Christ. Fourth, Christ goes to the cross to receive the just wrath of the Father upon His own body in payment and satisfaction for man's sin. Fifth, by God's common grace and His Word, man sees his moral and spiritual bankruptcy before God and may accept forgiveness and eternal life as a one hundred percent free gift from God. Sixth, the righteousness of Christ is imputed to the sinner, pronouncing him sinless before God—

> For he hath made him to be sin for us, who knew no sin; that we might be made the righteousness of God in him (II Cor. 5:21)

In the next chapter we will demonstrate that there has been only one plan of salvation throughout all ages, dispensations, and under all the various covenants of the Bible

---

[28] Stephen J. Wellum defines the paedobaptist position in *The Compromised Church*, John H. Armstrong, Editor (Wheaton, Illinois: Crossway Books, 1998), p. 161—"Those who advocate a paedobaptist position admit that even though there is no explicit command in the New Testament to baptize infants, the practice is still legitimate...Since infants were included in the Old Covenant through circumcision, which was an outward sign of entrance into the covenant community, and since circumcision has been replaced by baptism in the New Covenant, then believing parents are required to administer the New Covenant sign—baptism—to their children..."

Chapter Three
One Plan Of Salvation For All Ages

> The covenant of salvation, reaching down to us from the foundation of the world, through different generations and times, is one—although it is conceived as different in respect of the gift. For it follows that there is one unchangeable gift of salvation given by one God, through one Lord, benefiting in many ways.
>
> *Clement of Alexandria (c. 195, E), 2.504.*

When searching out the true nature of the saving gospel, the honest Christian seeker can easily become bogged down and overwhelmed in a debate regarding the different ways God required sinners lay hold of eternal life throughout the divisional periods of scriptural history. How were people saved from Adam through Noah and on to Abraham? Were Gentiles and children of Abraham saved differently until Moses? Could Gentiles be saved during the Mosaic period without becoming Jewish proselytes? How were people saved in the era of the synagogue when observance of Mosaic ceremonialism during the exilic period was an impossibility? Was the thief on the cross saved under an intermediate gospel between the Mosaic system and the New Testament system? These are deep questions that are taken very seriously by many contemporary theologians.

It will be the purpose of this chapter to demonstrate that there never has been but one plan of salvation for all time. There will be deliberate absence of extensive discussion about covenants, dispensations, degrees of Calvinism, etc. These various concepts do not alter the principle of the imputed righteousness of Christ for salvation. This plan was illustrated differently for educational and testimonial purposes in various divisions of biblical history, but the plan was eternal and unchanging.

God is omniscient (all-knowing), which means that He has nothing to learn, and there is nothing of which He can be ignorant. He is infinite and eternal and therefore knew before all other existence what would transpire as a result of creation. If God is not infinite (without limitation) then He may be supernatural but certainly not God. God knew in eternity past and determined that only one means would be used to ransom fallen man from His fiery wrath—crucifixion of His only begotten Son.[1] From Adam to eternity future the only saving power will have been Christ the crucified Messiah—*The counsel of the LORD standeth for ever, the thoughts of his heart to all generations* (Psa. 33:11). The Psalmist knew that the council of God had established salvation from eternity past when he petitioned Him saying:

> Grant thee according to thine own heart, and fulfil all thy counsel. We will rejoice in thy salvation, and in the name of our God we will set up our banners: the LORD fulfil all thy petitions. Now know I that the LORD saveth his anointed; he will hear him from his holy heaven with the saving strength of his right hand (Psa. 20:4-6).

---

[1] Lewis Sperry Chafer, *Systematic Theology* (Dallas, Texas: Dallas Seminary Press, 1964), 42: "*The Covenant of Redemption* (Titus 1:2; Heb. 13:20) into which, it is usually thought by theologians, the Persons of the Godhead entered before all time and in which each assumed that part in the great plan of redemption which is their present portion as disclosed in the Word of God. In this covenant the Father gives the Son, the Son offers Himself without spot to the Father as an efficacious sacrifice, and the Spirit administers and empowers into the execution of this covenant in all its parts. This covenant rests upon but slight revelation. It is rather sustained largely by the fact that it seems both reasonable and inevitable."

One Plan Of Salvation For All Ages

This plan of salvation in eternity past has been called other names such as: *covenant of redemption, covenant of grace,* or *promise of redemption*. Nothing can be added to this plan nor taken away from it, though the plan's promise of eternal life can be integral to other covenants and contained within other promises. This will be graphically illustrated in a later portion of this book. For all practical purposes, we will refer to it as *the plan of salvation*.

THE PLAN OF SALVATION IN ETERNITY PAST

The purpose of God to save men by grace through faith in Christ the Messiah is the basis of the Trinitarian council held in eternity past—

> …to make all men see what is the fellowship of the mystery, which from the beginning of the world hath been hid in God, who created all things by Jesus Christ: To the intent that now unto the principalities and powers in heavenly places might be known by the church the manifold wisdom of God, According to the eternal purpose which he purposed in Christ Jesus our Lord: In whom we have boldness and access with confidence by the faith of him (Eph. 3:9-12).

So the declaration of this plan of salvation was called the *counsel of God* (Acts 20:27-28). The Apostle Paul declared to the Corinthians:

> For I determined not to know any thing among you, save Jesus Christ, and him crucified…Howbeit we speak wisdom among them that are perfect: yet not the wisdom of this world, nor of the princes of this world, that come to nought: But we speak the wisdom of God in a mystery, even the hidden wisdom, which God ordained before the world unto our glory (I Cor. 2:2, 6, 7).

God the Son was in ready agreement with this eternal plan and said, *lo, I come to do thy will, O God* (Heb. 10:7, 5; Ps. 40:6-8) and again, *a body hast Thou prepared for me*[2]

> For *it is* not possible that the blood of bulls and of goats should take away sins. Wherefore when he cometh into the world, he saith, Sacrifice and offering thou wouldest not, but a body hast thou prepared me: In burnt offerings and *sacrifices* for sin thou hast had no pleasure (Heb. 10:4-6).

If the person presently reading this book is a Christian, he should stop and fathom, for a moment, how far back infinity extends prior to Creation. It is without end, and yet there never was a moment in which Christ did not know and love you by name and plan to die on the cross for your sins. The Apostles and Prophets understood their salvation to have been established before the foundation of the earth— *And all that dwell upon the earth shall worship him, whose names are not written in the book of life of the Lamb slain from the foundation of the world. If any man have an ear, let him* hear (Rev. 13:8, 9) cf. Rev. 17:8.

It was within the eternal council of God that it was predetermined to transfer the guilt of the sinner to Christ, and to transfer the innocence of Christ to the sinner (transferred meaning *imputed*). Isaiah, who prophesied from 790 B.C., expressed imputation very clearly when he said:

---

[2] *The Bible Knowledge Commentary: New Testament Edition*, John F. Walvoord & Roy B. Zuck, Editors (USA: Victor Books, 1983), pp. 803, 804. "The phrase **a body you prepared for Me** is one Septuagint rendering of the Hebrew expression 'You have dug ears for Me'. The Greek translator whose version the author of Hebrews used (obviously translating with the help of the Holy Spirit), construed the Hebrew text as a kind of figure of speech (technically called synecdoche) in which a part is put for the whole. If God is to 'dig out ears' He must 'prepare a body.' This interpretation is both valid and correct as its quotation in Hebrews proves. In the 'body' which He assumed in Incarnation, Christ could say that He had come to achieve what the Old-Covenant sacrifices never achieved, the perfecting of New-Covenant worshipers. In this sense He did God's will."

One Plan Of Salvation For All Ages

> All we like sheep have gone astray; we have turned every one to his own way; and the LORD hath laid on him the iniquity of us all (Isa. 53:6).

And just as Isaiah expressed the imputation of the sinner's iniquities upon Christ, the Apostle proclaims the imputation of Christ's righteousness upon the sinner who believes—*For he hath made him to be sin for us, who knew no sin; that we might be made the righteousness of God in him* (II Cor. 5:21).

Hence He was declared and promised, and expected as the Redeemer, long before He came into the world to do this service. Job knew him as his living Redeemer, and numerous Old Testament saints waited for Him as such, having had a promise of it, which was founded on the eternal council of the Trinity before the foundation of the world. To doubt this truth is to doubt Christ Himself when He said: *Search the scriptures; for in them ye think ye have eternal life: and they are they which testify of me* (Jn. 5:39). And again, when He said:

> Do not think that I will accuse you to the Father: there is one that accuseth you, even Moses, in whom ye trust. For had ye believed Moses, ye would have believed me: for he wrote of me. But if ye believe not his writings, how shall ye believe my words? (Jn. 5:45-47).

The Savior proved this point when He spoke to the doubting disciples on the Emmaus road saying:

> ...O fools, and slow of heart to believe all that the prophets have spoken: Ought not Christ to have suffered these things, and to enter into his glory? And beginning at Moses and all the prophets, he expounded unto them in all the scriptures the things concerning himself (Lk. 24:25-27).

This truth of one unified plan of salvation for all ages was also expressed by the Apostles. The Apostle Peter spoke of it when he said: *To him give all the prophets witness, that through his name whosoever believeth in him shall receive remission of sins* (Acts 10:43). The Apostle Paul spoke of it when he said:

> Therefore by the deeds of the law there shall no flesh be justified in his sight: for by the law is the knowledge of sin. But now the righteousness of God without the law is manifested, being witnessed by the law and the prophets; Even the righteousness of God which is by faith of Jesus Christ unto all and upon all them that believe: for there is no difference (Rom. 3:20-22).

The rituals of any age are only meant to be instructional or educational illustrations pointing to the finished work of Christ on the Cross. The writer of the Epistle of Hebrews called Mosaic rituals the *shadow* of the coming Messiah and His salvation:

> For the law having a shadow of good things to come, and not the very image of the things, can never with those sacrifices which they offered year by year continually make the comers thereunto perfect. For then would they not have ceased to be offered? because that the worshippers once purged should have had no more conscience of sins. But in those sacrifices there is a remembrance again made of sins every year. For it is not possible that the blood of bulls and of goats should take away sins. Wherefore when he cometh into the world, he saith, Sacrifice and offering thou wouldest not, but a body hast thou prepared me: In burnt offerings and sacrifices for sin thou hast had no pleasure. Then said I, Lo, I come (in the volume of the book it is written of me,) to do thy will, O God (Heb. 10:1-7).

This is precisely why there never was a time when animal sacrifices could have taken away sin, not even in the daily sacrifices of the Mosaic priests—

> By the which will we are sanctified through the offering of the body of Jesus Christ once for all. And every priest standeth daily ministering and offering oftentimes the same sacrifices, which can never take away sins: But this man, after he had offered one sacrifice for sins for ever, sat down on the right hand

of God; From henceforth expecting till his enemies be made his footstool. For by one offering he hath perfected for ever them that are sanctified (Heb. 10:10-14).

THE PLAN OF SALVATION BEFORE THE FLOOD

Concerning Christ and His saving grace, Zacharias, the father of John the Baptist, prophesied before the New Testament was ever written, saying:

> Blessed *be* the Lord God of Israel; for he hath visited and redeemed his people, And hath raised up an horn of salvation for us in the house of his servant David; As he spake by the mouth of his holy prophets, which have been since the world began: That we should be saved from our enemies, and from the hand of all that hate us; To perform the mercy *promised* to our fathers, and to remember his holy covenant; The oath which he sware to our father Abraham, That he would grant unto us, that we being delivered out of the hand of our enemies might serve him without fear, In holiness and righteousness before him, all the days of our life. And thou, child, shalt be called the prophet of the Highest: for thou shalt go before the face of the Lord to prepare his ways; To give knowledge of salvation unto his people by the remission of their sins, Through the tender mercy of our God; whereby the dayspring from on high hath visited us (Lk. 1:68-78; cf. Ps. 89:2,3.).

Eternal life was indeed made known in the earliest writings of the Old Testament and was believed, looked for, and expected by the multitudes of saints from the beginning. In the Old Testament, many saints looked forward to the Christ that was to come, but in the New Testament believers look backwards to Christ as having already come.

Adam and Eve first received the promise while overhearing God's words to the serpent in Gen. 3:15. Adam and Eve discovered that they were not to die immediately, but that a seed should be of the woman Who would be the ruin of Satan and the Savior of them. Here we see the incarnation of the son of God signified by the *seed of the woman*. We see the sufferings and death of Christ signified by the serpent's *bruising his heel.* The crucifixion of Jesus is sometimes expressed by his being bruised for his people.[3] Again, the victory that Christ would accomplish over Satan is prophesied by *bruising his head.*

The plan of salvation by grace was illustrated again when the Lord made coats of skin for Adam and Eve. These were the skins of slain beasts, thus pointing to the sacrifice of Christ, the woman's Seed, which would be offered up. These sins covered their nakedness but only pointed to the true covering of their sin. The fact that God would not allow them to cover their own nakedness with fig leaves demonstrated man's helplessness to make himself righteous before God.

Consider Adam's son, Abel. He is called *righteous* Abel. Not his own righteousness; otherwise, he would not have needed a sacrifice for his sins in the first place. It was the righteousness of faith which he possessed before he performed the sacrifice. This was nothing less than the righteousness of Christ received by faith. He was looking to Christ for eternal life, as when the writer of Hebrews said:

> By faith Abel offered unto God a more excellent sacrifice than Cain, by which he obtained witness that he was righteous, God testifying of his gifts: and by it he being dead yet speaketh (Heb. 11:4).

His sacrifice was a more excellent one by being a lamb, and thus typified the Lamb of God. It was also more excellent by the manner in which it was offered—by faith. He did not offer the sacrifice to obtain faith but, offered it by faith, in view of a better sacrifice—the sacrifice of Christ.

Skipping over to the days of Enos we see the effects of divine grace when *Men began to call upon the name of the Lord* (Gen. 4:25-26). In doing this they met the Lord, Who is the only literal mediator between God and man—*For whosoever shall call upon the name of the Lord shall be saved* (Rom. 10:13).

Though perhaps thousands were made partakers of the grace of God at this time, the Bible takes special notice of Enoch. He had a testimony that he pleased God, which he could not have without faith,

---

[3] See Isa. 53:5, 10

for...*without faith it is impossible to please him* (Heb. 11:6a). He drew near and walked with God, thus enjoying communion with Him. He was even anointed with a spirit of prophecy with which he foretold of a future judgment and the coming of Christ to perform it.[4] If he was conversant with the second coming of Christ, he would have understood the aspects of His first coming, for the Old Testament foresaw all of the advent of the Messiah as one coming. It could only have been God's grace that took Enoch from the earth before the judgment of the flood. He was translated in faith and the object of his faith was Christ.[5]

THE PLAN OF SALVATION FROM NOAH TO ABRAHAM

Lamech, Noah's father, foresaw something remarkable in his son saying: *This same shall comfort us concerning our work and toil of our hands, because of the ground which the Lord hath cursed* (Gen. 5:29). Therefore Lamech called his name *Noah,* meaning *comfort.* Noah was perhaps divinely gifted to be an inventor of tools, not only for carpentry, but for cultivating the earth and facilitating progress in agriculture, whereby the curse upon the earth was lightened. This indeed was a gift of God's grace in that no fallen man ever deserved to have his curse lightened.

Perhaps Lamech had something even more spiritual in mind by his words toward Noah. Might he have been hoping that Noah would be the promised seed, the Messiah, the Consolation from whom all comfort flows, the Savior of men from their evil works, and from the curses of the fall? Was he the promised *seed* who would ease them from the toil

---

[4] (Jude 14) "And Enoch also, the seventh from Adam, prophesied of these, saying, Behold, the Lord cometh with ten thousands of his saints, To execute judgment upon all, and to convince all that are ungodly among them of all their ungodly deeds which they have ungodly committed, and of all their hard *speeches* which ungodly sinners have spoken against him." Though Jude is quoting from the apocryphal *Book of Enoch* the concept is inscripturated under Divine inspiration and must be allowed to factor into the Genesis record.

[5] (Heb. 11:5,6) "By faith Enoch was translated that he should not see death; and was not found, because God had translated him: for before his translation he had this testimony, that he pleased God. But without faith *it is* impossible to please *him*: for he that cometh to God must believe that he is, and *that* he is a rewarder of them that diligently seek him."

and labor of their hands? This is precisely what the Messiah will do at His second coming when he lifts the curse from the ground.[6]

Noah was at least a type of Christ in Whom was a rich display of the eternal saving grace of God. When God determined to destroy the earth and the inhabitants thereof, it was said: *"But Noah found grace in the eyes of the LORD"* (Gen. 6:8). This means that he was an heir of the righteousness of faith, which is nothing less than the imputed righteousness of Christ—

> By faith Noah, being warned of God of things not seen as yet, moved with fear, prepared an ark to the saving of his house; by the which he condemned the world, and became heir of the righteousness which is by faith (Heb. 11:7).

This was the unmerited favor of God which Noah found before he ever cut the first timber to build the ark in obedience to God's command. He was a justified man, a perfect man and one who shared communion with God.[7] We know that he could not have justified nor perfected himself before God in his own righteousness. Therefore, his communion with God was grounded on the imputed righteousness of Christ.

In his public ministry Noah was a *Preacher of righteousness* in three regards: that which is done between man and man, the righteousness of God in bringing a flood upon the world to destroy it, and also of the righteousness of Christ; for he must have been a preacher of that of which he was a heir.[8] During his 120 years in which he had preached, God's longsuffering was being manifest with eternal consequences.[9]

---

[6] (Rev. 22:3) "And there shall be no more curse: but the throne of God and of the Lamb shall be in it; and his servants shall serve him."

[7] (Gen. 6:9) "…Noah was a just man *and* perfect in his generations, *and* Noah walked with God."

[8] (II Pet. 2:5) "And spared not the old world, but saved Noah the eighth *person*, a preacher of righteousness, bringing in the flood upon the world of the ungodly."

[9] (I Pet. 3:19, 20) "By which also he went and preached unto the spirits in prison; Which sometime were disobedient, when once the longsuffering of God waited in the days of Noah, while the ark was a preparing, wherein few, that is, eight souls were saved by water."

The ark itself would become a grand illustration of God's grace. The ark became a type of Christ, the shelter from the tempest of divine wrath and vindictive justice, and in whom spiritual rest is to be had for weary souls. When the dove was let out of the ark it found no rest until it returned. Although the flood was not God's eternal wrath, and the ark was not His eternal justification, eternal salvation was typified when the temporal boat saved eight people from a temporal judgment.[10] Noah's salvation by grace from temporal judgment became a type of his salvation from eternal judgment—a salvation that was his when he found grace, justification, perfection, and communion from God before he ever entered the ark.

Noah's sacrifices upon exiting the ark became a picture of the sacrifice of Christ in the fact that they were clean animals (Gen. 8:20); expressing the purity of Christ as a Lamb who offered Himself without spot to the Father for the sins of the undeserving, of whom Noah was numbered. It was a picture of the sacrifice of Christ in respect to God's acceptance of it...*And the Lord smelled a sweet savour* (Gen. 8:21a), meaning that God was well-pleased with the sacrifices and graciously accepted them. This is the same phrase used of Christ's sacrifice when Paul told the Ephesians to, *walk in love, as Christ also hath loved us, and hath given himself for us an offering and a sacrifice to God for a sweetsmelling savour* (Eph. 5:2).

Noah again displayed God's grace as he blessed his son saying: *Blessed be the LORD God of Shem* (Gen. 9:26). To be the personal God of any person is the sum and substance of eternal salvation by grace, which God expresses when he says, *I will be their God.*

THE PLAN OF SALVATION FROM ABRAHAM TO MOSES

Abraham is a dynamic example of God's saving grace. He was justified by faith in the righteousness of Christ. His faith was not an act of saving righteousness, but it was *counted to him for righteousness* (Gen. 15:6b). Not the act of faith, but the object of faith imputed perfect righteousness to him, and what was imputed to him is imputed to all in all ages who believe in the imputed righteousness of Christ. Abraham's

---

[10] (I Pet. 3:20) "...while the ark was a preparing, wherein few, that is, eight souls were saved by water." Note that they were saved in the ark and through the water, not by the water. (The NIV reads *saved through water*).

faith was not a meritorious work of any kind, as the Apostle Paul confirms when he asks:

> What shall we say then that Abraham our father, as pertaining to the flesh, hath found? For if Abraham were justified by works, he hath whereof to glory; but not before God. For what saith the scripture? Abraham believed God, and it was counted unto him for righteousness. Now to him that worketh is the reward not reckoned of grace, but of debt. But to him that worketh not, but believeth on him that justifieth the ungodly, his faith is counted for righteousness (Rom. 4:1-5).

This was a righteousness of faith which Abraham had before he ever obeyed God in circumcision, as Paul asked: *How was it then reckoned? when he was in circumcision, or in uncircumcision? Not in circumcision, but in uncircumcision* (Rom. 4:10).

The faith that Abraham possessed, independent of his works and acts of obedience, was the same faith that made him the father of all believers in all ages—

> And he received the sign of circumcision, a seal of the righteousness of the faith which he had yet being uncircumcised: that he might be the father of all them that believe, though they be not circumcised; that righteousness might be imputed unto them also (Rom. 4:11).

When Paul spoke of Abraham's faith being independent of Law, he was not speaking of the Mosaic in particular, but of any law of works:

> For the promise, that he should be the heir of the world, was not to Abraham, or to his seed, through the law, but through the righteousness of faith (Rom. 4:13).

One Plan Of Salvation For All Ages

Adding a law of works to faith makes faith void and the promise of God of none effect—

> For if they which are of the law be heirs, faith is made void, and the promise made of none effect (Rom. 4:14).

When Paul was speaking to the Galatians of Abraham's saving faith, he mentioned its relationship to law when he said:

> ...for if there had been a law given which could have given life, verily righteousness should have been by the law. But the scripture hath concluded all under sin, that the promise by faith of Jesus Christ might be given to them that believe (Gal. 3:21b, 22).

Make no mistake, Abraham staggered often. He was told to leave his kindred in Ur of the Chaldees, but he began instead in disobedience by taking his father and nephew with him. Instead of following God to the Promised Land, he stopped in Haran, the capital of moon worship, until his father died. We will not even begin to list the times that he lied about his marital status in order to save his life. Why was this disobedient man saved? Because—

> He staggered not at the promise of God through unbelief; but was strong in faith, giving glory to God; And being fully persuaded that, what he had promised, he was able also to perform. And therefore it was imputed to him for righteousness (Rom. 4:20-22).

It is essential to know that Abraham's faith was not an act of saving virtue (cf. 4:5; II Pet. 1:5), but rather, the sinless virtue of Christ was imputed to him because of his faith in Christ as redeemer. That Christ was the object of his faith is made clear as we are taught to accept eternal life on the same grounds, for—

> ... it was not written for his sake alone, that it was imputed to him; But for us also, to whom it shall be imputed, if we believe on him that raised up Jesus our Lord from the dead; Who was delivered for our offences, and was raised again for our justification (Rom. 4:23-25).

Are we reading into the story of Abraham when we say that the object of his faith was a coming redeemer? Certainly not. Abraham was personally visited by Christ and given the gospel, with the promise that it would be for Gentiles as well as his own seed. The Apostle Paul cited this very fact when he said:

> And the scripture, foreseeing that God would justify the heathen through faith, preached before the gospel unto Abraham, saying, In thee shall all nations be blessed (Gal. 3:8).

When God told Abraham that all the families of earth would be blessed in his *seed* he understood this to be the person of Christ and not the nation that would proceed from his loins—

> Now to Abraham and his seed were the promises made. He saith not, And to seeds, as of many; but as of one, And to thy seed, which is Christ (Gal. 3:16).[11]

The Apostle Paul wanted every believer to know that the saving gospel promise is unconditional, and therefore cannot be disannulled. This he communicated to the Galatians when he wrote:

> Brethren, I speak after the manner of men; Though it be but a man's covenant, yet if it be confirmed, no man disannulleth, or addeth thereto (Gal. 3:15).[12]

Absolutely nothing about the Mosaic Law was to be considered an addition to the plan of salvation promised to Abraham. Again, Paul writes:

---

[11] It is not our purpose in this present chapter to discuss all the ramifications of the Abrahamic Covenant, but only to discern the gospel aspect within it.

[12] Now the Laws of Moses did not constitute such an unconditional promise and therefore can be annulled— (Heb. 7:18,19) "For there is verily a disannulling of the commandment going before for the weakness and unprofitableness thereof. For the law made nothing perfect, but the bringing in of a better hope *did*; by the which we draw nigh unto God."

One Plan Of Salvation For All Ages

> And this I say, that the covenant, that was confirmed before of God in Christ, the law, which was four hundred and thirty years after, cannot disannul, that it should make the promise of none effect. For if the inheritance be of the law, it is no more of promise: but God gave it to Abraham by promise (Gal. 3:17-18).

When God presented the Gospel of the heathen to Abraham, He was able see the coming of Christ the redeemer, as the Savior Himself testified when He said:

> Your father Abraham rejoiced to see my day: and he saw it, and was glad. Then said the Jews unto him, Thou art not yet fifty years old, and hast thou seen Abraham? Jesus said unto them, Verily, verily, I say unto you, Before Abraham was, I am (Jn. 8:56-58).

It was in the salvation of the Gentiles, who would follow in the steps of Abraham's faith, that he knew that he would be the *father of many nations*—

> Therefore *it is* of faith, that *it might be* by grace; to the end the promise might be sure to all the seed; not to that only which is of the law, but to that also which is of the faith of Abraham; who is the father of us all, (As it is written, I have made thee a father of many nations), (Rom. 4:16, 17a; cf. Gen. 22:18).

Actually, God manifested the Gospel to Abraham several times. The first was when he was told to leave Ur of the Chaldees (Gen. 12:1-3); cf. Gal. 3:18—

> For if the inheritance *be* of the law, *it is* no more of promise: but God gave *it* to Abraham by promise.

The second was in Gen. 15:1 when God spoke to him in a vision saying: *I am thy shield, and thy exceeding great reward*, speaking of his reward in this life and the life to come. His reward in this life was his natural seed and a promise of the land of Canaan to his posterity, but his eternal reward was a city in the eternal state of Palestine after the resurrection— *For he looked for a city which hath foundations, whose builder and maker is God* (Heb. 11:10). The third manifestation took place when

Abraham was ninety-nine years of age (Gen. 17). Then he was told that he would be the father of many nations. The fourth manifestation was in the plains of Mamre (Gen. 18), where three angels appeared to him in human form. One of the three was Jehovah, the Son of God, who told Abraham of His plans to destroy Sodom. God graciously allowed Abraham to stand before him and plead for the wicked city, which showed him to be the friend of God indeed.

As a parenthesis let us look at Lot, the nephew of Abraham. Is this the man who chose to live in that wicked city and who gave his virgin daughters to its men to be molested? Is this the same man who impregnated the same two daughters and fathered the Ammonites and Moabites? And yet, while living in Sodom he was a possessor of justification by faith in the coming Redeemer—

> And turning the cities of Sodom and Gomorrha into ashes condemned them with an overthrow, making them an ensample unto those that after should live ungodly; And delivered just Lot, vexed with the filthy conversation of the wicked: (For that righteous man dwelling among them, in seeing and hearing, vexed his righteous soul from day to day with their unlawful deeds;) The Lord knoweth how to deliver the godly out of temptations, and to reserve the unjust unto the day of judgment to be punished (II Pet. 2:6-9-).

The fifth manifestation of God's grace took place in God's command for Abraham to sacrifice his only son on a mountain in Moriah (Gen. 22). Isaac was carrying the wood even as Christ carried His wooden cross toward His crucifixion. But Isaac queried about the absence of any sacrificial animals for this trip, at which point Abraham made his great prophetic utterance: *My son, God will provide himself a lamb for a burnt offering* (Gen. 22:8). When the moment came for Abraham to thrust the knife into the heart of his son, God then restrained him from the actual performance of the task and drew his attention to a ram caught in a thicket to be used as a sacrifice instead. Abraham therefore called the name of that place *Yahweh Jireh,* (the Lord will provide), (Gen. 22:14). Abraham was no doubt made to understand his own prophetic words when God exclaimed in verse 18a: *And in thy seed shall all the nations of the earth be blessed....* Abraham knew full well that God would provide Himself (in the form of His son Jesus Christ) as

One Plan Of Salvation For All Ages

the only acceptable sacrifice for sin. Again, Paul proves this very fact when he affirms:

> Now to Abraham and his seed were the promises made. He saith not, And to seeds, as of many; but as of one, And to thy seed, which is Christ (Gal. 3:16).

Abraham was so certain of God's promise of a redeemer that he knew it would be impossible for Isaac to remain dead. He believed that, even if he were successful in killing and burning his son, the boy would be immediately raised from the dead and they would walk home together. Therefore, in a sense, he did receive Isaac from the dead, as the Scriptures said:

> By faith Abraham, when he was tried, offered up Isaac: and he that had received the promises offered up his only begotten son, Of whom it was said, That in Isaac shall thy seed be called: Accounting that God was able to raise him up, even from the dead; from whence also he received him in a figure (Heb. 11:17-19).

And let us not forget the interview Abraham had with Melchizedek, who met him on his return from the slaughter of the kings (Gen. 19), and blessed him in the name of the Most High God. This man was an eminent type of Christ. His name and title agree with Christ—*king of righteousness* and *peaceable king*; a priest continually, and of whose order Christ was; and the eternity of Christ shadowed forth in the fact of his genealogy being unknown. Thus we can say that Melchisedek was made like unto the Son of God—

> For this Melchisedec, king of Salem, priest of the most high God, who met Abraham returning from the slaughter of the kings, and blessed him; To whom also Abraham gave a tenth part of all; first being by interpretation King of righteousness, and after that also King of Salem, which is, King of peace; Without father, without mother, without descent, having neither beginning of days, nor end of life; but made like unto the Son of God; abideth a priest continually (Heb. 7:1-3).

Concerning Jesus Christ, the writer of Hebrews says:

> And it is yet far more evident: for that after the similitude of Melchisedec there ariseth another priest, Who is made, not after the law of a carnal commandment, but after the power of an endless life. For he testifieth, Thou art a priest for ever after the order of Melchisedec (Heb. 7:15-17).

And again, he writes:

> But this man, because he continueth ever, hath an unchangeable priesthood. Wherefore he is able also to save them to the uttermost that come unto God by him, seeing he ever liveth to make intercession for them. For such an high priest became us, who is holy, harmless, undefiled, separate from sinners, and made higher than the heavens; Who needeth not daily, as those high priests, to offer up sacrifice, first for his own sins, and then for the people's: for this he did once, when he offered up himself. For the law maketh men high priests which have infirmity; but the word of the oath, which was since the law, maketh the Son, who is consecrated for evermore (Heb. 7:24-28).

Returning once more to Abraham's willingness to sacrifice his son, we see in Isaac an excellent type of Christ. He was Abraham's only son. Isaac went without reluctance, carrying the wood on which he was to be laid. Jesus went as a lamb to the slaughter, bearing on his shoulders the wooden cross on which he was to be sacrificed, and was not spared by his divine father, but delivered up for us all. Isaac was delivered, as from the dead, and went home alive unto his father's house on the third day from the time Abraham reckoned him as a dead man. So Christ was put to death in the flesh, quickened in the Spirit, and ascended again unto His Father's house.

Obviously, we could make the same illusions to the Gospel of grace in the life of Jacob regarding the prediction that the *elder shall serve the younger* (Gen. 25:23), by the ladder reaching into heaven (Gen. 28:12), by Christ appearing in human form to wrestle with him, with whom he so prevailed as to obtain a blessing—getting the name *Israel* (Gen 32:24-28). He even prophesied of the Messiah under the name of Shiloh (*the prosperous* and *the peaceable*), in whose hands the pleasure of the Lord prospered, and who made peace for all men by the blood of his cross, that he should come forth from his son Judah—

> ...The sceptre shall not depart from Judah, nor a lawgiver from between his feet, until Shiloh come; and unto him shall the gathering of the people be (Gen. 49:10)...(also, vs. 18) I have waited for thy salvation, O LORD.

However, we are excited to move forward to the time when the children of Israel were in Egypt, before the time of Moses. Here we have the story of Job and his friends. First, we must note who they were. Eliphaz was the eldest son of Esau and father of several Edomite clans, including Teman (Gen. 36:15-16; I Chron. 1:35). He was the first and, presumably, oldest of Job's three friends (Job 2:11; 4:1; 15:1; 22:1; 42:7, 9). Eliphaz's designation, the Temanite, suggests he was from the area settled by the Edomite clan of Teman. Bildad was a Shuhite (Job 2:11). The meaning of his name is obscure, but may be related to the Edomite king Bedad (Gen. 36:35). The name is compounded with the theophoric element *dad*. *Dad* is the name of the Edomite god. Zophar was a Naamathite (Job. 2:11). We cannot be certain where his home was, except that it was presumably East of Jordan.[13]

Though these three friends were not of Israel, but of the race of Esau, they were thoroughly conversant with the principles of salvation by grace. This had been made known to them as a pledge and earnest of what would be done in later times. Though they misjudged Job's case and misdiagnosed the cause of his afflictions, they knew much of gospel truth. In their speeches we see their understanding of the corruption of nature (25:4-6); of vanity and self-righteousness (4:17-19; 15:14-16); of the great Redeemer as the *Messenger* of the covenant, the uncreated Angel, Christ; as *an interpreter* of His Father's mind and will; *One among a thousand,* whose office it is to *shew unto men his uprightness*; and to be found as a ransom (33:23, 24).

The question arises: Why would such gospel wisdom reside in descendents of Esau? We know that Esau did not inherit the physical blessings of the Abrahamic Covenant, but do we know that God did not

---

[13] In the Septuagint, Zophar is called "king of the Minaeans."

personally desire for him to know the grace of salvation? God made Esau the father of the Edomites and recorded his descendents in Gen. 36: *these be the dukes of Edom, according to their habitations in the land of their possession: he is Esau the father of the Edomites* (vs. 43). Although Esau had no place in the Abrahamic Covenant, God, in His grace, provided a place for him—*And I gave unto Isaac Jacob and Esau: and I gave unto Esau mount Seir, to possess it* (Josh. 24:4).

In Deuteronomy God had clearly expressed his gracious oversight over the descendents of Esau. When Israel departed from Egypt, God warned them not to disturb the Edomites or the possession that He had given them—

> And command thou the people, saying, Ye are to pass through the coast of your brethren the children of Esau, which dwell in Seir; and they shall be afraid of you: take ye good heed unto yourselves therefore: ⁵Meddle not with them; for I will not give you of their land, no, not so much as a foot breadth; because I have given mount Seir unto Esau for a possession (Deut. 2:4, 5).[14]

Just as God used Israel to drive out the Canaanites, He used the offspring of Esau to drive out the Horims—

> The Horims also dwelt in Seir beforetime; but the children of Esau succeeded them, when they had destroyed them from before them, and dwelt in their stead; as Israel did unto the land of his possession, which the LORD gave unto them (Deut. 2:12).

God actually destroyed the Horims from before the Edomites—

---

[14] The Lord says the same of the descendents of Lot: "And the LORD said unto me, Distress not the Moabites, neither contend with them in battle: for I will not give thee of their land for a possession; because I have given Ar unto the children of Lot for a possession" (Deut. 2:9).

> As he did to the children of Esau, which dwelt in seir, when he destroyed the Horims from before them; and they succeeded them, and dwelt in their stead (Deut. 2:22).

And God commanded the Israelites saying: *Thou shalt not abhor an Edomite* (Deut. 23:7). Though God eventually destroyed the Edomites because of their enmity against Israel, yet He determined before the world began to reveal His saving grace to them.

Should we therefore conclude that Isaac had taught both of his sons about the blessings of eternal life when the writer of *Hebrews* says: *By faith Isaac blessed Jacob and Esau concerning things to come* (Heb. 11:20)? Could this be how Job's three friends could have known so much about redemption?

And what of Job himself: *a perfect and upright man,* justified by the righteousness of Christ. In his walk and conversation he was *one that feared God and eschewed evil* (Job 1:8). He also was deeply knowledgeable of the impurity of nature, the insufficiency of man's righteousness to justify himself before God (9:1, 2, 20, 30-31; 14:4), and of the doctrine of redemption and salvation by Christ. Think of all the doctrines of grace that are contained in his words: *I know that my redeemer liveth.* He knew that his redeemer existed; that he would be incarnate, dwell among men on earth; come (as we now understand as the second time) to judge the world; that there would be a resurrection of the body, and a beautiful vision of God in a future state (19:25-27).

Now imagine, dear reader, how that all of this knowledge of redemption, apart from ritual of any kind, existed and was openly discussed by Edomites and Job before Moses ever penned the first verse of Genesis. Think hard about this when you wonder if ritualistic sacraments really do impart the saving grace of God.

THE PLAN OF SALVATION FROM MOSES TO DAVID

When we think of Moses, we think of laws and rituals and ceremonies. Yet we often forget that Moses had a great knowledge of Christ; of His Person, offices, and grace; and of salvation by grace through faith. This knowledge was so obvious that Jesus said: *For had ye believed Moses, ye would have believed me: for he wrote of me* (Jn. 5:46).

Moses was an illustration, or type, of Christ. As one reads Hebrews chapter three, the writer parallels them in that they were both concerned about the house of God and both were faithful therein (with Moses as a servant and Christ as a Son in His own house). Moses was a mediator when the covenant on Sinai was given. At the request of the people, and by the permission of God, Moses stood between God and the people to deliver His word to them—

> I stood between the LORD and you at that time, to shew you the word of the LORD: for ye were afraid by reason of the fire, and went not up into the mount... (Deut. 5:5).

In this Moses was a type of Christ, the mediator of a new and better covenant and the mediator between God and man—

> Wherefore then serveth the law? It was added because of transgressions, till the seed should come to whom the promise was made; and it was ordained by angels in the hand of a mediator (Gal. 3:19).

Moses was a prophet to whom all Israelites were to hearken. When Moses, Elijah and Christ appeared on the Mount of Transfiguration, a voice was heard saying, *This is my beloved Son, in whom I am well pleased, hear ye him* (Matt. 17:5). Christ was the great prophet of the church—

> ...The LORD thy God will raise up unto thee a Prophet from the midst of thee, of thy brethren, like unto me; unto him ye shall hearken; I will raise them up a Prophet from among their brethren, like unto thee, and will put my words in his mouth; and he shall speak unto them all that I shall command him. And it shall come to pass, that whosoever will not hearken unto my words which he shall speak in my name, I will require it of him (Deut. 18:15,18-19).

The writer of Hebrews said it well when he affirmed:

> God, who at sundry times and in divers manners spake in time past unto the fathers by the prophets, Hath in these last days spoken unto us by his Son, whom he hath appointed heir of all things, by whom also he made the worlds (Heb. 1:1, 2).

Moses was an officiating priest even before Aaron's appointment (Ex. 29:1). He was also a king and lawgiver under God (Deut. 33:4,5). In comparison, Jesus Christ is the king (Ps. 149:2), the lawgiver and judge (Isa. 33:22), and—

> Of the increase of his government and peace there shall be no end, upon the throne of David, and upon his kingdom, to order it, and to establish it with judgment and with justice from henceforth even for ever. The zeal of the LORD of hosts will perform this (Isa. 9:7).

Moses was also a deliverer of Israel out of a state of Egyptian bondage (Acts 7:35), and thus a type of Christ Who redeems sinners from the bondage of sin, Satan and the Law of Moses.

The whole ceremonial law was nothing else but a shadowy exhibition of Christ's finished work on the cross. It was the Israelite schoolmaster teaching them the Gospel of Christ. It would be much too tedious to survey all of those particulars, though we will look at just a few.

The first Passover was the tenth plague pronounced upon Egypt, for the purpose of persuading Pharaoh to let the Israelites go from Egyptian slavery. The angel of death would pass over Egypt, killing the firstborn of every family and of livestock. To protect the firstborn in Israel, a lamb had to be slain, roasted with fire, eaten whole with bitter herbs, and its blood sprinkled on the door posts of the houses of the Israelites. When the destroying angel passed through Egypt, he would pass by the houses sprinkled with blood and leave them unharmed. Thus began the ceremony called the Passover (Ex. 12). The lamb had to be a young male without blemish, examined for four days from selection to the sacrifice. It was publicly slain without breaking any bones before the sprinkling of its blood was applied to the door posts.[15] *And the Lord said: When I see the blood I will pass over you* (Ex. 12:13).

All of this was a picture of the coming Messiah. In Christ's humanity He was sinless and perfect. He was a young male in the prime of His life. He lived a meticulously examined life. He died publicly and yet not one bone in his body was broken.[16] Finally, through the price of His blood, He has paid 100 percent of what it would cost for anyone to have forgiveness of sin and eternal life. Paul told the Ephesian Elders to, *feed the church of God, which he hath purchased with his own blood* (Acts 20:28b).[17] Christ and His grace are fed upon by faith alone— *Therefore we conclude that a man is justified by faith without the deeds of the law* (Rom. 3:28). Also, the public profession of Him is often accompanied with bitter afflictions, reproaches, and persecutions. His blood will from henceforth be called the *blood of sprinkling*—

> And to Jesus the mediator of the new covenant, and to the blood of sprinkling, that speaketh better things than that of Abel (Heb. 12:24).

Therefore the redeemed are—

> Elect according to the foreknowledge of God the Father, through sanctification of the Spirit, unto obedience and sprinkling of the blood of Jesus Christ: Grace unto you, and peace, be multiplied (I Pet. 1:2).

It is no wonder that John the Baptist announced Jesus as *the Lamb of God who takes away the sin of the world* (Jn. 1:29b); that the Apostle Paul wrote: *Christ our Passover, was sacrificed for us* (I Cor. 5:7b); and that the Apostle Peter identified Him as *the lamb without blemish and without spot* (I Pet. 1:19b).

Moving on, the manna from heaven was another great object lesson depicting the saving grace of Christ. Speaking of the manna and

---

[15] See Ex. 12:3-13; Nu. 9:12.

[16] (Jn. 19:36) "For these things were done, that the scripture should be fulfilled, A bone of him shall not be broken."

[17] See Rom. 5:9; Eph. 2:13; Col. 1:14; Heb. 9:22; 10:19; I Pet 1:2; I Jn. 1:7; Rev. 1:5; 7:14.

of Himself, Christ said, *My Father giveth you the true bread from heaven* (Jn. 6:32), meaning that Himself was the truth of which the manna was only a shadow. Therefore, He is called *the hidden manna* (Rev. 2:17) of which every believer in Christ has a right to eat through faith. Thus, the Old and New Testament saints all *eat of the same spiritual meat* (I Cor. 10:3).

Most carefully now, let us consider the water out of the rock, which the Israelites drank in the wilderness, as an emblem and objective lesson of Christ and His grace. The Israelites, wanting water, murmured, and Moses was ordered by the Lord to smite the rock, resulting in the gushing forth of water.[18] God told Moses that He would be on the Rock as Moses smote it with his rod. Thus, he would be smiting God Himself. The second occasion, Moses was commanded only to speak to the rock, but instead he struck it twice. Because of this disobedience, Moses corrupted a beautiful picture of the redemptive work of Christ. Moses' punishment was that he forfeited his life's ambition to take the children into the Promised Land.[19]

Even though pictures are only shadows of the real thing, God has not authorized us to alter them in any way. In the first instance, not only was Christ symbolized by the rock, but He was also symbolized by the rod. The picture is one of God the Father smiting Himself in the incarnation of His Son Who bears the punishment for our sins—

> Surely he hath borne our griefs, and carried our sorrows: yet we did esteem him stricken, smitten of God, and afflicted. But he was wounded for our transgressions, he was bruised for our iniquities: the chastisement of our peace was upon him; and with his stripes we are healed. All we like sheep have gone astray, we have turned every one to his own way; and the Lord has laid upon Him the iniquity of us all (Isa. 53:4-6).

And is this not what the Apostle Paul affirms when he says: *For he hath made him to be sin for us, who knew no sin; that we might be made the righteousness of God in him* (II Cor. 5:21)? And did not David see this

---

[18] See Ex. 17:1-8.
[19] See Nu. 20:1-13.

truth when he said: *For they persecute him whom thou hast smitten* (Ps. 69:26)? And let us not think for a moment that Moses did not understand the picture of the rock being smitten as well as its name. Listen to his words as he says:

> Give ear, O ye heavens, and I will speak; and hear, O earth, the words of my mouth. My doctrine shall drop as the rain, my speech shall distil as the dew, as the small rain upon the tender herb, and as the showers upon the grass: Because I will publish the name of the LORD: ascribe ye greatness unto our God. *He is* the Rock, his work *is* perfect: for all his ways *are* judgment: a God of truth and without iniquity, just and right *is* he.... But Jeshurun waxed fat, and kicked: thou art waxen fat, thou art grown thick, thou art covered *with fatness*; then he forsook God *which* made him, and lightly esteemed the Rock of his salvation... Of the Rock that begat thee thou art unmindful, and hast forgotten God that formed thee...O that they were wise, *that* they understood this, *that* they would consider their latter end! How should one chase a thousand, and two put ten thousand to flight, except their Rock had sold them, and the LORD had shut them up? For their rock *is* not as our Rock, even our enemies themselves *being* judges... And he shall say, Where *are* their gods, *their* rock in whom they trusted (Deut. 32:1-4, 15, 18, 29-31, 37).

Again, we can see illusions of this divine picture in the Prayer of Hanna—

> And Hannah prayed, and said, My heart rejoiceth in the LORD, mine horn is exalted in the LORD: my mouth is enlarged over mine enemies; because I rejoice in thy salvation. There is none holy as the LORD: for there is none beside thee: neither is there any rock like our God. (I Sam. 2:1, 2).

This picture can be understood also in the Song of David—

> And he said, The LORD is my rock, and my fortress, and my deliverer; The God of my rock; in him will I

One Plan Of Salvation For All Ages

> trust: he is my shield, and the horn of my salvation, my high tower, and my refuge, my saviour; thou savest me from violence... For who is God, save the LORD? and who is a rock, save our God?... The LORD liveth; and blessed be my rock; and exalted be the God of the rock of my salvation (II Sam. 22:2, 3, 32, 47).

David repeated this concept many times in his Psalms:

> The LORD *is* my rock, and my fortress, and my deliverer; my God, my strength, in whom I will trust; my buckler, and the horn of my salvation, *and* my high tower... For who *is* God save the LORD? or who *is* a rock save our God?... The LORD liveth; and blessed *be* my rock; and let the God of my salvation be exalted (Psa. 18:2, 31, 46).

> Unto thee will I cry, O LORD my rock; be not silent to me: lest, *if* thou be silent to me, I become like them that go down into the pit. (Psa. 28:1).

> Bow down thine ear to me; deliver me speedily: be thou my strong rock, for an house of defence to save me. For thou *art* my rock and my fortress; therefore for thy name's sake lead me, and guide me (Psa. 31:2, 3).

> He brought me up also out of an horrible pit, out of the miry clay, and set my feet upon a rock, *and* established my goings. And he hath put a new song in my mouth, *even* praise unto our God: many shall see *it*, and fear, and shall trust in the LORD (Psa. 40:2, 3).

> Hear my cry, O God; attend unto my prayer. From the end of the earth will I cry unto thee, when my heart is overwhelmed: lead me to the rock *that* is higher than I (Psa. 61:1, 2).

> Truly my soul waiteth upon God: from him *cometh* my salvation. He only *is* my rock and my salvation; *he is* my defence; I shall not be greatly moved... He only *is*

> my rock and my salvation: *he is* my defence; I shall not be moved. ⁷In God *is* my salvation and my glory: the rock of my strength, *and* my refuge, *is* in God (Psa. 62:1, 2, 6, 7).
>
> Be thou my strong habitation, whereunto I may continually resort: thou hast given commandment to save me; for thou *art* my rock and my fortress (Psa. 71:3).
>
> He shall cry unto me, Thou *art* my father, my God, and the rock of my salvation (Psa. 89:26).
>
> Those that be planted in the house of the LORD shall flourish in the courts of our God. They shall still bring forth fruit in old age; they shall be fat and flourishing; To shew that the LORD *is* upright: *he is* my rock, and *there is* no unrighteousness in him (Psa. 92:13-15).
>
> But the LORD is my defence; and my God *is* the rock of my refuge (Psa. 94:22).
>
> Come, let us sing unto the LORD: let us make a joyful noise to the rock of our salvation (Psa. 95:1).[20]

Because such an important and eternal gospel truth is presented in the picture of Christ standing upon the rock that is to be smitten, let us observe its manifestation into the prophecies of Isaiah:

> Sanctify the LORD of hosts himself; and *let* him *be* your fear, and *let* him *be* your dread. And he shall be for a sanctuary; but for a stone of stumbling and for a rock of offence to both the houses of Israel, for a gin and for a snare to the inhabitants of Jerusalem. And many among them shall stumble, and fall, and be broken, and be snared, and be taken (Isa. 8:13-15).
>
> Behold, a king shall reign in righteousness, and princes shall rule in judgment. And a man shall be as

---

[20] See Psa. 42:9; 78:34-37.

One Plan Of Salvation For All Ages

> an hiding place from the wind, and a covert from the tempest; as rivers of water in a dry place, as the shadow of a great rock in a weary land (Isa. 32:1, 2).

> The LORD hath redeemed his servant Jacob. And they thirsted not *when* he led them through the deserts: he caused the waters to flow out of the rock for them: he clave the rock also, and the waters gushed out (Isa. 48:20b, 21).

When the Apostle Peter confessed to Jesus that He was *the Christ, the Son of the living God*, Jesus immediately referred to this statement about Himself as being the *Rock* upon which the Church would be built: *and upon this rock I will build my church; and the gates of hell shall not prevail against it* (Matt. 16:18b). It has been argued for centuries that the *rock* in this passage is a reference to Peter as the first Pope. The question can be easily resolved by asking Peter himself, who answers:

> Wherefore also it is contained in the scripture, Behold, I lay in Sion a chief corner stone, elect, precious: and he that believeth on him shall not be confounded. Unto you therefore which believe he is precious: but unto them which be disobedient, the stone which the *builders* disallowed, the same is made the head of the corner, And a stone of stumbling, and a rock of offence, even to them which stumble at the word, being disobedient: whereunto also they were appointed (I Pet. 2:6-8).

The Apostle Paul tells of how Israel literally stumbled over the Rock of their salvation:

> But Israel, which followed after the law of righteousness, hath not attained to the law of righteousness. Wherefore? Because they sought it not by faith, but as it were by the works of the law. For they stumbled at that stumblingstone; As it is written, Behold, I lay in Sion a stumblingstone and rock of offence: and whosoever believeth on him shall not be ashamed (Rom. 9:31-33).

Paul clearly understood the rock that Moses struck to be Christ when he affirmed:

> Moreover, brethren, I would not that ye should be ignorant, how that all our fathers were under the cloud, and all passed through the sea; And were all baptized unto Moses in the cloud and in the sea; And did all eat the same spiritual meat; And did all drink the same spiritual drink: for they drank of that spiritual Rock that followed them: and that Rock was Christ (I Cor. 10:1-4).

Just as God wanted Israel to see Him in the rock, He wanted them to clearly see Him in the rod that was striking the rock as well. Jesus was God in the flesh, and He was the rod of God's wrath upon sin—

> And there shall come forth a rod out of the stem of Jesse, and a Branch shall grow out of his roots: and the spirit of the LORD shall rest upon him, the spirit of wisdom and understanding, the spirit of counsel and might, the spirit of knowledge and of the fear of the LORD; And shall make him of quick understanding in the fear of the LORD: and he shall not judge after the sight of his eyes, neither reprove after the hearing of his ears: But with righteousness shall he judge the poor, and reprove with equity for the meek of the earth: and he shall smite the earth with the rod of his mouth, and with the breath of his lips shall he slay the wicked (Isa. 11:1-4).

King David makes the same declaration when he writes:

> I will declare the decree: the LORD hath said unto me, Thou art my Son; this day have I begotten thee. Ask of me, and I shall give thee the heathen for thine inheritance, and the uttermost parts of the earth for thy possession. Thou shalt break them with a rod of iron; thou shalt dash them in pieces like a potter's vessel (Psa. 2:7-9).

One Plan Of Salvation For All Ages

Jeremiah saw His work first hand when he said: *I am the man that hath seen affliction by the rod of his wrath* (Lam. 3:1). The Prophet Micah preached it when he proclaimed: *The Lord's voice crieth unto the city, and the man of wisdom shall see thy name: hear ye the rod, and who hath appointed it* (Micah 6:9).

This was a unique picture of God sacrificing Himself for our sins. Christ died to save each Christian only once, and that *once-for-all* (Heb. 10:10). Moses interfered with that picture when he struck the rock twice, and for this he did not miss heaven, but he forfeited his goal to lead the children of Israel into the Promised Land. Even so, God wants the Christian today to understand that salvation is *once for all*, and is, therefore, secure in the finished work of Christ, where God the Father smote God the Son on the cross of Calvary in punishment for our sin—

> By the which will we are sanctified through the offering of the body of Jesus Christ once *for all*. And every priest standeth daily ministering and offering oftentimes the same sacrifices, which can never take away sins: But this man, after he had offered one sacrifice for sins for ever, sat down on the right hand of God; From henceforth expecting till his enemies be made his footstool. For by one offering he hath perfected for ever them that are sanctified (Heb. 10:10-14).

The example of Moses should serve as a warning to Christians not to warp the picture of baptism and the Lord's Supper in the same way. These are testimonies to the Gospel but they are not the gospel in themselves. Those who have never been saved should understand the meaning of the rod smiting the rock and receive God's gift of salvation before reading any further.

However, for those of us who are redeemed, we should see, in the second occasion of Moses striking the rock, a pictorial contrast between the eternal security of the believer and his divine chastisement. Those who believe in the security of the believer are often falsely charged with teaching that there are no consequences when a child of God disobeys. When Moses struck the rock instead of speaking to it, in Numbers chapter 20, he still went to heaven when he died. However, as punishment, God took his life's ambition from him. He died on the wilderness side of the Jordan River and could only watch as someone else led the children of Israel into the Promised Land—

> And Moses lifted up his hand, and with his rod he smote the rock twice: and the water came out abundantly, and the congregation drank, and their beasts *also*. And the LORD spake unto Moses and Aaron, Because ye believed me not, to sanctify me in the eyes of the children of Israel, therefore ye shall not bring this congregation into the land which I have given them (Nu. 20:11, 12).[21]

Another picture of the grace of the gospel was that of the brazen serpent. The Israelites during the exodus were being bitten with fiery serpents and many died. God commanded Moses to make a brass fiery serpent and set it on a pole. Any bitten Israelite would only have to look at it and live (Nu. 21:6-9). All of the ceremonies, commandments and rituals of Moses were impotent, and the sinner was impotent to help himself. Looking at the brass serpent was not an act of virtue but it was an act of faith.

Our Lord Jesus Christ mentions this same significant type and applies it to Himself when He says:

> And as Moses lifted up the serpent in the wilderness, even so must the Son of man be lifted up: That whosoever believeth in him should not perish, but have eternal life (Jn. 3:14, 15).

Moses' serpent had the form of a serpent, but not the nature. So, likewise, Christ was in the likeness of sinful flesh, but He did not have a sinful, fleshly nature. He was totally without the corruption of the world, the flesh or the devil. It was a fiery brass serpent even as Christ, in the likeness of sinful flesh, bore the fiery wrath of God on His own wooden pole (the cross). This is why Jesus said:

---

[21] See Deut. 32:48-52 for the fulfillment of this chastisement. See also Deut. 34:1-12.

> And I, if I be lifted up from the earth, will draw all men unto me. This he said, signifying what death he should die (Jn. 12:32, 33).

And, just as the Israelites could look to the brass serpent on a pole and live, those who are envenomed with the poison of sin and incurably condemned, might, through looking to Christ by faith, live spiritually and eternally. Jesus expressed as much in Jn. 6:40 when He exclaimed:

> And this is the will of him that sent me, that every one which seeth the Son, and believeth on him, may have everlasting life: and I will raise him up at the last day.

Bypassing several other precious types of the grace of Christ, let us proceed to Joshua who led the Israelites into the Promised Land and settled them there. So also Christ, Who by His blood and righteousness, has opened the way for sinners into heaven, giving them an entrance into His glorious kingdom. Joshua did not provide true heavenly rest in Canaan, for then another and more glorious rest would not have been proclaimed. Joshua's ministry was a typical one pointing to Christ as our spiritual Joshua, giving us spiritual rest here, and everlasting rest in heaven. Even both names, (Joshua and Jesus) signify a savior. Joshua is actually called Jesus in (Heb. 4:8).[22]

And finally we must look at Rahab the harlot, the Canaanite woman of Jericho, outside the covenant of Israel, already condemned to die by God's command to exterminate the inhabitants of the land, but spared when she identified her house by the scarlet rag in her window. Even so were we condemned to eternal wrath but for the scarlet blood of Jesus Christ, which brought us peace, pardon, righteousness, and salvation; through which we have security from eternal wrath, ruin, and destruction How else could Rahab become a distant grandmother to Jesus Christ Himself...*And Salmon begat Booz of Rachab; and Booz begat Obed of Ruth* (Matt. 1:5). She was not of them that believed not, but of those who had faith in the mercy of the coming Messiah—

---

[22] (vss. 8-10) "For if Jesus had given them rest, then would he not afterward have spoken of another day. There remaineth therefore a rest to the people of God. For he that is entered into his rest, he also hath ceased from his own works, as God *did* from his."

> By faith the harlot Rahab perished not with them that believed not, when she had received the spies with peace (Heb. 11:31).

THE PLAN OF SALVATION FROM DAVID TO CHRIST

Christ has been spoken of by all *the holy prophets which have been since the world began* (Lk. 1:71).[23] Now we come to consider David, who was a prophet through whom the Spirit spoke abundantly of Christ and the plan of salvation made with Him—

> Men *and* brethren, let me freely speak unto you of the patriarch David, that he is both dead and buried, and his sepulchre is with us unto this day. Therefore being a prophet, and knowing that God had sworn with an oath to him, that of the fruit of his loins, according to the flesh, he would raise up Christ to sit on his throne (Acts 2:29-30).[24]

David was such an eminent type of Christ that Christ is often called by David's name.[25] David was speaking the words of the Father to the Son when he wrote: *I will declare the decree: the LORD hath said unto me, Thou art my Son; this day have I begotten thee* (Psa. 2:7). David speaks of the humanity of Christ; of a body being prepared for him which would be Christ in flesh; of the formation of that body in the womb of a virgin; of the Messiah being the offspring of his seed.[26]

> The LORD hath sworn *in* truth unto David; he will not turn from it; Of the fruit of thy body will I set upon thy throne (Psa. 132:11; see vs. 17).[27]

---

[23] (Heb. 1:1, 2a) "God, who at sundry times and in divers manners spake in time past unto the fathers by the prophets, Hath in these last days spoken unto us by *his* Son…"

[24] See also Acts 1:16 and II Sam. 23:2-5.

[25] See Psa. 89:3, 20; Ezek. 34:23, 24; 37:24; Hos. 3:5.

[26] See Psa. 40:6

[27] See Heb. 10:5; Ps. 139:15, 16.

One Plan Of Salvation For All Ages

Of this man's seed hath God according to *his* promise raised unto Israel a Saviour, Jesus (Acts 13:23).

David describes expressly the sufferings and death of Christ in the twenty-second Psalm, using the very words which Christ uttered on the cross: *My God, my God, why hast thou forsaken me...* He speaks of the Messiah as being a Priest like Melchizedek (110:4);[28] of His rejection by the Jews (2:2);[29] of His betrayal by a friend (41:9);[30] of Judas' office being taken by another (109:7, 8);[31] of false witnesses accusing Him (27:12; 35:11);[32] of being silent when accused (38:13, 14);[33] of being hated without a cause (69:4; 109:3-5);[34] of the piercing of His hands and feet (22:16);[35] of His being mocked and insulted (22:6-8);[36] of being given gall and vinegar (69:21);[37] of hearing His prophetic words repeated in mockery (22:8)[38]; of His praying for His enemies (109:4);[39] of soldiers casting lots for His coat (22:18);[40] of not a bone in His body being broken (34:20);[41] of His resurrection (16:10);[42] of His ascension (68:18);[43] and of His being seated at the right hand of God (110:1).

The royal Covenant which God made with David, and confirmed with his son, Solomon, is a picture of eternal salvation and of the chastisement of an eternally secure believer—

---

[28] See Heb. 6:20; 5:5, 6; 7:15-17 for fulfillment.
[29] See John 1:11; 5:43; Lu. 4:29; 17:25; 23:18 for fulfillment.
[30] See Mk. 14:10; Mt. 26:14-16; Mk. 14:43-45 for fulfillment.
[31] See Acts 1:16-20 for fulfillment.
[32] See Mt. 26:60, 61 for fulfillment.
[33] See Mt. 26:62, 63 for fulfillment.
[34] See Jn. 15:23-25 for fulfillment
[35] See Jn. 20:25-27; 19:37 for fulfillment.
[36] See Mt. 27:39-44; Mk. 15:29-32 for fulfillment.
[37] See Jn. 19:29 for fulfillment.
[38] See Mt. 27:43 for fulfillment.
[39] See Lk. 23:34 for fulfillment.
[40] See Mk. 15:24; Jn. 19:24 for fulfillment.
[41] See Jn. 19:33 for fulfillment.
[42] See Mt. 28:9 for fulfillment.
[43] See Lk. 24:50, 51; Acts 1:9 for fulfillment.

I will be his father, and he shall be my son. If he commit iniquity, I will chasten him with the rod of men, and with the stripes of the children of men: But my mercy shall not depart away from him, as I took *it* from Saul, whom I put away before thee. And thine house and thy kingdom shall be established for ever before thee: thy throne shall be established for ever (II Sam. 7:14-16). Cf. 4-16. [44]

Some might say that David, though writing under inspiration of the coming Messiah, was blind to the true significance of what he was foreseeing. In response to this charge, it would be good to look at what might be considered the dirtiest story in the Bible. This would be no less than the ugly story of David's adulterous sin with Bathsheba, and the subsequent murder of her husband, Uriah, to cover it up. He then takes Bathsheba to be his wife.[45] When David is confronted by Nathan the prophet, he admits to the sin. Nathan responds by saying: *The LORD also hath put away thy sin; thou shalt not die* (II Sam. 12:13b). Nathan could say this because he knew the king to be a born again man. This sin was put away before a priest could be consulted and before any animal could be sacrificed. David needed more than forgiveness, more than pardon, and more than a covering for his sin. He needed to be innocent of having committed it in the first place. This kind of justification (or being pronounced innocent) is not something the Mosaic Law could provide—

> ...he said on this wise, I will give you the sure mercies of David. Wherefore he saith also in another *psalm*, Thou shalt not suffer thine Holy One to see corruption. For David, after he had served his own generation by the will of God, fell on sleep, and was laid unto his fathers, and saw corruption: But he, whom God raised again, saw no corruption. Be it known unto you therefore, men *and* brethren, that through this man is preached unto you the forgiveness of sins: And by him all that believe are justified from

---

[44] See I Chron. 17:3-15; Psa. 89:20-37. In the declaration of this covenant, God may interrupt the actual reign of David's sons if chastisement is required.

[45] See II Sam. 11.

all things, from which ye could not be justified by the law of Moses (Acts 13:34b-39).[46]

So we can see the extent of David's understanding when he assumes direct access to God's mercy. He composes his prayer of confession and repentance regarding this matter, seeking much more than forgiveness, pardon and covering. He calls upon God directly (not through a priest or a sacrifice) to... *Hide thy face from my sins, and blot out all mine iniquities* (Psa. 51:9).[47] David appeals directly to God's mercy, supplied by the coming Messiah, to remove this transgression completely from his record. David knew the difference between forgiveness, covering and outright justification—

> Even as David also describeth the blessedness of the man, unto whom God imputeth righteousness without works, *Saying*, Blessed *are* they whose iniquities are forgiven, and whose sins are covered. Blessed *is* the man to whom the Lord will not impute sin (Rom. 4:6-8) cf. Psa. 32:1, 2.

And even though II Samuel 12 spells out the severe chastisement imposed upon David in this life, he knows that the record of this sin will not be waiting in heaven for him. Bathsheba also must have gone to the Lord for justification in this matter, for she is recognized by God as David's legitimate wife. She becomes the mother of King Solomon and the distant grandmother of Jesus Christ—*And Jesse begat David the king; and David the king begat Solomon of her that had been the wife of Urias* (Matt. 1:6).

---

[46] The Prophet Isaiah understood this implicitly when he said: "Incline your ear, and come unto me: hear, and your soul shall live; and I will make an everlasting covenant with you, *even* the sure mercies of David. Behold, I have given him *for* a witness to the people, a leader and commander to the people" (Isa. 55:3, 4).

[47] Isaiah defines the blotting out of sin as nothing less than Justification: "I, *even* I, *am* he that blotteth out thy transgressions for mine own sake, and will not remember thy sins" (Isa. 43:25) and "I have blotted out, as a thick cloud, thy transgressions, and, as a cloud, thy sins: return unto me; for I have redeemed thee" (Isa. 44:22).

And what did King Solomon know of the coming Messiah? He writes of him under the name of Wisdom, as a divine Person, the same with the Logos, the Word, and Son of God; of his eternal existence; of the eternal generation of him; of his being brought forth, and brought up as a Son with his Father from everlasting.[48]

Solomon (or Agur) speaks of Christ under the names of Ithiel (signifying *God is with me*) and Ucal (signifying *The mighty one* or *I am able*). He speaks of the infinite, omnipresent, and omnipotent Being, Whose name (or nature) is incomprehensible and ineffable; a divine Son distinct in person from His Father; same in nature with the Father; and co-essential, co-eternal, and co-equal with Him:

> The words of Agur the son of Jakeh, *even* the prophecy: the man spake unto Ithiel, even unto Ithiel and Ucal, Surely I *am* more brutish than *any* man, and have not the understanding of a man. I neither learned wisdom, nor have the knowledge of the holy. Who hath ascended up into heaven, or descended? who hath gathered the wind in his fists? who hath bound the waters in a garment? who hath established all the ends of the earth? what *is* his name, and what *is* his son's name, if thou canst tell? Every word of God *is* pure: he *is* a shield unto them that put their trust in him (Prov. 30:1-5).[49]

Continuing with the Old Testament prophets, we can see Zechariah speaking of the Divine Persons who entered into the covenant of grace (or plan of salvation), which would last forever; and of Jehovah and the Branch, between whom the council of peace was conducted (Zech. 6:12, 13).

---

[48] All this is declared in the eighth chapter of Proverbs. If one did not know better, he would be tempted to think that Solomon was plagiarizing from the first chapter of John because of the similarity of diction, sentiment, and doctrine.
[49] The book of Canticles, believed to have been written by Solomon, is replete with illusions of the glories and excellencies of Christ, of His blessings of grace bestowed upon His people.

Isaiah speaks of the sure mercies of David in the Messiah, and whose blood is said to be the ratification and confirmation of the covenant, and Who is the messenger of it (the plan of salvation), even proclaiming salvation to the Gentiles.[50] He identifies the recipients of the plan of salvation as the elect of God, both Jews and Gentiles.[51]

The Old Testament prophets (from the times of the kings forward) speak even more plainly of the mercies of grace than in previous periods.[52] They speak of God's pardon as flowing from His mercy in that there is none like Him.[53] They proclaim that He pardons abundantly anyone who applies to him for it.[54] They talk of the freeness of pardon, as the effect of the unmerited favor, love, grace and mercy of God.[55] They proclaim this grace to be grounded upon the sufferings, redemption, reconciliation, atonement, and satisfaction accomplished by the crucifixion of Christ.[56]

Justification by the imputed righteousness of Christ is something that could be studied solely from the Old Testament prophets:

> But now the righteousness of God without the law is manifested, being witnessed by the law and the prophets; Even the righteousness of God which is by faith of Jesus Christ unto all and upon all them that believe: for there is no difference (Rom. 3:21, 22).

Daniel calls it an *everlasting righteousness* (Daniel 9:24). Isaiah says that the Lord is well pleased with the righteousness of the Son because it answers all of the demands of the Law, magnifying its requirements and thus honoring it (Isa. 42:21). He is the Justifier of them that know Him, because His righteousness is imputed to them as a result of their iniquities having been imputed to Him (Isa. 53:6, 11). He literally clothes us with the robe of His righteousness (Isa. 61:10). He will be a light to the Gentiles and bring salvation to the ends of the earth (Isa.

---

[50] See Isa. 42:6; 49:8; 55:3; Zech. 9:11; Mal. 3:1.
[51] See Isa. 49:5-8.
[52] See Heb. 8:10-13; Jer. 31:31-34.
[53] See Dan. 9:9; Mic. 7:18.
[54] See Isa. 1:18; 55:7.
[55] See Isa. 43:25.
[56] See Isa. 44:22; Dan. 9:24.

49:6). It is an *everlasting salvation* to the true Israel of God, both Jews and Gentiles who look to Christ alone for salvation (Isa. 45:17, 22). Jeremiah said that the Jews would someday call Him *The Lord our Righteousness* (Jer. 23:6; cf. Isa. 45:24, 25). His incarnation and virgin birth are spoken of as if they had already occurred (Isa. 9:6; 7:14). The Angel of the Lord used these same two verses when announcing the birth of Christ to Joseph:

> Now all this was done, that it might be fulfilled which was spoken of the Lord by the prophet, saying, Behold, a virgin shall be with child, and shall bring forth a son, and they shall call his name Emmanuel, which being interpreted is, God with us (Matt. 1:22, 23).

Isaiah spoke of the particular geographical locations where Christ would live, teach and minister (Isaiah 9:1).[57] The fifty-third chapter of Isaiah speaks of His humiliation, sufferings, and death. Hosea speaks of Gentiles becoming the adopted sons of God (Hos. 1:10). Malachi tells us that divine righteousness will originate from Him as light from the sun, thus calling Him the *Sun of Righteousness* (Mal. 4:2), and speaks of His forerunner, and that Christ would come suddenly into His temple (Mal. 3:1; 4:5).. Micah tells of the place of His birth (Mic. 5:2).[58]

Many people will travel to the "Holy Land" thinking to get in touch with God and His salvation. But if they had only consulted the prophets, they would have found, *Truly in vain is salvation hoped for from the hills, and from the multitude of mountains: truly in the LORD our God is the salvation of Israel.* (Jer.3:23). Jeremiah spoke of the massacre of infants in Bethlehem (Jer. 31:15) and Hosea spoke of Christ being carried to Egypt (Hos. 11:1).[59] Zechariah spoke of the Messiah riding into Jerusalem on a colt, the foal of an ass proclaiming true salvation (Zech. 9:9). Now we know that Christ did not ride into town that day to liberate Israel politically. Therefore, Zechariah was foreseeing salvation by the imputed righteousness of Christ the Son.

---

[57] See Matt. 4:13-16 for fulfillment.
[58] See Matt. 2:4-6; Jn. 7:41, 42.
[59] See Matt. 2:13-23 for fulfillment.

Zechariah also saw Jehovah the Son being crucified and pierced in the side with a spear—

> ...and they shall look upon me whom they have pierced, and they shall mourn for him, as one mourneth for his only son (Zech. 12:10b).

Zechariah foretold His being forsaken for thirty pieces of silver and ultimately forsaken by all of His disciples (Zech. 11:12, 13; 13:7; cf. Psa. 118).[60]

Most of the Old Testament prophets clearly understood the WHAT of our salvation, but they did not understand the WHEN of the suffering of the Messiah and subsequent glorification. But, because they knew the gracious salvation of the imputed righteousness of God, they became ministers to us as they were inspired by the Spirit to speak:

> Receiving the end of your faith, *even* the salvation of *your* souls. Of which salvation the prophets have enquired and searched diligently, who prophesied of the grace *that should come* unto you: Searching what, or what manner of time the Spirit of Christ which was in them did signify, when it testified beforehand the sufferings of Christ, and the glory that should follow. Unto whom it was revealed, that not unto themselves, but unto us they did minister the things, which are now reported unto you by them that have preached the gospel unto you with the Holy Ghost sent down from heaven; which things the angels desire to look into (I Pet. 1:9-12).

However, some of the prophets do speak of the time of His coming and sufferings. Daniel fixes the exact time from a particular date (Dan. 9:24-26).

Years before any of the New Testament was written, Simeon of Jerusalem received a revelation from the Lord that he would live to see the *Lord's Christ*. And when Joseph and Mary brought the baby Jesus to the temple, Simeon held the child in his arms and said:

---

[60] See Matt. 27:3-10; 26:31; Jn. 19:34-37 for fulfillment.

> Lord, now lettest thou thy servant depart in peace, according to thy word: For mine eyes have seen thy salvation, Which thou hast prepared before the face of all people; A light to lighten the Gentiles, and the glory of thy people Israel (Lk 2:29-32).

Then there was the eighty-four-year-old prophetess named Hanna who served, fasted, and prayed in the temple daily. She immediately followed up the words of old Simeon *and spake of him to all them that looked for redemption in Jerusalem* (Lk 2:36-38).

Before leaving this chapter we must take particular note of Jewish people approaching God's grace while in Babylonian exile. The Temple, center of Jewish religious life and ceremony, was lost. Ezekiel may have anticipated the concept of the synagogue where people could meet God's grace completely apart from Mosaic ritual when he said:

> Therefore say, Thus saith the Lord GOD; Although I have cast them far off among the heathen, and although I have scattered them among the countries, yet will I be to them as a little sanctuary in the countries where they shall come (Ezek. 11:16).

Nehemiah mentions the public reading of the Torah (Neh. 8).[61] The very fact that prophecies were being written, and people were in relationship with God during the exile, speaks clearly that the Mosaic Law was never meant to impart salvation through its sacrifices and rituals. Jeremiah prophesied of a coming day when the Jews would know this like never before, when God said through him:

> And I will give you pastors according to mine heart, which shall feed you with knowledge and understanding. And it shall come to pass, when ye be multiplied and increased in the land, in those days, saith the LORD, they shall say no more, The ark of the covenant of the LORD: neither shall it come to mind:

---

[61] See also I Maccabees 3:48 "And laid open the book of the law, wherein the heathen had sought to paint the likeness of their images."

neither shall they remember it; neither shall they visit it; neither shall that be done any more (Jer. 3:15, 16).

So, from what we have observed, it becomes clear that the plan of salvation (by the imputed righteousness of Christ, accomplished by His crucifixion) reaches from eternity past through the fall of Adam to the coming of Christ Himself. It was taught and testified to by types, figures, shadows, sacrifices, promises and prophecies that are now fulfilled in Christ, but Christ was the sum and substance of this great plan of salvation for all time and eternity. To Him alone be glory forever.

We conclude this chapter by returning again to the prophet Zechariah. God told Joshua the priest of the Son of God coming as *a branch* (Zech. 3:8). But before this, Zechariah saw a vision of Joshua standing before the Angel of the Lord, and Satan standing at his right hand to resist him. Here we see Christ as our Advocate (I Jn. 2:1) and Satan as our adversary (I Pet. 5:8). Joshua, clothed in filthy garments, is standing before Christ, Who said:

> Take away the filthy garments from him. And unto him he said, Behold, I have caused thine iniquity to pass from thee, and I will clothe thee with change of raiment (Zech. 3:4).

Isaiah said it when he exclaimed:

> I will greatly rejoice in the LORD, my soul shall be joyful in my God; for he hath clothed me with the garments of salvation, he hath covered me with the robe of righteousness…(Isaiah 61:10a).

Is this not the imputed righteousness of Christ?

> *I sinned, and straightway, posthaste, Satan flew*
> *Before the presence of the most high God*
> *And made a railing accusation there.*
> *He said, "This soul, this thing of clay and sod,*
> *Has sinned. 'Tis true that he has named thy name*
> *But I demand his death, for thou hast said,*
> *'The soul that sinneth, it shall die.' Shall not*
> *Thy sentence be fulfilled? Is justice dead?*

Send now this wretched sinner to his doom.
What other thing can a righteous ruler do?"
And thus he did accuse me day and night,
And every word he spoke, oh God, was true.

Then quickly one arose from God's right hand
Before whose glory the angels veiled their eyes.
He spoke, "Each jot and tittle of the law
Must be fulfilled: the guilty sinner dies!
But wait—suppose his guilt were all transferred
To me, and that I paid his penalty.
Behold my hands, my side, myfeet. One day
I was made sin for him, and died that he
Might be presented faultless at Thy throne."
And Satan fled away. Full well he knew
That he could not prevail against such love
For every word my dear Lord spoke, Oh God , was true.

<u>**MY ADVOCATE**</u> *(author unknown)*

The Lord himself, who is Emmanuel from the virgin, is the sign of our salvation. It was the Lord Himself who saved them. For they could not be saved by their own instrumentality, Therefore, when Paul explaines human infirmity, he says, "For I know that there dwells in my flesh no good thing" [Rom. 7:18]. He thus shows that the "good thing" of our salvation is not from us, but from God. And again: "Wretched man that I am, who will deliver me from the body of this death?"[Rom. 7:24]…Here we see that we must be saved by the help of God, not by ourselves.

Irenaeus (c. 180, E/W), 1.499

This makes it perfectly certain that the ministry of John was the very same as that which was afterwards delegated to the apostles. For the different hands by which baptism is administered do not make it a different bptism, but sameness of doctrine proves it to be the same. John and the apostles agreed in one doctrine.

John Calvin's *Institutes Of The Christian Religion* **(Book IV 15.7)**

Chapter Four
The Gospel And Baptism Of John The Baptist: Was It Christian?

Before we address the question of whether John the Baptist was a gospel preacher and whether his baptism was Christian baptism, we must establish that he was a prophet of God; that his baptism was not a Jewish proselyte ritual; that his baptism was not an Essene proselyte baptism; that his ministry was not a separate dispensation; and finally, that his gospel and baptism were one and the same with that of Christ and the apostles after Pentecost. The necessity for this direction of study is occasioned by the stress of some ritual salvationists in either tracing Christian baptism as far back as the Genesis record or by factoring the Old Testament and the ministry of John the Baptist out of the gospel equation altogether. They demonstrate these errors primarily through the allegorical method of interpretation, of which we will define and discuss in the context of this chapter.

Jesus called John the greatest prophet (even more than a prophet) that had ever been born of a woman (Lk. 7:26-28; Matt. 11:9-12). He said that John was the fulfillment of the Old Testament prophecy that a prophet like unto Elijah would appear (Matt. 11:13-15; 7:10-13).[1] Let us consider it established, therefore, that John the Baptist was a prophet.

The Apostle Peter proclaimed that there never was a prophet of God who did not preach the gospel of Christ, when he said: *To him give all the prophets witness, that through his name whosoever believeth in him shall receive remission of sins* (Acts 10:43). Mark said that John's arrival as the forerunner of Christ, in fulfillment of prophecy, was the beginning of the Gospel of Christ:

> The beginning of the gospel of Jesus Christ, the Son of God; As it is written in the prophets, Behold, I send my messenger before thy face, which shall prepare thy

---

[1] Of course, Jesus proclaimed His own witness through His works to be greater than that of John the Baptist (Jn. 5:36).

way before thee. The voice of one crying in the wilderness, Prepare ye the way of the Lord, make his paths straight. John did baptize in the wilderness, and preach the baptism of repentance for the remission of sins (Mk. 1:1-3).

John did not restore temporal Israel to its political autonomy in the land of Palestine, but he did preach a repentance that would receive remission of sin—*John did baptize in the wilderness, and preach the baptism of repentance for the remission of sins* (Mk. 1:4). John knew full well that there was only one source for the remission of sin and admitted this when he said: *Behold the Lamb of God, which taketh away the sin of the world* (Jn. 1:29b, 36)—not just the sin of the corporate nation of Israel.

Zacharias, the father of John the Baptist, proclaimed that every prophet since the beginning of the world preached the gospel of Christ:

> As he spake by the mouth of his holy prophets, which have been since the world began…To give knowledge of salvation unto his people by the remission of their sins, Through the tender mercy of our God; whereby the dayspring from on high hath visited us, (Lk. 1:70, 77, 78).

When the rich man in hell requested for Lazarus to return to earth from Paradise to give the plan of salvation to his lost brothers, Abraham replied that they already had the written gospel—*They have Moses and the prophets; let them hear them* (cf. Lk. 16:29-31). This was not referring to the Law of Moses, but rather, to his gospel.

Jesus told His disciples that all the things that would befall Him in Jerusalem were spoken by the prophets (Lk. 18:31-33). He told the two disciples on the road to Emmaus that they were fools for not discerning all things concerning Himself in the Old Testament prophets (Lk. 24:25-27). And when Jesus, in disguise, explained the gospel to them from Moses and the prophets it burned within their hearts (Lk. 24:32). When Jesus met with all the disciples in Jerusalem He rehearsed the gospel to them in this wise:

The Gospel And Baptism Of John the Baptist: Was It Christian?

> These are the words which I spake unto you, while I was yet with you, that all things must be fulfilled, which were written in the law of Moses, and in the prophets, and in the Psalms, concerning me (Lk. 24:44).

The Apostle Peter proclaimed to the Jews at the temple that all of the prophets preached the coming of a suffering Messiah Who could blot out their sins:

> But those things, which God before had shewed by the mouth of all his prophets, that Christ should suffer, he hath so fulfilled. Repent ye therefore, and be converted, that your sins may be blotted out, when the times of refreshing shall come from the presence of the Lord (Acts 3:18, 19).

It was this Jesus Christ Whom the prophets preached— *And he shall send Jesus Christ, which before was preached unto you* (vs. 20). It was this same Jesus Whom the prophets had been preaching since the world began—*Whom the heaven must receive until the times of restitution of all things, which God hath spoken by the mouth of all his holy prophets since the world began* (vs. 21; cf. Ps. 51:1). Christ is the prophet that Moses prophesied would be like unto Him—

> For Moses truly said unto the fathers, A prophet shall the Lord your God raise up unto you of your brethren, like unto me; him shall ye hear in all things whatsoever he shall say unto you (vs. 22).

And it is failure to believe in Him that results in destruction—

> And it shall come to pass, *that* every soul, which will not hear that prophet, shall be destroyed from among the people. Yea, and all the prophets from Samuel and those that follow after, as many as have spoken, have likewise foretold of these days. Ye are the children of the prophets, and of the covenant which God made with our fathers, saying unto Abraham, And in thy seed shall all the kindreds of the earth be blessed. Unto you first God, having raised up his Son Jesus, sent him

to bless you, in turning away every one of you from his iniquities.(vs. 23-26).

Jesus Christ Himself was in all of those prophets as they predicted and inquired into the Gospel of Grace—

> Of which salvation the prophets have enquired and searched diligently, who prophesied of the grace *that should come* unto you: Searching what, or what manner of time the Spirit of Christ which was in them did signify, when it testified beforehand the sufferings of Christ, and the glory that should follow. Unto whom it was revealed, that not unto themselves, but unto us they did minister the things, which are now reported unto you by them that have preached the gospel unto you with the Holy Ghost sent down from heaven; which things the angels desire to look into (I Pet. 1:10-12).

The false prophets of old and new are damned because they deny the only Lord God that bought them—

> But there were false prophets also among the people, even as there shall be false teachers among you, who privily shall bring in damnable heresies, even denying the Lord that bought them, and bring upon themselves swift destruction (II Pet. 2:1).

The apostles were preaching the same word that had been spoken by the prophets—*That ye may be mindful of the words which were spoken before by the holy prophets, and of the commandment of us the apostles of the Lord and Saviour* (II Pet. 3:2).

The Apostle Paul affirmed before Felix that his hope toward God was built upon his belief in the things written in the Law and the Prophets:

> But this I confess unto thee, that after the way which they call heresy, so worship I the God of my fathers, believing all things which are written in the law and in the prophets: And have hope toward God, which they

themselves also allow, that there shall be a resurrection of the dead, both of the just and unjust (Acts 24:14-15).

He testified before Agrippa that he hadn't preached anything that had not been prophesied by the prophets and Moses:

> Having therefore obtained help of God, I continue unto this day, witnessing both to small and great, saying none other things than those which the prophets and Moses did say should come: That Christ should suffer, *and* that he should be the first that should rise from the dead, and should shew light unto the people, and to the Gentiles (Acts 26:22, 23).

When Paul was taken to Rome, after he had appealed to Caesar, he was allowed to lodge in a home under house arrest. It was there that the Jews appointed him a day wherein he could preach. From morning to evening he preached Jesus Christ from Moses and the prophets:

> And when they had appointed him a day, there came many to him into *his* lodging; to whom he expounded and testified the kingdom of God, persuading them concerning Jesus, both out of the law of Moses, and *out of* the prophets, from morning till evening (Acts 28:23).

When writing to the Roman church, he reminded them that the gospel of God had been promised by His prophets in the holy Scriptures:

> Paul, a servant of Jesus Christ, called *to be* an apostle, separated unto the gospel of God, (Which he had promised afore by his prophets in the holy scriptures,) Concerning his Son Jesus Christ our Lord, which was made of the seed of David according to the flesh; And declared *to be* the Son of God with power, according to the spirit of holiness, by the resurrection from the dead: By whom we have received grace and apostleship, for obedience to the faith among all

nations, for his name: Among whom are ye also the called of Jesus Christ (Rom. 1:1-6).

The Scriptures of the prophets had predicted a gospel for all nations:

> But now is made manifest, and by the scriptures of the prophets, according to the commandment of the everlasting God, made known to all nations for the obedience of faith (Rom. 16:26).

The things Christ preached about Himself are those which were spoken to the Jewish fathers by the prophets—

> God, who at sundry times and in divers manners spake in time past unto the fathers by the prophets, Hath in these last days spoken unto us by *his* Son, whom he hath appointed heir of all things, by whom also he made the worlds (Heb. 1:1, 2).

Some scholars of dispensationalism may be apprehensive of the path we are taking in this line of reasoning about a unified plan of salvation. They see the gospel of the kingdom as uniquely Jewish, announced by John the Baptist, offered by Jesus, and the offer withdrawn by Jesus. They understand the good news of the kingdom to be the literal restoration and establishment of the nation of Israel in the Promised Land. To all of this, we agree also. However, integral within this message of the kingdom was the same simple plan of salvation that is the same for all men since the fall of Adam, (cf. Chapter 3 of this present work). Though the visible church on earth is not the literal nation of Israel established, the present form of God's kingdom is spiritual and is entered into by both Jews and Gentiles alike upon reception of the Gospel of Jesus Christ. J. Dwight Pentecost explains the present form of the kingdom as follows:

> Notice too that the kingdom of God in this present age formed through the preaching of the Gospel would be made up of Jews, of Samaritans, and of Gentiles...
>
> Paul's life was dedicated to the preaching of the grace of God. But then he went on to say, "Now I know that

none of you among whom I have gone about preaching the kingdom will ever see me again (Acts 20:25). Paul clearly equated preaching the Gospel of the grace of God with the preaching of the kingdom of God. Once again we see that the two terms are used interchangeably, as in 28:23 when Paul arrived in Rome and "they arranged to meet Paul on a certain day, and came in even larger numbers to the place where he was staying. From morning till evening he explained and declared to them the kingdom of God and tried to convince them about Jesus from the Law of Moses and from the Prophets." Again the preaching of Gospel was referred to as testimony concerning the kingdom of God. And in verses 30-31 this identification was again made where "for two whole years Paul stayed there in his own rented house and welcomed all who came to see him. Boldly and without hindrance he preached the kingdom of God and taught about the Lord Jesus Christ."

Thus as we survey Paul's ministry as recorded in the Book of Acts, we see that he was an ambassador of the kingdom of God—but his message was salvation through the death and the resurrection of Jesus Christ. No reference is made to support the notion that the earthly Davidic kingdom had been established. Rather, the message concerns entrance into a present form of the kingdom of God by faith in Jesus Christ.[2]

Philip's evangelism of the Samaritans is described as follows:

But when they believed Philip preaching the things concerning the kingdom of God, and the name of Jesus Christ, they were baptized, both men and women (Acts 8:12).

---

[2] J. Dwight Pentecost, *Thy Kingdom Come: Tracing God's Kingdom Program And Covenant Promises Throughout History* (Grand Rapids, MI: Kregel Publications, 1995), pp. 278, 280-281.

When Paul preached in Iconium, a great number of Jews and Greeks believed (Acts 14:1). When he returned again to Iconium, Luke tells us that he spoke words…

> Confirming the souls of the disciples, and exhorting them to continue in the faith, and that we must through much tribulation enter into the kingdom of God (Acts 14:22).[3]

So, all prophets preached the gospel of Christ; John the Baptist was a prophet who preached the one true gospel; therefore, all of the apostles preached the same gospel as did John the Baptist—

> That ye may be mindful of the words which were spoken before by the holy prophets, and of the commandment of us the apostles of the Lord and Savior (II Pet. 3:2).

If there is only one plan of salvation that will remit sins and take them away, and if John the Baptist preached it, can we therefore call his baptism a Christian New Testament Baptism? Before we can approach the answer to this question there must be an unmistakable understanding of what John's baptism was not. If the next several pages are too difficult for some Christians to understand, they may wish to skip to the end of the chapter regarding the gospel that John the Baptist preached. However, it is strongly advised that one familiarize himself with all the material in this chapter.

We begin by affirming that John's baptism was neither a continuation of Jewish proselyte baptism nor a transition into Christianity. There is a very informative article by Wm. Sanford La Sor in the Biblical Archaeology Review analyzing the various discoveries of ancient Jewish baptismal immersion pools. He points out that archaeologists have discovered forty-eight such ritual baths, and he includes several excellent photographs. La Sor does state that Christian *Initiatory baptism, however, has its parallels in Jewish Proselyte baptism* and further states, *Now—with all this newly available*

---

[3] For a further study of *kingdom of God* in the NT, see Acts 1:3; 19:8; Rom. 14:17; I Cor. 4:20; 6:9, 10; 15:24, 50; Gal. 5:21; Eph. 5:5; Col. 1:13; 4:11; I Thess. 2:12; II Thess. 1:5; II Tim. 4::1, 18; James 2:5; II Pet. 1:11.

evidence—we can ask what these miqvoat [baptistries] can tell us about Christian baptism, for almost surely these Jewish miqvoat provided the background for Christian baptism.[4] If this thesis is correct, it creates a great challenge for Christianity and the Gospel. We will now address this challenge, trusting that the reader will see its relevance.[5]

If there ever was such a rite as proselyte baptism, it should be mentioned at least once in Scripture. In the Old Testament we read of many proselytes to the Jewish nation. There were the Shechemites in Jacob's time (Gen. 34); the multitude that came out of Egypt with the Israelites (Numbers 21:4); Jethro, Moses's father-in-law (Ex. 18:6,7); Shua (Gen. 38:2); Ruth (Ruth 1:6); and many inhabitants of Persia (Esth. 8:17). But in all of these cases, not a word is mentioned of admitting proselytes by baptism. There was indeed a law listing the qualifications for admitting proselytes to the Jewish religion so that they might enjoy the ordinances and privileges there—they must be circumcised with all their males (Ex. 12:48).

There were proselytes in the times of Hezekiah who came out of the land of Israel to eat the Passover at Jerusalem (II Chron. 30:25). They, therefore, had to be circumcised, but there was no mention of proselyte baptism. Among the families to have come out of Babylon, proselytes are one sort; but they say nothing of their baptism (Ezra 6:21). There was a law regarding marriage of a woman taken captive in a war (Deut. 21:10-14). She had to first become a proselyte by shaving her head, cutting her nails, and putting off the raiment of her captivity; but not a word was written about proselyte baptism for her.

There were many different bathings, baptisms, or dippings required of the Israelites, and these would be equally incumbent, after the fact, upon proselytes as well; yet none of these served to initiate a proselyte. They were for purification from some form of uncleanness in

---

[4] William Sanford La Sor, *Discovering What Jewish Miqvoat Can Tell Us About Christian Baptism*, Biblical Archaeological Review, January/February, 1987, pp. 57, 59.

[5] Emil Schurer D.D., M.A., *A History of the Jewish People in the Times of Jesus Christ* (Edinburgh: T & T Clark, 1901), Division II, Vol. 2, pp. 321-324. Schurer argues that it should be obvious to all that Christian baptism is the same as Old Testament bathings going back to the Levitical ritual bathing requirements.

a ceremonial sense. These purification rites were actually baths where people scrubbed for sanitation as well as ceremonial purposes.[6]

If there was such a ritual as proselyte baptism, it would certainly appear in the Apocryphal writings, written between the Old and New Testaments. These were supposedly written by Jews about Jews. Though mention is made of proselytes, there is not a mention of proselyte baptism. One example is Achoir the Ammonite, in the times of Judith, when he cut off the head of Holophernes— *And when Achior had seen all that the God of Israel had done, he believed in God greatly, and circumcised the flesh of his foreskin, and was joined unto the house of Israel unto this day* (Judith 14:10).[7] Here we see Achoir becoming a proselyte for life, but read nothing of his being baptized.

And with all of the mention of proselytes in the New Testament, one would expect at least one reference to proselyte baptism (Matthew 23:15; Acts 2:10; 6:5; 13:43). In fact, one would expect to see traces of this custom in the literature surrounding the times of John, Christ and the Apostles. But there is no mention of proselyte baptism in Philo the Jew, who lived in first century Alexandria where there should have been more proselytes than in Judea. He mentions proselytes, but speaks nothing of their baptism.[8]

Josephus, the Jewish historian, who lived a little after Philo, was immensely knowledgeable of Jewish affairs. He had been a Jewish priest and understood their rites and ceremonies. He spoke of many

---

[6] *Encyclopedia of Religion and Ethics*, Ed., James Hastings (New York: Charles Scribner's Sons), Vol. 2, pp.408, 409. "In one passage of the Mishna, proselyte baptism seems to be merely a bath of ceremonial purification, which the proselyte must take as one who 'comes from the foreskin.' The ceremonial of the practice likewise would be developed gradually… We find, however, that proselyte baptism was regarded also as a bath of purification, designed to remove the uncleanness of heathenism…thus, in the case of a woman who was desirous of embracing Judaism, and who had taken the bath required after menstruation, this act was credited to her by a certain Rabbi Joshua as equivalent to the bath required of proselytes." But Christian baptism does not purify one physically or spiritually.

[7] KJV Aprcrypha.

[8] See regulations concerning proselytes. *Philo, The Works of: complete and updated*; Translated by C.C. Younge (Peabody, Massachusetts: Hendrickson Publishers, 1993), pp. 38, 39.

The Gospel And Baptism Of John the Baptist: Was It Christian?

Gentile proselytes, and speaks of whole nations becoming Jews by circumcision. He mentions the Idumaeans, whom Hyrcanus conquered and allowed to remain in their own land on condition that they be circumcised and conform to the laws of the Jews.[9] He writes of the Itureans whom Aristobulus fought against, adding part of their country to Judea. Again, the inhabitants could remain in their country if they were circumcised and conformed to the laws of the Jews. In the context, Josephus quotes Strabo, who, upon the authority of Timogenes, says that he enlarged the country of the Jews, and made part of the country of Iturea theirs, joining them to them by the bond of circumcision.[10] He writes of Helena, queen of Adiabene, and her son Izates, embracing the Jewish religion. He also speaks of another Helena who became married to Monobazus, the king of Adiabene, but not a word is written about proselyte baptism in either case.[11] However, Josephus does speak of the Baptism of John the Baptist and how the Jews used it, *not in order to the putting away, [or the remission] of some sins [only] but for the purification of the body; supposing still that the soul was thoroughly purified beforehand by righteousness.*[12] Whatever Josephus conceived baptism to mean, he seems to have understood faith and remission of sin to be a prerequisite (Josephus refers to faith and remission as righteousness).

One would also suppose that if such a thing as proselyte baptism existed in the time of John, Jesus and the apostles, there would be some record of it in the Jewish Targums. These were translations of the Hebrew Scriptures into Aramaic when Aramaic was the common language of Palestine after the Babylonian Exile (about 250 B.C. and A.D. 300). After the reading of the Scriptures there would be an oral rendering of them into Aramaic for the worshipers. This practice began at least as early as the prophet Ezra—*So they read in the book in the law of God distinctly, and gave the sense, and caused them to understand the reading* (cf. Neh. 8:5-8).[13]

---

[9] *Josephus, Antiquities*, Book XIII, chap. 9.1, William Whiston: translator (Grand Rapids, Michigan: Kregel Publications, 1966) p. 279.

[10] Ibid., *Antiquities*, Book XIII, chap. 11.3, p. 282.

[11] Ibid., *Antiquities*, Book XX, chap. 2.1, p. 415.

[12] Ibid., *Antiquities*, Book XIII, chap. 5.1, p382. Note: In Scripture, John the Baptist's baptism was never for physical purification as Josephus thought.

[13] For an easily readable study consult *The Aramaic Bible: The Targums*, twelve volumes. Project Director, Martin Mc Namara, M.S.C. *(Continued on next page)*

The next step in the development of targums was to record these oral renditions into writing. The earliest existing material of such like is from Qumran about the second century B.C. In the centuries following the return from exile, Judaism was centered in Babylonia and in Palestine. In Babylonia, the Targum Onkelos was a word-for-word rendering of the Hebrew Pentateuch. Targum Jonathan Ben Uzziel became authoritative from the fourth century A.D. as the official Babylonian version of The Prophets. The only complete version of the Palestinian Targum in existence is Neofiti I from about the third century A.D. Only fragments of the Palestinian Targum on the Pentateuch are in existence among the Cairo Genizah scrolls. There are individual targums on Job-Psalms, Proverbs, the Five Scrolls and Chronicles which were never official and were later in origin than the targums of the Law and the Prophets.[14]

These targums are valuable in that they educate us regarding Jewish modes of expression, exegetical methods and interpretation in the early centuries of Christianity. In the Jonathan Ben Uzziel of the prophets, and the Onkelos of the Pentateuch, nothing is mentioned of Jewish proselyte baptism.

Various incomplete targums are extant, some of which would mention a dipping for servitude. This would not be a proselyte of choice, but a proselyte by compulsion in accordance with Gen. 17:12, 13, and would have nothing to do with Christian baptism.

When an incomplete targum comments on Deut. 21:13 regarding the conditions required for a beautiful captive woman being married to an Israelite, it requires that she dip herself and become a proselytess in his house. But such dipping is not mentioned in the Deuteronomy passage itself, nor is it mentioned in the Targum Onkelos. The mention of dipping comes after the Talmud via an allegorical

---

(Collegeville, Minnesota: The Liturgical Press, 1992). [separate volumes have distinct publication dates]. Mc Namara is professor of Sacred Scripture at Milltown Institute of Theology and Philosophy, Doublin.

[14] For an extensive discussion of the targums and the talmuds, see Emil Schurer, D.D., M.A., *A History of the Jewish People in the Time of Jesus Christ*, Translated by Rev. John Macpherson, M.A., (U.S.A.: Hendrickson Publishers, Inc., 1998), First Division, Vol I., pp. 117-166.

method of interpretation and does not come within the time of the targums under consideration.

Neither is there any mention of such a custom in the *Book of Traditions*, a collection of all the traditions among the Jews from age to age. It was written by Judah Hakkadosh around 150 A.D. (some say around 220 A.D.), and speaks of proselytes, but not of their baptism into Judaism. Now, if there is mention of a proselytized stranger dipping himself on the evening of the Passover, this is not proselyte baptism. He is unclean from being just circumcised and must bathe for the same reason any Jew would have to bathe if he had contacted anything unclean before eating the Passover. So this rule, according to Shammai, was concerning one already made a proselyte, and therefore the dipping or baptism prescribed to him by Hillell was for ceremonial uncleanness. His circumcision and commitment to Jewish Law made him a proselyte, but being just circumcised made him unclean, as if he had touched a dead body.[15] This dipping was not on account of proselytism, but was common to, and obligatory upon, a circumcised Israelite in order to eat the Passover. Therefore he had to wait seven days until he was purified.[16] This required a body washing which had both symbolic as well as literal, sanitary significance (Nu.19:11-19).

It was an ablutionary *(immersion)* washing of the body that was prescribed on a number of occasions in the Old Testament. It was required for defilement of lepers (Lev. 14:8,9);[17] of those having a

---

[15] Augustus Hopkins Strong, *Systematic Theology* (Valley forge, Pa.: The Judson Press, 1969), p. 931. Strong's Theology quotes Edersheim's *Life and Times of Jesus,* 2,742-744 regarding this exact exchange: "We have positive testimony that the baptism of proselytes existed in the times of Hillel and Shammai. For, whereas the school of Shammai is said to have allowed a proselyte who was circumcised on the eve of the Passover, to partake, after baptism, of the Passover, the school of Hillel forbade it."

[16] Allbert M. Shulman, *Gateway to Judaism: An Encyclopedic Guide to the Doctrines, Ceremonies, Customs, Languages, and Community Life of the Jews* (S. Brunswick; New York; London: Thomas Lyoseloff, 1971) Vol. 1, p. 458. "The founders of Judaism were among the first to realize the value of circumcision to the hygiene and health of the people."

[17] For sanitation purposes it was required that there be two washings of clothes and body and two head shavings, seven days apart. This had not only spiritual significance but also hygienic, removing scales and flakes that might have passed on contagious diseases.

bloody issue (Lev. 15:5-13);[18] of those having eaten that which had died (Lev. 17:15,16); of women before marriage (Esther 2:12); after childbirth (Lev. 12:6-8; Lk. 2:22); [19] after menstruation (Lev. 15:19-23; II Sam. 11:4);[20] of those who came in contact with the dead (Num. 19:11-22; 31:19-20);[21] of the high priest bathing himself before performing the rituals of the Day of Atonement (Lev. 16:4) and of Jews before the Passover (Jn.11:55).[22]

The proof that purification rules were for hygienic as well as ceremonial purposes is clearly seen in Deuteronomy 23:12, 13. When a soldier in a military camp went out to defecate at night, he had to take with him a small paddle for digging. He was then required to bury his excrement.[23] Having to defecate was not a sin, but the soldier was to realize the Lord's holiness and omnipresence in the camp at all times. Even in his most private moments the holy God was with him, observing his behavior. But also, digging latrines had much to do with proper hygiene and to prevent disease from spreading through the camp.

---

[18] This is a man who is probably infected with gonorrhea. The passage deals with ceremonial uncleanness as well as hygienic. This is why the passage addresses the contamination of his bed (vss. 4, 5), his chair (v.6), his person (v.7), his spittle (v.8), his saddle (v.9), and anything contacted from his discharge (v.10). The concern was that his uncleanness was infectious. There was a seven-day waiting period after the disease and then a bathing and washing of his clothes (15:13-15).

[19] Having a baby was a fulfillment of a divine command (Gen. 1:28) and therefore not a sin from which to be purified. Thus, the ritual cleansing had a sanitary purpose as well as a ceremonial significance.

[20] Though this was a periodic rather than a chronic uncleanness (vss. 25-27), the woman was considered unclean for seven days, the same as the man with venereal disease (vss. 2-12). Sexual intercourse was forbidden during menstruation (18:19; 20:18); 15:24 could mean that if a wife's period commenced while having intercourse, the husband would be unclean also and would also be a source of secondary pollution.

[21] It is easy to see the sanitary as well as the spiritual significance of these rules.

[22] The symbolic, spiritual significance of such purification is recorded in Psalms 26:6; 5:17; Ezekiel 36:25; Hebrews 10:22, but sanitary purposes should not be overlooked.

[23] Ibid. *Josephus*, *Wars* Book II, Chap. 8.7, p.477. Josephus notes that the Essenes had the same requirement for the members of their communities.

Why are we discussing the sanitary significance of purification baths in the Old Testament? Because it is important for those who believe in ritual salvation to stress spiritual cleansing when referring to these purification rituals. This is why *they of the circumcision* in the early church considered circumcision essential to salvation. Maimonides, a twelfth century Jewish exegete, taught that the bathing pool [*Jewish Miqvaot*] was definitely not for hygienic cleansing when he wrote: *Now 'uncleanness' is not mud or filth which water can remove but is a matter of scriptural decree and dependent on the intent of the heart.*[24] Maimonides observed that the water of a spring *imparts cleanness however little its quantity.*[25] Whatever may be said of Maimonides as an industrious and judicious compiler of things out of the Talmud, he should not be considered of greater and higher authority than those writings from which he has compiled them. In Jewish interpretation there is a *Hierarchy of Authority* with an assumption that every later group of scholars is inferior to an earlier one, and is therefore bound by the decrees of its predecessors. This principle should be applied to anything originating with Maimonides.

The allegorical method of interpretation has allowed later Jewish Scholars and Christian theologians through the Reformation to take extreme liberties with the text of Scripture when it served their purposes. Maimonidies says of allegorizing that the intention was not to destroy the Biblical reading, but to add to it a poetic figure. And so, if the scholar wishes to glorify the Sabbath, he will read Isaiah 56:2: *Blessed is the man that keepeth the Sabbaath, and he shall be pardoned*, instead of: *That keepeth the Sabbaath from polluting it.* Hence the

---

[24] *Code of Maimonides, Book Ten, the Book of Cleanness*, transl., Herbert Danby (New Haven: Yale University Press, 1954), p. 526. See also, William Sanford La Sor, "Discovering What Jewish Miqvoat Can Tell Us About Christian Baptism" (*Biblical Archaeology Review*, Jan.-Feb. 1987) p. 52. Also, Frederic W. Ferrar, *History of Interpretation* (Grand Rapids, Michigan: Baker Book House, 1979) pp. 275,463. Maimonides believed in the allegorical method of interpretation; was a rationalist and a Kabbalist. He practically rejected much Talmudism and attempted to show by Aristotelian and Alexandrian methods that the written Law was founded on immutable reason. Some of his contemporary rabbis charged him with *selling the Scriptures to the Greeks*. When Scriptures were incompatible with his reason he held that the Scriptures were to be allegorically explained.

[25] Ibid., Maimonides *Book of Cleanness*, p. 526

incessant Rabinic formula: *Read not so, but so.*[26] Even though Old Testament ablution also had a spiritual significance, that meaning was metaphysical and not made real by the physical rite itself. The only spiritual significance was in pointing to a literal reality of the coming of a suffering Messiah. This precise point has always been a stumbling block for those who believed in ritual regeneration. Ablution was a picture of the literal fact that God's grace and mercy washes away our spiritual filth through the blood of Christ: (Rev. 1:5) *unto him that loved us, and washed us from our sins in his own blood.*[27]

Again, one would expect to read of some form of proselyte baptism in the Jewish Mishnah which defines all matters of civil and religious interest for the Jews. It is regarded as the *corpus juris* of Judaism. The Mishnah addressed agricultural tithes, public feasts, marriage, torts, Temple sacrifices, and ritual purity. It was organized into sixty-three tractates and six orders and was created around 200 A.D. under Rabbi Judah the Prince in Palestine. The text evolved in its exposition and interpretation by the Babylonian and Palestinian Talmuds. But, according to some scholars, there is no mention in them

---

[26] Ibid. Ferrar, *History of Interpretation*, pp. 104,105: "Concerning allegorization, Ferrar says: "Besides all these methods there was yet another which consisted in altering the words of the text into others which resembled them. It is strange that this absolutely arbitrary device for making the Scriptures say exactly what the interpreter wished to make them say was defended on the same principle of letter-worship as that which lay at the root of the whole system. The method was indefinitely facilitated by the plasticity of words in which the vowel-points could be altered in many ways. Thus the Bible was forced to imply thousands of things of which its writers never dreamed. On the pretence that every word of it was supernaturally communicated by God, it was asserted that if words sounded at all like other words, that secondary meaning must all be implied." Remember in the *Music Man* the famous line: *"Pool" starts with "P" and "P" rhymes with "T" and "T" spells "Trouble" right here in River City."*

[27] See also Ps. 51:2, 7; 65:3; 73:13; 79:9; Prov. 16:6; 20:9; Isa. 1:16, 18; 4:3,4; Dan. 12:10; Acts 22:16; I Cor. 6:11; Tit. 3:5; Heb. 1:3; 9:14; 2 Pet. 1:9; I Jn. 1:7, 9; Rev. 7:14. When the New Testament tells us to clean ourselves it is not speaking of physical sanitation but of spiritual self-discipline (James 4:8; I Cor. 5:7). Peter reminds us that baptism is *not the putting away of the filth of the flesh* (I Pet. 3:21), but OT bathing was the putting away of the filth of the flesh. Yet, OT bathing did not put away the filth of the spirit.

of a proselyte baptism.[28]   However, other scholars equally contend that the Mishnah does teach a proselyte baptism dating from the first century A.D., which is still too late to have its antecedent in ancient Judaism.[29] Usually such passages speak of the baptism of one who is already a proselyte as a prerequisite to eating the Passover. This again is not a dipping to become a proselyte, but a dipping for ceremonial uncleanness. If he had just been made a proselyte by such a bath, there would have been no reason for a second dipping to qualify him for the Passover. Just coming out of heathenism and circumcision made him a ceremonially unclean Jewish proselyte, and therefore he had to undergo a purification rite the same as was common to and obligatory upon a circumcised Israelite in order to eat the Passover (See footnote 3). And though female proselytes had to undergo a ritual bathing also, nothing is said of that baptism making them proselyte Jewesses.

If there had been such a ritual as proselyte baptism in the time of John, Christ and the Apostles, we should look for it in the writings of the Christian Fathers of the first four centuries. They, especially converted Jews, would certainly not be ignorant of this if from Judaism Christian baptism was taken.

The Epistle of Barnabas speaks of Jewish rites as being a type of the Christian gospel and of their having their fulfillment in it.[30] His

---

[28] Ibid. *Strong syst. Theo.* P. 931. Quoting Broadus in his *American Commentary* on Matt. 3:6…"Proselyte baptism is not mentioned in the Mishna (A. D. 200); the first distinct account of it is in the Babylonian Talmud (Gemara) written in the fifth century; it was not adopted from the Christians, but was one of the Jewish purifications which came to be regarded, after the destruction of the Temple, as a peculiar initiatory rite. There is no mention of it, as a Jewish rite, in the OT, NT, Apocrypha, Philo, or Josephus."

[29] *The Interpreter's Dictionary of the Bible* (New York: Abingdon Press, 1962), Vol. 1, p. 348. "There is no reference to proselyte baptism in the OT or the Apoc., nor in Josephus or Philo. Some have therefore disputed whether this rite was practiced early enough to have influenced the origin of Christian baptism. It is now generally agreed, however, that the references in Epictetus, the Sibylline Oracles, and the Mishnah enable us, with some confidence, to date the beginnings of the practice not later than from the first century A.D." But these baptisms were for physical and spiritual purification. Christian baptism was for neither of these purposes.

[30] *Epistle of Barnabas, Ante-Nicene Fathers*, chaps. 6-12 (Grand Rapids, Michigan: Wm. B. Eerdmans Publishing Co., 1977), pp. 140-145.

goal is to find out what was beforehand said concerning the ordinance of baptism, but does not speak of a proselyte baptism, though he had ample opportunity if he knew anything about it.[31]

Justin Martyr lived in the second century and was a Samaritan who had knowledge of Jewish affairs. He had a great dispute with Trypho the Jew and Tarphon, a Jewish doctor—both frequently mentioned in the Mishnah. Neither of these Jews bring up the subject of proselyte baptism.[32] In fact, in answer to a question by Justin regarding what Jewish rites were necessary to be observed, Trypho replies: *to keep the Sabbath; to be circumcised; to observe the new moons; to be baptized or dipped, whoever touches any of these things forbidden by Moses.* This spoke of ceremonial uncleanness from touching a dead body, or bone, or grave.[33] Justin himself makes mention of Jewish proselytes, and calls them circumcised proselytes, but does not mention baptism.[34] He does speak of a certain sect, whom he does not consider truly Jews, and calls them Baptists.[35] If it was a universal Jewish tradition to receive proselytes by baptism, why would a certain sect be stigmatized by such a name as *Baptists*?

Origen, of the beginning of the third century, lived in Alexandria with a great numbers of Jews, and must have known their customs. In his opposition to Heracleon the heretic, he says that *he was not able to shew that ever any prophet baptized.*[36] If none of these baptized, except for John the Baptist, then what is the foundation for believing that there was such a baptism of proselytes before John and Christ?

---

[31] Ibid. *Epist. of Barn*, Chap.11, p. 144..
[32] Ibid. *Ante-Nicene Fathers* Vol. 1: Justin Martyr, *Dialogue with Trypho*, Chap. 13, p. 200. "For Isaiah did not send you to bath, there to wash away murder and other sins, which not even all the water of the sea were sufficient to purge; but as might have been expected, this was that saving bath of the olden time which followed those who repented, and who no longer were purified by the blood of goats and of sheep, or by the ashes of an heifer, or by the offerings of fine flour, but by faith through the blood of Christ, and through His death, who died for this very reason..."
[33] Ibid. *Dialogue with Trypho*, Chap. 46, Vol. 1, p. 217.
[34] Ibid. *Dialogue with Trypho*, Chaps. 122,123, Vol. 1, PP. 260-261.
[35] Ibid. *Dialogue with Trypho*, Chap. 80, Vol. 1, p. 239.
[36] Ibid. *Origen's Commentary on John*, Chap. 13, *Ante-Nicene Fathers*, Vol. 10, PP. 362,363.

The Gospel And Baptism Of John the Baptist: Was It Christian?

Jerome, living in the same century, spent much time in Judea, having Jews for his teachers, yet he never mentions admitting proselytes by baptism or dipping. In defense of his doctrine of Christian baptism he attempts to take almost every reference to water in the Old Testament and make it a type of baptism. He promises to do this *with all the skill of a rhetorician* to *sing the praises of water and of baptism.* He argues that the Spirit's moving over the face of the waters to produce the infant world is a type of the *child drawn from the laver of baptism.* The Genesis firmament between heaven and earth teaches that the sinner must go through baptism to enter heaven. The first living beings coming out of the waters pictures believers soaring *out of the laver with wings to heaven.* The fountain in the midst of the Garden of Eden which parts into four river heads is Ezekiel's fountain which flows out of the temple *towards the rising of the sun until it heals the bitter waters and quickens those that are dead. When the antediluvian world falls into sin, nothing but a flood of waters can cleanse it again. But as soon as the foul bird of wickedness is driven away, the dove of the Holy Spirit comes to Noah as it came afterwards to Christ in the Jordan, and, carrying in its beak a branch betokening restoration and light, brings tidings of peace to the whole world.* Jerome uses the crossing of the Red Sea as a type of baptism. As the sweet waters of Marah watered the seventy palm trees, *so the cross makes the waters of the law lifegiving to the seventy who are Christ's apostles.* Baptism is pictured by Abraham's and Isaac's digging of wells. The cities of Beersheba and Gihon derive their names from springs, and thus become types of baptism. It is beside a well that Eliezer finds Rebekah; and Rachel, as a drawer of water, *wins a kiss* from Jacob. Jerome leaps from these illustrations directly into the ministries of John the Baptist, Christ and the apostles.[37] Clever allegorist that Jerome was, one would think that he would find Christian baptism somewhere in an Old Testament proselyte baptism, if indeed there was such a rite. Yet he does not mention admitting proselytes into Judaism by baptism or dipping.

Mentions of baptism from Tertullian, Cyprian, Gregory Nazianzen, and Basil only speak of the figurative baptism of the Israelites at the Red Sea; or of ritual bathings by immersion for purification from ceremonial uncleanness.

---

[37] *The Principle Works of St. Jerome, The Nicene And Post-Nicene Fathers,* (Grand Rapids, Michigan: Wm. B. Eerdmans Publishing Company, 1975) Chap. 69.6, Vol. 6, p. 145.

Where did church history first hear of proselyte baptism? It is claimed that it first appears in the Jewish Talmuds, one called *Jerusalem* and the other called *Babylonian*. The Jerusalem Talmud was for Palestinian Jews in the Jerusalem dialect. The Babylonian was for Jews in Babylon according to their dialect. The Talmud is composed of the *Mishnah*—the oral law which was in existence by the end of the second century A.D., and was collected by Rabbi Judah the Prince, and the *Gemara*—the commentaries of the Rabbis on the Mishna from A.D. 200 to 500. There was a strong practice of allegorism in interpretation so as to relativise the Scriptures. It was thought that the law of Moses had to be adapted to changing conditions in Israel. The sixth part of the Mishnah (*Purification*) enumerates laws regarding Levitical cleanness and uncleanness, clean and unclean persons and objects, and purifications (see footnote 4). The Mishnah became a textbook in rabbinical academies. The Talmud represents the work of Judaism from Ezra to the sixth century.

The Talmuds contain several passages referring to dipping of Israelites and proselytes as well. There is still some serious debate among scholars as to whether these referred to dipping for servitude, for physical pollution, etc., or whether there was a proselyte immersion practiced throughout Jewish history. This debate will continue for years to come, yet neither side will alter the point that John's baptism was from God and not from Jewish tradition. But, from a Bible student's point of view, it must be said that the Talmuds are of too late a date to prove that such a custom existed before and during the ministries of John and Christ, since they were written several centuries after those times.

The *Encyclopedia Judaica Jerusalem*, regarding *Laws of Conversion*, comments on Ex. 12:49: *There shall be one law for the citizen and for the stranger that dwelleth amongst you*, saying that *the sages interpreted to mean that the stranger (proselyte) was the equal of the citizen concerning all the precepts of the Torah*. It would seem, therefore, that if a proselyte underwent a ceremonial immersion [*tevilah*] in a baptistry [*miqvoat*], this would be the same Old Testament sanitary/ceremonial bathing that any Jew would undergo in

The Gospel And Baptism Of John the Baptist: Was It Christian?

case of uncleanness.[38] Still, this has been an ongoing debate since the first century—

> Rabbi Eliezer and Rabbi Joshua disagreed as to whether someone who immersed himself but was not circumcised or vice versa could be considered a proselyte. According to R. Eliezer, he is a proselyte even if he performed only one of these commandments. R. Joshua however, maintained that immersion was indispensable. The halakhic[39] conclusion is that *he is not a proselyte unless he has both been circumcised and has immersed himself.*[40]

The *Interpreter's Dictionary of the Bible* speaks of baptism as a purification rite for Jews and proselytes alike.[41] Also, *The New Standard Jewish Encyclopedia* takes the view that baptism is, *An essential part of the rite of conversion to Judaism in case of either sex is immersion in water to the accompaniment of special prayers. The rite,*

---

[38] *Encyclopedia Judaica Jerusalem* (Jerusalem, Israel: Keter Publishing House Jerusalem Ltd., 1972), Vol. 13, p. 1183.

[39] Geoffrey Wigoder, Editor-In-Chief, *The Encyclopedia of Judaism* (New York: Collier Macmillan Publishers, 1989), pp. 308-311. "*Halakhah* is rabbinnic jurisprudence. It is used to indicate a definitive ruling in any particular area of Jewish law. It was held that in certain areas the Torah did not prescribe any specific legislation, but left the matter to the sages to lay down specific legislation. In the early days of the Sanhedrin, the Sadducees questioned the validity of the whole concept of the oral law, halakhic rulings based upon hermeneutic interpretation."

[40] Ibid. *Encycl. Judaica Jer.*, p. 1183.

[41] *Interpreter's Dictionary of the Bible* (Abingdon Press) Vol. 1, p.p. 348, 349. Note also, *The Oxford Dictionary of the Jewish Religion* (New York-Oxford: Oxford University Press, 1997), p. 98. "…ritual purification by total immersion in water (tevilah). During the Second Temple period, baptism was practiced by many pietist groups and sects (see Essenes; John the Baptist). It was required of converts to Judaism and became the distinctive conversion rite of the Christian church (Mk. 1:9; Acts 2:38, 19:3-5). The practice of total immersion has largely given way in Christianity to a ceremonial sprinkling of water. See also Ablution; Hemerobaptists; Miqveh." Here again the assumption is made that baptism regenerates and purifies which is not the case either in the OT or the NT.

followed by John the Baptist, was subsequently taken over by the Christian Church.[42]

But what is the authority for these halakhic interpretations referring to proselyte baptism? In the eighth century, a group called the *Karaites* contended that Jewish Law can be inferred only from a literal interpretation of the Scripture. They repudiated the whole concept of Oral Law, from whence we learn of proselyte baptism. The heirs of the anti-kalakhists of modern times were the founders of Reform Judaism in the early nineteenth century.[43] If one is confused about these later references to proselyte baptism, he should consult again the principle called *hierarchy of Authority.* Within this hierarchy there is the assumption in halakhah that every later group of scholars is inferior to an earlier one and is therefore bound by the decrees of its predecessors. Therefore, we must consider that earlier sources for these proselyte baptism inferences are wanting, thus creating a lack of authority for these latter statements.

However, if the Bible is the final arbiter for the common Christian, he will realize that God never ordained a requirement for proselytes separate from that required of natural-born Jews. The Old Testament dippings for Jews, and especially priests, were not one-time events, but were repeated for sanitation as well as ceremonial purposes.[44] There was only one law for Jews and proselytes—

> One ordinance shall be both for you of the congregation, and also for the stranger that sojourneth with you, an ordinance for ever in your generations: as ye are, so shall the stranger be before the Lord (Nu. 15:15).

Moving on in our discussion, one of the strongest contemporary arguments for proselyte baptism is that Christian baptism

---

[42] *The New Standard Jewish Encyclopedia* (New York-Oxford: Facts On File, 1992), p. 112. Here again we have the assumption that Christian baptism had the same significance as OT bathing, which is impossible to defend.

[43] Ibid. *Encyclopedia of Judaism*, pp. 308-311.

[44] The *Hemerobaptists* were a sect of Jews who practiced daily ritual baptism.

sprang from the Essene community at Qumran. In 1962 the Rev. Dr. Charles Francis Potter released the second printing of his popular work, *The Lost Years Of Jesus Revealed*. The back cover of the book explained the sum and substance of the challenge under consideration:

> For centuries Christian students of the Bible have wondered where Jesus was and what he did during the so-called "eighteen silent years" between the ages twelve and thirty.
>
> The amazing and dramatic scrolls of the great Essene library found in cave after cave near the Dead Sea have given us the answer at last.
>
> That during those "lost years" Jesus was a student at this Essene school is becoming increasingly apparent. Scholars are gradually admitting the startling parallels between his doctrines and vocabulary and those of the Essenes and their "Teacher of Righteousness," who was evidently executed nearly a century before the birth of Jesus. It is to his title and authority that Jesus probably succeeded.[45]

Dr. J. L. Teicher published several articles to this effect in issues of *Journal of Jewish Studies* between 1950 and 1955. We know from history that the catalyst for Essene theology was the "Teacher of Righteousnes". Dr. Dupont-Sommer wrote: *the Galilean Teacher, as he is presented to us in the New Testament writings, appears in many respects as an astonishing reincarnation of the Teacher of Righteousness.*[46] J. M. Allegro said: *It now seems probable that the Church took over the sect's way of life, their discipline, much of their doctrine, and certainly a good deal of their phraseology, in which it is now seen that the New Testament abounds.*[47] These very same views

---

[45] The Rev. Dr. Charles Francis Potter, *The Lost Years of Jesus Revealed*, (Greenwich, Conn.: Fawcett Publications, 1966), Back cover of the book.

[46] Cited in: F. F. Bruce, *Second Thoughts on the Dead Sea Scrolls* (Great Britain: Paternoster Press, 1966) p. 139.

[47] Ibid. Bruce, *Second Thoughts,* p. 139, quoting *The Radio Times*, January 13, 1956, p. 9.

became popular in the book *The Scrolls from the Dead Sea* (1955) written by Edmund Wilson, wherein he affirms that Khirbet Qumran is perhaps more than Bethlehem or Nazareth, the cradle of Christianity.[48] The *Illustrated London News* of September 3, 1955 printed:

> John the Baptist was almost certainly an Essene, and must have studied and worked in this building; he undoubtedly derived the idea of ritual immersion, or baptism, from them. Many authorities consider that Christ Himself also studied with them for some time. If that be so, then we have in this little building something unique indeed, for alone of all the ancient remains in Jordan, this has remained unchanged—indeed, unseen and unknown, to this day. These, then, are the very walls He looked upon, the corridors and rooms through which he wandered and in which He sat...[49]

Heinrich Hirsch Graetz believed firmly that Christianity arose out of Essenism. He had a great deal to say about this point in the course of his research.[50] His main evidence consisted in the fact that John the Baptist was an Essene in all his manner of life and had all of their traits. In fact, he believed that the whole church behaved in all respects like an Essene community. In Vol. II of his famous six-volume work on the History of the Jews he wrote:

---

[48] Edmund Wilson, *The Scrolls from the Dead Sea* (New York: Oxford University Press, 1955), p. 94. "But what was the relation of Jesus to the ritual and doctrine of the sect, which the Gospels so persistently echo? Could he have been actually a member of the sect during those early years of his life when we know nothing about him—where he was or how he occupied himself—or was his contact with it, as Albright believes, chiefly by way of John the Baptist.".

[49] Ibid. Cited in : *Second Thoughts*, p. 139.

[50] Heinrich Hirsch Graetz, *History of the Jews* (Philadelphia: Jewish Publication Society of America, 1893), Vol. II: *From the Reign of Hyrcanus (135 B.C.E.) to the Completion of the Babylonian Talmud (500 C.E.)*, pp. 219, 220: "The Essenes, who had no families, were obliged to augment their numbers from without. They could only add to the community by dint of mystical persuasions, and, as believing followers of Jesus, they continued their propaganda and attracted new adherents from the lower classes, whom the leaders of the Pharisees had neglected or avoided."

> Jesus must, from the idiosyncrasies of his nature, have been powerfully attracted by the Essenes, who led a contemplative life apart from the world and its vanities. When John the Baptist—or more correctly the Essene—invited all to come and receive baptism in the Jordan, to repent and prepare for the Kingdom of Heaven, Jesus hastened to obey the call, and was baptized by him. Although it cannot be proved that Jesus was formally admitted into the order of the Essenes, much in his life and work can only be explained by the supposition that he had adopted their fundamental principles.[51]

Dr. Joseph Klausner was a great Jewish scholar of the first half of the twentieth century. He was a leading thinker in Jewish circles of rabbinical studies. Taking exception with the Essene connection view of John the Baptist and Jesus he wrote:

> Many Scholars, and especially Graetz, have wished to see in Christianity a purely Essene movement. This is not true. Jesus' object was not to form a community of solitaries, nor, as we shall see later, did he consistently practice monasticism and asceticism. Furthermore, even the early Nazarenes were no Jewish nationalists as were the Essenes, for whereas the latter played their own part in the war between Judaea amd Rome, the former fled from Jerusalem to Pella, beyond Jordan. The Christians seek to save the soul of the

---

[51] Ibid., Graetz, *History of the Jews*, Vol. II, p. 150. See also, Joseph Klausner, *Jesus of Nazareth: His Life, Times, and Teaching*, (Boston: Beacon Press, 1964), p. 110. Klausner cites the works of the famous Jewish author H. Graetz in his complete works about Jesus. It was originally written in German but it never appeared in its original form, since it was almost all embodied in his "History of the Jews" (III[5] Leipzig, 1905, pp. 376, 407-415). The French translator and editor was Moses Hess. Its French title is: H. Graetz, *Sinai et Golgotha, ou les origines du judaisme et du christianisme, suivi d'un examen critique des Evangiles anciens et modernes. Traduit et mis en ordre par Maurice Hess*, Paris, 1867. Pages 270-362 deals with the life of Jesus and his teaching, the history of subsequent Christianity being touched on briefly.

individual: the Essenes sought to save the community by social means.[52]

It will be the next task of this current study to demonstrate that the beliefs and practices of both John and Jesus would have disqualified both of them from the disciplines of the Qumran sect. If they had joined, they would no doubt have been expelled for heresy, ritual uncleanness and unseparate practices. We will enumerate fifteen contradistinctions between Christianity and the Essene sect, although it would be possible to list many more.

(1) Although there were married Essenes living in the world, the strict Essene communities practiced celibacy.[53] Philo stated that they were a celibate order, writing that *they repudiate marriage; and at the same time they practice continence in an eminent degree; for no one of the Essenes ever marries a wife.*[54] Josephus states that they shun marriage in order to guard themselves from the wantonness of woman and *are persuaded that none of them preserve their fidelity to one man.*[55] Albert M. Shulman said: *They were essentially a celibate people, frowning upon all association with women, although some did marry.*[56]

Though Christ was not married, He associated with several women such as Mary and her sister, Martha (Matt. 27, 28); the Samaritan woman at the well (Jn. 4); and the woman taken in adultery (Jn. 8). Neither John nor Jesus required their disciples to be unmarried.

---

[52] Ibid. Klausner, *Jesus of Nazareth*, P. 211.
[53] Ibid., Graetz, *History of the Jews*, Vol. II, p. 24. "It was almost impossible for Essenes to mix with women, as by the slightest contact with them they risked coming under the Levitical condemnation of uncleanliness, and, led on from one deduction to another, they began to avoid, if not to despise, the married state."
[54] Ibid. *The Works of Philo*, p. 746, *Hypothetica* 11, 14-17.
[55] Ibid. *Josephus, Complete Works, Wars of the Jews*, Book II, chap. 8.2. Also, Frank M. Cross points out that there was an order within the movement that married. *The Ancient Library of Qumran And Modern Biblical Studies* (Garden City, New York: Doubleday & Company, Inc., 1958), p. 72
[56] Albert M. Shulman, *Gateway to Judaism: An Encyclopedic Guide to the Doctrines, Ceremonies, Customs, Languages, and Community Life of the Jews* (South Brunswick-New York-London: Thomas Yoseloff, 1971), Vol. II, P. 621.

The Gospel And Baptism Of John the Baptist: Was It Christian?

In Matt. 8:14, 15 Jesus heals Peter's mother-in-law at his house. In Christianity there is neither male nor female (Galatians 3:28). Therefore, Christ's close, yet virtuous, association with women would have disqualified Him from association with the Essene sect.

(2) The Essenes required the practice of communism, as states Josephus: *These men are despisers of riches and so very communicative as raises our admiration. Nor is there any one to be found among them who hath more than another; for it is a law among them, that those who come to them must let what they have be common to the whole order.*[57] Shulman states that *Only those who would subscribe to the vow of poverty could be admitted to the order.*[58]

Although the Jerusalem church practiced community of goods, it was never prescribed by God (Acts 5). The experiment was not successful, and Paul spent much time raising money during his missionary journeys to assist the saints of Jerusalem in their poverty (II Cor. 8). The Apostle John spoke of the "haves" and "have-nots" and the need for the former to have compassion on the latter (I Jn. 3:17). Paul was speaking of degrees of wealth in the church when he said: *He which soweth sparingly shall reap also sparingly; and he which soweth bountifully shall reap also bountifully* (II Cor. 9:6). Paul did not mandate a vow of poverty but advised: *Every man according as he purposeth in his heart, so let him give; not grudgingly, or of necessity: for God love a cheerful giver* (9:7). The fact that there was both bounty and poverty in Christianity was the very basis of Paul's collections (II Cor. 8). Therefore, it is doubtful that the founders of Christianity would have been qualified members of the Essene sect.

(3) Essene custom seems to have required morning prayer facing the rising sun. Cross translates the passage in *Wars of the Jews* (Book II, Chap. 8.5) to mean, not that they worshipped the Sun, but that they prayed toward the Sun.[59] When the Prophet Daniel would pray at sun up he would face the Temple (Dan. 6:10). Jesus taught praying in secret (Matt. 6:6), and praying in Christ's name (Jn. 14:13). There is only one mediator between God and man, Who is omnipresent, and

---

[57] Ibid. *Josephus*, p. 476, *Wars of the Jews* (Book II, Chap. 8.3).
[58] Ibid. *Gateway to Judaism*, p. 621.
[59] Frank M. Cross, *Ancient Library of Qumran And Modern Biblical Studies*, Garden City, New York: Doubleday & Company, Inc., p. 77.

therefore direction is not important (I Tim. 2:5). There is no mechanical formula for prayer in the teachings of Christianity. Christ prayed early in the morning (Mk. 1:35), with others (Lk. 11:1), and on a mountain (Matt. 14:23). In the Bible one could pray standing (Neh. 9:5); kneeling (Ezra 9:5); sitting (I Chron. 17:16-27); bowing (Ex. 24:8); or with hands uplifted (I Tim. 2:8). The early church could pray in the upper room (Acts 1); in a house (Acts 12:5-17); by a river (Acts 16:13); or on a beach (Acts 21:5). What mattered was the condition of the heart and the mediation of Jesus Christ (I Jn. 5:14; Matt. 21:22; Jn. 14:13). When the question arose as to where true worship took place (on Mt. Gerizim or Mt. Zion), Jesus replied: *But the hour cometh, and now is, when the true worshippers shall worship the Father in spirit and in truth: for the Father seeketh such to worship him. God is a Spirit: and they that worship him must worship him in spirit and in truth* (Jn. 4:23, 24). Because they did not teach mechanical or ritualistic prayer, there is reason to doubt that Christ and John would have been compatible with Essenes in their worship.

(4) The Essenes were a counter-Israel cult with a counter priesthood. They were a dissident priestly sect. According to Cross, *The priests of Qumran regarded the Jerusalem sanctuary as defiled, its priests false, its calendar unorthodox.*[60] Josephus stated that: *when they send what they have dedicated to God into the temple, they do not offer sacrifices, because they have more pure lustrations of their own; on which account they are excluded from the common court of the temple, but offer their sacrifices themselves.*[61]

But, in the New Testament, no explanation is needed for the function of the non-Zadokian priest in the story of the *good Samaritan* (Luke 10:31). Essenes would not have recognized the priesthood of John the Baptist's father, Zechariah, a priest of the division of Abijah who served, according to lot, in the Jerusalem Temple (Luke 1:5, 9). Jesus recognized the legal functions of priests at Jerusalem in declaring lepers clean (Matt. 8:4; Mk. 1:44; Lk. 5:14; 17:14; see Lev. 14:3). He had no basic quarrel with the prescribed function of the temple and the priesthood of His day. When Mary and Joseph brought the baby Jesus to the Temple to be circumcised, they offered a sacrifice and placed Him in the arms of Simeon the priest. Simeon had received revelations

---

[60] Ibid. *Ancient Libraary of Qumran*, p. 96, 97.
[61] Ibid. *Josephus*, p. 377, *Antiquities* (Book XVIII, Chap. 1.5).

from the Holy Spirit about the arrival of the Messiah and prophesied to Joseph and Mary concerning the child (Lk. 2:21-35). Jesus celebrated the Passover with His disciples (Matt. 26:17-19).

Jesus was neither a Zadokian nor an Aaronic priest. His priesthood surpassed these (Hebrews 7:11); reaching back to Melchizedek (7:15-17); containing the perfection missing in the Aaronic system (7:18); being based on God's oath (7:20-22); being permanent (7:23-25); having no need to purge Himself as did the sons of Aaron (7:26-28); continuing in heaven where God has erected the true sanctuary of which Moses' tent was but a shadow (8:1-7); fulfilling the promise of a New Covenant (8:8-13); its sacrifice needing no repeating for it was once-for-all (7:27; 9:12); its offering not being animal but the body and blood of Jesus Christ (10:4, 10-14); resulting in access to God for all Christians, not just the priestly order (10:11-22); and its effectiveness in the lives of God's people being guaranteed by Christ's constant intercession (7:25). Therefore, John and Jesus could not have been a part of a separatist Zadokian-Essene sect.

(5) The Essenes lived mostly to themselves in a monastic communal environment that was fortified with walls and stringent membership requirements. Anyone seeking admission to their brotherhood underwent three years probation. During the first year, he wore the white linen habit and loin-cloth (characteristic of the sect)[62] and carried the small trowel which every Essene used to dig a latrine, as prescribed in Deut. 23:12-14. At the end of the first year, the novice was admitted to their baptismal water of purification, but two more years would elapse before he could be admitted to the communal meal. Even then there was a swearing of a list of tremendous oaths before he could touch their food.[63]

---

[62] Ibid. Graetz, *History of the Jews*, Vol. II, p. 26: "The Essenes were distinguished also by other peculiarities, they were always clothed in white linen." Ibid., But Klausner notes a contrast in clothing in *Jesus of Nazareth*, p. 243: "From his clothing of camel's hair it would seem that he [John the Baptist] looked upon himself as a prophet, for it is said of the prophets that they 'wore camel's hair;' and from his wearing a leathern girdle, that he supposed himself to be Elijah."

[63] Ibid. *Josephus*, p. 477, *Wars* (Book II, Chap. 8.7). Josephus describes the long lists of requirements for joining the Essene sect.

John baptized people as soon as he saw that they had repented or believed (Acts 19:4, 5). There was no probation period on the Day of Pentecost (Acts 2:37, 38). There was no waiting period of instruction for the Apostle Paul (Acts 9:18). John baptized publicans (possibly Gentile money handlers) without requiring them to become Jews (Lk. 3:12). John felt that he needed to be baptized, a need he would not have felt if he were an Essene and if his baptism was Essene baptism (Matt. 3:14). Luke said that any who *gladly received his word were baptized* the same day (Acts 2:41). Philip baptized the Ethiopian eunuch as soon as he believed (Acts 8:36-39). Jesus told His disciples to present the gospel to all nations, baptize believers, and then teach them to observe all things (Matt. 28:18-20). Therefore, John and Jesus required disciples to be baptized too soon after conversion to be a part of an Essene tradition.

(6) The Essenes would not anoint themselves with oil. Again, Josephus says: *They think that oil is a defilement; and if one of them be anointed without his own approbation, it is wiped off his body; for they think to be sweaty is a good thing.*[64] But the disciples of Christ went out two by two laying hands on the sick and anointing them with oil (Mk. 6:13). When Jesus was eating in the home of a Pharisee, a woman in the city, *which was a sinner* [i.e. Mary Magdalene, John 11:2], anointed Him with oil (Lk. 7:46; cf Mk. 16:6-13). See also Mary, sister of Martha in John 12:2-5. Jesus described the Good Samaritan as one who poured oil into the wounds of the man left by the side of the road (Lk. 10:34). The writer of Hebrews describes the Son as having been anointed by the Father with the *oil of gladness* (Heb. 1:9). The Apostle James told the sick to call the elders to pray for him and anoint him with oil (James 5:14). Most ointments in the Bible contained an oil base, to which aromatic spices, especially myrrh, were added (Ex. 30:23-25). Therefore, Jesus would have been seen as having unclean skin that was not rough enough and sweaty enough to be considered an Essene.

(7) We see a contrast with Essene baptism, as we have noted above, in the three-year probation before admission to the sect. Essene baptism was for physical and spiritual purification. The Baptism of John, Jesus and the apostles was for neither. The New Testament rite was believer's baptism (Acts 2:41). John's baptism was called the *Baptism of repentance for the remission of sins* (Lk. 3:3). John did not

---

[64] Ibid. *Josephus*, p. 476, *Wars* (Book II, Chap. 8.3).

baptize people so that they would repent and have remission of sins but only if they already had done so. Christians in the New Testament were added to the visible church the same day they were ritually immersed (Acts. 2:41). A key difference to be noted well is that Old Testament ritual bathings and Essene ablution were self-administered (Lev. 14:8, 9; Nu. 19:7,8), whereas John's and Apostolic baptism required an administrator (Acts 8:38, 39; Matt. 3:13, 14; 28:19; Jn. 3:23). Therefore, John and the disciples would have made themselves ceremonially unclean by touching their candidates for baptism, thus disqualifying themselves from Essene communion.

(8) Another point of difference was that of physical separatism.[65] Hippolytus said that Essenes would not handle a coin which bore the likeness of the emperor or any other man, for the very act of looking at such a thing was regarded by them as one of the forms of idolatry forbidden in the Second Commandment.[66] When the Pharisees tried to entrap Jesus on the subject of taxes He said: *Shew me the tribute money* (Matt. 22:19), then He made particular note of Caesar's image and superscription on the coin (22:20, 21). Jesus often associated with publicans who were tax collectors handling many coins for the Roman government (Matt. 9:10). Among Jews they were also rejected because they had contact with Gentiles and were, therefore, ritually unclean. *Publicans and sinners* are cited together as examples of undesirable types (Matt. 9:11; 11:19; Luke 15:1). Jews regarded Publicans as ceremonially unclean, on account of their continual contact with Gentiles, and their need to work on the Sabbath. Thus the rabbis taught that their pupils should not eat with such persons. This explains

---

[65] Ibid. Graetz, *History of the Jews*, p. 24. Of Essene separation he writes: "...an Essene, was consequently obliged to avoid any intercourse with those who were less strict than himself, lest he should be contaminated by their proximity. Such considerations compelled him to frequent the society of, and to unite himself with, those only who shared his views. To keep their purity unspotted, the Essenes were thus induced to form themselves into a separate order, the first rule of which commanded implicit obedience to the laws of scrupulous cleanliness."

[66] Ibid. *Ante-Nicene Fathers,* Vol 5, p. 136. Hippolytus, *The Refutation Of All Heresies*, Chap. 21: "Wherefore no one of those goes into a city, lest (by so doing) he should enter through a gate at which statues are erected, regarding it a violation of law to pass beneath images....And if they happen to come in contact with them (of another party) they immediately resort to ablution, as if they had touched one belonging to an alien tribe."

the expressions *tax collectors and sinners* (Matt. 9:10f.; 11:19; Mk. 2:15f.; Lk. 5:30; 7:34; 15:1) and *tax collectors and harlots* (Matt. 21:31). Matthew, one of the twelve, was himself a publican (Mtt. 10:3). The Scribes and Pharisees complained that Jesus ate with publicans and sinners (Lk. 5:30).[67] He was called a *friend of publicans* (Matt. 11:19). Jesus said that publicans would go to heaven before the Pharisees (Matt. 21:31, 32). John baptized publicans and told them to continue collecting taxes, but fairly this time (Lk. 3:12, 13). Publicans felt free to draw near to Jesus (Lk. 15:1). Jesus abode in the home of Zacchaeus the publican (Lk. 19:5). He told Peter that he would find a coin in the mouth of a fish with which to pay tribute (Matt. 17:27). The Scribes and Pharisees complained that Christ's disciples did not wash their hands when they ate bread (Matt. 15:2). Jesus was always laying hands on the sick (Mk. 5:23; 6:5; 8:25). He prophesied that his followers would lay hands on the sick (Mk. 16:18). Therefore, the Essenes would have considered Jesus an unclean, unseparate idolator and unqualified for Essene communion.

(9) We see a huge difference in their observance of the Sabbath laws.[68] In the Gospels, even the strictest rabbis would allow a domestic animal to be rescued from a pit on the Sabbath. But in the Zadokite *Laws*, a human may be rescued but not an animal. About twenty-five Sabbath regulations are listed among the Zadokite *Laws*, and they are a total contrast from the words of Jesus when He said: *The sabbath was made for man, not man for the sabbath* (Mk. 2:27). Christ's interpretation was based on the purpose for which the Sabbath was originally instituted. In addition, the New Testament Christians do not have a Sabbath day, for Christ Himself is their rest. Note the words of the Apostle Paul to the Colossian church: *Let no man therefore judge you in meat, or in drink, or in respect of an holyday, or of the new moon, or of the sabbath days* (Col. 2:16). Jesus and His disciples gleaned corn on the Sabbath (Matt. 12:1), He healed on the Sabbath

---

[67] Ibid. Graetz, *History of the Jews*, p. 25. Of the Essenes he writes: "It was only those whose views coincided with their own who could be allowed to cook food for them, and from such likewise had to be procured their clothes, tools, implements of trade and other things, in order to ensure that, in their manufacture, the laws of cleanliness had been duly carried out."

[68] Ibid. Graetz, *History of the Jews*, p. 24. Of the Essene Sabbath he writes: "In their eyes the mere act of moving a vessel from one place to another would count as a desecration of that holy day. Even the calls of nature were not attended to on that day."

(Matt. 12:10), performed miracles on the Sabbath, and was considered a Sabbath-breaker (John 9:16). Therefore, the Essenes would have considered Christ to have been in an unclean violation of their strict Sabbath laws and unqualified for communion with their sect.

10. The Qumran sect bound themselves to the old covenant of Moses. Bruce states: *What the people as a whole had failed to do, they themselves would do as a righteous Israel within Israel, and do it so faithfully that their obedience would compensate for their brethren's disobedience.*[69] Many scholars see Israel the nation as the suffering servant in Isaiah chapter fifty-three. Contrast this thought with the words of the Apostle Paul: *For as by one man's disobedience many were made sinners, so by the obedience of one shall many be made righteous* (Romans 5:19). Philip taught the Ethiopian eunuch that the suffering servant of Isaiah 53 was none other than Jesus Christ (Acts 8:32-35). Paul confronted Peter, saying: *Knowing that a man is not justified by the works of the law, but by the faith of Jesus Christ, even we have believed in Jesus Christ, that we might be justified by the faith of Christ, and not by the works of the law: for by the works of the law shall no flesh be justified* (Gal. 2:16). Paul affirmed to the Romans: *Therefore we conclude that a man is justified by faith without the deeds of the law* (Rom. 3:28). Therefore, Jesus and John would not have been committed to the Law of Moses according to the dictates of Essene standards of discipline, disqualifying them from communion with the sect.

(11) The Essenes looked for a reinstatement of the Aaronic priesthood and a new temple made with hands with a worthy priesthood.[70] In the early days of the Jerusalem church *a great many of the priests were obedient to the faith* (Acts 6:7), but there is no indication that they retained their priestly status within the Christian community. Christians were taught that they were all *a royal priesthood, to offer spiritual sacrifices acceptable to God through Jesus*

---

[69] Ibid. Bruce, *Second Thoughts*, p. 147.
[70] Miller Burrows, *Burrows on the Dead Sea Scrolls* (Grand Rapids, Michigan: Baker Book House, 1978), Vol. 2, pp. 69, 70: "In calling Jesus the Christ, the New Testament presupposes the messianic expectation of the average Jew, not the special two-Messiah concept of the Essenes... The Christian belief that several different forms of the Messianic hope were fulfilled in Jesus does not seem to have any parallel in the Qumran texts."

Christ (I Peter 2:5). They, and not the Essenes, were the true *Israel of God*, the *chosen race*, and God's own people. The Essenes saw themselves as the *Israel of God* by law and the Christians were the *Israel of God* by grace. Therefore, Jesus would have been training early Christians to be totally distinct from the Essene sect.

(12) The Qumran sect cannot he distinguished from their *Teacher of Righteousness,* who was a Zadokian priest.[71] Cross quotes 1QS9:9-11 as it speaks of *the Messiahs of Aaron and Israel.*[72] But in the Bible, Christ is a Priest forever after the order of Melchizedek (Ps. 110:4; Heb. 7:17, 21), which has its roots in the days of Abraham, 430 years before the Law of Moses (Heb. 5:6, 10; 6:20; 7:1, 10). When Jesus asked His disciples: *Whom do men say that I the Son of man am?*, the disciples responded with what they had heard: John the Baptist, Elijah, Jeremiah or one of the Old Testament prophets (Matt. 16: 13-16). But no one seems to have heard that He was the Essene *Teacher of Righteous* returned to restore Israel.[73] Therefore, Christ's own priesthood disqualified Him from association in the Essene sect. The same would be true of John's descent from the priestly line of Abijah.

(13) The Essenes expected a militant Davidic Messiah who would deliver Israel politically.[74] Jesus repudiated this concept from the days of His temptations in the wilderness right up to His death. Yes, He

---

[71] Dr. Hugh J. Schonfield *The Passover Plot: A New Interpretation of the Life and Death of Jesus* (New York: Bantam Books, 1967), p. 59. "The nearest individual approach to the achievement of Jesus is the prophetic and didactic power of the Essenes associated with the unnamed Teacher of Righteousness."

[72] Ibid. *Ancient Library of Qumran*, p. 168.

[73] Ibid. *Burrows on the Dead Sea Scrolls*, p. 68. Miller Burrows writes: "To the very end, in spite of all his efforts to instill a very different conception (Mark 8:31-33; 9:31f), the disciples hoped that he would 'restore the kingdom to Israel' (Luke 24:21; Acts 1:6). This was what the Qumran sect expected of the Davidic Messiah; he was to be, as Bruce says, 'the victorious captain of the sons of light in the final conflict with the sons of darkness'; but, Bruce adds, 'Jesus repudiated this kind of Messiahship'; indeed, he 'rejected the whole conception of such a warfare.'"

[74] Ibid. Klausner, *Jesus of Nazareth*, p. 245. "Had not the movement [Christianity] from the very beginning been impregnated with some seed, no matter how minute, of anti-Jewish nationalism, there never could have arisen the religion which so definitely tears away national barriers. *Ex nihilo nihil fit.*"

was the Messiah of David's line and will establish Israel at His second coming. But He refused to accept the kingship which the Jews of Galilee tried to force upon Him, even though this caused considerable disillusionment among many who had followed Him up to that point (Jn. 12:12-16). If He had called for a holy war, thousands would have followed Him, but instead, *Jesus answered, My kingdom is not of this world: if my kingdom were of this world, then would my servants fight, that I should not be delivered to the Jews: but now is my kingdom not from hence* (John 18:36). Therefore, Christ's rejection of any form of Zealotism disqualified Him as an Essene Messiah.

(14) As stated above, the Qumran citizens saw themselves as the suffering servant of Isaiah 53. They did not appear to have seen this fulfillment in any of their messianic figures. Jesus, on the other hand, became the *Suffering Servant,* which was the very essence of His messianic role. When the Essenes finally had to abandon their fortress, some of them might have found their way to the Jerusalem Church. There they would have learned that their hopes were fulfilled, not in the militant way in which they expected, but by the crucifixion and resurrection of Jesus Christ of Nazareth.[75] Therefore, Christ's refusal to recognize the Essenes as the *suffering servant* would have alienated Him from their sect.

(15) The role of *suffering servant* could never have been fulfilled by a total withdrawal from contact with the sinful world. Philo affirmed that the Essenes separated themselves physically from other Jews and, in so far as possible, eschewed all contact with non-Essenes.[76] Jesus was condemned because He welcomed sinners; accepted invitations to their homes, and ate their food. But even the Pharisees who condemned Him were not nearly as separate as the Qumran sect. Jesus would lay hands on the sick, thus making Himself ceremonially

---

[75] For *suffering servant* see Mk. 8:31; 9:12; Lk. 22:15; 24:26; Acts 3:18; 26:23; 17:3; Phil. 3:10; Heb. 5:8; 9:26; 13:12; I Pet 1:11; 2:121-23; 3:18; 4:1; 5:1.

[76] Ibid. *Works of Philo, (quod omnis Probus Liber Sit)* XII(76), p. 689: "These men, in the first place, live in villages, avoiding all cities on account of the habitual lawlessness of those who inhabit them, well knowing that such a moral disease is contracted from association with wicked men, just as real disease might be from an impure atmosphere, and that this would stamp an incurable evil on their souls."

unclean by Essene standards. He has always been known to Christians as the *friend of sinners*. The true *suffering servant* of Old Testament Prophecy would not be separate from Gentiles but, on the contrary, the Father said I will call Christ *a light of the Gentiles* (Isa, 42:6; Lk. 2:32). Jesus commissioned His disciples to take the gospel to all nations (Matt. 28:18-20; Acts 1:8). Obedience to such a commission would have defiled an Essene and disqualified him from communion with the sect.

The proliferation of published material connecting Christian baptism with Mosaic ritual or Essene purification has made this discussion necessary to the study of the issues under present consideration.[77] Many who espouse an Old Testament or Essene proselyte baptism stress the sacramental saving nature of the rite.[78] Therefore, a few more questions need to be asked. First, if John took up this ritual as he found it among the Jews, then why do the Scriptures represent him as the first administrator of Christian baptism?[79] Why do

---

[77] Dr. Charles F. Potter, *Did Jesus Write This Book?* (Greenwich, Conn.: Fawcett Publications, Inc., 1967), p. 143. Potter writes: "However, of all the *'ologies* and *'ists* involved in the serious riddle of Qumran and its caves, theology takes the lead because of the relationship between the Essenes, Jesus Christ and early Christianity. Bishop Lightfoot and his followers thought they had settled the question in the nineteenth century by dismissing the Essenes as having nothing to do with Christ and Christianity. A hundred years earlier, during the Age of Enlightenment, discussions frequently revolved around these questions: Was Jesus God? Was he or wasn't he an Essene? Wasn't Christianity the product of Essenism? Debates were long and hot and volumes pro and con were printed and distributed…Illustrative of that rationalistic age is a sentence from a letter (dated October 17, 1770) written by Frederick the Great to encyclopedist d'Alembert: 'Jesus was really an Essene; he was imbued with the Essene ethics, which, in their turn, owe much to Zeno [a Greek stoic philosopher].'"

[78] Ibid. *Interpreter's Dictionary of the Bible, pp.* 348, 349: "Some have maintained that the significance of proselyte baptism was purely ceremonial, but in view of the fact that commandments of the Law were read during the administration of the rite, it is probable that we should, with H. H. Rowley, see proselyte baptism as *not an act of ritual purification alone but an act of self-dedication to the God of Israel, involving spiritual factors as well as physical, with a fundamentally sacramental character.*" But Christian baptism does not have a sacramental character in that it is not a means of saving grace and does not purify the recipient in any physical or spiritual way.

[79] John's baptism is called, *the baptism of repentance*, because a change of mind was required previous to his baptism (Matt. 3:6, 7, 8; Mk. 1:4). *(Continued on next page)*

the Scriptures single him out as *the baptist* if his baptism was a common ritual in Israel? John 1:6, 33 tells us that he was sent from God with direct instructions to baptize with water. The Jews thought it was some new thing and sent a committee to confront him concerning it saying: *Why baptizest thou then, if thou be not that Christ, nor Elias, neither that prophet?* (Jn 1:25). What was so strange about this if it was a common thing among Jews?

Jesus affirmed that John's baptism was commissioned straight from Heaven and not from the traditions of men:

> The baptism of John, whence was it? from heaven, or of men? And they reasoned with themselves, saying, If we shall say, From heaven; he will say unto us, Why did ye not then believe him? But if we shall say, Of men; we fear the people; for all hold John as a prophet. And they answered Jesus, and said, We cannot tell. And he said unto them, Neither tell I you by what authority I do these things (Matt. 21:25-27).[80]

But if it was from the tradition of men, the Jews could have readily proclaimed: *of men.*

Also, if Christian baptism is Jewish proselyte baptism, why baptize natural Jews? Why did the Pharisees and Sadducees, who were natural Jews, come to be baptized of John? The Pharisees, of all people, would have been fit for a Jewish baptism, but were declared unfit for John's—

> But when he saw many of the Pharisees and Sadducees come to his baptism, he said unto them, O generation of vipers, who hath warned you to flee

---

So also, the apostles of Christ exhorted men to repent, to profess their repentance, and give evidence of it, previous to their baptism (Acts 2:38; 26:20).

[80] Jesus was baptized by John (Matt. 3:13-17). Christ's disciples were baptized by John, since Jesus baptized no one (Jn. 4:2). So, the baptism of John, and the baptism of Christ and His apostles, were simultaneous. One did not succeed the other, and there were not three Bible baptisms being administered at the same time with different meanings. It was all one ritual (Jn. 3:22, 23, 26; 4:1, 2).

from the wrath to come? Bring forth therefore fruits meet for repentance: And think not to say within yourselves, We have Abraham to *our* father: for I say unto you, that God is able of these stones to raise up children unto Abraham (Matt. 3:7-9).[81]

When the Pharisees rejected the baptism of John, they were not rejecting the tradition of men, but the very counsel of God—*But the Pharisees and lawyers rejected the counsel of God against themselves, being not baptized of him* (Lk. 7:30). The *Bible Knowledge Commentary* has a unique comment about John 3:25 regarding John's baptism:

> The zealous disciples of John the Baptist found themselves at a disadvantage in an argument. A certain Jew asked why he should join John's group. He (and others; cf. "They" in v. 26) argued about ceremonial washing. Since there were Essene lustrations and Pharisaic washings, why should Jews follow another washing, John's baptism? Besides, the group following Jesus was larger (v. 26).[82]

Why did Jesus commission His disciples to baptize all nations indiscriminately and without circumcision? Really, could anyone become a Jewish proselyte and be baptized without first being circumcised? And, *Then went out to him Jerusalem, and all Judaea, and all the region round about Jordan, And were baptized of him in*

---

[81] In the phrase *works meet for repentance*, the word *meet* (*axois*) means "worthy", or "appropriate" as in I Cor. 16:4; or "deserving" as in Matt. 10:10; or "worth" considering or accepting as in (I Tim. 1:15). In the NT the thought of merit is excluded; we are recipients of the gospel only as we receive it (Matt. 10:11, 13; 22:8; Acts 13:46; Heb. 11:38; Rev. 3:4). The *meet* John wanted was a demonstration that they had changed their minds about his gospel of Christ. Paul admonishes his readers to walk worthy of the gospel, their calling, and the Lord (I Th. 2:12; Phil. 1:27; Col. 1:10; Eph. 4:1; 3 Jn. 6), thus linking the motive and goal of Christian action, the motivating power residing in God's prior action. Hence the warning not to receive the Lord's Supper unworthily (*anaxios*) does not refer legalistically to a moral quality but to an attitude determined by the gospel.

[82] Ibid. *Bible Knowledge Commentary,* New Testament Edition, pp. 282, 283.

Jordan (Matt. 3:5). Why such a multitude if John's baptism was such a common thing?

Many scholars have used Isa. 1:16; Ezek. 16:9 and 26:29 as predictions of Christian baptism, but they refer to pursuits of personal righteousness, or else an act of God in bestowing salvation apart from any ritual. One would have to experience divine inspiration in order to get baptismal regeneration from these passages. And if the Old Testament does not speak of being admitted to Judaism by baptism, then such a Jewish practice would have been a tradition and doctrine of men. Would Jesus have condemned the traditions of men and then have proceeded to establish one of them as a divine ordinance? Instead, Jesus said to the Scribes and Pharisees: *Why do ye also transgress the commandment of God by your tradition?... Thus have ye made the commandment of God of none effect by your tradition...But in vain they do worship me, teaching for doctrines the commandments of men* (Matt. 15:3, 6, 9). Nothing can make a rite a Christian ordinance but by its being instituted by God Himself. John's ministry was based on the Word of God as it came to him—*but he that sent me to baptize with water, the same said unto me* (John 1:33), and—*the word of God came unto John the son of Zacharias in the wilderness. And he came into all the country about Jordan, preaching the baptism of repentance for the remission of sins* (Lk. 3:2, 3).

The Ethiopian Eunuch had come to Jerusalem to worship (Acts 8:27). If he was already a Jewish proselyte and had undergone their proselyte baptism, how did he know that he needed to undergo a Christian believer's baptism (Acts 8:36)? Many of the Jews on the Day of Pentecost were proselytes (Acts 2:10). If proselyte baptism and Christian baptism were the same, why did Peter command those who believed to be baptized (Acts 2:38)? Why do we assume that any proselytes became converted on the Day of Pentecost? Because the Grecians, or Hellenists, whose widows were neglected in the daily ministration, no doubt included widows of Jewish proselytes whose husbands had been members of the Jerusalem church and had been baptized. This is why Nicholas the *proselyte of Antioch* was one of the men appointed to administer the benevolent fund to these widows (Acts 6:1, 5)? Why then would he, as one of the first deacons of the Jerusalem church, have submitted to Christian baptism?

Finally, if baptism and circumcision always co-existed, where did Christianity get the idea that baptism replaces circumcision? This question will be discussed more thoroughly in the next section of this study.

Some scholars, admitting the point we have made regarding proselyte baptism, will argue that John the Baptist's ministry was a parenthetical bridge between the Old and New Testaments. Is there a *dispensation of John* in the Bible? As we have noted before, the Holy Spirit proclaimed John's ministry as *The beginning of the gospel of Jesus Christ, the Son of God* (Mk. 1:1). When Peter was called to present the Gospel to Gentiles, he professed the same, saying:

> In every nation he that feareth him, and worketh righteousness, is accepted with him. The word which God sent unto the children of Israel, preaching peace by Jesus Christ: (he is Lord of all:) That word, I say, ye know, which was published throughout all Judaea, and began from Galilee, *after the baptism which John preached* (Acts 10:35-37).

Jesus said: *The law and the prophets were until John: since that time the kingdom of God is preached, and every man presseth into it* (Lk. 16:16). John did not foretell the imminent coming of the Messiah, but announced that the Messiah/King was present—*In those days came John the Baptist, preaching in the wilderness of Judaea, And saying, Repent ye: for the kingdom of heaven is at hand* (Matt. 3:1, 2). The phrase *is at hand* is in the perfect tense and therefore it was before the crucifixion, resurrection, or Day of Pentecost that John knew that he must decrease and that Christ must be preeminent (Jn. 3:30).

A simple resolution to the whole debate can be accomplished by comparing the gospel of John the Baptist with that of Christ, and again with that of the apostles. John said: *repent ye: for the kingdom of heaven is at hand* (Matt. 3:2); Jesus said: *Repent: for the kingdom of heaven is at hand* (Matt. 4:17); and Luke said concerning Paul that he, *dwelt two whole years in his own hired house, and received all that came in unto him, Preaching the kingdom of God, and teaching those things which concern the Lord Jesus Christ, with all confidence, no man forbidding him* (Acts 28:30, 31).

The Gospel And Baptism Of John the Baptist: Was It Christian?

The Apostle Paul equated his gospel and baptism with John the Baptist when he said: *John verily baptized with the baptism of repentance, saying unto the people, that they should believe on him which should come after him, that is, on Christ Jesus* (Acts 19:4). And John the Evangelist said of Jesus: *that whosoever believeth in him should not perish, but have eternal life* (Jn. 3:15).

John the Baptist said: *Behold the Lamb of God, which taketh away the sin of the world* (Jn. 1:29, 36); Phillip identifies the lamb of Isaiah 53, who is dumb before his shearer, as none other than Jesus Christ (Acts 8:32-35); Peter calls Christ *a lamb without blemish and without spot* (I Pet. 1:19); and in the book of Relevation Christ Himself *stood a Lamb as it had been slain* (Rev. 5:6).

John the Evangelist records John the Baptist as saying:[83] *He that believeth on the Son hath everlasting life: and he that believeth not the Son shall not see life; but the wrath of God abideth on him* (Jn. 3:36);[84] Paul said of John the Baptist: *John verily baptized with the*

---

[83] Most theologians will not allow John the Baptist to have said or understood the statement in v. 36, and therefore insist that these are the words of John the Evangelist. Though John the Evangelist is recording these words, they could be considered the testimony of John the Baptist. This would be perfectly consistent with Paul's description of the Baptist's gospel in Acts 19:4. Tertullian was certain of this in the third century when he said: "Moreover, when John (the Baptist) was asked what he happened *to know* of Jesus, he said: *The Father loveth the Son, and hath given all things into His hand. He that believeth on the Son hath everlasting life; and he that believeth not the Son shall not see life, but the wrath of God abideth on him.*" Ibid., *Ante-Nicene Fathers*, *[Against Praxeas, Chapter XXI]* Vol. III, p., 616, see also p. 674. Also, Victorinus of fourth century Africa, perhaps the first systematic theologian of the Trinity, said: "Moreover, John the Baptist had also anticipated this, by saying to his disciples: *For God giveth not the Spirit by measure <u>unto him</u>. The Father*, says he, *loveth the Son, and hath given all things into His hands.*" Ibid., *[Commentary on the Apocalypse of the Blessed John, From the First Chapter] Ante-Nicene Fathers*, Vol. VII, p. 345.

[84] Henry M. Morris, *Defenders Study Bible: King James Version* (Grand Rapids, Michigan: Word Publishing, 1995), p. 1138. (Note on Jn. 3:31) "Since there is no contextual break after John 3:30, it is reasonable to infer that the testimony of John the Baptist continues through John 3:36, These words demonstrate still further the remarkable understanding he had concerning the person and work of Jesus Christ. In John 3:31, the phrase *from above* is the *(Continued on next page)*

baptism of repentance, saying unto the people, that they should believe on him which should come after him, that is, on Christ Jesus (Acts 19:4); John the Evangelist records Jesus as saying: *He that believeth on him is not condemned: but he that believeth not is condemned already, because he hath not believed in the name of the only begotten Son of God* (Jn. 3:18); yet the Apostle Peter said: *To him give all the prophets witness, that through his name whosoever believeth in him shall receive remission of sins* (Acts 10:43). John the Baptist's plan of personal salvation and John the Evangelist's were the same.

John the Baptist *came for a witness, to bear witness of the Light, that all men through him might believe* (Jn. 1:7); Simeon the Priest called Jesus *A light to lighten the Gentiles, and the glory of thy people Israel* (Lk. 2:32); Jesus said of Himself: *And this is the condemnation, that light is come into the world, and men loved darkness rather than light* (Jn. 3:19); yet when Paul was called into the ministry, God commanded that he would be *a light of the Gentiles, that thou shouldest be for salvation unto the ends of the earth* (Acts 13:47; cf, 26:18, 23). Paul shows us that even the devil knows this to be true when he says: *In whom the god of this world* [Satan] *hath blinded the minds of them which believe not, lest the light of the glorious gospel of Christ, who is the image of God, should shine unto them* (II Cor. 4:4). Jesus said of Himself: *I am the light of the world: he that followeth me shall not walk in darkness, but shall have the light of life* (Jn. 8:12); and, *As long as I am in the world, I am the light of the world* (Jn. 9:5); and again: *believe in the light, that ye may be the children of light...I am come a light into the world, that whosoever believeth on me should not abide in darkness* (Jn. 12:36, 46).

John the Baptist, Christ, and the Apostles taught salvation by grace through faith in Christ, and therefore John's gospel was not a parenthetical plan of salvation. When Apollos joined the ministries of Aquila and Priscilla, he knew only the baptism of John but was never asked to be rebaptized (Acts 18:24-28).[85] John's baptism was

---

same Greek word as *again* in John 3:3. Thus to be *born again* is to be *born from above*."

[85]Ibid., p. 1211. (Acts 19:4) "...John verily baptized with the baptism of repentance, saying unto the people, that they should believe on him which should come after him, that is, on Christ Jesus" See note: "...Not even Apollos, who also had known *only the baptism of John* until Aquila and Priscilla gave *(Continued on next page)*

considered Christian. It was John who baptized Jesus Christ (Matt. 3:13-16). So, when a Christian follows the Lord in baptism, it is John's baptism. Christian baptism is a profession of faith in the death, burial and resurrection of Christ. When the Jerusalem Church felt it was necessary to replace Judas, the betrayer of Christ, the replacement had to be someone who had been with them since John's ministry—*Wherefore of these men which have companied with us all the time that the Lord Jesus went in and out among us, Beginning from the baptism of John, unto that same day that he was taken up from us, must one be ordained to be a witness with us of his resurrection* (Acts 1:21, 22).[86]

If John's baptism was parenthetical, then so was that of the disciples before Pentecost (Jn. 3:22-24). If this was not Christian baptism, then why were none of these rebaptized in order to enter the New Testament church? It was said that the disciples of Christ baptized more converts than the disciples of John (Jn. 4:1, 2; cf. Jn. 3:26). If John's converts were not rebaptized, and if the disciples themselves were not rebaptized, then the New Testament church began with a multitude of "converts" who refused to embrace Christian baptism—if John's baptism was not Christian.

If the reader does not yet understand the import of this question, he will when he later sees how essential it is for many baptismal regenerationists to factor the dying thief out of the gospel equation. They will admit that he was saved without being baptized because Christian baptism was not essential to salvation until Pentecost and thereafter.[87] But, as we have seen, the gospel is not one of the things that changed at Pentecost, and no one saved and baptized during the ministries of John and Christ were required to be rebaptized. For those theologians who believe that regeneration happens by or at baptism, it is fundamental to factor John the Baptist out of the gospel equation. Why? Because John the Baptist required regeneration and proof of it prior to his baptism. This is why the next chapter of this present work will be fundamentally important to the reader for

---

him further instruction (Acts 18:25, 26), needed to be rebaptized. The same is true of the twelve apostles.

[86] See footnotes 78 & 79.

[87] Ibid. *Interpreter's Dictionary of the Bible*, p. 349: "The rite of baptism with water as the symbol of entry into the Christian community was practiced from the day of Pentecost onward."

demonstrating that salvation in the NT was independent of, and prior to, ritual baptism..

So, in summarization, we have seen that Jewish proselyte baptism cannot be cited prior to and during the establishment of Christianity except through the allegorical method of interpretation.[88] We have observed that John and Jesus could not have been members of the Essene sect. We have noted that there is no *Jonic*, parenthetical dispensation of the gospel. We have established that many Jewish proselytes joined the Jerusalem church and were required to be baptized. We have failed to see where any born-again converts baptized by John or the disciples needed rebaptism after Pentecost.[89] And, we have documented that the gospels of John the Baptist, Jesus, and the apostles were one and the same.

---

[88] For a most informative study of first century Jewish proselytism see: *Jewish Proselytism at the Time of Christian Origins: Chimera or Reality*, in Journal for the Study of the New Testament, Francis Watson, Editor (Sheffield, England: sheffield Accademic Press, 62, 1996), pp. 62-103.

[89] In chapter nine of this present work we will discuss the "so-called" disciples of John the Baptist who were rebaptized (Acts 19).

Chapter Five

Does Baptism Replace Circumcision?

Let the one who contends that... circumcision on the eighth day is still to be observed because of the threat of death,... prove to us that in ancient times righteous men kept the Sabbath or practiced circumcision, and were thereby made "friends of God." God created Adam uncircumcised and non-observant of the Sabbath. Why did God not circumcise him—even after his sinning—if circumcision purges?... Furthermore, God freed from the deluge Noah, who was uncircumcised and did not observe the Sabbath. Enoch, too, God transported from this world, even though that most righteous man was uncircumcised and did not observe the Sabbath.... Melchizedek also, "the priest of the most high God," although uncircumcised and not observing the Sabbath, was chosen to the priesthood of God.

Turtullian (c. 197, W), 3.153

Evangelical theology is long overdue for a fresh discussion regarding the place of circumcision in the Old Testament plan of salvation. For logical reasons, there will be a repetition of certain concepts in this chapter. The redundancy will be essential to the flow of the argument being set forth. The theory that baptism imparts the saving grace of Christ is most often a product of the belief that circumcision imparted the saving grace of God throughout the Old Testament. It will be the purpose of this chapter to cite the theory of circumcisional regeneration among Jewish scholars; to show from Scripture that at no time has circumcision been a means of saving grace; and to cite the history of the theory that baptism replaced circumcision in the New Testament. We intend to show that the call of Abraham, the Abrahamic Covenant, and the covenant of circumcision were three separate propositions and should be understood separately as well as compositely. We will observe that the plan of salvation by grace was only a part of the Abrahamic Covenant. In chapter nine of this work we will demonstrate from Scripture the error of the baptismal regeneration theory.

We begin by asking the question: *What was the covenant of circumcision and its relationship to personal salvation in the Old Testament?* If some Christians find it difficult to concentrate on this section of the chapter, they may wish to skip toward the end where Dr. Alexander Carson discusses Col. 2:11, 12. However, it is strongly advised that one familiarize himself with the material in this entire section. We learned in the previous chapters that God's plan of salvation has been the same throughout all divisions of the Bible. The plan is based on a covenant of redemption (the plan of salvation) made within the Trinity before the world began (Titus 1:2).

From a purely historical perspective, we cannot presently resolve the debate concerning whether the Jews considered circumcision to be that which imparted the regenerating power of God, or whether it was a separate covenant of works pointing to (but not imparting) the regenerating grace of God. It can, as we shall observe, be defended both ways from Jewish tradition. But from a purely biblical slant, we will deny that circumcision ever imparted the eternally saving grace of God.

Does Baptism Replace Circumcision?

We should consider, for historic perspective, the second century invasion of Jerusalem by Antiochus Epiphanes.[1] On the fifteenth day of Kislev, 168 B.C.E., he erected the statue of Zeus in the Jewish temple sanctuary and ordered a pig to be sacrificed on the altar. Jews were forced to join a parade in honor of Dionysus. Antiochus decreed the death penalty for loyalty to the Jewish faith, and thus circumcision became a capital crime.[2] Several mothers who had their sons circumcised suffered martyrdom. It is recorded that two women had their babies bound to their breasts and then were cast headlong from the wall.[3] That Jews were willing to give their lives for the sake of circumcision implies that, in the minds of some, eternity was at stake.

Yet many Hellenistic Jews did not consider circumcision a matter of eternal life and death. Some of those who participated in athletics at the gymnasium had an operation performed to conceal the fact of their circumcision.[4] This procedure to obliterate circumcision

---

[1] (I Maccabees 1:44-50) "For the king had sent letters by messengers unto Jerusalem and the cities of Judah that they should follow the strange laws of the land, and forbid burnt offerings, and sacrifice, and drink offerings, in the temple; and that they should profane the sabbaths and festival days: And pollute the sanctuary and holy ordinances. And people: Set up altars, and groves, and chapels of idols, and sacrifice swine's flesh, and unclean beasts: That they should also leave their children uncircumcised, and make their souls abominable with all manner of uncleanness and profanation: To the end they might forget the law, and change all the ordinances. And whosoever would not do according to the commandment of the king, he said, he should die."

[2] "Jerusalem became a desolate city inhabited by strangers. The Chassidim fled to the hills and sought refuge in the caves. One Sabbath day a thousand of them were surprised in their retreats by soldiers of the king, and all the thousand perished. In the court of the Temple, beside the altar, stood 'the abomination of desolation,' the statue of Zeus, symbol of the triumph of Hellenism and the subjugation of the Hebrew spirit and nation." Rufus Learsi, *Israel: A History of the Jewish People*, (Cleaveland: World Publishing Company, 1949), p. 131.

[3] (II Maccabees 6:10) "For there were two women brought, who had circumcised their children; whom when they had openly led round about the city, the babes handing at their breasts, they cast them down headlong from the wall."

[4] (I Maccabees 1:14, 15) "Whereupon they built a place of exercise at Jerusalem according to the customs of the heathen: And made themselves uncircumcised, and forsook the holy covenant, and joined themselves to the heathen, and were sold to do mischief."

was called *epispasm*. Circumcision was widely neglected in Hellenistic times, and accordingly, uncircumcision was proclaimed an unforgivable, damnable error of eternal consequence.[5]

Under the persecution of Hadrian we find that the Emperor sought to transform Jerusalem into a pagan city and was determined to destroy Judaism altogether. He also made it a capital crime to follow the practice of circumcision. Roman officials were zealous in capturing the sages and their pupils. It was a reign of terror. The surviving teachers of the Jews held a secret meeting in a garret in Lydda and voted to differentiate between laws of primary and laws of secondary importance. It was determined that the secondary laws could be broken in order to escape death and torture.[6] This would include circumcision.

---

[5] *The Old Testament Pseudepigrapha: Expansions of the "Old Testament" and Legends, Wisdom and Philosophical Literature, Prayers, Psalms, and Odes, Fragments of Lost Judeo-Hellenistic Works*, James H. Charlesworth, Editor (Garden City, New York: Doubleday & Company, Inc., 1985), Vol. 2, p. 87. (*Book of Jubilees 15:33-34*) "And now I shall announce to you that the sons of Israel will deny this ordinance and they will not circumcise their sons according to all of this law because some of the flesh of their circumcision they will leave in the circumcision of their sons. And all of the sons of Beliar will leave their sons without circumcising just as they were born. And great wrath from the Lord will be upon the sons of Israel because they have left this covenant and have turned aside from his words. And they have provoked and blasphemed inasmuch as they have not done the ordinance of this law because they have made themselves like the Gentiles to be removed and be uprooted from the land. And there is therefore for them no forgiveness or pardon so that they might be pardoned and forgiven from all of the sins of this eternal error." See also *Encyclopedia Judaica Jerusalem* (Jerusalem, Israel: Keter Publishing House Ltd., 1971), p. 567, an excellent article on the history of Jewish circumcision.

[6] "Amongst the members present at this assemblage were Akiba, Tarphon, and Joseph the Galilean. Doubtless Ishmael, who resembled R. Joshua in character, was also present on that occasion. The strict elements appear to have considered that every Jew, rather than become guilty of the slightest infringement of the law, however heavy or light, should be ready to die the death of a martyr. Ishmael supported the opposite view. He considered that, outwardly and under compulsion, one might transgress the Law in order to preserve one's life, for the Torah enacted that its followers should live by it and not die through it. The assembly at Lydda, as usual, adopted the middle course, that a difference should be made between important precepts and those which were less weighty. The matter was put to a vote, and the decision was reached, that in order to avoid death by torture, all laws might be broken, with the
(Continued on next page)

Does Baptism Replace Circumcision?

Learsi documents for us that, *the laws of primary importance were declared to be those that prohibited murder, adultery, and idolatry, and were declared inviolable.*[7]

Action was sometimes taken during the Hadrianic persecution to conceal the appearance of circumcision. But in order to prevent the possibility of obliterating the traces of circumcision altogether, certain procedures were added by the rabbis so that recognition would be unmistakable.[8]

Yet with many Jewish scholars, circumcision was so important that it was allegorically read into the Scriptures where it is not there. F. W. Farrar cites Rabbi Nathan in his view that Adam, Noah, Jacob, Joseph, Moses, and Balaam had all been born circumcised (Abhoth, ch. ii). Farrar gives another example wherein circumcision is substituted in Scripture for the Abrahamic covenant of grace in Jeremiah 33:25— *But for circumcision, heaven and earth could not exist; for it is said, "save for (the sign of) my covenant, I should not have made day and night the ordinances of heaven and earth"* (*Nedarim*, f. 32, col. 1, referring to Jerem. xxxiii.25). The same remark is made about the whole Law when Rabbi (Juda Hakkadosh) speaks of how great circumcision is, since it is equivalent to all the commandments of the Law, for it is said, *behold the blood of the covenant which the Lord hath made with you, concerning all* (Heb., *above* all) *these words* (Ex. xxiv, 8—*Nedarim*, f. 32, 1). Again, Farrar illustrates the belief that angels so detested an uncircumcised person that, when God spoke to Abraham before

---

exception of those prohibiting idolatry, adultery, and murder." H. Graetz, *History of the Jews: From the Reign of Hyrcanus (135 B.C.E.) to the Completion of the Babylonian Talmud* (Phildelphia: Jewish Publication Socitey of America, 1893), pp. 423, 424.

[7] Ibid., Learsi, *A History of the Jewish People*, p. 194.

[8] *The Oxford Dictionary of the Jewish Religion*, R. J. Zwi Werblowsky and Geofrey Wigodor, Editors (New York and Oxford: Oxford University Press, 1997), p. 161. "The rabbis added the requirement of *peri'ah* (laying bare the glans). To this was added a third requirement, *metsitsah* (sucking of the blood). This was originally done by the *mohel* (circumciser). For hygienic reasons, a glass tube with a wad of cotton wool inserted in the middle is now generally employed, or the blood is simply drawn off by the use of some absorbent material."

circumcision, He spake in Aramaic, which, it appears, the angels do not understand (*Yalkuth Chadash*, f. 117, 3).[9]

Thus, we see both the primary (circumcision saves) and secondary (circumcision testifies) views of circumcision in Jewish history. Yet, from a purely biblical perspective, we know that the Judaizers of Paul's day did believe that circumcision was essential to personal salvation or eternal life, for they said of Gentile converts, *Except ye be circumcised after the manner of Moses, ye cannot be saved* (Acts 15:1).

Nevertheless, from a biblical viewpoint, we know that God preached the gospel of Jesus Christ to Abraham with the same terms for Jews and Gentiles—*And the scripture, foreseeing that God would justify the heathen through faith, preached before the gospel unto Abraham, saying, in thee shall all the nations be blessed* (Gal. 3:8). A crucial question is: *When was this gospel presented to Abraham*?

The unconditional gospel of Jesus Christ was received either while he was living in Ur of the Chaldees or when he was first called to leave that city. One thing we know for certain, he left that city in saving faith—*By faith Abraham, when he was called…went out* (Heb. 11:8). This refers to Genesis chapter 12 and his original call. This call (Gen. 12:1-3) was accompanied by a package of promises:

1. I will make of thee a great nation.
2. I will bless thee.
3. I will make thy name great.
4. Thou shalt be a blessing.
5. I will bless them that bless thee.
6. I will curse him that curseth thee.
7. In thee shall the families of the earth be blessed

---

[9] For documentation of the above citations see Frederic W. Farrar, D.D., F.R.S., *The Life and Work of St. Paul* (London, Paris & New York: Cassell & Company, Limited, 1884), pp. 428, 429.

Does Baptism Replace Circumcision?

Verse one describes this call of Abraham as past tense. He received this call while living in Ur of the Chaldees. The call of Abraham and the covenant with Abraham are separate propositions. The Call was conditional and required Abraham to:

1. Leave his country.
2. Leave his kindred.
3. Leave his father's house.
4. Proceed to a promised land.

Abraham moved from Ur of the Chaldees in disobedience. Actually, his father led him out of town with Lot, Abraham's nephew, and took up residence in Haran.[10] The family remained in Haran until Terah died (Gen. 11:31, 32). Terah probably preferred this city because he was a worshiper of other gods than Jehovah (Joshua 24:2). Terah was seventy years old when Abraham was born, but was two-hundred and five when he died in Haran. Therefore, the family must have lived in Haran for many years in disobedience to God's call.

Abraham finally did follow God further, but it was not in complete obedience. He was told to leave his kindred but he took his nephew, Lot (Gen. 12:5). When Abraham arrived in the land that God had promised to show him, God appeared again and added an eighth promise to the package: *Unto thy seed will I give this land* (Gen. 12:7).

But when famine came to the *Promised Land*, Abraham sought security in the land of Egypt (Gen. 12:10). He introduced his wife to Pharaoh as his sister. When the Egyptian king took Sarah into his house with plans for marriage, God put a plague upon him (Gen. 12:11-20). Abraham and his wife used this same routine again in Gen. 20 with Abimelech, king of Gerar.[11]

There is a great difference between making a promise and repeating a promise.[12] There is a great difference between the making

---

[10] Haran was approximately 700 miles N.W. of Ur and about 60 mi. from the Euphrates River. The city was a center of moon god worship.

[11] Abraham's son, Isaac, will follow this same bad example by lying about his wife Rebekah (Gen. 26).

[12] Twersky incorrectly affirms that, "in connection with circumcision, thirteen covenants were made with our ancestor Abraham. *And I will make My*
(Continued on next page)

of a promise and the subsequent illustrations of that promise.[13] When Abraham and Lot returned to the land of Canaan and parted from each other, God reappeared to Abraham repeating the promise, adding that He would make his *seed as the dust of the earth* (Gen. 13:16). We need to ask a fundamental question at this point. When did God's oath to Abraham become immutably based upon the fact that God cannot lie? We find the answer in the sixth chapter of Hebrews as follows:

> For when God made promise to Abraham, because he could swear by no greater, he **sware by himself, Saying, Surely** blessing I will bless thee, and **multiplying** I will multiply thee. And so, after he had patiently endured, he obtained the promise. For men verily swear by the greater: and an oath for confirmation *is* to them an end of all strife. Wherein God, willing more abundantly to shew unto the heirs of promise the **immutability of his counsel, confirmed** *it* **by an oath:** That by two immutable things, in which *it was* **impossible for God to lie**, we might have a strong consolation, who have fled for refuge to lay hold upon the hope set before us: Which *hope* we have as an anchor of the soul, both sure and stedfast, and which entereth into that within the veil (Heb. 6:13-19). *Emphasis added.*

The two immutable things that confirmed the promise were God's oath and His Word. An unconditional promise from God is *sure, confirmed,*

---

covenant between Me and thee (Gen 17:2); *As for Me, behold, My covenant is with thee* (Gen. 17:4); *And I will establish My covenant between Me and thee* (Gen. 17:7); *for an everlasting covenant* (ibid.); *And as for thee, thou shalt keep My covenant* (Gen. 17:9); *This is my covenant which ye shall keep* (Gen. 17:10); *And it shall be a token of a covenant* (Gen. 17:11); *And My covenant shall be in your flesh* (Gen. 17:13), *for an everlasting covenant* (ibid.); *He hath broken My covenant* (Gen. 17:14); *And I will stablish My covenant with him* (Gen. 17:19); *for an everlasting covenant* (ibid.); *But my covenant I will establish with Isaac* (Gen. 17:21), (see MN, III, 49)." Isadore Twersky, *Introduction to the Code of Maimonides (Mishneh Torah)* (New Haven: Yale University Press, 1980), pp. 52, 53.

[13] Circumcision was a token of a promise that was already sure and certain apart from and prior to any ritual.

and *immutable* the very first time God makes it because it is impossible for Him *to lie.*

In Genesis 15:1-21 God appeared to Abraham again and said, *Fear not, Abram: I am thy shield, and thy exceeding great reward* (vs. 1). Once again God promised to multiply Abraham's seed as the stars of heaven (15:5). In vs. 6 the Bible says: *and he believed the Lord, and he counted it to him for righteousness.* In the New Testament, the word *counted* is translated *imputed.* Today we often use the word *blame.* The plan of salvation involves three major imputations or blames:

1. The sin of Adam is blamed upon the human race (Rom. 3:23; 5:12).
2. The sin of the race is blamed upon Christ (Isa. 53:5, 6; Heb. 2:9; II Cor. 5:14-21; I Pet. 2:24).
3. The righteousness of Christ is blamed upon the believing sinner (Phil. 3:9; Jas. 2:23; Rom. 4:6, 8, 11, 22, 23, 24).

It is in this third blame that the believing sinner becomes clothed with the righteousness of Christ (II Cor. 5:21). The Bible declares that all sinners are naked before God (Gen. 3:10; Heb. 4:13). Some will attempt to deal with sin by applying their own spiritual clothes, but the best of this wardrobe is as filthy rags in the sight of God (Isa. 64:6).

Abraham did not lack belief at this point, but he did lack assurance. There is a difference between believing and knowing, as the Apostle John writes: *These things have I written unto you that believe on the name of the Son of God; that ye may know that ye have eternal life...*(I Jn. 5:13a). The Bible does not teach that salvation faith equals a total absence of doubt. Even John the Baptist became agnostic as he waited for his execution and sent two of his disciples to Jesus with the question: *Art thou he that should come, or do we look for another?*

(Matt. 11:3).[14] So also, Abraham, standing in the imputed righteousness of Christ, asks: *Whereby shall I know that I shall inherit it?* (Gen. 15:8).

Now, God was telling the absolute truth back in chapter twelve where His promises were sure and unconditional at that point. Nothing can make those promises more unconditional or more certain to be fulfilled. However, God was going to teach Abraham to be more certain in his own knowledge.

First, God instructed Abraham to take a three-year-old heifer, a three-year-old she goat, a three-year-old ram, a turtle dove and one young pigeon. He was to cut everything but the birds in half, piling them beside each other. And when the scavenger birds flew down upon the carnage, Abraham drove them away (Gen. 15:9-11). And as the sun was going down, God put Abraham into a deep sleep. God then prophesied the four-hundred year sojourn in Egypt and assured Abraham that it would not be in his lifetime, but after four generations they shall return with great substance (vss. 13-16).

When it became dark, God passed between the two piles of carnage by Himself (vs. 17) in the form of a smoking fire pot and a torch. This is reminiscent of an ancient sacrificial ritual performed to consummate a contract between two parties. It would require both parties to join hands and walk together between the pieces. This constituted a pledge of their commitment to keep the terms of this contract, in the presence of blood, suffering and death. It is known in the Bible as a *covenant of blood* (cf. Jer. 34:18-19). The fact that God passed between the parts alone illustrates the unconditional nature of this covenant. But the covenant was already unconditional from chapter twelve and was only being illustrated by the ceremony of chapter fifteen. Reading the life of Abraham makes it easy to know that this covenant was not in any way contingent upon Abraham's faithfulness. This object lesson helped Abraham's understanding, but it didn't make the promises of God more true or more unconditional than they were in the twelfth chapter.

And now we come to the seventeenth chapter of Genesis where God repeats the covenant. If the covenant was sure, confirmed, and

---

[14] In the twenty-fourth chapter of Luke all of Christ's closest friends and associates had fallen into a state of absolute doubt.

immutable, it never needed to be renewed but only repeated and reillustrated.[15] Abraham was ninety years old when God appeared to him again. This time God gave Abraham something to help him remember. He changed his name from *Abram* to *Abraham* (17:5). God called it an *everlasting covenant*, which it had been since chapter twelve. God then promised that the covenant would be established with Abraham's seed after him, which had been true since chapter twelve (vs.7).

Then God made another covenant with Abraham which was conditional while, at the same time, serving as a reminder and illustration of the unconditional covenant. The unconditional covenant is one that God alone keeps (like that of the rainbow). The covenant of circumcision is one that man keeps—

> This *is* my covenant, which ye shall keep, between me and you and thy seed after thee; Every man child among you shall be circumcised. And ye shall circumcise the flesh of your foreskin; and it shall be a token of the covenant betwixt me and you (Gen. 17:10,11).

Circumcision served as a conditional covenant of works as well as a *token* of the unconditional covenant of grace given in chapter twelve.[16]

We can be absolutely certain of several things at this point. Abraham was not regenerated by his circumcision. Saving faith was not

---

[15] How many times do Christians repeat the broken bread and the cup of wine in remembrance of Christ. These do not impart life, but are repeated illustrations of the sacrifice of Christ which has already imparted life.

[16] The rainbow was a *token* of God's covenant with Noah (Gen. 9:12). It was not the covenant but a *token* of the covenant (9:13, 17). The privilege of serving God on Mt. Sinai was a *token* to Moses that God was with him (Ex. 3:12). The blood of the first Passover lamb became a *token* on the doorposts of the Israelite's houses. (Ex. 12:13; 13:16). Aaron's rod became a *token* against the murmurings of rebels (Nu. 17:10). The scarlet thread in the window of Rahab the harlot became a token that she and her family would not be destroyed with Jericho (Josh. 2:12). See Ps. 86:13; Mk. 14:44; Phil. 1:28; II Thess. 3;17. The word is *owth* in the Hebrew and means a sign, a monument, a beacon, a flag. Its root is *uwth* meaning to assent or consent. It is God's way of saying *amen* to something that is already true.

imparted to him by his circumcision. Circumcision did not make the promise of God more immutable, more sure, or more confirmed than it was in chapter twelve. It was an experience that made God's unconditional promise also unforgettable.

Consider the statement about circumcision in 17:13b, *and my covenant shall be in your flesh for an everlasting covenant.* Every Christian needs to decide if vs. 13 proclaims circumcision to be an everlasting covenant, or if it proclaims the rite to be a *token, sign,* or *seal* of an everlasting covenant. It will help if one realizes that the everlasting covenant cannot be abolished, but that circumcision of the flesh has definitely been abolished (Gal. 5:1-4, 6; Eph. 2:11-15; Col. 3:11).

God had said to Abraham: *in thee shall all the families of the earth be blessed* (Gen. 12:1-3). The seed of Abraham has blessed all of the families of the earth in the Person of Jesus Christ who said: *Your father Abraham rejoiced to see my day: and he saw it, and was glad* (Jn. 8:56). Paul affirmed that the promised Seed was Jesus Christ when he wrote: *Now to Abraham and his seed were the promises made. He saith not, And to seeds, as of many; but as of one, And to thy seed, which is Christ* (Gal. 3:16). This promise became certain and unconditional to Abraham in Genesis chapter 12. The covenant of circumcision did not exist until five chapters later. Abraham was eternally saved through the faith he had in Jesus Christ before he ever received the covenant of circumcision—

> And he received the sign of circumcision, a seal of the righteousness of the faith which he had yet being uncircumcised: that he might be the father of all them that believe, though they be not circumcised; that righteousness might be imputed unto them also (Rom. 4:11).[17]

---

[17] A debate has existed throughout church history regarding the meaning of the words *sign* and *seal*. It will not be necessary to discuss all of the possible usages of these two words. What we must determine is how they are not being used in this chapter. They do not mean that Abraham's personal salvation was unconfirmed and unreal prior to the *sign* and *seal*.

Does Baptism Replace Circumcision?

It was prior to his circumcision that Abraham became the father of all them that believe, including all those who were never circumcised—

> And the father of circumcision to them who are not of the circumcision only, but who also walk in the steps of that faith of our father Abraham, which he had being yet uncircumcised (Rom. 4:12).

This is the exact same righteousness of faith that Noah, Enoch, and Abel had before him (Heb. 11:4-7). There were not two plans of salvation from Genesis seventeen onward—one of circumcision and one without.

Now the covenant of circumcision was a law of works, and therefore not a part of the plan of salvation for Abraham—

> For the promise, that he should be the heir of the world, *was* not to Abraham, or to his seed, through the law, but through the righteousness of faith. For if they which are of the law *be* heirs, faith is made void, and the promise made of none effect: Because the law worketh wrath: for where no law is, *there is* no transgression. Therefore *it is* of faith, that *it might be* by grace; to the end the promise might be sure to all the seed; not to that only which is of the law, but to that also which is of the faith of Abraham; who is the father of us all (Rom. 4:13-16).

The plan of salvation did not change in chapter seventeen when God gave Abraham the covenant of circumcision. In many great theological works of both Catholic and Reformed traditions, it seems that the covenant of circumcision is the actual covenant of grace. But we see that Abraham was standing by faith in the covenant of grace five chapters before Gen. 17:10-14. We should not conclude that any subsequent covenant made with Abraham was the covenant of salvation by grace. Neither should we conclude that the covenant of grace or plan of salvation is a composite of all of the agreements and promises made with Abraham.

The Abrahamic covenant of Gen. 12, 13, and 15 contains the plan of salvation, yet it is more than just that. It was an unconditional covenant (Gen. 15), but the covenant of circumcision was a conditional covenant of works. When God passed alone through the two mounds of animal parts in Gen. 15, he proclaimed that the promises of His covenant with Abraham were conditioned solely upon the faithfulness of His own promises. It was a covenant that only God could keep.

Not so with the covenant of circumcision. It was a covenant that Abraham and his descendents were to keep in order to inherit its blessings—*This is my covenant, which ye shall keep, between me and you and thy seed after thee; Every man child among you shall be circumcised* (Gen. 17:10). The promises of chapters 12-15 can only be broken by God Who cannot break a promise. But the covenant of circumcision can be broken by man (17:14). The covenant promises of chapters 12-15 were confirmed before circumcision and cannot be broken or added unto— *...though it be but a man's covenant, yet if it be confirmed, no man disannulleth, or addeth thereunto* (Gal. 3:15). And, *for we say that faith was reckoned to Abraham for righteousness. How then was it reckoned? When he was in circumcision, or in uncircumcision? Not in circumcision, but in uncircumcision* (Rom. 4:9).

The covenant of circumcision can be amended to become part of the Mosaic covenant of works. Actually, the covenant of circumcision was not added to the Mosaic Law, but the Mosaic Law was added to the covenant of circumcision (Ex. 12:44, 48; Lev. 12:3). But there can be no additions to the covenant of salvation made with Abraham (Gal. 3:15). Abraham's covenant of circumcision became a part of the Law of Moses. There were not two physical circumcisions for Israel from the Law of Moses, but only one; having amended the covenant of circumcision made with Abraham. Abraham's circumcision was four hundred and thirty years before the Law of Moses (Gal. 3:17), but from the time of Moses anyone who is circumcised is obligated to keep the whole Law, which is impossible (Gal. 3:3; Rom. 2:25). So, if there has never been a law which could have given life, then there never was and never will be a time when circumcision can give eternal life to one who receives it—

> ...for if there had been a law given which could have given life, verily righteousness should have been by the law. But the scripture hath concluded all under sin, that the promise by faith of Jesus Christ might be given to them that believe (Gal. 3:21b-22).

Yet the promises made to Abraham in Gen. 12-15 cannot be broken or annulled—

> And this I say, that the covenant, that was confirmed before of God in Christ, the law, which was four hundred and thirty years after, cannot disannul, that it should make the promise of none effect (Gal. 3:17).

Nevertheless, the Mosaic Law can be annulled and broken—

> For there is verily a disannulling of the commandment going before for the weakness and unprofitableness thereof. For the Law made nothing perfect…(Heb. 7:18, 19a).

Though the covenant of circumcision was a covenant of the flesh which could be broken, it was indeed a commandment of the law of God and served several purposes, two of which we will mention. It was a conditional covenant, and yet it was also a badge or symbol of the unconditional covenant. However, there were consequences for being uncircumcised—

> And the uncircumcised man child whose flesh of his foreskin is not circumcised, that soul shall be cut off from his people; he hath broken my covenant (Gen. 17:14).[18]

The penalty for violating the covenant of circumcision was physical death (not eternal death), either executed by God or by civil authority.[19]

---

[18] See such expressions as "from his people" (Lev. 17:4, 10; Num. 15:30), "from Israel" (Ex. 7:15; Num. 19:13), "from the congregation of Israel" (Ex. 12:19); and instead of "that soul," in Lev. 17:4-9 (cf. Ex. 30:33,38), we find "that man."

[19] Ex. 31:14 equates the phrase *cut off* as being put to death by civil authority. It is very interesting to study the histories of those who were put to death in Christian history for withholding baptism from their infants. It was assumed that infant baptism replaced circumcision and that disobedience required the death penalty. This concept will be discussed at length in chapter seven of this present work (cf. Ex. 12:15, 19; Lev. 7:20, 21, 25, etc.). In Lev. 17:9,10 the phrase *cut off* refers to an act of God in destroying a violator of His commandment.

We must not fail to distinguish between the theocratic death penalty and eternal condemnation. In Ex. 4:24-26 God was going to kill Moses for having failed to circumcise his son. Moses' wife, Zipporah, circumcised the boy and threw the bloody foreskin at Moses' feet and he lived. But, if Moses had died at that moment, he would have gone to Paradise, because Moses was in salvation faith when he left Egypt the first time—

> By faith Moses, when he was come to years, refused to be called the son of Pharaoh's daughter (Heb. 11:24).

To illustrate the difference between the theocratic death penalty and eternal damnation, the writer of Hebrews clearly describes a saint who forsakes the assembly as one who is worthy of physical death but who is, at the same time, eternally sanctified by the unconditional covenant of salvation. Hebrews 10:10-14 describes the saved person as sanctified *once for all* and *forever* by the *offering of the body of Jesus Christ*. This same saint is warned not to forsake the visible assembly of God in verse 25. If he does forsake the assembly, no sacrifice (including the sacrifice of Christ) will protect him from what could happen next (vs. 26). What will happen to this saint is described as the *judgment* and *fiery indignation* of God which shall devour (vs. 27). Now the writer of Hebrews clearly connects what he is saying to the Mosaic theocratic death penalty: *He that despised Moses law died without mercy under two or three witnesses* (vs. 28).[20] We are not guaranteed that the unfaithful church member is going to drop dead at the hand of God, but there is a guarantee that the unfaithful are worthy of such a death—*of how much sorer punishment, suppose ye, shall he be thought worthy* (vs. 29). The fuller context here is speaking of much more than just unfaithfulness to the local assembly, but for present purposes we will discuss this one point to illustrate our case. The saint who violates this precept, whether he knows it or not—

> ...hath trodden under foot the Son of God, and hath counted the blood of the covenant, wherewith he was

---

[20] This verse is not authorizing the visible church to execute unfaithful members, but it is a warning of the judgment of God. cf. I Cor. 11:30 "For this cause many are weak and sickly among you, and many sleep."

sanctified, an unholy thing, and hath done despite unto the Spirit of grace (vs. 29b).

This man is in trouble with God. He is cut off from communion with God, cut off from a list of blessings from God, cut off from fellowship with the saints, cut off from rewards in heaven, perhaps cut off from physical life or health on earth, but *he was sanctified* when he once accepted the grace of Christ. The phrase *wherewith he was sanctified* refers this disobedient saint back to verses 10-14 wherein God has *perfected forever them that are sanctified.*[21]

Likewise, Israelites were to be cut off from citizenship in physical Israel, with all of the privileges of that citizenship, if they were not circumcised. They were supposed to be disqualified from eating the Passover (Ex. 12:48).[22] But they were not necessarily cut off from eternal salvation by the absence of circumcision.[23] Under the leadership

---

[21] In II Pet. 1 the saint is told to add to his faith: virtue, knowledge, temperance, patience, godliness, brotherly kindness, and charity. But in vs. 9 he is told that if he lacks these additions he is "blind and cannot see afar off" and "hath forgotten that he was purged from his old sins." This man is in trouble, cut off from many things, but not cut off from eternal life.

[22] We know that the children of Israel in the wilderness journey were commanded to celebrate the Passover beginning with the second year after they came out of Egypt. It was to be celebrated on the fourteenth day of the month of Abib (Nu. 9:1-14; Deut. 16:1-6). However, at the end of the Journey, the Israelites, with their infants at Horeb, had not been circumcised; nor were they when they entered into covenant with the Lord under the leadership of Moses (Deut. 29:10-15; Josh. 5:7-9).

[23] Concerning the circumcision of a proselyte, Moore writes: "The significance of its initiatory rite was not entrance into a religious community, it was naturalization in the Jewish nation, that is—since the idea of nationality was racial rather than political—adoption into the Jewish race, the convert entering into all the rights and privileges of the born Jew and assuming all the corresponding obligations." Moore also cites the regenerationist view of circumcision and baptism when he refers to Rabbi (Judah, the Patriarch) who marked "the correspondence between the admission of a proselyte and the experience of Israel. As the Israelites came into the covenant only by three things, circumcision, baptism, and sacrifice, precisely so the proselyte comes into the covenant by the same three things. For the proselyte is equally a 'son of the covenant' with the born Jew." George Foot Moore, *Judaism in the First Centuries of the Christian Era: The Age of the Tannaim* (Cambridge: Harvard University Press, 1927), Vol. I, pp. 232, 234.

of Moses, children were not circumcised during the forty-year wilderness journey. Does this mean that no one in Israel was truly saved during those fourty years?[24] What was the fate of any who died in infancy? Were they not truly Jews?

In chapter one of the book named for him, Joshua prepares these uncircumcised Israelites (who had supposedly kept the Passover for thirty-eight years) to cross the Jordan River into the land of rest— *Remember the word which Moses the servant of the Lord commanded you, saying, The Lord your God hath given you rest, and hath given you this land* (1:13). In chapter 2, Rahab the harlot says of the uncircumcised Israelites: *I know that the Lord hath given you the land, and that your terror is fallen upon us, and that all of the inhabitants of the land faint because of you* (vs.9). The two spies return to Joshua saying: *Truly the Lord hath delivered into our hands all the land; for even all the inhabitants of the country do faint because of us* (vs. 24). In chapter 3 Joshua presents proof to the people that God is with them as the waters of the Jordan part, enabling the people to cross on dry ground (vss. 9-17). As the nation passes over the Jordan, a stone monument is built in the midst of the river as a memorial that God was with the nation when they crossed the river and, *On that day the Lord magnified Joshua in the sight of all Israel; and they feared him, as they feared Moses, all the days of his life* (4:14). The demonstration of God's mighty presence among the people melted the hearts of the inhabitants of the land (5:1). This all happened while the Children of Israel were in uncircumcision. Subsequent to this, God commands Joshua to circumcise all male Israelites, for this had not been practiced throughout the forty-year wilderness journey (5:2-9).

Absolutely nowhere in God's word is it stated that a soul becomes eternally condemned if he refuses circumcision, or that circumcision places one into the covanant of saving grace.[25] The

---

[24] Joseph C. Dillow, *The Reign of the Servant Kings: A Study of Eternal Security and the Final Significance of Man* (Hayesville, NC: Schoettle Publishing Co, 1993), pp. 344, 448, 453. Dillow gives a scholarly argument that many who left Egypt after the first Passover were saved Israelites. The price they paid for unbelief was that they experienced physical death in the wilderness without living to see the promised land.

[25] In II Sam. 12 Nathan the prophet tells King David that his first son with Bathsheba will die (vs. 14). On the seventh day the child dies (apparently uncircumcised) (vs. 18). Yet, David is certain that he will see his son in the *(Continued on next page)*

circumcision required of Abraham is the same as required of Moses, and yet the Mosaic law never placed anyone into the covenant of saving grace by an act of works.[26] If there ever was a time when circumcision could bring one into the covenant of saving grace, then Abraham could not have been the father of all uncircumcised believers from the time before he was circumcised—

> And he received the sign of circumcision, a seal of the righteousness of the faith which he had yet being uncircumcised: that he might be the father of all them that believe, though they be not circumcised; that righteousness might be imputed to them also (Rom. 4:11).

The covenant of circumcision is not the covenant of grace.[27] There were men living who were left out of the covenant of circumcision, who were nevertheless in the covenant of grace, such as Adam, Abel, Enoch, Enos, Noah, Shem, Arphaxad, Melchizedek, Lot, and others.[28] The covenant of salvation was made with Christ in

---

hereafter when he says, "But now he is dead, wherefore should I fast? Can I bring him back again? I shall go to him, but he shall not return to me (vs. 23).

[26] We must also note that circumcision was to be forced upon anyone bought with money or of any stranger in a Jewish house which is not of the seed of Abraham (Gen. 17:12). This same principle is repeated in Ex. 12:44, 48. It has never been God's will to compel a salvation decision upon anyone.

[27] Ibid., *Ante-Nicene Fathers*, Vol. I, p. 481…Irenaeus connected the New Testament circumcision made without hands (Col. 2:11) to the circumcision of the heart spoken by Jeremiah (Jer. 4:3,4). He then uses Lot, Noah and Enoch as examples of circumcised hearts before the establishment of circumcision of the flesh… "Moreover, all the rest of the multitude of those righteous men who lived before Abraham, and of those patriarchs who preceded Moses, were justified independently of the things above mentioned [works of the law], and without the law of Moses." (*Against Heresies*, Book IV. Chap xvi.1, 2).

[28] In the third century A.D., Cyprian will make this precise argument (*The Treatises of Cyprian*, 12, 8). He spoke of Jeremiah's reference to the circumcision of the heart (Jer. 4:3, 4) and Moses' prophecy of the circumcision of the heart (Deut. 30:6). Cyprian then draws a direct connection from these passages to the reference to circumcision made without hands in Col. 2:11. He argues that Adam, Abel, Enoch, Noah, and Melchizedek had the salvation that results from circumcision of the heart, yet none of these men had the circumcision of the flesh. *Ante-Nicene Fathers: Fathers of the Third Century*, *(Continued on next page)*

eternity past, as the federal head of all believers in Him (Titus 1:2). That the temporal blessings of the covenant of circumcision belonged to Abraham's natural seed is beyond question. But we deny that the spiritual and eternal blessings of the covenant of salvation by grace belonged to Abraham's seed after the flesh by physical circumcision.[29] God, who cannot lie (Heb. 6:18), guaranteed that the promises made to Abraham would be established in Isaac before the boy was even conceived (Gen. 17:18,19).[30] The same God was not lying when he declared that the identical promises were intended for Jacob before he was born (Gen. 25:23). The promise of eternal life was totally independent of circumcision from before the creation of the world, as the Apostle Paul stated: *In hope of eternal life which God, that cannot lie, promised before the world began* (Titus 1:2).

We also deny that salvation came to Abraham's natural seed of Jews or Gentiles through a physical, fleshly ordinance. Regardless of whether one is Jew or Gentile, he becomes Abraham's spiritual seed without circumcision made with hands. Many Jews who believed on Christ had always thought that their souls were free because they were of the fleshly seed of Abraham. Jesus said: *And ye shall know the truth, and the truth shall make you free* (John 8:32) . They responded by saying: *We be Abraham's seed, and were never in bondage to any man: how sayest thou, Ye shall be made free?* Christ's response was that *If the Son therefore shall make you free, ye shall be free indeed* (vs. 33). Jesus knew that He was not talking to truly saved Jews and proclaimed: *I know that ye are Abraham's seed; but ye seek to kill me, because my word hath no place in you* (John 8:31-37). The spiritual promise that

---

Rev. Alexander Roberts, D. D., and James Donaldson, LL.D., Editors (Grand Rapids, Michigan: Wm. B. Eerdmans Publishing Company, 1975), Vol. 5, p. 510.

[29] Question: If the spiritual blessings of the Abrahamic covenant were conferred and confirmed by fleshly circumcision, then why did not Ishmael receive title to them when Abraham circumcised him (Gen. 17:25)? If circumcision constituted a promise from God that the child would be saved, then why were so many thousands of circumcised Jews in Christ's day declared to be lost? Why did Paul declare them to be lost? Why? Because circumcision never did confer eternal life on anyone and never constituted a promise that the recipient would someday trust the grace of God for salvation.

[30] Abraham's faith that God would raise up Isaac from the dead after being sacrificed was based on God's promise to Abraham about Isaac before the boy was ever conceived (Heb. 11 17-19).

Does Baptism Replace Circumcision?

Abraham would be the heir of the world in eternity was not given to Abraham or his seed through the righteousness of the law of circumcision, but through the righteousness of faith (Rom. 4:13). Abraham possessed this righteousness of faith before the covenant of circumcision (Rom. 4:10, 11). The same is true of all Gentiles who are the spiritual seed of Abraham (vss. 11, 16).

The Apostle Paul wanted so passionately to see the fleshly seed of Abraham saved that he was willing to be cursed in exchange for their conversion (Rom. 9:1-3). Paul then began to list the temporal privileges of being a natural Jew after Abraham's fleshly seed:

> ...who are Israelites; to whom pertaineth the adoption, and the glory, and the covenants, and the giving of the law, and the service of God, and the promises; Whose are the fathers, and of whom as concerning the flesh Christ came, who is over all, God blessed forever. Amen (vss. 4, 5).

Yet these same people with such great blessings are eternally lost, and Paul longs for their salvation (vss. 1-3).

But then Paul contrasted spiritual Israel from fleshly Israel when he said: *for they are not all Israel, which are of Israel* (vs. 6:b). Paul continued by describing how God selected Isaac, and then Jacob, to be the forefathers of the promised seed of Abraham. God did this so that He could make known the riches of His glory to the saved (vs. 23). Just as there was nothing in Isaac or Jacob to recommend God's grace to them, so there is nothing in saved Jews or Gentiles which deserve the saving grace of God—

> And that he might make known the riches of his glory on the vessels of mercy, which he had afore prepared unto glory, Even us, whom he hath called, not of the Jews only, but also of the Gentiles? As he saith also in Osee, I will call them my people, which were not my people; and her beloved, which was not beloved. And it shall come to pass, *that* in the place where it was said unto them, Ye *are* not my people; there shall they be called the children of the living God. Esaias also crieth concerning Israel, Though the number of the

children of Israel be as the sand of the sea, a remnant shall be saved (9:23-27).

It was a pure act of God's sovereign, common grace to be born into fleshly Israel—

> Speak not thou in thine heart, after that the LORD thy God hath cast them out from before thee, saying, For my righteousness the LORD hath brought me in to possess this land: but for the wickedness of these nations the LORD doth drive them out from before thee. Not for thy righteousness, or for the uprightness of thine heart, dost thou go to possess their land: but for the wickedness of these nations the LORD thy God doth drive them out from before thee, and that he may perform the word which the LORD sware unto thy fathers, Abraham, Isaac, and Jacob. Understand therefore, that the LORD thy God giveth thee not this good land to possess it for thy righteousness; for thou *art* a stiffnecked people (Deut. 9:4-6).

But it is an act of God's saving grace (received by faith) that makes one within fleshly Israel a part of the remnant of truly saved Israel—

> What shall we say then? That the Gentiles, which followed not after righteousness, have attained to righteousness, even the righteousness which is of faith. But Israel, which followed after the law of righteousness, hath not attained to the law of righteousness. Wherefore? Because *they sought it* not by faith, but as it were by the works of the law (Rom. 9:30-32a).

When *they of the circumcision* came to Corinth they taught that there was something redemptive about being of the physical seed of Abraham. Paul responded to their foolishness by saying: *are they Hebrews? So am I. Are they Israelites? So am I. Are they the seed of Abraham? So am I* (II Cor. 11:22). On this point Paul had to repeat himself many times but he never tired of doing so—*To write the same things to you, to me indeed is not grievous, but for you it is safe* (Phil. 3:1b). He called Jews who had confidence in the flesh *dogs* and *evil workers* (vs. 2). Then he contrasted spiritual Israel with Israel after the flesh when he said:

> For we are the circumcision, which worship God in the spirit, and rejoice in Christ Jesus, and have no confidence in the flesh. Though I might also have confidence in the flesh. If any other man thinketh that he hath whereof he might trust in the flesh, I more: Circumcised the eighth day, of the stock of Israel, *of the tribe of Benjamin, an Hebrew of the Hebrews*; as touching the law, a Pharisee; Concerning zeal, persecuting the church; touching the righteousness which is in the law, blameless (Phil. 3:3-6).

Paul discounted all of these things as a grounds for entering the covenant of saving grace—

> But what things were gain to me, those I counted loss for Christ. Yea doubtless, and I count all things *but* loss for the excellency of the knowledge of Christ Jesus my Lord: for whom I have suffered the loss of all things, and do count them *but* dung, that I may win Christ, And be found in him, not having mine own righteousness, which is of the law, but that which is through the faith of Christ, the righteousness which is of God by faith (Phil. 3:7-9).

Paul became a recipient of the covenant of saving grace on the same ground that Abraham did when the latter became the father of all them that believe, whether circumcised or uncircumcised (Rom. 4:11, 12).

There has been an argument throughout church history that the "sacrament" of baptism replaces circumcision in the New Testament. The argument is almost always as follows: *Just as circumcision placed an infant into the Abrahamic covenant of grace, so also does baptism place the infant of Christian parents into the bond of the covenant of grace.*

But we are challenged to observe that baptism was used and in force before circumcision was abolished, which was not until the death of Christ. *They of the circumcision* at the Jerusalem Council in Acts 15 were baptized members of the first church of that city. It was radically incumbent upon the apostles to refute the heresy that Gentiles must be circumcised in order to be saved. It should seem strange to the reader that these Jews had never heard that the baptism of these Gentiles replaced circumcision. It was argued that converts should be both circumcised and baptized. This debate plagued the church throughout the New Testament. What a perfect time it would have been to simply explain the substitution of baptism for circumcision. It was *no small disputation and dissension* (15:2), resulting in a letter of clarification being sent to Gentiles in Antioch, Syria and Cilicia, but with no explanation that baptism was the reason that circumcision was not incumbent upon Gentile converts.

When Paul went to great lengths to explain that circumcision avails nothing he missed a tremendous opportunity to explain that baptism was the procedure that made circumcision obsolete. To the Galatians he said: *For in Jesus Christ neither circumcision availeth anything, nor uncircumcision; but faith which works by love* (Gal. 5:6). It could have added much clarity to the subject if he had just said: *but by baptism which replaces circumcision.* Paul told the Colossians that in Christ, *There is neither Greek nor Jew, circumcision nor uncircumcision, Barbarian, Scythian, bond nor free: but Christ is all, and in all* (Col. 3:11). This would have been a strategic time to explain that baptism replaces circumcision in the Church of Christ.

When addressing the heresy of *they of the circumcision*, Paul said to the Corinthians: *And so ordain I in all churches* (I Cor. 7:17b). Surely he would have mentioned how baptism had been ordained to replace circumcision, but he did not. Without even mentioning baptism he ordains:

> Is any man called being circumcised? Let him not become uncircumcised. Is any called in uncircumcision? Let him not be circumcised. Circumcision is nothing, and uncircumcision is nothing, but the keeping of the commandments of God (I Cor. 7:18-19).

When circumcising Timothy for the sake of the Jews, Paul could have noted that his partner was already baptized in place of circumcision—but he did not. When the same apostle refused to circumcise Titus, he could have explained that the young evangelist was already baptized in place of circumcision—but he did not. Again, when

Does Baptism Replace Circumcision?

Paul appointed Titus to ordain elders in every city of Crete, he listed some of the qualifications that Titus was to look for in such leaders as follows:

> Holding fast the faithful word as he hath been taught, that he may be able by sound doctrine both to exhort and to convince the gainsayers. For there are many unruly and vain talkers and deceivers, specially they of the circumcision: Whose mouths must be stopped, who subvert whole houses, teaching things which they ought not, for filthy lucre's sake (Titus 1:9-11).

These heretics were teaching baptism and circumcision. Titus could have been instructed to teach these elders how to explain that baptism had replaced circumcision—but he was not.

We have just cited several instances where the shift could have been explained, but was not. Nevertheless, we are reminded that it is dangerous to argue from what the Bible does not say, so we must be cautious. We must also remind ourselves that in the theory which affirms that baptism saves us or imparts the saving grace of God to us, we are instructed that the substitution of baptism for circumcision was so self-evident that it didn't need to be explained in the Bible. Theologians throughout church history constantly used the phrases: *it is only natural to infer* or *it must logically be presumed* when referring to the substitution of baptism for circumcision. Calvin makes this very point forthrightly by saying:

> Now, the first access to God, the first entrance to immortal life, is the remission of sins. Hence it follows, that this corresponds to the promise of our cleansing in baptism…We have, therefore, a spiritual promise given to the fathers in circumcision, similar to that which is given to us in baptism, since it figured to them both the forgiveness of sins and the mortification of the flesh. Besides, as we have shown that Christ, in whom both of these reside, is the foundation of baptism, so must he also be the foundation of circumcision. For he is promised to Abraham, and in him all nations are blessed. To seal this grace, the sign of circumcision is added.

4. There is now no difficulty in seeing where the two signs agree and wherein they differ. The promise, in which we have shown that the power of the signs consists, is one in both—viz. **The promise of the paternal favour of God, of forgiveness of sins, and eternal life. And the thing figured is one and the same—viz. Regeneration**. The foundation on which the completion of these things depends is one in both. Wherefore there is no difference in the internal meaning, from which the whole power and peculiar nature of the sacrament is to be estimated. The only difference which remains is in the external ceremony, which is the least part of it, the chief part consisting in the promise and the thing signified. Hence we may conclude, that everything applicable to circumcision applies also to baptism, excepting always the difference in the visible ceremony. To this analogy and comparison we are led by that rule of the apostle, in which he enjoins us to bring every interpretation of Scripture to the analogy of faith (Rom. 12:3-6). **And certainly in this matter the truth may almost be felt.** For just as circumcision, which was a kind of badge to the Jews, assuring them that they were adopted as the people and family of God, was their first entrance into the Church, while they, in their turn, professed their allegiance to God, so now we are initiated by baptism, so as to be enrolled among his people, and at the same time swear unto his name. **Hence it is incontrovertible, that baptism has been substituted for circumcision, and performs the same office** [emphasis added].[31]

Calvin is drawing his conclusion *incontrovertibly* from his interpretation of Colossians 2:11, 12. This is the controversial one-of-a-kind passage that has been the pivotal point of debate for almost two thousand years—

---

[31] John Calvin, *Institutes of the Christian Religion* (Grand Rapids, Michigan: Wm. B. Eerdmans Publishing Company, 1972), Vol. II, pp. 530, 531.

Does Baptism Replace Circumcision?

> In whom also ye are circumcised with the circumcision made without hands, in putting off the body of the sins of the flesh by the circumcision of Christ: Buried with him in baptism, wherein also ye are risen with him through the faith of the operation of God, who hath raised him from the dead (Col. 2:11, 12).

Calvin is so certain that the heart is circumcised in ritual baptism that he uses Titus 3:5 as his commentary on the Colossian passage—

> Not by works of righteousness which we have done, but according to his mercy he saved us, by the washing of regeneration, and the renewing of the Holy Ghost (3:5).[32]

Confusion regarding the Colossian passage exists as far back as Justin Martyr in the second century. In his *Dialogue with Trypho* [Chapter XIX] he asserts that Christian baptism does not have its roots in O. T. ablutions and, *Even you, who are the circumcised according to the flesh, have need of our circumcision; but we having the latter, do not require the former.* In defense of Christian circumcision of the heart Justin refers to Adam, Abel, Enoch, Lot and Melchizedek. It didn't seem to connect with Justin that these men had neither fleshly circumcision nor baptism, though they had spiritual circumcision.[33] We can see his utter confusion on the matter in the forty-third chapter of his *Dialogue with Trypho* when he affirms:

> And we, who have approached God through Him, have received not carnal, but spiritual circumcision, which Enoch and those like him observed. And we have received it through baptism, since we were

---

[32] Ibid., *Institutes of the Christian Religion*, Vol. II, p. 515... "that we are circumcised, and put off the old man, after we are buried in Christ by baptism (Col. ii.12). And in this sense, in the passage which we formerly quoted, he calls it 'the washing of regeneration, and renewing of the Holy Ghost' (Tit. iii. 5). We are promised, first, the free pardon of sins and imputation of righteousness; and secondly, the grace of the Holy Spirit, to form us again to newness of life."

[33] Ibid., *Ante-Nicene Fathers*, Vol. I, pp. 203, 204.

sinners, by God's mercy; and all men may equally obtain it.[34]

It would seem then, that Justin sees circumcision of the heart and justification as independent of ritual altogether in the O. T. yet completely contingent on ritual baptism in the New Testament.

During the Protestant Reformation there were some Christians who contended that baptism does not regenerate the sinner. They believed in justification by faith, and they affirmed that faith was a prerequisite to scriptural baptism. This position is known as *believer's baptism*. Key reformers considered the doctrine of believer's baptism to be an even greater threat to the purity of the church than Romanism itself. Calvin discards them as *frenzied spirits* who *continue to raise, great disturbance in the Church on account of paedobaptism*. He comments that their arguments are *not founded on the institution of God, but was introduced merely by human presumption and depraved curiosity, and afterwards, by a foolish facility, rashly received in practice*. He further describes their position as destitute of Christ's authority and as an insult to the Savior Himself. He says: *let us beware of discarding the sacred institution of God, and thereby insulting their author.*[35] Describing his own position on the matter, Calvin says: *In the first place, then, it is a well-known doctrine, and one as to which all the pious are agreed.*[36]

---

[34] Ibid., *Ante-Nicene Fathers*, Vol. I, p. 216.

[35] Contemporary reformed theologian R. C. Sproul uses much the same wording when answering the question: "Would you encourage an adult who has just come to Christ to be baptized if he or she had already been baptized?" His answer is: "The reason I wouldn't encourage them is that if indeed this is the sign of God's promise that certain things would happen if you put your trust in Christ, why would you now come before God and say 'would you run that promise by me again?' to do so in a sense casts a shadow on the integrity of that original promise that God has just fulfilled in full magnificence. Logically, I would say the repetition of the act would be a thinly veiled insult to God's integrity, though I fully recognize that not one person in a million who undergoes a second baptism intends it to be an insult. R.C. Sproul, *Now That's A Good Question* (Wheaton, Illinois: Tyndale House Publishers, 1996), pp. 341, 342.

[36] Ibid., Calvin, *Institutes of the Christian Religion*, Vol. II, p. 529.

Does Baptism Replace Circumcision?

Martin Luther, in the preface to his commentary on Galatians, had even stronger words for those who taught that *baptism is nothing unless the person is a believer*. He argues that from the "believer's baptism" position *it must follow that all the works of God are nothing if a man is not good.*[37] He illustrates his point by affirming: *If baptism, which is a work of God, ceases to be a work of God when man is evil, it follows that the married state, the office of magistrate, and the station of a servant, which are works of God, are no longer works of God because men are evil.* He then compares baptism with the common grace of God upon the entire human race as an argument that baptism regenerates an unbelieving soul—*The ungodly have the sun, moon, earth, water, air, and all that is subject to man; yet since they are not godly, it must follow that the sun is not the sun, and moon, earth, water, air, are not what they are.* Luther is characterizing the position of "believer's baptism" as teaching that nothing about God is true prior to belief, saying that those who held this position, *had bodies and souls before they were rebaptized, but because they were not godly, they had not real bodies and souls.* Next, he argues that their position implies that there are no institutions of God prior to belief, thus confessing themselves as bastards if their parents were not saved when first married—*Similarly, their parents were not really married—as they admit—because they were not re-baptized, and therefore the Anabaptists themselves are all illegitimate and their parents were adulterers and fornicators. Yet they inherit their parents' property, although they admit themselves to be illegitimate and without right of inheritance.* Luther describes the advocates of believer's baptism as not only *possessed by demons, but demons themselves possessed by worse demons.* He equates this position with the error of the Papists, describing them as foxes *tied together by the tails, even though their heads look in opposite*

---

[37] Martin Luther, *A Commentary on St. Paul's Epistle to the Galatians: Based on Lectures Delivered at the University of Wittenberg in the Year 1531 and First Published in 1535* (London: James Clarke & Co. LTD., 1956), pp. 18, 19. See also, *Luther's Works: Church and ministry III*, Eric W. Gritsch, Editor; Helmut T. Lehmann, General Editor (Philadelphia: Fortress Press, 1966), Vol. 41, p.336. Luther often imputes words to the one he is writing against and then lets these imagined words become a self-evident refutation. This has never been a valid form of logical argumentation. He uses this method of logic with rebaptizers and also the Pope of Rome: "*Oh, no, speaks the most hellish father, Christ is drunken, raving, and mad; he has forgotten what great power he, with the keys, gave me to bind—namely, I have the authority to bind and to forbid that:*"

directions.[38] He says that this teaching is *against our one and only Savior Christ* and felt that if Anabaptists were to be saved, God could do it through some other plan than that proclaimed by Scripture—

> Then there was talk about the blood of the Anabaptists that Ferdinand had spilled and about the constancy of the Anabaptists. Peter Weller asked whether they would be saved. The doctor [Martin Luther] replied, "We judge according to the gospel: he who doesn't believe in Christ can't be saved (John 3:18]. Therefore we must be sure that they are in error, etc. However, God can also act outside the prescribed rule, although we can't judge otherwise."[39]

Luther concludes his comments regarding the advocates of believer's baptism by saying: *Let him who can, then, hold fast to this one article; and let the rest, who make shipwreck, be driven by the wind and waves until they either return to the ship or swim to the shore.*[40]

The late Princeton theologian Benjamin Warfield affirmed the probability that Jewish proselyte baptism and Christian baptism were one because the nation of Israel and the Church of Christ are the same entity:[41]

---

[38] Ibid., Martin Luther, *A Commentary on St. Paul's Epistle to the Galatians*, pp. 18, 19. Also see Ibid., *Luther's Works*, Vol. 41, pp. 336, 337. Not only does he equate rebaptizers with the papacy in the preface to his commentary on Galatians, elsewhere Luther uses very crude charicatures and strong pejorative language as a logical argument against the Pope of Rome. The actual words used on these pages are far too vile to print in a Christian work, but the reader should look at them and draw his own conclusion. Although we must consider the times in which Luther lived, we should still remind ourselves that pejorative language and character assassination are never valid arguments.

[39] Luther was sure that they were in error. *Luther's Works: Table Talk*, Theodore G. Tappert, editor/translator; Helmut T. Lehmann, general editor (Philadelphia: Fortress Press, 1967), Vol. 54, p.152.

[40] Ibid., Martin Luther, *A Commentary on St. Paul's Epistle to the Galatians*, pp. 18, 19.

[41] *New Dictionary of Theology*, Sinclair B. Ferguson, David F. Wright, J.I. Packer, Editors (Downers Grove, Illinois: Intervarsity Press, 1988), pp. 716-718. "Benjamin Breckinridge Warfield (1851-1921), was the last great theologian of the conservative Presbyterians at Princeton Theological Seminary,
(Continued on next page)

Does Baptism Replace Circumcision?

> It might be *a priori* possible, indeed, that the Jewish rite was borrowed from the Christians or that the Christian was based upon the Jewish, And we may judge the similarity too close to admit the likelihood of their being of wholly independent origin.[42]

Warfield believed baptism did not replace circumcision until Acts fifteen where, *we see the change formally constituted at the so-called Council of Jerusalem—*

> How fully Paul believed that baptism and circumcision were but two symbols of the same change of heart, and that one was instead of the other, may be gathered from Col. ii. 11, when, speaking to a Christian audience of the Church, he declares that "in Christ ye were also circumcised"—but how?--"with a circumcision not made with hands, in putting off the body of the flesh,"—that is, in the circumcision of Christ. But what was the Christ-ordained circumcision? The Apostle continues: "Having been buried with Him in baptism, wherein also ye were raised with Him through faith in the working of God, who raised Him from the dead." Hence in baptism they were buried with Christ, and this burial with Christ was the circumcision which Christ ordained, in the partaking of which they became the true circumcision. This falls little, if any, short of a direct assertion that the Christian Church is Israel, and has Israel's circumcision, though now in the form of baptism.[43]

Warfield goes to great lengths in an attempt to refute the *Systematic Theology* of Dr. Augustus H. Strong—the formidable

---

New Jersey...Warfield distinguished himself as a scholarly defender of Augustinian Calvinism."

[42] Benjamin Warfield, *The Works of Benjamin Warfield: Studies in Theology* (Grand Rapids, Michigan: Baker Book House, 1932), Vol. IX, p. 380, cf. 377-380.

[43] Ibid., *Works of B. Warfield*, Vol. IX, p.405.

advocate of believer's baptism.[44] He argues that Strong's position is based on, *the illegitimate use it makes of the occasional character of the New Testament declarations.*[45] And it is Strong's, *unmeasured zeal to make all texts which have been appealed to by paedobaptists—not merely fail to teach paedobaptism—but teach that children were not baptized, that has led him so far astray here.* He discards all of Strong's arguments as based on an unscholarly *foregone conclusion.* Warfield illustrates his rebuttal of Strong as follows:

> I am prepared to allow in general the validity of Dr. Strong's first argument—when thus softened to reasonable proportions. It is true that there is no express command to baptize infants in the New Testament, no express record of the baptism of infants, and no passages so stringently implying it that we must infer from them that infants were baptized. If such a warrant as this were necessary to justify the usage we should have to leave it incompletely justified. But the lack of this express warrant is something far short of forbidding the rite; and if the continuity of the Church through all ages can be made good, the warrant for infant baptism is not to be sought in the New Teatament but in the Old Testament...[46]

Warfield's final rebuttal is: *But Strong has omitted to give the chapter and verse where Christ's command not to baptize infants is to be found.* He then concludes by saying: *The argument in a nutshell is simply this: God established His Church in the days of Abraham and put children into it. They must remain there until He puts them out. He has nowhere put them out.*[47]

But the Old and New Testaments reveal that physical circumcision did not accomplish spiritual circumcision. It is easy to see that many circumcised Jews of Christ's day were not only

---

[44] For an excellent study of *believer's baptism* see Agustus Hopkins Strong, *Systematic Theology* (Valley Forge, Pa.: The Judson Press, 1969), Three Volumes in One, pp. 931-959.
[45] Ibid., *Works of B. Warfield,* Vol. IX, p. 393.
[46] Ibid., *Works of B. Warfield,* Vol. IX, p. 399.
[47] Ibid., *Works of B. Warfleld,* Vol. IX, p. 408.

Does Baptism Replace Circumcision?

uncircumcised of heart but out (not put out) of spiritual Israel. They were out because they were never in, as Jesus said: *And then will I profess unto them, I never knew you: depart from me, ye that work iniquity.*

The nation of Israel was a visible, corporate entity. The belief that the Church of Jesus Christ is Israel has led to the belief that the universal Body of Christ should be a visible, organized entity with a headquarters staffed by men on earth. Many reformers were strong believers in the state church concept of dominion theology, or *theonomy* as it is sometimes called. It is believed that the Old Testament prophecies of the restoration of Israel were fulfilled on the Day of Pentecost rather than in some future millennium. We believe that Christ clearly addressed this question just prior to the Day of Pentecost. The disciples asked the Lord: *Wilt thou at this time restore again the kingdom to Israel* (Acts 1:6)? Jesus forthrightly tells them that it is none of their business to know when that will happen: *And he said unto them, It is not for you to know the times or the seasons, which the Father has put in his own power* (vs. 7). However, there is something that is your business to know: *But ye shall receive power, after that the Holy Ghost is come upon you: and ye shall be witnesses unto me both in Jerusalem, and in all Judaea, and in Samaria, and unto the uttermost part of the earth* (vs. 8). Now, it cannot be the disciples' business to know this and, at the same time, none of their business to know when the kingdom will be restored to Israel, if they indeed are both the same thing. Therefore, the Day of Pentecost was not the restoration of the earthly kingdom of Israel.

Jesus considered corporate Israel (i.e. *the commonwealth of Israel*) to be the *lost sheep of the house of Israel* (Matt. 10:6). Even in their lost state, God gave the Scriptures; made covenants and promises; and gave us Christ through them (Rom. 9:1-5). But a Jew is not saved by being in the commonwealth of Israel (Eph. 2:12, 17), nor is an Old Testament Gentile unsaved by being outside the commonwealth of Israel (cf. discussion of Job and friends in chapter three). Both Jews and Gentiles equally need Christ as Savior and find Him in the Gospel (Eph. 2:18,19). Personal salvation makes anyone a member of the *household of God*, but fleshly birth and circumcision makes one a member of the *commonwealth of Israel*. It is not the *commonwealth*, but *household of God...built on the foundation of the apostles and prophets* (Eph. 2:19, 20) that a Christian becomes a part of at conversion (Gal. 6:16)—*For we are the circumcision, which worship God in the spirit, and rejoice in*

Christ Jesus, and have no confidence in the flesh (Phil. 3:3). We were afar off from Christ and made nigh to Christ by the blood of Christ (Eph. 2:13). But so also were many in the commonwealth of Israel (Rom. 9:1-5). It is only in Christ that the middle wall of partition between Jews and Gentiles has been removed (Eph. 2:14; Gal. 3:28). A believer does not become one new man with a lost citizen of political Israel, but becomes one in Christ with a saved Jew in a new entity called the *Household of God*, comprised only of saved people.

Before proceeding we should note that numerous Baptists are currently embracing the *baptismal salvationist* view, whereas many Reformed theologians never adopted such a view. The *New Dictionary of Theology*, with J. I. Packer as consulting editor, says of Baptists:

> Suspicious of sacramentalism, most Baptists have until comparatively recently interpreted believer's baptism primarily in symbolic terms and as an individual act of personal witness. However, the past two decades have witnessed in many places an increasing desire to regard baptism as integral to the gospel (so that it becomes part of their proclamation of Christ), conversion (regarding it as the outward ratification of an inward turning to God) and church membership (so that baptism is viewed not solely in personal terms as "into Christ" but also corporately as into his body, the church).[48]

If one would walk into the theology departments of many Baptist seminaries and colleges today and ask if it is appropriate to believe that baptism regenerates, or at least imparts the saving grace of God as the primary means of saving grace, they would hear that this is just a semantically different way of expressing the same gospel that Baptists have always preached.

However, traditional Baptists would be pleased to find that there were Reformed theologians who never believed that baptism

---

[48] Ibid., *New Dictionary of Theology*, P. 75.

regenerates the sinner or imparts the saving grace of Christ.[49] Charles Hodge describes Zwingli thusly:[50]

> According to the doctrine of Zwingli afterwards adopted by the Remonstrants, the sacraments are not properly "means of grace." They were not ordained to signify, seal, and apply to believers the benefits of Christ's redemption. They were indeed intended to be significant emblems of the great truths of the Gospel. Baptism was intended to teach the necessity of the soul's being cleansed from guilt by the blood of Christ and purified from the pollution of sin by the renewing of the Holy Ghost. They were further designed to be perpetual memorials of the work of redemption, and especially to be the means by which men should, in the sight of the Church and of the world, profess themselves to be Christians…The sacraments,

---

[49] Karl Barth, *The Christian Life (Fragment): Baptism as the Foundation of the Christian Life (Church Dogmatics)* (Edinburgh: T. & T. Clark, 1969), Vol. IV, 4, pp. 128, 129… Barth describes Huldrych Zwingli thusly: "Zwingli's understanding and doctrine of baptism are worked out in the *Commentarius*, the book *Vom touf…*, the reply to the *Toufbuchlein* of Balthasar Hubmaier, the *Elenchus in catabaptistarum strophas* (all 1525), and the *Quaestiones de Sacramento Baptismi* aimed at Schwenkfield (1530). His teaching departs from the tradition which we have considered in its Roman Catholic, Lutheran and Calvinistic forms. It does so first in a way which brings it close to that represented in the present work, for Zwingli very definitely dissociates himself from the sacramental view of baptism, which he also, not unjustly, thought he could detect among his Anabaptist adversaries. Among his contemporaries he was a lonely figure… In Zwingli everything finally stands or falls with the principle, which is more philosophical than theological, that an external thing cannot do an internal work, that a material thing cannot accomplish or reveal what is spiritual… According to Zwingli, the founder of baptism was not Jesus Christ—He simply confirmed it in Mt. 28:19—but John the Baptist (Germ. 366, 424)."

[50] Ibid., *New Dictionary of Theology*, pp. 312, 313. "Hodge, Charles (1797-1878) was the best-known proponent of the conservative Calvinistic theology that came from the Presbyterian seminary in Princeton, New Jersey, from its founding in 1812 to its reorganization in 1929…but his work remains the most effective 19th century American presentation of Calvinism."

therefore, are "badges of Christian men's profession."[51]

Although Baptist theology would differ with Hodge regarding the mode of baptism and the proper candidates for baptism,[52] they would concur with his distinction between ritual and reality when he writes:

> Circumcision did not make a man a Jew. It gave him neither the knowledge nor the grace necessary to his being one of the true children of Israel. It was the appointed means of avowing that he was a Jew; it was the sign of his being included among the worshippers of the true God; and it secured for him the privileges of the theocracy. In like manner, baptism does not make a man a Christian. It is the appointed means of avowing that he is a Christian; it is the badge of his Christian profession before men, it secures for him the privileges of membership in the visible Church, and it is a pledge on the part of God that, if sincere and faithful, he shall partake of all the benefits of the redemption of Christ. It is only in this sense that the Reformed Church teaches the necessity of baptism. It has the necessity of a divine precept. It is the condition of salvation, in the same sense in which confession is, and in which circumcision was. The uncircumcised child was cut off from among the people, he forfeited his birthright. But he did not forfeit his salvation. The Apostle teaches us that if an uncircumcised man kept the law, his uncircumcision

---

[51] Charles Hodge, *Systematic Theology* (Grand Rapids, Michigan: Wm. B. Eerdmans Publishing Company, 1977), Vol. III, p. 498.

[52] Ibid., Hodge, *Systematic Theology*, Vol. III, p. 537... "It is not denied that *Baptizo* means to immerse, or that it is frequently so used by the fathers as by the classic authors; it is not denied that the Christian rite was often administered, after the apostolic age, by immersion; it is not even denied that during certain periods of the history of the Church, and in certain regions, immersion was the common method in which baptism was administered. But it is denied that immersion is essential to baptism; that it was the common method in the apostolic Churches; that it was at any time or in any part of the Church the exclusive method; and more especially it is denied that immersion is now and everywhere obligatory or necessary to the integrity of Christian baptism."

Does Baptism Replace Circumcision?

was counted for circumcision. To this the Jews objected by asking, What profit then is there in circumcision? Paul answered, Much every way. It is not useless, because not essential. The same is true of baptism. Although not the means of salvation or necessary to its attainment, its benefits are great and manifold.[53 & 54]

One contemporary and popular view of the gospel is that salvation is purely by grace, but that the sovereign grace of God will irresistibly cause an elect one to obey all the commandments and sacraments of Christ.[55] Hodge responds to this view forthrightly when he writes:

---

[53] Ibid., Hodge, *Systematic Theology*, Vol. III, p. 585. Also, p. 583: "The Jewish Church in the time of Christ, had become completely ritualistic. Rites and ceremonies had usurped the place of truth and holy living... The Reformation was in its essential character a protest against ritualism. It proclaimed salvation by a living faith which purified the heart, in opposition to the doctrine of salvation by rites and ceremonies... Ritualism is a broad, smooth, and easy road to heaven, and is always crowded."

[54] Ibid., *Church Dogmatics*, Vol. IV, 4, p. 129...According to Barth, Zwingli affirms this same position: "According to Zwingli himself all teachers from the days of the apostles had greatly erred. Through a misunderstanding of John. 3:5 they had sought to ascribe to the water something which it cannot have. Christ has taken from us all external justifying (ed. Schuler and Schulthess, Germ. III, 238). Water baptism, in spite of the opinion of the earliest fathers, does not cleanse or save a man (255f.). He can be saved without baptism (241f.). It has no *vis mutandi* (Lat. III, 229). Nor does it serve—the core of Calvin's teaching is here rejected in advance—to give assurance or confirmation to faith (Germ. 243, Lat. 229f.). Only the direct work of God, Christ and the Holy Spirit can do these things. This alone is the basis of faith in the elect."

[55] John MacArthur, *The Gospel According to Jesus* (Grand Rapids: Zondervan Publishing House, 1989), p. 33. " Thus salvation cannot be defective in any dimension. As a part of His saving work, God will produce repentance, faith, sanctification, yieldedness, obedience, and ultimately glorification. Since He is not dependent on human effort in producing those elements, an experience that lacks any of them cannot be the saving work of God."

Also, John MacArthur, *Faith Works: The Gospel According to the Apostles* (Dallas, London, Vancouver, Melborne: Word Publishing, 1993), p. 106. "Nowhere in Scripture do we find positional righteousness set against righteous behavior, as if the two realities were innately disconnected."

> For any one, therefore, to say that although a man truly believes the record God has given of his Son, yet that he is not a Christian, unless he belongs to some particular church organization, unless he is baptized with water, unless he comes to the Lord's table, contradicts not the general teaching of the Bible only, but the fundamental principle of the gospel method of salvation. Even Gabriel would not dare to shut the gates of paradise on the thief converted on the cross, because he had not been baptized.[56]

However, not all Reformed theologians would agree with Hodge. Michael S. Horton is the founder and president of Christians United for Reformation (CURE). He reiterated a popular view regarding why many are missing the experience of God's forgiveness when he wrote:

> Sealed with the Holy Spirit through baptism, faith, and the Word, we are forgiven people...
> ...the Lord's Supper is a sacrament. That is, it is a sign and seal through which He gives us what He promises us in the Gospel...This is not a Roman Catholic notion; it is the traditional evangelical view much lost to us today.
> One of the reasons people seem to experience so little "forgiveness" today is because of the diet of the preaching and the lack of confirmation through the sacraments. In fact, many evangelical churches have abandoned the use of sacraments altogether, which of course means that they no longer fit the evangelical definition.[57]

---

[56] Ibid., Hodge, *Systematic Theology*, Vol. III, p. 601.

[57] Michael S. Horton, *Beyond Culture Wars: Is America a Mission Field or Battlefield?* (Chicago: Moody Press, 1994), p. 219. In support of his view, Horton quotes *The Scots Confession* of 1560 which declares: "And so we utterly condemn the vanity of those who affirm the sacraments to be nothing else than naked and bare signs. No, we assuredly believe that by baptism we are engrafted into Christ Jesus, to be made partakers of his righteousness, by which our sins are covered and remitted, and also that in the supper rightly used, Christ Jesus is so joined with us that he becomes the very nourishment and food of our
(Continued on next page)

Horton speaks of the sign and the real thing as being interchangeable and often indistinguishable:

> In every sacrament, two things are involved: the sign and the thing signified. The sign in baptism, for instance, is water; in the Lord's Supper, bread and wine. The thing signified in baptism is regeneration; in the Lord's Supper it is the body and blood of Christ. As the *Westminister Confession* puts it, "There is in every sacrament a spiritual relation, or sacramental union, between the sign and the thing signified; whence it comes to pass that the names and effects of the one are attributed to the other."
>
> In other words, the union between water and regeneration is so close in baptism that Scripture will often speak of both interchangeably, as if the water cleansed in baptism or as if the bread and wine in Communion were truly the body and blood of Christ.[58]

If Horton's position is correct, then it could be said that the Anabaptist view (that the efficacy of Christ's saving grace must be evident before the ordinances) is an undermining of the saving grace of Christ—

> The Roman Church undermined the importance of God's ordained sacraments by adding sacraments of their own. The Anabaptist enthusiasts undermined them by reducing the efficacy of the two sacraments

---

souls." Again, Horton reminds us that *The Heidelberg Catechism* agrees with these definitions and quotes the *Westminister Confession*... "Sacraments are holy signs and seals of the covenant of grace". Michael Horton, *In The Face Of God* (Dallas: Word Publishing, 1996), pp. 139, 140.

[58] Ibid. *In The Face Of God*, P. 140. See also p. 141: "It was for this reason that the Protestant Reformers followed such great church fathers as St. Augustine in calling the sacraments 'God's visible word.' The sacraments serve the same purpose as the Word itself, not only offering or exhibiting God's promise, but actually conferring his saving grace by linking us, through faith, to Christ and his benefits."

Christ instituted. We see both extremes in our own day as well.[59]

Horton holds the same sacramental view regarding Old Testament circumcision of the flesh when he writes: *Did this mean that circumcision was an invalid sacrament? Hardly, After all, it was through this sign and seal of God's covenant of grace that the believing Israelites were incorporated into one redeemed people.*[60]

Those who hold to a pure gospel of grace often have a friendly disagreement regarding the source of salvation faith. Both views hold that, apart from God's grace, no man could draw his first breath. One view holds that faith is possible because of God's common grace upon all humanity. The other view holds that faith can only exist as a fruit of being already regenerated and saved. Both views hold that faith alone in Christ alone must be present in order to experience salvation independently of baptism. Hodge punctuates his view in a way that should attract the attention and respect of anyone committed to a pure-grace view of the gospel of Christ:

---

[59] Ibid., Horton, *In The Face Of God*, p. 142. Horton oversteps the boundaries of logic when he says that God does not, yet does work outside His ordained means of saving grace (Word and Sacraments). See also pp. 219, 220, "In the face of super-spirituality, it is always necessary to stress God's objective, ordained and formal means of bringing us into fellowship with Himself. Nevertheless, even the biblical sacraments cannot be viewed magically, as if God were *bound* to means. **It is true that he does not work outside these means, but it is equally true that he does not *have* to work through them**" [emphasis added].

[60] Ibid., Horton, *In The Face Of God*, p. 220. Also Ibid., p. 220— "Furthermore, a sacrament not only reveals; it confers. Through Word and sacrament, God actually gives that which he promises in his gospel— forgiveness of sins, freedom from the tyranny of sin, and eternal life. The sacraments not only testify to or signify divine activity in salvation, but are part of that divine redemptive activity…A sacrament is a means of saving rather than common grace. Just as there can be no salvation apart from a miraculous new birth (John 3:3), so there can be no impartation of the new birth apart from the Spirit working through ordained means (Titus 3:5)…a sacrament…proclaims and seals divine forgiveness, reconciliation, adoption, justification, and sanctification. Nothing other than the Word, baptism, and the Lord's Supper are given this place by God as a means of grace."

Does Baptism Replace Circumcision?

> It is plain that Baptism cannot be the ordinary means of regeneration, or the channel of conveying in the first instance the benefits of redemption to the souls of men, because, in the case of adults, faith and repentance are the conditions of baptism. But faith and repentance, according to the Scriptures, are the fruits of regeneration. He who exercises repentance towards God and faith in our Lord Jesus Christ is in a state of salvation before baptism and therefore in a state of regeneration. Regeneration consequently precedes baptism, and cannot be its effect, according to the ordinance of God. That the Apostles did require the profession of faith and repentance before baptism, cannot be denied. This is plain, not only from their recorded practice but also from the nature of the ordinance. Baptism is a profession of faith in the Father, and the Son, and the Holy Spirit; not of a faith to be obtained through the ordinance, but of a faith already entertained.[61]

What confuses many common Christian readers is the ambivalence of some scholars when questioned about the ability of sacraments to regenerate and save the soul of the sinner. The answer is often *yes*, and *no*, and *maybe*, and *actually either way*.

To be *saved* is to become a born again member of God's family. J. I. Packer writes:

> Since Pentecost, becoming a member of God's family according to his revealed will—Christian initiation, to use the technical phrase—has involved three factors: repentance and faith, plus Christian baptism, plus the coming of the Spirit for new covenant ministry...The order scarcely matters; what matters is that all three links between us and Jesus Christ—faith, baptism, Spirit—should actually be there.[62]

---

[61] Ibid. Hodge, *Systematic Theology*, Vol. III, p. 601.
[62] J. I. Packer, *I Want to Be a Christian* (Wheaton, Illinois: Tyndale House Publishers, Inc., 1977), p. 138.

Packer's definition of *initiation* is given more explicitly when he writes:

> Baptism is and always was the church's initiation-rite ("Initiation," from a Latin word for "beginning," means reception and entrance into committed membership).[63]

Accordingly, in Packer's view, the baptism of the Spirit into the mystical body of Christ and ritual water baptism are one single act of Christ—

> When Paul says that in the one *Spirit* we were all *baptized* (that is, by Christ) into his one *body* (I Corinthians 12:13), he thinks of water-baptism and the gift of the Spirit as two complementary aspects of a single act of Christ, who claims and incorporates or ingrafts us (Paul's image, Romans 11:17-24) into vital union with himself...In God's revealed purpose for our lives, water-baptism and Spirit-baptism are joined. Let not any of us in thought or practice put them asunder.[64]

Putting the two asunder is precisely what Packer thinks the *believer's baptism* doctrine does:

> To safeguard the importance of conversion, some proponents of infant baptism argued that the regeneration which baptism in some sense mediates is a different thing from the regeneration into which the converted man has come; and some Baptists affirmed

---

[63] J. I. Packer, *Growing in Christ* (Wheaton, Illinois: Crossway Books, 1994), p. 95. Published originally under the above title *I Want to Be a Christian*. See P. 100: "Paul writes to First-generation converts whose baptism, according to New Testament custom, would have followed directly on their professing faith; so that believing and being baptized were already linked in their minds as two aspects of the single reality of becoming a Christian."

[64] Ibid., Packer, *I Want To Be A Christian*, pp. 138, 139. See Ibid. *Growing in Christ*, p. 136: "In the New Testament baptism signifies all aspects of entering new life in Christ, including the gift of the Spirit (Acts 2:38; I Corinthians 12:13)."

that true water-baptism (as opposed to the Spirit baptism of conversion) is the believer's witness to his response to grace, rather than a sign or means of God's work of grace itself. Thus people have put asunder what God had joined.[65]

The *believer's baptism* doctrine sees ritual baptism as the profession of faith of one already regenerated and born again. Thus, the rite is a sign or token of something that is already real. This is quite different from Packer, who writes:

> The sacraments are rightly viewed as means of grace…Knowing this, Christ and the apostles not only speak of the sign as if it were the thing signified but speak too as if receiving the former is the same as receiving the latter…As the preaching of the Word makes the gospel audible, so the sacraments make it visible, and God stirs up faith by both means…Sacraments function as means of grace on the principle that, literally, seeing is (i.e., leads to) believing.[66]

However, after proclaiming that the doctrine of *believer's baptism* puts asunder what God has joined together, Packer can affirm that the "Baptist" way can bring a sinner into union with Christ prior to, or even without, ritual baptism—[67]

> …no Christian tradition—Protestant, Catholic, or Orthodox—allows that baptized persons capable of faith can be saved without faith, or that genuine believers can be lost for being unbaptized.[68] …When

---

[65] Ibid., Packer, *Growing in Christ*, p.p. 93, 94.
[66] J. I. Packer, *Concise Theology: A Guide to Historic Christian Beliefs* (Wheaton, Illinois: Tyndale House Publishers, Inc., 1993), pp. 210, 211.
[67] Usually, if an advocate of *believer's baptism* is leading one to Christ on his deathbed, he will bring him to faith in the finished work of Christ but not baptize him. He will assure him of salvation the same as the thief on the cross.
[68] Ibid., Packer, *Growing in Christ*, p. 100.

are we thus washed? When we believe—that is, commit ourselves to Christ...[69]

Accordingly, as can be seen, we can get the answer *yes, no, maybe* or *either way* when asking for a direct response regarding the efficacy of ritual baptism in personal salvation.

Regarding the position that the Church is Israel and that, therefore, baptism replaced circumcision, we will let nineteenth century pastor/theologian, Alexander Carson [1776-1884] give us the *believer's baptism* response. In his lengthy work on the baptism debate he could find, *no plausible foundation in the word of God* for baptism replacing circumcision.[70] The advocates of baptismal regeneration placed the burden of proof on their opponents, challenging them to find a verse that commands not to baptize infants into the mystical body of Christ. However, Carson properly placed the burden of proof on them, in that their position was so generally received and taken for granted as a first principle. Look again at the problem passage:

> In whom also ye are circumcised with the circumcision made without hands, in putting off the body of the sins of the flesh by the circumcision of Christ: Buried with him in baptism, wherein also ye are risen with him through the faith of the operation of God, who hath raised him from the dead (Col. 2:11, 12).

Carson is correct when he says: *This passage says not a word about the subject, either expressly or by implication.* They represent *the apostle as saying, 'being buried with Christ by the washing of baptism, they are circumcised with the circumcision without hands.*[71] But this is not how the passage is constructed.

Carson points out that the *apostle himself minutely explains how they were circumcised in Christ. It is a circumcision made without hands. It cannot then, be baptism; for it is not without hands...*

---

[69] Ibid., p. 116.
[70] Alexander Carson, *Baptism: Its Mode and Subjects* (Grand Rapids, Michigan: Kregel Publications), p. 228.
[71] Ibid.

> This circumcision consists in putting off the body of the sins of the flesh. The external circumcision cut off a part of the flesh; the circumcision without hands puts off the body of the sins of the flesh. This is the circumcision of Christ; the other was the circumcision of the law…It is called the circumcision made without hands to distinguish it from its type, the circumcision of the flesh: it is called the circumcision in which is put off the body of the sins of the flesh, to distinguish it from the typical circumcision, which did not cut off sin, but flesh: it is called the circumcision of Christ, to distinguish it from the circumcision of Moses. No language can be more express, or less capable of perversion. The circumcision here spoken of, could not possibly be baptism; because it is a circumcision which Christians are not only said to have without any external operation, but which they have in Christ: *"In whom* ye are circumcised." Christ himself performs this circumcision, and we have it in him.[72]

Yes, something did replace circumcision. *The circumcision made without hands, came in the room of the circumcision made with hands; the putting off the body of the sins of the flesh came in the room of the cutting off the foreskin; the circumcision of Christ came in the room of the circumcision of Moses…The Christian ordinances do not come in the room of the Jewish ordinances.*[73] So, according to Carson, Jewish typical ordinances were literally fulfilled in the Christ event, not in corresponding ordinances, such as baptism and communion. Carson illustrates this precise point, using the Lord's Supper as an example:

> The Lord's supper and the passover have a resemblance still more close; yet the one is not said to come in the room of the other. Christ himself has come in the room of the passover; for it is said, "Christ our Passover is sacrificed for us." The Lord's supper is a feast of like nature, but with this fundamental

---

[72] Ibid., p. 229.
[73] Ibid.

difference, which equally applies to baptism and circumcision—it does not belong to the same persons. The Lord's supper, as well as baptism, belongs solely to the true Israel of God: the passover belonged to the carnal Israel, without respect to their faith or character. The persons whom John drove from his baptism, had as good a right to all the Jewish ordinances as John the Baptist himself. The Scribes, and Pharisees, and Sadducees, with the whole unbelieving body of the Jewish nation, enjoyed all the ordinances of the Jewish dispensation, by as valid a title as the apostles of Christ. Neither Jesus nor his apostles ever forbade this, nor made any observations on it as an impropriety. The ministrations of the priests were never objected to; because they were carnal men, and rejected the Messiah when he manifested himself to Israel. This is the grand distinction between Jewish ordinances and the ordinances of the Church of Christ. The former shadowed good things to come, and were appointed for the nation in general, which had only a typical holiness; the latter are appointed only for the true holy people, and take it for granted, that all who partake of them, enjoy the thing figured by them.[74]

Carson continues by arguing that if baptism replaced circumcision, it would not have commenced until the former had ceased, and it would not have applied to circumcised persons. He then asks: *Why did John baptize the circumcised Jews before the manifestation of Christ? Why did Jesus baptize before the end of the Jewish dispensation?*[75] Carson places the burden of proof on his opponents and points out that their highest authority is *the saying of the divines.*[76]

It has been argued that only the children of believers have the right to baptism based on the faith of the immediate ancestor. But Carson argues that *the child of a Jew must be circumcised without any respect to the faith of the parent. If, then, none but believers have a*

---

[74] Ibid., pp. 229, 230.
[75] Ibid., p. 230. Actually, Jesus authorized his disciples to baptize.
[76] Ibid.

right to obtain baptism for their children, the law of circumcision does not apply to it. He also questions why slaves are not required to be baptized with their masters as the law of circumcision requires (Gen. 17:10-13), and, if the baptized will obtain an earthly Canaan.[77]

Carson wonders why, being excluded from circumcision, females had equal spiritual privileges with males. There was no spiritual distinction between male and female. He called circumcision *a part of that yoke, from which the spiritual Israelites were delivered by Christ.*[78] It is strange for Him to hear Christians speaking of fleshly circumcision as a ritual privilege. Regarding two separate OT gospels, he states:

> Had circumcision, then, been appointed to designate the heirs of the everlasting inheritance, it must have been extended to females. It is said, the Abrahamic covenant contained spiritual blessings: infants had its seal; why, then, shall not infants have baptism? I reply, the one half of Jewish infants had not the seal, which demonstrates that the seal had no personal application to the individual.[79]

A casual reading of the New Testament will convince anyone that fleshly circumcision never bestowed eternal salvation on a Jewish person. Otherwise Paul was wasting his time longing for their salvation. But if baptism is circumcision under a different form, why is it considered to bestow eternal salvation? Carson asks:

> But are we for this reason to infer, that as infants under the Jewish dispensation received circumcision, a rite that supposed no character in the person circumcised, they should under the Christian dispensation receive baptism, which supposes that all baptized persons are washed from sin through the belief of the truth.[80]

---

[77] Ibid.
[78] Ibid., p. 231. He noted a unique contrast when he said: "The church of Israel had the circumcision of the flesh,—the church of the New Testament has the circumcision of the heart."
[79] Ibid., Carson is speaking of personal, spiritual application.
[80] Ibid., p. 233.

Jews in New Testament times could not unite with a church without a profession of faith in Christ as the Messiah/Savior. John the Baptist would not baptize a Jew until he believed in Jesus. This causes Carson to ask the question:

> Is the Christian church that rejected the great body of the Jewish nation, the same with the Jewish church, which, by God's own appointment, contained the whole nation? Was the church into which its members were born, the same with the church whose members must be born from above.—born, not of blood, nor of the will of the flesh, nor of the will of man, but of God? Was the church that admitted every stranger to its passover, without any condition of faith or character, merely on complying with a certain regulation that gave circumcision to their males, without any condition of faith or character, the same with the church that requires faith and true holiness in all who enjoy its ordinances? Was the church that contained the scribes, and Pharisees, and Sadducees—the most cruel, determined, open, and malignant enemies of Christ—the same with that church into which such persons could not enter without a spiritual birth? The church of Israel was the nation of Israel, and as a whole could no more be called the church of Christ, in the sense of that phrase in the New Testament, than the nation of England can be called the church of Christ. It is said that a similar corruption has taken place in the church of Christ. But this observation proceeds on a fundamental mistake. The very constitution of the Jewish church recognized the membership of carnal persons. It did not make the distinction between those born after the flesh, and those born after the Spirit. There was no law to exclude the Pharisees, or even the Sadducees, from the Jewish church. Their doctrines and practices were condemned by the Old Testament; but it was no corruption of the constitution of the church to contain them. On the other hand, the constitution of the

churches of Christ rejects such persons, and provides for their expulsion.[81]

Carson makes strong note of the fact that the ordinances of the Jewish church were abolished in Christ Himself Who could not have been a priest in it. But He is the only mediator between God and man in the Christian church, *For the priesthood being changed, there is made of necessity a change also of the law"* (Heb. 7:12). The Jewish church, by its constitution, included carnal members; the Christian Church, by its constitution, admits spiritual members.[82]

Carson continues by noting that the theory which affirms *that baptism and the Lord's supper are seals of the covenant, is a doctrine so common, and a phraseology so established, that it is received without question as a first principle.* Without being too disrespectful of the ancients he said: *Let our ancestors have all the esteem and gratitude to which they are entitled—but that esteem is much misplaced, if it leads us to follow them in anything in which they have not followed Christ.* Therefore, he questions again:

> Is there any Jewish tradition more void of scriptural authority, than that which designates baptism and the Lord's supper *seals of the new covenant*? There is not in the New Testament any single portion that can bear such a meaning...God...has not said that baptism is a seal. Circumcision was a seal of the righteousness of the faith of Abraham. This was God's seal to the truth, till the letter was abolished. The Spirit of truth is the seal, and the circumcision of the heart by him is the thing signified by circumcision in the flesh. The circumcised nation was typical of the church of Christ, for the apostle says, "we are the circumcision, which worship God in the spirit;" and "circumcision is that of the heart, in the spirit, and not in the letter." The circumcision of the Jews was the letter, of which the circumcision of the heart in Christians is the spirit. The Christian, then, has a more exalted seal than circumcision—he has the Spirit of God, "whereby he

---
[81] Ibid., p. 233.
[82] Ibid., p. 234.

is sealed unto the day of redemption." Ephes. iv. 30. When sinners believe in Christ, they are sealed with that Holy Spirit of promise, which is "the earnest of their inheritance until the redemption of the purchased possession." Eph. i.13. The seal, then, that comes in the room of circumcision, is the seal of the Spirit. Circumcision sealed God's truth to Abraham, and all who ever shall have the faith of Abraham. It was applied to the typical nation without respect to character; but the seal of the Spirit is applied to none but believers, and to believers of all nations as well as Jews. When the Holy Spirit himself, in the heart of the believer, is the seal of God's truth, there is no need of any other seal...He that is once sealed by the Spirit, is secured to eternity.[83]

How can Carson be right and almost two thousand years of tradition be wrong? Sometimes error has a long history. Paul told the Ephesians that error would begin immediately after his departure. Carson reminds us, *How soon was the Lord's supper corrupted by the church at Corinth.* We saw from chapter one of this present work how strong and quick *they of the circumcision* were in the apostolic period to dominate with error every environment they entered. If baptism is simply circumcision in another form, then every argument of *they of the circumcision* can be equally argued in favor of baptismal regeneration.

Is there a single window through which we could look for an understanding concerning the Apostle Paul's meaning when he pinned the words: *Buried with him in baptism, wherein also ye are risen with him through the faith of the operation of God, who hath raised him from the dead?* The answer is explicitly "yes"—it would be the window of Paul's personal conversion to Christ. When was he regenerated, born again, illuminated and justified in God's saving grace? When can it first be said that he was *in* or *with* Christ? Was Paul already with Christ as he was being baptized or was he baptized to get "with Christ"?

Many scholars date his new birth from his meeting with Ananias in Damascus—

---

[83] Ibid., p. 235

Does Baptism Replace Circumcision?

> And he said, The God of our fathers hath chosen thee, that thou shouldest know his will, and see that Just One, and shouldest hear the voice of his mouth. For thou shalt be his witness unto all men of what thou hast seen and heard. And now why tarriest thou? arise, and be baptized, and wash away thy sins, calling on the name of the Lord (Acts 22:14-16).

Two questions revolve around this passage—was Paul saved on the Damascus Road or at Judas' house?

Several factors suggest he was saved on the Damascus Road. First, the gospel was presented to him directly by Christ—*For thou shalt be his witness unto all men of what thou hast seen and heard.* (Acts 11:15). The gospel that converted Paul came straight to him from Jesus Christ—*But I certify you, brethren, that the gospel which was preached of me is not after man. For I neither received it of man, neither was I taught it, but by the revelation of Jesus Christ* (Gal. 1:11-12; Eph. 3:1-4)—not later by Ananias.

Paul had already submitted in faith to Christ before he met Ananias—

> And I said, Who art thou, Lord? And he said, I am Jesus whom thou persecutest. But rise, and stand upon thy feet: for I have appeared unto thee for this purpose, to make thee a minister and a witness both of these things which thou hast seen, and of those things in the which I will appear unto thee; Delivering thee from the people, and *from* the Gentiles, unto whom now I send thee, To open their eyes, *and* to turn *them* from darkness to light, and *from* the power of Satan unto God, **that they may receive forgiveness of sins**, and inheritance among them which are sanctified by faith that is in me. Whereupon, O king Agrippa, **I was not disobedient unto the heavenly vision**: But shewed first unto them of Damascus, and at Jerusalem, and throughout all the coasts of Judaea, and *then* to the Gentiles, **that they should repent and turn to God, and do works meet for repentance**. For these causes the Jews caught me in the temple, and went about to kill *me*. Having therefore obtained help of God, I

continue unto this day, witnessing both to small and great, saying none other things than those which the prophets and Moses did say should come: That Christ should suffer, *and* that he should be the first that should rise from the dead, and should shew light unto the people, and to the Gentiles." (Acts 16:15-23). [emphasis added]

This is precisely why Paul referred to the Damascus Road experience as the moment in which he became reborn: *And last of all he was seen of me also, as of one born out of due time* (I Corinthians 15:8).

The Greek aorist participle, *epikalesamenos,* translated (*calling on His name*) refers either to action which is simultaneous with or before that of the main verb. Here Paul's calling on Christ's name (for salvation) preceded his water baptism. The participle may therefore be translated: *having called on His name.*

What then do the words (*wash your sins away*) mean? Do they teach that salvation comes by water baptism? Because Paul was already cleansed spiritually:

> But rise, and stand upon thy feet: for I have appeared unto thee for this purpose, to make thee a minister and a witness both of these things which thou hast seen, and of those things in the which I will appear unto thee; Delivering thee from the people, and *from* the Gentiles, unto whom now I send thee, To open their eyes, *and* to turn *them* from darkness to light, and *from* the power of Satan unto God, that they may receive forgiveness of sins, and inheritance among them which are sanctified by faith that is in me. (Acts 26:16-18).

In order to be a light of the Gospel to the Gentiles, one must, first of all, be a recipient of the light of the Gospel, as was the Apostle Paul prior to his baptism—

> And the next sabbath day came almost the whole city together to hear the word of God. But when the Jews saw the multitudes, they were filled with envy, and spake against those things which were spoken by Paul, contradicting and blaspheming. Then Paul and

Does Baptism Replace Circumcision?

> Barnabas waxed bold, and said, It was necessary that the word of God should first have been spoken to you: but seeing ye put it from you, and judge yourselves unworthy of everlasting life, lo, we turn to the Gentiles. For so hath the Lord commanded us, *saying*, I have set thee to be a light of the Gentiles, **that thou shouldest be for salvation unto the ends of the earth**. And when the Gentiles heard this, they were glad, and glorified the word of the Lord: and as many as were ordained to eternal life believed. And the word of the Lord was published throughout all the region (Acts 13:44-49). [emphasis added]

What is the "Light" that brings forgiveness to men? Why not ask Paul himself, Simeon the priest and then John the evangelist—

> But if our gospel be hid, it is hid to them that are lost: In whom the god of this world hath blinded the minds of them which believe not, lest the light of the glorious gospel of Christ, who is the image of God, should shine unto them. For we preach not ourselves, but Christ Jesus the Lord; and ourselves your servants for Jesus' sake. For God, who commanded the light to shine out of darkness, hath shined in our hearts, to *give* the light of the knowledge of the glory of God in the face of Jesus Christ (II Cor. 4:3-6).

> For ye were sometimes darkness, but now *are ye* light in the Lord: walk as children of light (Eph. 5:8).

> Ye are all the children of light, and the children of the day: we are not of the night, nor of darkness (I Thess. 5:5).

> The people which sat in darkness saw great light; and to them which sat in the region and shadow of death light is sprung up (Matt. 4:16).

> Lord, now lettest thou thy servant depart in peace, according to thy word: For mine eyes have seen thy salvation, Which thou hast prepared before the face of

all people; A light to lighten the Gentiles, and the glory of thy people Israel (Lk. 2:29-32).

In him was life; and the life was the light of men. And the light shineth in darkness; and the darkness comprehended it not. There was a man sent from God, whose name *was* John. The same came for a witness, to bear witness of the Light, that all *men* through him might believe. He was not that Light, but *was sent* to bear witness of that Light. *That* was the true Light, which lighteth every man that cometh into the world (Jn. 1:4-9).

He that believeth on him is not condemned: but he that believeth not is condemned already, because he hath not believed in the name of the only begotten Son of God. And this is the condemnation, that light is come into the world, and men loved darkness rather than light, because their deeds were evil (Jn. 3:18-19).

Ye sent unto John, and he bare witness unto the truth. But I receive not testimony from man: but these things I say, that ye might be saved. He was a burning and a shining light: and ye were willing for a season to rejoice in his light. But I have greater witness than *that* of John: for the works which the Father hath given me to finish, the same works that I do, bear witness of me, that the Father hath sent me (Jn.. 5:33-36).

Then spake Jesus again unto them, saying, I am the light of the world: he that followeth me shall not walk in darkness, but shall have the light of life (Jn. 8:12).

As long as I am in the world, I am the light of the world (Jn. 9:5).

Then Jesus said unto them, Yet a little while is the light with you. Walk while ye have the light, lest darkness come upon you: for he that walketh in darkness knoweth not whither he goeth. While ye have light, believe in the light, that ye may be the children of light. These things spake Jesus, and departed, and did hide himself from them...

Jesus cried and said, He that believeth on me, believeth not on me, but on him that sent me. And he that seeth me seeth him that sent me. I am come a light into the world, that whosoever believeth on me should not abide in darkness. And if any man hear my words, and believe not, I judge him not: for I came not to judge the world, but to save the world. He that rejecteth me, and receiveth not my words, hath one that judgeth him: the word that I have spoken, the same shall judge him in the last day (Jn. 12:35, 36, 44-48).

Now the question is, *Did Paul distinguish the Gospel Light from baptism? Listen to him as he describes the baptisms of the Corinthians*:

I thank God that I baptized none of you, but Crispus and Gaius; Lest any should say that I had baptized in mine own name. And I baptized also the household of Stephanas: besides, I know not whether I baptized any other. For Christ sent me not to baptize, but to preach the gospel: not with wisdom of words, lest the cross of Christ should be made of none effect. For the preaching of the cross is to them that perish foolishness; but unto us which are saved it is the power of God (I Cor. 1:14-18).

But if Paul did not baptize them, how could he have begotten them in the Lord as he said:

I write not these things to shame you, but as my beloved sons I warn you. For though ye have ten thousand instructors in Christ, yet have ye not many fathers: for in Christ Jesus I have begotten you through the gospel. Wherefore I beseech you, be ye followers of me (I Cor. 4:14-16)?

So, is a person saved when he is begotten (*or born again*) or when he is baptized? Let the Apostle Peter give us the answer:

Blessed *be* the God and Father of our Lord Jesus Christ, which according to his abundant mercy hath begotten us again unto a lively hope by the resurrection of Jesus Christ from the dead, To an inheritance incorruptible, and undefiled, and that fadeth not away, reserved in heaven for you, Who are kept by the power of God through faith unto salvation ready to be revealed in the last time (I Pet. 1:3-5).

The Apostle John tells us that to be *born of God* is synonymous with being *begotten of God* when he says: *Whosoever believeth that Jesus is the Christ is born of God: and every one that loveth him that begat loveth him also that is begotten of him* (I Jn. 5:1). The Bible teaches that God *begets* us when we receive the Word of Truth: *Of his own will begat he us with the word of truth, that we should be a kind of firstfruits of his creatures* (James 1:18). It is through the "Word of God" that we are born again (or begotten)—*Being born again, not of corruptible seed, but of incorruptible, by the word of God, which liveth and abideth for ever* (I Pet. 1:23).

We can objectively see from where water is coming and to where it is flowing, but not so with spiritual birth—

That which is born of the flesh is flesh; and that which is born of the Spirit is spirit. Marvel not that I said unto thee, Ye must be born again. The wind bloweth where it listeth, and thou hearest the sound thereof, but canst not tell whence it cometh, and whither it goeth: so is every one that is born of the Spirit (Jn. 3:6-8).

How could Paul have espoused the Corinthians to Christ if he did not baptize them?—

For I am jealous over you with godly jealousy: for I have espoused you to one husband, that I may present you as a chaste virgin to Christ. But I fear, lest by any means, as the serpent beguiled Eve through his subtilty, so your minds should be corrupted from the simplicity that is in Christ (II Cor. 11:2, 3).

To espouse means to "join someone to." It is the same concept as the word "betroth," as in Hosea 2:19-20:

> ... And I will betroth thee unto me for ever; yea, I will betroth thee unto me in righteousness, and in judgment, and in lovingkindness, and in mercies. I will even betroth thee unto me in faithfulness: and thou shalt know the LORD.

In New Testament times, engaged couples were so joined that a legal divorce had to transpire in order to undo an espousement, as in Matt. 1:18, 19:

> Now the birth of Jesus Christ was on this wise: When as his mother Mary was espoused to Joseph, before they came together, she was found with child of the Holy Ghost. Then Joseph her husband, being a just man, and not willing to make her a public example, was minded to put her away privily.[84]

Thus, even though the marriage of the Lamb will not take place until after the rapture of the Church, saints are forever Christ's now because they are espoused, betrothed, begotten and born of God and joined to Him in eternal life, as Paul told the Corinthians: *But he that is joined unto the Lord is one spirit* (I Cor. 6:17); and as he said to the Romans:

> The Spirit itself beareth witness with our spirit, that we are the children of God: And if children, then heirs; heirs of God, and joint-heirs with Christ; if so be that we suffer with him, that we may be also glorified together (Rom. 8:16,17).

What then do the words *wash away thy sins* mean in Acts 22:16? They refer to the symbolism of baptism. Why? Because baptism is a picture of God's inner work of washing away sin. Paul's conscience was clear the moment he believed, as the Apostle Peter said: *...not the putting away of the filth of the flesh, but the answer of a good conscience toward God.* Paul's conscience was clear before he was baptized, and his baptism was his answer of a good conscience toward God.

---

[84] cf. Matt. 5:31, 32; 19:9.

Based upon Paul's use of the words *begotten, espoused,* and *joined* and his distinction between the *light* of the gospel and the ordinance of baptism, why not let him interpret his own words in Titus 3:5—... *Not by works of righteousness*[85] *which we have done, but according to his mercy he saved us, by the washing of regeneration, and renewing of the Holy Ghost.* Perhaps Paul would ask us by what authority the church divines have substituted "ritual baptism" for "washing" in this verse when it is not there—especially in light of the fact that he received God's mercy before he was baptized (Acts 26:19); received the fullness of the Holy Spirit before he was baptized (Acts 9:17)[86]; was washed by the gospel in the Word of God before he was baptized (9:6; Eph. 5:26); was a chosen vessel before baptism (Acts 9:6); confessed Christ as Lord before baptism (9:6); called to preach the gospel before baptism (Acts 26:15-18); obeyed the Lord before baptism (Acts 9:6-9; 26:19); had a praying relationship with God before baptism (Acts 9:11); was ordained to suffer for Christ's sake before baptism (Acts 9:16); and was Ananias' brother in Christ before baptism (Acts 9:17).[87]

Paul sees no difference between the putting away of sin, the washing away of sin or the washing of regeneration. But how are sins put away?

(Heb. 9:26) for then must he often have suffered since
the foundation of the world: but now once in the end

---

[85] Obeying the Law of Moses is a work of righteousness and circumcision was such a work. If baptism replaced circumcision, then baptism is a work of righteousness.

[86] Paul had received the baptism of the Holy Spirit but he was not yet filled with the Spirit. Paul often told saved Christians how to be filled with the Holy Spirit. Compare Acts 10:43-47. The filling of the Holy Spirit is distinct from the baptism of the Holy Spirit. The filling can be observed before Pentecost (Ex. 28:3; 31:3; 35:31; Lk. 1:15, 41, 67; 4:1). In the N.T., everyone who had the baptism of the Spirit could be filled by the spirit if he met the conditions (Acts 2:4; 4:8, 31; 6:3, 5; 7:55; 9:17; 11:24; 13:9, 52; Eph. 5:18).

[87] Controversy exists regarding whether the reference to Paul as *brother* is a cultural greeting as a fellow Jew or a recognition as a brother in Christ. The N. T. uses the term either way throughout. Knowing what Paul had the legal authority to do with Christians it seems doubtful that the greeting meant *brother Jew.*

of the world hath he appeared to put away sin by the sacrifice of himself.

This is experienced as a reality in the life of the believer at the moment of faith through the proclamation of the word of the gospel (Eph. 5:26).

In Mark 16:16 we see that belief and baptism are two separate acts: *He that believeth and is baptized shall be saved; but he that believeth not shall be damned.* Most of the clear presentations of the gospel in the Bible do not even mention ritual baptism. But the New Testament does teach that a person is in union with Christ the moment he trusts Christ as his savior (John 1:12; 3:18; 3:36; 5:24; 6:47; 20:30; Acts 10:43-49, compare Acts 11:15-18).

It is totally legitimate to separate "belief" from "baptism," without minimizing either, and still call it the saving gospel. In Mark 16:16 there is no question but that "belief" and "baptism" are listed separately and are not synonymous. But notice what "believers" are in the New Testament. They are *sons of God* (Jn. 1:12, 13); have *eternal life* (Jn. 3:14-16, 18; 5:24; 6:47; I Jn. 5:13); have *passed from death unto life* (Jn. 5:24); are *alive in Christ* (Jn. 11:25); shall *never die* (Jn. 11:26); have *remission of sins* (Acts 10:43-47; 15:7-11; 13:39; Rom. 3:27, 28; 4:5-8); are *purified* (Acts 15:9); sin is not *imputed* to them (Rom. 4:8); have *peace with God* (Rom. 5:1); have the *righteousness of God* (Rom. 10:3, 4); are *sealed by the Holy Spirit* (Eph. 1:13); sealed *unto the day of redemption* (Eph. 1:13); are *born of God* (I Jn. 5:1); are *indwelt* by God (I Jn. 4:15); have *overcome the world* (I Jn. 5:5); and have God *working within* (Phil. 1:6); are *predestinated* (Eph. 1:5; Rom. 8:28-30). It is God's will for all believers to be ritually baptized, but it is their faith, independent of baptism, that receives Jesus Christ (John 1:12).

We will discuss, in chapter nine of this work, other verses that are used to teach baptismal regeneration. In this chapter we have studied the OT covenant of circumcision, and found that it was not to be the plan of salvation or a means of saving grace. We have traced the history of the Jewish belief in circumcisional regeneration. We have traced, in church history, the belief that baptism is circumcision in another form. We have demonstrated this to be false. And we have demonstrated that the Apostle Paul was regenerated, born again, justified, and called to preach before he was ritually baptized.

If the reader has trusted baptism to save him or to bestow salvation upon him, he needs to ask: *was I really trusting Christ alone for salvation?* Or, *Was I thinking that my faith could receive the grace of Christ only because my baptism as an infant placed me eternally into the body of Christ?* In chapter six we will discuss the controversy of infant baptism vs. believer's baptism.

> For if, as we believe, baptism is right and useful and brings the children to salvation, and I then did away with it, then I would be responsible for all the children who were lost because they were unbaptized—a cruel and terrible thing. If baptism is not right, that is, without value or help to the children, then I would be guilty of no greater sin that that the Word of God had been spoken and his sign given in vain. I would not be responsible for the loss of any soul, but only of an effectual use of the word and sign of God.

Martin Luther

Chapter Six

Infant Baptism and Believer's Baptism

We observed in the previous chapter that there are those who take a regenerationist view of infant baptism and those who do not. Let us now attempt to diffuse a potential point of unnecessary offense. Because *baptismal regeneration* is such a common view among many Protestant groups, there is a misunderstanding when one of their members is required to be rebaptized by those of the *believer's baptism* position. The outrage stems from the judgment that the rebaptizers are attempting to deChristianize everyone in Christendom who had been baptized as an infant. This judgment would be correct when referring to those baptismal regenerationists who require immersion for salvation.[1] Even though these groups affirm *believer's baptism* by immersion, they do not hold that belief alone appropriates salvation. Many theologians of the Restoration movement (usually independent Christian churches) will distinguish between regeneration and forgiveness in a way that enables them to deny that they teach baptismal regeneration and yet affirm that no one is saved or forgiven until they are immersed into the *true Church*.[2] This would mean that a regenerate person could be damned for lack of baptism by immersion. Accordingly, this tradition is seen to be saying that all who are baptized as infants are not born again Christians until they are rebaptized by immersion.

It seems strange that most Protestants are not nearly as outraged at this position (baptismal salvation by immersion only) as they are those of the *baptistic* tradition. Most theologians of the Baptist

---

[1] (e.g. The Oneness or "Jesus Only" Pentecostal movement and the Restoration movement).

[2] Isaac Errett, *Our Position* (Cincinnati, Ohio: The Standard Publishing Company), pp. 16, 17. "Baptists say that they baptize believers *because they are forgiven*, and they insist that they shall have the evidence of pardon before they are baptized. But the language used in the Scriptures declaring what baptism is for, is so plain and unequivocal, that the great majority of Protestants, as well as Roman Catholics, admit it in their creeds to be, in some sense, for the remission of sins...But *forgiveness* is something distinct from *regeneration*...In baptism he *appropriates God's promise of forgiveness*..."

tradition hold that no form of baptism contributes to personal salvation. The baptistic view of *believer's baptism* is not an attempt to deChristianize anyone baptized as an infant, and no such offense need be taken. That is why the baptistic view can recognize many paedobaptists as brothers in Christ. However, their theological tradition does require that only believers are to be baptized. This is the only baptism they can find in the New Testament.[3] Though disagreeing with most Protestants regarding *mode* and *candidates* of Christian baptism, they recognize anyone as *brother in Christ* who professes that faith alone appropriates the saving grace of Christ. They do not see themselves as rebaptizing anyone, for they judge the baptism of an unbeliever to be no baptism at all.[4] They are not proclaiming unbaptized believers to be lost and unforgiven. Nevertheless, it is their firm belief that rituals never impart the saving grace of God—a position that has sparked contempt from many paedobaptist traditions against them.

So also, this present work does not deny the salvation of anyone who was baptized as an unbeliever, but we are saying that no one was saved by or through baptism. Many in the New Testament, who believed that circumcision appropriated salvation, came to this belief after they were redeemed by grace alone through faith alone in the finished work of Christ. So, even though they were now professing an apostate gospel, they were originally born again—

---

[3] This view is held today by a great number of churches and some organizations of churches which would never define themselves as *Baptists* (e.g. many Community churches and all independent Bible churches affiliated with the *Independent Fundamental Churches of America*). Therefore, we are not just talking about the Baptist tradition. Neither does it require becoming a Baptist to embrace *believer's baptism*.

[4] The Seventh Council of Carthage, under Cyprian in the third century, concerned the baptism of heretics. It was determined by the majority of the eighty-seven bishops attending that an heretical baptism that was not an identification with the true Gospel was no baptism at all. Therefore the requirement of Christian baptism should not be considered *rebaptism*. One of the bishops, Adelphius of Thasvalte, said: "Certain persons without reason impugn the truth by false and envious words, in saying that we rebaptize, when the Church does not rebaptize heretics, but baptizes them." Cyprian, *Seventh Council of Carthage* in *Ante-Nicene Fathers: down to A.D. 325*, Alexander Roberts, D.D., and James Donaldson, LL.D., Editors (Grand Rapids, Michigan: Wm. B. Eerdmans Publishing Company, 1975), Vol. V, p. 569.

> (e.g. Gal. 1:6-9) I marvel that ye are so soon removed from him that called you into the grace of Christ unto another gospel: Which is not another; but there be some that trouble you, and would pervert the gospel of Christ. But though we, or an angel from heaven, preach any other gospel unto you than that which we have preached unto you, let him be accursed. As we said before, so say I now again, If any *man* preach any other gospel unto you than that ye have received, let him be accursed.

However, the one who had never believed anything but the position that circumcision saves, had therefore not trusted the finished work of Christ alone for eternal life. So, there were *saved* and *unsaved* advocates of *circumcisional salvation*. We must not attempt to determine which ones were saved or lost; but they, for their own sakes, needed to make that determination for themselves—

> This only would I learn of you, Received ye the Spirit by the works of the law, or by the hearing of faith? Are ye so foolish? having begun in the Spirit, are ye now made perfect by the flesh? (Gal. 3:2, 3).

We can only determine that circumcision was not the gospel or an essential part of the gospel.[5]

Strong makes the point that, *the rise of infant baptism in the history of the church is due to sacramental conceptions of Christianity, so that all arguments in its favor from the writings of the first three centuries are equally arguments for baptismal regeneration.*[6]

---

[5] We are often asked, "Who cares what people believe about circumcision as long as they believe in Jesus also?" Christ plus works is not the gospel. It is belief in the work of Christ alone that is the faith that appropriates salvation. To further study this question one should re-read Chapter One of this present work.

[6] August Hopkins Strong, *Systematic Theology* (Valley Forge, PA.: The Judson Press, 1907), p. 953.

Infant baptism must have been practiced as early as the third century where we find Tertullian arguing against it when he says:[7]

> ...And so, according to the circumstances and disposition, and even age, of each individual, the delay of baptism is preferable; principally however, in the case of little children. For why is it necessary—if (baptism itself) is not so necessary—that the sponsors likewise should be thrust into danger? Who both themselves, by reason of mortality, may fail to fulfil their promises, and may be disappointed by the development of an evil disposition, *in those for whom they stood?* The Lord does indeed say, "forbid them not to come unto me."[8] Let them "come," then, while they are learning, while they are learning whither to come;[9] Let them become Christians when they have become able to know Christ...Let them know how to "ask" for salvation, that you may seem (at least) to have given "to him that asketh"...If any understand the weighty import of baptism, they will fear its reception more than its delay: sound faith is secure of salvation.[10]

Cyprian,[11] on the other hand, believed that ritual infant baptism was spiritual circumcision and therefore should never be delayed till the eighth day like circumcision of the flesh—

> But in respect of the case of the infants, which you say ought not to be baptized within the second or third

---

[7] Ibid., *New Dictionary of Theology*, p. 675. "Tertullian began writing in Carthage, North Africa, towards the end of the 2nd century, his undisputed works dating from c. A.D. 196 to c. A.D. 212."

[8] Matt. 19:14; Mk. 10:14; Lk18:16.

[9] Or, "whither they are coming."

[10] Tertullian, *On Baptism [Chapter xviii], Ante-Nicene Fathers, Latin Christianity: Its Founder, Tertullian* (Grand Rapids, Michigan: Wm. B. Eerdmans Publishing Company, 1976), Vol. III, p. 678. Perhaps his view was evolving for in Chapters vii and xii he argues that ritual baptism is necessary to salvation, Vol. III, pp. 672, 674, 675.

[11] Ibid., *New Dictionary of Theology*, p. 184. Cyprian was a, "Latin church father, and Bishop of Carthage from about 249 until his death."

day after their birth, and that the law of ancient circumcision should be regarded, so that you think that one who is just born should not be baptized and sanctified within the eighth day, we all thought very differently in our council. For in this course which you thought was to be taken, no one agreed; but we all rather judge that the mercy and grace of God is not to be refused to any one born of man.

For in respect of the observance of the eighth day in the Jewish circumcision of the flesh, a sacrament was given beforehand in shadow and in usage; but when Christ came, it was fulfilled in truth. For because the eighth day, that is, the first day after the Sabbath, was to be that on which the Lord should rise again, and should quicken us, and give us circumcision of the spirit, the eighth day, that is, the first day after the Sabbath, and the Lord's day, went before in the figure; which figure ceased when by and by the truth came and spiritual circumcision was given to us.

For which reason we think that no one is to be hindered from obtaining grace by that law which was already ordained, and that spiritual circumcision ought not to be hindered by carnal circumcision, but that absolutely every man is to be admitted to the grace of Christ...[12]

In the following pages we will now list the reasons which have been offered throughout church history in defense of the affirmation that infants are to be baptized in order to receive the saving grace of God. Along with these reasons we will offer a biblical and theological response and then conclude with a Scriptural and historical defense of the *believer's baptism* position.

Reason # 1: Infant baptism is believer's baptism because an infant in the womb of a believer is also a believer. Martin Luther said: *Since our baptizing has been thus from the beginning of Christianity and the custom has been to baptize children, and since no*

---

[12] Cyprian, *The Epistles of Cyprian LVIII, Ante-Nicene Fathers: Fathers of the Third Century* (Grand Rapids, Michigan, Wm. B. Eerdmans Publishing Co., 1975), Vol. V, pp. 253, 254.

one can prove with good reasons that they do not have faith, we should not make changes and build on such weak arguments.[13] Concerning rebaptizers he comments: *When they say, "Children cannot believe," how can they be sure of that? Where is the Scripture by which they would prove it and on which they would build? They imagine this, I suppose, because children do not speak or have understanding. But such a fancy is deceptive, yea, altogether false, and we cannot build on what we imagine.*[14] Luther uses Scripture to prove that infants can believe, though they do not speak or understand:

> So, Ps. 72 [106:37f.], describes how the Jews offered their sons and daughters to idols, shedding innocent blood. If, as the text says, it was innocent blood, then the children have to be considered pure and holy—this they could not be without spirit and faith. Likewise the innocent children whom Herod had murdered were not over two years of age [Matt. 2:16]. Admittedly they could not speak or understand. Yet they were holy and blessed. Christ himself says in Matt. 18 [19:14], "The kingdom of heaven belongs to children."

---

[13] *Luther's Works: Church and Ministry II*, Conrad Bergendoff, Editor; Helmut T. Lehmann, General Editor (Philadelphia: Muhlenberg Press, 1958), Vol. 40, p. 241. The introduction to this volume states that *there is no later or more elaborate treatise on the subject* [of rebaptism] *by Luther. But the controversy seems to have stimulated him to deeper study of the significance of baptism...*, pp. 227, 228. In defense of Luther and contemporary Lutheranism we must say that in this volume Luther gives the impression that he does not know sufficiently what the teachings of the Anabaptists were, p. 261. Balthasar Hubmaier had written a book in defense of the Anabaptist doctrine in 1525 but there is no evidence that Luther had read it. Hubmaier, who had claimed Luther as a friend, was a former Roman Catholic who had studied theology at the University in Freiburg. In 1512 he became professor of theology at Ingolstadt. He served as cathedral preacher at Regensburg in 1519, where he declared himself in favor of the Reformation. However, upon further study, he associated with, and embraced the cause of, the Anabaptists at Waldshut. Denying the validity of infant baptism, he became a heretic in Catholic and Protestant territories. He fled for his life from Waldshut in Austria to Zurich in Switzerland and then to Moravia. He was finally burned at the stake for this heresy in Vienna in 1528. It would be wise for the interested reader to study his life and work.

[14] Ibid., *Luther*, Vol. 40, p. 242.

Infant Baptism And Believer's Baptism

> And St. John was a child in his mother's womb [Luke 1:41] but, as I believe, could have faith.
>
> Yes, you say, but John was an exception. This is not proof that all baptized children have faith. I answer, wait a minute. I am not yet at the point of proving that children believe. I am giving proof that your foundation for rebaptism is uncertain and false inasmuch as you cannot prove that there may not be faith in children. Inasmuch as John had faith, though he could not speak or understand, your argument fails, that children are not able to believe. To hold that a child believes, as St. John is an example, is not contrary to Scriptures. If it is not contrary to the Scripture to hold that children believe, but rather in accord with Scripture, then your argument, that children cannot believe, must be unscriptural. That is my first point.
>
> Who has made you so sure that baptized children do not believe in the face of what I here prove that they can believe? But if you are not sure, why then are you so bold as to discard the first baptism, since you do not and cannot know that it is meaningless? ...Now it is up to you to bring forth a single Scripture verse which proves that children cannot believe in baptism. I have cited these many verses showing that they can believe, and that it be reasonable to hold that they do believe.[15]

It is a fallacy of logic to ask someone to prove a negative (e.g. if you cannot disprove the existence of green men on Mars then I have therefore proven their existence). Luther placed the burden of proof on those who did not find that John The Baptist was a believer in his mother's womb. But when the burden of proof was placed on him he would respond as follows:

> On the other hand we cannot prove that children do believe with any Scripture verse that clearly and expressly declares in so many words, or the like, "you are to baptize children because they also believe." Whoever compels us to produce such a statement has

---

[15] Ibid., *Luther*, Vol. 40, pp. 242, 243.

> the upper hand and wins, for we cannot find such words. But sincere and sensible Christians do not require such proof. The quarrelsome, obstinate rebellious spirits do in order to seem to be clever. But on their side they can produce no statement which says, "you are to baptize adults but no children." We are however persuaded by many good reasons to hold that child baptism is right and that children do believe.[16]

Luther's comments are based on his belief that OT infants were brought into the covenant of grace through their circumcision and that infant baptism serves the same function—

> If the old covenant and the sign of circumcision made the children of Abraham believe that they were, and were called the people of God, according to the promise, I will be the God of thy descendants [Gen. 17:7], then this new covenant and sign must be much more effectual and make those a people of God who receive it.[17]

Luther thought that the advocates of *believer's baptism* were literally withholding the saving grace of God from infants for whom Christ died—

> For if, as we believe, baptism is right and useful and brings the children to salvation, and I then did away with it, then I would be responsible for all the children who were lost because they were unbaptized—a cruel and terrible thing. If baptism is not right, that is, without value or help to the children, then I would be guilty of no greater sin than that the Word of God had been spoken and his sign given in vain. I would not be responsible for the loss of any soul, but only of an effectual use of the Word and sign of God.[18]

---

[16] Ibid., *Luther*, Vol. 40, p. 254.
[17] Ibid., *Luther*, Vol. 40, pp. 257, 258.
[18] Ibid., *Luther*, Vol. 40, p. 254.

Luther uses I Jn. 2:14 as further proof of infant baptism where St. John writes to little children, that they know the Father.[19] And again he says of rebaptizers that, *They are indeed regular thieves and murderers of souls, blasphemers, and enemies of Christ and his churches.*[20]

The advocates of *believer's baptism* hold that all unborn and born infants are in the saving grace of God. What they cannot understand is the logic of arguing for the faith and salvation of infants in the womb while simultaneously arguing that only ritual baptism can wash away original sin.

Reason # 2: (Mt. 18:10) *Take heed that ye despise not one of these little ones; for I say unto you, That in heaven their angels do always behold the face of my Father which is in heaven.* All believers seem to have guardian angels (Ps. 34:7). The argument is that if these *little ones* have guardian angels, then they must have been brought into the covenant of grace by their infant baptism. But the angels of these *little ones* (*mikron touton;* cf. 18:6, 14) are entrusted to their care and are in constant communication with the heavenly Father (cf. Ps. 91:11; Acts 12:15; Heb. 1:14). This passage is telling us that either all children are under God's special care or that only believing children have special guardian angels. Vss. 12-14 seem to indicate believing children having gone astray.[21] However, most advocates of *believer's baptism* hold that all infants are alive in Christ (see Reason #3). Regardless of which view one holds, this passage does not teach nor authorize paedobaptism. It should be considered dangerous, however, to treat a believer or an infant with contempt if God and the angels are so actively involved in their well-being.

---

[19] Ibid., *Luther*, Vol. 40, p. 245.
[20] Ibid., *Luther*, Vol. 40, p. 384.
[21] Jamieson, Fausset & Brown, *Commentary On The Whole Bible* (Grand Rapids, Michigan: Zondervan Publishing House, 1961), pp. 933, 934. "Among men, those who nurse and rear the royal children, however humble in themselves, are allowed free entrance with their charge, and a degree of familiarity which even the highest state ministers dare not assume. Probably our Lord means that, in virtue of their charge over His disciples (Heb. 1:13; John 1:51), the angels have *errands* to the throne, a *welcome* there, and a *dear familiarity* in dealing with 'His father which is in heaven,' which on their own matters they could not assume."

Reason # 3: (Mtt. 19:14) *But Jesus said, Suffer little children, and forbid them not, to come unto me: for of such is the kingdom of heaven.* **Thus, withholding baptism from infants can keep them from the kingdom of heaven.** The Greek word for "little Children" is *paidia* and can refer to those ranging from babies to preteens. Notice how the same word is translated *damsel* in Mk. 5:39 [a twelve-year-old girl, vs. 42]. However, the word *brephos* is used in the parallel passage of Luke 18:15.[22] This word could refer to an "embryo," "young," "infant," or "small child."[23] So from a language perspective of this passage, the ages of the children could be argued both ways. Yet Jesus gives us the clue in Lk. 18:17 when He says, *Verily I say unto you, Whosoever shall not receive the kingdom of God as a little child [paidion] shall in no wise enter therein.* Jesus is saying that, like children, we need to come realizing that we are not sufficient in ourselves to rescue ourselves. We must realize that we are totally dependent on another for deliverance. Jesus is describing an intelligent childlike realization and attitude in adults which, if not there, will mean that they cannot enter the kingdom of heaven.[24]

---

[22] It is notable that John uses *brephos* in vs. 15 and *paidion* in vs. 17 as if to make them interchangeable in this passage.

[23] Paul uses this word for "baby" referring to one who had known the Scriptures at that age: "And that from a child [*brephous*] thou hast known the holy scriptures, which are able to make thee wise unto salvation through faith which is in Christ Jesus" (II Tim. 3:15).

[24] This is the sense in which Origen refers to the children in his Commentary on Matthew: "...as, for example, that, if any one be converted, and, though a man, such an one becomes as a child in respect of anger; and, as is the child in relation to grief, so that sometimes he laughs and plays at the very time that his father or mother, or brother is dead, he who is converted would become such an one as little children...as, for example, in the case of children there is a forgetfulness of their evils at the very time of their tears, for they change in a moment, and laugh and play along with those who were thought to grieve and terrify them, but in truth had wrought in them no such emotion...Wherefore you may see those who are not altogether infants, up to three or four years of age, like to those who are of mean birth, though they may seem to be of noble birth, and not appearing at all to love rich children rather than the poor." *Origin's Commentary on Matthew* [Book III, 16], *Ante-Nicene Fathers: The Writings of the Fathers down to A.D. 325* (Grand Rapids, Michigan: Wm. B. Eerdmans Publishing Company, 1974), Vol. X, p. 484. Origen (c. 185-c. 254) was considered a master exegete. He was imprisoned and tortured during the Decian persecution and died shortly thereafter at Tyre.

Infant Baptism And Believer's Baptism

The point we must face is that the passage is not about baptism or circumcision. These children were not brought to Christ to be baptized by Him; for Christ baptized no one, young or old. If they had been brought for baptism, they would have been brought to the disciples and not to Christ. And if the disciples were practicing infant baptism, it would not have been their business to forbid it. Mothers, fathers, and other adults were bringing these children to Jesus that He might touch them and confer a blessing on their lives (Mtt. 19:15). This could refer to a centuries old custom with Jews (Gen. 48:14, 15) of the laying on of hands for blessing of the young, which had nothing to do with circumcision or bestowing personal salvation. Mark and Luke say that they were brought to Him, *that he would touch them,* as when he healed the diseased. These children might have been diseased and brought for healing.

If these children were newborn infants, they did not need to be brought to Jesus for salvation for the Kingdom of Heaven was already made up of their like. Most contemporary advocates of *believer's baptism* take the position that all infants are saved regardless of their baptism or circumcision. David's son by Bathsheba died before being circumcised, but David knew he would see him again saying, *But now he is dead, wherefore should I fast? can I bring him back again? I shall go to him, but he shall not return to me* (II Sam. 13:23). David was not finding consolation in the thought that he would someday be buried in the plot next to his son.

Most advocates of *believer's baptism* deny that there are any babies or aborted fetuses in Hell.[25] For this position, they have often been falsely accused of *Pelagiunism.* Pelagius believed that infants were born without an Adamic nature and in a state of perfect innocence. This is the primary reason why Pelagius believed departed infants were in heaven. It would be difficult to find an advocate of *believer's baptism* who thought that infants were void of original sin.

Most contemporary advocates of *believer's baptism* recognize the imputed Adamic sin nature in all infants. They deny that it [original

---

[25] In chapter seven we will discuss the fact that advocates of *believer's baptism* were executed as baby-killers in that they withheld baptism from their infants. They were looked upon as casting their children into hell, and therefore worthy of death.

sin] is removed by circumcision or baptism. But if it is not removed, then upon what grounds are they entitled to heaven? Before answering that question we should ask, upon what grounds does anyone go to hell? If people go to hell for having a sin nature, then everyone is going there. If people go to hell for sinning or for having a disposition to sin, then everyone is going there. No one ever completely stops sinning before or after salvation (I Jn. 1:9). People still have a disposition to sin after salvation, which is why they are challenged to, *Let not sin therefore reign in your mortal body, that ye should obey it in the lusts thereof* (Rom. 6:12) and, *Neither Yield ye your members as instruments of unrighteousness* (6:13a). This is why the saved are told to, *through the spirit...mortify the deeds of the body...*(8:13b) and to *...Present your bodies a living sacrifice...and be not conformed to this world...*(12:1b, 2a.). Some brothers in Christ have failed to do this (I Cor. 3:1-3) and will experience the severe discipline of God but not His condemnation (Rom. 8:1). People go to hell because of unbelief (Mk. 16:16; Jn. 3:18, 36).[26] Jesus said to Martha:

> ... I am the resurrection, and the life: he that believeth in me, though he were dead, yet shall he live: And whosoever liveth and believeth in me shall never die. Believest thou this? (Jn. 11:25b, 26).

Martha's response was: *...Yea, Lord: I believe that thou art the Christ, the Son of God, which should come into the world.* (vs. 27b; cf. I Jn. 5:1).

Back to the question, upon what grounds are infants entitled to heaven? Those who believe that all infants are saved regardless of circumcision or baptism are sternly admonished against building an encompassing doctrine from David's statement regarding his uncircumcised, dead son in II Sam. 12. However, those who hold to the *believer's baptism* position struggle with the idea that the departed infants of all lost people and the unbaptized infants of all advocates of *believer's baptism* are burning in hell or confined to *limbo*. They are struggling with the more than thirty-million aborted babies in the United States alone. One popular American history text book quotes Johnathan Edwards as believing that hell was *paved with the skulls of unbaptized*

---

[26] See Jn.8:24, 25; 10:26; 12:37-40, 48; Rom. 11:20; II Thess. 1:8, 9; 2:11, 12.

infants.[27] Though Edwards cannot be found to have said it in those words, his writings reflect this to be the view of both the reformed and holiness divines of his day. Volume III of the AGES edition of his works contain lengthy discussions affirming that infant baptism brings the children of true Christians into the invisible as well as the visible church and that the infants of unconverted adults should not be baptized—which would of course leave them outside the covenant relationship of the invisible church.[28]

Responding to the challenge against building their position from II Sam. 12, some have taken a fresh look at Romans chapter seven. Here the Apostle Paul explicitly states: *For I was alive without the law once: but when the commandment came, sin revived and I died.* When was this? He was not without the law as a growing child because he was the son of a Pharisee (Acts 23:6), and lived in stringent conformity to the traditions of this sect (Acts 26:5). Paul was speaking of a time before he was cognizant of or could have known the law (Mosaic or natural)—*What shall we say then? Is the law sin? God forbid. Nay, I had not known sin, but by the law: for I had not known lust, except the law had said, Thou shalt not covet.* Some take the position that this is describing infancy. John A. Witmer addresses this question in his commentary on Romans as follows:

> Evidently the apostle was speaking of his personal experience as a child and perhaps even as a youth prior to the awareness and understanding of the full impact of God's commandments. The clause, **but when the commandment came**, does not speak of the giving of the Mosaic Law, but the dawning of the significance

---

[27] Thomas A. Bailey & David M. Kennedy, *The American Pageant: A History of the Republic*, Eighth Edition (Lexington, Massachusetts; Toronto: D. C. Heath and Company, 1987), p. 65. We cannot find this statement by Edwards in the works available to us. There is room for doubt that he ever said it. However, as we will demonstrate in a later chapter, it was a common belief among early American colonial Puritans that Baptists were worthy of death for withholding baptism from infants and consigning them to hell. This view of infants in hell is clearly Augustinian in its content, as we will study from Augustines writings in chapter seven of this present work.

[28] *Jonathan Edwards, The Works of* (Albany, Or: AGES Software [*The Master Christian Library* version 6], 1977), Vol. III, pp. 205, 331-334, 355-357, 469-473.

of the commandment ("Do not covet") on Paul's mind and heart before conversion. The result was that the principle of sin within made its presence and power known (it **sprang to life**) in his volitions of the **commandment**. As a result Paul **died** spiritually (cf. 6:23a) under the sentence of judgment by the Law he had broken.[29] [Emphasis added].

This is not a denial of original sin or of the sin nature in infants and therefore not subject to the false charge of *Pelagianism*. People in hell are bearing the eternal consequences of their inherited Adamic natures, their sins, and particularly the sin of willful unbelief. But it is their willful unbelief that kept them from salvation. Paul speaks of the damnation of Tribulation citizens as resulting from their willful rejection of the truth prior to the rapture:

> *Even him*, whose coming is after the working of Satan with all power and signs and lying wonders, And with all deceivableness of unrighteousness in them that perish; because they received not the love of the truth, that they might be saved. And for this cause God shall send them strong delusion, that they should believe a lie: That they all might be damned who believed not the truth, but had pleasure in unrighteousness (II Thess. 2:9-12).[30]

Unable to comprehend the consignment of billions of babies in hell, some cautiously construct the position that Christ, in His work on the cross, forgives all infants of having an Adamic nature. He does not eradicate the imputed sin of Adam (Pelagianism), but he forgives it. Therefore, all infants are *alive without the law* and will be under condemnation only when they become willful unbelievers and sinners against the Law. Original sin is there, and still worthy of condemnation,

---

[29] *The Bible Knowledge Commentary: An Exposition of the Scriptures by Dallas Seminary Faculty*, New Testament edition; John F. Walvoord & Roy B. Zuck, Editors (USA, Canada, England: Victor Books, 1983), pp. 646, 647.

[30] "They all" in this passage refers to those who had the opportunity to believe prior to the rapture but refused and now find themselves in the 70th week of Daniel. But during this same week of years, 144 thousand Jews will be saved and a multitude of Gentiles that no man can number (Rev. 7:4, 9).

but it is forgiven. The *believer's baptism* view denies that original sin is removed through an outward ritual. Where would Paul have spent eternity if he had died when he was *alive without the Law*? Many in the *believer's baptism* camp will argue that he would have gone to heaven.[31]

One thing of which we can be reasonably certain is that Matt. 19:14 does not teach infant baptism either literally or by special illumination.

Reason # 4: (Mtt. 28:19) *Go ye therefore, and teach all nations, baptizing them in the name of the Father, and of the Son, and of the Holy Ghost.* The idea that the citizens of nations are to be required to submit to baptism stems from the national-church theory. Some variations of this theocratic view hold that the people of any province or nation are bound together into a provincial or national organization, and that this organization has jurisdiction over all church matters. So, just as one born in a particular province is automatically and naturally a citizen of that territory, he is also under the authority of the organized, established church there. This is the pretext upon which laws have been decreed which required the baptism of all infants within the boundaries of a particular nation. In the case of the Roman church, the boundaries were the world, which, of course, would require conquest in order to implement enforcement. In the year 346 non-Christian temples were ordered closed in the Roman Empire and the death penalty was imposed for sacrifices. Theodosius' edict of 392 forbade even the simplest offerings to household gods.[32]

When Augustine was a young advocate of orthodoxy in North Africa, an area controlled by heretics, he pled for freedom of conscience. But when orthodoxy became favored by the state, he called on the civil power to suppress the dissidents in the church. He felt that it was better for heretics to be punished and purged from their error, than that they should die unsaved. Compulsion in such cases was considered benevolent, for what is a worse killer of the soul than

---

[31] An exception can be found in some reformed Baptists who hold the view that only the infants of the elect are saved and all other infants proceed to Hell upon death.

[32] M. Searle Bates, *Religious Liberty: An Inquiry* (New York and London: International Missionary Council, 1945), p. 134.

freedom to err?[33] C. J. Alexander writes that because of Augustine, more than any other person, *the Medieval Church was intolerant, was the source and author of persecution, justified and defended the most violent measures which could be taken against those who differed from it.*[34] Augustine and Thomas Aquinas taught that salvation could be achieved through compulsion, and that oppression and persecution of heretics was the holy duty of the Church—(e.g. *In Iceland in the year 1000, the entire population was made Christian by law, and all who had not previously accepted baptism were required to do so*).[35] The knights who conquered the Baltic seacoast likewise forced Christianity upon the natives there.[36] Persecution and oppression of heretics became universal and systematic under Pope Innocent III in the thirteenth century as he *called on secular princes to organize a crusade against the heretical Albigenses* [rebaptizers], *and the result was mass executions. This was followed by the establishment of the Inquisition about the second quarter of the thirteenth century.*[37] The Spanish Inquisition, established by Ferdinand and Isabella in 1480, lasted for centuries longer than any other. It burnt heretics at the stake as late as 1781 and was not abolished until 1834.

Church historian, W. W. Sweet writes:

> There is widespread notion among Protestant groups that the separation of Church and State, and thus religious liberty, was one of the immediate products of the Reformation, that the early Protestants were advocates of a large tolerance, and that religious liberty was but the logical development of the principles held by all of the reformers. Just where this notion arose is difficult to say, and no reputable historian of our times would endorse it. The fact is that the rise of Protestantism was accompanied by an

---

[33] Ibid., Bates, pp. 137, 138.
[34] Carlyle J. Alexander, *The Christian Church and Liberty* (London: J. Clarke, 1924), p. 96.
[35] Leo Pfeffer, *Church, State, and Freedom* (Boston: The Beacon Press, 1953), p. 18.
[36] Ibid., Bates, pp. 142, 143.
[37] Ibid., Pfeffer, p. 19.

unprecedented outburst of intolerance and cruelty in which both Protestants and Catholics participated.[38]

When expecting excommunication and assassination, Luther pleaded for separation of Church and state and for religious toleration. Declaring that heretics were to be converted with the Scriptures, and not by fire, he wrote:

> I say, then, neither pope, nor bishop, nor any man whatever has the right of making one syllable binding on a Christian man, unless it be done with his own consent. Whatever is done otherwise is done in the spirit of tyranny….I cry aloud on behalf of liberty and conscience, and I proclaim with confidence that no kind of law can with any justice be imposed on Christians, except so far as they themselves will; for we are free from all.[39]

But once Luther became allied with the secular state and was no longer a hunted heretic, his position changed completely as he wrote:

> Heretics are not to be disputed with, but to be condemned unheard, and whilst they perish by fire, the faithful ought to pursue the evil to its source, and bathe their hands in the blood of the Catholic bishops, and of the Pope, who is a devil in disguise.[40]

Luther's disciple, Melanchthon, *taught that dissenting sects ought to be put down by the sword, and that any person who started new opinions ought to be punished with death.*[41]

The theocratic element was strongest in Calvin. Like Augustine and Luther, his earliest writings proclaim tolerance. But when he established his theocracy in Geneva, absenteeism from church

---

[38] William Warren Sweet, *Religion in Colonial America* (New York: Charles Scribner's Sons, 1941), p. 320.
[39] Henry Wace and C. A. Bucheim, *Luther's primary works* (Philadelphia: Lutheran Publication Society, 1885), pp. 194, 195.
[40] Ibid., Pfeffer, p. 21.
[41] Ibid., Pfeffer, p. 21.

services was a crime, and missing the sacrament was penalized by banishment for a year. Criticism of the clergy was a blasphemy punishable by death. In fact, denial that blasphemy was punishable by death was itself blasphemy—

> Whoever shall now contend that it is unjust to put heretics and blasphemers to death, will, knowingly and willingly, incur their very guilt. This is not laid down on human authority; it is God that speaks and prescribes a perpetual rule for His Church.[42]

During the Reformation, Calvin extended the authority and duty of civil government to *cherish and support the external worship of God, to preserve the true doctrine of religion, to defend the constitution of the Church and to regulate our lives in a manner requisite for the social welfare.*[43] This became the pretext upon which persecution by the State was justified. Offenses against the Church/State were punishable by fines, imprisonment, exile, and, if necessary, by death. On this ground the execution of Servetus and other heretics was justified.[44] According to Schaff, Calvin aimed at the sole rule of Christ and His Word both in Church and State, but without mixture and interference. The law for both church and State, for Calvin, was the revealed will of God in the Holy Scriptures.[45]

The Peace of Augsburg (1555) was a compromise between Lutherans and Catholics in the German states whereby the religion of a province was determined by the religion of its prince. The Peace of Westphalia (1648) ended the terrible thirty years of religious war and extended a modified Augsburg principle to the Calvinist states. The Edict of Nantes granted a limited freedom of conscience, and was therefore condemned by Pope Clement VIII. It became limited further under Henry's successors until it was completely revoked by Louis XIV

---

[42] Ibid., Pfeffer, p. 22, referring to Calvin and his close associate Beza.

[43] Philip Schaff, *History of the Christian Church* (Grand Rapids, Michigan: Wm. B. Eerdmans Publishing Company, 1972), Vol. 8, p. 462.

[44] Servetus was an Anabaptist tried by the Inquisition in France. Calvin provided the Inquisitors with the evidence that helped secure his condemnation. Servetus escaped to Geneva, where he was denounced by Calvin and sentenced to death by the town council.

[45] Ibid., Schaff, Vol. 8, pp. 471-473.

when he launched a campaign of forced conversion against the Huguenots. The persecution of Protestants finally abated in France when a more conservative form of the Nantes edict was revived in 1787 (the eve of the French Revolution).

When Henry VIII established the Church of England, he retained almost all of Catholicism except the Pope. The *Bloody Statute* enacted by Parliament in 1539 made the denial of the doctrine of transubstantiation punishable by burning at the stake and confiscation of goods. The constitution established by Oliver Cromwell in 1647 granted liberty to all Protestant sects, but denied all toleration to Catholics

A similar theocratic concept followed the Church of England and the Puritans to the early American Colonies. Looking at colonial America, it is easy to see why the colony of Massachusetts could not tolerate Roger Williams' views. Consider the words of its *Body of Liberties* (December 10, 1641, Section 58, 59, 94):

> Civill Authoritie hath power and libertie to see the peace, ordinances and Rules of Christ observed in every church according to his word. So it be done in a Civill and not in an Ecclesiastical way...(Section 59) Civill Authoritie hath power and libertie to deale with any Church member in a way of Civill Justice, notwithstanding any Church relation, office or interest...(Section 94) If any man after legal conviction shall have or worship any other god, but the lord god, he shall be put to death, if any man shall blaspheme the name of god, the Father Sonne, or Holie ghost, with direct, expresse, presumptious or high handed blasphemie, or shall curse god in the like manner, he shall be put to death.[46]

In 1635 Massachusetts Bay Colony banished Roger Williams for advocating the separation of church and state and for denying the

---

[46] Massachusetts *Body of liberties* (December 10, 1641, Sections 58, 59, 94) in Richard L. Perry, *Sources Of Our Liberties* (Chicago: American Bar Foundation, 1959), pp. 154-158.

right of civil authorities to punish citizens for, among other things, withholding infant baptism—

> That if any Christian within this jurisdiction, shall go about to subvert and destroy the Christian faith and religion, by broaching and maintaining any damnable heresies; as denying the immortality of the soul, or resurrection of the body, or any sin to be repented of in the regenerate, or any evil done by the outward man to be accounted sin, or denying that Christ gave Himself a ransom for our sins, or shall affirm that we are not justified by His death and righteousness, but by the perfections of our own works, or shall deny the morality of the fourth commandment, **or shall openly condemn or oppose the baptising of infants, or shall purposely depart the congregation at the administration of that ordinance**, or shall deny the ordinance of magistracy, or their lawful authority to make war, or to punish the outward breaches of the first table, or shall endeavor to seduce others to any of the errors or heresies above mentioned; **every such person continuing obstinate therein, after due means of conviction, shall be sentenced to banishment …And if any person so banished, be taken the second time within this jurisdiction upon lawful trial and conviction, he shall be put to death.**[47] [Emphasis added].

In 1646, at the Bay colony, anyone expressing contempt toward an established clergyman was punished by standing four feet high on a block wearing a placard with the words, *An Open and Obstinate Contemner of God's Holy Ordinances*.[48]

Ann Hutchinson was a Boston Congregationalist who defied the religious establishment by holding meetings in her home, preaching a *covenant of grace* grounded on an individual's direct intuition of

---

[47] *American State Papers on Religious Freedom* (Washington D. C.: Review and Herald Publishing Association, 1949), pp. 32-34.
[48] Sanford H. Cobb, *The rise of Religious Liberty in America* (New York: The Macmillan Co., 1902), pp. 176, 177.

God's grace and love. This flew in the face of the established religion based on obedience to the laws of church and state. She was tried and condemned in 1638 and was exiled and excommunicated. She fled with her children to Rhode Island, and then migrated to New York, where, in 1642, she and most of her children were killed by the Native Americans.

Myers writes: *Puritans have put many Quakers to death, of other provinces. First they banished them as Quakers upon pain of death, and then executed them for returning. They have beaten some of them to jelly and been exceedingly cruel to others.*[49]

The royal charters testified to their missionary aim of colonization in America. Captain John Smith declared that the first duty of Virginians was to *preach, baptise into the Christian religion and by the propagation of the Gospel to recover out of the arms of the devil, a number of poor and miserable souls wrapt up unto death in almost invincible ignorance.*[50] The Anglican Church became established in Virginia where Governor Thomas Dale in 1612 decreed the *Laws Divine, Moral and Martial*. Sanford Cobb gives us the substance of the religious sections and in number eight he states:

> Every person in the colony, or who should come into it, was required to repair to the minister for examination in the faith. If he should be unsound, he was to be instructed. If any refused to go to the minister, he should be whipt; on a second refusal he should be whipt twice and compelled to "acknowledge his fault on Sabath day in the assembly of the congregation"; for a third refusal he should be "whipt every day until he makes acknowledgment."[51]

Under Peter Stuyvesant, the Dutch Reformed Church was established and supported by the state in New York. Law required the baptism of all children to be performed only by an established minister

---

[49] Gustavus Myers, *History of Bigotry in the United States* (New York: Random House, 1943), p. 5.
[50] Charles A. Beard and Mary R., *The Rise of Amrican Civilization* (New York: The Macmillan Co., 1947) Vol. I, p. 10.
[51] Ibid., Cobb, p. 78.

of the Reformed church.[52] Baptists who held religious services in their homes were subject to arrest, fine, whipping, and banishment.[53]

Sir William Blackstone (1723-1780) was an English jurist who in the 1760s wrote a famous work called *Commentaries on the Law of England.* By the time the *Declaration of Independence* was signed, there were probably more copies of his commentaries in America than in Britain. His works shaped the perspective of American law at that time and will serve to enlighten us regarding the English background of Colonial Anglican and Puritan political thought. In chapter 5 of his *Commentary* Blackstone lists the offences against God and religion in English law such as apostasy; failure to express belief in a future state of rewards and punishments when taking judicial oaths; heresy; **reviling the ordinances of the Church**; absence from Divine worship; gross impieties; blasphemy; cursing; witchcraft and sorcery; Sabbath-breaking; drunkenness; open lewdness and bearing bastard children.[54]

Often when advocates of *believer's baptism* would rebaptize a believer within the territory of an established state church, it was considered the equivalent of walking into a church building and disrupting the service. It was believed that the Church was to exercise dominion over the world and therefore require the baptism of all nations.

So, just as the Jews of the intertestamental period assumed the divine right to force proselytism and circumcision on whole heathen nations, many Puritan, Anglican and Reformed churches believed that God's Church was equally a theocracy of God whose doctrines must be forced by coercion. However, God does not command the baptizing of all nations; but the baptism only of such who are taught or made disciples by teaching of the Word of God. If infants are to be baptized because they are a part of all nations, then this would require the forceful baptism of the infants of heathens, Moslems, Hindus, Jews, etc., since they are a large part of all nations. Disciples and learners are the same, and one must be a learner in order to be a disciple. Disciples

---

[52] Ibid., Cobb, p. 315.
[53] Ibid., Cobb, pp. 317, 318.
[54] William Blackstone, *Blackstone's Commentaries On The Law*, Edited by Bernard C. Gavit, Dean, Indiana University School of Law (Washington, D. C.: Washington Law Book Co., 1941), pp. 770-779.

ought to learn something of Christ before they are baptized in his name. Aathanasius (c. 297-373) said it best:[55]

> For not he who simply says, 'O Lord,' gives Baptism; but he who with the Name has also the right faith. On this account therefore our Saviour also did not simply command to baptize, but first says, 'Teach;' then thus: 'Baptize into the Name of Father, and Son, and Holy Ghost;' that the right faith might follow upon learning, and together with faith might come the consecration of Baptism.[56]

Just because the State is the "mother" of the children born within its territorial boundaries, it does not follow that the church is no less the mother of all children born within the boundaries of its parish or diocese.

Reason # 5: The Bible teaches by example the baptism of whole households, and it is certain that there were infants in these families. John Calvin stressed this point in his *Institutes of the Christian Religion* when he wrote:

> Every one must now see that paedobaptism, which receives such strong support from Scripture, is by no means of human invention. Nor is there anything plausible in the objection, that we nowhere read of even one infant having been baptized by the hands of the apostles. For although this is not expressly narrated by the Evangelists, yet as they are not expressly excluded when mention is made of any baptized family (Acts xvi. 15, 32), what man of sense will argue from this that they were not baptized?[57]

---

[55] Athanasius, Bishop of Alexandria, was the great defender of the deity of Christ and the doctrine of the Trinity against the heretical Arians.

[56] St. Athanasius, *Select Works and Letters: Nicene and Post-Nicene Fathers* (Grand Rapids, Michigan: Wm. B. Eerdmans Publishing Company, 1978), p. 371.

[57] John Calvin, *Institutes of the Christian Religion* (Grand Rapids, Michigan: Wm. B. Eerdmans Publishing Company, 1972), Vol. II, p. 534.

There is, indeed, reference to whole housholds, or families, being baptized during apostolic times. However, if we are going to rest the personal, eternal salvation of millions of souls on a doctrine, it would be most advantageous if we could be certain that there were infants in these families and that they were baptized. It is not as if this is one of those peripheral doctrinal controversies, such as *mode* of baptism, which will not affect one's personal salvation either way.

There are usually three families in the New Testament that are cited to make this point. The first is that of Lydia and her household—

> (Acts 16:14, 15) And a certain woman named Lydia, a seller of purple, of the city of Thyatira, which worshipped God, heard *us*: whose heart the Lord opened, that she attended unto the things which were spoken of Paul. And when she was baptized, and her household, she besought *us*, saying, If ye have judged me to be faithful to the Lord, come into my house, and abide *there*. And she constrained us.

Again, if we are going to build the personal assurance of salvation for millions of souls on such a passage, should we not wonder whether she was single or married, maid or widow; and if married, whether she had any children, or ever had any; and if so, were they living and were they infants, adolescents, or adults? And if infants, did she bring them with her from Thyatira to Phillipi, where she seems to have been on a business trip? Was she the bread-winner in her family, and was her husband traveling with her? If she was there on business, did she have a hired house for the duration of her stay? Could her household have constituted menial servants brought along to assist her in business? From vss. 14, 15 we cannot satisfy any of these queries. What then can we know? When Paul and Silas came out of prison they again entered her house and met the brethren and were able to comfort them—*And they went out of the prison, and entered into the house of Lydia: and when they had seen the brethren, they comforted them, and departed.* These *brethren* may have been distressed and troubled about the recent social upheaval regarding the apostolic ministry (vss. 22-24). At best, this is not a passage upon which to build a soul-saving gospel for infants.

The second instance is the jailer and his household, which consisted of adult persons; for the apostle Paul spoke the word of the

Lord to *all* that were in his house (Acts 16:33). Were they not capable of hearing and understanding? The jailer *rejoiced* at the good news of salvation and everyone in his house *rejoiced* and *believed* with him— *And when he had brought them into his house, he set meat before them, and rejoiced, believing in God with all his house* (Acts 16:32-34). Again, this is not a passage upon which to build the assurance of salvation by the infant baptism of millions of souls.

The third instance is the household of Stephanus (I Cor. 1:16). They of his household were the first fruits of Achaia, the first converts of those parts, who had *addicted themselves to the ministry of the saints* (I Cor. 16:15). Is this something that infants do? There are too many unanswered questions regarding all three of these instances to allow us to read into them an absolute mandate to baptize infants, believing that the ritual will wash away original sin, regenerate their souls, and place them into the Body of Christ..

Reason # 6: Infants of believers in the Old Testament were taken into the covenant of grace by their circumcision, and in the New Testament infant baptism replaces circumcision. Luther admits that, according to his view, females were saved differently than males in the OT:

> With regard to the girls among the Jews the answer is easy. For because this sign was prescribed only for the male sex, it does not pertain to the girls. Nevertheless, since the girls are Abraham's descendants, they are not excluded from Abraham's righteousness; they attain it through faith. But those adults who despised circumcision or who despise Baptism are surely damned.[58]
>
> It cannot be denied that Ps.77 [106:37] speaks of girls and uncircumcised when it says that they were offered to the idols of Canaan. Yet they were described as innocent blood. And surely Moses in Lev. 12 [:15] included girls in the regulation of offerings for purification and atonement. Everybody knows that

---

[58] *Luther's Works: Lectures on Genesis, Chapters 15-20*, Jeroslav Pelikan, Editor (St. Louis: Concordia Publishing House, 1961), Vol. 3, p. 103.

boys alone were subjected to circumcision, but that girls participated in its benefits also by virtue of the saying spoken by God to Abraham (Gen. 17 [:7]): "I will be the God of thy descendants, and circumcision shall be a covenant between me and you and your descendants after you." Surely girls are the descendants of Abraham, and through this promise God is indeed their God, though they are not circumcised as are the boys.[59]

If the old covenant and the sign of circumcision made the children of Abraham believe that they were, and were called the people of God, according to the promise, I will be the God of thy descendants [Gen. 17:7], then this new covenant and sign must be much more effectual and make those a people of God who receive it.[60]

Calvin discounts those who would argue with this position as *furious madmen*—

Let us now discuss the arguments by which some furious madmen cease not to assail this holy ordinance of God. And, first, feeling themselves pressed beyond measure by the resemblance between baptism and circumcision, they contend that there is a wide difference between the two signs, that the one has nothing in common with the other. They maintain that the things meant are different, the covenant is altogether different, and that the persons included under the name of children are different...The Jews they depict as so carnal as to resemble brutes more than men, representing the covenant which was made with them as reaching no farther than a temporary life, and the promises which were given to them as dwindling down into present and corporeal blessings[61]

---

[59] Ibid., *Luther*, Vol. 40, p. 244.
[60] Ibid., *Luther*, Vol. 40, pp. 257, 258.
[61] Ibid., *Institutes of the Christian Religion*, Vol. II, p. 535.

Infant Baptism And Believer's Baptism

If Calvin would take his view one step further, it would logically follow that NT baptism was, in a sense, rebaptism, for what was supposed to have really happened at circumcision (removal of sin and placing into the covenant of grace) was to be repeated under a different form. If this be the case, then why such harsh words for the *rebaptizers*? Why condemn rebaptism if NT baptism itself was nothing more than a repetition of circumcision?

We recommend that the reader, at this point, review again the previous chapter of this work wherein we demonstrated that the call of Abraham, the Abrahamic covenant, and the covenant of circumcision were three separate propositions. It was shown that circumcision never brought a soul into the bonds of eternal life, but did entitle the recipient to the temporal blessings of Jewish citizenship within the promised land of Palestine. We must recall that Jewish males were not to be circumcised until the eighth day. If performed sooner, it would have been unlawful. But David's son, who died uncircumcised before the eighth day, was in the grace of God from birth, or even from conception (II Sam. 12). Israelites and their infants at Horeb had not been circumcised and were still uncircumcised when they entered into covenant with Jehovah in Deut. 29:10-15. If circumcision insured the grace of salvation in the OT, then the human race must have been without a plan of salvation from Adam to Abraham, or under a different plan of salvation.

NT baptism, on the other hand, is administered to Jews and Gentiles, to male and female, and to believers only. Circumcision was used to distinguish the natural seed of Abraham from others. If circumcision made one the spiritual seed of Abraham, the Bible would not be constantly confronting unregenerate, yet circumcised, Jews with their lost condition. Neither would the Bible so clearly distinguish, in both testaments, between fleshly circumcision and circumcision of the heart, if so they are one and the same. Circumcision was a badge for the fleshly seed of Abraham, whereas baptism is a badge of the spiritual seed of Christ, and the answer of a good conscience towards God. The conscience of an infant is not altered by a ritual.

Also, baptism was established before circumcision was disestablished (after the death of Christ). Can that which is established before the other is disestablished be said to succeed or replace the other?

Peter, on the Day of Pentecost, said to the Jews: *For the promise is unto you, and to your children, and to all that are afar off, even as many as the Lord our God shall call* (Acts 2:39). Peter is not promising this multitude that they are already saved because they are circumcised. In fact, he is certain that they are lost, saying: *save yourselves from this untoward generation* (2:40). Neither is Peter referring to salvation promised through baptism. The *promise* is no other than the promise of life and salvation by Christ, and remission of sins by his blood, and of an increase of grace from his Spirit.[62] And though the audience was guilty of the blood of Christ, they were told that the promise would be made good to their posterity also, provided that they did as directed. This would be true of Jews afar off in distant lands and future ages who would look on Christ and believe. This promise is for those who would be called by grace—*as many as the Lord our God shall call*. If there never was a time when circumcision saved a soul for eternity, why is it thought that infant baptism (which is said to be circumcision under a different form) will do a work of salvation that circumcision could not?

Reason # 7: (Rom. 11:16) *For if the firstfruit be holy, the lump is also holy: and if the root be holy, so are the branches.* **Thus, the children of believers are also in the covenant of grace by their baptism.** Does this mean that if parents are saved, their children are also saved? If it does, then it also means that the infant fatalities of all heathen are burning in hell at this very moment. This passage must be studied in the full context of Romans 9, 10, and 11. The firstfruits and the root are the patriarchs of Israel and Abraham in particular. The lump and the branches represent Israel. Thus, Israel is set apart or sanctified unto God as a nation. This does not guarantee eternal life to all individual Israelites, for Paul speaks of some who were broken off because of unbelief (11:20), and that their only possibility of being saved was if they *abide not still in unbelief* (11:23). But even though most of Israel are broken off, the nation as a *lump* will be saved at the revelation of Jesus Christ in His second coming (11:26-27). There is

---

[62] The OT promise was not a prediction of the institution of the NT ritual of baptism, though the OT does repeatedly promise salvation by Christ. The NT writers use the Red Sea and the Flood as types of baptism by way of illustration, but no OT Jewish scholar understood these literal stories as a prophecy of ritual baptism.

not one word or syllable about baptism, much less infant baptism, in this passage; and such should not be concluded from it.

We contend that all infants are in the grace of God regardless (Rom. 7:9). But if we say that children are saved because their parents are in the faith, then we are declaring the infants of all heathen to be lost and outside the bounds of God's grace. This is a declaration which most advocates of believer's baptism refuse to make. Neither do they excuse themselves by declaring limited agnosticism on this point for if only the baptized are saved, then the unbaptized are certainly lost.

Reason # 8: (I Cor. 7:14) *For the unbelieving husband is sanctified by the wife, and the unbelieving wife is sanctified by the husband; else were your children unclean, but now are they holy.* **This gives a claim to covenant privileges, and therefore, baptism.**

But if children, by virtue of parental holiness, have a claim to baptism, then so also does the unbelieving spouse who is sanctified by the faith of the believing yokefellow. Why is it commonly interpreted that the faith of a wife entitles an infant to baptism but not an unbelieving husband? Again, it is assumed that the children of unbelieving parents are unsanctified, and therefore, damned.

It would be much more coherent with all of Scripture if the words of 7:14 were understood as matrimonial holiness. The Jews often expressed the very act of marriage as being *sanctified*. The Hebrew often expresses the word *sanctified* as *espoused*. In this case the passage would read: *for the unbelieving husband is espoused to the wife, and the unbelieving wife is espoused to the husband.* They are legally married to each other and should not separate because of their different religious persuasions. Now if they are not truly married (or *sanctified*) to one another, their children are born out of wedlock and are therefore illegitimate. This is the sense of the following words: *else were your children unclean, but now are they holy.* And if they separate because one becomes converted, the departure would declare to all the world that their children were illegitimate; which is a reason why they ought to get legally married and stay together. Paul wanted them to avoid divorce because the Christian spouse was a channel of God's blessing in the marriage. God's blessings on the believer affected the family as a whole.[63] So Paul is saying that as the parents are legitimately espoused, so also, the children are holy (*sanctified*) in a civil and legal sense, that is, legitimate. John Gill has an extensive discussion giving the same sense to this passage that we are suggesting here:

> The sense I have given of this passage, is agreeable to the mind of several interpreters, ancient and modern, as Jerom, Ambrose, Erasmus, Camerarius, Musculus, etc. which last writer makes this ingenuous confession: formerly, says he, I have abused this place against the Anabaptists, thinking the meaning was, that the children were holy for the parents' faith; which though true, the present place makes nothing for the purpose: and I hope, that, upon reading this, every one that has abused it too such a purpose will make the like acknowledgment; I am sure they ought.[64]

The subject of baptism is not addressed in the I Cor. 7:14 passage and should never be imposed upon it.

Reason # 9: The New Testament records that those who believed were baptized, but it is nowhere written that they were the only ones. Where is the verse that says that infants were not baptized? In response to this question we might ask, where is the verse that forbids the baptism of pets, corpses, and livestock? Were not the first born of Israelite livestock spared at the first Passover when God said, *When I see the blood I will pass over you* (Ex. 11:5-7)? Unquestionably, infants and livestock were spared at the first Passover. However, the Passover lamb did not spare them from eternal condemnation. It was earthly life that was spared. The first Passover served as a picture of the coming suffering Savior, but only the Savior could take away sin and deliver from condemnation (I Cor. 5:7; Jn. 1:29, 36). But if we were to use the Passover as a soul-saving ordinance, we would have as much ground to baptize livestock and dogs

---

[63] (e.g. Jacob in Laban's household [Gen. 30:27] and Joseph in Potiphar's household (Gen. 39:5).
[64] John Gill, D. D., *Exposition: The New Testament* (London: William Hill Collingridge, 1852) Vol. 2, p. 192. Gill was a great Baptist theologian who was born at Kettering, in Northamptonshire, Nov. 23, 1697.

as we do for the baptism of infants. Actually, we should not use the Passover as grounds for the baptism of either.

As discussed previously, it is not logically legitimate to place the burden of proof on someone to prove a negative. The burden of truth is upon him who affirms. The question is not, *where is the verse that forbids baptism of infants?*, but rather, *where is the verse that commands the baptism of unbelievers?*

Reason # 10: In the Old Testament, unbelieving infants were not cut off from the seal of the covenant, and therefore, not cut off from the covenant. So also with infant baptism in the New Testament. We observed previously in this study that OT infants who were uncircumcised were not thereby cut off from the covenant of personal salvation (e.g. Abel, Seth, Enoch, Enos, Noah, Lot, descendents of Esau, David's son by Bathsheba, etc.). Thus, we affirm again: if circumcision never removed original sin, and if baptism is circumcision under a different form, why should we conclude that baptism removes original sin?

Reason # 11: Infant baptism is an older tradition than believer's baptism in the history of the Church; therefore, it is a tradition received from the apostles. Luther wrote: *since our baptizing has been thus from the beginning of Christianity and the custom has been to baptize children, and since no one can prove with good reasons that they do not have faith, we should not make changes and build on such weak arguments.*[65] When challenged to prove his position from the Bible, Luther replies:

> You say, this does not prove that child baptism is certain. For there is no passage in Scripture for it. My answer: that is true. From Scripture we cannot clearly conclude that you could establish Child baptism as a practice among the first Christians after the apostles. But you can well conclude that in our day no one may reject or neglect the practice of child baptism which has so long a tradition, since God actually not only has permitted it, but from the beginning so ordered, that it has not yet disappeared.

---

[65] Ibid., *Luther*, Vol. 40, p. 241.

> ...if the first, or child, baptism were not right it would follow that for more than a thousand years there was no baptism or any Christendom, which is impossible...For over a thousand years there were hardly any other but child baptisms. If this baptism is wrong then for that long period Christendom would have been without baptism, and if it were without baptism it would not be Christendom...But the fact that child baptism has spread throughout all the Christian world to this day gives rise to no probability that it is wrong, but rather to a strong indication that it is right.[66]

It is commonly contended that infant baptism is a tradition of the church received from the apostles, yet no other proof can be given but the testimony of Origen (c. 185-c. 254) and none before that. Gill states that the Origen references are not in his genuine Greek writings, but only from some Latin translations—*confessedly interpolated, and so corrupted, that it is owned, one is at a loss to find Origen in Origen.*[67] Gill further contends that no mention of infant baptism is made in the first two centuries. It first appears in the third century when Tertullian speaks against it.[68]

Reason # 12: Ritual must precede reality by divine order before the inner work of God's saving grace can take place. Luther comments:

> Now when God sends forth his holy gospel he deals with us in a twofold manner, first outwardly, then inwardly. Outwardly he deals with us through the oral word of the gospel and through the material signs, that is, baptism and the sacrament of the altar. Inwardly he deals with us through the Holy Spirit, faith, and other gifts. But whatever their measure or order the outward factor should and must precede. The inward

---

[66] Ibid., *Luther*, Vol. 40, pp. 256, 257.
[67] John Gill, *Body of Divinity* (Atlanta, Georgia: Turner Lassetter, 1965), p. 909.
[68] Ibid., Gill, p. 909. Also, "The antiquity of a custom, is no proof of the truth and genuineness of it; *The customs of the people are vain*, Jer. X. 3".

> experience follows and is effected by the outward. God has determined to give the inward to no one except through the outward. For he wants to give no one the Spirit or faith outside the outward Word and sign instituted by him, as he says in Luke 16 [:29], "Let them hear Moses and the prophets." Accordingly Paul can call baptism a "washing of regeneration" wherein God "richly pours out the Holy Spirit" [Titus 3:5]...Observe carefully, my brother, this order, for everything depends on it. However cleverly this factious spirit makes believe that he regards highly the Word and Spirit of God and declaims passionately about love and zeal for the truth and righteousness of God, he nevertheless has as his purpose to reverse this order. His insolence leads him to set up a contrary order and, as we have said, seeks to subordinate God's outward order to an inner spiritual one.[69]

Packer uses Acts 10:43, 44 to prove that baptism of the Spirit into the Body of Christ preceded faith—

> Since Pentecost, becoming a member of God's family according to his revealed will—Christian initiation, to use the technical phrase—has involved three factors: repentance and faith, plus Christian baptism, plus the coming of the Spirit for new covenant ministry (cf. Acts 2:38; Romans 8:9ff.; Ephesians 1:13ff.). In experience, the order has varied; apparently it was faith-baptism-Spirit at Pentecost (Acts 2:38-42), Spirit-faith-baptism at the "Gentile Pentecost" (Acts 10:44-48), faith-Spirit-baptism at Galatia (Galatians 3:2); certainly, it has been baptism-faith-Spirit for all those Christians down the centuries who were baptized as infants. The order scarcely matters; what matters is that all three links between us and Jesus Christ—faith, baptism, Spirit—should actually be there.[70]

---

[69] Ibid., *Luther*, Vol. 40, pp. 146, 147.
[70] J. I. Packer, *Growing in Christ* (Wheaton, Illinois: Crossway Books, 1994), pp. 124, 125.

Actually, there are no examples in the NT of the baptism of the Spirit prior to faith, and no examples of Scriptural water baptism prior to faith.

We respond to Luther and J. I. Packer by asking several questions. Why did John the Baptist require evidence of an inward change before he would baptize the Pharisees (Matt. 3:7, 8)? Why does faith precede baptism in Mark 16:16 if the outward sign must always precede inward grace? Why did the house of Cornelius receive the baptism of the Holy Spirit before ritual baptism (Acts 10:47; 11:15, 16)? Why did Peter liken this occasion to his own salvation and to that of the church of Jerusalem (Acts 11:17)? Why did the Jerusalem church recognize the experience of Acts 10:43, 44 to be a *repentance unto life* (Acts 11:18)? Why did Peter argue at the Jerusalem council that their [house of Cornelius] baptism of the Spirit into the Body of Christ was an inward work of the Spirit in their hearts prior to their ritual baptism (Acts 15:8, 9)? Why did Peter insist that our salvation experience must be the same as theirs in order to be real (Acts. 15:11)? Why does Paul refer to the gospel of Christ as *the power of God unto salvation to every one that believeth; to the Jew first, and also to the Greek* (Rom. 1:16)? And if the imputed righteousness of God is revealed from baptism to faith, why does Paul say, *for therein is the righteousness of God revealed from faith to faith…*?

Reason # 13: Submitting to rebaptism as an adult could bring damnation to one's soul through blasphemy. Luther writes: *for whoever permits himself to be rebaptized rejects his former faith and righteousness, and is guilty of sin and condemnation. Of all things such behavior is most horrible. As St. Paul, says, the Galatians have severed themselves from Christ [Gal. 5:4], even making Christ a servant of sin, when they circumcise themselves.*[71] Thus, Luther believed that the rebaptizers represented salvation by works and were the same as the *Judaizers* of Paul's day—

> It is the devil's masterpiece when he can get someone to compel the Christian to leave the righteousness of faith for a righteousness of works, as he forced the Galatians and Corinthians on to works though, as St.

---

[71] Ibid., *Luther*, Vol. 40, p. 249.

Paul writes, they were doing well in their faith and running rightly in Christ [Gal. 5:7].[72]

True, one should add faith to baptism. But we are not to base baptism on faith [believer's baptism]... Whoever allows himself to be baptized on the strength of his faith, is not only uncertain, but also an idolater who denies Christ. For he trusts in and builds on something of his own, namely, on a gift which he has from God, and not on God's Word alone...But on a baptism on the Word and command of God even when faith is not present is still a correct and certain baptism if it takes place as God commanded.[73]

They [rebaptizers] are guilty also of blaspheming and denying the commandment and work of God...
Since then these baptizers are altogether unsure of themselves and reveal that they are lying, and thereby deny and blaspheme the ordinance of God...every devout Christian, convinced that they are misleading, uncertain, and perverted spirits, should avoid them at the peril of his soul's salvation. May Christ, our Lord, grant this and help us. Amen.[74]

In sum, the Anabaptists are too frivolous and insolent...They attract a great many people by using great, high-sounding words of slander against baptism...The Jews do the same to this day. In order to keep their children in their faith they blaspheme Christ shamelessly, refer to him as "the hanged one" and confidently lie about him...
Since then, as far as I have been able to see and hear, the Anabaptists have no argument but high-sounding words of sacrilege, everyone ought properly to shun and avoid them as messengers of none other than the devil, sent out into the world to blaspheme the Word and ordinance of God so that people might not believe

---

[72] Ibid., *Luther*, Vol. 40, p. 249.
[73] Ibid., *Luther*, Vol. 40, p. 252.
[74] Ibid., *Luther*, Vol. 40, pp. 260, 261.

> therein and be saved. For they are the birds who eat the seed sown by the wayside (Matt. 13 [:4]).[75]

It seems strange, therefore, that the twelve "so-called" disciples of John the Baptist in Ephesus were not damned when they submitted to rebaptism. Not only were they not damned, but they received the Holy Ghost and spoke in tongues when Paul subsequently laid hands on them (Acts 19:4-7). There has never been a scriptural grounds to say that those who submit to *believer's rebaptism* are condemned for doing so.

Reason # 14: If we do not bring babies into the Body of Christ, our chances of persuading them as adults are statistically diminished to the extent that Christians will be reduced to an insignificant minority in the nations of the world. Luther again makes the following comments:

> It seems to me to be the result of God's special counsel and providence that we baptize infants in all of Christendom throughout the world and do not wait until they grow up and reach the age of discretion. If we were now to baptize them as grownups and older persons, I am certain that a tenth of them would not let themselves be baptized. Indeed, if it were up to us, we would surely long, long ago have become nothing but Turks [Moslems]. For those who were not baptized would not go to church and would despise all its doctrine and practice because the church seeks to make them holy, godly people. In fact, this is what they are doing now, although they have been baptized and claim to be Christians. .. If such an unbaptized multitude would gain the upper hand, what could the result be but a Turkish kingdom or heathenism?...
> Indeed, I am willing to make a substantial wager that the devil, through the activity of the factious spirits and the Anabaptists [rebaptizers], has all this in mind

---

[75] Ibid., *Luther*, Vol. 40, pp. 259, 260.

so that he might put an end to infant baptism, and would want only adults to be baptized...[76]

However, one of the qualifications for bishop on the island of Crete was the ability to persuade those in error (Titus 1:9-11). Those of the synagogue of the Libertines and Cyrenians and Alexandrians *were not able to resist the wisdom and spirit by which he* [Stephen] *spake* (Acts 6:9, 10). Paul said, *knowing therefore the terror of the Lord, we persuade men* (II Cor. 5:11a). The writer of Hebrews speaks of OT saints as a *persuaded* people (Heb. 11:13). Jude exhorts us all to *earnestly contend for the faith which was once delivered unto the saints* (Jude 3b).

This is why the Apostle Peter exhorts us to, *sanctify the Lord God in your hearts: and be ready always to give an answer to every man that asketh you a reason of the hope that is in you with meekness and fear* (I Pet. 3:15). It was Paul's manner to reason with the unconverted Jews *out of the Scriptures* (Acts 17:2b). In Corinth, Paul *reasoned in the synagogue every sabbath, and persuaded the Jews and the Greeks* (Acts 18:4). He did the same when he came to Ephesus (Acts 18:19). Paul, when on trial for his life, *reasoned of righteousness, temperance, and judgment to come* to governor Felix (Acts 24:25a). He did the same with King Agrippa who said, *Almost thou persuadest me to be a Christian* (Acts 26:28b).

Advocates of *believer's baptism* do not doubt the sufficiency of Scripture and the gospel to persuade men to believe, *for the preaching of the cross is to them that perish foolishness; but unto us which are saved it is the power of God* (I Cor. 1:18). How can anyone say that we would all be Jews or Turks if we had not been placed into Christ by infant baptism? We believe that the gospel of Christ is *the power of God unto salvation to every one that believeth; to the Jew first, and also to the Greek* (Rom. 1:16b). Paul wonders how anyone can call on the Lord if they do not believe; and how can they believe if they don't hear; and how can they hear without a preacher (Rom. 10:14). But how can they preach except they be sent (vs. 15)? All Christians have been sent

---

[76] *Luther's Works: Word And Sacrament, IV*, Martin E. Lehmann, Editor; Helmut T. Lehmann, General Editor (Philadelphia: Fortress Press, 1971), Vol. 38, p. 97.

to proclaim the gospel. Those who obey this call are those with *beautiful feet* in the sight of God (Rom. 10:15)—

> For the weapons of our warfare are not carnal, but mighty through God to the pulling down of strong holds; casting down imaginations, and every high thing that exalteth itself against the knowledge of God, and bringing into captivity every thought to the obedience of Christ (II Cor. 10:4, 5).

Yes, Christ did send us to make believers and disciples in all nations (Mk. 16:15, 16; Matt. 28:18-20).

Reason # 15: The *infant baptism* position is often based upon a special divine illumination which its theological proponents possessed, and of which the proponents of the *believer's baptism* did not. Therefore, the latter lack the proper credentials to be ministers of the truth and interpreters of the Bible. This *divine illumination* defines itself as a direct, extra-biblical revelation enabling one to derive infant baptism from passages that do not even remotely discuss the subject of baptism. It is contradictory to define *illumination* thusly and still affirm the *Sole Authority of Scripture*. Let us look again at Luther's comments:

> Satan does these things against us, in order to make our teaching seem contemptible, as if we could not have the right spirit or teaching because we had not been rightly baptized. But we know the tree by its fruits [Matt. 7:16f.]. For neither among the papists nor among these rebellious spirits do we find men who can handle and interpret Scripture as skillfully as do those on our side by the grace of God. This is not the least of the Spirit's gifts (I Cor. 12 [:10]).[77]

> Having made up their minds concerning their peculiar notions, they attempt to make the Scriptures agree with them by dragging passages in by the hair. But

---

[77] Ibid., *Luther*, Vol. 40, pp. 249, 250.

Christ has faithfully stood by our side up to this point and will continue to trod Satan under our foot.[78]

It is proper for officials, judges, and those concerned with government to be certain of their right to suspect these infiltrators not only of false teaching, but also of violence and revolt, realizing that the devil occupies the driver's seat in these people. Through their lieutenants they should assemble their subjects and call attention to and warn against such villains. They should sternly command their people to inform on these intruders on peril of heavy penalty, and make clear their duties as subjects if they do not wish to be regarded as accomplices in murder and revolt, which is the devil's purpose. Like the church officials they should press the matter of the call, questioning the infiltrator or his host, as mentioned previously, whence do you come? Who sent you? And the host should be asked, who has bidden you to give this intruder lodging, or to listen to his clandestine preaching? How do you know that he is authorized to teach you or you to learn of him? Why have you not notified the parish pastor or us? Why do you slouch in dark corners and forsake the church where you were baptized, instructed, went to communion and where you belong, in the order of God? Why, secretly and without commission, do you start something new? Who has given you right to divide this parish and cause dissentions among us? Who has commanded you to despise your pastor, to judge and condemn him behind his back without a charge or a fair hearing? Since when are you a judge of your pastor, or for that matter, your own judge?[79]

The illumination of God is not something that shines on the words of Scripture, but is the words of Scriptures itself—*Thy word is a lamp unto my feet, and a light unto my path* (Ps. 119:105). A theologian seeks to make his position untouchable when he claims that God has

---

[78] Ibid., *Luther*, Vol. 40, p. 262.
[79] Ibid., *Luther*, Vol. 40, pp. 385, 386.

granted him a special interpretation of a passage that is beyond the actual words and refutes all challengers on the grounds of their lack of his *special illumination.*

The question is often asked of us, *do you believe in the verbal, plenary inspiration of Scripture?* whereupon we answer spontaneously in the affirmative. *Plenary* means *full* and *verbal* means *words.* Therefore, the full message of God is in the words. We do not really believe this when we claim divine insight beyond the words. Paul knew that unbelievers had minds designed by a sovereign God to comprehend the light of His Word. How else could they *hold the truth in unrighteousness* (Rom. 1:18), and know God while glorifying Him not as God (Rom. 1:21)? Why else would Luke call the unbelieving Bereans noble for receiving the Word with *all readiness of mind* and for searching *the scriptures daily, whether those things were so*; and why does Luke conclude that, *therefore, many of them believed* (Acts 17:11b, 12a)? Why else could Paul say to lost Agrippa:

> For the king knoweth of these things, before whom also I speak freely: for I am persuaded that none of these things are hidden from him; for this thing was not done in a corner. King Agrippa, believest thou the prophets? I know that thou believest (Acts 26:26, 27)?

Why was the gift of tongues given as a sign to unbelieving Jews if unbelievers are unable to deduce anything of eternal value from them (I Cor. 14:21, 22)? Why is it that if the *unlearned* and *unbelievers* come into the church and hear the forthtelling of the Word of God, that they are convinced of all (I Cor. 14:24)? Are we attributing saving virtue to lost man by this line of reasoning? Not unless the Bible calls such mental comprehension a saving virtue, which it does not. Peter tells the redeemed to add virtue to their faith (II Pet. 1:5). Personal virtue requires works and obedience to law which, by definition, salvation by faith does not—

> But to him that worketh not, but believeth on him that justifieth the ungodly, his faith is counted for righteousness. Even as David also describeth the blessedness of the man unto whom God imputeth righteousness without works (Rom. 4:5, 6).

Infant Baptism And Believer's Baptism

The ability of a lost soul to comprehend objective truth does not originate from him, but from the common grace of God upon all mankind. Were it not for God's sovereign common grace, lost man could never have drawn his first breath, learned to read, or planted a garden. Apart from God's sovereign grace (both common and effectual) man can do nothing.

Satan knows full well that God has designed the human mind to comprehend objective truth and subjectively internalize it. Satan knows that if he doesn't work hard to blind them that they will indeed see the light—

> In whom the God of this world hath blinded the minds of them which believe not, lest the light of the glorious gospel of Christ, who is the image of God, should shine unto them (II Cor. 4:4).

The gospel does not need *lit* because it is *light* (cf. Ps. 119:105).

Yes, lost people can read and diagram sentences and look up words, but if there is no extra-biblical divine illumination, how do we explain I Cor. 2:14, 15a?—

> But the natural man receiveth not the things of the Spirit of God: for they are foolishness unto him: neither can he know them, because they are spiritually discerned. But he that is spiritual judgeth all things.

First of all, this passage describes natural man as being spiritually unreceptive to divine truth, but he is not an intellectual box of rocks. All messages directed to the lost in the NT presuppose their ability to comprehend what is being preached. Though natural man, by God's sovereign, common grace, can understand the message, it is spiritual descernment that receives it. Discernment is accepting rather than rejecting what you understand of spiritual things.

Secondly, the natural man cannot *know* these spiritual things. The word *know* does not refer to the intellect here but rather to experience. Spiritual knowledge cannot be experienced until one exercises the discernment to receive it (Jn. 1:12). When the virgin Mary said to the angel, *How shall this be, seeing I know not a man* (Lk. 1:34), what did she mean? She knew men (her father, uncle Zechariah, her espoused Joseph), but she had never received a man into a personal experience that would result in pregnancy. When Jesus finally says, *I never knew you: depart from me, ye that work iniquity* (Matt. 7:22), there will be nothing about them that He will not omnisciently understand. What He will mean is that He had never received them into an experiential relationship with Himself.

What does Paul mean when he says that, *There is none that understandeth, there is none that seeketh after God* (Rom. 3:11). If we qualify this statement with verse 10, we know that no one understands and seeks God in righteousness for, *there is none righteous, no, not one*. But Agrippa understood (Acts 26), the Bereans understood (Acts 17), the unbelievers who would wander into the Corinthian church would understand (I Cor. 14:24, 25), and the devil knows that if he doesn't blind them, they will understand (II Cor. 4:4). Jesus said to the lost: *But that ye may know that the Son of man hath power on earth to forgive sins, (then saith he to the sick of the palsy,) Arise, take up thy bed, and go unto thine house.* Jesus said that Tyre and Sidon would have repented had they seen the objective works that He performed in Chorazin and Bethsaida (Matt. 11:21). Abraham told the rich man in hell that his five lost brothers could avoid coming there if they would hear Moses and the prophets (Lk. 16:28-31).

We understand Christ's parables because we have His personal interpretation recorded in the Scriptures. In His day He related His personal interpretation privately to the disciples so that the public would not understand. Had he relayed this information publicly, it could have been publicly understood—

> And his disciples asked him, saying, What might this parable be? And he said, unto you it is given to know the mysteries of the kingdom of God: but to others in parables; that seeing they might not see, and hearing they might not understand (Lk. 8:10).

The public did not hear that the *seed is the word of God*; or who they were that fell by the *way side*; or that the *fowls of the air* were the devil *taking the word out of their hearts, lest they should believe and be saved* (8:12). The public did not know that they on the rock are believers who fall away into temptation; and that those who fell *among thorns* are those who are *choked with the cares and riches and pleasures of this life*; or that the *good ground* is the believer that brings *forth fruit* (8:13-15). Now that we have Christ's parables plus His private interpretation in writing, the information is public and understandable, as the libraries of apostate seminaries will demonstrate.

This claim of special illumination, enabling one to confirm infant baptism from passages which do not even discuss the subject, is nothing short of a claim of apostolic inerrancy and direct revelation from God. We, on the other hand, declare the all sufficiency of God's Word as it is written.

Reason # 16: Those who forsake their Christian baptism for rebaptism as believers would have been more likely to have remained saved under the Pope in Catholicism. Luther said:

> They take a severe stand against the pope, but they miss their mark and murder the more terribly the Christendom under the pope. For if they would permit baptism and the sacrament of the altar to stand as they are, Christians under the pope might yet escape with their souls and be saved, as has been the case hitherto. But now when the sacraments are taken from them, they will most likely be lost, since even Christ himself is thereby taken away.[80]

The Council of Trent was not only the Roman Catholic Church's response to the Reformation, but was also a response to Anabaptists who were practicing *believer's baptism*.[81] In *The Canons and Dogmatic Decrees of the Council of Trent, A.D. 1563*, referring to the Seventh Session held March 3, 1547, *Decree on the Sacraments,* we read:

---

[80] Ibid., *Luther*, Vol. 40, p. 233.
[81] That the Acts of the Council of Trent still stands, was affirmed by Pope John XXIII in 1962 during his opening speech to the Vatican II Ecumenical Council when he said, "The salient point of this Council is not, therefore, a discussion of one article or another of the fundamental doctrine of the Church which has repeatedly been taught by the Fathers and by ancient and modern theologians, and which is presumed to be well known and familiar to all. For this a council was not necessary…as it still shines forth in the Acts of the Council of Trent and First Vatican Council…" *The Documents of Vatican II*, Walter M. Abbott, S.J. and Joseph Gallagher, Editors (New York: Guild Press, 1966), p. 715.

[Canon IX]--If any one saith, that, in the three sacraments, to wit, Baptism, Confirmation, and Order, there is not imprinted in the soul a character, that is, a certain spiritual and indelible sign, on account of which they can not be repeated: let him be anathema.[82]

[On Baptism, Canon III]--If anyone saith, that in the Roman Church, which is the mother and mistress of all churches, there is not the true doctrine concerning the sacrament of baptism: let him be anathema.[83]

[Canon V]--If any one saith, that baptism is free, that is, not necessary unto salvation: let him be anathema.[84]

[Canon XIII]—If any one saith, that little children, for that they have not actual faith, are not, after having received baptism, to be reckoned amongst the faithful; and that for this cause, they are to be rebaptized when they have attained to years of discretion: or, that it is better that the baptism of such be omitted, than that, while not believing by their own act, they should be baptized in the faith alone of the Church: let him be anathema.[85]

The Novationists were third century rebaptizers (perhaps the first anabaptists) whose doctrinal viewpoints continued through the Council of Trent.[86] During the Fourteenth Session, held November 25, 1551, Chapter one states:

---

[82] *The Creeds of Christendom With a History and Critical Notes,* Philip Schaff, Editor; Revised by David S. Schaff (Grand Rapids, Michigan: Baker Books, 1996), Vol. II *The Greek and Latin Creeds*, p. 121.

[83] Ibid., *Creeds*, Vol. II, p. 122.

[84] Ibid., *Creeds*, Vol. II, p. 123.

[85] Ibid., *Creeds,* Vol. II, pp. 124, 125.

[86] Novation flourished from 249-251 A.D. as a highly educated priest, theologian and writer. During the Decian persecution many believers lapsed and denied the faith. Novation demanded a correct profession of faith and rebaptism before he would readmit them to the church. For this, he was proclaimed a heretic and excommunicated by a Roman synod. He set up his own anabaptist church, which lasted to the eighth century. We will discuss Novation and his followers at length in the next chapter.

> And the Catholic Church with great reason repudiated and condemned as heretics the Novations, who of old obstinately denied that power of forgiving. Wherefore, this holy synod, approving of and receiving as most true this meaning of those words of our Lord, condemns the fanciful interpretations of those who, in opposition to the institution of this sacrament, falsely wrest those words to the power of preaching the Word of God, and of announcing the Gospel of Christ.[87]

According to the preceding citations from Luther and Catholicism, one is expected to conclude that all advocates of *believer's baptism*, and therefore *rebaptism*, are hopelessly condemned to hell without remedy. According to the *Catholic Encyclopedia*: *An anathema is different from excommunication for, according to Gratian, the latter excluded one only from the sacraments while anathema signified total separation from the faith.*[88]

Most advocates of believer's baptism hold that it is an ordinance and not a sacrament. Ryrie distinguishes between the two concepts as follows:

> The Council of Trent defined a sacrament as "something presented to the sense, which has the power, by divine institution, not only of signifying, but also of efficiently conveying grace."
> By contrast, "ordinance" (though a synonym of sacrament in the dictionary) does not incorporate the

---

[87] Ibid., *Creeds,* Vol. II, p. 141.

[88] *Our Sunday Visitor's Catholic Encyclopedia*, Rev. Peter M.J. Stravinskas, Ph.D., S.T.L., Editor (Huntington, Indiana: Our Sunday Visitor Publishing Division, Inc., 1991), p. 67. Some Catholic authorities say that anathemas were abolished after the Second Vatican Council but we have not found where the canons and decrees of the Council of Trent have been repealed. However, we can find many contemporary authorities who proclaim that the Church still stands by the documents of the Council of Trent.

idea of conveying grace but only the idea of a symbol.[89]

Advocates of *believer's baptism* are quick to point out that John the Baptist only baptized believers (Matt. 3:2-6). But when Pharisees and Sadducees came to him for baptism, he turned them away until they showed proof that they had changed their minds about Christ (Matt. 3:7, 8). Jesus commanded that only the discipled were to be baptized (Matt. 28:19). Jesus commanded belief and then baptism (Mk. 16:16). On the Day of Pentecost, Peter told the Jews to repent and then to be baptized (Acts 2:37, 38). On that Day of Pentecost it was *they that gladly received his word* that were *baptized* (Acts 2:41). The Samaritans were baptized after they believed the preaching of Philip (Acts 8:12). Even Simon the sorcerer had to make a profession of faith before he could be baptized (Acts 8:13). The Ethiopian Eunuch asked Phillip: *what doth hinder me to be baptized?* (Acts 8:36b), to which Philip replied, *If thou believest...thou mayest*. The Apostle Paul was a believer before he was baptized (Acts 9:18; 26:19). The House of Cornelius believed before they were baptized (Acts 10:43-47).[90] Lydia was baptized after she believed (Acts 16:14, 15). Paul and Silas preached the Word to all that were in the Philippian jailer's house; they all believed and then Paul baptized them (Acts 16:31-33). Crispus, the chief ruler of the synagogue in Corinth, with his whole house, and many Corinthians, *hearing believed, and were baptized* (Acts 18:8). Paul said that John the Baptist would baptize only those who believed *on him which should come after him, that is, on Christ Jesus* (Acts 19:4b). The disciples of Jesus were baptized but not by Christ (Jn. 4:1, 2), therefore, they must have had John's baptism (c.f. Jn. 3:22, 23). Regardless, they were believers before they were baptized. The Apostle Paul had *begotten, espoused, and fathered* many believers in Corinth (I Cor. 4:15; II Cor. 11:2) without baptizing them (I Cor. 1:14). Throughout the Scriptures, the gospel is presented in terms of belief alone in the death,

---

[89] Charles C. Ryrie, *Basic Theology: A Popular Systematic Guide To Understanding Biblical Truth* (USA, Canada, England: Victor Books, 1987), P. 421.

[90] No one in the book of Acts received the baptism of the Spirit into the Body of Christ until after belief. No one but believers had the gift of tongues, *And these signs shall follow them that believe...they shall speak with new tongues* (Mk. 16:17). The house of Cornelius spoke in tongues and received the baptism of the Spirit before water baptism (Acts 10: 45-48), c.f. Acts 11:15, 16 with 10: 44.

burial and resurrection of Christ, or more simply, belief in Christ as the supplier of salvation (I Cor. 15:1-4; Rom. 8:1; Jn. 3:15-18, 36; Acts 16:31).

It seems strange indeed to advocates of *believer's baptism* when Luther and Calvin insist that these *satanic, demonic, heretical, schismatics* are only imagining the Bible to teach the baptism of believers only and that they are dragging the Scriptures *by the hair* in order to find this doctrine when it is not actually there. The actuality is that the *believer's baptism* advocates cannot find any other baptism in the NT, except for those who were rebaptized because their faith was not in Jesus Christ at their first baptism (as with the so-called disciples of John in Acts 19:1-7).[91] Not only in the NT, but the *believer's baptism* persuasion finds its position to be of greater antiquity in history than that of infant baptism. They are not moved by the fact that theirs has been the minority position because the terms *mainstream* and *fringe* have seldom been a factor in their search for the truth of this matter.

Clement of Alexandria supposedly died about A.D. 220. He had been the head of the Catechetical School at Alexandria at the close of the second century. In his work called *The Instructor* he writes: *And since knowledge springs up with illumination, shedding its beams around the mind, the moment we hear, we who were untaught become disciples...For instruction leads to faith, and faith with baptism is trained by the Holy Spirit.*[92]

Tertullian flourished from about 196 through 212 A.D. and began writing in Carthage, North Africa towards the end of the second century. In his work *Against Praxeas*, in which he affirms the doctrine of the Holy Trinity, he claims to be a defender of the *rule of faith* that *has come down to us from the beginning of the gospel even before any of the older heretics.*[93] Concerning baptism, he said that: *preaching is*

---

[91] We will discuss this passage as an example of anabaptism in chapter nine of this present work.

[92] Clement of Aleandria, *The Instructor* [chapter 5] in *Ante-Nicene Fathers: Fathers of the Second Century*, Rev. Alexander Roberts, D.D., and James Donaldson, LL.D., Editors (Grand Rapids, Michigan: Wm. B. Eerdmans Publishing Company, 1977), Vol. II, p.217.

[93] Tertullian, *Against Praxeas* [chapter 2] *Ante-Nicene Fathers: Latin Christianity: its Founder Tertullian* (Grand Rapids, Michigan: Wm. B. Eerdmans Publishing Company, 1976), Vol. III, p. 597.

the prior thing, baptizing the posterior.[94] Concerning candidates for baptism he said: *the delay of baptism is preferable; principally, however, in the case of little children.*[95] Regarding preparation for baptism he writes:

> They who are about to enter baptism ought to pray with repeated prayers, fasts, and bendings of the knee, and vigils all the night through, and with the confession of all bygone sins, that they may express the meaning even of the baptism of John: "They were baptized," saith (the Scripture), "confessing their own sins."[96]

Tertullian understood John's baptism to be from God but he denied that it was celestial. Using the words of John the Baptist:

> He who is from the earth speaketh concerning the earth; He who comes from the realms above is above all" and again, by saying that he "baptized" in repentance only, but One would shortly come who would baptize in the spirit and fire.[97]

His point is that baptism is earthly and does not remit sins. He insists that *repentance is antecedent, remission subsequent—*

> But if repentance is a thing human, its baptism must necessarily be of the same nature: else, if it had been celestial, it would have given both the Holy spirit and remission of sins. But none either pardons sins or freely grants the Spirit save God only.[98]

---

[94] Ibid., Tertullian, *On Baptism* [chapter 14] *Ante-nicene Fathers*, Vol. III, p. 676.
[95] Ibid., Tertullian, *On Baptism* [chapter 19] Vol. III, p. 678.
[96] Ibid., Tertullian, *On Baptism* [chapter 20] Vol. III, pp. 678, 679.
[97] Ibid., Tertullian, *On Baptism* [chapter 10] Vol. III, p. 674.
[98] Ibid., Tertullian, *On Baptism* [chapter 10] Vol. III, p. 674. Note also his work *The Chaplet, or De Corona* on p. 94: "To deal with this matter briefly, I shall begin with baptism. When we are going to enter the water, but a little before, in the presence of the congregation and under the hand of the president, we solemnly profess that we disown the devil, and his pomp, and his *(Continued on next page)*

Infant Baptism And Believer's Baptism

Tertullian is a unique example of one who advocated believer's baptism yet still believed that baptism was necessary to salvation (c.f. discussion in chapter seven).

At the Seventh Council of Carthage under Cyprian, one Felix of Bussacene said: *In the matter of receiving heretics without the baptism of the Church, let no one prefer custom to reason and truth, because reason and truth always exclude custom.*[99] And *The Teaching of the Twelve Apostles*, written at least as early as the first half of the second century, states: *But before the baptism let the baptizer fast, and the baptized, and whatever others can; but thou shalt order the baptized to fast one or two days before.*[100] In the Psuedo-Clementine literature, purporting to be authored by Clement of Rome, there is a work called *Recognitions of Clement.* In the chapter entitled *Baptism must be preceded by Fasting* it states:

> When Niceta had spoken thus, our mother fell down at Peter's feet, entreating and beseeching him that both herself and her hostess might be baptized without delay...But she must fast at least one day first, and so be baptized; and this because I have heard from her a certain declaration, by which her faith has been made manifest to me, and which has given evidence of her belief; otherwise she must have been instructed and taught many days before she could have been baptized.[101]

---

angels." Again, we must remind ourselves that Tertullian makes baptism essential to salvation on other pages of his writings, Vol. 3, pp. 672, 674, 675.

[99] Cyprian, *The Seventh Council of Carthage: Concerning the Baptism of Heretics, The Judgment Of Eighty-Seven Bishops On The Baptism Of Heretics* In *Ante-Nicene Fathers: Fathers of the Third Century,* Alexander Roberts, D.D., and James Donaldson, LL.D., Editors (Grand Rapids, Michigan: Wm. B. Eerdmans Publishing Company, 1975), Vol. 5, p. 571.

[100] *The Teaching Of The Twelve Apostles* in *Ante-Nicene Fathers: Fathers down to A.D. 325,* Alexander Roberts, D.D., and James Donaldson, LL.D., Editors (Grand Rapids, Michigan: Wm. B. Eerdmans Company, 1975), Vol. VII, p. 379.5

[101] Psuedo Clementine, *Recognitions of Clement* in *Ante-Nicene Fathers: Down to A.D. 325,* Alexander Roberts, D.D., and James Donaldson, *(Continued on next page)*

Philip Schaff introduces us to the life and work of St. John Chrysostom as *The greatest pulpit orator and commentator of the Greek Church*. Schaff divides his life into five periods the first of which is: *His youth and training till his conversion and baptism, A. D. 347-370.* He was born in 347 at Antioch, the capital of Syria, where the church of Antioch had sent out the first Gentile mission and where the disciples were first called Christians. He had a very godly Christian mother, Anthusa, whom Schaff describes as *among the most pious mothers of the fourth century*[102]—

> Anthusa gained general esteem by her exemplary life. The famous advocate of heathenism, Libanius, on hearing of her consistency and devotion, felt constrained to exclaim: "Bless me! What wonderful women there are among the Christians."[103]

Chrysostom was not converted from cultural heathenism, because his heathen father died in his infancy, and his mother dedicated herself to planting *in his soul the germs of piety, which afterwards bore the richest fruits for himself and the church. By her admonitions and teachings of the Bible, he was secured against the seductions of heathenism.*[104] Why then did she postpone his baptism till the age of maturity? If she was so respected by the church, why hadn't she brought her son as an infant to be baptized? Schaff says:

> Even Christian parents, as the father and mother of Gregory Nazianzen, the mother of Chrysostom, and the mother of Augustin, put off the baptism of their offspring.

LL.D., Editors (Grand Rapids, Michigan: Wm. B. Eerdmans Publishing Company, 1974), Vol. VIII, p. 164.

[102] Philip Schaff, D.D., LL.D., *Prolegomena: The Life and Work of St. John Chrysostom,* in *Nicene and Post-Nicene Fathers,* Philip Schaff, Editor (Grand Rapids, Michigan: Wm. B. Eerdmans Publishing Company, 1975), Vol. IX, p. 5.

[103] Ibid., Schaff, *Nicene and Post-Nicene Christianity*, Vol. IX, p. 5.

[104] Ibid., Schaff, *Nicene and Post-Nicene Christianity*, Vol. IX, p. 5

Infant Baptism And Believer's Baptism

This is not to be associated with the superstitious heresy of putting off baptism till the end of life, thinking that sins after baptism cannot be covered by baptism—

> e.g. The Emperor Constantine who favored Christianity as early as 312, and convened the Council of Nicea in 325, who postponed baptism till 337, shortly before his death. The orthodox Emperor Theodosius the Great was not baptized till the first year of his reign (380), when attacked by a serious illness.[105]

Chrysostom often rebukes this superstition, but he never renounced his own baptism. Schaff says: *His baptism was, as in the case of St. Augustin, the turning point in his life, an entire renunciation of this world and dediction to the service of Christ.*[106]

Augustine was born Nov. 13, 354, of Christian parents, but he did not receive baptism from Ambrose in Milan until Easter Sunday of the year 387.[107] St. Jerome (c. 347-420), author of the Vulgate Translation of the Bible into Latin, was not baptized in infancy, even though his father, Eusebius and his mother were Catholic Christians.[108]

The reader should not see this chapter as an attack on all who are baptized as infants. Our concern is with the belief that infant baptism regenerates and saves one's soul. There are innumerable parents throughout Christendom who had their infants baptized as a public commitment on their part to live for the day that this child would profess faith in the gospel of Christ's grace and become born again. There are many in the Reformed tradition who practice infant baptism with this in view. And even though there may still be disagreements over the candidates and mode of Christian baptism, their gospel is one

---

[105] Ibid., Schaff, *Nicene and Post-Nicene Christianity*, Vol. IX, p. 6.
[106] Ibid., Schaff, *Nicene and Post-Nicene Christianity*, Vol. IX, p. 6.
[107] Philip Schaff, *Prolegomena: St Augustin's Life and Work* in *Nicene and Post-Nicene Fathers*, Phillip Schaff D.D., LL.D., Editor (Grand Rapids, Michigan: Wm. B. Eerdmans Publishing Company, 1974), Vol. I, p. 4.
[108] *Prolegomena to Jerome* in *Nicene and Post-Nicene Fathers*, Philip Schaff, D.D., LL.D. & Henry Wace, D.D., Editors (Grand Rapids, Michigan: Wm. B. Eerdmans Publishing Company, 1975), Vol. VI, p. xvi.

of grace alone (without works), by faith alone in the finished work of Christ on the cross (not in the water).[109] Just as there were thousands of circumcised infants in the OT who never embraced the grace of God as adults, but instead trusted their circumcision to save their souls, so also there are many who were baptized as infants who never grew to embrace the saving grace of Christ. Their only testimony is something like, *I know I'm going to heaven; that was settled when my parents had me baptized as an infant.*

In the following chapter we will discuss the history of the *baptismal regeneration* position and offer cross-examining questions from Scripture, in order that the reader may acquire his own conclusions.

---

[109] From an historical perspective, these truly Christian parents should consider the fact that the *dedication* rather than the *regeneration* view of infant baptism is relatively new. Almost every argument for infant baptism in ancient and medieval church history is an argument for baptismal regeneration.

Chapter Seven

Historical Overview Of The Baptismal Regeneration Tradition

> ...That Christ by baptism has made us partakers of his death, ingrafting us into it. And as the twig derives substance and nourishment from the root to which it is attached, so those who receive baptism with true faith truly feel the efficacy of Chist's death in the mortification of their flesh, and the efficacy of his resurrection in the quickening of the Spirit.
>
> **John Calvin's** *Institutes Of The Christian Religion* **(Book IV 15.4)**

Cardinal Hosius Stanislos presided over the Council of Trent [1545-1563], which was a response of the Roman Catholic Church to the Reformation and to the Anabaptist movements as well as an attempt to reform the Catholic Church from within. Several church histories credit Cardinal Hosius with a unique statement (and admission) about anabaptism [rebaptism]. The statement is supposedly cited from pp. 112, 113 of his *Letters Apud Opera*. We have been unable to find such a work by him in the libraries of the United States. There are those who have conducted research in Europe who claim to have located it but they do not give us a complete citation. Historian John T. Christian gives us the alleged quotation as follows:

If the truth of religion were to be judged by the readiness and boldness of which a man of any sect shows in suffering, then the opinion and persuasions of no sect can be truer and surer than that of the Anabaptists since there have been none for these twelve hundred years past, that have been more generally punished or that have more cheerfully and steadfastly undergone, and even offered themselves to the most cruel sorts of punishment than these people. *Baptist Magazine* CVIII, 278, May, 1826.[1]

Although we must consider the possibility that Hosius never made such a statement, we should also consider the fact that it would have been an accurate declaration for anyone to have made at that moment in history.[2] The term *Anabaptist* refers to any person or sect that requires a rebaptism for any reason. This may, or may not, refer to an advocate of salvation by grace alone through faith alone. Although *anabaptism* can be successfully traced backward to the third century and the Novationists, the history of the Anabaptists should not necessarily be considered a history of the doctrine of salvation by grace.

---

[1] John T. Christian, *A History Of Baptists* (Texarkana, Ark.-Tex.: Bogard Press, 1922), Vol. I, pp. 85, 86. If anyone knows of a clearer reference to this quotation, it would be deeply appreciated if that person would forward it to the author of this present work. Notwithstanding, the *Fourteenth Session* of the Council of Trent verified the facts of this quotation [See footnote reference 139 of this present chapter and footnote reference 87 in chapter 6].

[2] Rev. Francis J. Zdrodowski, M.A., S.T.L., *The Concept of Heresy According to Cardinal Hosius: A Dissertation Submitted to the Faculty of the School of Sacred Theology of the Catholic University of America in Partial Fulfillment of the Requirements for the Degree of Doctor of Sacred Theology* (Washington, D. C.: The Catholic University of America Press, 1947), p. 62…"Hosius emphasizes the fundamental fact of heresy; the heretic falls back upon the Bible as the sole source of salvation…thus insisting upon the right of the individual to interpret all truths for himself. Heretics regard the right of private judgment as a special immunity from ecclesiastical or civil supervision in matters of conscience, and join therewith a freedom to ascertain what the word of God teaches on every point of doctrine and practice. Notwithstanding the alterations that the Bible suffers at his hands, the heretic will insist on the Bible as the sole authoritative and sufficient norm concerning things necessary to salvation, and denies that Catholic tradition likewise serves as a necessary and integral element of the rule of faith…"

Historical Overview Of The Baptismal Regeneration Tradition

Some Baptist history books attempt to trace a gospel tradition backward through Catabaptists, Waldensians, Berengarians, Arnaldists, Henricians, Petrobrusians, Albigensians, Bogomils, Paulicians, Donatists and finally to Novationists.[3] One of the primary common denominators connecting these groups was the practice of rebaptism. Most contemporary advocates of a pure grace gospel would find little affinity with the gospel conceptions of many of the above named sects. However, their existence does dispel the notion that rebaptism and believer's baptism was an innovation of non-traditional origin.[4]

Actually, the history of the pure grace gospel (independent of ritual and law) was a view often found outside the ancient Anabaptist circles. Many of the Anabaptists, of whom we will mention, were also believers in baptismal regeneration. Their distinction was that they required a profession of faith prior to their baptism. Some of them advocated a *works* salvation and some of them were mystics.[5] Though a contemporary advocate of *believer's baptism* and salvation by grace alone will find references to his position in many Anabaptists of the Reformation period and following, the real theological task for the preacher of a pure grace gospel is to find its roots in Scripture alone, for the Bible is the final arbiter in any debate over the nature of the true gospel.[6] But first we will look at the history of the *baptismal regeneration* view.

For present purposes, we will begin to trace the history of *baptismal regeneration* from the earliest of post-apostolic times. We begin with an inspection of the *Apostles' Creed* which, though certainly not compiled by the Apostles, was indeed purely apostolic in its content. Phillip Schaff gives us the earliest *old Roman* form as given by Rufinus in Latin [c. 390 A.D.], also by Marcellus in Greek [336-341 A.D.] and then the *Received* form which came into general use in the seventh or

---

[3] It would be advisable for the reader to research the doctrinal distinctives of each of these divergent groups.
[4] The tradition began officially with the rebaptism of the so-called disciples of John the Baptist in Acts 19.
[5] We will discuss the concept of *mystical illumination* in chap. 8 of this present work.
[6] This we will endeavor to do in chaps. 8 & 9 of this present work.

eighth century. He records the eleven articles of the *old Roman* and the additions of the *Received Form* in brackets as follows:

1. I believe in God the Father Almighty [*Maker of heaven and earth*].
2. And in Jesus Christ, his only Son, our Lord;
3. Who was [*conceived*] by the Holy Ghost, born of the Virgin Mary;
4. [*Suffered*] under Pontius Pilate, was crucified [*dead*], and buried [*He descended into Hell (Hades)*];
5. The third day he rose from the dead;
6. He ascended into heaven; and sitteth on the right hand of [*God*] the Father [*Almighty*];
7. From thence he shall come to judge the quick and the dead.
8. [*I believe*] in the Holy Ghost;
9. The Holy [*Catholic*] Church [*The communion of saints*];
10. The forgiveness of sins;
11. The resurrection of the body (flesh);
12. [*And the life everlasting*].[7]

Schaff, quoting from Dr. Shedd (Presbyterian, *History of Christian Doctrine,* II, p. 433), writes:

> The Apostle's Creed is the earliest attempt of the Christian mind to systematize the teachings of the Scripture, and is, consequently, the uninspired foundation upon which the whole after-structure of symbolic literature rests. All creed development proceeds from this germ.[8]

But to search back even further we see traces of the leading articles of this Creed in Ignatius [A.D. 30-107], Chapter IX of his *Epistle to the*

---

[7] *The Creeds of Christendom: With a History and Critical Notes,* Edited by Philip Schaff; Revised by David S. Schaff (Grand Rapids, Michigan: Baker Books), Vol. I, pp. 21, 22.

[8] Ibid., *Creeds of Christendom*, Vol. I, p. 16.

Trallians.[9] Tradition tells us that Ignatius and Polycarp were direct disciples of the Apostle John. Ignatius was the bishop of Antioch during the time of Trajan. The *Catholic Encyclopedia* admits the Apostles' Creed is the—

> formula of belief in twelve articles and contains the fundamental doctrines of Christianity. Its authorship comes from being a summary of apostolic teachings, not from being written by the Apostles...[10]

The *Apostles' Creed* is a distillation of the apostolic teaching. Schaff says:

> As the Lord's Prayer is the Prayer of prayers, the Decalogue the Law of laws, so the Apostles' Creed is the Creed of creeds. It contains all the fundamental articles of the Christian faith necessary to salvation, in the form of facts, in simple Scripture language...[11]

He describes the Creed as the profession of faith *of candidates for baptism and church membership. It is not a logical statement of abstract doctrines, but a profession of living facts and saving truths.*[12] Schaff refers to Tertullian as teaching the Creed to be a *summary of the Gospel.*[13]

We began with this review of the *Apostles' Creed* in order that the reader might notice the conspicuous fact that neither *baptismal regeneration* nor the necessity of baptism for salvation is anywhere

---

[9] *Ante-Nicene Fathers: The Writings of the Fathers down to A.D. 325*, Editors, Rev. Alexander Roberts, D.D. and James Donaldson, LL.D., (Grand Rapids, Michigan: Wm. B. Eerdmans Publishing Company), Vol. 1, pp. 69, 70. Ignatius speaks of Christ as truly born "of the Virgin Mary," "Suffered under Pontius Pilate," "Was Crucified and died," and "was raised from the dead." The same articles can be traced in Justin Martyr's [A.D. 110-165] *First Apology* Chapters X, XIII, XXI, XLII, XLVI, L. Ibid. Vol. 1, PP. 165-179.

[10] *Our Sunday Visitor's Catholic Encyclopedia*, Rev. Peter M. J. Stravinskas, Ph.D., S.T.L., Editor (Huntington, Indiana: Our Sunday Visitor Publishing Division, Our Sunday Visitor, Inc.), p. 85.

[11] Ibid., *Creeds Of Christendom*, Vol. I, p. 14.

[12] Ibid., *Creeds Of Christendom*, Vol. I, p. 15.

[13] Ibid., *Creeds of Christendom*, Vol. I, pp. 16, 17.

mentioned in the twelve articles. If baptism were the centerpiece of the true gospel, one would think that it would not have been left to assumption, but rather conspicuously written into the context, as in the *Nicene Creed* of A.D. 325 [Article 10] which states: *We [I] acknowledge one baptism for the remission of sins.*[14]

However, we will note that most of the Church Fathers of the second through the fifth centuries taught baptismal regeneration to be the essential grounds for entering the kingdom of Heaven. Concerning Ezekiel 47:12 the *Epistle of Barnabas* [A.D. 100] says: *This meaneth that we indeed descend into the water full of sins and defilement, but come up, bearing fruit in our heart, having the fear [of God] and trust in Jesus in our spirit.*[15]

Justin Martyr [A.D. 110-165] was an advocate of both *believer's baptism* and *baptismal regeneration*. Chapter LXI of his *First Apology* is entitled *Christian Baptism*, wherein he states:

> As many as are persuaded and believe that what we teach and say is true, and undertake to be able to live accordingly, are instructed to pray and to entreat God with fasting, for the remission of their sins that are past, we praying and fasting with them. Then they are brought by us where there is water, and are regenerated in the same manner in which we were ourselves regenerated. For, in the name of God, the Father and Lord of the universe, and of our Savior Jesus Christ, and of the Holy Spirit, they then receive the washing with water. For Christ also said, "Except ye be born again, ye shall not enter the kingdom of heaven...And this washing is called illumination

---

[14] Ibid., *Creeds of Christendom*, Vol. I, p. 28.
[15] *Ante-Nicene Fathers: Down to A.D. 325*, The Rev. Alexander Roberts, D. D., and James Donaldson, LL.D., Editors (Grand Rapids, Michigan: Wm. B. Eerdmans Publishing Company, 1977), Vol. I, p. 144. The writer of the *Epistle of Barnabas* is alleged to be an Alexandrian Jew of the times of Trajan and Hadrian [A.D. 100].

Historical Overview Of The Baptismal Regeneration Tradition

because they who learn these things are illuminated in their understandings.[16]

Chapter XLIII of his *Dialogue With Trypho* [the Jew] Justin argues that, *we, who have approached God through Him, have received not carnal, but spiritual circumcision, which Enoch and those like him observed. And we have received it through baptism...*[17]

Hermas, a brother of Pius, the ninth Bishop of Rome [c. 140] composed an allegory entitled *The Shepherd,* or *The Pastor.* Irenaeus quotes him as Scripture.[18] Clement of Alexandria [c. A.D. 150-215] seems to quote Hermas as Scripture also.[19] Nevertheless, *The Shepherd* was excluded from the NT canon because of the late date of its authorship and its non-apostolic beliefs. Hermas taught that water-baptism was essential to salvation even for OT souls in Hades who were baptized by the apostles after the latter had died:

> "Accordingly, those also who fell asleep received the seal of the Son of God. For," he continued, "before a man bears the name of the Son of God he is dead; but when he receives the seal he lays aside his deadness, and obtains life. The seal, then, is the water: they descend into the water dead, and they arise alive, and to them, accordingly, was this seal preached, and they made use of it that they might enter into the kingdom of God... These apostles and teachers who preached the name of the son of God, after falling asleep in the power and faith of the son of God, preached it not only to those who were asleep, but themselves also gave them the seal of the preaching. Accordingly they descended with them into the water, and again ascended. [But these descended alive and rose up

---

[16] Ibid., Vol. I, p. 183. There is a great contradiction between the view that illumination of understanding cooresponds with the need to believe the gospel prior to baptism and the view that illumination happens only at baptism.

[17] Ibid., Vol. I, p. 216.

[18] Ibid., *Against Heresies*, Book IV, xx, 2, *Ante-Nicene Fathers*, Vol. I, p.488.

[19] Ibid., Clement of Alexandria, *Stromata*, Book I, xxix, Vol. II, p.341.

again alive; whereas they who had previously fallen asleep descended dead, but rose up again alive.]... For they slept in righteousness and in great purity, but only they had not this seal..."[20]

Clement of Alexandria quotes this passage but goes one step further by supposing that Christ also baptized in Hades.[21]

Irenaeus [A.D. 120-202] was the disciple of Polycarp who was himself the disciple of the Apostle John. He was bishop of Lyons, in France, during the last quarter of the second century. His greatest work was *Against Heresies*. Chapter XXI of Book One discusses the views of redemption entertained by heretics and affirms:

> And when we come to refute them, we shall show in its fitting-place, that this class of men have been instigated by Satan to a denial of that baptism which is regeneration to God, and thus to a renunciation of the whole [Christian] faith.[22]

Tertullian [A.D. 145-220] is another example of one who advocated *believer's baptism* yet still believed in baptismal salvation. He believed that no one could obtain salvation without ritual baptism. In chapter VII of his work *On Baptism* he writes: *The act of baptism itself too is carnal, in that we are plunged in water, but the effect spiritual, in that we are freed from sins.* Chapter XII of the same work entitled *Of The Necessity Of Baptism To Salvation*, he writes: *When, however, the prescript is laid down that "without baptism, salvation is*

---

[20] Ibid., *Shepherd of Hermas* [*Similitude* xvi], Ante-Nicene Fathers, Vol. II, p. 49. The fragment known as the *Muratorian Canon* became the basis for assigning the date A.D. 160 to this work. The fragment found by Muritori in Milan in the seventeenth century, says that "Very recently in our own times, in the city of Rome, Hermas compiled *The Shepherd*; his brother, Bishop Pius, then sitting in the *cathedra* of the Roman Church." Ibid. (Introduction to *The Shepherd*) Vol. II, pp. 3, 4.

[21] Ibid., Clement of Alexandria, *Stromata* II.9, Vol. 2, p. 357; VI.6, Vol. II, p. 490.

[22] Ibid., Vol. I, p. 345.

Historical Overview Of The Baptismal Regeneration Tradition

attainable by none" (chiefly on the ground of that declaration of the Lord, who says, "Unless one be born of water, he hath not life").[23]

Cyprian [A.D. 200-258], in contrast to Tertullian, believed in infant baptism, baptismal regeneration, and rebaptism of heretics. He held that withholding baptism from an infant was to withhold God's saving grace:

> But in respect of the case of the infants, which you say ought not to be baptized within the second or third day after their birth, and that the law of ancient circumcision should be regarded, so that you think that one who is just born should not be baptized and sanctified within the eighth day, we all thought very differently in our council. For in this course which you thought was to be taken, no one agreed; but we all rather judge that the mercy and grace of God is not to be refused to any one born of man [Epistle XVIII.2].[24]

When Cyprian was in council with forty-nine other bishops, he prescribed the re-baptism of those baptized by heretics outside the Catholic Church because only the one true Church could bestow remission of sins through baptism:

> But, moreover, the very interrogation which is put in baptism is a witness of the truth. For when we say, "Dost thou believe in eternal life and remission of sins through the holy Church?" we mean that remission of sins is not granted except in the Church, and that among heretics where there is no Church, sins cannot be put away.[25]

Cyprian denied that this was a rebaptism, for the former was not a baptism in the first place:

---

[23] Ibid., *Ante-Nicene Fathers: Latin Christianity: its Founder, Tertullian*, Part III, *On Baptism*, Chapters vii and xii, Vol. III, pp. 672, 674, 675.
[24] Ibid., *Ante-Nicene Fathers*, Vol. V, pp. 353, 354.
[25] Ibid., Cyprian, Epistle LXIX, *To Januarius And Other Numidian Bishops, On Baptizing Heretics*, Vol. V, p. 376.

> But we say that those who come thence are not rebaptized among us, but are baptized. For indeed they do not receive anything there, where there is nothing.[26]

> And therefore it behooves those to be baptized who come from heresy to the Church, that so they who are prepared, in the lawful, and true, and only baptism of the holy Church, by divine regeneration, for the kingdom of God may be born of both sacraments, because it is written, "Except a man be born of water and of the Spirit, he cannot enter into the kingdom of God."[27]

The *rebaptism* conflict can be traced to the persecution of Christianity by the Roman emperor Decius who reigned from A.D. 249-251. His persecution threatened Christianity more than any which had preceded it. The extent of its execution can be observed in the reports from North Africa, Rome, Egypt, and Asia Minor. It was held by Anabaptists of that period that public profession was a mechanical contingency to a saving gospel.[28] A public recantation either meant the loss of salvation or that the recanting soul was never a born again Christian in the first place. The Epistle to the Hebrews; the First Epistle of Peter and the letters to the seven churches of Asia in the Apocalypse exhort faithfulness, even unto death, under sufferings and persecutions. God will have a special crown, reward, and inheritance for those who are faithful unto death.. However, the Scriptures never taught that martyrdom would purchase eternal life for its victim.

Believing that martyrdom will save one's soul for eternity is a greater error than the public denial of the faith. Though Cyprian

---

[26] Ibid., *Epistle LXX.1, To Quintus, Concerning the Baptism of Heretics*, Vol. V, p. 377.

[27] Ibid., *Epistle LXXII.21, To Jubaianus, Concerning the Baptism of Heretics*, Vol. V, p. 385.

[28] This concept was derived from a misinterpretation of (Matt. 10:33; Mk. 8:38; Lk. 9:26; 12:9). Later in this chapter we will show from Scripture that public denial does not result in the loss of salvation but rather in loss of communion with the Savior.

correctly spoke of special reward, crown, glory and inheritance that awaited martyrs in heaven, he made many statements implying that martyrdom would save one's soul from hell. In his treatise *On The Glory Of Martyrdom* he wrote:

> For assuredly you ought to consider what glory there is in expiating any kind of defilement of life, and the foulness of a polluted body, and the contagions gathered from the long putrefaction of vices, and the worldly guilt incurred by so great a lapse of time, by the remedial agency of one stroke, whereby both reward may be increased, and guilt may be excluded. Whence every perfection and condition of life is included in martyrdom. This is the foundation of life and faith, this is the safeguard of salvation, this is the bond of liberty and honor.[29]

Cyprian even suggested that the spilt blood of the martyr is that which would present him spotless before God at his judgment:

> For there is no doubt how much they obtain from the Lord, who have preferred God's name to their own safety, so that in that judgment-day their blood-shedding would make them better, and the blood spilt would show them to be spotless.[30]

> Heaven lies open to our blood; the dwelling-place of Gehenna gives way to our blood; and among all the attainments of glory, the title of blood is sealed as the fairest, and its crown is designated as most complete.[31]

It was thought that if one lived a long life he might backslide and lose his salvation. Dying a martyr's death would insure such a person against this possibility; as Cyprian said: *If you fear to lose salvation, know that you can die...*[32] It was even implied that

---

[29] Ibid., Treatises Attributed to Cyprian, *On The Glory Of Martyrdom*, Vol. V, p. 579.
[30] Ibid., Vol. V, p. 580.
[31] Ibid., Vol. V, p. 581.
[32] Ibid., Vol. V, p. 581.

martyrdom was the ground of God's election of some—*And that either their body is thrown to wild beasts, or the threatening sword is not feared, is shown as the reason of their dignity, is manifested as the ground of their election.*[33] It was also implied that Christ is crucified afresh every time a martyr is slain—*In Isaiah He was sawn asunder, in Abel He was slain, in Isaac He was offered up, in Joseph He was sold into slavery, in man He was crucified.*[34] And because it was believed that baptism saved the soul, it was also believed that martyrdom would substitute for baptism if one was slain before he could receive the ritual—

> Then, that they are certainly not deprived of the sacrament of baptism who are baptized with the most glorious and greatest baptism of blood…But the same Lord declares in the Gospel, that those who are baptized in their own blood, and sanctified by suffering, are perfected, and obtain the grace of the divine promise, when He speaks to the thief believing and confessing in His very passion, and promises that he would be with Himself in paradise.[35]

Some congregations developed a contempt of death and a passion for martyrdom, but there were also individuals who considered it legitimate to flee from persecution and martyrdom. The *Shepherd* of Hermas contains many examples of the effects which the persecutions of Trajan and Hadrian had on the congregation of Rome, noting that the faith of many had lapsed. The persecutions of Antoninus Pius and Marcus Aurelius resulted likewise in a lapse of faith among many professed Christians. One can read of the influence of the Decian and Valerian persecutions from the letters of Cyprian and his treatise *De lapsis*.[36] Denial was frequent during the persecution instituted by Julian, but the lapsed were soon permitted to reenter the churches.

---

[33] Ibid., Vol. V, p. 585.
[34] Ibid., Vol. V, p. 587.
[35] Ibid., Cyprian, Epistle LXXII.22, *To Jubaianus, Concerning the Baptism of Heretics*, Vol. V, p. 385.
[36] Ibid., Vol. V, pp. 437-447 [Treatise III, *On The Lapsed*]. See also Cyprian [Epistle X], pp. 290-292; and [Epistle XXVI, *Cyprian To The Lapsed*], pp. 305, 306; and [Epistle LIII, *To Cornelius, Concerning Granting Peace To The Lapsed*], pp. 336-338.

After the Decian persecution the lapsed were categorized and distinguished. The *sacrificati* were those who had sacrificed to the gods. The *thurificati* had burned incense to the gods. The *libellatici* had paid bribes to obtain certification that they had already fulfilled all requirements. Following the Diocletian persecution [A.D.303], a new term was coined.[37] The *traditores* had either actually surrendered their sacred books and vessels or had created the appearance that they had done so by substituting other books and vessels for them.[38] By so doing, they spared themselves from torture and martyrdom. Schaff writes:

> In the second century it was generally accepted throughout the Church that a Christian who had relapsed into idolatry could not be readmitted to the congregation. The most sincere repentance was not sufficient; only open profession under a new trial and martyrdom could blot out the guilt. In the middle of the third century milder views were adopted. In 250 Cyprian and the Roman clergy still felt uncertain about the question, but gradually a more lenient practice prevailed in the churches of Carthage, Rome, Alexandria, and Antioch, and between 251 and 325 a complete system of penitential rules was elaborated by the bishops.[39]

Novation became a leader in the controversy over readmitting the lapsed into the Church. He agreed with Cyprian and with the general opinion of Christendom, that though a lapse into paganism was

---

[37] Diocletian issued three edicts and Maximian, a co-regent, issued a fourth. Churches were to be destroyed; sacred writings were to be burned; Christians were to be deprived of public office and civil rights and all were to sacrifice to the gods or die a painful death. In A.D. 308 a fifth edict required every member of families, including servants, to sacrifice and taste the offerings. All provisions in the markets were to be sprinkled with the sacrificial wine. This would leave Christians with a choice of apostasy or starvation.

[38] This may be why the earliest of the NT codices belong to the fourth century when the State was at peace with the Church.

[39] *The New Schaff-Herzog Encyclopedia of Religious Knowledge*, Samuel Macauley Jackson, D. D., LL. D., Editor in Chief (Grand Rapids, Michigan: Baker Book House, 1950), Vol. VI, p, 416.

a great sin, it was not unpardonable.[40] But after he separated from the Catholic Church over a dispute regarding whether he or Cornelius was the duly ordained bishop of Rome, he detected fresh errors in the church that had rejected him.[41] He came to teach that the Church was defiled by restoring those who had been guilty of lapsed faith or profession.

When Stephen became bishop of Rome a new conflict developed with Carthage regarding whether the fallen should be rebaptized in order to reenter the Church. Seventy-one bishops convened at Carthage and affirmed the doctrine of rebaptism. Stephen would readmit apostates to communion without rebaptism, but not Cyprian. The bishops of Africa and Asia Minor sided with Cyprian. So, Stephen excommunicated the church at Carthage while the churches of Asia Minor agreed with Cyprian. The council of Arles [A.D. 314] was comprised of Western bishops of York, Lincoln, and London, in Britain. This council decided against Carthage and for Rome.

From a purely scriptural perspective, all parties to this conflict were in error. Rome was wrong in believing that the sacrament, the bishop, and the Church could absolve the *lapsi* of the sin of apostasy.[42] Any Christian can confess any sin to Christ at any time; experience forgiveness; and be restored to fellowship with Him (I Jn. 1:9). The Novationists and the followers of Cyprian were wrong in assuming that

---

[40] Cyprian and Carthage had a stiffer attitude toward clergy who had lapsed. The lapsed were not to be reinstated. Basilides and Martialis, two Spanish bishops, had been deprived of their bishoprics and Stephen of Rome reinstated them.

[41] He disagreed with Cornelius, who, after the Decian persecution, was nominated bishop of Rome and readmitted to the Church the repentant Christians who had lapsed. Those who opposed the restoration of the lapsed chose Novation to be the bishop. Cornelius excommunicated Novation. Cyprian sided with Cornelius. Novation formed a sect known as the *Cathari*, or Pure Ones, who held that no clemency should be extended to the apostates. This sect propagated itself in the West and the East down to the sixth century. They were known to rebaptize those who were thought to have been baptized by heretics.

[42] Richard P. McBrien, *Catholicism* [Study Edition] (Minneapolis, MN: Winston Press, Inc., 1981), pp, 777, 778... "The first to deny the Church's and the bishop's right to forgive those guilty of serious sins were the *Montanists* and the *Novationists*, both arguing that certain sins (e.g., apostasy, murder, adultery) were outside the Church's powers."

the lapsed could not be restored without a rebaptism and that lapsed clergy could not be restored at all. Rome was wrong in assuming that Christians could be damned to Hell by the excommunication of the Church. It is not necessary to enter into a voluminous study of history on this point in order to resolve the essential question regarding a Christian whose faith experiences a lapse to the extent that he may even embrace apostasy. The final authority on this question should be resolved by the Scriptures themselves, which predate all of the *Ante-Nicene Fathers*.

Jesus told Peter that Satan desired to *have* him and to *sift* him *as wheat* (Lk. 22:31). Even though the Lord knew that Peter's faithfulness and public profession would fail, He prayed that his faith would not fail. And, without suggesting a long period of trial and probation or a rebaptism, Jesus told Peter that as soon as he had recovered from this experience he must resume an ordained ministry to *strengthen thy brethren* (Lk. 22:32). Peter presumptuously and vehemently corrected the Lord, claiming that he was ready to go to prison and die for his Master (22:33; Mk. 14:31), whereupon the other disciples made the same boast. Christ then prophesied that Peter would publicly deny Him three times before the cock would crow twice (22:34; Mk. 14:30).

When Jesus was on trial, Peter sat outside the palace, following *afar off* (Mk. 14:54), where a woman recognized him as a follower of Jesus. Peter openly denied that there was any truth to the accusation (Matt. 26:69, 70). When he went out onto the porch he was identified by another woman as a follower of Jesus of Nazareth, whereupon he publicly denied, with an oath, even knowing Christ (26:71, 72). When a third person made the same accusation, Peter tried to become more convincing by swearing and cursing in his denial of knowing Christ—

> ...And immediately the cock crew. And Peter remembered the word of Jesus, which said unto him, Before the cock crow, thou shalt deny me thrice. And he went out, and wept bitterly (26:74b, 75; also, Mk. 14:71, 72).

It was precisely at this moment that Jesus was within sight of Peter and suddenly turned and looked at him as he uttered his denial (Lk. 22:60, 61).

Peter was not a unique exception in his lapse of public profession and faithfulness, because all of the other disciples forsook Jesus as well (Mt. 26:56; Mk. 14:50). Cowardice, doubt, and unbelief became a common experience among the followers of Christ, but none were rebaptized because of it, and none had to wait for restoration to communion upon repentance. Let us review briefly the state of faith in the followers of Jesus after His death.

Mary Magdalene, Joanna, Mary the mother of James and other women had stopped believing in the resurrection of Christ when they went to the tomb on the third day to anoint His body (Lk. 23:55, 56; 24:1, 10). Upon arrival, they found the stone rolled away and the tomb empty. Instead of believing that He had risen from the dead, they were *much perplexed* about what had taken place (24:4). Suddenly two angels appeared and asked, *Why seek ye the living among the dead* (24:5)? It wasn't that they hadn't been told, for the angels said:

> He is not here, but is risen: remember how he spake unto you when he was yet in Galilee, saying, The Son of man must be delivered into the hands of sinful men, and be crucified, and the third day rise again (24:6, 7).

They remembered that Jesus had said these things but they hadn't come to the tomb that day in belief.

The women returned and reported to the eleven apostles and to all the rest of the disciples with them. Their response was that the women were spreading *idle tales* and they also professed unbelief that He had risen from the dead (24:9, 11). But, just in case there might be some truth to the report, Peter ran toward the sepulchre to investigate their story. When he found the tomb empty, with the linen wraps laid neatly, he still did not consider the probability of a resurrection; instead, he walked away *wondering in himself at that which was come to pass* (Lk. 24:12).

Next, we see two disciples on the road to Emmaus recounting the recent events that led to the crucifixion of Christ (Lk. 24:13, 14). Jesus suddenly appeared to them in supernatural disguise and inquired about their conversation and their apparent sadness (24:16, 17). The two disciples professed to Him that Jesus was at least a prophet

(24:19).[43] This was the wrong answer. To add insult to injury, the two then professed that they had at a previous time believed that He would be the prophesied redeemer of Israel (24:21). Their sadness also betrayed their unbelief in the reports of the women and that their own inspection of the empty tomb had left them unconvinced of His resurrection (24:22-24). At this point Jesus called them *fools* and *slow of heart* to believe the OT prophets—*Ought not Christ to have suffered these things, and to enter into his glory* (24:25, 26)? Then Jesus began to expound all these truths to them from Moses and the Prophets.

When they came to the village of Emmaus, they constrained Jesus to be their guest for the evening (24:28, 29). Then suddenly a strange development occurred. As He sat as their guest at the evening meal, instead of waiting for the blessing and the food to be passed, He took the bread, *and blessed it, and brake, and gave to them* (24:30). Suddenly, something about this moment seems familiar. Ah, yes! The last Supper before Jesus died, *he took bread, and gave thanks, and brake it, and gave unto them, saying, This is my body which is given for you: this do in remembrance of me* (Lk. 22:19). As disciples, they would have doubtlessly heard of the events of the last supper from the other apostles. Instantly their eyes were opened; they recognized Him, and He disappeared before their eyes (24:31). The lapse of faith had ended and they were back into intimate communion with the Savior.

Subsequently, the two disciples returned to Jerusalem and reported their experience to the eleven apostles and the disciples who were with them. This group was still wallowing in their own unbelief when Jesus suddenly appeared in the midst of them and said, *Peace be unto you* (24:33-36). Still, instead of being uplifted and strengthened in faith, they were fearful and concluded that they were seeing a ghost (24:37). Jesus read their minds and questioned their unbelief. Then He offered them objective, empirical evidence that he was not a ghost, saying: *Behold my hands and my feet, that it is I myself: handle me, and see; for a spirit hath not flesh and bones, as ye see me have* (24:39, 40).

---

[43] When Jesus had previously asked the disciples whom men said that He was, they answered that it was generally thought that He was a prophet (Matt. 16:13, 14). This was the wrong answer. But when Jesus asked: *whom say ye that I am?*, Peter gave the only correct answer: *Thou art the Christ, the Son of the living God* (16:15, 16). Jesus had previously said to the scribes and Pharisees: *...if ye believe not that I am he, ye shall die in your sins* (Jn. 8:24).

This is embarrassing indeed, for after investigating the empirical evidence, they were still in a state of unbelief: *And while they yet believed not...*(24:41). Then Jesus asked for a piece of their broiled fish and a honeycomb and ate it before them as further proof that He was not a spirit (24:41-43). Jesus reminded the disciples that He had predicted all of this to them before His crucifixion, including His death and resurrection (24: 44-47). At this point Jesus told these *lapsed* disciples that they are to be *witnesses of these things* without mentioning a period of probation.

For some reason, Thomas was not with them on this occasion (Jn. 20:24), but when the disciples reported to him that they had seen the Lord he said: *except I shall see in his hands the print of the nails, and put my finger into the print of the nails, and thrust my hand into his side, I will not believe* (Jn. 20:25). Eight days later, Jesus walked through a closed door and invited Thomas to indeed put his finger into the nail prints and thrust his hand into His side. Then He said to Thomas: *be not faithless, but believing* (Jn. 20:27).

When the Apostle Paul was given legal authority to punish and even execute Christians, he successfully compelled many of them to blaspheme Christ (Acts 26:10, 11), but there is no scriptural record of their rebaptism. Paul had personally won the Galatians to the grace of Christ, but they later left him and embraced another gospel (Gal. 1:6, 7). There is no record of their rebaptism upon returning to fellowship with Paul.

These men had not lost their salvation; they had no need of rebaptism; they had not forfeited their ministries; but they had fallen into a state of unbelief and denial. Yet Jesus said: *And this is the Father's will which hath sent me, that of all which he hath given me I should lose nothing, but should raise it up again at the last day* (Jn. 6:39). This describes a permanent transaction that was certain to the believer at the moment of faith—

> And this is the will of him that sent me, that every one which seeth the Son, and believeth on him, may have everlasting life: and I will raise him up at the last day (Jn. 6:40).

Numerous contemporary evangelical scholars argue that the NT uses the Greek term for the verb *belief* in the present tense, meaning that, by God's sovereign will, it cannot lapse. It is argued that if the original act of belief in Christ as the sole source of saving grace and mercy were a one-time transaction, it would be in the aorist tense.[44] But John 4:39, 41; 10:42; and 11:45 do use the term *pisteuo* ("believe") in the aorist tense as if it were a one time, permanent transaction. We observe the aorist of the same verb again in Acts 14:1; 16:31; Rom. 4:3; I Cor. 15:11; Gal. 3:6; and James 2:23. This question cannot be resolved by studying the tenses of the verb, for both tenses are used interchangeably. The solution is in the dozens of cases of lapsed faith we have just observed in Lk. 24 and Jn. 20.

Jesus said that there was never a greater prophet born of woman than John the Baptist. He saw the Holy Spirit descend on Jesus and proclaimed Him to be the Lamb of God which would take away the sin of the world. He was a confirmed believer. Yet, being overwhelmed with doubt, he became agnostic in his prison cell. Therefore, he sent two of his disciples to ask Jesus if He was the Christ or whether they should be looking for someone else (Matt. 11:2, 3). This was a lapse of faith, but if he had died at that moment he would have awakened in Paradise. His salvation was not contingent upon an unbroken continuation of his original act of faith. And again, what of the Galatians who were *so soon removed from him that called you into the grace of Christ unto another gospel*? This is not a continuing faith in the one true gospel.

A slight breath of fresh air surfaces in the Cyprian/Novation controversy through *A Treatise Against The Heretic Novation By An Anonymous Bishop* found in the appendix of Vol. V, *Ante-Nicene Fathers*. The writer was certainly a contemporary of Cyprian and wrote in the early part of the reign of Valerian (A.D. 254-256). Most scholars believe him to have been an African. We will call him the *Unknown Bishop*. He attempts to cite all the major Bible cases of lapses in faith, illustrates the fact that God was willing to restore them to communion

---

[44] John F. MacArthur, Jr, *The Gospel According To Jesus* (Grand Rapids, Michigan: Academie Books, Zondervan Publishing House, 1988), p. 172..."The continuing nature of saving faith is underscored by the use of the present tense of the Greek verb *pisteuo* ('believe') throughout the gospel of John (cf. 3:15-18, 36; 5:24; 6:35, 40, 47; 7:38; 11:25-26; 12:44, 46; 20:31; also Acts 10:43; 13:39; Romans 1:16; 3:22; 4:5; 9:33; 10:4, 10-11). If believing were a one-time act, the Greek tense in those verses would be aorist."

immediately upon repentance, and then concludes with an exhortation to Novation:

> And now blush if thou canst, Novation; cease to deceive the unwary with thy impious arguments; cease to frighten them with the subtlety of one particular. We read, and adore, and do not pass over the heavenly judgment of the Lord, where he says that He will deny him who denies Him. But does this mean the penitent? And why should I be taking pains so long to prove individual cases of mercies? Since the mercy of God is not indeed denied to the Ninevites, although strangers, and placed apart from the law of the Lord, when they beseech it on account of the overthrow announced to their city. Nor to Pharoah himself, resisting with sacrilegious boldness, when formerly he was stricken with plagues from heaven, and turning to Moses and to his brother, said, "Pray to the Lord for me, for I have sinned." At once the anger of God was suspended from him. And yet thou, O Novation, judgest and declarest that the lapsed have no hope of peace and mercy.[45]

However, the greatest breath of fresh air for this period comes from another *Anonymous Treatise On Re-baptism*. Internal evidence indicates that the writer was a bishop. It was probably written while the baptismal controversy was still in contest. The treatise is an attack on the definition of a heretic and upon the rebaptism of anyone who had been baptized as a believer. The writer understands the difference between ritual baptism and Holy Spirit baptism into the Body of Christ and affirms that belief, and not ritual baptism, appropriates remission of sins from Christ:

> And further, as you are not ignorant, the Holy Spirit is found to have been given to men who believe, by the Lord without baptism of water, as is contained in the Acts of the Apostles after this manner: "While Peter was still speaking these words, the Holy Ghost fell

---

[45] Ibid., *Ante-Nicene Fathers, A Treatise Against The Heretic Novation By an Anonymous Bishop*, Vol. V, pp. 660, 661.

upon all them who heard the word. And they who were of the circumcision which believed were astonished, as many as came with Peter because that on the Gentiles also was poured out the gift of the Holy Spirit. For they heard them speak with their tongues, and they magnified God. Then answered Peter, Can any man forbid water, that these should not be baptized who have received the Holy Ghost as well as we? And he commanded them to be baptized in the name of Jesus Christ." Even as Peter also subsequently most abundantly taught us about the same Gentiles, saying: "And He put no difference between us and them, their hearts being purified by faith." And there will be no doubt that men may be baptized with the Holy Ghost without water,--as thou observest that these were baptized before they were baptized with water; that the announcements of both John and of our Lord Himself were satisfied,-- forasmuch as they received the grace of the promise both without the imposition of the apostle's hands and without the laver, which they attained afterwards. And their hearts being purified, God bestowed upon them at the same time, in virtue of their faith, remission of sins; so that the subsequent baptism conferred upon them this benefit alone, that they received also the invocation of the name of Jesus Christ, that nothing might appear to be wanting to the integrity of their service and faith.[46]

This unknown author uses the Apostles themselves as an argument against Cyprian's and Novation's concepts of rebaptismal salvation when he writes:

...but all the disciples, to whom, though already baptized, the Lord afterwards says, that "all ye shall be offended in me," all of whom, as we observe, having amended their faith, were baptized after the Lord's resurrection with the Holy Spirit...the baptism of

---

[46] Ibid., *Ante-Nicene Fathers, A Treatise on Re-Baptism By An Anonymous Writer*, Vol. V, pp. 669, 670.

water, which is of less account provided that afterwards a sincere faith in the truth is evident in the baptism of the Spirit, which undoubtedly is of greater account.[47]

We will now give the reader a lengthy quotation which will be redundant to this present chapter. This quotation is such a rare find for this period of history in that it demonstrates why believers, who are subsequently ritually baptized, need never be rebaptized—

> And so there was this same presumption concerning Christ in the mind of the disciples, even as Peter himself, the leader and chief of the apostles, broke forth into that expression of his own incredulity. For when he, together with the others, had been asked by the Lord what he thought about Him, that is, whom he thought Him to be, and had first of all confessed the truth, saying that He was the Christ the Son of the living God, and therefore was judged blessed by Him because he had arrived at this truth, not after the flesh, but by the revelation of the heavenly Father; yet this same Peter, when Jesus began to show His disciples that He must go to Jerusalem, and suffer many things from the elders, and priests, and scribes and be killed, and after the third day rise again from the dead; nevertheless that true confessor of Christ, after a few days, taking Him aside, began to rebuke Him, saying, "Be propitious to thyself: this shall not be;" so that on that account he deserved to hear from the Lord, "Get thee behind me, Satan; thou art an offence unto me, because he savoured not the things which are of God, but those things which are of men." Which rebuke against Peter became more and more apparent when the Lord was apprehended, and, frightened by the damsel, he said, "I know not what thou sayest, neither know I thee;" and again, when using an oath, he said this same thing; and for the third time, cursing and swearing, he affirmed that he knew not the man, and not once, but frequently denied Him. And this

---

[47] Ibid., Vol. V, p. 671.

disposition, because it was to continue to him even to the Lord's passion, was long before made manifest by the Lord, that we also might not be ignorant of it. Again, after the Lord's resurrection, one of His disciples, Cleopas, when he was, according to the error of all his fellow-disciples, sorrowfully telling what had happened to the Lord Himself, as if to some unknown person, spoke thus, saying of Jesus the Nazarene, "who was a prophet mighty in deed and in word before God and all the people; how the chief priests and our rulers delivered Him to be condemned to death, and fastened Him to the cross. But we trusted that it had been He which should have redeemed Israel." And in addition to these things, all the disciples also judged the declaration of the women who had seen the Lord after the resurrection to be idle tales; and some of them, when they had seen Him, believed not, but doubted; and they who were not then present believed not at all until they had been subsequently by the Lord Himself in all ways rebuked and reproached; because His death had so offended them that they thought that He had not risen again, who they had believed ought not to have died, because contrary to their belief He had died once. And thus, as far as concerns the disciples themselves, they are found to have had a faith neither sound nor perfect in such matters as we have referred to; and what is much more serious, they moreover baptized others, as it is written in the Gospel according to John.[48]

To prove that belief in Christ alone appropriates salvation prior to ritual baptism, this unknown author uses the case of one who believes and is martyred before he can be baptized:

> And what wilt thou determine against the person of him who hears the word, and haply taken up in the name of Christ, has at once confessed, and has been punished before it has been granted him to be baptized with water? Wilt thou declare him to have perished

---

[48] Ibid., Vol. V, p. 672.

> because he has not been baptized with water? Or, indeed, wilt thou think that there may be something from without that helps him to salvation, although he is not baptized with water? They thinking him to have perished will be opposed by the sentence of the Lord, who says "Whosoever shall confess me before men, him will I also confess before my Father which is in heaven;" because it is no matter whether he who confesses for the Lord is a hearer of the word or a believer, so long as he confesses that same Christ whom he ought to confess..."[49]

Arguing that the baptism of the Holy Spirit is independent of and distinct from ritual baptism, the unknown author writes:

> Which Spirit also filled John the Baptist even from his mother's womb; and it fell upon those who were with Cornelius the centurion before they were baptized with water. Thus, cleaving to the baptism of men, the Holy Spirit either goes before or follows it; or failing the baptism of water, it falls upon those who believe.[50]

He also argues that salvation through faith suffices for future sins as well, without the necessity of another salvation and that souls are washed through faith in Christ's blood and not by water baptism:

> But neither should I omit that which the Gospel well announces. For our Lord says to the paralytic man, "Be of good cheer, my son, thy sins are forgiven thee." That he might show that hearts were purified by faith for the forgiveness of sins that should follow. And this remission of sins that woman also which was a sinner in the city obtained, to whom the Lord said, "Thy sins are forgiven thee." And when they who were reclining around began to say among themselves,

---

[49] Ibid., Vol. V. p. 673. The unknown author qualifies this statement by affirming that the mere speaking of the name of Jesus will count for nothing unless the speaker already has Christ within, having received Him as personal Savior: "Therefore nobody can confess Christ without His name, nor can the name of Christ avail any one for confession without Christ Himself."

[50] Ibid., Vol. V, p. 676.

> "Who is this that forgiveth sins?"—because concerning the paralytic the scribes and Pharisees had murmured crossly—the Lord says to the woman, "Thy faith hath made thee whole; go in peace." From all which things it is shown that hearts are purified by faith, but that souls are washed by the Spirit; further, also, that bodies are washed by water, and moreover that by blood we may more readily attain at once to the rewards of salvation.[51]

One thing this document demonstrates for certain is that the view of salvation by grace through faith, totally distinct from ritual baptism, is a tradition as old as the *baptismal regenerationist* view itself. This unknown author, as pertaining to the gospel, had more in common with contemporary Baptists and numerous other advocates of *believer's baptism* than the Anabaptists, Cyprian and Novation.

Another point that should be made before moving forward in our discussion, is that fleeing to escape persecution and martyrdom is not necessarily an act of cowardice or a denial of our Lord. This point was eloquently addressed by Peter, Bishop of Alexandria [A.D. 260-300-311] in his *Canonical Epistle*:

> Hence neither is it lawful to accuse those who have left all, and have retired for the safety of their life, as if others had been held back by them. For at Ephesus also they seized Gaius and Aristarchus instead of Paul, and rushed to the theatre, these being Paul's companions in travel [Acts 19:26-30], and he wishing himself to enter into the people, since it was by reason of his having persuaded them, and drawing away a great multitude to the worship of the true God, that the tumult arose. "The disciples suffered him not," he says, "Nay, moreover, certain of the chief of Asia,

---

[51] Ibid., Vol. V, p. 677. His reference to forgiveness of sins that were to follow pertains to salvation rather than to fellowship with Christ and chastisement. Unrepentant Christians who have been born again will lose fellowship with Christ and bring upon themselves His severe chastisement but they do not lose their salvation for they are still brethren in Christ (I Cor. 3:1-3; Rom. 12:1, 2).

who were his friends, sent unto him, desiring him that he would not adventure himself into the theatre." But if any persist in contending with them, let them apply their minds with sincerity to him who says, "Escape for thy life; look not behind thee" [Gen. 19:17]. Let them recall to their minds also how Peter, the chief of the apostles "was thrown into prison, and delivered to four quaternions of soldiers to keep him" [Acts 12:4]; of whom, when he had escaped by night, and had been preserved out of the hand of the Jews by the commandment of the angel of the Lord, it is said, "As soon as it was day, there was no small stir among the soldiers, what was become of Peter. And when Herod had sought for him, and found him not, he examined the keepers and commanded that they should be put to death" [Acts 12:18, 19], on account of whom no blame is attributed to Peter; for it was in their power, when they saw what was done, to escape, just as also all the infants in Bethlehem [Matt. 2:13-16], and all the coast thereof, might have escaped, if their parents had known what was going to happen. These were put to death by the murderer Herod, in order to secure the death of one infant whom he sought, which infant itself also escaped at the commandment of the angel of the Lord... The Magi... "being warned of God in a dream," he says, "that they should not return to Herod, they departed into their own country another way" [Matt. 2:11-13]... Together with whom, having sought to kill another infant that had been previously born, and not being able to find him, he slew *the child's* father Zacharias between the temple and the altar, the child having escaped with his mother Elisabeth [Matt. 23:35]. Whence these men that have withdrawn themselves are not at all to be blamed.[52]

Notwithstanding, the *baptismal regeneration* theory continued to dominate church history. When Dionysius [A.D. 200-265] was

---

[52] Ibid., *Ante-Nicene Fathers, The Canons of the Blessed Peter, Archbishop of Alexandria, As They Are Given In His Sermon On Penitence*, Vol. VI, pp. 277, 278.

Historical Overview Of The Baptismal Regeneration Tradition

bishop of Alexandria he spoke of the decisions of the councils on the subject of baptism:

> For, indeed, in the most considerable councils of the bishops, as I hear, it has been decreed that they who come from heresy should first be trained in Catholic doctrine, and then should be cleansed by baptism from the filth of the old and impure leaven.[53]

We have the remains of an uncommon work called *The Acts Of Xanthippe And Polyxena*.[54] Section XXI describes the conversion of one Probus as follows:

> Then Probus arising from the ground fell again upon the couch, and arising early he came to Paul, and finding him baptising many in the name of the life-giving Trinity, he said, My lord Paul, if only I were worthy to receive baptism, behold the hour. Paul said to him, Son, behold the water is ready for the cleansing of those that come to Christ. Therefore immediately taking off his garments, and Paul laying hold of him, he leapt into the water, saying, Jesus Christ, son of God, and everlasting God, let all my sins be taken away by this water.[55]

Methodius [A.D. 260-312] had served simultaneously as bishop of Olympus and Parara, in Lycia before becoming a martyr. The only complete work of his that we have is his *Banquet of the Ten Virgins*, wherein he praises the *virginal life*. Chapter VI addresses *the works of the Church, the bringing forth of children in baptism; the moon in baptism, the full moon of Christ's passion*. Of baptism he wrote:

---

[53] Ibid., *Ante-Nicene Fathers, Works of Dionysius—Extant Fragments, Part II—containing Epistles, or Fragments of Epistles [Epistle vi—To Sixtus, Bishop]*, Vol. VI, p. 102.

[54] This work was edited from the original Greek text in *Text and Studies*, Vol. II, No 3 (1893), by Montague Rhodes James, M.A., from an eleventh century manuscript originating from Paris.

[55] Ibid., *Ante-Nicene Fathers, The Acts Of Xantheppe and Polyxena*, Vol. X, p. 211. This work is a religious novel based upon the belief that St. Paul actually did visit Spain according to the intention expressed by him in Romans 15:24.

> Now the statement that she stands upon the moon, as I consider, denotes the faith of those who are cleansed from corruption in the laver *of regeneration...*
>
> [Chapter VII] So that you also must confess that the Church labours and gives birth to those who are baptized.[56]

There is also an ancient work entitled *Constitutions Of The Holy Apostles.* The first six books are the oldest. The seventh and eighth books are later but it is generally agreed that the entire work is not later than the fourth century. In section xv of Book VI it is written:

> Nay, he that, out of contempt, will not be baptized, shall be condemned as an unbeliever, and shall be reproached as ungrateful and foolish. For the Lord says: "Except a man be baptized of water and of the spirit, he shall by no means enter into the kingdom of God" [Jn. 3:5].[57]

Section xliii of Book VII describes how a priest is to pray that Christ and His saving grace will enter the water of baptism and thus regenerate the candidate there:

> Moreover, he adores the only begotten God Himself, after His Father, and for Him giving Him thanks that He undertook to die for all men by the cross, the type of which He has appointed to be the **baptism of regeneration**... Him, therefore, let the priest even now call upon in baptism, and let him say: Look down from heaven, and sanctify this water, and give it grace and power, that so he that is to be baptized, according to the command of Thy Christ, may be crucified with Him and may die with Him, and may be buried with Him, and may rise with Him to the adoption which is

---

[56] Ibid., *Ante-Nicene Fathers, Methodius: Concerning Chastity* [chaps. VI, VII], Vol. VI, pp. 336, 337.
[57] Ibid., *Ante-Nicene Fathers, Constitutions Of The Holy Apostles*, Book VI, Section XV, Vol. VII, pp. 456, 457.

in Him, that he may be dead to sin and live to righteousness.[58] [Emphasis added].

There is within the Psuedo-Clementine Literature no definite conclusion as to who the author is. A passage from the *Recognitions of Clement* is quoted by Origen in his *Commentary on Genesis* [A.D. 231]. Chapter VIII of *Recognitions* states:

> For he who is regenerated by water, having filled up the measure of good works, is made heir of Him by whom he has been regenerated in incorruption... And do you suppose that you can have hope towards God, even if you cultivate all piety and all righteousness, but do not receive baptism.

> [Also Chapter IX] ...When you are regenerated and born again of water and of God, the frailty of your former birth, which you have through men, is cut off, and so at length you shall be able to attain salvation; but otherwise it is impossible.[59]

Again in the *Clementine Homilies*, Chapter VIII we read:

> And this is the service He has appointed: To worship Him only, and trust only in the Prophet of truth, and to be baptized for the remission of sins, and thus by this pure baptism to be born again unto God by saving water...[60]

Eusebius of Caesarea [c. 265-c. 339] was famous for his *Ecclesiastical History* [c. 325]. His greatest influence was perhaps his defense of the *Constantinian revolution.* In his *Life of Constantine*, [Chap. LXII.] he quotes Constantine requesting baptism and making his own comment:

---

[58] Ibid., *Ante-Nicene Fathers, Constitutions Of The Holy Apostles,* Book VII, Section XLIII.
[59] Ibid., *Ante-Nicene Fathers, Recognitions of Clement*, Vol. VIII, pp. 154-155.
[60] Ibid., *Ante-Nicene Fathers, The Clementine Homilies*, Vol. VIII, p. 269.

> "The time is arrived which I have long hoped for, with an earnest desire and prayer that I might obtain the salvation of God. The hour is come in which I too may have the blessing of that seal which confers immortality; the hour in which I may receive the seal of salvation. I had thought to do this in the waters of the river Jordan, wherein our Saviour, for our example, is recorded to have been baptized: But God, who knows what is expedient for us, is pleased that I should receive this blessing here. Be it so, then, without delay." ...Thus was Constantine the first of all sovereigns who was regenerated and perfected in a church dedicated to the martyrs of Christ.[61]

Gregory of Nyssa [C. 335-95] was the youngest of three Cappadocian Fathers and helped to bring about the victory of Nicene orthodoxy over Arianism. Concerning Arians who denied the deity and perfection of Christ, he wrote:

> Why are they baptized into Christ, if He has no power of goodness of His own? God forgive me for saying it! Why do they believe in the Holy Ghost if the same account is given of Him? How are they regenerate by baptism from their mortal birth, if the regenerating power does not pass in its own nature infallibility and independence.[62]

Gregory of Nazainzen [c. 329-390], also known as Gregory the Theologian, was another of the three great Cappadocian Fathers (Basil being the third). His forty-five orations leaves him a legacy of being one of the best orators of antiquity. In his Oration XL, *On Holy Baptism* [Sections ii & iv] he states:

---

[61] *Nicene and Post-Nicene Fathers: Eusebius*, Philip Schaff, D.D., LL.D., and Henry Wace, D.D., Editors (Grand Rapids, Michigan: Wm. B. Eerdmans Publishing Company, 1979), Vol. 1, p. 556.

[62] Ibid., *Nicene and Post-Nicene Fathers*, Gregory of Nyssa: *Dogmatic treatises, etc.* [Book I.23] *Against Eunomius*, Vol. V, p. 62.

> The Word recognizes three Births for us; namely, the natural birth, that of Baptism, and that of the Resurrection...
>
> We call it, the Gift, the Grace, Baptism, Unction, Illumination, the generation, the Seal, and everything that is honourable...[63]

Ambrose [c. 339-397], Bishop of Milan, was one of the four Latin doctors of the Church. His life became a pattern of the discharge of episcopal duties. In his work entitled *Of The Holy Spirit* [Book III, Chap. XVIII.138] he wrote: *And it is not doubtful that sin is forgiven by means of baptism, but in baptism the operation is that of the Father and of the Son and of the Holy Spirit.*[64] In *Concerning Repentance* [Book II, Chap. II.8] he wrote: *...we are renewed by means of the laver of baptism...as we being dead to sin are through the Sacrament of Baptism born again to God, and created anew.*[65]

John Chrysostom [347-407] was Patriarch of Constantinople and a renowned preacher and commentator of the Bible. There was a time in his ministry where he appears to affirm that remission of sins is received directly from God to the believer without human mediation of any kind. In his *Two Instructions To Candidates For Baptism* [Second Instruction.4] he writes:

> And not only is this the wonderful thing that he remits our sins, but that he not even reveals them nor makes them manifest and patent, nor compels us to come forward into the midst, and to tell out our errors, but bids us make our defense to him alone, and to confess ourselves to him...But one thing alone he seeks, that he who enjoys this remission should learn the greatness of the gift.[66]

---

[63] Ibid., *Nicene and Post-Nicene Fathers*, Gregory of Nazainzen [Oration XL. 1, 4, *On Holy Baptism*] Vol. VII, p. 360.

[64] Ibid., *Nicene and Post-Nicene Fathers,* St. Ambrose [*Of The Holy Spirit*—Book III, Chap. XVIII.138] Vol. X, p. 154.

[65] Ibid., Vol. X, p. 346.

[66] Ibid., *Nicene and Post-Nicene Fathers: The Works Of St. Chrysostom*, Vol. IX, p. 168.

Yet, in his *Third Homily On First Corinthians* Chrysostom states: *and without baptism it is impossible to obtain the kingdom.*[67] In his *Seventh Homily* [19.] he calls baptism the *Laver of regeneration*[68] and in his *Second Homily On Second Corinthians* [9.], *the regeneration of the laver.*[69] In the *Sixth Homily* he calls it a life-giving grace[70] and in the *Seventh Homily* he taught that baptism confers righteousness upon sinners.[71] His *Commentary on Galatians* states that baptism regenerates, washes and makes us sons of God.[72] In his *Fourth Homily on Ephesians* he states that *He doeth away iniquity here, both by the laver of Baptism, and by penitence.*[73] In his *Second Homily on I Timothy* he calls baptism an anointing and a sweet savor perfume.[74] In his *Thirty-Fourth Homily on St. John* he affirms that baptism buries sin.[75] In the *Fifty-Third Homily* this washing is the only cure for sin,[76] and finally in *Homily LXXIII* it is the *font* that *cleanseth* and wipes off filthiness.[77]

Gregory the Great (c. 540-603), the See of Rome, played an active role in the expansion of the church to England, Spain, Gaul and North Italy. In his *Epistle XLV* he affirmed:

> But, if there are any who say that sins are only superficially put away in baptism, what can be more against the faith than such preaching, whereby they would fain undo the very sacrament of faith, wherein principally the soul is bound to the mystery of heavenly cleanliness, that, being completely absolved from all sins, it may cleave to Him alone of Whom the Prophet says, *But it is good for me to cleave to God*

---

[67] Ibid., Vol. XII, p. 12.
[68] Ibid., Vol. XII, p. 43.
[69] Ibid., Vol. XII, p. 284.
[70] Ibid., Vol. XII, p. 307.
[71] Ibid., Vol. XII, p. 310.
[72] Ibid., Vol. XIII, p. 4.
[73] Ibid., Vol. XIII, p. 69.
[74] Ibid., Vol. XIII, p. 415.
[75] Ibid., Vol. XIV, p. 121.
[76] Ibid., Vol. XIV, p. 190.
[77] Ibid., Vol. XIV, p. 270.

(Ps. lxxii, 28)?[78] ...Whosoever says, then, that sins are not entirely put away in baptism, let him say that the Egyptians did not really die in the Red Sea. But, if he acknowledge that the Egyptians really died, he must needs acknowledge that sins die entirely in baptism...In the Gospel the Lord says, *He that is washed needeth not to wash, but is clean every whit* (Joh. xiii.10). If therefore sins are not entirely put away in baptism, how is he that is washed clean every wit?[79]

The *Seven Ecumenical Councils of the Undivided Church* issued a mass of canons and dogmatic decrees. With these canons, several local synods received ecumenical acceptance. The *Synod of Laodicea*, in the fourth century in Phrygia Pacatiana, called *Laodicea of Lyeum* (not to be confused with *Laodicea in Syria*), established Canon III which stated: *He who has been recently baptized ought not to be promoted to the sacerdotal order.* But a note declaring an exception to this rule was also a statement regarding the belief in baptismal regeneration:

> Notwithstanding this provision, that light, Nectarius, just separated from the flock of the catechumens, when he had washed away the sins of his life in the divine font, now pure himself, he put on the most pure dignity of the episcopate, and at the same time became bishop of the Imperial City, and president of the Second Ecumenical Synod.[80]

Jerome [c. 347-420] was the author of the Vulgate Translation of the Bible into Latin. His writings portray the general, as well as the ecclesiastical, life of his time. It was the age of Ambrose and Augustine in the West, of Basil, the Gregories, and Chrysostom in the East. In his *Letter XVII* he repeats his own profession of faith to Marcus the presbyter saying: *Every day I am asked for my confession of faith, as*

---

[78] In *English Bible, lxxiii.28*.
[79] Ibid., *Nicene and Post-Nicene Fathers,* Part II, *Epistles Of St. Gregory The Great* [Epistle XLV] Vol. XIII, p. 66.
[80] Ibid., *Nicene and Post-Nicene Fathers: The Seven Ecumenical Councils*, Vol. XIV, p. 126.

though when I was regenerated in baptism I had made none.[81] In his *Letter LXXIX* to Salvina [a lady of the imperial court] he spoke of sins being done away in baptism and of the *old man* being eradicated in Baptism. In this same letter he calls salvation the *grace of baptism.*[82] In *Letter CVII*, to a woman named Laeta who had written to Jerome regarding how she ought to bring up her infant daughter, he writes in return: *The truth is that, as baptism ensures the salvation of the child, this in turn brings advantage to the parents. Whether you would offer your child or not lay within your choice, but now that you have offered her, you neglect her at your peril.*[83] In *Letter CXXIII* to a woman named Ageruchia he affirms that regeneration is *through the baptismal laver.*[84] And in his *Letter CXLIV* to Optatus, regarding the origin of the soul, he affirmed that *it is necessary even for babies to be born anew in Christ by the grace of regeneration.*[85]

Augustine was born *Aurelius Augustinus* on Nov. 13, A.D. 354; began the study of rhetoric at Carthage in 371; converted to Christianity in 386; was baptized by Ambrose at Milan in 387; was ordained a priest at Hippo, North Africa in 391; and became the bishop of Hippo in 396. He was the intellectual head of the North African as well as the entire Western church of his time. R.C. Sproul says of Augustine:

> The influence of Augustine's thought on Luther is a matter of record. In Luther's account of his famous "tower experience," when he was awakened to the gospel of Justification by faith alone, He said this experience was triggered by reading a comment Augustine had written centuries earlier regarding the righteousness of God in Romans 1. The person John Calvin quoted more frequently than any other extra-biblical writer was Augustine. His teaching on grace fueled the Reformation and shaped Protestant theology for centuries. Augustine is generally regarded as the

---

[81] Ibid., *Nicene and Post-Nicene Fathers: The Principal Works of St. Jerome*, Vol. VI, p. 21.
[82] Ibid., Jerome, Vol. VI, pp. 163-168.
[83] Ibid., Jerome, Vol. VI, p. 192.
[84] Ibid., Jerome, Vol. VI, p. 234.
[85] Ibid., Jerome, Vol. VI, p. 287.

greatest theologian of the first millennium of Christian history, if not of all time.[86]

The Reformers would claim to be the true interpreters of Augustinianism which was to become the heart of the Protestant gospel. He was their theological champion. Perhaps this is why *baptismal regeneration* is the heart of many Protestant versions of the gospel of Christ. Even those who deny that they teach *baptismal regeneration* find in Augustine a champion for their faith. The *New Dictionary of Theology* says of Benjamin Warfield:

> When at the end of the century American Presbyterians debated whether to amend the Westminster Confession, ...Warfield responded with a series of careful studies on the meaning of that document. His own opinion never wavered: the Reformers of the 16th and 17th centuries had provided sound guidelines for the church...Warfield penned several careful monographs on the Confession, many penetrating studies of Calvin's thought, and a number of academic treatises on figures in the early church **(especially Augustine)**. All testified to his belief that the theological principles of these earlier periods were fully sufficient for the present. In 1904 he summed up the burden of these historical exercises: "Calvinism is just religion in its purity. We have only, therefore, to conceive of religion in its purity, and that is Calvinism" (*Selected Shorter Writings, I, p. 389*).[87]

Warfield wrote a lengthy introduction to Augustine's *Anti-Pelagian writings* wherein he strongly identifies with the fourth century theologian. He noted in his introduction that:

> Late in 417, or early in 418, the African bishops assembled at Carthage, in number more than two

---

[86] R.C. Sproul, *Willing to Believe: The Controversy Over Free Will* (Grand Rapids, Michigan: Baker Books, 1997), p. 50.
[87] *New Dictionary Of Theology*, Sinclair B. Ferguson, David F. Wright, Editors; J. I. Packer, Conculting Editor (Downers Grove, Illinois; Leicester, England: InterVarsity Press, 1988), p. 717.

hundred...The synod's nine canons part naturally into three triads. The first of these deals with the relation of mankind to original sin, and anathematizes in turn those who assert that physical death is a necessity of nature, and not a result of Adam's sin; those who assert that new-born children derive nothing of original sin from Adam to be expiated by the laver of regeneration;[88] and those who assert a distinction between the kingdom of heaven and eternal life, for entrance into the former of which alone baptism is necessary.[89]

Of the Pelagian debate Warfield said: *Both by nature and by grace, Augustin was formed to be the champion of truth in this controversy.*[90] Warfield analyses Augustine's treatise *On the Merits and Remission of Sins and on the Baptism of Infants*, consisting of two books written in 412.[91] He does not consider Augustine's *baptismal regenerationist* view as an offensive obstacle to his version of the gospel of grace. However, this does not imply that Warfield is to be associated with every minute view of Augustine's theology, even as Warfield himself writes:

> The saddest corollary that flowed from this doctrine was that by which Augustin was forced to assert that all those who died unbaptized, including infants, are finally lost and depart into eternal punishment. He did not shrink from the inference, although he assigned the place of lightest punishment in hell to those who were

---

[88] Ibid., In the *Nicene and Post-Nicene Fathers* [series I] Augustine refers to ritual baptism as the *laver of regeneration* some fifty-five times. Perhaps to inspire a research paper on this concept, we will list the citations as follows: Vol. II, 18, 246, 429, 436, 464, 487; III, 386, 499: V, 24, 48, 195, 211, 237, 238, 244 253, 263, 268, 272, 273, 279, 284, 318, 329, 336, 339, 349, 350, 351, 361, 385, 386, 396, 404, 415, 417, 420, 432, 439, 449, 476, 513, 532, ; VI, 277, 320; VIII, 367, 573, 630. A laver is a container for water. In the OT it was a large copper vessel used in the tabernacle and the temple for priestly ablutions (Ex. 30:17-21). Solomon's Temple had 10 lavers made by Hiram of Tyre (I Ki. 7:30, 38).
[89] Ibid., *Nicene and Post-Nicene Fathers* [Series I], Vol. V, p. xx.
[90] Ibid., p. xxi.
[91] Ibid., p. xxiv.

> guilty of no sin but original sin, but who had departed this life without having washed this away in the "laver of regeneration." This is the dark side of his soteriology; but it should be remembered that it was not his theology of grace, but the universal and traditional belief in the necessity of baptism for remission of sins, which he inherited in common with all of his time, that forced it upon him.[92]

Although he considers Augustine his partner in the gospel of grace, Warfield takes a different view of the eternal destiny of unbaptized infants. He contrasts himself with Augustine on this point as follows:

> ...he believed that baptism and incorporation into the visible Church were necessary for salvation. And it is only because of Augustin's theology of grace, which places man in the hands of an all-merciful Saviour and not in the grasp of a human institution, that men can see that in the salvation of all who die in infancy, the invisible Church of God embraces the vast majority of the human race,--saved not by the washing of water administered by the Church, but by the blood of Christ administered by God's own hand outside of the ordinary channels of his grace. We are indeed born in sin, and those that die in infancy are, in Adam, children of wrath even as others; but God's hand is not shortened by the limits of his Church on earth, that it cannot save. In Christ Jesus, all souls are the Lord's, and only the soul that itself sinneth shall die (Ezek. xviii. 1-4).[93]

However, Warfield does not see a gospel conflict in this contrast of views but instead gives Augustine his highest endorsement when he wrote:

> No other of the fathers so conscientiously wrought out his theology from the revealed Word; no other of them so sternly excluded human additions... "We just first

---

[92] Ibid., p. lxx.
[93] Ibid., p. lxxi.

bend our necks to the authority of Scripture," he [Augustine] insists, "in order that we may arrive at knowledge and understanding through faith." And this was not merely his theory, but his practice. No theology was ever, it may be more broadly asserted, more conscientiously wrought out from the Scriptures.[94]

In Warfield's work on *Augustine and His "Confessions,"* he writes:

> But his doctrine of the Church and Sacraments had not yet given way before his doctrine of grace when he was called away from this world of partial attainment to the realms of perfect thought and life above…he touched on the problem raised by the notions of baptismal regeneration and the necessity of the intermediation of the Church for salvation in the face of his passionately held doctrine of the free grace of God, and worked out a sort of compromise between them. In one way or another he found a measure of contentment for his double mind. But this could not last. We may say with decision that it was due only to the shortness of human life; to the distraction of his mind with multifarious cares; to the slowness of his solid advance in doctrinal development—that the two elements of his thought did not come to their fatal conflict before his death. Had they done so there can be no question what the issue would have been.[95]

So, Warfield felt that if Augustine had lived one more decade he would no longer have held to baptismal regeneration:

> Had he been granted, perhaps, ten years longer of vigorous life, he might have thought his way through this problem also. He bequeathed it to the Church for solution, and the Church required a thousand years for

---

[94] Ibid., p. lxxi.
[95] Benjamin Warfield, *The Works of: Studies In Tertullian And Augustine* (Grand Rapids, Michigan: Baker Book House, 1981), Vol. IV, p. 284.

the task. But even so, it is Augustine who gave us the Reformation.[96]

In his work entitled *Augustine and the Pelagian Controversy*, Warfield writes:

> When Augustine comes to speak of the *means of grace*, i.e., of the channels and circumstances of its conference to men, he approaches the meeting point of two very dissimilar streams of his theology—his doctrine of grace and his doctrine of the Church... But he teaches that those who are thus lost out of the visible Church are lost because of some fatal flaw in their baptism, or on account of post-baptismal sins; and that those who are of the "called according to the purpose" are predestinated not only to salvation, but to salvation by baptism. Grace is not tied to the means in the sense that it is not conferred save in the means; but it is tied to the means in the sense that it is not conferred without the means. Baptism, for instance, is absolutely necessary for salvation: no exception is allowed except such as save the principle—baptism of blood (martyrdom), and, somewhat grudgingly, baptism of intention. And baptism, when worthily received, is absolutely efficacious: "if a man were to die immediately after baptism, he would have nothing at all left to hold him liable to punishment." In a word, while there are many baptized who will not be saved, there are none saved who have not been baptized;[97] it is the grace of God that saves, but

---

[96] Ibid., *Augustine And His "Confessions"*, Vol. IV, p. 285.

[97] John F. MacArthur, Jr., *Faith Works: The Gospel According to the Apostles* (Dallas: Word Publishing, 1993), pp. 207, 208. Although MacArthur affirms that baptism is not a condition of salvation but an act of obedience, he quotes C.H. Spurgeon thusly in defense of his position: "If the professed convert distinctly and deliberately declares that he knows the Lord's will, but does not mean to tend to it, you are not to pamper his presumptions, but it is your duty to assure him that he is lost." MacArthur makes this same point again when he writes: "Nevertheless, one can hardly read the New Testament without noticing the heavy stress the early church placed on baptism. They simply *assumed* that every genuine believer would embark on a life of obedience and discipleship. *(Continued on next page)*

baptism is a channel of grace without which none receive it...but it should be remembered that it was not his theology of grace, but the universal and traditional belief in the necessity of baptism for remission of sins, which he inherited in common with all of his time, that forced it upon him...he believed that baptism and incorporation into the visible Church were necessary for salvation.[98]

In contrast to Warfield, Augustine believed that the unbaptized infants of believers and unbelievers alike, who died in infancy, would spend eternity in hell because only baptism could remove original sin. In his *Treatise on the Merits and Forgiveness of Sins, and on the Baptism of Infants* [Book I, Chapter 33] he states: *Let there be then no eternal salvation promised to infants out of our own opinion, without Christ's baptism.*[99] [Book III, Chapters 21, 22] states:

> That there is no other valid means of making Christians and remitting sins, except by men becoming believers through the sacrament according to the institution of Christ and the Church...[22] But if we are taught to render help to orphans, how much more ought we to labour in behalf of those children who, though under the protection of parents, will still be left more destitute and wretched than orphans, should that grace of Christ be denied them, which they are all unable to demand for themselves?[100]

That was nonnegotiable. Therefore they viewed baptism as the turning point. Only those who were baptized were considered Christians. That is why the Ethiopian eunuch was so eager to be baptized (Acts 8:36-39). Unfortunately, the church today takes baptism more casually. It is not unusual to meet people who have been professing Christians for years but have never been baptized. That was unheard of in the New Testament church. Unfortunately, we have lost the focus on initial obedience."

[98] Ibid., Warfield, *Augustine And The Pelagian Controversy*, Vol. IV, p. 409-411.
[99] Ibid., *Nicene and Post-Nicene Fathers*, Vol. V, p. 29.
[100] Ibid., Vol. V, p. 78.

In fact, Augustine would have considered Warfield a heretic for believing that unbaptized infants would go to heaven upon death. In his treatise *On Marriage And Concupiscence* [Chapter 22] he wrote:

> Now the Christian faith unfalteringly declares, what our new heretics have begun to deny, both that they who are cleansed in the laver of regeneration are redeemed from the power of the devil, and that those who have not yet been redeemed by such regeneration are still captive in the power of the devil, even if they be infant children of the redeemed, unless they be themselves redeemed by the self-same grace of Christ...until they are redeemed therefrom by the laver of regeneration and the blood of Christ, and pass into their Redeemer's kingdom.[101]

In his work *On The Soul And Its Origin* [Chapter 12] Augustine says, *If you wish to be a catholic, refrain from believing, or saying, or teaching that 'infants which are forestalled by death before they are baptized may yet attain to forgiveness of their original sins.*[102] In refuting the errors of Victor [Chapter 20] he says:

> You, on the contrary, acknowledge that infants have original sin, and yet you absolve them from it without the laver of regeneration, and send them for a temporary residence in paradise, and subsequently permit them to enter even into the kingdom of heaven.[103]

Augustine was probably the most aggressive defender of *baptismal regeneration* in the ancient church. He calls baptism the *bath of regeneration*[104]; *baptismal regeneration*[105]; the *Sacrament of our*

---

[101] Ibid., Vol. V, p. 273. See also *On the Soul and its Origin* [Chap. 10], p. 319.
[102] Ibid., Vol. V, p. 348.
[103] Ibid., Vol. V, p. 351. See also *Against Two Letters Of The Pelagians* [Chaps. 6, 7, 11] Vol. V, pp. 394, 396.
[104] Ibid., Vol. V, pp. 122, 124.
[105] Ibid., Vol. I, pp. 131, 407, 408; Vol. IV, pp. 419, 497; Vol. V, pp. 47, 371, 394.

regeneration[106]; The *font of regeneration*[107]; and the *washing of regeneration.*[108] He insists that baptism is essential to salvation.[109] In *On The Soul And Its Origin* [Chapter 17] he states: *It is enough to find that no one can enter into the kingdom of God, except he be washed in the laver of regeneration*[110]; and that *...regeneration makes Christians.*[111]

Augustine is so certain of the efficacy of baptism that he affirmed the regeneration of one who was baptized for the wrong reason altogether:

> Some, indeed, bring their little ones for baptism, not in the believing expectation that they shall be regenerated unto life eternal by spiritual grace, but because they think that by this as a remedy the children may recover or retain bodily health; but let not this disquiet your mind, because their regeneration is not prevented by the fact that this blessing has no place in the intention of those by whom they are presented for baptism.[112]

However, according to Augustine, one can lose the grace of baptism by his own impiety—

> And thus, when the grace of Christ has been once received, the child does not lose it otherwise than by his own impiety, if when he becomes older, he turn out so ill. For by that time he will begin to have sins of his own, which cannot be removed by regeneration, but must be healed by other remedial measures.[113]

---

[106] Ibid., Vol. IV, pp. 189, 461; Vol. V, pp. 62, 63, 274, 322.
[107] Ibid., Vol. II, p. 487.
[108] Ibid., Vol. IV, p. 181; Vol. V, pp. 27, 320, 382, 392, 394, 404, 414, 426, 427, 432.
[109] Ibid., Vol. V, pp. 78, 337.
[110] Ibid., Vol. V, p. 350.
[111] Ibid., Vol. V, p. 75.
[112] Ibid., *Nicene and Post-Nicene Fathers, Letters of St. Augustin* [Letter xcviii.5] Vol. I, p. 408.
[113] Ibid., *Letters of St. Augustin* [Letter xcviii.2],Vol. I, p. 407.

Historical Overview Of The Baptismal Regeneration Tradition

This view is based on his belief in mortal and venial sin. Mortal sin must be avoided in order to guard one's baptism—

> When ye have been baptized, hold fast a good life in the commandments of God, that ye may guard your Baptism even unto the end. I do not tell you that ye will live here without sin; but they are venial, without which this life is not.[114]

Actually, for Augustine, there were three ways to remit sins—

> In three ways then are sins remitted in the Church; by Baptism, by prayer, by the greater humility of penance; yet God doth not remit sins but to the baptized. The very sins which He remits first, he remits not but to the baptized. When? When they are baptized. The sins which are after remitted upon prayer, upon penance, to whom He remits, it is to the baptized that He remitteth.[115]

Augustine believed that there was one other way to obtain remission of sins—i.e. the public confession of Christ by someone being martyred prior to the opportunity to be baptized, would wash away sin the same as baptism could have done.[116] In his sermon to the catechumens entitled *On The Creed* he could say: *Be baptized, and ye will be His temple* and *"forgiveness of sins." Ye have [this article of] the Creed perfectly in you when ye receive Baptism.*[117]

---

[114] Ibid., *Nicene and Post-Nicene Fathers, On The Creed: A Sermon to the Catechumens*, [Section 15] Vol. III, p. 374.

[115] Ibid., *On The Creed: A Sermon to the Catechumens*, [Section 16] Vol. III, p. 375.

[116] "For whatever unbaptized persons die confessing Christ, this confession is of the same efficacy for the remission of sins as if they were washed in the sacred font of baptism." *St Augustin's City Of God*, Translated by Rev. Marcus Dods, D.D., of Glasgow in *Nicene and Post-Nicene Fathers* [First Series], Philip Schaff, D.D., LL.D., Editor (Grand Rapids, Michigan: Wm. B. Eerdmans Publishing Company, 1977), Vol. II, p.248.

[117] Ibid., *Nicene And Post-Nicene Fathers* [First Series], Vol. III, p. 374.

Calvin favored Augustine partially because of his strong views on predestination. Augustine believed that all whom God elected in eternity past were also predestined to be baptized. In his work *On The Soul And Its Origin* [Chapter 38] he rebukes Victor for saying in effect that, *"They whom the Lord has predestinated to be baptized can be taken away from His predestination, or die before that has been accomplished in them which the Almighty had predetermined."* [118]

Describing the deathbed experience of a man named Curma, who had been having dream-like visions of Paradise, Augustine recorded his testimony as follows:

> He narrated how he had, moreover, been led into Paradise, and how it was there said to him, when he was thence dismissed to return to his own family, "Go, be baptized, if thou wilt be in this place of the blessed." Thereupon, being admonished to be baptized by me, he said it was done already. He who was talking with him replied, "Go, be truly baptized; for that thou didst but see in the vision." After this he recovered, went his way to Hippo. [119]

But what about the thief on the cross? He was not baptized, yet he was promised Paradise by the Lord Himself. Augustine will not let us use this argument because, he says it is credible to assume that when Christ was pierced in the side, some of the bodily fluid splashed onto the thief, thus baptizing him. Again, in his argument against Victor he wrote:

> Besides all this, there is the circumstance, which is not incredibly reported, that the thief who then believed as he hung by the side of the crucified Lord was sprinkled, as in a most sacred baptism, with the water which issued from the wound of the Saviour's side...only let no rule about baptism affecting the Saviour's own precept be taken from this example of the thief; and let no one promise for the case of unbaptized infants, between damnation and the

---

[118] Ibid., Vol. V, p. 371.
[119] Ibid., *On Care To Be Had For The Dead*, Vol. III, pp. 546, 547.

Historical Overview Of The Baptismal Regeneration Tradition

> kingdom of heaven, some middle place of rest and happiness, such as he pleases and where he pleases [*On The Soul And Its Origin,* Chapter 11].[120]

> As for the thief, although in God's judgment he might be reckoned among those who are purified by the confession of martyrdom, yet you cannot tell whether he was not baptized. For, to say nothing of the opinion that he might have been sprinkled with the water which gushed at the same time with the blood out of the Lord's side, as he hung on the cross next to Him, and thus have been washed with a baptism of the most sacred kind [Chapter 12].[121]

These were Augustine's arguments against Victor who had assured parents of dead children that their infants were with God—

> But when he wished to answer with respect, however, to those infants who are prevented by death from being first baptized in Christ, he was so bold as to promise them not only paradise, but also the kingdom of heaven,--finding no way else of avoiding the necessity of saying that God condemns to eternal death innocent souls, which, without any previous desert of sin, He introduces into sinful flesh. He saw, however, to some extent what evil he was giving utterance to, in implying that without any grace of Christ the souls of infants are redeemed to everlasting life, and the kingdom of heaven, and that in their case original sin may be cancelled without Christ's baptism, in which is effected the forgiveness of sins...no one becomes a member of Christ except it be either by baptism in Christ, or death for Christ [Chapter 10].[122]

It was not that ordinary water had the power to save. Augustine believed that when the priest consecrated the water, Christ and His Word entered the laver of liquid, thus waiting to regenerate the

---

[120] Ibid., Vol. V, p. 319.
[121] Ibid., Vol. V, p. 348.
[122] Ibid., Vol. V, p. 319.

unwilling infant. He writes: *"This is the word of faith which we preach,"* whereby baptism, doubtless, is also consecrated, in order to its possession of the power to cleanse *[On The Gospel Of John*, Tractate LXXX.3].[123]

Many theologians throughout church history were correct in their doctrines of election and predestination. However, it seems that some would interpret their own election as placing them above the laws of logic, enabling them to pontificate with totally contradictory premises and conclusions. When anyone pointed out the inconsistencies, they were informed of the smallness of their minds and addressed with degrading pejorative language. In the *Prolegomena* of the first of the eight volumes of Augustine's works,[124] we have this unique illustration:

> In great men, and only in great men, great opposites and apparently antagonistic truths, live together. Small minds cannot hold them. The catholic, churchly, sacramental, and sacerdotal system stands in conflict with the evangelical Protestant Christianity of subjective, personal experience. The doctrine of universal baptismal regeneration, in particular, which presupposes a universal call (at least within the church), can on principles of logic hardly be united with the doctrine of an absolute predestination, which limits the decree of redemption to a portion of the baptized. Augustine supposes, on the one hand, that every baptized person, through the inward operation of the Holy Ghost, which accompanies the outward act of the sacrament, receives the forgiveness of sins, and is translated from the state of nature into the state of grace, and thus, *qua baptizatus,* is also a child of God and an heir of eternal life; and yet, on the other hand, he makes all these benefits dependent on the absolute will of God, who saves only a certain number out of the "mass of perdition," and preserves these to the end. Regeneration and election, with him, do not, as with Calvin, coincide. The former may exist without the

---

[123] Ibid., Vol. VII, 345.
[124] Taken from Schaff's Church History, Revised Edition, New York 1884. Vol. III, pp. 988-1028.

latter, but the latter cannot exist without the former. Augustine assumes that many are actually born into the kingdom of grace only to perish again; Calvin holds that in the case of the non-elect baptism is an unmeaning ceremony.[125]

One can easily see that the evidence for *baptismal regeneration* is overwhelming in the writings of almost all the Church Fathers of the second through the fifth centuries. This provides cause for great confidence to those current advocates of ritual salvation as they see themselves as mainstream insiders while labeling advocates of *believer's baptism* as radical fringe groups. It is often assumed that these fringe sects are spin-offs of the mainstream and that their arguments are unsophisticated and based on inadequate biblical scholarship. Therefore, at this point of our study, we will evaluate some of the theological questions that advocates of *believer's baptism* ask as they search the Scriptures regarding this issue. But first, if regeneration can only take place in baptism or in martyrdom, then let us examine what biblical regeneration is in actuality.

We know from the Bible that regeneration is a point of translation from a state of nature to a state of grace (Eph. 2:1-6; Rom. 11:24; I Cor. 2:14,15). This translation occurs when one becomes born again and born from above (John 3:3, 7; I Pet. 1:3, 23). It is the moment when we are begotten of God (James 1:17, 18; I Pet. 1:3; I Jn. 5:1). It is the moment we receive the grace of God (Jn. 3:27; Eph. 2:8, 9). It is the moment when one partakes of the heavenly and high calling of God in Christ Jesus (II Pet. 1:3, 4; Heb. 3:1; Phil. 3:14). It is when one becomes a new creation, a new man, and a new born babe (Titus 3:5; II Cor. 5:17; Eph 4:24; I Pet. 2:2). It is when one receives a new heart (Jer. 24:7; Ez. 11:19; Acts 2:37; 4:32; 16:14; Rom. 10:10; Heb. 10:22). It is when one is *quickened* (Eph. 2:1; I Cor. 15:45; Jn. 6:63; Ps. 119:50, 93; I Pet. 3:18; Col. 2:13), previous to which one is spiritually dead while he yet lives. It is passing from death to life (Jn. 5:24). Prayer is the spiritual breath of a regenerate man. When Paul was regenerated it was observed, *Behold he prayeth* (Acts 9:11), who just before had been breathing out threatenings and slaughter against the disciples of Christ (Acts 9:1). Regeneration is when Christ is imprinted in the heart wherein the image of the second Adam is stamped (I Cor. 15:47-49).

---

[125] Ibid., *Nicene and Post-Nicene Fathers* [First Series], Vol. I, p. 23.

This is a conforming which takes place in regeneration (Rom. 8:29; Col. 3:10). It is when one becomes a partaker of the divine nature (II Pet. 1:4). It is when faith occurs (Acts 15:9). Without regeneration, no man can be translated into the kingdom of God. It is when the heart is circumcised (Rom. 2:29). It is God's gift of grace wherein He gives us life (Eph. 2:4, 5). It happens by the sovereign will of God (James 1:18). It is the result of God's abundant mercy (I Tim. 1:14). The instrumental cause of regeneration is the presentation of the Word of God (Rom. 10:17; I Pet. 1:23; James 1:18; I Cor. 4:15; Gal. 3:2). Three thousand were regenerated on the Day of Pentecost (Acts 2:37). The Samaritans were regenerated at the preaching of Philip (Acts 8:6).The Ethiopian Eunuch was regenerated in a chariot (Acts 8:36). The Philippian jailer was regenerated in the prison (Acts 16:29-31). The house of Cornelius was regenerated during the beginning of Peter's sermon (Acts 10:44-47).

Regeneration is an instantaneous event. It is not like progressive sanctification which is a work that carries on gradually. Faith grows, hope and love abound more and more, and spiritual light and knowledge increase by increments, till they come to the perfect day. But regeneration is an instantaneous event. Just as a natural infant is generated at an instance and is born on a particular day, so it is in spiritual regeneration. One man cannot be more regenerated than another, though he may be more experientially sanctified. One cannot be more regenerated at one time than at another.

The whole old man is unregenerate and remains the same even after regeneration takes place. However, the old man loses his right to dominion (Rom. 6:9, 14). The new man is wholly regenerate and remains the same. There is no sin in the new man, nor committed by him (I Jn. 3:9).

The grace of regeneration can never be lost, just as one born in the physical sense cannot return to his mother's womb and become unborn (Jn. 3:4), neither can one born again become un-born again for he is born of an incorruptible and immortal seed (I Pet. 1:23). And all such who are begotten again unto a lively hope of a glorious inheritance, are kept by the power of God, through faith unto salvation (I Pet. 1:3, 4, 5, 23; Jn. 10:27-29; Heb. 10:10-14).

If, as the majority of the Fathers of the second through the fifth centuries agree, regeneration cannot exist prior to baptism, then we should not expect anyone to be acting regenerated prior to that event.[126] We should never see the words *faith, believe,* or *repentance* applied to anyone in the NT prior to the *laver of regeneration*. Then why were all candidates for baptism in the NT required to believe and show signs of regeneration before the ritual would be administered? If Fathers of the second through the fifth centuries represent the true gospel of Christ, then why was not the NT adjusted to accommodate their view?

How could Jesus have said of the unbaptized centurian in Capernaum, *I have not found so great faith, no, not in Israel* (Matt. 8:10)? Why did He forgive the sins of the sick of the palsy without his baptism (9:6; Mk. 2:5)? Why did He say to the woman with the diseased issue, as she touched the hem of His garment, *thy faith hath made thee whole* (9:22)? How could He have touched the two blind men saying, *According to your faith be it unto you* (9:29)? When the woman of Canaan asked Him for mercy, how could he have said, *O woman, great is thy faith: be it unto thee even as thou wilt* (15:28)? How can these things be if it is so that no one can respond to Jesus in regeneration prior to baptism?

How could Simon and Andrew have forsaken all to become fishers of men prior to a "baptismal regeneration" (Mk. 1:15-18)? How

---

[126] John F. MacArthur, Jr., *Faith Works: The Gospel According to the Apostles* (Dallas: Word Publishing, 1993)...(p. 61) "But by transforming the heart, grace makes the believer wholly willing to trust and obey." (p. 62) "Furthermore, because of human depravity, there is nothing in a fallen, reprobate sinner that desires God or is capable of responding in faith." (Footnote 8, p. 62) "From the viewpoint of reason, regeneration logically must initiate faith and repentance. But the saving transaction is all a single, instantaneous event." (p. 65) "Unregenerate sinners have no life by which they can respond to spiritual stimuli. No amount of love, beseeching, or spiritual truth can summon a response. People apart from God are the ungrateful dead, spiritual zombies, death-walkers, unable to understand the gravity of their situation. They are lifeless."
See also: MacArthur, *The Gospel According to Jesus* (Grand Rapids, Michigan: Zondervan Publishing House, 1989), p. 33: "Thus salvation cannot be defective in any dimension. As a part of His saving work, God will produce repentance, faith, sanctification, yieldedness, obedience, and ultimately glorification. Since He is not dependent on human effort in producing those elements, an experience that lacks any of them cannot be the saving work of God."
Note: These statements accurately portray the positions of many, but not all, contemporary Reformed theologians.

could James and John have left their ship, nets, hired servants, and father to go after Jesus prior to their "baptismal regeneration" (1:19, 20)? Why did Jesus heal the son with the foul deaf and dumb spirit when the father cried, *Lord, I believe; help thou mine unbelief* (Mk. 9:24)? How could Jesus have placed belief before baptism in Mk. 16:16 if so be that regeneration cannot take place until baptism? How could Jesus have said *believe only* to the parents of the dead daughter when He raised her from the dead (Lk. 8:50)? Shouldn't the regeneration of baptism have factored somewhere into these faith experiences rather than afterwards?

Why does John equate *received* with *believe* if so be that one can only receive Christ in ritual baptism (Jn. 1:12)? Why did John say that belief results in not perishing and in taking possession of eternal life (3:15, 16)? Why is condemnation the result of not believing rather than the result of not being baptized (3:18; Mk. 16:17)? Why does the wrath of God abide on those who believe not rather than on those who are baptized not (3:36)? Why did Jesus offer the gift of the living water of everlasting life to the Samaritan woman at the well and how could she have accepted it without being baptized (4:10-15); and how could she have won others to Christ prior to her own "baptismal regeneration" (vs. 39)? How can it be said that those who hear the Word and believe on Christ have everlasting life; have escaped condemnation, and have passed from death unto life if this can only happen in baptism (5:24)? How can belief alone partake of the bread of life and the water of life (6:35)? How could Christ guarantee the glorious resurrection of those who believed on Him (5:40)? How could He have promised that to believe is to possess eternal life (6:47)? How could *many people* have *believed on Him* without a "baptismal regeneration" (7:31)? How can rivers of living water flow from the belly of one who simply believes on Christ (7:38)? How could Jesus tell the Jews that the truth would make them free without mentioning baptism (8:31, 32)? Why did He accept the faith and worship of the man born blind without him first being baptized (9:38)? How could He have said to Martha: *Whosoever liveth and believeth in me shall never die* without mentioning baptism (11:25, 26)? How could Jesus have promised that believing the written Word of God would bring life through His name if eternal life requires belief and literal water (20:30, 31)? How could so many Jews become believers on Him at the raising of Lazarus without their becoming baptized first (11:45; 12:11)? How could Jesus tell people that they had the Light, could believe the Light, and become children of the Light without mentioning baptism (12:36)?

Historical Overview Of The Baptismal Regeneration Tradition

How did the three thousand souls on the Day of Pentecost gladly receive God's word before they were baptized (Acts 2:41)? How did the lame man find wholeness on the Temple steps through faith without first being baptized (3:16)? How did thousands believe on Jesus when Peter and John, the preachers through whom they believed, were in jail and could not immediately baptize them (4:4)? How could the Samaritans have responded in belief to Philip's preaching without first being baptized (Acts 8:12)? How could so many people believe on the Lord upon hearing that Peter had raised Dorcas from the dead (9:36-42)? How could the house of Cornelius respond to Peter's gospel message and receive the baptism of the Holy Spirit before ritual baptism is even mentioned (10:43-48; 11:15, 16; 15:7-9)? How could they have been saved under Peter's preaching if they could only be saved under water? How did deputy Sergius Paulus of Paphos believe the doctrine of the Lord simply upon seeing Paul pronounce blindness upon the evil sorcerer, Bar-jesus (13:6-12)? How could Paul promise justification to all believers without mentioning baptism (13:39)? How could Paul describe Gentiles who gladly heard the Word as believers who were ordained to eternal life without mentioning baptism (13:48)? How could a multitude of Jews and Greeks become believers inside the Iconium synagogue without a baptismal service being held there (14:1)? Where did Paul get the perception that the crippled man in Lystra had the faith to be made whole (14:8-10)? How could Paul promise the Philippian jailer that he and his house could be saved if they only believed (16:30, 31)? How could a great multitude of devout Greeks and chief women, in a Thessalonian synagogue, have become believers upon simply responding to Paul's and Silas' preaching of the suffering, death and resurrection of Jesus (17:1-4)? How could the noble Bereans (honorable Greek women and many men) receive the word with readiness of mind in a synagogue, search the Scriptures to verify Paul's preaching and become believers before being baptized (17:10-12)? How could Dionysius the Areopagite and the woman Damaris and others become believers in Athens under Paul's Mars' Hill sermon rather than under the water of baptism (17:34)? When Paul preached in the house of Justus, which was joined to the synagogue in Corinth, how did Crispus, the chief ruler of the synagogue, become a believer with many other Corinthians before they were baptized (18:8)? How could so many in Ephesus have believed, confessed, showed their deeds and burned their magic books before being baptized (19:18, 19)? How could Paul testify to Agrippa that he was obedient to his heavenly vision before he was baptized (26:15-19)? When Paul was under house arrest in Rome, awaiting his trial, he preached the gospel and people became believers, yet there was no baptistry in the house (26:23, 24). Baptismal regenerationists seem to lay all these questions aside by reminding us that all of these aforementioned examples were baptized shortly thereafter. So, are we supposed to assume that they all became believers, received Christ, and took possession of eternal life without experiencing the regeneration of baptism, if so be that regeneration only takes place in baptism? Can we see the contradiction here?

If circumcision is part of the Law and baptism replaces circumcision (as the reformers insisted), then baptism is law. So, how could Paul affirm that the righteousness of God by faith is upon all who believe (Rom. 3:22, 28)? How could he affirm that propitiation, the righteousness of Christ and remission of sins past are imputed upon faith in Christ's blood (3:25)? Why does God justify through faith (3:31) if faith and baptism are two separate acts (Mk. 16:16)? How can the gospel of Christ be the power of God unto salvation to everyone that believeth (1:16)? Why is the righteousness of God revealed from faith to faith rather than from baptism to faith (1:17)? If baptism is circumcision, it is works and it is law. How then could Paul speak of justification by faith without works (4:2, 3, 5, 16)? How could Paul call *Christ the end of the law for righteousness to every one that believeth* (10:4)? Why does Paul call *faith* our access into the grace of God and His justification (5:1, 2)? And how can a man believe *unto righteousness* with his heart prior to his baptism, if so be that the righteousness of Christ is imputed only at the laver of regeneration (10:10, 11)?

Why did God ordain that men would become saved believers under the preaching of the gospel rather than under the water of baptism (I Cor. 1:21)? How can an unbeliever walk into the Corinthian church, hear the forthtelling of the Word of God, become convinced of all, fall down on his face, and worship God, if regeneration transpires only in the laver of baptism (14:24, 25)? If baptism saves, then the devil would know it. But his chief task on earth is not to stop infants from being baptized but to blind unbelievers lest they should see the gospel light (II Cor. 4:4). But if baptism is illumination, why does Satan not know this and make prevention of infant baptism his chief objective?

How could the Galatians have received the Spirit by the hearing of faith if the baptism of the Spirit and ritual baptism are one and the same (Gal. 3:2)? How could God have preached the gospel of Christ to Abraham without mentioning baptism or circumcision (3:6-9)?

If ritual baptism is the seal of salvation and the promise of eternal life, how did the Ephesians become sealed with the Holy Spirit of promise after they believed the gospel and trusted Christ (Eph. 1:13)? How were the Ephesians saved by grace through faith and not by grace through baptism (Eph. 2:8, 9)?

Why did Paul tell the Thessalonians that people would be damned for not believing the truth of the Gospel when he could have mentioned that they would be damned for not being regenerated in baptism (II Thess. 2:12)? Why did Paul tell Timothy that hereafter people should believe on Christ to life everlasting (I Tim. 1:16)?

How could the writer of *Hebrews* declare that we have entered into God's rest by simply believing the preaching of the gospel (Heb. 4:3)? How could he speak of *them that believe to the saving of the soul* if no soul is saved through belief apart from *baptismal regeneration* (Heb. 10:39)?

How could the Apostle Peter affirm that we are *kept by the power of God through faith unto salvation* if it is our baptism wherein lies the power of God to save us (I Pet. 1:5)? How could he affirm that one who believes in the chief corner stone [Jesus Christ] *shall not be confounded* (2:6)?

It was John the Evangelist who recorded the words of Jesus: *except a man be born of water and of the Spirit, he cannot enter into the kingdom of God* (Jn. 3:5). Who is more qualified to interpret those words than John himself? Then how could he say that *whosoever believeth that Jesus is the Christ is born of God* (I Jn. 5:1)? How could he proclaim that we have overcome the world by believing that Jesus is the Son of God (5:5)?

Of course we have belabored our point by these sweeping questions, but the fundamental question is: does the belief that salvation can only take place in the visible church and in the *sacred* water of baptism constitute a saving gospel? To help answer this question, let us consider some graphic parallels as illustrations. Suppose you attended church this Sunday where the minister explained perfectly the sovereign grace of God and justification by faith in the finished work of Christ but then added one point: *that this gift is only for those who will stand up in this Baptist church and confess that he too is a Baptist and that no one is saved until he makes this confession that he is a Baptist.* Is this a saving Gospel? If you attended the church of Jerusalem and the preacher explained the Gospel perfectly but added that no one is saved until he is circumcised and keeps the whole law, would this still be the saving gospel (Gal. 1:6-9)? Then, if you attended the Augustinian church at Hippo and heard the sovereign grace of God explained perfectly with the addition that no one on earth can receive this by grace through faith but only through the laver of regeneration followed by faith, would this still be the saving gospel of Jesus Christ?

Paul calls the gospel of circumcision *another gospel* (Gal. 1:6, 7). And if baptism is circumcision under another form, it is law and we need to ask ourselves: is baptism our profession of faith in the completed gospel or is it the gospel itself? And if it is proclaimed as the gospel itself, is it not another gospel the same as the gospel of circumcision? Especially is this question relevant if baptism is circumcision under a different form. There is a difference between believing in Jesus Christ and believing that His finished work was only the down payment for your salvation to be paid in full by your baptism and your personal post-baptismal righteousness (Heb. 12:2; Rom. 3:28; 4:5).

Yet the doctrine of *baptismal regeneration* dominated the Roman Catholic Church throughout medieval history. Perhaps the most influential theologian of the medieval church was Thomas Aquinas [1225-74]. This thirteenth-century scholastic theologian embraced what was true in Aristotle and revised what he could not accept as reasonable. He correctly believed that there could be no conflict between faith and reason. When addressing issues he would consistently quote the works of the Church Fathers and ancient philosophers, just as the Apostle Paul quoted the Greek poets Aratas and Epiminides. He became the doctor of the Dominican order. He was canonized in 1323 and by the time of the Reformation in the sixteenth century Thomism became the leading school of thought in Catholicism. The Jesuits [approved in 1540] became Thomists, and we can see the words of Thomas in the pronouncements of the Council of Trent.

Historical Overview Of The Baptismal Regeneration Tradition

In Volume III of his *Summa Theologica* [Question LXVI], Aquinas writes: *Therefore Baptism is not the mere washing; but rather is it the regeneration, the seal, the safeguarding, the enlightenment.*[127] He agrees with and quotes Augustine as having said: *As soon as Christ was plunged into the waters, the waters washed away the sins of all.*[128] In his work *Of God And His Creatvres* [Chapter LIX—*Of Baptism*], he states his clear position on *baptismal regeneration* as follows:

> The generation of a living thing is a change from not living to life. Now a man is deprived of spiritual life by original sin; and whatever sins are added thereto go still further to withdraw him from life. Baptism therefore, or spiritual generation, was needed to serve the purpose of taking away original sin and all actual sins. And because the sensible sign of a Sacrament must be suited to represent the spiritual effect of the Sacrament, and the washing away of filth is done by water, therefore Baptism is fittingly conferred in water sanctified by the word of God. And because what is brought into being by generation loses its previous form and the properties consequent upon that form, therefore Baptism, as being a spiritual generation, not only takes away sins, but also all the liabilities contracted by sins,--All guilt and debt of punishment: therefore no satisfaction for sins is enjoined on the baptized.[129]

We sometimes hear an objection in his defense, arguing that he calls baptism a *sign* and, therefore, he does not mean that it really remits sins. This objection is resolved by the footnote in this same chapter, which reads as follows:

---

[127] St. Thomas Aquinas, *The Summa Theologica*, Literally translated by Fathers of the English Dominican Province (New York: Benziger Brothers, 1914), Vol. III, p. 93.

[128] Ibid., *The Summa Theologica,* Vol. III, p. 95.

[129] St. Thomas Aquinas, *Of God And His Creatvres: An Annotated Translation of the SVMMA Contra Gentiles*, Translated by Joseph Rickaby S.J. (Westminister, Maryland: The Carroll Press, 1950), p. 385.

Hence the axiom, a cardinal principle in the theology of the Sacraments: "The sacraments effect what they signify," *sacramenta efficiunt quod significant.* It bears upon the Edwardine Ordinal. To spoil the significance is to spoil the effect.[130]

Thus, Aquinas could say: *And therefore the baptised, if they die fresh from baptism, are immediately caught up into bliss: hence it is said that baptism opens the gate of heaven.*[131]

Aquinas was no doubt responding to Anabaptists [*rebaptizers*] when he wrote:

> One and the same thing can be generated only once: therefore, as Baptism is a spiritual generation, one man is to be baptised only once. The infection that came through Adam defiles a man only once: hence Baptism, which is directed mainly against that infection, ought not to be repeated.[132]

With the exception of some scattered Anabaptist testimonies throughout the world, the dominant position held by Christendom throughout the Dark Ages regarding baptism was that of the sacramental view of baptismal regeneration. And, with the exception of Zwingli and many Anabaptists, the Protestant Reformation continued a thousand years of tradition which had held to baptismal regeneration.[133] These Anabaptists, who held that there was never any saving efficacy in ordinances, were known as the *Radical Reformation*.

Without repeating the ground we have already covered in the works of Luther, let us focus on his view of baptism by quoting his *Small Catechism* [A.D. 1529]—

---

[130] Ibid., *Of God and His Creatvres*, p. 385.
[131] Ibid., *Of God and His Creatvres*, p. 385.
[132] Ibid., *Of God and His Creatvres*, p. 385.
[133] *Luther's Works: Church and Ministry II,* Conrad Beregendoff, Editor; Helmut T Lehmann, General Editor (Philadelphia: Muhlenberg Press, 1958), Vol. 40, p. 147. "...If the first, or child, baptism were not right it would follow that for more than a thousand years there was no baptism or any Christendom, which is impossible...For over a thousand years there were hardly any other but child baptisms."

Part IV.
II. What does Baptism give, or of what use is it? Answer:
It worketh forgiveness of sins, delivers from death and the devil, and gives everlasting salvation to all who believe, as the Word and promise of God declare.

III. How can water do such great things? Answer:
It is not water, indeed, that does it, but the Word of God which is with and in the water, and faith which trusts in the Word of God in the water. For without the Word of God the water is nothing but water, and no baptism; but with the Word of God it is a baptism—that is, a gracious water of life and a washing of regeneration in the Holy Ghost, as St Paul says, Titus, third chapter [iii.5-7]: *by the washing of regeneration, and renewing of the Holy Ghost, which he shed on us abundantly through Jesus Christ our Saviour; that being justified by his grace, we should be made heirs according to the hope of eternal life.* [134]

And again, without repeating all that we have discussed regarding the works of Calvin, let us reiterate his view that the baptismal symbol and that which is symbolized are one and the same thing and indistinguishable. In arguing the equivocation of OT circumcision with NT baptism he states:

> The promise, in which we have shown that the power of the signs consists, is one in both—viz. The promise of the paternal favour of God, of forgiveness of sins, and eternal life. And the thing figured is one and the same—viz. Regeneration. The foundation on which the completion of these things depends is one in both. Wherefore, there is no difference in the internal

---

[134] *The Creeds of Christendom: With a History and Critical Notes,* Philip Schaff, Editor; Revised by David S. Schaff (Grand Rapids, Michigan: Baker Books, 1983) Vol. III *The Evangelical Protestant Creeds*, pp. 85, 86.

meaning, from which the whole power and peculiar nature of the sacrament is to be estimated. [135]

We began this chapter with an alleged quotation from Cardinal Hosius who presided over the Council of Trent [1545-1563] wherein he allegedly antedated the Anabaptist movement by twelve hundred years. Regarding the doctrine of baptism, we can observe that *The Canons and Dogmatic Decrees of the Council of Trent, A.D. 1563* were as much a response to the Radical Reformation (*Anabaptists*) as they were to Lutheranism and Calvinism. The *Fifth Session* held June 8, 1546 was a response to a movement that denied the efficacy of baptism to remove original sin—

> If any one denies, that, by the grace of our Lord Jesus Christ, which is conferred in baptism, the guilt of original sin is remitted; or even asserts that the whole of that which has the true and proper nature of sin is not taken away; but says that it is only rased, or not imputed; let him be anathema. For in those who are born again, there is nothing that God hates; because, *There is no condemnation to those who are* truly *buried together with Christ by baptism into death; who walk not according to the flesh,* but, *putting off the old man, and putting on the new who is created according to God,* are made innocent, immaculate, pure, harmless, and beloved of God, *heirs indeed of God, but joint heirs with Christ;* so that there is nothing whatever to retard their entrance into heaven...And if any one is of a contrary sentiment, let him be anathema. [136]

On The Sacraments In General, Canon VI is more of a response to the Anabaptists than to Lutheranism and Calvinism—

> If any one saith, that the sacraments of the New Law do not contain the grace which they signify; or, that they do not confer that grace on those who do not

---

[135] John Calvin, *Institutes of the Christian Religion* (Grand Rapids, Michigan: Wm. B. Eerdmans Publishing Company, 1972), Vol. 2, p. 531.
[136] Ibid., *Creeds of Christendom*, Vol. II, pp. 87, 88.

Historical Overview Of The Baptismal Regeneration Tradition

place an obstacle thereunto; as though they were merely outward signs of grace or justice received through faith, and certain marks of the Christian profession, whereby believers are distinguished amongst men from unbelievers: let him be anathema.

Canon VIII.—If any one saith, that by the said sacraments of the New Law grace is not conferred through the act performed, but that faith alone in the divine promise suffices for the obtaining of grace; let him be anathema.

Canon IX.—If any one saith that, in the three sacraments, to wit, Baptism, Confirmation, and Order, there is not imprinted in the soul a character, that is, a certain spiritual and indelible sign, on account of which they can not be repeated: let him be anathema.[137]

On Baptism, Canon V was again a response to the Anabaptist position—

If anyone saith, that baptism is free, that is, not necessary unto salvation: let him be anathema.

Canon XIII.—If any one saith, that little children, for that they have not actual faith, are not, after having received baptism, to be reckoned amongst the faithful; and that for this cause, they are to be rebaptized when they have attained to years of discretion; or, that it is better that the baptism of such be omitted, than that, while not believing by their own act, they should be baptized in the faith alone of the Church: let him be anathema.[138]

During the *Fourteenth Session* held November 25, 1551, the Council professed that it was responding to an ancient Anabaptist conviction that the Church does not have the power to forgive sins—

---

[137] Ibid., *Creeds of Christendom*, Vol. II, pp. 120, 121.
[138] Ibid., *Creeds of Christendom*, Vol. II, pp. 123-125.

Chapter I: ...And the Catholic Church with great reason repudiated and condemned as heretics the Novations, who of old obstinately denied that power of forgiving. Wherefore, this holy Synod, approving of and receiving as most true this meaning of those words of our Lord, condemns the fanciful interpretations of those who, in opposition to the institution of this sacrament, falsely wrest those words to the power of preaching the Word of God, and of announcing the Gospel of Christ.[139]

Meanwhile, the Anglican Church published its "39 Articles" [1563] where we see a reformed view of baptism with even stronger sacramental language. Puritans held more to a Calvinist view of baptism. Baptists rejected child Baptism, while Quakers rejected ritual baptism completely in favor of inward Spirit-baptism.

Now we will move forward in time to the early colonial period of American history. We know much of Roger Williams and the Rhode Island experiment with its *freedom of religion* and s*eparation of church and state*, but we know much less of his associate, John Clarke. It was Clarke who petitioned Charles II in 1662 to grant a charter for Rhode Island, stating: *A most flourishing Civil State may stand, yea, and best be maintained...with full liberty in religious concernments.*[140] The charter was obtained in 1663 and provided that *no person within the said colony...shall be in any way molested, punished, disquieted, or called in question, for any differences in opinion in matters of religion...*[141] The controversy over baptism was highlighted in [John Clarkes: *Ill Newes from New England:* or *A Narrative of New England's Persecution* (London: 1652)]. The narrative describes Clarke, Obadiah Holmes and John Crandall visiting Massachusetts Bay on May 16, 1651. On the 19th they came into the town of Lynn and lodged with William Witter. While discussing religion, two constables entered the house, arrested them, and took them to Boston for sentencing. Holmes

---

[139] Ibid., *Creeds of Christendom*, Vol. II, p. 141.
[140] William Warren Sweet, *Religion in Colonial America*, (New York: Charles Scribner's Sons, 1942), p. 130.
[141] Anson Phelps Stokes, *Church and State in the United States* (New York: Harper and Brothers, 1950), p. 205.

was to pay a thirty pounds fine or be *well whipped* and Crandall was to pay five pounds or be well whipped. When Clark asked what law they had transgressed, Governor John Endecott—*stepped up, and told us we had denied Infant Baptism, and being somewhat transported, broke forth and told me I had deserved death, and said, he "would not have such trash brought into their jurisdiction."*[142]

Clark included in his book a letter by Obadiah Holmes giving his version of what happened on that occasion. Holmes reported that Mr. Cotton gave a sermon before the court just before the sentencing, affirming that *denying Infant Baptism would overthrow all; and this was a capital offense, and, therefore, they were foul murderers.* Holmes also reported that Governor Endecott told them: *"You deserve to die, but this we agreed upon, that Mr. Clark shall pay twenty pounds fine, and Obadiah Holmes thirty pounds fine, and John Crandall five pounds fine, and to remain in prison until their fines be either paid, or security given for them, or else they are all of them to be well whipped..."*[143]

Moving forward still to the seventeenth century, we must consider the works of John Wesley [1703-1791] who was a leader in the evangelical revival of that time. He sent Methodist preachers to North America from 1769 through the post-revolutionary war with Britain. Studying his works is a difficult exercise in semantics and logical consistency. In his work: *The Principles Of A Methodist*, he defines *Justification by faith* as follows:

> 2. First. That I believe Justification by faith alone. This I allow. For I am firmly persuaded, that every man of the offspring of Adam is very far gone from original righteousness, and is of his own nature inclined to evil; that this corruption of our nature, in every person born into the world,

---

[142] Irwin H. Polishook, Roger Williams, John Cotton and Religious Freedom: *A Controversy in New and Old England* (Englewood Cliffs, New Jersy: Prentice-Hall, Inc., 1967), pp. 111, 112. Polishook records for us the actual wording of this narrative.

[143] Ibid., Polishook, p. 112. Again, the author records the actual wording of the narrative. This work contains the actual exchanges in the debates between John Cotton and Roger Williams as well as excerpts from Governor John Winthrop's Diary.

deserves God's wrath and damnation; that therefore, if ever we receive the remission of our sins, and are accounted righteous before God, it must be only for the merit of Christ, by faith, and not for our own works or deservings of any kind. Nay, I am persuaded, that all works done before justification, have in them the nature of sin; and that, consequently, till he is justified, a man has no power to do any work which is pleasing and acceptable to God.

3. To express my meaning a little more at large: I believe three things must go together in our justification: Upon God's part, his great mercy and grace; upon Christ's part, the satisfaction of God's justice, by the offering his body, and shedding his blood; and upon our part, true and living faith in the merits of Jesus Christ. So that in our justification there is not only God's mercy and grace, but his justice also. And so the grace of God does not shut out the righteousness of God in our justification; but only shuts out the righteousness of man, that is, the righteousness of our works.[144]

Such a definition of justification is most commendable if taken at face value. But here is the exercise in semantics. Wesley meant by these words that one cannot front-load the gospel with human works of righteousness. However, his position holds that if one does not back-load *justification by faith alone* with absolute personal holiness, then the said justification ceases to exist in his life and he is again in need of a born again experience— *But it should also be observed, what that faith is whereby we are Justified. Now, that faith which brings not forth good works, is not a living faith, but a dead and devilish one.*[145] *...No ungodly man hath or can have this 'sure trust and confidence in God,*

---

[144] *The Works of Wesley* (Grandrapids, Michigan, Baker Book House, 1978), Vol. VIII, pp. 361, 362.

[145] Ibid., *Works of Wesley*, Vol. VIII, p. 363. In chapter nine of this present work we will have a lengthy discussion regarding the back-loading of the gospel with human righteousness and whether this alters the saving grace nature of the plan of salvation.

that by the merits of Christ his sins are forgiven, and he reconciled to the favour of God. This is what I believe (and have believed for some years) concerning justification by faith alone).[146]

But when some accused Wesley of teaching sinless perfection in this life he would forthrightly deny the charge.[147] But what did Wesley mean by the term *a perfect man*? He wrote:

> (4.) " 'But whom then do you mean by *one that is perfect*?' We mean one in whom 'is the mind which was in Christ,' and who so 'walketh as Christ walks;' a 'man that hath clean hands and a pure heart,' or that is 'cleansed from all filthiness of flesh and spirit;' one in whom 'is no occasion of stumbling, and who accordingly 'doth not commit sin.' To declare a little more particularly: We understand by that scriptural expression, 'a perfect man,' one in whom God hath fulfilled his faithful word, 'From all your filthiness and from all your idols will I cleanse you: I will also save you from all your uncleannesses.' We understand hereby one whom God hath 'sanctified throughout, in body, soul, and spirit;' one who 'walketh in the light as he is in the light, in whom is no darkness at all; the blood of Jesus Christ his Son having cleansed him from all sin.'
>
> (6.) "This it is to be 'a perfect man,' to be sanctified throughout: Even 'to have a heart so all-flaming with the love of God,' to use Archbishop Usher's words, 'as continually to offer up every thought, word, and work, as a spiritual sacrifice, acceptable to God through Christ.' In every thought of our hearts, in every word of our tongues, in every work of our hands, to 'show forth his praise, who hath called us out of darkness into his marvelous light.' O that both we, and all who seek the Lord Jesus in sincerity, may thus be made perfect in one?"[148]

---

[146] Ibid., *Works of Wesley*, Vol. VIII, p. 363.
[147] Ibid., *Works of Wesley*, Vol. VIII, p. 364.
[148] Ibid., *Works of Wesley*, Vol. VIII, pp. 364, 365.

Though Wesley correctly distinguished between baptism and regeneration, he clearly believed that regeneration and salvation began at baptism. In his sermon, *Awake, Thou That Sleepest* he states:

> Now, "they that sleep, sleep in the night." The state of nature is a state of utter darkness; a state wherein "darkness covers the earth, and gross darkness the people." The poor unawakened sinner, how much knowledge soever he may have as to other things, has no knowledge of himself: In this respect "he knoweth nothing yet as he ought to know." He knows not that he is a fallen spirit, whose only business in the present world is, to recover from his fall, to regain that image of God wherein he was created. He sees *no necessity* for the *one thing needful*, even that inward universal change, that "birth from above," figured out by baptism, which is the beginning of that total renovation, that sanctification of spirit, soul, and body, "without which no man shall see the Lord."[149]

Though he believed that an infant was born again at his baptism, he affirmed that an adult who is not demonstrating an entire change of heart has lost that born again experience and is in need again of a salvation experience—

> It is certain our Church supposes that all who are baptized in their infancy are at the same time born again; and it is allowed that the whole Office for the Baptism of Infants proceeds upon this supposition.[150]

> I tell a sinner, "You must be born again." "No," say you: "He was born again in baptism. Therefore he cannot be born again now." Alas, what trifling is this! What, if he was *then* a child of God? He is *now* manifestly a child of the devil; for the works of his

---

[149] Ibid., *Works of Wesley* [Sermon III, First Series of Sermons 1-39] (Peabody, Massachusetts: Hendrickson Publishers, Inc., 1994), Vol. V, p. 25.

[150] Ibid., *Works of Wesley* [Sermon XLV: *The New Birth*], Vol. VI, p. 74.

Historical Overview Of The Baptismal Regeneration Tradition

> father he doeth. Therefore, do not play upon words. He must go through an entire change of heart.[151]

> Lean no more on the staff of that broken reed, that ye were born again in baptism. Who denies that ye were then made children of God, and heirs of the kingdom of heaven? But, notwithstanding this, ye are now children of the devil. Therefore ye must be born again.... And if ye have been baptized, your only hope is this,--that those who were made the children of God by baptism, but are now the children of the devil, may yet again receive "power to become the sons of God;"[152]

But the question of quantification always arises: At what point does one lose his born again state and become lost? According to Wesley, that point is at the moment of any willful sin—

> What must one who loves the souls of men, and is grieved that any of them should perish, say to one whom he sees living in sabbath-breaking, drunkenness, or any other willful sin? What can he say, if the foregoing observations are true but, "You must be born again?"

> And do you glory in this, that you once belonged to God? O be ashamed! Blush! Hide yourself in the earth! I answer, Secondly, You have already denied your baptism; and that in the most effectual manner. You have denied it a thousand and a thousand times; and you do so still, day by day. For in your baptism you renounced the devil and all his works. Whenever, therefore, you give place to him again, whenever you do any of the works of the devil, then you deny your baptism. Therefore you deny it by every willful sin; by every act of uncleanness, drunkenness, or revenge:

---

[151] Ibid., *Works of Wesley: Addresses and Essays,* "A Partial Appeal to Men of Reason and Religion", Vol. VIII, p. 48.

[152] Ibid., *Works of Wesley* [Sermon XVIII: *The Marks of the New Birth*], Vol. V, pp. 222, 223.

by every obscene or profane word; by every oath that comes out of your mouth. Every time you profane the day of the Lord, you thereby deny your baptism; yea, every time you do anything to another which you would not he should do to you...Without inward as well as outward holiness, you cannot be happy, even in this world, much less in the world to come.[153]

Can a Christian live in perfect obedience to the commandments of God? Can it be said that he cannot be saved unless he does? Regarding the sacrament of the Lord's Table Wesley states:

> For all that you profess at the Lord's table, you must both profess and keep, or you cannot be saved. For you profess nothing there but this, --that you will diligently keep his commandments. And cannot you keep up to this profession? Then you cannot enter into life.
>
> Think then what you say, before you say you cannot live up to what is required of constant communicants. This is no more than is required of any communicants; yea, of every one that has a soul to be saved. So that to say, you cannot live up to this, is neither better nor worse than renouncing Christianity. It is in effect renouncing your baptism, wherein you solemnly promised to keep all his commandments. You now fly from that profession. You willfully break one of his commandments, and, to excuse yourself, say, you cannot keep his commandments; Then you cannot expect to receive the promises, which are made only to those that keep them.
>
> What has been said on this pretence against constant communion, is applicable to those who say the same thing in other words: "We dare not do it, because it requires so perfect an obedience afterwards as we cannot promise to perform." Nay, it requires neither more nor less perfect obedience than you promised in

---

[153] Ibid., *Works of Wesley: The New Birth*, Vol. VI, pp. 75, 76.

your baptism. You then undertook to keep the commandments of God by his help; and you promise no more when you communicate.[154]

Regarding baptism as a means or channel of God's saving grace into the human soul, Wesley identifies with the position held in ages past—

> Are there, under the Christian dispensation, any *means ordained* of God, as the usual channels of his grace? This question could never have been proposed in the apostolical church, unless by one who openly avowed himself to be a heathen; the whole body of Christians being agreed, that Christ had ordained certain outward means, for conveying his grace into the souls of men.[155]

> By "means of grace" I understand outward signs, words, or actions, ordained of God, and appointed for this end, to be the ordinary channels whereby he might convey to men, preventing, justifying, or sanctifying grace.

> I use this expression, means of grace, because I know none better; and because it has been generally used in the Christian Church for many ages,--in particular by our own Church, which directs us to bless God both for the means of grace, and hope of glory; and teaches us, that a sacrament is "an outward sign of inward grace, and a means whereby we receive the same."[156]

> Yet once more: we allow, though it is a melancholy truth, that a large proportion of those who are called

---

[154] Ibid., *Works of Wesley* [Sermon CI: *The Duty of Constant Communion*], Vol. III, pp. 253, 254. Wesley is here addressing those who were baptized as adults.

[155] Ibid., *Works of Wesley* [Sermon XVI: *The Means of Grace*], Vol. V, p. 185.

[156] Ibid., *The Means of Grace*, Vol. V, pp. 187, 188.

Christians, do to this day abuse the means of grace to the destruction of their souls.

But the main question remains: "We know this salvation is the gift and the work of God; but how (may one say who is convinced he hath it not) may I attain thereto?" If you say, "Believe, and thou shalt be saved! He answers, "True: but how shall I believe?" You reply, "Wait upon God." "Well; but how am I to wait? In the means of grace, or out of them? Am I to wait for the grace of God which bringeth salvation, by using these means, or by laying them aside?"

It cannot possibly be conceived, that the word of God should give no directions in so important a point; or, that the Son of God, who came down from heaven for us men and for our salvation, should have left us undetermined with regard to a question wherein our salvation is so nearly concerned.

And, in fact, he hath not left us undetermined; he hath shown us the way wherein we should go. We have only to consult the oracles of God; to inquire what is written there; and, if we simply abide by their decision, there can no possible doubt remain.

According to this, according to the decision of holy writ, all who desire the grace of God are to wait for it in the means which he hath ordained; in using, not in laying them aside.[157]

Noted previously was the fact that Wesley insisted upon complete obedience to the commandments of God in order to commune at the Lord's Table. But then he tells us that we may experience the saving grace of God in the Lord's Table—

---

[157] Ibid., *The Means of Grace*, Vol. V, pp. 189, 190. By *Means of Grace* Wesley enumerates constant prayer; searching the Scriptures; partaking of the Lord's supper.

> Is not the eating of that bread, and the drinking of that cup, the outward, visible means, whereby God conveys into our souls all that spiritual grace, that righteousness, and peace, and joy in the Holy Ghost, which were purchased by the body of Christ once broken and the blood of Christ once shed for us? Let us all, therefore, who truly desire the grace of God, eat of that bread, and drink of that cup.[158]
>
> And thus he continues in God's way, in hearing, reading, meditating, praying, and partaking of the Lord's supper, till God, in the manner that pleases him, speaks to his heart, "Thy faith hath saved thee. Go in peace."[159]
>
> Whenever opportunity serves, use all the means which God has ordained; for who knows in which God will meet thee with the grace that bringeth salvation.[160]

The next large movement to emerge in North America was that of the *Disciples of Christ*. Thomas Campbell of the Seceder Presbyterian Church in Northern Ireland was assigned to work as a minister in the Presbytery of Cartiers, Western Pennsylvania and arrived in America in 1807. Splitting with the Church, he formed the *Christian Association of Washington, Pa.*

His minister-son, Alexander, joined him after having been trained for the ministry at Glasgow, Ireland. Their goal was the restoration of the primitive Christian church in order to create Christian oneness. They rejected infant baptism and affusion [*pouring*] and established their first congregation [1811] at Brush Run, Pa.

---

[158] Ibid., *The Means of Grace*, Vol. V, p. 195.
[159] Ibid., *The Means of Grace*, Vol. V, p. 199.
[160] Ibid., *The Means of Grace*, Vol. V, p. 200. Wesley cautions everyone not to confuse the means of grace with the grace itself. He argues throughout the remainder of this sermon that there is no merit in using the means of grace: "Remember also, to use all means, *as means*; as ordained, not for their own sake, but in order to the renewal of your soul in righteousness and true holiness", p. 201.

The Campbells, Barton W. Stone, and Walter Scott were the chief advocates of the new message. Their belief in immersion brought them into relationships with Baptists. In 1823, Alexander Campbel began publishing *The Christian Baptist*. In the first seven years he issued 46,000 volumes of his works. The Redstone Baptist Association and the Mahoning Association received them into fellowship. These were Baptist organizations in Western Pennsylvenia and Ohio. Their separation from Baptists eventually took place primarily over the Campbellite insistence that baptism by immersion was essential to salvation.

Consequently, the Disciples of Christ became a separate body. It was taught that only the immersed should be admitted to the churches. Their assemblies are known as *Christian Churches* or *Churches of Christ*. In 1829, Alexander began publication of the *Millennial Harbinger* magazine, which continued until his death. Currently, the descendents of the Campbellite influence exists in the denomination called the *Christian Church* (*Disciples of Christ*); in the non-instrumental *Churches of Christ*; and in independent Christian churches. A main point of contention still being the essentiality of baptism in salvation.

We conclude this historical overview of *baptismal regeneration* with a discussion of *Fundamentalism* as a movement. The *fundamentals* were considered to be the bare essentials which would serve as a collective common denominator for traditional denominations to distinguish themselves as truly Christian as opposed to rationalism, modernism, and theological liberalism. This movement can be traced to the academic renaissance which occurred in the last half of the 19th century. It was believed that Imanuel Kant, G. F. Hegel, F. C. Baur, Albrecht Ritschl, and G. F. Schleiermacher were responsible for launching German philosophy and theology onto the North American continent. Several within the scientific revolution developed a view of quantum physics and materialism which denied the existence of any metaphysical reality in the universe. Anyone denying the proposition that <u>time multiplied by space multiplied by motion multiplied by matter multiplied by chance = existence</u> was perceived by many to be *anti-education*, *anti-intellectual*, and *irrational*. Many universities and seminaries cowered to this intimidation and sought to develop a secularized theology that discounted much of the supernatural contained within traditional Christian beliefs.

Historical Overview Of The Baptismal Regeneration Tradition

Such thinking was in direct contradiction to what had previously been affirmed by traditional Christianity within both Catholic and Protestant traditions. The result was such a challenge to the authority of the sacred Scriptures that orthodoxy itself seemed to collapse as many traditional theological institutions failed to react in defense of historic Christian beliefs.

Fundamentalism was therefore a semi-ecumenical movement that led to a partial return to orthodoxy. The term *fundamental* can be explained by using an automobile as an analogy. The motor is fundamental to its operation, whereas the mirrors are important, yet not essential. One can drive home without mirrors, but not without a motor. Although the modern media has applied the term *fundamentalist* to anything considered radically extreme in Christianity, the original usage meant that there are five doctrines which are fundamental to being considered a part of true Christianity: (1) the inerrancy of the Sacred Scriptures; (2) the virgin birth and deity of Christ; (3) the substitutionary nature of His atoning death; (4) His bodily resurrection; and (5) His literal, physical return to establish His kingdom on earth.

Contrary to contemporary media perceptions, not only are these five affirmations not radical or extreme, they predate fundamentalism beyond the beginning of Roman Catholicism and remained principles of orthodoxy throughout the establishment of all mainline Protestant denominations. It was a semantic maneuver for the academic community to classify those who believed these five affirmations as *fringe* while portraying the denial of these affirmations as *mainstream*.

The difficulty in understanding fundamentalism as a movement is in the fact that a large variety of gospel traditions can fit within the framework of the five affirmations. Although the five fundamentals affirm the inerrancy of the Sacred Scriptures, they do not affirm the sole authority of the Bible. Therefore, just as Catholicism affirmed the inerrancy of Scripture and proclaimed *tradition* to be of equal authority, so also many fundamentalists could affirm inerrancy while proclaiming experience and the *inner voice of God* to be equally reliable. This would leave room for heterodox, extra-biblical concepts to be proclaimed as the inerrant mind of God. Also, just as Roman Catholicism has always affirmed the substitutionary nature of Christ's atoning death while insisting that works, penance and other sacraments are essential to salvation, so also a fundamentalist can subscribe to the substitutionary atonement of Christ while front-loading or back-loading Christ's finished work with sacraments and/or personal righteousness. The common denominator in Fundamentalism was more *anti-modernism* than a precise understanding of God's terms for granting eternal life.

Although many within *fundamentalism* have held to a pure grace view of the gospel, a precise definition of the gospel was not listed as one of the fundamentals. This is why we have called *fundamentalism* a semi-ecumenical movement. To illustrate this weakness let us use a NT illustration. The gospel of circumcision was prompt to profess belief in the death, burial and resurrection of Jesus Christ; otherwise, its advocates could never have participated in or have had a voice at the Council of Jerusalem (Acts 15). And yet the gospel of circumcision is called *soul perverting* (Acts 15:24) and *another gospel* which is *accursed* (Gal. 1:6-9), of which the advocates thereunto (*who subvert whole households*) must have their *mouths stopped* by the truth (Titus 1:9-11).

They of the Circumcision were not denying any of the five *fundamentals*. Their error was that they added personal righteousness and ritual to the gospel apart from which they said no soul could be saved (Acts 15:1, 5). The writer of *Hebrews* saw the distinction between believing in the atoning death of Christ as a portion of the price of salvation in contrast to faith in Christ's finished work on the cross as the total price, saying: *looking unto Jesus the author and finisher of our faith*...(Heb. 12:2). Thus, Paul could proclaim that if the righteousness that saves the soul is personal, rather than the imputed righteousness of Christ, then the death of Christ was nothing more than an act of suicide, saying: *I do not frustrate the grace of God: for if righteousness come by the law, then Christ is dead in vain* (Gal. 2:21).

So, *fundamentalism* was a broad, separatist, anti-modernist coalition which began to fragment again into two variant directions in the 1940s. One major group softened its position in order to retain contact with mainline denominations, and thus made sacramentalism and works salvation *nonessential* issues in the mass evangelism of the world. At first they called themselves *neo-evangelicals*, but from the 1950s they were known simply as *evangelicals*. Some within this category would preach a pure grace only view of the gospel apart from ritual or human righteousness. However, their broader testimony was that the gospel of sacraments and personal righteousness was a saving plan of salvation as well. Liberals often refer to them as the *inclusivist wing* of ex-fundamentalists.

Other groups separated in the opposite direction on the basis of legalistic standards of personal holiness. These standards often became annexed to the definition of what a *true fundamentalist* really is.

Still others separated on the basis of a clear definition of the terms of the NT gospel. These went further than the original five affirmations and believed also that the foremost fundamental of the faith should be a clear affirmation of a gospel of grace totally distinct from sacraments and personal righteousness. It was not, as they were almost universally accused, that ordinances and personal holiness were insignificant, it is just that they were not an integral part of the saving gospel of Christ. In the early part of the twentieth century when a number of great conservative scholars published a set of tracts entitled *THE FUNDAMENTALS*, most of the contributors would have insisted that baptism is not a part of the gospel or a *means/channel* of saving grace. Rev. George W. Lasher, D.D., LL.D., of Cincinnati, delivered the paper on *Regeneration—Conversion—Reformation.* Herein he described how many stumble over John 3:5 in that—

> They accept the doctrine of regeneration, but couple it with an external act without which, in their view, the regeneration is not and cannot be completed. In their rituals they distinctly declare that water baptism is essential to and is productive of the regeneration which Jesus declares must be from heaven. They stumble over, or pervert the words used, and make "born of water" to be baptism, of which nothing is said in the verse in the chapter, and which the whole tenor of Scripture denied.[161]

---

[161] *The Fundamentals For Today*, Charles L. Feinberg, Editor (Grand Rapids, Michigan: Kregel Publications, 1964), pp. 396, 397. Rev. Lasher wrote: "The lexicographers, the grammarians and evangelical theologians are all pronounced against the interpretation put upon the words of Jesus when he said: 'Except a man [any one] be born of water *kai* spirit, he cannot enter into the kingdom of God.' The lexicographers tell us that the conjunction *kai* (Greek) may have an exegetical meaning and may be (as it frequently is) used to amplify what has gone before; that it may have the sense of 'even,' or 'namely.' And thus they justify the reading: 'Except a man be born of water, even [or namely] *(Continued on next page)*

Lasher referred to the Apostle Paul as the best interpreter of Jesus in the N.T. and noted that: *never once, in all his discussions of the way of salvation, does Paul intimate that the new creation is effected by a ritual observance. He always and everywhere regarded and treated it as a spiritual experience wrought by the Spirit of God.*[162]

Today, the terms *fundamentalist* and *evangelical* are painted with such a broad spectrum of descriptions that they almost defy definition. This is why we must affirm the Bible itself to be the final arbiter in any debate regarding the clarity of the Gospel.

Throughout this entire overview, the Scriptural passage that emerges most often in defense of *baptismal regeneration* is John 3:5—*Jesus answered, Verily, verily, I say unto thee, Except a man be born of water and of the Spirit, he cannot enter into the kingdom of God.* Baptismal regenerationists insist that the water in this verse means *born of baptism*, apart from which no one will enter the kingdom of God.

The first question that must be considered before interpreting this verse is: *Does the phrase born of water appear anywhere else in the New Testament?* The answer is unmistakably in the negative. This makes our job slightly more difficult.

Can we take any reference to *water* in the NT and authoritatively use it to teach baptism? The swine that perished in the waters of the sea did not perish in baptism (Matt. 8:32). The evil spirit that cast its victim into the water was not throwing him toward regeneration (Mk. 9:22). When the Apostle Paul was in *perils of water* (II Cor. 11:26) he was not speaking of baptism. When the Apostle John described God's voice as *the sound of many waters* (Rev. 1:15; 14:2) he

---

spirit, he cannot enter into the kingdom of God.' The grammarians tell us the same thing, and innumerable instances of such usage can be cited from both classic and New Testament Greek. The theologians are explicit in their denial that regeneration can be effected by baptism. They hold to a purely spiritual experience, either before baptism, or after it, and deny that the spiritual birth is effected by the water, no matter how applied. And yet some who take this position in discussions of the 'new birth' fall away to the ritualistic idea when they come to treat of baptism, its significance and place in the Christian system."

[162] Ibid., *The Fundamentals For Today*, pp. 397, 398.

was not speaking of many baptisms. When John further describes tribulation saints already in heaven as being led to *living fountains of water*, he was not speaking of blood-washed saints getting baptized when they get to heaven (Rev. 7:14-17). When John describes a heavenly object falling to earth onto fountains of waters he was not speaking of interrupted baptismal services (Rev. 8:10). And when this event results in many men dying because of the waters becoming bitter he was not speaking of men being baptized to death. When the two witnesses of the tribulation period demonstrate the power to turn waters into blood, they will not be practicing some form of baptism in so doing (Rev. 11:6). When the angel glorifies God for making the *fountains of water*, he is not referring to baptism (Rev. 14:7). When the third angel pours out his vial on the fountains of waters so that *they became blood*, he is not polluting baptistries in particular (Rev. 16:4), and the *angel of the waters* is not the angel of baptism (Rev. 16:5). The whore that sits on many waters is not sitting on many baptisms (Rev. 17:1), because the waters there represent masses of people (Rev. 17:15). Later, the *voice of many waters* is that of a multitude in Heaven worshiping God, not being baptized (Rev. 19:6). In the same sense, we need one clue that mandates that the water of John 3:5 must be interpreted to mean *born again in baptism.*

But what clues do we have in John 3? First of all, how did Jews understand baptism at that point in the life of Christ? They were aware only of John's baptism which required belief in Christ and a public demonstration of having been regenerated. That concept does not fit into the context of John 3.

We cannot help but notice that Nicodemus thought that Christ was talking about a repetition of physical birth—*How can a man be born when he is old? Can he enter the second time into his mother's womb, and be born?* (Jn. 3:4). Of course, Jesus was not talking about that kind of a birth, but rather of a second kind of birth. So He qualifies Himself to Nicodemus by contrasting fleshly birth with spiritual birth—*That which is born of flesh is flesh and that which is born of spirit is spirit* (Jn. 3:6). Jesus does not say *born again and again* as though there are three births in this passage. The *born again* experience is a second birth. So if John 3:5 refers to two births (*born of water and of the Spirit*), the first must refer to fleshly birth. Otherwise, the context is saying that one must be born of the flesh, born of the water, and born of the spirit (which was the precise position taken by John Wesley).

Now the context tells us that we are contrasting physical birth with spiritual birth, without the ritual of baptism even being mentioned. Add to this the fact that the disciples were born again before they were baptized and the fact that the thief was not baptized at all, and we can easily conclude that the water birth in John 3:5 refers to physical birth. There is nothing in the Greek to substantiate the substituting of the word *baptism* for the word *water*. This would require pure speculation or else a special revelation from God.

But does the Bible qualify itself any further regarding the meaning of the new birth? Paul tells the Corinthians that he had *begotten* them *through the gospel* (I Cor. 4:15), but he had not baptized them (I Cor. 1:14). James proclaimed that God *begat* us with the *word of truth* (Jas. 1:18). The Apostle Peter proclaimed that we are *born again* by the *incorruptible seed* of the *Word of God* (I Pet. 1: 23). So, one must be born physically and then spiritually in order to enter the kingdom of heaven.

The only time one can authoritatively use an unrelated reference to water as an illustration of baptism is at a moment of divine inerrancy and inspiration, as in Peter's use of Noah's flood (I Pet. 3:21), and as in Paul's use of the Red Sea crossing (I Cor. 10:2).

Speaking for many in the independent Christian Church (*restoration*) movement, Isaac Errett distinguishes regeneration from forgiveness saying that the former occurs at the moment of faith but that the latter is contingent upon baptism by immersion.[163] However, if *born of water* in John 3:5 means baptism, and if forgiveness cannot transpire prior to baptism, then several questions need to be answered. How could Jesus immediately say to the sick of the palsy, *Thy sins be forgiven thee* (Matt. 9:2; Mk. 2:5; Lk. 5:20)? While dining in the house of an unbelieving Pharisee wherein a woman anointed His feet with ointment from an alabaster box, how could Jesus proclaim, *Her sins which are many are forgiven* (Lk. 7:47, 48) and *Thy faith hath saved thee; go in peace* (vs. 50)? When the publican went to the temple to pray, How could Jesus say, *I tell you this man went down to his house justified* (Lk. 18:14)? How could Jesus have said to Zacchaeus, *This day is salvation come to this house* (Lk. 19:9)? How could these things be true if God's forgiveness is contingent upon baptism?

---

[163] See Chapter 6, footnote 2.

So, in this chapter we have searched the Ante-Nicene, Nicene and Post-Nicene Church Fathers. We have studied the works of Thomas Aquinas, the Reformers and the Canons and Decrees of the Council of Trent. We have noted English and American Puritanism; the emergence of John Wesley; the rise of the Campbellite movement; the development of Fundamentalism and the evolution of Evangelicalism. We have used brutal honesty in observing that the dominant position of Christendom throughout church history regarding the sacrament of baptism has been that of *baptismal regeneration.* The question we are confronted with most often relates to how we can persist in affirming that these great figures of Church history could all have been wrong in contradistinction to our own position. The answer to such a question was clearly noted by Karl Barth as he surveyed the writings of Zwingli in their German and Latin editions—

> According to Zwingli himself all teachers from the days of the apostles had greatly erred. Through misunderstanding of John 3:5 they had sought to ascribe to the water something which it cannot have. Christ has taken from us all external justifying (ed. Shuler and Schulthess, Germm. III, 238). Water baptism, in spite of the opinion of the earliest fathers, does not cleanse or save a man (255f.). He can be saved without baptism (241f.). It has no *vis mutandi* (Lat. III, 229). Nor does it serve—the core of Calvin's teaching is here rejected in advance—to give assurance or confirmation to faith (Germ. 243, Lat. 229f.). Only the direct work of God, Christ and the Holy Spirit can do these things. This alone is the basis of faith in the elect.[164]

---

[164] Karl Barth, *Church Dogmatics: The Doctrine of Reconciliation*, Editors: Rev. G. W. Bromiley, Ph.D., D.Litt. and Rev. Prof. T. F. Torrance, D.D., D.Theol. (Edinburgh: T. & T. Clark, 1980), Vol. IV, p. 129.

Chapter Eight

Subjective And Extra-biblical Arguments For Baptismal Regeneration

Being baptized, we are illuminated, we become sons....This work is variously called grace, illumination, perfection, and washing. Washing, by which we cleanse away our sins. Grace by which the penalties accruing to transgressions are remitted. Illumination, by which that holy light of salvation is beheld, that is, by which we see God clearly.

Clement of Alexandria (c. 195, E) 2.215.

    The controversy over *baptismal regeneration* will fall into two major categories for those making affirmations in its defense. There are those who insist that their views on sacramentalism have been derived objectively from the Scriptures alone, and those who proclaim authority for their position on mystical, emotional, or other extra-biblical grounds. We will discuss the latter group in this present chapter and the former in the forthcoming chapter. (see Reason # 15 in Chapter 6 of this present work).

    There has always existed, within Christendom, a superstitious view of biblical authority and interpretation which can lead to a *talismanic* view of one's own heart, conscience, intuition or of the consensus of the Church as a community. We have observed this same error among the Jewish leaders in the NT. In addition to the written Torah, the Pharisees and rabbis recognized an oral Torah which comprised specific applications of the general principles of the written Torah. In Christ's day the oral traditions went beyond application to the establishment of an extra-textual orthodoxy which was assigned equal authority with the Scriptures. According to Christ, this practice literally resulted in the cancellation of the written Word of God (Matt. 15:2; Mark 7:9, 13; Col. 2:8).

This same error is being committed today in the name of *The Living Logos* or the *inner illumination of the Holy Spirit*. Some contemporary theologians attribute to themselves, or to the community of believers, the same authority that was possessed by the apostles. This present work, on the other hand, interprets the words *dynamis* (ability, power) and *exousia* (right, power, authority) within their contextual usage and not merely by their lexical definitions. In so doing, we can observe that the power and authority of the sacred text is of a different domain and thus not the same as the *exousia* of government (cf. Lk. 19:17), the Sanhedrin (Acts 9:14), or Pilate (Lk. 20:20). It is also different from the God-given power of self-determination in the believer (Acts 5:4) the satanic power of kings (Rev. 17:12), and the *powers that be* (Lk. 12:11; Rom. 13:1). It is not the same as the sphere of the state's dominion (Lk. 23:7), the domain of spirits (Eph. 2:2), nor of the spiritual powers (I Cor. 15:24; Eph. 1:21; Col. 1:16; I Pet. 3:22).

First, God possesses *exousia* as the source of all power and legality (Lk. 12:5; Acts 1:7; Jude 25; Rom. 9:21). Secondly, all natural forces derive their *exousia* from God (Rev. 6:8; 9:3, 10, 19; 16:9; 18:1). Thirdly, God's will also encompasses Satan's sphere of dominion (Acts 26:18; Col. 1:13). Fourthly, God's *exousia* and *dynamis* are fully possessed by Jesus Christ in His deity (Matt. 28:18; Rev. 12:10).

That the Church has a power of self-determination is clearly seen in Acts 15. But this is a freedom to embrace as well as to reject error. When Christ prophesied the immediate entering in of false prophets, He was declaring that God would not with force prohibit error in the church (Mt. 7:15, 22, 23). It was the Church's task to defend itself from error (Jude 3). But by what rule? If there was not a rule distinct from the body of saints that would serve as an effective tool, then either the will of the saints would become the rule or else the will of the ecclesiastical hierarchy would become the authoritative canon law for the Church. In the latter case we would have a repetitious parallel to the Pharisees and Scribes negating the *exousia* of the sacred writings (Matt. 15:6, 9).

We hold that the Bible is the rule or canon for the Church. Because of our fleshly natures, we are not an extremely humble race. Therefore, we must take steps to protect ourselves from our own pride. Thus doing, we should attempt to require that none of our Christian doctrines will have originated with ourselves or our denomination. They must have originated with Christ and have been delivered to the Church via the original apostles and passed down through the Scriptures. Although the redeemed of the Church Age are universally *in Christ*, doctrines which originated from within that body, since the death of the apostles, are not catholic (universal).

Thus, the doctrinal *exousia* chain of command begins with the entire Trinity and is delivered to the Church through Christ and the Holy Spirit to the original apostles. Even before the Scriptures were complete the *apostolic tradition* had become a closed system of doctrine—

> Now I beseech you, brethren, mark them which cause divisions and offences contrary to the doctrine which ye have learned; and avoid them (Rom. 16:17).

> Now we command you, brethren, in the name of our Lord Jesus Christ, that ye withdraw yourselves from every brother that walketh disorderly, and not after the tradition which he received of us (II Thess. 3:6).

> Beloved, when I gave all diligence to write unto you of the common salvation, it was needful for me to write unto you, and exhort *you* that ye should earnestly contend for the faith which was once delivered unto the saints (Jude 3; cf. Gal. 1:6-9).

It is the nature of a canon to be closed. But upon what grounds was the NT canon closed and how were the twenty-seven books therein chosen? *The Cambridge History Of The Bible* summarizes the process as follows:

> ...The Canon of the New Testament was the result of a long and gradual process in the course of which the

books regarded as authoritative, inspired, and apostolic were selected out of a much larger body of literature. Such a process of selection necessarily involved both selectors and grounds on which the selection would be made.

...Selection thus involved not only comparison among books but also comparison with a norm viewed as relatively fixed. Before this norm, among early Christians regarded as the faith of the apostles, reached a relative fixity of expression it was not possible for a definite Canon to come into existence. About A.D. 170, when opponents of the enthusiastic movement known as Montanism endeavored to cut the ground from under it by rejecting the Gospel and Revelation of John, their own theological ideas had not incorporated Johannine insights, and their rejection of the Johanine books was destined to fall because the theology of the Church as a whole was coming to be increasingly Johannine. This is to say that the development of the Canon and the development of Christian theology were closely interrelated, and supported one another.

...The question of canonicity or, to put it more historically, authority—since the term *canon* was not used until the fourth century—did not and could not arise until the idea of orthodoxy had clearly arisen out of the second-century anti-gnostic debates.[1]

The early post-apostolic church sought to protect itself from error with a closed system of pre-canon orthodoxy known as the *apostolic tradition*. Since the actual term *canon* was not in use until the fourth century, instead we will use the word *authority*. The recognition of doctrinal authority can indeed be observed in the second-century anti-gnostic debates. The primary criterion in such debates was the usage of

---

[1] *The Cambridge History Of The Bible: From the Beginnings to Jerome*, P. R. Ackroyd And C. F. Evens, Editors (Cambridge, London, New York, Melbourne: Cambridge University Press, 1970), Vol. I, pp. 284- 285.

this closed system of doctrine among groups known to have held the traditional *faith of the apostles.*

Jn. 14:26 was spoken by Christ to the Apostles when He proclaimed that the Holy Ghost would *teach you all things, and bring all things to your remembrance, whatsoever I have said unto you.* In John 16:13 Christ said that the Spirit of Truth would guide the apostles into *all truth.* This was a promise of total accuracy based upon total recall of what was spoken by Christ. We understand that neither we nor the community of believers possess such an authority today. We only have the information that was delivered to us through the apostles, as Paul said to Timothy: *And the things that thou hast heard of me among many witnesses, the same commit thou to faithful men, who shall be able to teach others also* (II Tim. 2:2). Therefore believers are members *of the household of God; and are built on the foundation of the apostles and prophets, Jesus Christ himself being the chief corner stone* (Eph. 2:19b-21). Jude called the NT body of doctrines *the faith* and exhorted Christians to *...earnestly contend for the faith which was once delivered unto the saints* (Jude 3). Therefore, the concept of a closed system of apostolic doctrine will be fundamental to the pursuit of Christian truth. Let us illustrate this from the earliest Ante-Nicene Fathers.

Clement of Rome, the third bishop of the congregation at the city of Rome, who was conversant with the apostles, refers to a pre-canon closed system of orthodoxy in his First Epistle to the Corinthians:

> [Chap. XLII] The apostles have preached the Gospel to us from the Lord Jesus Christ; Jesus Christ has done so from God. Christ therefore was sent forth by God, and the apostles by Christ. Both these appointments, then, were made in an orderly way, according to the will of God. Having therefore received their orders, and being fully assured by the resurrection of our Lord Jesus Christ, and established in the word of God, with full assurance of the Holy Ghost, they went forth proclaiming that the kingdom of God was at hand.[2]

---

[2] *The Ante-Nicene Fathers: First Epistle of Clement* [Chap. XLII], Rev Alexander Roberts, D.D. and James Donaldson, LL.D., Editors (Grand Rapids, Michigan: Wm. B. Eerdmans Publishing Company, 1977), Vol. I, p. 16.

Ignatius of the church of Antioch in Syria is remembered as a co-disciple of the Apostle John along with Polycarp. He also refers to a pre-canon orthodoxy in his Epistle to the Magnesians:

> (Chap. XIII) Study, therefore, to be established in the doctrines of the Lord and of the apostles, that so all things, whatsoever ye do, may prosper, both in the flesh and spirit, in faith and love....[3]

Thus, true catholic unity must be based on a closed system of apostolic doctrine.

In his Epistle to the Romans, Ignatius distinguishes between his authority as a bishop and the authority of the apostles:

> (Chap. IV.) I do not, as Peter and Paul, issue commandments unto you. They were apostles of Jesus Christ, but I am the very least [of believers].[4]

Irenaeus, the disciple of Polycarp, states the case for us in the preface to his third book *Against Heresies* wherein he points out that his truth is qualified in that it did not originate with himself:

> But in this, the third book, I shall adduce proofs from the Scriptures, so that I may come behind in nothing of what thou hast enjoined; yea, that over and above what thou dist reckon upon, thou mayest receive from me the means of combating and vanquishing those who, in whatever manner, are propagating falsehood. For the love of God, being rich and ungrudging, confers upon the suppliant more than he can ask from it. Call to mind, then, the things which I have stated in the two preceding books, and, taking these in connection with them, thou shalt have from me a very copious refutation of all the heretics; and faithfully and strenuously shalt thou resist them in defence of the

---

[3] Ibid., *Ante-Nicene Fathers: Epistle of Ignatius to the Magnesians*, [Chap. XIII "To Be Established In Faith And Unity"], Vol. 1, p. 64.

[4] Ibid., *Ante-Nicene Fathers: Epistle of Ignatius to the Romans*, [Chap. IV "Allow Me To Fall Prey To The Wild Beasts"], Vol. 1, p. 75.

only true and life-giving faith, which the Church has received from the apostles and imparted to her sons. For the Lord of all gave to His apostles the power of the Gospel, through whom also we have known the truth, that is, the doctrine of the Son of God; to whom also did the Lord declare: "He that heareth you, heareth Me; and he that despiseth you, despiseth me, and Him that sent Me.[5]

Again in (Chap. I) Irenaeus states that:

We have learned from none others the plan of our salvation, than from those through whom the Gospel has come down to us, which they did at one time proclaim in public, and, at a later period, by the will of God, handed down to us in the Scriptures, to be the ground and pillar of our faith.[6]

He describes heretics as those who claimed to have received new truth from God to be added to the apostolic tradition and demonstrates the task of the presbyters as that of keeping the system closed:

(Chap. II.) But, again, when we refer them to that tradition which originates from the apostles, [and] which is preserved by means of the successions of

---

[5] Ibid., *Ante-Nicene Fathers: Irenaeus Against Heresies, Book III* [Preface], Vol. 1, p. 414. See also p. 331, *Book I, Chap. X.1*: "Nor will any one of the rulers in the Churches, however highly gifted he may be in point of eloquence, teach doctrines different from these (for no one is greater than the master); nor, on the other hand, will he who is deficient in power of expression inflict injury on the tradition. For the faith being ever one and the same, neither does one who is able at great length to discourse regarding it, make any addition to it, nor does one, who can say but little, diminish it."

[6] Ibid., [Book III, Chap.I.1], Vol. 1, p. 414. Contrasting orthodoxy, as a closed system of doctrine, with heresy, he states in [Chap. XVI.1], p. 440: "I Judge it necessary therefore to take into account the entire mind of the apostles regarding our Lord Jesus Christ, and to show that not only did they never hold any such opinions regarding Him; but still further, that they announced through the Holy Spirit, that those who should teach such doctrines were agents of Satan, sent forth for the purpose of overturning the faith of some, and drawing them away from life."

presbyters in the Churches, they object to tradition, saying that they themselves are wiser not merely than the presbyters, but even than the apostles, because they have discovered the unadulterated truth.[7]

Irenaeus tells us that it is this closed system that makes Christian doctrine public and therefore catholic (universal):

> (Chap. III.) It is within the power of all, therefore, in every Church, who may wish to see the truth, to contemplate clearly the tradition of the apostles manifested throughout the whole world; and we are in a position to reckon up those who were by the apostles instituted bishops in the Churches, and [to demonstrate] the succession of these men to our own times; those who neither taught nor knew of anything like what these [heretics] rave about. For if the apostles had known hidden mysteries, which they were in the habit of imparting to "the perfect" apart and privily from the rest, they would have delivered them especially to those to whom they were also committing the Churches themselves.[8]

He further illustrates the principle of II Timothy 2:2 by listing in succession the first twelve bishops of the Church at Rome in relation to their obligation to keep the system closed:

> (Chap. III.) ...In this order, and by this succession, the ecclesiastical tradition from the apostles, and the preaching of the truth, have come down to us. And this is most abundant proof that there is one and the same vivifying faith, which has been preserved in the Church from the apostles until now, and handed down in truth.[9]

Irenaeus continues by using Polycarp to illustrate the *sole authority* of the apostolic tradition:

---

[7] Ibid., [Book III, Chap.II.2], Vol. 1, p. 415.
[8] Ibid., [Book III, Chap. III.1], Vol. 1, p. 415.
[9] Ibid., [Book III, Chap. III.3], Vol. 1, p. 416.

> (Chap. III.) But Polycarp also was not only instructed by apostles, and conversed with many who had seen Christ, but was also, by apostles in Asia, appointed bishop of the Church in Smyrna, whom I also saw in my early youth....and, when a very old man, gloriously and most nobly suffering martyrdom, departed this life, having always taught the things which he had learned from the apostles, and which the Church has handed down and which alone are true. To these things all the Asiatic Churches testify, as do also those men who have succeeded Polycarp down to the present time....He it was who, coming to Rome in the time of Anicetus caused many to turn away from the aforesaid heretics to the Church of God, proclaiming that he had received this one and sole truth from the apostles.[10]

This is precisely why Irenaeus considers it unnecessary to seek for extra-apostolic information regarding the will of God:

> (Chap. IV.) Since therefore we have such proofs, it is not necessary to seek the truth among others which it is easy to obtain from the Church; since the apostles, like a rich man [depositing his money] in a bank, lodged in her hands most copiously all things pertaining to the truth...[11]

This same idea of the sole authority of the apostolic tradition is equivalent to the belief in the *sole authority* of the Scriptures for faith and doctrine. Irenaeus makes this very conclusion:

---

[10] Ibid., [Book III, Chap. III.4], Vol. 1, p. 416. Also p. 417: "Suppose there arise a dispute relative to some important question among us, should we not have recourse to the most ancient Churches with which the apostles held constant intercourse, and learn from them what is certain and clear in regard to the present question? For how should it be if the apostles themselves had not left us writings? Would it not be necessary, [in that case,] to follow the course of the tradition which they handed down to those to whom they did commit the Churches?"

[11] Ibid., [Book III, Chap. IV.1], Vol. 1, p. 416.

(Chap. V.) Since, therefore, the tradition from the apostles does thus exist in the Church, and is permanent among us, let us revert to the Scriptural proof furnished by those apostles who did also write the Gospel, in which they recorded the doctrine regarding God, pointing out that our Lord Jesus Christ is the truth, and that no lie is in him.[12]

Sole authority would mean, for Irenaeus, a closed, fixed system of doctrine to which no theological truth claims could be added nor taken away:

True knowledge is [that which consists in] the doctrine of the apostles, and the ancient constitution of the Church throughout all the world, and the distinctive manifestation of the body of Christ according to the successions of the bishops, by which they have handed down that Church which exists in every place, and has come even unto us, being guarded and preserved, without any forgoing of Scriptures, by a very complete system of doctrine, and neither receiving addition nor [suffering] curtailment [in the truths which she believes]; and [it consists in] reading [the word of God] without falsification, and a lawful and diligent exposition in harmony with the Scriptures, both without danger and without blasphemy…[13]

We will note one final quotation wherein Irenaeus defines orthodoxy as the true Church standing for the closed system of apostolic tradition through the written Scriptures:

(Chap. XX.) Now all these [heretics] are of much later date than the bishops to whom the apostles committed the Churches; which fact I have in the third book taken all pains to demonstrate. It follows, then, as a matter of course, that these heretics aforementioned, since they are blind to the truth, and deviate from the [right] way, will walk in various roads; and therefore the

---

[12] Ibid., [Book III, Chap. V.1], Vol. 1, p. 417.
[13] Ibid., [Book IV, Chap. XXXII.8], Vol. 1, p. 508.

footsteps of their doctrine are scattered here and there without agreement or connection. But the path of those belonging to the Church circumscribes the whole world, as possessing the sure tradition from the apostles, and gives unto us to see that the faith of all is one and the same, since all receive one and the same God the Father, and believe in the same dispensation regarding the incarnation of the Son of God, and are cognizant of the same gift of the Spirit and are conversant with the same commandments, and preserve the same form of ecclesiastical constitution, and expect the same advent of the Lord, and await the same salvation of the complete man, that is, of the soul and body. And undoubtedly the preaching of the Church is true and steadfast, in which one and the same way of salvation is shown throughout the whole world. For to her is entrusted the light of God; and therefore the "wisdom" of God, by means of which she saves all men, "is declared in [its] going forth; it uttereth [its voice] faithfully in the streets, is preached on the tops of the walls, and speaks continually in the gates of the city." For the Church preaches the truth everywhere, and she is the seven-branched candlestick which bears the light of Christ.... Now, such are all the heretics, and those who imagine that they have hit upon something more beyond the truth.... It behoves us, therefore, to avoid their doctrines, and to take careful heed lest we suffer any injury from them; but to flee to the Church, and be brought up in her bosom, and be nourished with the Lord's Scriptures.[14]

Furthermore, the use of the *kerygma* (proclamation) as an overall term to denote the substance of the message of the New Testament, and a skeleton framework underlying it, is well founded. Paul's Gospel was the same as the preaching of Jesus (Rom. 16:25), and any departure from it was to be avoided (Rom. 16:17; II Thes. 3:6; Acts 20:25-31). Thus, the true *kerygma* was committed to the Church originally through the preaching of the apostles (Titus 1:3; II Tim. 4:17).

---

[14] Ibid., [Book V, Chap. XX.1], Vol. 1, pp. 547, 548.

Tertullian (*c. 160-230*) was a Christian writer in Carthage, North Africa who wrote apologies and works against heretics. In *The prescription Against Heretics* he discusses the boundaries of church doctrine thusly:

> They then in like manner founded the churches in every city, from which all the other churches, one after another, derived the tradition of the faith, and the seeds of doctrine, and are every day deriving them, that they may become churches. Indeed, it is on this account only that they will be able to deem themselves apostolic, as being the offspring of apostolic churches. Every sort of thing must necessarily revert to its original for its classification. Therefore the churches, although they are so many and so great, comprise but the one primitive church, (founded) by the apostles, from which they all (spring).[15]

---

[15] Ibid., *Ante-Nicene Fathers [The Writings of Tertullian, Part Second] On Prescription Against Heretics,* [Chap xx], Vol. III, p. 252. [Cf. Chap. XXXII]: "Let the heretics contrive something of the same kind. For after their blasphemy, what is there that is unlawful for them (to attempt)? But should they even effect the contrivance, they will not advance a step. For their very doctrine, after comparison with that of the apostles, will declare by its own diversity and contrariety, that it had for its author neither an apostle nor an apostolic man; because, as the apostles would never have taught things which were self-contradictory, so the apostolic men would not have inculcated teaching different from the apostles, unless they who received their instruction from the apostles went and preached in a contrary manner. To this test, therefore will they be submitted for proof by those churches, who, although they derive not their founder from apostles or apostolic men (as being of much later date, for they are in fact being founded daily), yet, since they agree in the same faith, they are accounted as not less apostolic because they are akin in doctrine. Then let all the heresies, when challenged to these two tests by our apostolic church, offer their proof of how they deem themselves to be apostolic. But in truth they neither are so, nor are they able to prove themselves to what they are not. Nor are they admitted to peaceful relations and communion by such churches as are in any way connected with apostles, inasmuch as they are in no sense themselves apostolic because of their diversity as to the mysteries of the faith."

Subjective And Extra-biblical Arguments For Baptismal Regeneration

This is the closed system of apostolic doctrine that Tertullian imposed upon the followers of Marcion.[16] Thus, true doctrine was deposited in the church only by the original apostles[17] and the prescription of any innovation was unlawful.[18] For Tertullian, there was no need of innovation because the apostles omitted nothing that we needed to know in order to carry out God's work.[19]

Cyprian was a third century bishop in Carthage, North Africa who wrote various treatises and epistles during a period of great persecution. In his *Epistle lXII.10 &11* he warned that we must not depart from apostolic doctrine nor innovate the ordinances delivered by them.[20]

---

[16] Ibid., [Part Second, *Against Marcion*, Book I, Chap. XXI], Vol. III, p. 286: "No other teaching will have the right of being received as apostolic than that which is at the present day proclaimed in the churches of apostolic foundation. You will, however, find no church of apostolic origin but such as reposes its Christian faith in the Creator. But if the church shall prove to have been corrupt from the beginning, where shall the pure ones be found? Will it be amongst the adversaries of the Creator? Show us, then, one of your churches tracing its descent from an apostle, and you shall have gained the day."

[17] Ibid., [Part Second, *Against Marcion*, Book IV, Chap. V], Vol. III, p. 249,250: "On the whole, then, if that is evidently more true which is earlier, if that is earlier which is from the very beginning, if that is from the beginning which has the apostles for its authors, then it will certainly be quite as evident, that that comes down from the apostles, which has been kept as a sacred deposit in the churches of the apostles."

[18] Ibid., Tertullian, *On Fasting* [Chap. XIII], Vol. IV, p. 111: "You lay down a prescription that this faith has its solemnities 'appointed' by the Scriptures or the tradition of the ancestors; and that no further addition in the way of observance must be added, on account of the unlawfulness of innovation."

[19] Ibid., Tertullian, *De Fuga In Persecutione*, 9, Vol. IV, p. 121: "The teaching of the apostles was surely in everything according to the mind of God: they forgot and omitted nothing of the Gospel." Cf. II Tim. 3:16, 17 "All scripture is given by inspiration of God, and is profitable…That the man of God may be perfect [*complete*], Throughly furnished unto all good works."

[20] Ibid., *Ante-Nicene Fathers* [Cyprian, *Epistle LXII, 10, 11*], Vol. V, p. 361: "…but that we must not at all depart from the evangelical precepts, and that disciples ought also to observe and to do the same things which the Master both taught and did…11. Since then, neither the apostle himself nor an angel from heaven can preach or teach any otherwise than Christ has once taught and His apostles have announced, I wonder very much whence has originated this
(Continued on next page)

Archelaus also was a third century bishop who publically debated Manes, the founder of Manichaeism. He believed that the sign of a false prophet or a false Christ was the attempt to teach beyond the boundaries of the apostolic tradition. He even notes that they will use Scripture to justify themselves to go beyond the Scriptures to establish new doctrine.

> You well understand, no doubt, that those who seek to set up any new dogma have the habit of very readily perverting into a conformity with their own notions any proofs they desire to take from the Scriptures. In anticipation, however, of this, the apostolic word marks out the case thus: 'If anyone preach any other gospel unto you than that which you have received, let him be accursed.' And consequently, in addition to what has been once committed to us by the apostles, a disciple of Christ ought to receive nothing new as doctrine.[21]

Therefore, there is not a divine extra-biblical *kerygma* to be recognized by the Church today. If there is, we will never have the inerrant ability to distinguish it from the claims of false apostles (II Cor. 11:13). Our only hope of getting close to the truth is the *sole authority* of the Bible. The contemporary game of *preacher roulette* is one wherein the sinner gambles his soul on a guess as to which *prophet* is really speaking the oracles of God.

The New Testament Church has an *exousia* (authority) which is a freedom for the community, but this is not a freedom to correct the Scriptures with spiritual authority in the name of the *Living Logos*.

---

practice, that contrary to evangelical and apostolical discipline, water is offered in some places in the Lord's cup."

[21] Ibid., *Ante-Nicene Fathers* [Archelaus, *The Acts Of The Disputation With The Heresiark Manes, 40*], Vol. VI, p. 213, 214. Cf. section 36, p. 210: "As Paul himself also seems to tell us, and, further, as we have learned likewise from the earlier account given in the Gospel, an introduction to preaching, or teaching, or evangelizing, or prophesying, is not in this life at least, held out on the same terms to any person in times subsequent *to the apostle's:* and if the opposite appears ever to be the case, the person can only be held to be a false prophet or a false Christ."

Subjective And Extra-biblical Arguments For Baptismal Regeneration

When the Apostle Paul spoke by *concession* or *permission* (*suggnome*), he was only offering personal advice and made it clear that this was not a commandment from God (I Cor. 7:6). Though Timothy and Irenaeus were indwelt by the *Living Logos*, they received no new doctrines that were not already handed down from the apostles—*And the things that thou hast heard of me among many witnesses, the same commit thou to faithful men, who shall be able to teach others also* (II Tim. 2:2). The Christian community is free to enter into error but not authorized to pontificate that the error is a *revelational mandate* from Christ. When the Christian community rejected the heliocentric view of the solar system, it proved to the world that the canon for the church was not the consensus of the community nor of the hierarchs. The community's freedom is from the curse of the law (Rom 6:14) and from the theological commandments of men (Col. 2:20-22), but not a freedom and authority to issue new commandments (I Tim. 4:1-4). Thus, community *exousia* is not intrinsic divine autonomy from the authority of Scripture. Contemporary Christian gnosticism seems to have developed a freedom along the lines of the extremists at Corinth (I Cor. 5:1 ff.) wherein men established their own autonomy in moral and theological issues as if God had certainly approved. In the apocryphal Acts, as is often the case today, *exousia* was a mystically extorted power deployed for one's own ends.

Although God reveals Himself in nature (Rom. 1:20) and in the conscience of man (Rom. 1:18, 19), these revelations contain no doctrines which are not already declared in Scripture (Rom. 2:14). We are often charged with limiting God to the content of the Scriptures and thus putting Him in a box. On the contrary, we know that God is infinite and therefore cannot be limited. However, we would be attempting to limit God if we proclaimed that He is incapable of placing scriptural boundaries on what He will allow us to know regarding His will for mankind. The Apostle Paul was a limited agnostic. Although there is infinitely more to God than is revealed in Scripture, we should consider with Paul that extrabiblical information about the will of God is past finding out (Rom. 11:33; James 4:13-16). So it is not that the infinite God is limited to this Book. The limitation is that we are small and finite, and therefore, our understanding is confined to the boundaries of the canon.

The Body of Christ has a mission and the Scriptures contain all the doctrinal furnishings necessary to perform every work within that objective:

> All scripture *is* given by inspiration of God, and *is* profitable for doctrine, for reproof, for correction, for instruction in righteousness: That the man of God may be perfect, throughly furnished unto all good works (II Tim. 3:16,17).

Never let it be once said that God cannot reveal new truth beyond the Scriptures. However, it would be limiting God to insist that He must reveal extrabiblical truth to us whether or not He desires to do so. It would be limiting God to say that He cannot close the canon.

But there is also the problem with the thousands of variant readings of the Greek manuscripts of the NT. We must understand that a variation does not constitute a corruption. Otherwise, Christ and the apostles would not have used the Septuagint and the Hebrew Text interchangeably. Geisler and Nix comment on how the variations are counted:

> There is an ambiguity in saying there are some 200,000 variants in the existing manuscripts of the New Testament, since these represent only 10,000 places in the New Testament. If one single word is misspelled in 3,000 different manuscripts, this is counted as 3,000 variants or readings.[22]

Church historian, Phillip Schaff, concluded that only 400 of the 150,000 variant readings caused doubt about the textual meaning, and only 50 of these were of great significance. In the manuscripts available in his day, he could not find one variation which altered, *an article of faith or a precept of duty which is not abundantly sustained by other and undoubted passages, or by the whole tenor of Scripture teaching.*[23]

Laying aside the issue of canonical authority, there is the question of interpretation. We should require of ourselves to refrain from a talismanic view of our own feelings or of the consensus of the

---

[22] Norman L. Geisler and William E. Nix, *A General Introduction to the Bible* (Chicago: Moody Press, 1968), p. 361.

[23] Philip Schaff, *Companion to the Greek Testament and the English Version*, Revised Edition (New York: Harper Brothers, 1883), p. 177.

Christian community. In order for the canon to be a public measuring rod, it must self-contain the key to its own interpretation. This is a concept that most of the earliest Church fathers failed to completely comprehend. We should require that our method of interpretation, as well as the revelation we use, be objectively outside ourselves. We should realize that a correct guess regarding biblical meaning is absolutely improbable. It is rational to conclude that the writers had a particular meaning in mind for each text. It is also reasonable to conclude that they intended for that meaning to be ascertained. We will live long enough to uncover only a portion of the answers to all Bible questions. However, this does not mean that the answers are not there. An objective historical-grammatical analysis of a text will give us more truth than any other alternative available. If we cannot find the hermeneutical key to the correct interpretation of a text, we should refuse to guess or look inside ourselves for a mystical key. The true meaning of a text must be contained within the text itself and within the coherent context of the entire canon. Otherwise, our correct understanding would require a further revelation which some contemporary scholars refer to as "illumination." On the contrary, the true Gospel does not need lighting, it is light—

> In whom the god of this world hath blinded the minds of them which believe not, lest the light of the glorious gospel of Christ, who is the image of God, should shine unto them. (II Cor. 4:4).

Furthermore, the Word of God does not need lighting, for it is the illumination of God when properly read and understood—*Thy word is a lamp unto my feet, and a light unto my path* (Ps. 119:105). It would be a wise course of action if each member of the Christian community were to read and hear the Scriptures with heed, caution and discretion, attempting to recognize when the preacher or the community is departing from textual authority.

Our hermeneutical approach to a text should not therefore be dialectic—i.e. we do not bring our objections to a text as an antithesis and work toward a compromise position between it and ourselves. There is a vast difference between assigning a new meaning to a text and deriving a further interpretation from it. If change or progression occurs in our understanding, it must be the text that changes us and not ourselves who change the text.

When contradictions seem apparent in the Bible, as in the case of Paul's *faith without works* and James' *faith plus works*, we must have confidence that God's true Word cannot be self-contradictory and that two contradictory positions cannot simultaneously be true. If the Bible is infallible and coherent in matters of faith and doctrine, then there is something that we may have failed to observe. Paul said we are *justified by faith without the deeds of the law* (Rom. 3:28) while James proclaimed that we are justified by works and *not by faith only* (James 2:24). Paul described faith without works as very much alive (Rom. 4:5) while James affirmed that the same faith without works is "dead" (James 2:17). Paul declared that Abraham was not justified by works in the sight of God (Rom. 4:2) while James proposes that Abraham was justified by works (James 2:21).

What are we missing here? The key to Romans chapter four is: *but not before God* (4:2), while the key to James chapter two is: *show me thy faith without thy works, and I will show thee my faith by my works* (James 2:18). Paul is speaking of justification in the sight of God while James is addressing justification in the sight of man: *show me...and I will show you.* God can see your faith when you are sitting silently on a bench, eating an apple. But others can recognize us as Christians only by our testimonies and deeds. Therefore, there is no contradiction between these texts.

Allegorizing the Bible in order to teach baptismal regeneration from every mention of moisture or water is a technique which, if valid, would require divine inspiration and inerrancy on the part of the interpreter. Again, *The Cambridge History of the Bible* traces the origin of this technique:

> But we may regard as certain the conclusion that the New Testament was first subject to allegorising, not within the bounds of the Catholic Church, but among the heterodox gnostic sects which flourished outside the Church or only on its periphery, and that orthodox Christian writers only adopted the allegorisation of the New Testament by way of defense, in order to extract orthodox doctrine from it...The Gnostics on the whole accepted such of the books of the New Testament as were in general circulation in the second century, and accepted them willingly, though they claimed the right to supplement them by their own secret traditions. It

is among them that we can first discern the allegorisation of the New Testament. Tertullian tells us that allegories, parables and riddles represent *par excellence* the heretics' way of interpreting the New Testament. The Valentinians in Irenaeus' day regularly allegorised the parable of the Workers in the Vineyard. The Gnostics interpreted the parable of the Foolish Virgins as referring to the five (deceptive) senses.[24]

We should also consider the fact that the inner witness of the *Living Logos* and the outer witness of the Scriptures are the same in content. I Jn. 5:10, 11 states:

He that believeth on the Son of God hath the witness in himself [inner witness]: he that believeth not God hath made him a liar because he believeth not the record [outer witness] that God gave of his son. And this is the record, that God hath given to us eternal life, and this life is in his son.

Verse 13 states: These things have I written [outer witness] unto you that believe on the name of the Son of God; that ye may know that ye have eternal life, and that ye may believe on the name of the Son of God.

The problem is this: if the Bible is not the sole authority for faith and doctrine, our only alternative is to find absolute information about God's will from another source. Many a self-proclaimed prophet today will arise and proclaim that the *Living Logos* has chosen to reveal this new information through him or through his denomination.

The *Church Fathers* of the earliest centuries of Christianity developed varied interpretations of the apostolic writings. Yet there was an understanding that the parameters of argument, within a legitimate debate regarding heresy, were the traditions of the original apostles. The larger question is one of whether the apostles left a clue regarding the interpretation of their traditions. We hold that Scriptures are self-

---

[24] Ibid., *The Cambridge History Of The Bible*, Vol. I, pp. 416, 417.

interpreting and do not require a further mystical, revelational key in order to be understood.

The most perplexing element of contemporary Christendom is its multi-varied doctrinal traditions. Most of the high points of Church history have arisen when great men of God made it their goal to stand as truly as they could upon the Word of God. But after experiencing a degree of success, and many seeming blessings from God, these same men often fell prey to the notion that the Holy Spirit wanted to use their personal opinions about almost everything as the new standard for the universal Church. From this fallacy there would arise a tradition among their followers based upon these extra-biblical *convictions*. The next generation of their followers would introduce this as a doctrinal tradition based upon a biographical analysis of the great man's life and personal testimony. This would establish into the movement a mystical *knowledge of God* which could not finds its source in Scripture. Thus arose the fallacy that *our critics must find a biblical prohibition against this teaching or a direct command not to teach this tradition*. The impossibility of proving a negative was considered an ultimate proof for the extra-biblical tradition.

After the dogma was well established, it honestly seemed ridiculous to suggest that it was not revealed by God Himself. Such traditional misconceptions became fixed dogmas resulting in exegetical blindness to certain key passages of Scripture.

It has been argued that those who have held to *baptismal regeneration* throughout the Church age have proven themselves by having been greatly endowed with spiritual gifts. The Apostle Paul taught that truth and spirituality could not be measured solely by the gifts of the Spirit. In I Cor. 1:4-7 he thanked God that the Corinthians were enriched in *all utterance* and *all knowledge* and that they had *come behind in no gift*. He then proceeded to discuss how the general church membership was carnal and unspiritual: *And I, brethren, could not speak unto you as unto spiritual, but as unto carnal, even as unto babes in Christ* (I Cor. 3:1). Thus, the most spiritually gifted church mentioned in the NT was also the most unspiritual and carnal, being plagued with heresies among them (I Cor. 11:19).

On the other hand, spirituality can be detected by the fruits of the Spirit—*But the fruit of the Spirit is love, joy, peace, longsuffering, gentleness, goodness, faith, meekness, temperance: against such there is no law* (Gal. 5:22, 23).[25] A further study of Scripture will reveal how each of these fruits can be convincingly feigned to the deception of many. Therefore, the searching Christian should look for them in a context of Scriptural truth, particularly as pertains to the purity of the Gospel.

Love is not only a fruit of the Spirit, but also one of the gifts of the Spirit. Where there is no godly love there is no serious degree of spirituality. In I Cor. 13:1 Paul stated that if he had the tongues of men and angels and had not love, he would *become as sounding brass or tinkling cymbal.* Obviously, such a gift is not the ultimate measure of spirituality. In verse two he proclaimed that if he had the gift of prophecy, inerrant knowledge, theological understanding, plus the faith to move mountains, he would be nothing without love. Again, these are not ultimate measures of spirituality. The value of faith is not measured by its intensity but by its object. If one had the greatest faith in the world that the air would support his weight, it would not. However, if he had the least amount of faith in the world that the ground would support him, it would. The smallest amount of faith will save a sinner if its object is the finished work of Christ accomplished upon the cross of Calvary. In verse three, Paul stated that if he gave all his goods to the poor and died a martyr's death, his life would be an insufficient standard for his followers if there was no true spirituality.

A key to detecting true spiritual love is its commitment to biblical truth, for love *rejoiceth not in iniquity, but rejoiceth in the truth* (I Cor. 13:6). A Christian should be suspicious when someone is always testifying of an intimate relationship with Jesus and the Spirit while simultaneously expressing apathy toward the doctrinal truths of God's Word. Christ wants to have an intimate relationship with us, but this experience is not to become a basis for theological or spiritual pontification about extra-biblical issues.

Likewise, spirituality and truth cannot be measured solely by the real, or feigned, power of the Spirit. Samson's Nazarite vows were three-fold: he was to abstain from strong drink; from touching dead carcasses, and from cutting his hair. Throughout his adult life we see

---

[25] There are many more than nine fruits of the spirit but it will not be our task to study or list them here.

him at drinking parties, gambling, living with ungodly women, eating honey out of a dead carcass. Almost all, if not all, of his supernatural victories were acts of personal vindication over losing a bet or over one of his women. But in each case the power of the Spirit came upon him. In Judges 15 he allowed Israel to bind him with new cords and deliver him to the Philistines. In verse fourteen *the Spirit of the Lord came mightily upon him* and he brake the cords, picked up the jawbone of a dead carcass (in defiance to God's revealed will), and slew a thousand Philistines. Could he have used the *power of the Spirit* on his life at that moment as proof of his spirituality, doctrinal accuracy, and devoted obedience? Certainly not. In Judges 16 his hair had been cut and his eyes had been gouged out by the Philistines. His last request to God was for the supernatural power to commit suicide while getting vengeance for his eyes: *And Samson called unto the Lord and said, O Lord God, remember me, I pray thee, and strengthen me, I pray thee, only this once, O God, that I may be at once avenged of the Philistines for my two eyes* (Judges 16:28). When did he ever use his supernatural strength for God and country? Yes, God used it for Israel and for His glory, but Samson's motive was always one of personal vengeance. Does his death constitute proof that it is sometimes God's will for a man to commit suicide? Certainly not.

One great shortcut to approaching truth is systematically to eliminate that which is not true. This can be partially accomplished by an understanding of the stumblingblocks to clear theological thinking. Negative thinking has gotten too much bad publicity of late. The Bible repeatedly contrasts that which is true with that which is not true (Gal. 2:16; Eph. 2:8, 9; Acts 13:39; Rom. 3:28; Ps. 1). Part of the definition of *positive* is that it is a solution to a negative alternative. Positive cancer research has to focus on the nature of the negative processes of malignant cells. With this in mind, let us remind ourselves of the factors which could mislead us in our theological thinking. The following will not be a study in proper hermeneutics as much as an identification of improper hermeneutics and invalid tests for theological authority.

Thinkers have often elevated feeling to a level of theological authority. Feelings are usually vague, ill-defined, lack precision and conflict with one another—e.g. mixed emotions. Without neglecting the fact that God created us with feelings, He has never established them as a theological authority. Therefore, we should never make authoritative theological affirmations on the basis of feelings.

Subjective And Extra-biblical Arguments For Baptismal Regeneration

Custom and acquired tradition can also be misleading. Traditions are customs which have been preserved for generations with deep cultural roots. They may or may not agree with truth, but they are not valid criterion for truth. We do not allow for the antiquity of ancient forms of cannibalism to argue for the validity of their tradition. It has been traditional in some ancient societies to place a living wife into the funeral fire of her deceased husband, but tradition is not an argument for the validity of the custom.

We often hear that a position is true because it has *stood the test of time*. Theology is often debated merely from this criterion. If this were a valid test for truth, then many false superstitions of the past would be ultimately vindicated. The geocentric theory of the universe is much older than the heliocentric theory, as well as the theory that the earth is flat.

Intuition, on the other hand, can result in the discovery of truth (as in the case of Thomas Edison), but it is the objective discovery of the truth that becomes the reliable test. In Edison's case, intuition was the source of truth but not the test of truth. Verification was not obtained in the intuitive experience, for there was no way of knowing whether or not the light bulb would work. The idea had to be tested in some nonintuitive manner in a laboratory. In the same sense, the apostolic message was received subjectively but was confirmed objectively through the apostolic gifts—

> How shall we escape, if we neglect so great salvation; which at the first began to be spoken by the Lord, and was confirmed unto us by them that heard *him*; God also bearing *them* witness, both with signs and wonders, and with divers miracles, and gifts of the Holy Ghost, according to his own will (Heb. 2:3, 4)?
>
> Truly the signs of an apostle were wrought among you in all patience, in signs, and wonders, and mighty deeds (II Cor. 12:12).
>
> Unto the angel of the church of Ephesus write; These things saith he that holdeth the seven stars in his right hand, who walketh in the midst of the seven golden candlesticks; I know thy works, and thy labour, and

thy patience, and how thou canst not bear them which are evil: and thou hast tried them which say they are apostles, and are not, and hast found them liars (Rev. 2:1, 2).

The false apostles would claim to receive revelations from God in addition to the doctrines delivered to the church by the original apostles. Thus, they could claim the inerrancy of the Scriptures plus the inerrancy of their additional revelations. Those who claim apostolic authority today fail to realize that legitimate revelation from God is a source of truth, but not a criterion for truth. There are thousands of revelation claims throughout Church history. All true revelations should offer a process of verification or criteria. The Bible offers a combination of tests for varification: fulfilled prophecy, apostolic sign gifts, and consistency and coherence with all the other claims of the sacred texts.

Jesus Christ did not expect hearers to believe Him apart from objective, coherent criteria. He claimed to be a source of truth, but professed that the claim alone was not conclusive:

> I can of mine own self do nothing: as I hear, I judge: and my judgment is just; because I seek not mine own will, but the will of the Father which hath sent me. If I bear witness of myself, my witness is not true (Jn. 5:30, 31).

Therefore, He offered a combination of criteria. First, the testimony of John the Baptist as fulfilled prophecy—

> There is another that beareth witness of me; and I know that the witness which he witnesseth of me is true (Jn. 5:32).

Secondly, there was His own objective works which could be empirically examined—

> But I have greater witness than that of John: for the works which the Father hath given me to finish, the

same works that I do, bear witness of me, that the Father hath sent me (Jn. 5:36).[26]

Thirdly, the testimony of God the Father—

> And the Father himself, which hath sent me, hath borne witness of me. Ye have neither heard his voice at any time, nor seen his shape (Jn. 5:37).

And finally, the test of coherency with the rest of the sacred Scriptures—

> Search the scriptures; for in them ye think ye have eternal life: and they are they which testify of me (Jn. 5:39).

Many modern claimants of direct revelation and personal inerrancy offer the claim alone as proof of authority. How many can offer the combination of criteria as did Christ and the Apostles?

The following discussion may seem elementary to a university graduate, but for the sake of the average Christian we will evaluate several of the roadblocks to sound biblical thinking.

---

[26] (e.g. Matt. 11:1-5; 20-23) "And it came to pass, when Jesus had made an end of commanding his twelve disciples, he departed thence to teach and to preach in their cities. Now when John had heard in the prison the works of Christ, he sent two of his disciples, And said unto him, Art thou he that should come, or do we look for another? Jesus answered and said unto them, Go and shew John again those things which ye do hear and see: The blind receive their sight, and the lame walk, the lepers are cleansed, and the deaf hear, the dead are raised up, and the poor have the gospel preached to them…Then began he to upbraid the cities wherein most of his mighty works were done, because they repented not: Woe unto thee, Chorazin! woe unto thee, Bethsaida! for if the mighty works, which were done in you, had been done in Tyre and Sidon, they would have repented long ago in sackcloth and ashes. But I say unto you, It shall be more tolerable for Tyre and Sidon at the day of judgment, than for you. And thou, Capernaum, which art exalted unto heaven, shalt be brought down to hell: for if the mighty works, which have been done in thee, had been done in Sodom, it would have remained until this day."

Rarely someone might appeal to instinct as a revelation from God. Yet the Adamic nature, which is instinctive, is not a revelation of God's will. A discrepancy may therefore occur when *instincts* seem to conflict, as with forms of oppression. Neither the *instinct* to oppress nor the *instinct* to be free of oppression can appeal to instinct as the test of truth.

Still others may cite the consensus of the *mainstream* as opposed to the *radical fringe*—e.g. *Seventy million Frenchmen cannot be wrong*. It is the old Latin proverb: *vox populi, vox dei* (the voice of the people is the voice of God). In America we have the *Bill of Rights* in order that an individual may defend himself against the will of the majority. These first ten amendments to the Constitution assume that the majority will at times be wrong. It is often falsely assumed that if a majority of accepted people hold to a theological position, it is *ipso facto* true. King David employed this fallacy in carrying out a most noble objective. First, he conducted a survey of the mainstream—*And David consulted with the captains of thousands and hundreds, and with every leader* (I Chron. 13:1). Secondly, he took a census of the citizens—

> And David said unto all the congregation of Israel, If it seem good unto you, and that it be of the LORD our God, let us send abroad unto our brethren every where, that are left in all the land of Israel, and with them also to the priests and Levites which are in their cities and suburbs, that they may gather themselves unto us (13:2).

Thirdly, he stated his noble objective: *And let us bring again the ark of our God to us: for we enquired not at it in the days of Saul* (13:3). Finally, his false premise was achieved— *And all the congregation said that they would do so: for the thing was right in the eyes of all the people* (13:5). From these factors of confirmation they proceeded to devise an unauthorized method of carrying out the objective—*And they carried the ark of God in a new cart out of the house of Abinadab: and Uzza and Ahio drave the cart* (13:7). If they had consulted the Scriptures they would have read:

> ...after that, the sons of Kohath shall come to bear it: but they shall not touch any holy thing, lest they die. These things are the burden of the sons of Kohath

Subjective And Extra-biblical Arguments For Baptismal Regeneration

> [Levites] in the tabernacle of the congregation (Nu. 4:15a; cf. Ex. 25:12-15).

David reinforced his judgment with pragmatism as he observed the success of the project being carried out by multitudes with pomp, dynamic music, mighty zeal, and magnificent ceremonial—

> And David and all Israel played before God with all their might, and with singing, and with harps, and with psalteries, and with timbrels, and with cymbals, and with trumpets (13:8).

In the NT, *they of the circumcision* will use the same reinforcement to confirm ritual salvation and salvation by personal righteousness—

> For I bear them record that they have a zeal of God, but not according to knowledge. For they being ignorant of God's righteousness, and going about to establish their own righteousness, have not submitted themselves unto the righteousness of God (Rom. 10:2, 3).

When the oxen stumbled, Uzzah put his hand on the ark to keep it from falling and was immediately stricken dead (13:9, 10). David was amazed that God would be so displeased over such a small technicality, and he fearfully began to question how this project should be executed (13:11, 12). So he went back to square one and consulted the Scriptures alone before proceeding. He determined that such an objective necessitated a prepared place (15:1), a prepared method (15:2, 15), and Scriptural instruction (15:12, 13). So with the priests in their proper places (15:14, 15), and sacrifices offered (5:26), the project became a success because the mind of God was properly consulted—

> And the children of the Levites bare the ark of God upon their shoulders with the staves thereon, as Moses commanded according to the word of the LORD (15:15).

Again, David used pomp singing, musical instruments, zeal and enthusiasm, but he did not use these as a test of truth (15:16). Doing the wrong thing with a noble motive will not transform it into the right thing—i.e. *The plowing of the wicked is sin* (Prov. 21:4b).

Pragmatism is the theory that an idea is true if it works. The argument has been made that great churches and movements were built from the doctrine of *baptismal regeneration*, whereas the advocates of *believer's baptism* constitute a radical fringe. It is argued that the workability of an idea validates it. Such a criterion is very useful in scientific research as one proceeds from theory to substantiation, but the theological difficulty is in the inadequate definitions of *workability* and *consequences*. In the final analysis, it is one's value system which determines the workability of an idea. If head-counts, magnificent buildings, and stained-glass windows are the measure, then there is an argument for sacramentalism. However, on the other hand, it is the scriptural assurance of eternal life that works for an advocate of *believer's baptism*—

> These things have I written unto you that believe on the name of the Son of God; that ye may know that ye have eternal life, and that ye may believe on the name of the Son of God (I Jn. 5:13).

Yet a communist, capitalist, socialist, Nazi, religious zealot, or an atheist can simultaneously appeal to the workability of his solution.

Theologians who claim extra-biblical doctrinal information from God will argue that additional revelation is appropriate as long as it is consistent with the Bible. It is argued that infant baptism is valid because we cannot find a Scripture verse that commands us to not baptize infants. It is claimed that any extra-biblical innovation which does not contradict the Bible is therefore authorized. Let us illustrate with a series of statements which do not contradict one another: *Our church baptizes infants; the sun shines; today is Sunday; chariots have wheels; the Roman Empire governs.* Although these statements do not contradict, they nevertheless do not cohere, and therefore, prove nothing about infant baptism. Discovering contradictions will most often prove falsehood, for the detection of falsehood is an important facet in the discovery of truth. However, much more than the mere elimination of contradiction is necessary for testing the validity of a truth claim.

We have referred to *coherence* which, in theology, requires that truth claims be more than consistent. They must cohere with an integrated whole (facts of Scripture and history), not just compatible within themselves, but with every other teaching of Scripture. A good theologian will use coherence as a prime criterion of a truth claim. Actually, coherence is the nature of truth as well as its criterion.

We can often observe someone using emotive language as an argument for a truth claim. If he can appear outraged or deeply convicted, people are supposed to assume the credibility of his assertion. Referring to one's dearly departed mother as having held this position, (e.g. *baptismal regeneration*), can throw his adversary off balance. Referring to advocates of *believer's baptism* as *radical, frivolous, unsophisticated, hateful, fringe, uneducated* and *unrecognized* is to use words which possess no value except to incite emotions against their truth claims. We are philosophically opposed to communism. But to call a man a *dirty communist* is not an argument but an expression of contempt. The word means *the common ownership of the means of production*, but this definition does not lend itself to the use of emotive language. Debaters learn to describe their own refusal to compromise as *conviction*, while their opponents refusal is *stubborn, rebellious, close-minded and stiff-necked*. In either case, a valid argument for truth has not been offered.

We must also learn to avoid the fallacy which reasons that what is true of any part separately is also true of the whole. It might be argued that if Augustine was so extremely correct about other theological affirmations, then his position on *baptismal regeneration* must also be reliable. Or, this fallacy might affirm that if Thomas Muncer, of Mulhausen, in Thuringia was a criminal anarchist and an Anabaptist, then all Anabaptists must be advocates of lawlessness and therefore incorrect in their views on baptism. Having the most outstanding Greek scholar on a faculty does not prove that your seminary has the most outstanding teaching staff.

On the other hand, there is also the opposite fallacy which reasons that whatever is true of the whole must also be true of each part separately. Because one is part of the nation's leading theological faculty does not make him the leading textual critic of the land. One cannot argue his point by reminding us that he was on the staff of such-and-such theological seminary.

Another fallacy is one which bypasses the issues under consideration by citing the fact that many advocates of the favored persuasion have been persecuted throughout the ages. This is an appeal to our sympathy and pity. Sympathy is virtuous and should guide many of our actions, but we should never let it obscure the truth of God's Word or be used as a test for truth.

We avoid still another pitfall when we observe someone departing from the point at issue to appeal instead to prestige, awe, or cultural elitism. This fallacy is committed when one argues that cultured and refined Christians of distinction will hold to a certain truth claim.

Almost everyone is familiar with the fallacy which shifts the discussion from the truth-claim under consideration to the assassination of the opponent's character. Even if one's own position is correct, this is never a valid form of argument. The personal character of a person has no essential relation to the factuality of his truth-claim. The level of a person's post-secondary education (if any) is totally unrelated to the credibility of his evidence. The reader should note again the number of times this fallacy has been used in the baptism debates cited in the previous chapters of this present work.

Then there is the argument from force when one reminds us that he has the power to persecute or ruin us if we do not embrace his position. Power and authority do not constitute criteria for a truth claim. The power to punish someone can corrupt thinking and logic almost effortlessly.

We have already observed, in previous chapters the contention that if one's adversary cannot disprove a thesis, it is therefore established as true. For instance, it has been argued that though the Bible does not command the baptism of infants, the burden of proof is on the advocates of *believer's baptism* to prove from Scripture that the Bible forbids it. The burden of proof should always fall upon the one who is proposing a thesis, and not the adversary. Under the U.S. Bill of Rights, one is presumed innocent until proven guilty beyond a reasonable doubt. But when putting forth a thesis, one cannot prove his affirmation valid on the grounds that it cannot be disproved. A proposition must be reinforced by positive evidence, not by the absence of it.[27] This fallacy results when arguing from possibility to actuality.

---

[27] John 10:27-29 affirms that no creature can pluck a believer out of Christ's or the Father's hand. The opponent of eternal salvation by grace through faith alone will argue that the passage does not say that the believer
(Continued on next page)

Subjective And Extra-biblical Arguments For Baptismal Regeneration

The fallacy begins by arguing the omnipotence of God. Who would deny that an all-powerful God could deliver the saving work of Christ to an infant through baptism? It is argued that if it is possible for God to do this then it is actual that He does. We should keep two principles in hand at all times: it is the one who affirms who must validate; and lack of evidence on one side does not constitute evidence for the contrary side of the question at hand. (e.g. A refutation of the theory of evolution does not establish creationism as a fact). Though disestablishment of an opposing view is a step toward the truth, it is not a test for truth.

We must also guard ourselves against an appeal to passions and prejudices, of which human reason is always vulnerable. Hence, we should not reject a truth claim simply because it would cause our dear old mothers and grandmothers to roll over in their graves. Many false religions hold their constituents captive by the use of this fallacy. No one desires to be shunned by his peers. One would like to see himself on the inside looking out rather than on the outside with his nose against the window viewing the mainstream dining in acceptability and dignity. The reason many post-secondary students so easily convert to atheism, agnosticism or pluralism when first entering college is that this is considered a badge of intelligence and abstract thinking .

Still another pitfall is the error in thinking wherein one establishes or disestablishes the wrong point. Instead of proving proposition (A), one proves affirmation (B)—i.e. *I once suffered as a missionary to China so therefore my position on baptism deserves the highest credibility.* Or, instead of overturning thesis (C), point (D) is impeached—e.g. *Pastor Smo's position on baptism is unworthy of consideration because he has spent his career in the comfort of a parsonage and has never undergone the test of hunger and hostile persecution.* This is a fallacy of irrelevance which, when committed in a court of law (i.e. answering a different question than the lawyer has asked) receives instruction from the judge to be responsive to the particular question that was put forth or else be held in contempt.

---

cannot jump out of the father's hand. Thus, a consuming viewpoint is dogmatically based on what the passage does not say and the burden of proof is placed on one who must prove from Scripture that the believer cannot bail out of God's love.

We should also be aware of the arguement that because thesis (B) followed incident (A) then the former was the root and cause of the latter—i.e. it has occasionally been argued that whereas the rebellion at Muncer was conducted by uneducated peasants who held to re-baptism, the thesis of *believer's baptism* is a position held primarily by a radical, uneducated, culturally deprived subculture who are an insignificant fringe outside the mainstream of religious society.

Then there is the compound question which assumes a previous question to have already been answered—e.g. *Have you stopped hating paedobaptists?* Either a positive or a negative answer is self-incriminating and a refusal to answer is deemed a denial. Another example is: *How do you account for your passion to divide the Body of Christ over this issue?*; or, *Who died and made you the judge of the universe?*; or, *Does your mother know that you condemn us all to hell?* This fallacy is usually followed with, *He could not look me in the eye and give me a "yes" or "no" answer.*

A pulpit orator will often use an analogy to illustrate a point in his sermon. But a fallacy is committed if the illustration is used to prove a truth claim. In such a case one would attempt to refute *believer's baptism* by pointing out that there are those who believe that baptism is the gospel and those who hold that ritual baptism is dispensationally not for today at all. The next step would be to depict the advocate of *believer's baptism* as an attempt at compromise between these two extremes— e.g. *This reminds me of the man during the Civil War who tried to be friends with both sides. So, he wore gray pants and a blue shirt. Instead of making peace, they shot at him from both directions.* Though this analogy may correctly illustrate the nature of compromise, it does not prove that *believer's baptism*, or any other proposition, is a compromise of the truth.

An equally dangerous fallacy is the attempt to overthrow a truth claim by tracing it to an embarrassing source. If a known fornicator insists that H_2O is water, could we overthrow his truth claim by pointing out that he is living in disobedience to God? Of course not. The source of a thesis is not relevant to its truthfulness.

We must also guard ourselves against the error of using an authority outside of his field as proof for a truth claim. We cannot prove the existence of God by pointing out that an internationally renowned scientist believed in Him. If he was not a theologian or a philosopher of religion, we would therefore need to review his reasons for believing in the existence of a deity.

On the other hand, we must also not use an authority even within his given field of expertise as proof for a truth claim on the basis of his degree and credentials. If anyone really is an expert on a given subject, he should be willing to provide documented evidence for his thesis and conclusion. No one is right simply because he is a recognized authority. In theology, he must justify his position with the facts of Scripture.

We would be most wise to also watch for contradictions which completely cancel each other out. Self-contradiction is almost always self-refuting—e.g. *What if an irresistible force met an immovable object?* If there exists an irresistible force, there cannot exist an immovable object. If an immovable object exists, then there is no such thing as an irresistible force. We see this fallacy committed when one insists: *We do not believe that baptism saves you, but you are not saved until you are baptized.* Or, *We believe that salvation is 100% free but you must forsake everything and commit everything in order to obtain it.*[28] If someone in a college or university setting contradicts himself completely, he will not impress his professor by labeling the contradiction a *qualification* of his original premise. One should refrain from using the term *qualification* in a self-contradictory manner.

Finally, we must beware of reasoning in a circle by using a premise as ultimate proof for itself as a conclusion. We support

---

[28] John F. MacArthur, Jr., *The Gospel According To Jesus* (Grand Rapids: Zondervan Publishing House, 1988), p. 31... "They set up a concept of faith that eliminates submission, yieldedness, or turning from sin, and they categorize all the practical elements of salvation as human works. They stumble over the twin truths that salvation is a gift, yet it costs everything." P. 140... "Eternal life is indeed a free gift (Romans 6:23). Salvation cannot be earned with good deeds or purchased with money. It has already been bought by Christ, who paid the ransom with His blood. But that does not mean there is no cost in terms of salvation's impact on the sinner's life. This paradox may be difficult but it is nevertheless true: salvation is both free and costly... Thus in a sense we pay the ultimate price for salvation when our sinful self is nailed to the cross...It is an exchange of all that we are for all that Christ is. And it denotes implicit obedience, full surrender to the lordship of Christ. Nothing less can qualify as saving faith."

proposition (A) with proposition (B) then support proposition (B) with (C) and finally support (C) with the original proposition (A) –e.g. *Are you the king? Yes, I am the king. How is it that you are the king? Because I'm wearing the king's hat. How is it that you are wearing the king's hat? Because I'm the king, dummy.* The Bible gives us several objective criteria upon which to support its claim of Divine inspiration, such as prophecy, the miracles of Christ and His resurrection; apostolic miracles, absence of self-contradiction, etc. The world is understandably skeptical when one proclaims that, *The Bible is the Word of God because it says so and we know it is true when its says so because it is the Word of God and that settles it.* If that settles it then there was never a need for prophecies, miracles and internal coherence.

Because we find ourselves in a world of spiritual and theological confusion, we must consult the Bible alone for our knowledge of the Holy Spirit rather than claiming to have consulted the Holy Spirit directly. There are hundreds of truth claims about the ministry of the Holy Spirit that fly in the very face of the scriptural authority. But before discussing what the ministry of the Spirit is not, we should review what are His functions in the world and the life of the believer. The Holy Spirit is God (Acts 5:3, 4); came into the world to glorify Christ (Jn. 16:14); does not speak for Himself (Jn. 16:13; Acts 13:2); imparts eternal life by regeneration (Jn. 3:3-7; Titus 3:5); baptizes the believer into the Body of Christ (I Cor. 12:13); indwells the believer (Rom. 8:9); seals the believer to eternal life (Eph. 1:13; 4:30); fills the believer who walks in Him (Eph. 5:18); bestows gifts to believers, not in relation to our spirituality or theological accuracy, but according to the grace that is in us (Rom. 12:6); convicts the world of sin, righteousness and judgment (Jn. 16:7-11); intercedes for the believer (Rom. 8:26, 27); works in the believer's sanctification (Heb. 10:14, 15); is the earnest of the believer's inheritance (Eph. 1:13, 14); is the Comforter (Jn. 13:1, 17, 26); and enables believer's to be receptive to spiritual things (I Cor. 2:14). In the past He was at work in creation (Gen. 1:1), was the source of the divine inspiration of the Bible writers (II Tim. 3:16; II Pet. 1:20, 21), and generated the virgin birth of Christ (Lk. 1:35).

We often hear the accusation that one is blasphemously limiting the Holy Spirit unless he agrees that all He has done in the past He must still be doing today. This accusation is usually leveled against those who believe that continuing revelation, divine inspiration, and personal inerrancy ceased with the original apostolic office. It is said that such an one is altogether denying the immutability of God and the ministry of the Holy Spirit.

On the contrary, the providential activity of the entire Trinity is present in every moment of our lives and on all occasions. However, we would be limiting the Holy Spirit if we insisted that He must be generating virgin births, raising the dead, or inspiring new doctrines today whether or not He desires to do so. Therefore, let us distinguish the Bible doctrine of the Holy Spirit from dogmas which have developed from traditional misconceptions. These misconceptions are often used to proclaim sacramentalism as the authorized Gospel of Christ. Remember, when seeking to determine what the truth is, an important step is to determine what it is not.

The *witness of the Spirit* and the *leading of the Spirit* are subjects which are usually discussed side-by-side. However, we will deal with them separately throughout the remainder of this chapter.

"The Spirit itself beareth witness with our spirit, that we are the children of God" (Rom. 8:16). Some will claim the Spirit to have witnessed to their hearts that they were indeed reborn in baptism and therefore conclude that *baptismal regeneration* is the revealed will of God. It would be incorrect to counter that argument by insisting that such a claim denies the inerrancy or inspiration of the Bible. This type of affirmation is, however, grounded on the belief in continuing extra-biblical revelation from God. It is the affirmation that God is conceptually communicating His inerrant will in addition to the content of Scripture. Those claiming continuing revelation may make themselves less conspicuous by calling their new information a *Holy Spirit conviction* or a *burden* divinely placed on their hearts. By this semantic they can avoid an embarrassing association with some charismatics who do not mince words about their claim to be prophets receiving direct revelation from God. But it must be remembered that most of the Scriptures were not delivered through the audible voice of God, but rather through *inerrant Holy Spirit convictions* or the *burden of the Lord*. This is why the personal vocabulary, literary style, and personality of each author can be observed. Yet, these *convictions* and *burdens* were in every sense revelations from God. Divine inspiration occurred when the Holy Spirit enabled the recipient to communicate this revelation to others in conceptual or propositional form either orally or in writing. The question to be addressed is one of whether or not individuals are receiving conceptual or propositional information from

God today in addition to the content of the Bible. Or, is the Bible the only source of information for Christian doctrine since the death of the Apostles?

When one speaks of having discovered the will of God, he should be careful to define his terms correctly. Though the full will of God is beyond our finite minds, we do know of two categories within God's will as it pertains to our lives. First, there is the revealed will of God, which is the Bible properly interpreted. The second is the unrevealed will of God, which is His sovereign desire for every other area of personal life. God has not simply abandoned us to the Bible alone. He has assured us that He is at work in every area of our lives. However, as long as a man possesses an Adamic nature, he cannot reach a level of personal inerrancy in discerning God's undeclared will. The fact that we are not stopped from fulfilling many or our own intentions does not constitute proof that we are fulfilling the perfect will of God in all that we do or proclaim. God may sovereignly permit us to fulfill a personal plan or express a false belief when another plan or proclamation would have been better from the beginning—e.g. *how often **would I*** [God's loving will] *have gathered thy children together, even as a hen gathereth her chickens under her wings, and **ye would not*** [God's permissive will] (Matt. 23:37, emphasis added). Though many faceted, all of God's will is sovereign. Some of the most outstanding Christians in history could have looked over their shoulders and identified how everything they accomplished could have been executed more accurately, efficiently and to the glory of God.

We can observe many Christians who are deeply distressed when they hear the testimonies of others describing how wonderful it is to be standing in the *perfect center of God's will* regarding every single aspect of their lives, including their extra-biblical beliefs. The distressed believers may come to doubt their very salvation or that God hears their prayers because, after all their attempts to confess sin and to obey God, they never experience *the perfect center of God's will* or hear *His voice*. They conclude that there is something desperately lacking in their lives about which they can do nothing. If they would study the Scriptures on this matter they would find that getting closer to and more intimate with God is accomplished through obedience to His *declared will*, (i.e. the Bible).

The Scriptures teach that, in the sight of God, right and wrong are absolute. Therefore, if one claims to be *convicted* or *burdened* that *believer's baptism* and *rebaptism* are heresy, he must affirm that this is heresy for all believers as well. One who makes such extra-biblical claims is relating in propositional form what he considers to be inerrant concepts from the Lord. He seems certain that he has spoken the *will of God* but may deny having received a verbal revelation. But there is no way a non-verbal burden can be verbally explained. One cannot non-verbally comprehend God's will without reducing it to verbal concepts. A non-verbal conviction or a non-verbal burden, informing one of God's inerrant extra-biblical will, cannot exist.

Occasionally, that which cannot be demonstrated from the Bible to be heresy or sinful is labeled *worldly*, and thus made heretical or sinful by the *inspired* will of the affirmer. Without citing a verse of Scripture, entire catalogues of acts and concepts have been labeled *sin* and *heresy* as if they were symbols of rebellion against the obvious *leading* and *convicting* of the Holy Spirit. It is all that a good Christian can do to hate what the Bible calls sin and heresy, yet these affirmers feel compelled of the Holy Spirit to invent new classifications of sin and heresy and to place upon Christians a burden which neither they nor their fathers were able to bear. The initial error was in failing to limit the word *worldly* to the biblical definitions of sin and heresy.

One is on dangerous ground when he proclaims the dictates of his own spirit as a message from God and then preaches the vision of his own imagination as a God-sent message—

> Thus saith the Lord God; Woe unto the foolish prophets, that follow their own spirit, and have seen nothing! Have ye not seen a vain vision, and have ye not spoken a lying divination, whereas ye say, The LORD saith it; albeit I have not spoken (Ezek. 13:3, 7)?

When the imagination and conscience are construed to be the voice of God in extra-biblical matters, they must be cast down—

> [For the weapons of our warfare are not carnal, but mighty through God to the pulling down of strong holds;] Casting down imaginations, and every high thing that exalteth itself against the knowledge of God, and bringing into captivity every thought to the obedience of Christ (II Cor. 10:4, 5).

It is critical that we learn to distinguish the revealed will of God from what we consider to be our own best judgment. How does one check his personal wisdom when it is in fact a subjective experience? The answer is in consulting the objective, sole authority of Scripture for faith, doctrine and practice. The canon of Scripture is closed and there is no continuing revelation. When confronted with several self-proclaimed prophets, one will ask, *How do I know which one to believe?* The answer is simple, *Don't believe any of them.* This standard will eliminate perhaps most of the confusion in contemporary Christianity.

If *Holy Spirit convictions* and *burdens* were inerrant revelations in Bible times, then we must assume that they would still be the same today. The *still small voice* inside of us is ourselves talking to ourselves and not the voice of God, unless an actual Bible concept is being subjectively brought to mind. Or, if it is not us talking nor the Bible internalized, we may have a more serious problem yet.

Rom. 8:16 is not saying that the Holy Spirit is witnessing to our spirit, but rather with our spirit. Thus, there are two witnesses in this verse: that of the Holy Spirit and that of our spirit. It is when the two witnesses agree that assurance of salvation can be rightfully claimed. When the witness of the believer's spirit, as to why he believes he is a child of God, agrees with the witness of the Holy Spirit (i.e. the apostolic gospel), then he knows that he is a child of God. Many advocates of the sacramental gospel claim the inner witness of the Spirit as the grounds of their assurance.

We have witnessed Reformers affirming that doctrinal concepts which do not contradict the Bible may be taught as God's will. If this affirmation is correct, the canon of Scripture should never have been closed and believers should have expected continuing revelation throughout the entire church age. If revelation and inspiration did not cease with the apostolic office, then we have no reason to believe that those who compiled the New Testament canon, and closed it, knew what they were doing or had any authority from God to do it.

Those claiming to possess an extra-biblical message from the Spirit will often try to make two separate categories out of one in order to open the door and step outside the bounds of Scripture. For example, in John 3:5, 6 Christ told Nicodemus that he must be *born of the Sprit* in

Subjective And Extra-biblical Arguments For Baptismal Regeneration

order to see the Kingdom of God. This is the second birth. However, in I Pet. 1:23 the Apostle Peter speaks of being born again of the incorruptible seed by the Word of God. This is not a third birth but is synonymous with the second birth. In like manner, the content of the Spirit's witness in the heart and the content of the Bible's witness to the heart are one—i.e. *The words that I speak unto you, they are spirit, and they are life* (John 6:63). Similarly, the quickening of the Holy Spirit and the quickening of the Word of God are one. In John 6:63 *It is the spirit that quickeneth...* (c.f. Eph. 2:1-5; Col. 2:13; I Cor. 15:45). On the other hand, it is the Word of God that is *quick* (Hebrews 4:12). David said: *Quicken thou me according to thy word* (Ps. 119:25); *...For thy word hath quickened me* (vs.50); *I will never forget thy precepts for with them thou hast quickened me* (vs. 93); *Quicken me, O Lord, according unto thy word* (vs. 107); and *...Quicken me according to thy word* (vs. 154). The same is true regarding the verbal communication of the leading of the Spirit. In Ps. 37:23 David said: *The steps of a good man are ordered by the Lord.* Yet in Ps. 119:133 he said: *Order my steps in thy word.* So, in a post-apostolic context, the verbally communicated leading of the Spirit and the verbal communication of the Scriptures are one in content. This is not to say that God does not providentially direct in our lives at all times, but He is not speaking to us about this beyond the content of the Bible.

In I Jn. 2:20 we see that the unction of the Holy Spirit is a source of information—*But ye have an unction from the Holy One, and ye know all things.* This passage is often cited as a biblical basis for extra-biblical knowledge. But where did the recipients of this epistle obtain this body of knowledge called *all things*? Does the phrase *all things* have parameters or does it mean *omniscience*? The answer lies in verse 24: *If that which ye have heard from the beginning shall remain in you, ye also shall continue in the Son, and in the Father.* Here we observe that the outer witness (i.e. that which they had heard from the apostles from the beginning, Heb. 2:3, 4), and the inward abiding of that same body of truth are one in content. Thus, the anointing or unction of the Holy Spirit and the inward abiding of (and agreement with) the apostolic teachings are one in content—

> But the anointing which ye have received of him abideth in you, and ye need not that any man teach you: but as the same annointing teacheth you of all things, **and is truth** and is no lie, and even as it hath

taught you, ye shall abide in him [emphasis added] (I Jn. 2:27).

So, the *unction* is the *anointing*; the anointing is *the truth*; and the truth is *that which was heard from the beginning* (i.e. the apostolic message)—

> *...And it is the Spirit that beareth witness, because the Spirit is truth* (I Jn. 5:6); *For the truth's sake which dwelleth in us, and shall be with us forever* (II Jn. 2).

Again, note the content of that which was heard from the beginning:

> That which we have seen and heard declare we unto you, that ye also may have fellowship with us: and truly our fellowship is with the Father and with his Son Jesus Christ. And these things **write** we unto you, that your joy may be full [emphasis added] (I Jn. 1:3, 4).

The word "we" in this instance refers to the apostolic office. One should not use this passage to affirm that fullness of joy is insufficiently obtained through commitment to the anointed truths of the apostolic writings.

Likewise, it is observed that all Scripture was given—*that the man of God may be perfect, throughly furnished unto all good works* (II Tim. 3:17). Every furnishing we need to carry out the work of God in our lives is contained in the information of Scripture. This written information will make us *perfect* (or complete) and thus there are not essential informational furnishings to be discovered elsewhere.

Again, we notice that I Jn. 5:9-11, 13 declares that the inner witness of God and the recorded witness of God are one:

> *If we receive the witness of men, the witness of God is greater: for this is the witness of God which he hath testified of his Son. He that believeth on the Son of God hath the **witness in himself*** [inner witness]*: he that believeth not God hath made him a liar; because he believeth not the **record*** [outer witness] *that God*

> *gave of his Son. And this is the record* [outer witness], *that God hath given to us eternal life, and this life is in his Son.... These things have I **written** [outer witness] unto you that believe on the name of the son of God; that ye may know that ye have eternal life...*[emphasis added].

Notice John's equation of this written knowledge and assurance with the inner witness of the Spirit: *...And hereby we know that he abideth in us, by the Spirit which he hath given us* (I Jn. 3:24b). The content of a last will and testament document and the will of the signator should be one and the same. The last will and testament that God has left on earth is the Scriptures. God's sovereign will is infinitely more vast than His revealed will. However, God's revealed will for the believer and the revealed will of His written Word are one in content. He may subjectively bestow duplicate information within (i.e. conscience and natural law, Romans 1), but not additional doctrine. Additional dogma should be considered the product of one's own judgment or, more seriously, from a demonic source. Although personal judgment can be very fruitful when walking in the spiritual truths of God's Word, it is not a valid basis for a theological truth claim. One's judgment in extra-biblical matters should not be called *the absolute revealed will of God*. The inner witness does not contain more information than the outer witness.

The scribes and Pharisees asked Christ: *Why do thy disciples transgress the tradition of the elders? For they wash not their hands when they eat bread* (Mtt. 15:2). Hand-washing is a fruitful act of personal judgment and a healthy practice, but the sin was in elevating the concept into an article of faith (i.e. the revealed will of God in doctrinal form). Christ answered them, saying: *why do ye also transgress the commandment of God by your traditions* (vs.3). Obviously, such an elevation of their personal preferences was a direct violation of God's will, not a revelation of it. In the case of the scribes and Pharisees, such a practice negated all of their attempts to worship God—*But in vain they do worship me, teaching for doctrines the commandments of men* (vs. 9). Also, though the scribes and Pharisees believed in the infallibility of the OT, this practice became the academic equivalent of negating the Bible altogether—*Thus have ye made the commandment of God of none effect by your tradition* (vs. 6). Good personal preferences are advisable but should never be elevated to the level of *God's revealed will*.

Spiritual illumination is often defined as a guiding light from within which enables one to see beyond the words of Scripture into a more divine message or to know the precise geographical location on earth where God's perfect will can be performed. The same principle is applied in both cases. The Bible does not speak of normal Christians knowing God's inerrant geographical will or merchandising will. The Apostle James addressed the issue of knowing God's mind in such applications:

> Go to now, ye that say, To day or to morrow we will go into such a city, and continue there a year, and buy and sell, and get gain: Whereas ye know not what *shall be* on the morrow. For what *is* your life? It is even a vapour, that appeareth for a little time, and then vanisheth away. For that ye *ought* to say, If the Lord will, we shall live, and do this, or that. But now ye rejoice in your boastings: all such rejoicing is evil. (James 4:13-16).

No one knows if it is the Lord's will that he will live for another twenty-four hours. How then can he know where God wants him to be geographically located for the next year? Perhaps some Christians were boasting of absolute knowledge in these areas. James said: *But now ye rejoice in your boastings: all such rejoicing is evil.*

All of life's circumstances are within the providential and permissive will of God. Circumstances surround the believer at all times. However, circumstantial advantages should not be set forth as evidence for a truth claim in extra-biblical matters. The question should be: upon what information is his path being illuminated? David said: *Thy word is a lamp unto my feet, and a light unto my path* (Ps. 119:105). *Damascus Road* experiences and *Macedonian calls* should not be expected by Christians of today. The Holy Spirit should not be expected to speak to local churches today saying, *Separate me Barnabas,*[the prophet] *and Saul* [the Apostle]. We often hear the challenging question: *if God verbally reveals His geographical and temporal will to believers, then why should we not conclude that He convicts us about extra-biblical doctrines which He wants delivered to the Church?*

Subjective And Extra-biblical Arguments For Baptismal Regeneration

A semantic maneuver used often in this regard is to refer to one's new dogma as a biblical principle, though not an explicit biblical precept. This will give the appearance of biblical authority to an extra-biblical idea. This is how *baptismal regeneration* has been extracted from almost every reference to water or moisture in the Bible. This is how some churches establish standards of *tradition vs. fad* rather than the biblical issue *of modesty vs. immodesty*. The error is in distinguishing *biblical principle* from *biblical precept* in Bible interpretation. There are no principles in the Bible which are not at the same time verbal, propositional precepts.

Whenever we hear someone speaking of implied principles between the lines of Scripture, we must remind them that the only thing between the lines of the Bible is white paper. Everything the Spirit intended to say is in the words of the lines—not between, not in the numerical value of the words, and not in secret computer codes. When we say that we believe in the *verbal* [words], *plenary* [full] inspiration of the Bible, we are affirming that the full message of God is in the words and not between or outside of them.

Does this approach to Bible interpretation constitute a dethroning of the Holy Spirit? Is this approach too cold, theological and academic? Does it lack the personal touch of God? Is it impractical for everyday life? The answer is *yes,* if the doctrinal truth of God's Word can be called impractical to our spiritual lives. That which is academically true in the Bible is never cold to a spiritual Christian, as God said to Jeremiah: *Is not my Word like as a fire? Saith the Lord...*(Jer. 23:29). We must allow our biblical theology to influence every area of our lives. The modern attempt to distinguish the practical from the theological in the Christian life is a cloaked attack on the content of the Bible, though not necessarily premeditated. God said to Israel through Hosea:

> My people are destroyed for lack of knowledge: because thou hast rejected knowledge, I will also reject thee, that thou shalt be no priest to me: seeing that thou hast forgotten the law of thy God, I will also forget thy children (Hosea 4:6).

The two disciples who had traveled with Jesus on the road to Emmaus said: *...Did not our heart burn within us, while he talked with us by the way, and while he opened to us the scriptures?*

Truth claims founded upon an affirmation of personal inerrancy can often be extremely intimidating. The individual making the affirmation must be trusted as the source of knowledge for God's extra-biblical will. God said to Jeremiah, *Cursed be the man that trusteth in man* (Jer. 17:5). It is not the task of the preacher to compel souls to lean on him for salvation and knowledge of God's will, but his task is to exhort souls to trust in Whom he is trusting. Each Christian should learn to distinguish between the preacher who is trusting in the truth of the Bible alone and the preacher who is certain of the inerrancy of his own personal judgments or preferences in extra-biblical matters. The idea of *continuing revelation* has been one of the most devastating challenges to the gospel of Christ throughout church history.

The claim of continuing revelation is often reinforced by the affirmation that we can definitely know God's perfect leading in our lives. That God is providentially directing us is obvious from the Scriptures. That we are precisely following that direction cannot be determined by a mortal apart from a propositional, inspired revelation. But does not Romans 8:14 say: *For as many as are led by the Spirit of God they are the Sons of God*? A popular interpretation of this verse is that assurance of sonship will be confirmed by the steady reception of extra-biblical, supernatural direction from the Holy Spirit about life's personal direction and doctrinal convictions. However, a closer study of the context will make it obvious that the subject is one of holiness of life through obedience to the righteous mandates of Scripture—

> For they that are after the flesh do mind the things of the flesh; but they that are after the Spirit the things of the Spirit…(vs.5); and (vss. 12, 13)—Therefore, brethren, we are debtors, not to the flesh, to live after the flesh. For if ye live after the flesh, ye shall die: but if ye through the Spirit do mortify the deeds of the body, ye shall live.

A Christian shows by such living that he has been led of God to do so.

Many contemporary saints are living in a state of constant anxiety and fear that they are not performing perfectly God's undeclared will for their lives in areas which are not covered in Scripture. The anxiety proliferates when they are assured by others that personal inerrancy in such matters should be normal if one is truly spiritual.

They are told that the only alternative is to live their lives carnally outside of the *perfect will of God.*

The Bible teaches personal responsibility for our own judgment. One may avoid such responsibility by affirming every personal decision to be one which God made for him and delivered directly to him. All who question his judgment will be made to appear to be challenging God Himself Who made the decision in the first place. If the idea leads to failure, one will simply redefine the catastrophe as a mysterious plan of God to teach him patience or to judge those who followed him into the failure. Complaining that the course of action or the truth claim was not well thought out will be made to appear as an attack upon the integrity of God's sovereign wisdom. But when the Bible is properly taught, there should be a Holy Spirit revival of critical thinking and personal responsibility in our service to God.

Another verse which is often used to support supernatural, extra-biblical guidance by inner feelings is Isa. 30:20, 21 which reads:

> And though the Lord give you the bread of adversity, and the water of affliction, yet shall not thy teachers be removed into a corner any more, but thine eyes shall see thy teachers: And thine ears shall hear a word behind thee, saying, This is the way, walk ye in it, when ye turn to the right hand, and when ye turn to the left.

This is the same advice that was given to Joshua, but in his case it was a reference to the Scriptures which Moses had received—

> Only be thou strong and very courageous, that thou mayest observe to do according to all the law, which Moses my servant commanded thee: turn not from it to the right hand or to the left, that thou mayest prosper whithersoever thou goest (Joshua 1:7).

However, in the Isaiah passage, the *word behind* will be the wise counselors who will be visibly present. The visible teachers will faithfully warn them when they sin against the Word of God and cause them to repent, thus delivering them from God's judgments (vss. 22-26). There is nothing here about an inward voice of any kind.

To know the perfect extra-biblical will of God regarding life and belief, one would have to possess personal inerrancy, and such a gift is not promised to post-apostolic believers. It is popular to cite instances of extraordinary guidance in the Bible, claim the same for oneself, and plead the unchangeableness and omnipotence of God in order to command the belief of others. In this case such a person would accuse doubters of limiting God—an act often referred to as blasphemy. He will remind us that Philip was infallibly directed to join himself to the Ethiopian eunuch's chariot (Acts 8:26). It was directly revealed to Peter that he must accept the invitation of Cornelius in Acts 10:1-23. In Acts 13 the Holy Spirit said to separate Barnabas and Saul for a special work. This was in fulfillment of a vision received in a trance by Paul earlier as recorded in Acts 22:17-21. Paul crossed into Europe after a vision in Acts 16:6-10. We must not fail to notice that each of these instances were the experiences of apostles and prophets and that they were all direct inerrant revelations from God. Such personal inerrancy had been promised to the apostles who were to hand down the doctrines of the NT. John 14:26 is a promise of personal inerrancy and total supernatural recall to those who were with Christ (i.e.the apostles)—

> But the comforter, which is the Holy Ghost, whom the Father will send in my name, he shall teach you all things, and bring all things to your remembrance, whatsoever I have said unto you.

There is no mention that this is a promise to contemporary believers—otherwise, we can write Scripture with inerrant inspiration and total recall as well as did the apostles.

Many will object to the above point by affirming that all of the believers of Rome were instructed to prove what is the *perfect will of God*—

> And be not conformed to this world but be ye transformed by the renewing of your mind that ye may prove what is that good, and acceptable, and perfect will of God (Rom. 12:2).

A quick study of the context will reveal that the thing which the believer is to prove is that the Word of God is right and that obedience to it works. Chapters 12, 13, and 14 describe what is being referred to as the *perfect will of God*. It is a clear reference to that which was taught by the apostles and prophets [now contained in the Bible] and not an injunction to experience personal inerrancy.

Those claiming divine extra-biblical knowledge about any matter may often refer to Col. 1:9 which reads:

> For this cause we also, since the days we heard it, do not cease to pray for you, and to desire that ye might be filled with the knowledge of His will in all wisdom and spiritual understanding.

But we should be careful to note that the knowledge was to be in *wisdom and spiritual understanding.* Wisdom and understanding are not sources of information, but rather proper reactions to God's truth. The phrase *His will* is qualified in vss. 10-13:

> That ye might walk worthy of the Lord unto all pleasing, being fruitful in every good work, and increasing in the knowledge of God; Strengthened with all might, according to His glorious power, unto all patience and longsuffering with joyfulness; giving thanks unto the Father, which hath made us meet to be partakers of the inheritance of the saints in light: Who hath delivered us from the power of darkness and hath translated us into the kingdom of His dear son.

Each item in this passage is a commonly occurring biblical precept. Therefore, *His will* in this context is a reference to God's declared will. It would not be prudent to use Col. 1:9 to affirm extra-biblical knowledge about the nature of baptism, nor of personal decisions regarding the purchase of an automobile or a home. Paul was not asking for them to have the knowledge of God's full will, but for them to be full *with the knowledge of His will.*

We are often challenged at this point with the affirmation that though we have no extra-biblical knowledge of doctrinal truth, we may know the mind of God in personal decisions of our lives. Such a view would not be a challenge to the authority of the Bible and Christians should not divide at that point. However, we commonly see the doctrinal and personal aspects of the affirmation in partnership. In fact, the personal dimension is often used as reinforcement for the claim of an extra-biblical doctrinal conviction.

Though discussed previously, we should look again at I Cor. 2:14, which states:

> But the natural man receiveth not the things of the Spirit of God: for thay are foolishness unto him: neither can he know them, because they are spiritually discerned.

Is this verse saying that natural men do not *understand*, or that they do not *receive*? We know of many unregenerate people who understand spiritual things in the Bible and then reject them. Many understand the Gospel but postpone a decision for Christ. Many understand six-day creationism, the virgin birth, deity of Christ, inerrancy of Scripture, and yet have not received eternal salvation from the Lord. Does this not contradict the phrase, *neither can he know them for they are spiritually discerned*? The Greek for *know* is *ginosko* and can have reference to personally experiencing a truth. It is the same idea that Christ used in Matt. 7:23 with the words: *And then will I profess unto them, I never knew you.* There is nothing regarding them that Christ does not intellectually comprehend. He simply meant that He had not received them into a personal relationship with Himself. The virgin Mary used this concept when she was told that she would give birth to the Son of God, saying: *How shall this be, seeing I know not a man?* She knew men. She knew her espoused, Joseph; her father; and her uncle Zechariah. She meant that she had never *received* a man into such a personal relationship as would result in pregnancy. The *things of the Spirit of God* in this passage refer to the *testimony of God* which is now declared in the Scriptures through the mouths of the Apostles. This is particularly true of the words of Paul as we look back to I Cor. 2:1 where we read: *And I, brethren, when I came to you, came not with excellency of speech or of wisdom, declaring unto you the testimony of God.* Vs. 14 does not teach that a saint possesses E.S.P. with God regarding His extra-biblical, undeclared will in doctrinal or personal matters.

The phrase, *they are spiritually discerned* is not a reference to inerrant, extra-biblical information originating from within the believer, but rather speaks of the believer's reaction to the *testimony of God*. An alcoholic knows that his strong drink will destroy his liver but, because of lack of discernment, he will disregard what he knows and choose to remain a drunkard. In the same sense, spiritual discernment is not a

Subjective And Extra-biblical Arguments For Baptismal Regeneration

revelational source of doctrinal or personal knowledge, but rather a correct reaction to God's revealed will in His Word.

Closely related to the term *discern* is the concept of *judging*. I Cor. 2:15 affirms: *He that is spiritual judgeth all things.* This means that spiritual discernment seeks to react to all things in accordance with Scripture—*But strong meat belongeth to them that are of full age, even those who by reason of use have their senses exercised to discern both good and evil* (Heb. 5:14). Is this a contradiction to Matt. 7:1 where Jesus said: *Judge not that ye be not judged*? Matt. 7 is exhorting us to judge nothing using ourselves as the standard of measurement. I Cor. 2 is exhorting the spiritual to judge all things solely by the measurement of God's testimony—i.e. His Word. This is spiritual discernment. It is interesting to note how many times in Matt. 7 Christ exhorts His followers to exercise sound judgment regarding dogs and swine (vs.6), entering at the strait gate (vss. 13), false prophets in sheep's clothing (vs. 15), fruit-bearing (vss. 16-20), being known by the Lord (vss. 21-23), building one's spiritual house upon a rock rather than sand (vss. 24-27), and doctrine (vss. 28, 29).

Instead of God anointing the thoughts and intents of one's heart with the inerrant ability to determine the mind of God in extra-biblical matters, it is the Word of God that discerns *the thoughts and intents of the heart* (Heb. 4:12).

The book of Proverbs speaks of two levels of understanding. First, there is a level of understanding based upon personal feelings apart from the Word of God. Prov. 3:5 says: *Trust in the Lord with all thine heart and lean not unto thine own understanding.* Secondly, there is an understanding based upon the Word of God—*O ye simple, understand wisdom: and, ye fools, be of an understanding heart* (Prov. 8:5). A popular interpretation of Prov. 3:5 is that the believer should trust in his heart and not in his understanding. But the verse does not say, *trust in thy heart*, but rather, *Trust in the Lord with all thine heart.* In fact, Prov. 28:26 states: *He that trusteth in his own heart is a fool.* One should not affirm that the counsel of his own heart, in extra-biblical matters, is the mind and thoughts of God. Prov. 19:21 states: *There are many devices in a man's heart; nevertheless the counsel of the Lord, that shall stand.* We should never refer to our extra-biblical thoughts as the mind of God and our way as the revealed way of God. Isa. 55:8, 9 affirms: *For my thoughts are not your thoughts, neither are your ways my ways, saith the Lord.* The Bible does not promise that we can know when we are standing in the perfect center of God's undeclared, extra-biblical will for our lives, or that we can even know where that spot is located. The Bible does, however, tell us to concern ourselves with obeying and understanding His declared will in the Scriptures. It is fashionable to condemn honest biblical scholarship and exalt the mystical pursuit of personal infallibility in determining the mind of the Spirit about extra-biblical concepts which seriously affect other people's lives.

Sometimes, a missionary will claim that he/she knows that God has geographically given a call to a specific mission field through a devotional study of Ps. 2:8 which promises: *Ask of me, and I shall give thee the heathen for thine inheritance, and the uttermost parts of the earth for thy possession.* In its context this verse is solely a reference to Christ during the millennium. But the missionary believes that there is a non-literal, yet spiritual, interpretation of this passage that personally applies to his life's geographical direction in a way that is not meant for other members of the Body of Christ at that moment. Though the passage called him/her to China, it does not call all Christians to that same field. The Bible nowhere justifies such use of the Scriptures. The only proof of this interpretation is the personal testimony of the person who practiced this method. Using this same hermeneutic, a missionary might cancel his plans to do a work for God in Egypt by flipping to verses in the OT which say, *go not into Egypt.*

Constituents of varied world religions gain a false confidence that God has bestowed an inward feeling which confirms their chosen beliefs about certain dogmas. They may call this a *burning in the bosom* or the *peace of the Spirit* about a matter. Although the Lord desires that the peace of God rule in the hearts of believers (Col. 3:15), He does not promise that feelings of peace will determine His extra-biblical will, and often asks believers to act in their absence. Daniel prophesied that the anti-Christ would *by peace destroy many* (Dan. 8:25). Feelings of peaceful euphoria can be very misleading, especially in the case of mystical cults. Unbelievers can experience such sensations in relation to physical or mental health. Such euphoria can also stem from the conscience; from the Adamic nature, and from the new nature. Christians should not exempt themselves from personal responsibility for their individual judgment in extra-biblical matters by saying that God has given them divine peace about the subject.. Christians should find their joy and peace in believing the Word of God. The three Hebrew children, in the book of Daniel, had no clue as to whether or not they would burn in the fiery furnace (Dan. 3:17). They only knew that they were not going to worship Nebuchadnezzar's image in either case (vs.18). The same is true of Daniel in the den of lions (Dan. 6).

Although feelings are not conclusive, they are not to be totally ignored. If we feel extremely uneasy about a course of action or a belief, we should stop and think it through again, seeking to refine our thinking on the matter.

It has been argued that personal plans for the future would be impossible without direct information from God. Even the apostles held themselves responsible to plan for the future. They would propose to do something and set out to do it fearlessly, recognizing at the same time that God might order things in a totally different way (cf. I Cor. 16:8, 9; II Cor. 1:15-24; Acts 15:36). In Acts 16:7 we read: A*fter they were come to Mysia, they essayed to go into Bithynia: but the Spirit suffered them not.* The apostles had no way of knowing in advance that their good and noble plans were not the perfect will of God. In II Cor. 1:15-17 we read:

> And in this confidence I was minded to come unto you before, that ye might have a second benefit; And to pass by you into Macedonia, and to come again out of Macedonia unto you, and of you to be brought on my way toward Judaea. When I therefore was thus minded, did I use lightness? or the things that I purpose, do I purpose according to the flesh, that with me there should be yea yea, and nay nay?

Paul had been charged with changeableness, but he argued that he had sound reasons for changing his plans. New facts had come to light and the situation had been drastically and unforeseeably altered. He never claimed that his original plans were anointed or that he *felt unmistakably led of the Spirit* in that direction. The Bible does not teach that the desire of one's heart is a revelation from God regarding what to believe or do. An excellent example in this light is II Chron. 6:8, 9, which reads:

> But the Lord said to David my father, Forasmuch as it was in thine heart to build an house for my name, thou didst well in that it was in thine heart: Notwithstanding

thou shalt not build the house; but thy son which shall come forth out of thy loins, he shall build the house for my name.

Sometimes the noble desire of one's heart and God's plans are not the same.

There are also those who feel that God, in answer to prayer, has given them a sign that their position on baptism, or some other subject, is the will of God. A favorite Bible story in this wise is that of Gideon's fleece (Judges 6). The story of this fleece and other guiding signs in the Bible have caused many to conclude that they have a right to ask God for a sign before they make an important decision. Gideon's fleece was put out twice after God had affirmed verbally that Israel would be delivered by His hand. The putting out of the fleece was actually a demonstration of lack of faith in God's Word and ability to perform. We must also remember that the purpose of the fleece was not to confirm Gideon's personal plans and thoughts, but to confirm a direct revelation that had been given him. Such personal revelations are not being received since the Bible has become complete. Truly spiritual Christians do not need signs to boost their faith in the recorded promises of God. If the cases of extraordinary guidance mentioned in Scripture (Peter and Cornelius, Philip and the Eunuch, Paul and the Macedonians) were intended to be a model for post-apostolic saints to follow, and not just uniquely for apostles and prophets, we should look for a statement of that fact in the NT. Yet, we have cited many passages that instruct Christians to pass on that which was received from the apostles (Rom. 16:17; II Thess. 3:6; II Tim. 2:2; Titus 1:9; Jude 3).

Many gifted and qualified Christians have hesitated to enter full time ministry because they have neither received a *call* to the ministry nor an inward *anointing* with a set of doctrinal convictions. In the NT God personally called apostles and prophets, but nowhere mentions an individual call to the pastorate, to the mission field, nor for any other type of full time Christian ministry. Timothy was to commit the ministry of the Gospel to faithful men. In I Tim. 3, Paul told Timothy that, if a man desired the office of bishop and met the list of qualifications, he desired a good thing. Every qualification in the list was simply something God wants to see exemplified in the life of every Christian. If the desire and qualifications exist, one should not wait for a personal, verbal divine call. If he desires full time service on God's terms, God will accept him. We cannot help but wonder how many missionary endeavors are being ignored in the face of the clearest opportunities simply because there is no sign nor personal revelation to assure that one should proceed. On the other hand, how often does some supposed sign justify a foolish or even unscriptural course of action? The second and third missionary journeys were undertaken because the churches needed the help. The need determined the course of action in such cases. Gary Friesen expressed it well when he said:

> I had become convinced that Scripture does not require some kind of mystical experience whereby one "hears" God's "inward" call....Rather than waiting for some kind of inward voice, a man should cultivate an inward response to the challenge to serve God in the fullest manner possible....According to the New Testament, a church leader must be a spiritually mature Christian man who desires a position of leadership in the church, and is able to lead God's people and teach God's Word....Where the traditional view speaks of a "call," the New Testament speaks of a "desire" or an "aspiration" for the pastoral office. Perhaps the question (about the call at the time of ordination) should be reworded: "Why do you desire to be set apart for the gospel ministry?" ...(The answer should be) I want to serve the Lord in the best and fullest way possible. God says that the office of pastor provides a good means for serving Him. So I have consciously aspired to become qualified for that position. The characteristics listed in I Timothy 3, Titus 1, and I Pet. 5 have been my personal goals.[29]

Occasionally a Christian will seek advice regarding how to be certain of God's call to the ministry. Such an one is often told to do anything to keep from it, for, if he is called, he will not be able to keep from it. This advice is dangerously false. As long as one is in possession of the fleshly nature, he has the power to keep from serving God in any way he wishes. There is no passage of Scripture that advises any Christian to avoid serving God in the ministry if desire and qualifications are there.

---

[29] Gary Friesen, *Decision Making and the Will of God* (Portland: Multnomah, 1980), pp. 315-319).

Christians are not encouraged in the NT to seek after signs. Satan uses signs and creates coincidences, especially with people whom he considers to be emotional cripples. Quite often, the testimony of one's *call* to the ministry is bound together with a *message* which God gave at the time.

What is even more controversial is the matter of interpreting signs. In multiple locations where Paul visited, he was warned by visions and prophecies that imprisonment, danger, and affliction awaited him if he proceeded to Jerusalem. Godly Christians felt that it would be wise for him to cancel his engagement there. But Paul did not for a moment interpret these as a sign that he should reconsider his duty to deliver the relief money which he had raised for the poor saints in the City of David, as well as his duties in other areas. His determination overruled the almost universal petitions of his friends (cf. Acts 20:22-24; 21:10-12).

Some Christians will use circumstances to proclaim God's purposes regarding a truth claim or a choice of action. But satanic forces are also allowed to arrange circumstances to bring about remarkable coincidences (II Thess. 2:9-11). Many wrong marriages and divorces have been pursued in this manner.

Nevertheless, God may often use circumstances to make some course of action impossible. Paul often made the decision to relocate when persecution became so intense that a public ministry was no longer possible. Paul's appeal to Caesar (Acts 25:11) was determined by circumstances which made it apparent that such an appeal might be his only escape from murder on his way to Jerusalem (Acts 25:10, 11, 20, 21). Paul also knew how to seize sudden and unexpected opportunities, as at Athens, where circumstances allowed for a one-time opportunity to speak on Mars Hill. Circumstances seem to have influenced godly wisdom in the NT only when they presented an opportunity for an honorable course of action or when they made a planned course of action impossible. Even then, the exact details of how God wanted the endeavor executed was not given.

David received what appeared to be remarkable *circumstantial guidance* to do the wrong thing. King Saul had been pursuing David in order to kill him (I Sam. 24). It had already been revealed to David that he was to be the next king and that God had taken the kingdom from Saul. Suddenly, Saul entered the cave alone wherein David and his men

Subjective And Extra-biblical Arguments For Baptismal Regeneration

were hiding. David's men felt that God was overruling circumstances to give opportunity to fulfill His divine plan. But David did not determine God's will by circumstances on that day, and refused to kill the king. Subsequently, circumstances were again seemingly miraculously overruled, but David took Saul's spear and his jar of water from beside him as he slept, instead of assuming supernatural guidance to kill the king (I Sam. 26:5-12).

We have already discussed James 4:13-18 regarding revelations of God's temporal, geographical, and merchandising will. Still, some may persist in using a claim of geographical, divine direction as reinforcement for a truth claim regarding baptism or some other doctrine. In fact, we often hear that God will not use us until we find the perfect center of God's geographical will. The biblical truth is that any and every place can be the place of triumph and victory when the Gospel is presented and the Bible is properly consulted.

The Apostle Paul came to Troas with the intention of preaching the Gospel. There he found an open door of service which he claimed was of the Lord—*Furthermore, when I came to Troas to preach Christ's Gospel, and a door was opened unto me of the Lord* (II Cor. 2:12). This would seem to be a clear opportunity for triumph indeed. However, he had no peace of spirit about the absence of an associate with whom he desired at his side in the work—*I had no rest in my spirit because I found not Titus my brother* (II Cor. 2:13a). Complicating matters further, he had a vision of a man in Macedonia requesting him to come over—

> And they passing by Mysia came down to Troas. And a vision appeared to Paul in the night; There stood a man of Macedonia, and prayed him, saying, Come over into Macedonia, and help us. And after he had seen the vision, immediately we endeavoured to go into Macedonia, assuredly gathering that the Lord had called us for to preach the gospel unto them (Acts 16:8-10).

Now he was confronted with two simultaneous open doors of opportunity which were apparently *of the Lord*. His decision was to leave the open door of the Lord at Troas and to proceed toward the direction of Macedonia—*But taking my leave of them, I went from thence into Macedonia* (II Cor. 2:13b). Did Paul walk out on God's perfect place of triumph when he left Troas? On the contrary, Paul tells us that anyplace and everyplace is the geographical location of triumph if the knowledge of Christ is being manifested: *Now thanks be unto God, which always causeth us to triumph in Christ, and maketh manifest the savour of his knowledge by us in **every place*** (II Cor. 2:14). This incident seems to contradict the truth claim that God reveals His will by providentially leaving only one geographical door of service open where triumph in Christ may be experienced. We do not need post-apostolic visions of *Macedonian calls,* yet, as we read Paul's account we should realize that we may at times choose among any number of open doors of opportunity and gain the victory through scriptural obedience. A wise Christian will, however, choose the direction that appears to offer him the best use of his talents and abilities for the Lord.

Quite frequently, we may hear someone proclaiming God's perfect will for another regarding a mission field or extra-biblical truth claim conviction. Even the Apostle Paul would not violate the personal preferences of Apollos in extra-biblical matters—

> As touching our brother Apollos, I greatly desired him to come unto you with the brethren: but his will was not at all to come at this time; but he will come when he shall have convenient time (I Cor. 16:12).

Why did Paul not impose his personal desire upon Apollos as a revelational mandate from God and, more importantly, why should any one of us attempt the same?

Some Christians will procrastinate through life, waiting for God to choose a vocation, career or a doctrinal position for them, but they never experience such a divine call. Some are postponing baptism because God has not personally directed them about that matter. It is not enough for them that God's Word commands all believers to be baptized. They have memorized Eph. 4:1 wherein Paul says: *I therefore the prisoner of the Lord, beseech you that ye walk worthy of the vocation wherein ye are called*. A clear exposition of this verse with the surrounding chapters will reveal that the vocation wherein they were called is *sonship*. This vocation was to be characterized by humility, meekness, longsuffering, holiness, unity, mutual forbearance, and brotherly love (cf. Eph. 4:2). The Bible does not teach that God will inform a saint regarding whether to be a fisherman, shepherd, carpenter, centurion, seller of purple, jailor or a bishop of a local church.

Subjective And Extra-biblical Arguments For Baptismal Regeneration

Sometimes an unsuspecting Christian will be putty in the hands of one who denies receiving a direct revelation from God but nontheless has an unmistakable *burden* or *conviction* from the Lord regarding a truth claim that must be heard. These two terms, (*burden* and *conviction*) when used in the Bible, almost always refer to a claim of having received an inspired revelation from God:

> And when this people, or the prophet, or a priest, shall ask thee, saying, What *is* the burden of the LORD? thou shalt then say unto them, What burden? I will even forsake you, saith the LORD. And *as for* the prophet, and the priest, and the people, that shall say, The burden of the LORD, I will even punish that man and his house. Thus shall ye say every one to his neighbour, and every one to his brother, What hath the LORD answered? and, What hath the LORD spoken? And the burden of the LORD shall ye mention no more: for every man's word shall be his burden; for ye have perverted the words of the living God, of the LORD of hosts our God (Jer. 23:33-36).

Christians should be keenly aware of self-proclaimed prophets who place God's stamp on their own wills by using the phrases *burden of the Lord* or *Holy Spirit conviction* in reference to extra-biblical dogma. These false prophets will often seek to place their hearers into a bondage to their *divine burdens*. If their hearers do not submit, they may be charicatured as having blasphemed the Holy Spirit Himself. They may be labeled *self-willed, opposed to God's will,* and *just the help Satan has been seeking.*

Paul taught that a Christian could be robbed of rewards if he submits to the legalistic mandates of another as if submitting to the will of God in an act of worship. Such a Christian may be told to not touch, taste, or handle that which God has not forbidden (cf. I Tim. 4:1-4). In such a case, he is not worshiping God but rather unknowingly worshipping the will of the false prophet—

> Let no man therefore judge you in meat, or in drink, or in respect of an holyday, or of the new moon, or of the sabbath *days*: Which are a shadow of things to come; but the body *is* of Christ. Let no man beguile you of your reward in a voluntary humility and worshipping

of angels, intruding into those things which he hath not seen, vainly puffed up by his fleshly mind, And not holding the Head, from which all the body by joints and bands having nourishment ministered, and knit together, increaseth with the increase of God. Wherefore if ye be dead with Christ from the rudiments of the world, why, as though living in the world, are ye subject to ordinances, (Touch not; taste not; handle not; Which all are to perish with the using;) after the commandments and doctrines of men? Which things have indeed a shew of wisdom in will worship, and humility, and neglecting of the body; not in any honour to the satisfying of the flesh (Col. 2:16-23).

The Christian must also be cautioned against being deceived by the improper use of the word *application* to teach with divine authority that which the Bible does not say. This clever semantic maneuver is designed to make one appear immune to the charge of misinterpreting or reading into the Bible. He simply affirms: *I was not interpreting, but simply applying.* All sound Bible applications must be within the parameters of sound interpretation. We must not allow someone to place us into bondage to an *application* that contains a principle which is not also a clear biblical precept.

Many of the fallacies of thinking which have been discussed within this chapter are committed by honest Christians whose characters should not be impugned on such grounds. However, this chapter was written to enable normal Christians to be familiar with some of the erroneous methods used to support extra-biblical truth claims. This understanding is particularly valuable in considering the truth claim of *baptismal regeneration* among the several mystical sects of Christianity.

However, there are other sects of Christianity which are not mystical nor subjective in their approach to Scripture. They cite numerous proof-texts in which they affirm that the Bible clearly and objectively teaaches *baptismal regeneration*. In chapter nine we will endeavor to discuss each of these proof-texts in determining the reliability of the affirmation that baptism imparts the saving grace of Christ to the sinner and places him within the Body of Christ.

Chapter Nine

Scriptural Arguments For Baptismal Regeneration Examined

Since Pentecost, becoming a member of God's family according to his revealed will—Christian Initiation, to use the technical phrase—has involved three factors: repentance and faith, plus Christian baptism, plus the coming of the Spirit for new covenant ministry...The order scarcely matters; what matters is that all three links between us and Jesus Christ—faith, baptism, Spirit—should actually be there.

When Paul says that in the one spirit we were all baptized (that is, by Christ) into his one body (I Corinthians 12:13), he thinks of water-baptism and the gift of the Spirit as two complementary aspects of a single act of Christ, who claims and incorporates or ingrafts us (Paul's image, Romans 11:17-24) into vital union with himself...In God's revealed purpose for our lives, water-baptism and Spirit-baptism are joined. Let not any of us in thought or practice put them asunder.

J. I Packer,
I Want To Be A Christian, pp. 38, 39.

It is a common argument that until one is in possession of all of the facts, he should not be dogmatic about his conclusions. But even a casual reading of Scripture reveals that God expects Christians to arrive at a limited number of unmistakable conclusions without being in possession of all of the facts. One unmistakable truth is that no finite person is in possession of all of the facts. When someone says, *Do not say that you know anything for certain until you certainly know everything*, we should ask in response, *From what vantage point were you standing when you concluded for certain that unmistakable conclusions are impossible?* We should then ask, *Are you certain that we cannot be certain?* When a proposition violates the same rule which it sets forth, it is contradictory and incoherent.

God, the Creator, has designed our minds with the capability of thinking in a linear fashion. The fact that the entire human race recognizes the same limited number of metaphysical moral boundaries constitutes logical evidence that there exists a God of righteousness and wrath—

> For the wrath of God is revealed from heaven against all ungodliness and unrighteousness of men, who hold the truth in unrighteousness; Because that which may be known of God is manifest in them; for God hath shewed *it* unto them (Rom. 1:18, 19; cf. 2:14, 15).

This evidence is so logically conclusive that it is said of the unregenerate that they *hold the truth in unrighteousness.* We will expand upon this concept in chapter ten.

Furthermore, the objective designs and purposes of physical things constitute conclusive evidence of a metaphysical Creator—

> For the invisible things of him from the creation of the world are clearly seen, being understood by the things that are made, *even* his eternal power and Godhead; so that they are without excuse: Because that, when they knew God, they glorified *him* not as God, neither were thankful; but became vain in their imaginations, and their foolish heart was darkened (Rom. 1:20, 21).

We have heard the comparison of the human anatomy to a watch found on a jungle trail. Though we cannot see the designer and creator of the watch, we may unmistakably conclude that he existed by the logical inescapability of the fact that the watch could not have designed and brought itself into existence. These are unmistakable conclusions at which we can arrive without knowing all of the facts of the universe.

Scriptural Arguments For Baptismal Regeneration Examined

We are indeed guilty of limiting God by concluding that an infinite being can reveal nothing to a finite being without revealing everything. Paul said of the unregenerate that *they knew God* (Rom. 1:21). This is a limited knowledge that God bestows upon the natural mind enabling the finite person to logically deduce the existence, righteousness, and wrath of God, thus bringing conviction of sin and of the righteous judgment of the Creator:

> And when he is come, he will reprove the world of sin, and of righteousness, and of judgment: Of sin, because they believe not on me; Of righteousness, because I go to my Father, and ye see me no more; Of judgment, because the prince of this world is judged (Jn. 16:8-10).

This is a description of a limited capacity for some conclusive information. It is toward this capacity that we are to target our presentation of the Gospel of Christ (c.f. Paul's sermon on Mars Hill in Acts 17). However, we must not mistake this mental capacity as a saving virtue, for the Scriptures assure us that men possess absolutely no saving virtue of their own (Rom. 3:10, 23).

But man has the option of rejecting this God-given capacity and exalting his imagination in its place, concluding this decision to be the ultimate act of wisdom— *Professing themselves to be wise, they became fools* (Rom. 1: 22). Christians are to avoid this same temptation in their theological conclusions because God has given us the way to accomplish this and bring our thoughts into godly obedience—

> Casting down imaginations, and every high thing that exalteth itself against the knowledge of God, and bringing into captivity every thought to the obedience of Christ (II Cor. 10:5).

Each Christian will choose whether to worship God with his imagination or in spirit and truth—

> But the hour cometh, and now is, when the true worshippers shall worship the Father in spirit and in truth: for the Father seeketh such to worship him. God

is a Spirit: and they that worship him must worship *him* in spirit and in truth (Jn. 4:23, 24).

God has also given us the tools for testing the logical coherence of our conclusions with the known facts. This will not reveal all truth, but it will serve as a fast track to the discovery of what is not true. If our conclusions are incoherent with our limited possession of known facts, then they may also be incoherent with all the facts of reality. When we interpret any text of Scripture, we must apply this principle of coherence. This we did in the case of Paul's baptism (Acts 22:16 cf. chapter five of this present work). The idea that baptism literally washed away Paul's sins was incoherent to his own proclamations of the Gospel. We saw an incoherence between Paul's gospel and the debate over the distinction between ritual and reality (cf. chapter one of this present work). We found the gospel of circumcision to be incoherent with the unified plan of salvation presented throughout every division of Scripture (cf. chapter three of this present work). We observed the particular incoherence of ritual salvation with the NT gospel as it was proclaimed by John the Baptist (cf. chapter four of this present work). The idea of ritual salvation was strongly incoherent with John the Evangelist's record of the gospel of Christ (cf. discussion of Jn. 3:5 in chapter seven of this present work).

With this same principle of coherence in mind, we now examine several of the proof texts used by baptismal regenerationists to affirm that ritual is essential to salvation and imparts the saving grace of Christ.

The argument that one cannot be saved prior to baptism is often taken from Mark 16:16— *He that believeth and is baptized shall be saved; but he that believeth not shall be damned.* Before applying the principle of coherence, we must first look at what is most obvious about the passage. We can see from the conjunction *and* that belief and baptism are two separate items. We also know that a person is in union with Christ from the moment of belief—

> (Jn. 1:12) But as many as received him, to them gave he power to become the sons of God, *even* to them that believe on his name.
>
> (3:18) He that believeth on him is not condemned: but he that believeth not is condemned already, because he

Scriptural Arguments For Baptismal Regeneration Examined

hath not believed in the name of the only begotten Son of God.

(3:36) He that believeth on the Son hath everlasting life: and he that believeth not the Son shall not see life; but the wrath of God abideth on him.

(5:24) Verily, verily, I say unto you, He that heareth my word, and believeth on him that sent me, hath everlasting life, and shall not come into condemnation; but is passed from death unto life.

(6:47) Verily, verily, I say unto you, He that believeth on me hath everlasting life.

(20:31) But these are written, that ye might believe that Jesus is the Christ, the Son of God; and that believing ye might have life through his name.

(Acts 10:43-47) To him give all the prophets witness, that through his name whosoever believeth in him shall receive remission of sins. While Peter yet spake these words, the Holy Ghost fell on all them which heard the word. And they of the circumcision which believed were astonished, as many as came with Peter, because that on the Gentiles also was poured out the gift of the Holy Ghost. For they heard them speak with tongues, and magnify God. Then answered Peter, Can any man forbid water, that these should not be baptized, which have received the Holy Ghost as well as we?

(13:39) And by him all that believe are justified from all things, from which ye could not be justified by the law of Moses.

(16:31) And they said, Believe on the Lord Jesus Christ, and thou shalt be saved, and thy house.

Looking closely at Mk. 16:16, one can base his interpretation on what the passage says or upon what it does not say. It does not say *he that is baptized not shall be damned*, but it does say *he that believeth not shall be damned.* From this point we should seek coherence with the many passages which affirm that they who believe are *sons of God* (Jn. 1:12, 13); have *eternal life* (Jn. 3:14-16; 5:24; 6:47; I Jn. 5:13); are not *condemned* (Jn. 3:18); have *passed from death to life* (Jn. 5:24); are *alive in Christ* (Jn. 11:25); shall *never die* (Jn. 11:26); have *remisson of sins* (Acts 10:43-47; 15:7-11); are *justified* (Acts 13:39); are *purified* (Acts 15:9); are *saved* (Acts 16:31); are *made righteous* (Rom. 3:24-28; 4:5-8; 10:3, 4); do not have sin *imputed* to them (Rom. 4:8); have *peace with God* (Rom. 5:1); are *sealed by the Holy Spirit* (Eph. 1:13) *unto the day of redemption* (Eph. 4:30); are *born of God* (I Jn. 5:1); are *indwelt* by God (I Jn. 4:15); have *overcome the world* (I Jn. 5:5); have God working within (Phil. 1:6, 7); and are predestinated (Eph. 1:5).

Is it legitimate to distinguish *belief* from *baptism* in the definition of salvation? In Mk. 16:16 there is no question that *belief* and *baptism* are listed separately. They are not synonymous. The following statement is true: *he that believeth and is baptized; has blue eyes; wears red ties; lives in a white house, etc., shall be saved. However, he that believeth not shall be damned.* He that *believeth not* shall be damned solely on that basis. Thus, the principle of coherence with the Bible as a whole disqualifies Mk. 16:16 as teaching *baptismal regeneration.*

Before examining the other proof texts used to defend *baptismal regeneration*, we need to expand on our discussion of *order* which took place in chapter five. Some will argue that the order in which faith, ritual baptism, and Spirit baptism occurs is irrelevant, but that all three are essential to salvation. J. I Packer states:

> Since Pentecost, becoming a member of God's family according to his revealed will—Christian initiation, to use the technical phrase—has involved three factors: repentance and faith, plus Christian baptism, plus the coming of the Spirit for new covenant ministry (cf. Acts 2:38; Romans 8:9ff.; Ephesians 1:13ff.). In experience, the order has varied; apparently it was faith-baptism-Spirit at Pentecost (Acts 2:38-42), Spirit-faith-baptism at the "Gentile Pentecost" (Acts 10:44-48), faith-Spirit-baptism at Galatia (Gal. 3:2); certainly, it has been baptism-faith-Spirit for all those Christians down the centuries who were baptized as infants. The order scarcely matters; What matters is

that all three links between us and Jesus Christ—faith, baptism, Spirit—should actually be there.

When Paul says that in the one *Spirit* we were all *baptized* (that is by Christ) into his one *body* (I Cor. 12:13), he thinks of water baptism and the gift of the Spirit as two complementary aspects of a single act of Christ, who claims and incorporates or engrafts us (Paul's image, Romans 11:17-24) into vital union with himself. So converts who have received the Spirit should seek baptism, and the baptized should seek conversion, so that they may receive the Spirit! In God's revealed purpose for our lives, water baptism and Spirit-baptism are joined. Let not any of us in thought or practice put them asunder.[1]

When Packer states: *certainly, it has been baptism-faith-Spirit for all those Christians down the centuries who were baptized as infants*, he is basing his certainty on that which cannot be found in Scripture. Thus *experience* becomes *His revealed will*—(cf. chapter eight of this present work). The fact is that, though water baptism could occur before the baptism of the Spirit, scriptural water baptism never occurred prior to saving faith. The original disciples were of course ritually baptized prior to the coming of the Spirit. We will argue later that the Jews on the Day of Pentecost were born again believers prior to their water baptism. In Acts 10, 11, 15 the Gentile believers experienced faith, baptism of the Holy Spirit, and then water baptism (10:47, cf. the Galatians, Gal. 3:2, 3). We will argue that the Ephesians who were so-called "disciples of John the Baptist" were not really born again at all, but were introduced to Christ by Paul and subsequently rebaptized. Rebaptism was not required of anyone else in Scripture who was saved and baptized during the lives of John and Jesus.

But many seem to stumble at the order in Acts 8 when Philip evangelizes the Samaritans—faith, water baptism, Spirit baptism (Acts 8:15, 16). God is not totally explicit as to why He changed the order in this case. Without being overly dogmatic on this point, let us consider several observations and suggestions.

---

[1] J. I. Packer, *Growing In Christ* (Wheaton, Illinois: Crossway Books, 1994), PP. 124, 125.

John the Baptist, Jesus Christ, the Apostle Peter, Philip the Evangelist and the Apostle Paul all preached the gospel of personal salvation through faith in Christ.[2] This is why Philip could preach Jesus Christ to the Ethiopian Eunuch from the fifty-third chapter of Isaiah even though Isaiah never mentions ritual baptism. Remember the problem that Jews had with Samaritans—they were considered the "mixed-breeds" of the ten northern tribes of Israel who were forced to marry the Assyrians during their captivity. There was potential controversy with the Jews in accepting Samaritans as brothers in Christ. Perhaps this is why the apostles (Peter and John) themselves needed to impart the gift of the Spirit to them. There was a longstanding predisposition for schism between Jews and Samaritans, and perhaps it was needful for the Samaritans to be officially introduced with full apostolic authority into the communion of fellowship with the Jerusalem saints.

Philip's sermon would indeed have introduced a controversy in Jerusalem. He preached *the things concerning the kingdom of God and the name of Jesus* (Acts. 8:12) to these Samaritans. When he preached Jesus as the Christ (literally, *the Messiah*), he was saying that the Samaritans would become heirs of the Millennium by faith in Jesus Christ, as Messiah. They were still Jews in God's eyes. The Millennium will be shared by twelve tribes of Israel. During the seventieth week of Daniel there will be 12,000 Jews saved from each tribe of Israel, totaling 144,000. There probably needed to be explicit apostolic authority for the idea of an equivocation of Samaritans and Jews in the Jerusalem church. In Acts 6 the Palestinian Jewish converts desired to withhold the benevolent fund from Grecian Jewish converts. The Grecians were mostly Jews who had come home from the dispersion (the evangelist, Philip, was a Grecian Jew and was, therefore, open-minded enough to take the gospel to the Samaritans). How much

---

[2] Many argue that it was John's purpose to preach the Kingdom of God to Israel (Lk. 16:16) rather than the NT plan of salvation. The fact is that John preached the Kingdom of God (Matt. 3:1, 2) and personal salvation through faith in Christ (Jn. 1:29, 36; Acts 19:4; 10:37, 43); Jesus did the same (Matt. 4:17; Acts 1:3, 6-9); and Peter (Acts 3:16; 10:37); and the evangelist Philip (Acts 8:12); and the Apostle Paul (Acts 14:22; 19:8; 20:25; 28:23, 31). The term *Kingdom of God* often spoke of a coming kingdom while personal salvation in Christ Jesus is here and now (Acts 1:3-8).

less would Jewish converts be inclined to extend the hand of fellowship to Samaritans?

It is interesting to note that the Apostle John would be one of the apostles to impart the Spirit to the Samaritans. When Jesus had sent messengers to a Samaritan village to make ready for His visit there, the Samaritans were not receptive. So James and John said: *Lord, wilt thou that we command fire to come down from heaven, and consume them, even as Elias did?* (Luke 9:54). For this they received a sharp rebuke from Jesus, Who then informed them of His intention to save and not destroy them (Luke 9:55, 56).

So with Philip being a Grecian Jew and not an apostle, it is easy to see why apostolic authority needed to be injected into the situation. Notwithstanding, regardless of the variation of order in the NT baptism accounts, there is no account of an individual being biblically baptized prior to faith and salvation.

When the Apostle Paul came to Ephesus, he met a group of men calling themselves disciples of John the Baptist. Paul asked them, *Have ye received the Holy Ghost since ye believed?* Actually, Paul was asking them if they had received the Spirit when they believed (Acts 19:2). Their answer was that they had not even heard that the Holy Spirit had been given.[3] At this point Paul inquired about their baptism and they responded that they had experienced John's baptism. Paul may have become suspicious of their having been personally associated with John, for the Baptist spoke often of the Holy Spirit (Matt. 3:11, 12; Mk. 1:7, 8; Lk. 3:16, 17; Jn. 1:32, 33). So Paul proclaimed to these men in Ephesus that John required belief in Jesus before he baptized anyone (19:4). Paul may have had a difficult time conceiving of any one being scripturally baptized and yet being so ignorant about the new birth. *When they heard this, they were baptized in the name of the Lord Jesus* (19:5). This would be the first case of *anabaptism* recorded in Church history. Then in 19:6 Paul laid hands on them and they received the Holy Ghost.

---

[3] It is therefore extremely doubtful that they had heard the Apostle Peter on the Day of Pentecost when the Holy Spirit was given with power and 3000 were saved and baptized. Among the seventeen nationalities present that day were men from Asia, of which Ephesus was the capital (Acts 2:9).

It is strange that no one else recorded in the NT, who was immersed with John's baptism, was required to submit to a rebaptism. The Apostles themselves were not required to submit to a rebaptism. Then why was it required of these "so called" disciples of John at Ephesus? That John required faith in Jesus seemed to be news to them. Perhaps they were disciples of disciples of John. It is possible that they trusted Christ for the first time that day, and, therefore, became baptized in the name of Jesus. This rebaptism became their Christian baptism. If they were baptized prior to faith in Christ for salvation, their baptism was invalid. The order, as in the case of the Samaritans, placed the giving of the Holy Ghost after ritual baptism but, as always, faith in Christ and salvation preceded the ritual baptism.

So, in the cases of the apostles prior to Pentecost, the Samaritans, and the so-called disciples of John, the baptism of the Spirit happened after ritual baptism but not before faith in Christ. But now, from Acts 10:47, the principle of Romans 8:9 must be understood— *Now if any man have not the Spirit of Christ, he is none of his.* We become His at the moment of faith, from which time Christ is in us— *And if Christ be in you, the body is dead because of sin but the Spirit is life because of righteousness* (Rom. 8:10).

The next major proof text for *baptismal regeneration* is found in the second chapter of Acts. It was the Day of Pentecost or *Feast of Weeks* (Lev. 23:15-22). It was a day when Jews of many languages met in Jerusalem for the holiday. Also, the Christian disciples were all gathered together in one place. These disciples were already regenerated, justified, and saved through faith in Christ's finished work on the cross.

Many books have been written to address questions surrounding Acts chapter 2. We will address the most important question of all: *Was the NT gospel of Jesus Christ preached that day, or was it a parenthetical gospel of some kind?* The answer to the first part of this question is *yes* and the answer to the second part is *no*. Peter did preach the same gospel as was preached by Paul and John the Baptist—

> Then said Paul, John verily baptized with the baptism
> of repentance, saying unto the people, that they should
> believe on him which should come after him, that is,
> on Christ Jesus (Acts 19:4).

Scriptural Arguments For Baptismal Regeneration Examined

> The word which *God* sent unto the children of Israel, preaching peace by Jesus Christ: (he is Lord of all:) That word, *I say*, ye know, which was published throughout all Judaea, and began from Galilee, after the baptism which John preached (Acts 10:36, 37).

John did not baptize anyone in order that they would repent, but only because they had already changed their minds about Christ (cf. chapter four of this present work regarding the NT nature of John's baptism).

Peter spoke of the OT prophecy of the death, burial, and resurrection of Christ (vss. 29-37). The promise of salvation and remission of sins was not just a Jewish gospel, but was for anyone called by the Lord—

> For the promise is unto you, and to your children, and to all that are afar off, *even* as many as the Lord our God shall call (Acts 2:39).

Later in the book of Acts when the angel of the Lord loosed Peter from prison, he was commanded to preach the same gospel again in the temple—

> But the angel of the Lord by night opened the prison doors, and brought them forth, and said, Go, stand and speak in the temple to the people all the words of this life (Acts 5:19, 20).

The Gospel he preached was distinct from his exhortations to be baptized—

> The God of our fathers raised up Jesus, whom ye slew and hanged on a tree. Him hath God exalted with his right hand *to be* a Prince and a Saviour, for to give repentance to Israel, and forgiveness of sins (Acts 5:30, 31).

When Peter preached to the Gentile house of Cornelius it was a gospel of faith alone in Jesus Christ (Acts 10:43), distinct from baptism—

> Can any man forbid water, that these should not be baptized, which have received the Holy Ghost as well as we (Acts 10:47)?

Just as he began his message, their minds changed, they received the baptism of the Holy Spirit, and were placed into the Body of Christ—

> And as I began to speak, the Holy Ghost fell on them, as on us at the beginning. Then remembered I the word of the Lord, how that he said, John indeed baptized with water; but ye shall be baptized with the Holy Ghost (Acts 11:15, 16).

Then Peter testified that these Gentiles received the same gift of the Holy Spirit that the disciples and the Jews had received on the Day of Pentecost:

> Forasmuch then as God gave them the like gift as *he did* unto us, who believed on the Lord Jesus Christ; what was I, that I could withstand God (Acts 11:17)?

That day the Jews of Jerusalem agreed with the Apostle Peter that Hebrews and Gentiles are granted eternal life on the same exact basis—

> When they heard these things, they held their peace, and glorified God, saying, Then hath God also to the Gentiles granted repentance unto life (Acts 11:18).

Later, the Apostle Paul would proclaim to the Jews that all (Jews and Gentiles) are saved by one and the same gospel:

> Be it known unto you therefore, men *and* brethren, that through this man is preached unto you the forgiveness of sins: And by him all that believe are justified from all things, from which ye could not be justified by the law of Moses (Acts 13:38, 39).

Note how Paul worded his gospel in a way similar to that presented by John the Baptist:

> Whereupon, O king Agrippa, I was not disobedient unto the heavenly calling: But shewed first unto them

of Damascus, and at Jerusalem, and throughout all the coasts of Judaea, and then to the Gentiles, that they should repent and turn to God, and do works meet for repentance (Acts 26:19, 20).

During the debate at the Council of Jerusalem Peter argued that if Jews were to be saved, it would have to be the same way the House of Cornelius received eternal life (i.e. distinct from baptism):

> And when there had been much disputing, Peter rose up, and said unto them, Men *and* brethren, ye know how that a good while ago God made choice among us, that the Gentiles by my mouth should hear the word of the gospel, and believe. And God, which knoweth the hearts, bare them witness, giving them the Holy Ghost, even as *he did* unto us; And put no difference between us and them, purifying their hearts by faith. Now therefore why tempt ye God, to put a yoke upon the neck of the disciples, which neither our fathers nor we were able to bear? But we believe that through the grace of the Lord Jesus Christ we shall be saved, even as they (Acts 15:7-11).

This is the same Gospel that Paul would later preach to King Agrippa as he explained his mission from Jesus Christ:

> To open their eyes, *and* to turn *them* from darkness to light, and *from* the power of Satan unto God, that they may receive forgiveness of sins, and inheritance among them which are sanctified by faith that is in me (Acts 26:18).

Thus Paul could proclaim that there are not various ethnic versions of the NT gospel, but only one plan of salvation for all nations and classes:

> There is neither Jew nor Greek, there is neither bond nor free, there is neither male nor female: for ye are all one in Christ Jesus. And if ye *be* Christ's, then are ye

Abraham's seed, and heirs according to the promise (Gal. 3:28, 29).[4]

The result of Peter's gospel sermon on the day of Pentecost was the conversion of three thousand individual Jews. This was not a national conversion, but rather a new birth experienced only by individuals who received the word of the Gospel—

> Then they that gladly received his word were baptized: and the same day there were added *unto them* about three thousand souls (Acts 2:41).

Notice that only believers were baptized and that they did not contact the Word in the water, but rather contacted the water only after having received the Word..

In arguing for *baptismal regeneration* much emphasis is placed on the order in which Peter listed his instructions to those who desired to be saved: (a) repent; (b) be baptized (c) receive remission of sins; and (d) receive the gift of the Holy Ghost (Acts 2:38). Is the order that Peter used here a prescription of the order in which full salvation will occur? It has been argued for centuries that the baptism of the Holy Ghost is (a) water baptism; (b) happens at water baptism or (c) happens only after water baptism.

We must approach this problem of the order in Acts 2:38 using the principle of coherence. By Peter's own testimony they were saved the same way the house of Cornelius was saved (Acts 15:7-9), which was unmistakably before and independent of ritual baptism (Acts 10:47). Thus, their salvation was prior to and distinct from their ritual baptism—

> And as I began to speak, the Holy Ghost fell on them, as on us at the beginning. Then remembered I the word of the Lord, how that he said, John indeed baptized with water; but ye shall be baptized with the Holy Ghost (Acts 11:15, 16).

---

[4] We will discuss Gal. 3:27 later in this chapter.

Scriptural Arguments For Baptismal Regeneration Examined

Baptismal regenerationists will often argue that Acts 10 was the other side of a transition in the gospel, and therefore a different set of terms for receiving eternal life. It is argued that the way of life for a Gentile was different than that of a Jew. It was regarding this very point of controversy that the Jerusalem council met to resolve in Acts 15. In applying the principle of coherence, we must look closely at a particular occurrence of salvation between Acts 2 and Acts 10.

It was the day after, or shortly thereafter, the Acts 2:38 occasion when this same Apostle Peter led the lame man at the temple gate into a born again experience without his being baptized. When the beggar asked alms, Peter said: *In the name of Jesus Christ of Nazareth rise up and walk* (Acts 3:6b). Peter not only presented healing, but also spoke eternal life to this man so that he was saved by grace through faith in Jesus Christ without yet experiencing ritual baptism:

> And his name through faith in his name hath made this man strong, whom ye see and know: yea, the faith which is by him hath given him this perfect soundness in the presence of you all (Acts 3:16).

Peter then preached to the Jews gathered at the temple, telling them that they needed a dose of the same gospel:

> Repent ye therefore, and be converted, that your sins may be blotted out (Acts 3:19a)

It is fundamental to notice at this point that Peter's gospel to these Jews and his gospel to the Gentiles was the same gospel predicted by the OT prophets—

> And he shall send Jesus Christ, which before was preached unto you: Whom the heaven must receive until the times of restitution of all things, which God hath spoken by the mouth of all his holy prophets since the world began. For Moses truly said unto the fathers, A prophet shall the Lord your God raise up unto you of your brethren, like unto me; him shall ye hear in all things whatsoever he shall say unto you. And it shall come to pass, *that* every soul, which will not hear that prophet, shall be destroyed from among

> the people. Yea, and all the prophets from Samuel and those that follow after, as many as have spoken, have likewise foretold of these days (Acts 3:20-24).
>
> (Cf. Acts 10:43) To him give all the prophets witness, that through his name whosoever believeth in him shall receive remission of sins.

Peter preached the same gospel and the same baptism that John the Baptist had preached to the Jews—

> The word which *God* sent unto the children of Israel, preaching peace by Jesus Christ: (he is Lord of all:) That word, *I say*, ye know, which was published throughout all Judaea, and began from Galilee, after the baptism which John preached (Acts 10: 36, 37).

Though the Jews were unique in many ways and had a package of separate promises that the Gentiles and the Church would not possess, the gospel of eternal life presented to Abraham was the same as that which was presented to Gentiles—

> Ye are the children of the prophets, and of the covenant which God made with our fathers, saying unto Abraham, And in thy seed shall all the kindreds of the earth be blessed (Acts 3:25).
>
> Now to Abraham and his seed were the promises made. He saith not, And to seeds, as of many; but as of one, And to thy seed, which is Christ (Gal 3:16).
>
> And the scripture, foreseeing that God would justify the heathen through faith, preached before the gospel unto Abraham, *saying*, In thee shall all nations be blessed (Gal.3:8).

If the reader will recall chapter three of this present work, he will note again that the plan of salvation through the ages was always distinct from ritual and always looked forward to the finished work of the suffering Messiah.

Returning our thoughts to Peter and Acts 3, his version of the gospel that day was not for Jews only, but for Jews first—

> Unto you first God, having raised up his Son Jesus, sent him to bless you, in turning away every one of you from his iniquities (Acts 3:26).

Looking again at Acts 2:38 we must interpret the clause, *be baptized every one of you in the name of Jesus Christ for the remission of sins.* The correct interpretation of these words will be largely determined by the meaning of the word *for* (Gr. *eis*) in this context. This little Greek preposition can mean *with reference to, because of, in relation to, concerning* or *unto.* Using the principle of coherence, we can narrow the meaning in this passage to either *in order to* or *because of.* In the case of *in order to*, we would have to conclude that ritual baptism is essential to receiving remission of sins. In *because of*, we would conclude that Peter is telling them to be ritually baptized because their sins are already remitted. It is the *because of* usage that coheres with all we know of the plan of salvation throughout the OT and throughout the remainder of the NT.

Is there any biblical precedent for using *eis* in this manner? First we will look at Matt. 3:11—

> I indeed baptize you with water unto (eis) repentance: but he that cometh after me is mightier than I, whose shoes I am not worthy to bear: he shall baptize you with the Holy Ghost, and *with* fire.

John the Baptist did not baptize them in order that they would repent, but only because they had repented.

In Matt. 12:41 we need to note that the Ninevites did not repent in order that Jonah would preach, but because he had already preached—

> The men of Nineveh shall rise in judgment with this generation, and shall condemn it: because they repented at (eis) the preaching of Jonas; and, behold, a greater than Jonas *is* here.

In Lk. 5:13, 14 the leper was to go to a priest and make an offering, not in order to be cleansed, but, because he had been cleansed—

> And he put forth *his* hand, and touched him, saying, I will: be thou clean. And immediately the leprosy departed from him. And he charged him to tell no man: but go, and shew thyself to the priest, and offer for (*eis*) thy cleansing, according as Moses commanded, for a testimony unto them.

If we said, *John was beheaded for (eis) his faithfulness*, would we be saying that he was executed in order that he would be faithful? If we said, *The criminal was hanged for (eis) his crime*, would we be saying that he was hanged in order that he would commit crime? If we said, *The people laughed for (eis) joy*, would we be saying that the people laughed in order to obtain joy? The interpretation we derive from Acts 2:38 must be consistent and coherent with the context of the entirety of Scriptures, or we have interpreted incorrectly. Baptism is not the gospel, but instead is a picture and a testimonial of the gospel from one who has already received it—

> Moreover, brethren, I declare unto you the gospel which I preached unto you, which also ye have received, and wherein ye stand; by which also ye are saved, if ye keep in memory what I preached unto you, unless ye have believed in vain. For I delivered unto you first of all that which I also received, how that Christ died for our sins according to the scriptures; And that he was buried, and that he rose again the third day according to the scriptures (I Cor. 15:1-4).

Ordinances have never, and can never, accomplish a literal remission of sins—

> By the which will we are sanctified through the offering of the body of Jesus Christ once *for all*. And every priest standeth daily ministering and offering oftentimes the same sacrifices, which can never take away sins: But this man, after he had offered one sacrifice for sins for ever, sat down on the right hand of God; from henceforth expecting till his enemies be

> made his footstool. For by one offering he hath perfected for ever them that are sanctified (Heb. 10:10-14).

Notice what the writer of Hebrews says about the saving faith of OT saints:

> And these all, having obtained a good report through faith, received not the promise: God having provided some better thing for us, that they without us should not be made perfect (Heb. 11:39, 40).

This *better thing* was not another ordinance; they had books of ordinances. The *better thing* was the literal *offering of the body of Jesus Christ once for all*. This is why we must look to Jesus as *the author and finisher of our faith* (Heb. 12:2a).

A key verse used in tandem with Acts 2:38 is Gal. 3:27—*For as many of you as have been baptized into Christ have put on Christ.* This text is used to affirm that we put on the robe of Christ's righteousness at the moment of ritual baptism. Although it is true that the righteousness of Christ is imputed to us, and put upon us, at the moment of salvation, we must remind ourselves again that Mk. 16:16 clearly distinguishes between *belief* and *baptism*. The moment of faith and the moment of ritual baptism are two separate occurrences—e.g. the house of Cornelius (Acts 10:47). The verses preceding Gal. 3:27 affirm that the moment of salvation is the moment of faith:

> But the scripture hath concluded all under sin, that the promise by faith of Jesus Christ might be given to them that believe. But before faith came, we were kept under the law, shut up unto the faith which should afterwards be revealed. Wherefore the law was our schoolmaster *to bring us* unto Christ, that we might be justified by faith. But after that faith is come, we are no longer under a schoolmaster. For ye are all the children of God by faith in Christ Jesus (Gal. 3:22-26).

The word *into (eis)* in vs. 27 can be interpreted to say *with reference to*, pointing retroactively to the work of Christ applied to the sinner at the moment of faith. Compare I Cor. 10:2—*And were all baptized unto (eis) Moses in the cloud and in the sea*. If *eis* means *put into Christ* in Gal. 3:27 then the Corinthian passage could mean *put into Moses* or *in order to obtain Moses*. However, if we interpret *eis* to mean *with reference to*, the passage becomes coherent with all else we know about the moment of salvation. Israel passed through the Red Sea *because of* the leadership of Moses, not *in order to* obtain his — leadership.

The phrase *put on* has several good applications in the NT. Compare Rom. 13:14, which was written to Christians who had already experienced salvation at the moment of faith—*But put ye on the Lord Jesus Christ, and make not provision for the flesh, to fulfil the lusts thereof.* *Put on* can literally mean the putting on of clothes (Matt. 6:25); or coats (Mk. 6:9); to *array* oneself in *royal apparel* (Acts 12:21); or to be *clothed in fine linen* (Rev. 19:14). Paul longed for the day that he would be *clothed* with a heavenly, glorified body (I Cor. 15:53, 54; II Cor. 5:3). Christians who have already had the salvation experience are to dress themselves in the *armour of light* (Rom. 13:12) by walking *honestly*; not in *rioting*, *drunkenness*, *chambering*, *wantonness*, *strife*, or *envy* (Rom. 13:13). In so walking, they will be putting on, or clothing themselves, with Jesus Christ (Rom. 13:14). This is a separate concept from the robe of Christ's righteousness which is imputed to the sinner at the moment of faith. Those who are saved through faith are exhorted to openly model that faith by putting on the *breastplate of faith and love*, and to model the *hope of salvation* by wearing that hope as a helmet (I Thess. 5:8). Those who are already *brethren* in Christ (Eph. 6:10) are to *put on the whole armour of God* in order to *stand against the wiles of the devil* (Eph. 6:11). Christians are to openly model their election by their open practice of godliness (Col. 3:12-25). When a sinner is born again, he becomes a new man on the inside, but his flesh is still carnal. Through mortification, he is to dress himself outwardly with the new man. But in doing this, he must undress himself of the outward appearance of the old man—

> Lie not one to another, seeing that ye have put off the old man with his deeds; And have put on the new *man*, which is renewed in knowledge after the image of him that created him (Col. 3:9, 10).

This same idea is portrayed by the Apostle Paul in his concept of ritual baptism. We become *children of God* and have Christ within at the moment of faith (Gal. 3:25, 26), and we publicly model this fact when we outwardly put on Jesus Christ at our baptism (3:27). Those who are saved by grace through faith are putting on Jesus Christ each time they obey His instructions. This is particularly true when they — model His grace and righteousness as a light to others.

The next powerful passage that is cited to demonstrate *baptismal regeneration* is:

> Husbands, love your wives, even as Christ also loved the church, and gave himself for it; That he might sanctify and cleanse it with the washing of water by the word (Eph. 5:25, 26).

It seems so certain that ritual baptism is in view here that *The Living Bible* paraphrases vs. 26 to read: *to make her holy and clean, washed by baptism and God's Word.*[5]

The Apostle Paul is comparing the husband's relationship to the wife with Christ's relationship to the Church. Just as Christ sacrificed Himself for the glorification of the Church, so also the Husband should be self-sacrificing toward the wife. But how and when does Christ sanctify the saint?

The term *sanctify* has a long list of separate applications throughout Scripture. The meaning in such cases carries the concepts of *separation*, *set apart*, *consecrate*, *dedicate* or *purify*. These meanings also have three separate applications to the saint (a *saint* is one who is sanctified).

The first application is what we refer to as *positional sanctification*. This is when Jesus Christ consecrates the believer to Himself, *without which no man shall see the Lord* (Heb. 12:14). This is when Christ's holiness and sanctity is imputed to the believer (II Cor. 5:21). This holiness is obtained through faith in Christ—

> To open their eyes, and to turn them from darkness to light, and from the power of Satan unto God, that they may receive forgiveness of sins, and inheritance

---

[5] *The Living Bible: Paraphrased* (Wheaton, Illinois: Tyndale House Publishers, 1971), p. 951.

among them which are sanctified by faith that is in me (Acts 26:18)

In this application, all believers are *saints* regardless of their level of maturity and spirituality (Rom. 1:7; I Cor. 1:2; Eph. 1:1; Phil 1:1; Col. 1:1; Jude 1, 3). The time of this sanctification is at the moment of faith (Acts 26:18) when God imputes the holiness of Christ to the sinner and proclaims him sanctified. The means through which this sanctification is made available is the blood of Christ (Heb. 13:12; Acts 20:28) at the offering of His body (Heb. 10:10-14). This is the application which Paul. had in view when he wrote Eph. 5:25, 26.

The second application of the sanctification concept has reference to the personal righteous acts of the saint wherein he separates himself, sets himself apart, consecrates himself, dedicates himself and purifies himself. This requires works of obedience to the commands of Christ, and is distinct from positional sancification. We call this second application *progressive sanctification*. One can be positionally sanctified and called a saint while at the same time practicing carnality and refusing to practice progressive sanctification. Paul told the Corinthians that they were *sanctified* (I Cor. 6:11) while declaring also that they were *yet carnal* (I Cor. 3:1-3). In his Second Epistle Paul told them that they had been *made the righteousness of God in Him* (positional sanctification (II Cor. 5:21), yet he exhorts them to *perfect holiness in the fear of God* (II Cor. 7:1). He calls the Ephesians *saints* (Eph. 1:1), meaning that they possessed the imputed righteousness of Christ. Yet, Christ gave them apostles, prophets, evangelists and pastor/teachers *for the perfecting of the saints* (Eph. 4:11, 12). He tells these positionally sanctified saints to walk as it *becometh saints* (Eph. 5:3). He tells the Thessalonians that they are already *sanctified* (positional sanctification, II Thess. 2:13), and yet he prays for their sanctification (I Thess. 5:23, 24).

This *progressive sanctification* is accomplished when the believer dresses himself with Christlikeness, as we discussed in Gal. 3:27. This should be practiced on a daily basis throughout the life of the believer. It is when the saint puts off the old man and puts on the new (Col. 3:8-12). It is when the saint yields his body as an instrument of righteousness (Rom. 6:13). It is when he presents his body as a living sacrifice (Rom. 12:2). It is when he cleanses himself *from all filthiness of flesh and spirit, perfecting holiness in the fear of God* (II Cor. 7:1). It is a lifelong pressing toward perfection. This is why Paul can speak of. himself as not yet perfect and yet, in another sense, perfect:

> Not as though I had already attained, either were already perfect: but I follow after, if that I may apprehend that for which also I am apprehended of Christ Jesus (Phil. 3:12).
>
> Let us therefore, as many as be perfect, be thus minded: and if in any thing ye be otherwise minded, God shall reveal even this unto you (Phil. 3:15).

Thiessen says:

> It is evident that one is positional perfection and the other experiential perfection. Positionally he was perfect since the day that he believed in Christ; experientially he was perfect only in a limited degree. The same Greek word is used in both verses; except that the first is a verb and the second an adjective. Col. 1:28; 4:12; Heb. 12:23 hold out perfection as a goal to be attained in the end, but not in this life. It is clear from these and other Scriptures that absolute perfection is not to be expected in this life.[6]

So, in the first application we are *set apart* from the condemnation of sin (Jn.5:24), and in the second application we are to *separate* ourselves from the *reign* of sin (Rom. 6:12). But in a third application, at the rapture of the saints, the believer will be *separated* from the very presence of sin (I Jn. 3:2; Heb. 9:28)—

> To the end he may stablish your hearts unblameable in holiness before God, even our Father, at the coming of our Lord Jesus Christ with all his saints (I Thess. 3:13).

---

[6] Henry Clarence Theissen, *Introductory Lectures In Systematic Theology* (Grand Rapids, Michigan: Wm. B. Eerdmans Publishing Company, 1971), pp. 381, 382.

This is when the believer will never have to struggle with sin again (Rev. 22:11). It is when the believer receives a glorified body which has flesh, but without a sinful nature (Rom. 8:23; I Cor. 15:53; Phil. 3:20, 21).

There are some who take the position that *positional* and *progressive/experiential* sanctification are one and that the godly behavior of the believer is indistinguishable from the imputed righteousness of Christ.[7] If personal obedience is 100% an act of God, we have a difficult time explaining degrees of obedience, degrees of heavenly inheritance, degrees of reward at the judgment seat of Christ, and degrees of ruling with Christ during the Millennium.[8]

Throughout the NT believers are told to decide how faithful and obedient they will become. Their faithfulness and obedience will never be saving virtues but they will be rewardable virtues at the judgment seat of Christ. There are no degrees of salvation. One is either saved or lost. Salvation is a free gift but the prize for which Paul pressed required perseverant, obedient striving—

---

[7] John MacArthur, *The Gospel According to Jesus* (Grand Rapids, Michigan: Academie Books, Zondervan Publishing House, 1988), p. 33 "We must remember above all that salvation is a sovereign work of God. Biblically it is defined by what it produces, not by what one does to get it. Works are not necessary to earn salvation, But true salvation wrought by God will not fail to produce the good works that are its fruit (cf. Matthew 7:17). We are God's workmanship. No aspect of salvation is merited by human works (Titus 3:5-7). Thus salvation cannot be defective in any dimension. As part of His saving work, God will produce repentance, faith, sanctification, yieldedness, obedience, and ultimately glorification. Since He is not dependent on human effort in producing those elements, an experience that lacks any of them cannot be the saving work of God."

[8] John F. MacArthur Jr., *Faith Works: The Gospel According To The Apostles* (Dallas: Word Publishing, 1993), pp. 182, 106. Again MacArthur states: "Any doctrine of eternal security that leaves out perseverance distorts the doctrine of salvation itself. Heaven without holiness ignores the whole purpose for which God chose and redeemed us, p. 182. And again, "Nowhere in Scripture do we find positional righteousness set against righteous behavior, as if the two realities were innately disconnected. In fact, the apostle Paul's teaching was diametrically opposed to the notion that *positional truth* means that we are free to sin", p. 106.

Scriptural Arguments For Baptismal Regeneration Examined

> Brethren, I count not myself to have apprehended: but *this* one thing *I do*, forgetting those things which are behind, and reaching forth unto those things which are before, I press toward the mark for the prize of the high calling of God in Christ Jesus (Phil. 3:13, 14).

Returning to Eph: 5:26, by what authority can anyone substitute the word *baptism* for the word *water*? The Greek reads *by the washing of water in the word*. The washing is in the Word, not in the water of ritual baptism. The baptismal regenerationist says that the Word is in the water, but the water of Eph. 5:26 is in the Word. Hence a literal washing but not literal water. The Water in the Word is none other than the saving grace of Jesus Christ Himself (Rev. 22:17). Jesus proclaimed the same truth to the woman at the well:

> Then saith the woman of Samaria unto him, How is it that thou, being a Jew, askest drink of me, which am a woman of Samaria? for the Jews have no dealings with the Samaritans. Jesus answered and said unto her, If thou knewest the gift of God, and who it is that saith to thee, Give me to drink; thou wouldest have asked of him, and he would have given thee living water. The woman saith unto him, Sir, thou hast nothing to draw with, and the well is deep: from whence then hast thou that living water? Art thou greater than our father Jacob, which gave us the well, and drank thereof himself, and his children, and his cattle? Jesus answered and said unto her, Whosoever drinketh of this water shall thirst again: But whosoever drinketh of the water that I shall give him shall never thirst; but the water that I shall give him shall be in him a well of water springing up into everlasting life. The woman saith unto him, Sir, give me this water, that I thirst not, neither come hither to draw (Jn. 4:9-15).

Sanctification and cleansing are blessings attributed to the sacrifice of Christ's body and blood (Acts 20:28; Heb. 10:10-14; Heb. 13:12) and the Word of God (Jn. 17:17). The washing of Eph 5:26 is not a ritual cleansing of the body, but rather a spiritual cleansing of the soul (Heb. 10:22). Jesus also referred to the Holy Spirit as *living water* (Jn. 7:38, 39). God the Father sanctifies the believer when He reckons the righteousness of Christ to him (I Cor. 1:30). Thus sanctification is the work of the entire Trinity, distinct from ritual baptism, but apprehended at the moment of faith (Acts 26:18; II Thess. 2:13, 14). It is when the believer becomes a brother in Christ and one in Christ with all other believers (Heb. 2:11). This was a choice God made before the foundation of the earth (I Pet. 1:2). Eph. 5:26 is not speaking of ritual baptism, but of salvation by grace through faith (cf. Eph. 2:8, 9).

But Eph. 5:26 sounds even more like baptismal regeneration when quoted in conjunction with Titus 3:5—

> Not by works of righteousness which we have done, but according to his mercy he saved us, by the washing of regeneration, and renewing of the Holy Ghost.

In Chapter five of this present work, we cited the prominent belief that ritual baptism replaced circumcision and that baptism is circumcision in a different form. We also endeavored to refute that position thoroughly from Scripture. However, if we were incorrect, the baptismal salvationists have then proven that baptism is a work of the law just as circumcision always was a Mosaic requirement for all males—infants and proselytes (Acts 13:39; Gal. 2:16; Rom. 4:5). Now if baptism is a righteous work of the law, then Titus 3:5 cannot be referring to ritual baptism. Unless, as some seem to hold, God irresistibly causes all of His elect to be ritually baptized.[9]

But we believe ourselves to be correct in the position that baptism did not replace circumcision. Yet still, baptism is a righteous work of obedience to one of the many commandments of the Lord Jesus Christ (Matt. 28:18-20). Therefore, the washing of Titus 3:5 cannot be ritual baptism. There is no textual basis upon which to substitute *baptism* for *washing* in this verse.

---

[9] Ibid., *Gospel According To Jesus*, p. 196—"...The contemporary teaching that separates discipleship from salvation springs from ideas that are foreign to Scripture...Every Christian is a disciple. The Lord's Great Commission was to go into all the world and *make disciples...teaching them to observe all that I have commanded you* (Matthew 28:19, 20)...Disciples are people who believe, those whose faith motivates them to obey all Jesus commanded. The word *disciple* is used consistently as a synonym for *believer* throughout the book of Acts (6:1, 2, 7; 11:26; 14:20, 22; 15:10). Any distinction between the two words is purely artificial."

Scriptural Arguments For Baptismal Regeneration Examined

Many *baptismal regenerationists* will strongly object to that label, saying that baptism saves us but does not regenerate us. But the moment of faith and the moment of regeneration are one moment and the *washing* of Titus 3:5 and the *regeneration* are the same event, and thus not ritual baptism. If regeneration and faith are two separate moments, then we would momentarily have regenerated, saved unbelievers.[10]

We studied in chapter seven that the moment of regeneration and the moment of faith are the same. There are no regenerate unsaved persons and there are no saved yet unregenerate persons. Again, study the vision of Cornelius in Acts 10 and 11:13, 14. How could he have been so interested in being saved when Peter had not yet given him the words *whereby thou and all thy house shall be saved* (11:14)? Notice exactly when Peter states that remission of sin is experienced—

> To him give all the prophets witness, that through his name whosoever believeth in him shall receive remission of sins (Acts 10:43).

The *washing of regeneration* in Titus 3:5 is the moment in which sins are remitted, when one is born again, the moment of belief in the finished work of Christ for our salvation, and the moment we receive the baptism of the Holy Spirit into the Body of Christ—*Now if any man have not the Spirit of Christ, he is none of his* (Rom. 8:9b; cf. Acts 11:15-18). This *washing* is bought for us by the fact of the physical death and shed blood of Jesus Christ—*feed the church of God, which he hath purchased with his own blood* (Acts 20:28b; cf. I Cor. 6:11). This *washing* is confirmed by the fact of His resurrection from the dead—

---

[10] This position would hold that regenerated unbelievers are spiritually alive and therefore, by sovereign decree, believe the light of the gospel. It holds that regenerated unbelievers believe the Gospel because they are already saved. Ibid., *Faith Works*, p. 69—"...Believing is therefore the first act of an awakened spiritual corpse; it is the new man drawing his first breath." Also, Ibid., p. 67—"...Of course! The unsaved are *dead*, incapable of any spiritual activity. Until God quickens us, we have no capacity to respond to Him in faith." Also, Ibid., p. 65—"...But by transforming the heart, grace makes the believer wholly willing to trust and obey."

> And from Jesus Christ, *who is* the faithful witness, *and* the first begotten of the dead, and the prince of the kings of the earth. Unto him that loved us, and washed us from our sins in his own blood (Rev. 1:5).

This is precisely why the saints of the *Great Tribulation* will be able to stand before the throne of God—

> And one of the elders answered, saying unto me, What are these which are arrayed in white robes? and whence came they? And I said unto him, Sir, thou knowest. And he said to me, These are they which came out of great tribulation, and have washed their robes, and made them white in the blood of the Lamb (Rev. 7:13, 14).

When the Apostle Paul said *And such were some of you: but ye are washed*, there is again no basis upon which to substitute the word *baptism* for *washed* (I Cor. 6:11). *Washed* is just another word for the *cleansing* which is accomplished by the literal blood of Christ (Rev. 1:5; Rom. 3:24, 25).

Perhaps the strongest argument for baptismal regeneration is the statement: *even baptism doth also now save us*—

> For Christ also hath once suffered for sins, the just for the unjust, that he might bring us to God, being put to death in the flesh, but quickened by the Spirit: By which also he went and preached unto the spirits in prison; Which sometime were disobedient, when once the longsuffering of God waited in the days of Noah, while the ark was a preparing, wherein few, that is, eight souls were saved by water. The like figure whereunto *even* baptism doth also now save us (not the putting away of the filth of the flesh, but the answer of a good conscience toward God, by the resurrection of Jesus Christ: Who is gone into heaven, and is on the right hand of God; angels and authorities and powers being made subject unto him (I Pet. 3:18-22).

Scriptural Arguments For Baptismal Regeneration Examined

There are many subjects which could be addressed from this passage, but for present purposes we will limit ourselves to the relationship of baptism to salvation.

Peter is discussing pictures of salvation and draws his first analogy by using the story of Noah as a figure. The Greek in vs. 20 should read *saved through water*. The water in Noah's day was the judgment of God and is used here as a figure of the judgment of God. Noah was saved from the judgment of his day in the ark, not by the flood. Thus the ark becomes a figure of Christ and His salvation.

The ark was made of wood. As Noah acquired the lumber, the life of the trees had to be cut off.. Even so, Christ is the *root out of dry ground* (Isa. 53:2), *the branch* (Zech. 3:8), and He was *cut off* (Dan. 9:26).

The ark was covered with pitch from without and from within. The same word for *pitch* (kapher) is translated *atonement* in Lev. 17:11 and means *covering*. Christ is our atonement or covering for sin—*And not only so, but we also joy in God through our Lord Jesus Christ, by whom we have now received the atonement* (Rom. 5:11). Christ not only covers, but he takes away our sin completely—*Behold the Lamb of God, which taketh away the sin of the world* (Jn. 1:29).

There was only one door into the ark and there is only one door into salvation from the eternal judgment of God—

> I am the door: by me if any man enter in, he shall be saved, and shall go in and out, and find pasture (Jn. 10:9).

> Jesus saith unto him, I am the way, the truth, and the life: no man cometh unto the Father, but by me (Jn. 14:6).

> For other foundation can no man lay than that is laid, which is Jesus Christ (I Cor. 3:11).

Just as the ark prefigures Christ's salvation, baptism postfigures the same. The Greek word for *figure* is *antitupon* meaning *a corresponding type*. Here we see two types. The ark was not a type of baptism but rather the ark and baptism are both types of Christ's salvation—the real thing. Both types point to salvation in Christ. Both types reveal that only those in Christ shall be delivered from God's coming wrath. The ark was only a type of Christ Who literally saved Noah from eternal judgment before he ever cut the first timber—*But Noah found grace in the eyes of the LORD* (Gen. 6:8). Noah was standing in the righteousness of faith as he was building the ark—

> By faith Noah, being warned of God of things not seen as yet, moved with fear, prepared an ark to the saving of his house; by the which he condemned the world, and became heir of the righteousness which is by faith (Heb. 11:7). cf. the discussion of Noah's faith in chapter three of this present work.

Baptism is also a picture, figure, or type of that which literally accomplishes our salvation—i.e. the death, burrial and resurrection of Christ (I Cor. 15:1-4; 20-23).

One thing that seems clear from I Pet. 3:21 is that baptism does not put away the *filth of the flesh*. But what is the *filth of the flesh* that baptism does not put away? We demonstrated in chapter four of this work that John's baptism was not a Jewish or Essene ritual for physical/ceremonial sanitation and cleansing. Physical sanitation was not the issue in NT discussions of the purpose of baptism. Most of John's converts had already experienced baptisms for such ritual cleansings. The three thousand converts on the Day of Pentecost were Jews who did not need a bath for physical cleansing, and Peter was not asking them to submit to such. The First Epistle of Peter is addressed to Christians of Asia Minor. The churches in the provinces therein were made up of Jews and Gentiles.

When there are two possible interpretations of a passage which may be coherent with the rest of Scripture, we should refrain from being overly dogmatic. Most commentators conclude that Peter is instructing the many Jewish converts by stressing that baptism is not a physical sanitation rite. This is an acceptable and coherent interpretation of this passage. However, Peter may not be dealing with such a misconception in that the Jewish ceremonial cleansings were scrubbings for physical sanitation and were self-administered.

An alternate coherent interpretation of this passage is one in which Peter uses the phrase *filth of the flesh* as a reference to the sins of the soul. When the New Covenant and personal salvation are being discussed, *filth* and *flesh* refer to sin and the *washing* of the body refers to the cleansing from sin by the blood of Christ—

> Let us draw near with a true heart in full assurance of faith, having our hearts sprinkled from an evil conscience, and our bodies washed with pure water (Heb. 10:22).

When the blood of Christ was applied to us at the moment of faith, our hearts were sprinkled and cleansed from the evil consciousness of sinful guilt that had not experienced atonement and removal.

Subsequent to our conversion, our fellowship with Christ is renewed daily by the same blood of Christ as we confess the sins of the flesh before Him—

> But if we walk in the light, as he is in the light, we have fellowship one with another, and the blood of Jesus Christ his Son cleanseth us from all sin. If we say that we have no sin, we deceive ourselves, and the truth is not in us. If we confess our sins, he is faithful and just to forgive us *our* sins, and to cleanse us from all unrighteousness. If we say that we have not sinned, we make him a liar, and his word is not in us (I Jn. 1:7-10).

Thus the washing of our bodies with pure water can be interpreted to mean the daily application of the blood of Christ to our confession of the sins of the flesh.

Even at initial conversion, the circumcision without hands put off from the body the sins of the flesh—

> In whom also ye are circumcised with the circumcision made without hands, in putting off the body of the sins of the flesh by the circumcision of Christ (Col. 2:11).

According to Peter, this is something that ritual baptism cannot do. Christ puts *away sin by the sacrifice of Himself* (Heb. 9:26).

How did Peter use the term *flesh* elsewhere in his epistles? He used it to refer to sins committed after conversion:

> That he no longer should live the rest of *his* time in the flesh to the lusts of men, but to the will of God (I Pet. 4:2).

He also uses the term *flesh* to describe the uncleanness and lust of the lost sinner:

> But chiefly them that walk after the flesh in the lust of uncleanness, and despise government (II Pet. 2:10).

> For when they speak great swelling *words* of vanity, they allure through the lusts of the flesh, *through much* wantonness (II Pet. 2:18a).

Christ used the term *flesh* as a reference to the sins of the soul (Matt. 26:41; Mk. 14:38; John 1:13; 6:63; 8:15). The Apostle Paul uses the term *flesh* as a reference to sin (Rom. 3:20; 6:19; 7:25; 8:1, 3-5, 12, 13; 13:14; I Cor. 10:2; Gal. 5:13, 16, 19, 24; 6:8; Eph. 2:3; Phil. 1:22; 3:3; I Jn. 2:16). If one consults the NIV he will notice how the term *filth* refers to sin in James 1:21 and Rev. 17:4. The NIV translates *flesh* as *sin nature* in Rom. 7:5, 18, 25; 8:3-5, 8, 9, 12, 13; 13:14; I Cor. 5:5; Gal. 5:13, 16, 17, 19, 24; 6:8; Eph. 2:3; Col. 2:11, 13; 3:5; II Pet. 2:10, 18.

Ezekiel did not predict the NT ordinance of baptism, but he did prophesy that the sprinkling of the blood of Christ on the heart would cleanse from the filth of the flesh:

> Then will I sprinkle clean water upon you, and ye shall be clean: from all your filthiness, and from all your idols, will I cleanse you. A new heart also will I give you, and a new spirit will I put within you: and I will take away the stony heart out of your flesh, and I will give you an heart of flesh. And I will put my spirit within you, and cause you to walk in my statutes, and ye shall keep my judgments, and do *them* (Ez. 36:25-27).

Scriptural Arguments For Baptismal Regeneration Examined

Ezekiel used the uncleanness of a removed woman to illustrate the spiritual filthiness of the nation of Israel:

> Moreover the word of the LORD came unto me, saying, Son of man, when the house of Israel dwelt in their own land, they defiled it by their own way and by their doings: their way was before me as the uncleanness of a removed woman (Ez. 36:16, 17).

It is this fleshly filthiness that Christ will put away through the shedding of His blood for the remission of their sins—*I will also save you from all your uncleannesses* (Ez. 36:29a). He repeatedly uses the term *filthiness* as a reference to the sins of the soul (Ez. 22:15; 24:13; 37:23). Ezekiel is speaking of the cleansing from sin in the New Covenant accomplished by the putting away of the sins of the flesh by the blood of Jesus Christ:

> Now the God of peace, that brought again from the dead our Lord Jesus, that great shepherd of the sheep, through the blood of the everlasting covenant (Heb. 13:20).

Proverbs is speaking of sin when it proclaims *There is a generation that are pure in their own eyes, and yet is not washed from their filthiness* (Prov. 30:12). Jeremiah spoke of washing the heart from wickedness (Jer. 4:14; cf. 33:8). David wanted to be *washed* from his iniquity (Ps. 51:2, 3). Isaiah spoke of the Lord washing away the *filth* of the daughters of Zion (Isa. 4:4).

When the terms *washing* and *cleansing* are used in the NT in relation to salvation and regeneration, they refer to the removal of sin by the blood of Jesus Christ (I Cor. 6:11; Eph. 5:26; Titus 3:5; Rev. 1:5). Even after salvation, the sins of the flesh are referred to as *filth* which is cleansed by the blood of Christ through the confession of those sins (I Jn. 1:7, 9). Christians also obtain reward and inheritance and avoid the chastising judgment of God by the extent to which they refrain from such filthiness in the first place—

> Having therefore these promises, dearly beloved, let us cleanse ourselves from all filthiness of the flesh and spirit, perfecting holiness in the fear of God (I Cor. 7:1).

So baptism does not put away the *filth of the flesh*, but it is a *like figure* with Noah's ark of what does put away the sins of the soul—i.e. the death, burial and resurrection of Christ (I Cor. 15:1-4).

But Peter says, *(not the putting away of the filth of the flesh, but the answer of a good conscience toward God,) by the resurrection of Jesus Christ* (I Pet. 3:21b). If baptism is the *answer* of a pure conscience or the *appeal* of a pure conscience, at what point does a lost person's conscience become purified before God? God makes it clear that the ordinances of the tabernacle in the OT could never heal the consciences of those who submitted to them—

> The Holy Ghost this signifying, that the way into the holiest of all was not yet made manifest, while as the first tabernacle was yet standing: Which *was* a figure for the time then present, in which were offered both gifts and sacrifices, that could not make him that did the service perfect, as pertaining to the conscience (Heb. 9:8, 9).

But if ordinances cannot purify the conscience, then what can? The answer is in Heb. 9:13-15—

> For if the blood of bulls and of goats, and the ashes of an heifer sprinkling the unclean, sanctifieth to the purifying of the flesh: How much more shall the blood of Christ, who through the eternal Spirit offered himself without spot to God, purge your conscience from dead works to serve the living God? And for this cause he is the mediator of the new testament, that by means of death, for the redemption of the transgressions *that were* under the first testament, they which are called might receive the promise of eternal inheritance.

Heb. 10:22 speaks of our hearts being sprinkled from an evil conscience, (cf. vs. 2). This is when we receive the good conscience that answers at baptism. But when is the conscience made pure? The conscience is made good by the application of the blood of Christ at the moment of faith—

Scriptural Arguments For Baptismal Regeneration Examined

> And to Jesus the mediator of the new covenant, and to the blood of sprinkling, that speaketh better things than *that of* Abel (Heb. 12:24).

> Wherefore Jesus also, that he might sanctify the people with his own blood, suffered without the gate (Heb. 13:12).

The Apostle Peter informs the readers of I Pet. 3:21 of the exact time in which this sprinkling from an evil conscience takes place:

> Peter, an apostle of Jesus Christ, to the strangers scattered throughout Pontus, Galatia, Cappadocia, Asia, and Bithynia, Elect according to the foreknowledge of God the Father, through sanctification of the Spirit, unto obedience and sprinkling of the blood of Jesus Christ: Grace unto you, and peace, be multiplied (I Pet. 1:1, 2).

Baptism does not purify the conscience; it is the answer of a conscience which has already been purified by the sprinkling of the blood of Christ in the heart at the moment of faith. It is this sprinkling that enables us to enter boldly and with assurance into the holiest of all when we commune with Jesus Christ—

> Having therefore, brethren, boldness to enter into the holiest by the blood of Jesus, By a new and living way, which he hath consecrated for us, through the veil, that is to say, his flesh. And *having* an high priest over the house of God; Let us draw near with a true heart in full assurance of faith, having our hearts sprinkled from an evil conscience, and our bodies washed with pure water. (Heb. 10:19-22).

So again, Peter is not saying that baptism saves us, but rather that baptism is a like figure with Noah's ark of what does save us; what does sprinkle our hearts from an evil conscience; what does make our consciences good and able to answer or appeal to God—i.e. the finished work of Jesus Christ for our salvation.

Again, John's baptism was a profession of repentance toward Jesus Christ—

> Then said Paul, John verily baptized with the baptism
> of repentance, saying unto the people, that they should
> believe on him which should come after him, that is,
> on Christ Jesus (Acts 19:4).

Christ's physical baptism was His identification with His own crucifixion—

> But I have a baptism to be baptized with; and how am
> I straitened till it be accomplished (Lk. 12:50).

Christ's submission to John's baptism was His consecration to die. It prefigured His death. He came to die for the remission of sins and the restoration of the nation of Israel (Lk. 1:67-79). It was this death to which He was referring when He said: *Ye know not what ye ask: can ye drink of the cup that I drink of? and be baptized with the baptism that I am baptized with?* (Mk. 10:38, cf. Lk. 12:50).[11] Christ's death was a sinking into and a being overwhelmed by the judgment of a holy God upon the sin of humanity. Christ's baptism expressed the purpose for which He came to earth in incarnate form. His ritual baptism at the beginning of His ministry prefigured the baptism of His literal death, burial and resurrection toward the end of His earthly ministry. He was made sin for us, and therefore suffered the judgment of our sin for us (II Cor. 5:21; Isa. 53:6). He became one in guilt with humanity—*made in the likeness of men* (Phil. 2:7); *in the likeness of sinful flesh* (Rom. 8:3) in order that we might be made one with God—

> And other sheep I have, which are not of this fold:
> them also I must bring, and they shall hear my voice;
> and there shall be one fold, *and* one shepherd.
> Therefore doth my Father love me, because I lay down
> my life, that I might take it again (Jn. 10:16, 17).
>
> Neither pray I for these alone, but for them also which
> shall believe on me through their word; That they all
> may be one; as thou, Father, *art* in me, and I in thee,
> that they also may be one in us: that the world may

---

[11] This literal baptism of Christ on the cross was foreseen by David— "… I am come into deep waters, where the floods overflow me (Ps. 69:2b).

believe that thou hast sent me. And the glory which thou gavest me I have given them; that they may be one, even as we are one: I in them, and thou in me, that they may be made perfect in one; and that the world may know that thou hast sent me, and hast loved them, as thou hast loved me (Jn. 17:20-23).

But not as the offence, so also *is* the free gift. For if through the offence of one many be dead, much more the grace of God, and the gift by grace, *which is* by one man, Jesus Christ, hath abounded unto many. And not as *it was* by one that sinned, *so is* the gift: for the judgment *was* by one to condemnation, but the free gift *is* of many offences unto justification. For if by one man's offence death reigned by one; much more they which receive abundance of grace and of the gift of righteousness shall reign in life by one, Jesus Christ. Therefore as by the offence of one *judgment came* upon all men to condemnation; even so by the righteousness of one *the free gift came* upon all men unto justification of life. For as by one man's disobedience many were made sinners, so by the obedience of one shall many be made righteous (Rom. 5:15-19).

For by one Spirit are we all baptized into one body, whether *we be* Jews or Gentiles, whether *we be* bond or free; and have been all made to drink into one Spirit (I Cor. 12:13).

When Jesus said to John the Baptist, *Thus it becometh us to fulfil all righteousness* (Matt. 3:15), He was testifying that only in the baptism of His literal death could He *make an end of sins* and *bring in everlasting righteousness* (Dan. 9:24). He could not be *the Lord our Righteousness* (Jer. 23:6) through His ritual baptism, but by His crucifixion (II Cor. 5:21). So Jesus had a baptism of water and a baptism of blood—

This is he that came by water and blood, *even* Jesus Christ; not by water only, but by water and blood. And it is the Spirit that beareth witness, because the Spirit is truth (I Jn. 5:6).

It was at Christ's baptism that the Holy Spirit bore witness and the Father spoke—

> And Jesus, when he was baptized, went up straightway out of the water: and, lo, the heavens were opened unto him, and he saw the Spirit of God descending like a dove, and lighting upon him: And lo a voice from heaven, saying, This is my beloved Son, in whom I am well pleased (Matt. 3:16, 17).

So, at His baptism, Christ was buried in the likeness of His coming death and raised in the likeness of His coming resurrection.

Apostolic New Testament baptism is the believer's profession of faith that his salvation was promised, accomplished and confirmed in the death, burial, and resurrection of Christ. Baptism professes in symbolic form that the believer has previously entered into the communion of Christ's death, burial and resurrection (Rom. 6:3). Because we were raised with Him from the moment of faith, we were, therefore, with Him at the moment of baptism. It was not Christ's ritual circumcision and ritual baptism that saves us from our trespasses, but rather His real circumcision and baptism on the cross of Calvary—

> In whom also ye are circumcised with the circumcision made without hands, in putting off the body of the sins of the flesh by the circumcision of Christ: Buried with him in baptism, wherein also ye are risen with *him* through the faith of the operation of God, who hath raised him from the dead. And you, being dead in your sins and the uncircumcision of your flesh, hath he quickened together with him, having forgiven you all trespasses; Blotting out the handwriting of ordinances that was against us, which was contrary to us, and took it out of the way, nailing it to his cross (Col. 2:11-14). (Cf. the lengthy discussion of this passage in chapter five of this present work.)

The believer experientially, and in fact, participates in the death and resurrection of Christ at the moment of faith and then portrays the *likeness* of Christ's death and resurrection when he is baptized—

> For if we have been planted together in the likeness of his death, we shall be also *in the likeness* of *his* resurrection (Rom. 6:5).

So Christ's ritual circumcision portrayed His spiritual circumcision on the cross (Col. 2:11), His ritual baptism portrayed His literal death and resurrection (Matt. 10:38), and the cup that He drank portrayed the literal shedding of His blood at the crucifixion of His body (Matt. 10:38). The benefits of all this becomes ours at the moment of faith in Him (Col. 2:13, 14) and is testified to at the moment of our baptism. Christ died to make it clear once for all that salvation was not through the keeping of any ordinance. And it is God's will that all born again believers publicly profess their faith in Jesus Christ and His finished work for our salvation. And, this they do when they obey the Lord in receiving ritual baptism according to the Scriptures.

Therefore, it is the conviction of this present work that ritual baptism is the obedient profession, in symbolic form, that salvation is by grace through faith in Jesus Christ provided by means of His death, burial and resurrection. We do not believe that ritual baptism ratifies our salvation. Salvation is ratified by the seal of the Holy Spirit at the moment of faith—

> Now he which stablisheth us with you in Christ, and hath anointed us, *is* God; Who hath also sealed us, and given the earnest of the Spirit in our hearts (II Cor. 1:21, 22).

> In whom ye also *trusted*, after that ye heard the word of truth, the gospel of your salvation: in whom also after that ye believed, ye were sealed with that holy Spirit of promise (Eph. 1:13).

> And grieve not the holy Spirit of God, whereby ye are sealed unto the day of redemption (Eph. 4:30).

> Nevertheless the foundation of God standeth sure, having this seal, The Lord knoweth them that are his (II Tim. 2:19a).

Ritual baptism is not a promise that we will be saved. The gospel itself is God's promise that believers will have everlasting life—

> That the blessing of Abraham might come on the Gentiles through Jesus Christ; that we might receive the promise of the Spirit through faith (Gal. 3:14).

> But the scripture hath concluded all under sin, that the promise by faith of Jesus Christ might be given to them that believe (Gal. 3:22).

> And if ye *be* Christ's, then are ye Abraham's seed, and heirs according to the promise (Gal. 3:29).

> That the Gentiles should be fellowheirs, and of the same body, and partakers of his promise in Christ by the gospel (Eph. 3:6).

> Paul, an apostle of Jesus Christ by the will of God, according to the promise of life which is in Christ Jesus (II Tim. 1:1).

> And this is the promise that he hath promised us, *even* eternal life (I Jn. 2:25).

Ritual baptism does not reinforce our faith or confirm our faith. Our faith is reinforced and confirmed by the fact of Christ's resurrection and the apostolic testimony to that fact—

> How shall we escape, if we neglect so great salvation; which at the first began to be spoken by the Lord, and was confirmed unto us by them that heard *him*; God also bearing *them* witness, both with signs and wonders, and with divers miracles, and gifts of the Holy Ghost, according to his own will? (Heb. 2: 3, 4).

Ritual baptism does not strengthen our faith, nor give us assurance of salvation. Our assurance is in the object of our faith as He is recorded in Scripture—

for I know whom I have believed, and am persuaded that he is able to keep that which I have committed unto him against that day (I Tim. 1:12b).

These things have I written unto you that believe on the name of the Son of God; that ye may know that ye have eternal life, and that ye may believe on the name of the Son of God (I Jn. 5:13).

Ritual baptism does not place us into the Body of Christ. We enter that Body by the baptism of the Holy Spirit at the moment of faith (Acts 10:43, 44; Rom. 8:9) and prior to ritual baptism—*Can any man forbid water, that these should not be baptized, which have received the Holy Ghost as well as we?* (Acts 10:47, cf. Eph. 3:6).

Therefore, when Paul said that we were *buried with him in baptism, wherein also ye are risen with him through the faith of the operation of God, who hath raised him from the dead,* he would have meant that we were already with Christ before the baptismal rite began and that is why we were still with Him when we were raised from the water. We did not get baptized in order to get with Him.

Having examined the major verses used to teach *baptismal regeneration*, we will proceed in the next chapter to discuss the proposition that the plan of salvation includes obedience to every commandment in the NT and every doctrine of Christ and the apostles.

Practical acknowledgement of Jesus' Lordship, yielding to His rule by following, is the very fibre of saving faith. It is only those who 'confess with the mouth the Lord Jesus' [Romans 10:9] that shall be saved. Believing and obeying are such parallel ideas that the New Testament interchanges the words...Believing is obeying. Without obedience, you shall not see life! Unless you bow to Christ's scepter, you will not receive the benefits of Christ's sacrifice...

Walter Chantry, *Today's Gospel— Authentic or Synthetic?* **P. 60**

Chapter Ten

Attaching Personal Righteousness To the Back-side Of The Gospel's Requirements

The absolute truth of the gospel needs to be identified within the boundaries of Scripture alone. Although it is helpful to read the works of others, we must stop where their reasoning goes beyond that of the sacred text. In this chapter we will not wrestle with the terms *Pelagian, Semi-Pelagian, Calvinistic*, or *Arminian*.[1] Most Christians who know enough to evoke these labels have never been substantially exposed to the writings of the men with whom the labels are identified. Instead, we will discuss the biblical paradigm of the gospel itself—what it is and what it is not.

Think of the gospel as a set of terms within a prescribed set of boundaries. Not all biblical truths are contingencies which belong inside these parameters. Though all scriptural truths are profitable (II Tim. 3:16), there are those which are more profitable, those that are less profitable, and those which are, or are not, essential to receiving the gospel. For instance, one's positions on the millennium, the rapture, or the length of days in creation do not fall within the parameters of what is essential to personal salvation. If we take a biblical concept that is important and profitably true and make it a contingency of the gospel when it is not, we have changed the gospel (Gal. 1:6-9). Remember, *they of the circumcision* believed in the shed blood, death, burial and resurrection of Christ, but then added ritual and personal righteousness to the back of the equation. Paul wrote that doing this constitutes a different gospel, as he said of Peter and Barnabas: *But when I saw that they walked not uprightly according to the truth of the gospel...*(Gal. 2:14a).

Placing ritual and works at the tail end of the plan of salvation still makes it a gospel of works. There are several good things which

---

[1] See R. C. Sproul, *Willing to Believe: The Controversy Over Free Will* (Grand Rapids: Baker Books, 1997), 221 pages. Sproul compares and contrasts the views of Pelagius, Augustine, Semi-Pelagians, Luther, Calvin, Arminius, Edwards, Finney and Chafer.

are God's will for every Christian, but they belong outside the boundaries of salvation contingencies. This subject could call for another whole book to be written, but we will cover what we consider several important errors in order that the reader can draw intelligent conclusions.

We will examine thirty-one separate affirmations used to defend the contention that personal works of righteousness must be included within the parameters of the gospel's definition. Those who use these arguments are often taken literally by their thousands of readers, although they may not have thoroughly meant what they implied. Occasionaly someone will affirm personal knowledge of one such author and assure us that our understanding of his words does not represent his position. We hope that this is the case and are even willing to assume the same. However, it still remains that we are dealing with thousands of readers who took their expressions at face value and made personal righteousness a contingent of saving faith in their own evangelistic affirmations. It is regarding these understandings that we are seeking to address in this chapter. Therefore, we caution the reader that this present work is not guaranteeing what the true heart positions of these authors are, but we are nonetheless responding to what multitudes of people have concluded to be true after having read their works. We would equally caution the reader to not conclude that this present work diminishes the responsibility of all believers to present themselves as *living sacrifices* to the cause of Christ as their *reasonable service*. Though believers make sacrifices, they should be assured that only the sacrifice of Christ has provided for their eternal redemption.

Argument #1: Total depravity means that unregenerate man is as lifeless as a literal cadaver.[2] This error is based on an incorrect definition of *total depravity*. The term should mean that lost

---

[2] John F. MacArthur Jr., *Faith Works: The Gospel According to the Apostles* (Dallas: Word Publishing, 1993), p. 64. "Because we were dead to God, we were dead to truth, righteousness, peace, happiness, and every other good thing, no more able to respond to God than a cadaver." **Note that this chapter does not address what Dr. MacArthur might have meant in the fuller context of his entire theology of salvation. No one should claim to know the heart of any author. However, the foregoing arguments are intended to deal with what multitudes of readers have concluded after reading the material on the "Lordship Salvation" debate from numerous authors.**

man is totally without saving virtue of his own. He is spiritually bankrupt before God. In this sense he is dead in sin—separated from God. But when it is said that he is the academic equivalent of a graveyard-dead cadaver, we have a difficult time cohering that affirmation with the rest of Scripture. Man's very existence is a sovereign act of God. Lost man's capacity to see the truth, comprehend it, and desire deliverance from condemnation, is not a saving virtue. But Jesus was presenting Himself to this capacity in man when He preached, performed miracles, rose from the dead, and instituted miraculous gifts in the apostles. Fulfilled prophecy is an appeal to this capacity. Satan is fully aware of this capacity and knows that he must work to prevent lost souls from seeing the light—*In whom the god of this world hath blinded the minds of them which believe not, lest the light of the glorious gospel of Christ, who is the image of God, should shine unto them* (II Cor. 4:4; cf. Jn. 1:7; 12:36). Luke referred to the Bereans as *noble*, as having *recveived the word with readiness of mind*, and as having *searched the scriptures daily, whether those things were so*. Then Luke concludes: *Therefore many of them believed* (Acts 17:11, 12).

In order to be regenerated, a man must first of all be generated. This is not a cadaver state. Though lost man possesses no saving virtue, the Bible describes him as created *after the similitude of God* (Jas. 3:8, 9; cf. I Cor. 11:7). In the OT, capital punishment was not just for the murder of redeemed individuals—yet, *who sheddeth man's blood by man shall his blood be shed: for in the image of God made he man* (Gen. 9:6). The Bible describes lost man as having *intellect* (which tells him right from wrong), *conscience* (which tells him what he ought to do about right and wrong) and *will* (which tells him what he shall do about right and wrong). Rom. 1:18 describes lost man as holding *the truth in unrighteousness*. The knowledge of God is manifest in him, for God has shown it to him (Rom. 1:19). God created lost man to observe objectively His power and Godhead to the extent that he actually knows Him (Rom. 1:21, 22).

Paul spoke the words of truth to lost Festus and then confronted him with the fact that he knew that these things were true in that none of these words of truth were hidden from him (Acts 26:25, 26). The resurrection of Christ was a sign to an evil and adulterous generation (Matt. 12:38-40). Christ's miracles were designed to persuade the unregenerate to believe (Matt. 9:6; Jn. 4:48; 20:30, 31). Jesus advises the lost to believe His works which will lead them to know who He is and could result in their believing *that the Father is in me and I in Him* (Jn. 10:37, 38). Tongues were a sign to them that believe not (I Cor. 14:22). Fulfilled prophecy is designed to motivate belief in those who believe not (Jn. 14:29). Remember the vision of Cornelius in Acts 10 and note all the things that he experienced before regeneration. Jesus said that when the Holy Spirit comes He will convict the world of unbelievers of sin, righteousness and of judgment (Jn. 16:8-11). In order to do this, God created unbelievers with a capacity for experiencing conviction of sin, understanding the righteousness of God and understanding the judgment of God. To attribute to unregenerate man a sovereignly God-given capacity to believe is not attributing a saving virtue to the sinner. Receiving deliverance from condemnation is a self-serving act and is not a saving virtue (Rom. 4:5; II Pet. 1:5).

This capacity in lost man was a gift of God's *common* grace, which is as sovereign as His *efficacious* grace. Therefore, we deny the charge that we are degrading the sovereign character of God by refusing to believe that lost man is a box of rocks.

Argument #2: Absolute holy obedience to all the commands of the NT is part of the definition of sovereign efficacious grace.[3] Personal holiness never reaches a state of perfection in this life, yet godliness is practiced by every believer in varying degrees. It is argued that if sovereign grace does not irresistibly cause a state of absolute obedience to the lordship of Christ, then a salvation experience has not yet occurred. Many of those making this argument deny that they are preaching salvation by personal righteousness in that God sovereignly accomplishes this through no effort on the part of the believer. It is said that the believer's will to do right is just as impotent as when he was lost and, therefore, his personal acts of righteousness are sovereign acts of God alone.

But, throughout the NT the believer is told to decide how faithful and obedient he will be. His faithfulness and obedience will never be saving virtues, but they will be rewardable virtues at the judgment seat of Christ. If faithfulness and obedience are God's act alone, then why are there degrees of reward and inheritance in heaven?

---

[3] Ibid., *Faith Works*, p. 61. "But by transforming the heart, grace makes the believer wholly willing to trust and obey."

There are no degrees of salvation. Count the number of times in the NT that believers are told to put forth effort to earn rewards as Paul did when he pressed *toward the mark of the prize*. Why do Christians need to decide to be steadfast, unmovable and abounding in the work of the Lord (I Cor. 15:58)? Why do Christians have to decide to forsake not God's assembly (Heb. 10:25)? Why are the *sanctified* (10:10-14), who do forsake the assembly (10:25) by their own decision, considered worthy of punishment (10:29)? Why do saints have to decide to *sanctify the Lord God* in their hearts (I Pet. 3:15)? Why do believers have to decide to be *meet for the Master's use* (II Tim. 2:21)? Why do saints need to decide to be *faithful unto death* (Rev. 2:10)? Why do Christians have to look to themselves in order not to lose rewards that they have already earned (II Jn. 8)? Why? Because God has made it their choice to do, or not to do, His revealed will.

Argument #3: *Faith* **and** *faithfulness* **are synonyms, so that where there is unfaithfulness, there has never been saving faith.**[4] Let us test this conclusion from an observation of Hebrews chapter eleven. Abraham left Ur *by faith*, yet he did so in disobedience, because he took his kindred with him and waited in Haran until his father died; he offered his wife to Pharaoh; and he had a son through Hagar. Were his faith and faithfulness synonymous?

By faith, Isaac blessed Jacob—but not intentionally. Isaac did not intend that the elder would serve the younger. Was his faith synonymous with his faithfulness when he lied to Abimelech about Rebekah and made a covenant with him (Gen. 26)? Was Jacob's faith

---

[4] John F. MacArthur, Jr., *The Gospel According To Jesus* (Grand Rapids: Academie Books, Zondervan Publishing House, 1988), p. 16: "By separating faith from faithfulness, it leaves the impression that intellectual assent is as valid as wholehearted obedience to the truth. Thus the good news of Christ has given way to the bad news of an insidious easy-believism that makes no moral demands on the lives of sinners. It is not the same message Jesus proclaimed." P. 47: "Thus the test of true faith is this: does it produce obedience? If not, it is not saving faith. Disobedience is unbelief. Real faith obeys." PP. 140, 141: "Saving faith…is an unconditional surrender, a willingness to do anything the Lord demands." P. 174: "Clearly, the biblical concept of faith is inseparable from obedience. 'Believe' is synonymous with 'obey' in John 3:36…Hebrews 11, the great treatise on faith, presents obedience and faith as inseparable."

synonymous with faithfulness in the way he obtained Esau's birthright and in his business dealings with his father-in-law?

By faith Moses—did Moses have to escape Egypt because of his faithfulness or because he had killed an Egyptian taskmaster and feared for his life? Was his faith also faithful as he gave God seven reasons why he should not lead Israel out of Egypt (Ex. 3:11, 13; 4:1, 10, 13, 14; 6:12, 30)? Was it Moses' faithfulness or unfaithfulness which prohibited him from entering the Pomised Land because he struck the rock twice in defiance of God's instructions?

It was *by faith* that Israel passed through the Red sea on dry land (Heb. 11:29); but was it their faithfulness that required them to wander in the wilderness for forty years?

Gideon had faith, but was the putting out of the fleece an act of faithfulness or doubt? Barak had faith, but was his cowardice to fight without Deborah an act of faithfulness (Judges 4:8)? Jephthah had faith, but was his misguided vow regarding his daughter an act of faithfulness and obedience? Name one thing that Samson did on purpose for God or country. He violated all of his Nazarite vows, and his dying prayer was for the strength to avenge himself of his eyes by committing suicide and taking his persecutors with him (Judges 16:28-30). He had faith, but was he faithful and perseverant?

King David had faith, but was his prayer in Ps. 51 about his faithfulness? Think about it! Heb. 11:39 tells us that these all obtained a good report *through faith* but not through perseverant faithfulness.

Argument #4: Just as efficacious grace is irresistible, so likewise is whole-hearted holiness in every dimension of life.[5] But if

---

[5] Ibid., *Gospel According To Jesus*, p. xiii: "Saving faith, repentance, commitment, and obedience are all divine works, wrought by the Holy Spirit in the heart of everyone who is saved…real salvation cannot and will not fail to produce works of righteousness in the life of a true believer." P. 33: "Thus salvation cannot be defective in any dimension. As a part of His saving work, God will produce repentance, faith, sanctification, yieldedness, obedience, and ultimately glorification. Since He is not dependent on human effort in producing those elements, an experience that lacks any of them cannot be the saving work of God." Ibid., *Faith Works*, pp. 236, 238, [quoting Martin Luther]: "Therefore, faith is something very powerful, active, restless, effective, *(Continued on next page)*

this means no defect in any dimension of life, then are we not talking about sinless perfection? Yet it is argued that: *every aspect of the Great Commission (Matt. 28:18-20) is an integral part of the plan of salvation.* Thus, it is said that one cannot be a believer without being a totally surrendered and obedient disciple. Obviously, this would make baptism essential to salvation.

Argument #5: Any act of obedience which comes from the believer is not of God but of the flesh.[6] Of course, no one is ever worth saving, but after salvation the believer must walk worthy of communion with the Lord. Rewardable virtues are decisions and acts carried out by the believer in the enabling power of the Holy Spirit. This is the worthiness that gauges one's reward at the judgment seat of Christ (I Cor. 11:27)—*Wherefore whosoever shall eat this bread, and drink this cup of the Lord, unworthily, shall be guilty of the body and blood of the Lord.* The disciples were not worthy of salvation, but they were proud to be counted *worthy to suffer shame* for the Lord (Acts 5:41). This is why saints must walk worthy of their vocation (Eph. 4:1). Fruitful good works are pleasing to the Lord and makes the believer worthy of communion with Him (Col. 1:10). Why else must *called* saints need to walk *worthy* of fellowship with God (I Thess. 2:12)? No one is worthy to enter the kingdom of God, but there is an inheritance in the kingdom of which a saint must be worthy in order to be rewarded (II Thess. 1:5). Why is the elder, that labors in word and doctrine, to be counted *worthy of double honor* (II Tim. 5:17)? No elder is worthy of salvation, but he can be worthy of an elder's reward (I Tim. 5:18). Why are the saints in Sardis, who have not defiled their garments, worthy to walk with Christ in white? They were not worthy of salvation itself (Rev. 3:4). Peter said: *And beside this, giving all diligence, add to your*

---

which at once renews a person and again regenerates him, and leads him altogether into a new manner and character of life, so that it is impossible not to do good without ceasing....Inasmuch as works naturally follow faith, as I said, it is not necessary to command them, for it is impossible for faith not to do them without being commanded, in order that we may learn to distinguish the false from the true faith."

[6] Ibid., *Faith Works*, p. 30: "No one who properly interprets Scripture would ever propose that human effort or fleshly works can be *meritorious*—worthy of honor or reward from God." P. 70: "Even our good works are works of *His* grace...They are the corroborating evidence of true salvation. These works, like every other aspect of divine salvation are the product of God's sovereign grace."

faith virtue; and to virtue knowledge (II Pet. 1:5). Such diligence is not a saving virtue, but neither is it a work of the flesh.

Count the number of times in the NT that Christians are exhorted to make right decisions and admonished against making wrong decisions. God does not force these decisions upon them. Though He does empower them to carry out right decisions, they still often make wrong choices. Why does Paul beseech and exhort brethren to walk as they ought and to please God (I Thess. 4:1)? Why do brethren have to be exhorted to warn them that are unruly (I Thess. 5:14)? Why do some saints have to be exhorted to work and eat their own bread (II Thess. 3:12)? Why should saints have to be exhorted to pray (I Tim. 2:1)? Why is it a primary task of all preachers to exhort the saints (II Tim. 4:2)? Why must we exhort the young to be sober-minded (Titus 2:6)? Why are saints to exhort one another daily (Heb. 3:13)? Why do elders need to be exhorted to feed the flock and not to act as lords over God's heritage (I Pet. 5:1-4)? Why must saints be exhorted to contend for the faith (Jude 3)? Why? Because these are decisions that saints must make. They will be rewarded in this life and in the life to come for right decisions and chastised for wrong decisions.

Argument #6: Logically, disobedience on the part of a believer would be a failure of God's sovereign grace—which cannot fail.[7] This would be true only if God's sovereign grace is a guarantee against human failure—which it is not.[8] God's grace is unmerited favor. Sin in the life of a believer is not a failure of God's grace. Otherwise, God's grace has failed in the life of every believer in that each one needs to confess sin daily (I Jn. 1:9). Note the distinction between God's sovereign desire for Jerusalem and His sovereign permissive will

---

[7] Ibid., *Faith Works*, p. 260: "*Irresistible grace*: grace that transforms the heart and thus makes the believer wholly willing to trust and obey. Saving grace is always irresistible." PP. 61, 62: "It is clear from all this that the sovereignty of God in salvation is at the heart of the lordship debate...But by transforming the heart, grace makes the believer wholly willing to trust and obey...Scripture makes clear that every aspect of grace is God's sovereign work...In no stage of the process is grace thwarted by human effort...If God's purposes were dependent on some self-generated response of faith or on human merit, then God Himself would not be sovereign and salvation would not be wholly His work." "

[8] Ibid.,*GospelAccording To Jesus*, p. 33: "But true salvation wrought by God will not fail to produce the good works that are its fruit."

for the same—*O Jerusalem, Jerusalem, thou that killest the prophets, and stonest them which are sent unto thee, how often would I* [God's sovereign desire] *have gathered thy children together, even as a hen gathereth her chickens under her wings, and ye would not!* [God allows them to resist His sovereign desire] (Matt. 23:37; cf. Lk. 13:34).

Including personal righteousness in the definition of irresistible grace would equally make heresy an impossibility on the part of the believer. Then why do so many of the authors of the *lordship salvation* view go to great length to quote historical figures who never held a scriptural view of baptism? Why would God not have irresistibly caused Jerome, Augustine, Luther, Calvin, and the Puritans to understand the nature of true baptism, the distinction between church and state, church and Israel, or circumcision and baptism? Why? Because doctrinal orthodoxy in all important areas is not a part of the definition of saving grace. When you take something which is good and important and make it a contingency of salvation, when it is not, you alter the gospel itself, and it becomes another gospel.

Argument #7: Irresistible grace means that the believer no longer has his old nature with which to contend. Regeneration is a wholesale transformation of the whole person in every dimension.[9] But why, then, does Paul beseech the brethren of Rome to not be conformed to this world, but rather to be transformed by the renewing of their minds (Rom. 12:1, 2)? In Rom. 6:6 the *old man* is nailed to the cross. Does this mean that he no longer exists and therefore the saint does not have to *put off the old man* daily (Eph. 4:22; Col. 3:9)? These passages are not speaking of eradication. The *new man* is also crucified with Christ, but he is definitely not graveyard dead (Gal. 2:20). The Bible speaks of the believer crucifying the flesh with its affections and lusts (Gal. 5:24, 25), yet the flesh is alive and wicked and must be

---

[9] Ibid., *Faith Works*, p. 116: "Nor is Paul describing a dualistic, schizophrenic Christian. The old man—the unregenerate person that was 'in Adam'—is dead...If the old self *isn't* dead, conversion hasn't occurred." P. 37, [quoting J. Gresham Machen]: "Faith...involves a change of the whole nature of man...The very first thing that the Christian does, therefore, is to keep the law of God...he keeps it joyously as a central part of salvation itself." P.45: "Saving faith, then, is the whole of my being embracing all of Christ. Faith cannot be divorced from commitment."

mortified daily (Rom. 6:11-14, 19; 8:13). The crucifixion of the flesh does not eradicate the lust of the flesh (Gal. 5:16, 17).

Argument #8: An elect person cannot fail to distinguish himself from the lost world.[10] Why then does Paul beseech them to not be conformed to this world (Rom. 12:2)? Why did Paul say that the Corinthians were walking *as men* (I Cor. 3:3)? Why does Paul admit that married men and women in the church care for the things of this world (I Cor. 7:33, 34)? Why does Paul warn the Colossians to beware of being *spoiled after the rudiments of the world* (Col. 2:8)? Why does Paul ask the Colossians why, if they are *dead with Christ from the rudiments of the world*, are they *subject to ordinances* as though they were *living in the world* (Col. 2:20)? Why does James tell believers that *friendship of the world is enmity with God* (James 4:4)? Why? Because there are such persons as worldly Christians.

---

[10] Ibid., *Gospel According To Jesus*, p. 124: "*The Worldly Heart:* Weedy soil represents a heart preoccupied with worldly matters...This is a perfect description of a worldly man—one who lives for the things of this world. He is consumed with the cares of this age. His chief pursuit is a career, a house, a car, a hobby, or a wardrobe. To him, prestige, looks, or riches are everything...Has such a person lost his salvation? No, he never had it." P. 140 "Thus in a sense we pay the ultimate price for our salvation when our sinful self is nailed to the cross...It is a total abandonment of self-will,...It is an exchange of all that we are for all that Christ is, and it denotes implicit obedience, full surrender to the lordship of Christ. Nothing less can qualify as saving faith. Geerhardus Vos articulates this principle when he writes, 'Jesus requires of his disciples the renunciation of all earthly bonds and possessions which would dispute God his supreme sway over their life...'" P. 187: "God will not declare a person righteous without making him righteous...One cannot pick and choose, accepting eternal life while rejecting holiness and obedience." P. 202: "A true believer is one who signs up for life....It means taking up the cross daily, giving all for Christ each day with no reservations, no uncertainty, no hesitation. It means nothing is knowingly held back, nothing purposely shielded from His lordship, nothing stubbornly kept from His control. It calls for a painful severing of the tie with the world....Having put his hand to the plow, he will not look back." Ibid., *Faith Works*, p. 115: "Paul's stress is not on the *immorality* of continuing to live the way we did before we were saved, but on the *impossibility* of it."

Argument #9: Election means that a believer cannot resist practicing perfect love at all times.[11] Included in the definition of love is keeping all the commandments of Christ, keeping the word of God, loving all brothers at all times, and walking in the light at all times. How then could the reformers, Roman Catholics and Puritans have hated the Anabaptists so vehemently? Why, then, was it necessary to tell the Romans to *let love be without dissimulation* (Rom. 12:9)? Why did the Corinthians have to be beseeched to confirm their love to a repenting brother (II Cor. 2:8)? Why did the Galatians have to be told to serve one another in love (Gal. 5:13)? Why did Paul have to pray for the Ephesians to be rooted and grounded in love (Eph. 3:17)? Why did Paul have to beseech the Ephesians to forbear one another in love (Eph. 4:1, 2)? Why did Paul have to tell Christian men to love their wives (Eph. 5:25)? And how could the Ephesian church, founded by Paul, have left its first love (Rev. 2:4)? Why did Paul need to tell the Thessalonians to put on the breastplate of love (I Thess. 5:8)? Why did he have to tell Timothy to follow after love (I Tim. 6:11; II Tim. 1:13)? Why do young Christian wives need to be taught to love their husbands (Titus 2:4)? Why do Christians need to provoke one another unto love (Heb. 10:24)? Why must Christians be told to let brotherly love continue (Heb. 13:1)? Why must Peter tell the saints to love one another as brethren (I Pet. 3:8)? Why does he tell Christians to be diligent to add charity and brotherly kindness to their faith (II Pet. 1:5-7)? Why must John tell the saints not to love the world (I Jn. 2:15)? Why was it necessary for him to tell the saints that they ought to love one another (I Jn. 4:11)? Why did Jude have to tell the beloved to keep themselves in the love of God (Jude 21)? Why? Because many saved believers can and do lack love, and thereby forfeit their fellowship with the Lord Jesus Christ. I Jn. 4:10, 11 says: *Herein is love, not that we loved God, but that he loved us, and sent his Son to be the propitiation for our sins. Beloved, if God so loved us, we ought also to love one another.* Love is an important and profitable attribute of a Christian, but it is God's love and not our own that saves us and keeps us saved.

---

[11] Ibid., *Faith Works*, p. 188: "There is no such thing as a Christian who lacks this love....No-lordship theology ignores this vital truth....Jesus said, 'if you love Me, you will keep my commandments.' 'He who has my commandments and keeps them, he is who loves me' (Jn. 4:21). Conversely, 'He who does not love Me does not keep My words' (v. 24)."

Argument #10: An elect person irresistibly cannot have a sinful habit.[12] Some will hold that there cannot exist a born again alcoholic nor a born again nicotine addict. Then why did Samson practice vindictiveness all the way through the moment of his death? Virtually every one of his supernatural demonstrations were acts of personal retribution. All he wanted from his final suicide was reprisal for his eyes. Why did some Corinthians persist in sin until God put them to death (I Cor. 11:30)? Does salvation mean that the flesh is incapable of addiction and that there can be no such an one as a regenerated over-eater—or that at least a saint will not die over-eating? Why do Christians have to *let not sin reign* in their mortal bodies (Rom. 6:12)? Why must they be told to *mortify the deeds of the body* (Rom. 8:13)? Why must they be told to cleanse themselves from all filthiness of the flesh (II Cor. 7:1)? Why must they be told to not use their liberty as an occasion to the flesh (Gal. 5:13)? Why must they be told to walk in the Spirit in order not to fulfill the lusts of the flesh, if true saints cannot fulfill the lusts of the flesh (Gal. 5:16)? Why do Christians need to know that they reap corruption when they sew to the flesh (Gal. 6:7, 8)? Why must they be told not to live the rest of their time in the flesh to the lusts of men, if it is impossible for a Christian to do this for the rest of his time (I Pet. 4:2)? Why must Peter beseech the saints to abstain from fleshly lusts, which war against the soul (I Pet. 2:11)? Why? Because Christians can have sinful problems that persist until their sin brings about the judgment of God in their death.

Argument #11: If one does not make obedience to the commands of Christ a contingency of salvation, he is therefore an antinomian in a state of apostasy and is consequently leading souls to an eternal hell.[13] Every Christian should pay the price of being an

---

[12] Ibid., *Faith Works*, p. 121: "No true believer will continue indefinitely in disobedience...Real Christians cannot endure perpetually sinful living." P. 114: "So it is impossible to be alive in Christ and still be alive to sin."

[13] Ibid., *Gospel According To Jesus*, p. xiv: "Several who disagree with my views have said in print that the lordship controversy is a matter of eternal consequence. This means that whoever is wrong on this question is proclaiming a message that can send people to hell. On that we agree. I went through a phase of thinking that the whole dispute might be a misunderstanding or a matter of semantics. But as I studied the issues, I discovered that this is simply not the case....I am now convinced that the two sides of this argument have distinctly different views of salvation." Ibid., *Faith Works*, p. 30: "The
(Continued on next page)

obedient disciple of the Lord. However, the blood of Christ is the 100 percent full price of salvation (Acts 20:28). When we offer our own obedience to the commands of Christ as our basis for assurance of heaven, we are missing the true meaning of the gospel message. If the believer is irresistibly like a glove on the hand of Jesus as Lord, then there is no need for temperance or self-control. A glove does not need self-control. Contrary to popular belief, the Bible does not speak of a *spirit-controlled* life. The will of the Spirit is that we practice self-control and, to the extent that we decide to do so, He will reward us. This is the fruit of the Spirit (Gal. 5:22, 23) rather than the control of the Spirit.

Argument #12: The believer irresistibly cannot fail to mortify the flesh.[14] But we think of the example of justified Lot in Sodom (II Pet. 2:7, 8). If a contemporary saint offered his two virgin daughters to a band of homosexuals, became drunk, and later impregnated both daughters, he would be judged to have failed to mortify his flesh.[15] Why must Christians be reminded to mortify their bodies in order to live (Rom. 8:13; Col. 3:5)? Why must Christians be

---

lordship controversy is a disagreement over the nature of true faith." P. 94: "Contemporary no-lordship doctrine is nothing but latter-day antinomianism..... Although most no-lordship advocates object to that term, it is a fair characterization of their doctrine." P. 233: "Dispensationalism is at a crossroads. The lordship controversy represents a signpost where the road forks. One arrow marks the road of biblical orthodoxy. The other arrow, labeled 'no-lordship' points the way to sub-Christian antinomianism."

[14] Ibid., *Faith Works*, p. 134: " 'In The Flesh' is descriptive of an unregenerate condition." PP. 190, 191: "Inevitably, the question is raised, 'how faithfully must one persevere....Ryrie suggests that if we cannot state precisely how much failure is possible for a Christian, true assurance becomes impossible. He wants the terms to be quantified....Jesus never quantified the terms of His demands; He always made them *absolute*. 'So therefore, no one of you can be My disciple who does not give up all his own possessions' (Lk. 14:33); 'He who loves father or mother more than Me is not worthy of Me; and he who loves son or daughter more than Me is not worthy of me' (Matt. 10:37); 'He who loves his life loses it; and he who hates his life in this world shall keep it to life eternal" (John 12:25)." Ibid., *Gospel According To Jesus*, p. 106: "...nor will He enter into partnership with one who loves to fulfill the passions of the flesh."

[15] Ibid., *Faith Works*, p. 128: "Lot was certainly not 'carnal' in the sense that he lacked spiritual desires. Though he lived in a wicked place, he was not wicked himself."

beseeched to present their bodies to Christ for service (Rom. 12:1, 2)? Why must Christians be told not to make provision for the flesh (Rom. 13:14)? Why must they be told not to lust after evil things and not to be idolaters (I Cor. 10:6, 7)? Why must they be instructed on how not to fulfill the lust of the flesh (Gal. 5:16)? Why must they be told not to live in the lust of concupiscence as the Gentiles do (I Thess. 4:3-5)? Why was it necessary to tell Timothy to flee youthful lusts (II Tim. 2:22)? Why must Peter beseech the beloved to abstain from fleshly lusts, which war against the soul (I Pet. 2:11)? Why? Because believers can fail to mortify the flesh.

Argument #13: Absolute obedience is either integral to the definition of faith or else an unmistakable by-product of it.[16] We do know that ritual baptism is the will of God for believers and that it is an act of faithfulness and obedience to the lordship of Christ. We know from Mk. 16:16 that *belief* and *baptism* are two separate occurrences. Are we therefore to understand that ritual baptism is a guaranteed by-product of faith? Does the sovereign grace of God take full responsibility for the believer's faithfulness and obedience to baptism, thus making failure to follow the Lord in baptism an impossibility? The answer to these questions is a resounding—*NO!*

Argument #14: Those who fail to back-load the gospel with personal righteousness are failing to instruct would-be converts to deny ungodliness and worldly desires and to live sensibly, righteously and godly in this present age.[17] This is a less than honest

---

[16] Ibid., *Gospel According To Jesus*, p. 173: "In other words, faith encompasses obedience...Yet faith is not complete unless it is obedient." P. 174: "Clearly, the biblical concept of faith is inseparable from obedience. 'Believe' is synonymous with 'obey' in John 3:36..."

[17] Ibid., *Faith Works*, p. 56: "No-lordship theology utterly ignores the biblical truth that grace 'instructs us to deny ungodliness and worldly desires and to live sensibly, righteously and godly in the present age' (Titus 2:12)." P. 228: "Chafer himself...paved the way for a brand of Christianity that has legitimized careless and carnal behavior. Chafer could rightly be called the father of twentieth-century no-lordship theology. He listed repentance and surrender as two of 'the more common features of human responsibility which are too often erroneously added to the one requirement of *faith* or *belief*.' He wrote 'to impose a need to surrender the life to God as an added condition of salvation is most unreasonable. God's call to the unsaved is never said to be unto the Lordship of Christ; it is unto His saving grace.'"

accusation, for though there is usually no failure to teach these things, they are not placed within the parameters of the gospel's definition. It is never a valid argument to use intimidating and pejorative language when referring to those who refuse to add personal righteousness to the gospel equation. Calling them *no-lordship* preachers states that they are actually opposed to any submission to the lordship of Christ. These accusers would not like to be called the *no-grace* crowd. Those who preach *free grace* are often accused of preaching *cheap grace*. This little quip of mockery is designed to portray them as cheapening the crucifixion of Christ if they fail to add personal righteousness to the righteousness of Christ. We are supposed to cower when accused of preaching *easy believism*. But the Bible does not coin a phrase like *easy believism* or *hard believism*. However, if obeying the lordship of Christ is not a part of the definition of saving faith, then this makes believing much easier. On the other hand, if absolute submission and obedience are an irresistible act of a sovereign God which requires no effort on the part of the believer, then nothing could be easier. However, believers are constantly warned that such a commitment will be costly and hard to carry out in the Christian life.

Argument #15: *Free-grace* preachers are teaching that the work of God in the believer's life stops at the moment of justification and that everything else is nothing but the believer's own effort apart from God's empowering.[18] We would like to have in our possession just a few of the names of these "many" who hold that justification is the only work of God in the believer's life. With very rare exception, almost all *free grace* preachers live godly lives and exhort all saints to do the same for the glory of Christ.

Argument 16: Some will refine their polemic by allowing temporary lapses and yet qualify themselves by affirming that any more than a temporary lapse would mean that salvation had never occurred in the first place.[19] But this assumes that no believer can die

---

[18] Ibid., *Gospel According To Jesus* [Revised Edition], pp. 201, 202: "Those who argue against lordship salvation often base their theology on the faulty assumption that the work of God in salvation stops with justification. The rest, many believe, is purely the believer's own effort…"

[19] Ibid., *Faith Works*, p. 121: "No true believer will continue indefinitely in disobedience, because sin is diametrically opposed to our new and holy nature. Real Christians cannot endure perpetually sinful living." P. *(Continued on next page)*

in one of these states of failure without first repenting. If this is correct, what do we do with Samson and some of the Corinthians (I Cor. 11:30)? Do we honestly believe that a Christian cannot die in a state of disobedience? If he dies in that condition, it was permanent in regard to his earthly life. As we surveyed in chapter three of this present work, the nature of salvation faith transcends all dispensations. This is why Abraham is the father of all them that believe. But Samson was carnal all of his life. He gambled for garments, yoked himself with heathen women, ate from a dead carcass, allowed his hair to be cut and commited suicide to gain personal vengeance for his eyes. Yet he is listed in Hebrews 11 as having lived by faith. Of course he was wrong and paid dearly for his unfaithfulness, but is the nature of his salvation faith that which transcends all dispensations?—Yes! How many OT saints lived their entire lives with multiple wives and concubines? Can it be said that none of these were saved in the first place?

The Davidic Covenant illustrates the difference between the security of a believer and God's chastisement of a believer when referring to David's son, Solomon—*He shall build an house for my name, and I will stablish the throne of his kingdom for ever. I will be his father, and he shall be my son. If he commit iniquity, I will chasten him with the rod of men, and with the stripes of the children of men: But my mercy shall not depart away from him, as I took it from Saul, whom I put away before thee* (II Sam. 7:13-15; cf. Ezek. 16).

Argument #17: An inventory of personal righteousness will determine if one is called and elected.[20] The Apostle Peter said:

181, quoting John Murray: "It is true that a believer sins; he may fall into grevous sin and backslide for lengthy periods. But it is also true that a believer cannot abandon himself to sin; he cannot come under the dominion of sin; he cannot be guilty of certain kinds of unfaithfulness." P. 182: "God's own holiness thus requires that we persevere....We cannot acquire 'the prize of the upward call of God in Christ Jesus' unless we 'press on toward the goal' (Phil. 3:14)." **Which is it? Are we regenerated before we actually believe or is salvation a goal we must press toward throughout life?**

[20] Ibid., *Gospel According To Jesus*, p. 217, 218: "Yet he [Peter] taught that the proof of faith's reality is the virtue it produces in the life of the believer (2 Peter 1:5-9). He wrote, 'Therefore, brethren, be all the more diligent to make certain about His calling and choosing you.'" Ibid., *Faith Works*, p. 162: "Should Christians seek assurance through clinging only to the *objective* promises of Scripture, or through *subjective* self-examination? If we opt for the *(Continued on next page)*

Attaching Personal Righteousness to the Back-side of the Gospel's Requirements

Wherefore the rather, brethren, give diligence to make your calling and election sure: for if ye do these things, ye shall never fall (II Pet. 1:10). It is commonly argued that the apostle is telling believers to look at their own righteousness for the assurance of salvation. But we must examine the context to see if the call to salvation and the election of grace is being addressed in this verse. Peter is addressing people that are born again—

> Simon Peter, a servant and an apostle of Jesus Christ, to them that have obtained like precious faith with us through the righteousness of God and our Saviour Jesus Christ (II Pet. 1:1).

Peter is speaking to those of *like precious faith* (vss. 5-8), who possess the imputed righteousness of Christ, telling them to add to their faith: *virtue* [knowing that faith is not a saving virtue], *knowledge, temperance, patience, godliness, brotherly kindness* and *charity*. But what of the believer who lacks these things?—*But he that lacketh these things is blind, and cannot see afar off, and hath forgotten that he was purged from his old sins* (II Pet. 1:9). Has such a person of like precious faith been purged from his old sins?—Yes! Peter is not talking about whether these brethren even go to heaven, but rather the degree in which a brother will abundantly enter into the kingdom of God—

> Wherefore the rather, brethren, give diligence to make your calling and election sure: for if ye do these things, ye shall never fall: For so an entrance shall be ministered unto you abundantly into the everlasting kingdom of our Lord and Saviour Jesus Christ (vss. 10, 11).

Then what is this *calling* of which we are to make sure? God has called all of the elect saints on earth to a *vocation* of practicing

---

objective promises only, those who profess faith in Christ while denying Him by their deeds (cf. Titus 1:16) can claim an assurance they have no entitlement to." P. 164: "Second Peter 1:5-10 lists several spiritual virtues that are essential to salvation: faith, moral excellence, knowledge, self-control, perseverance, godliness, brotherly kindness, and love. The person who lacks these virtues will also lack assurance…"

sonship which will involve humility; forbearance; unity; baptism; truth-speaking; love; putting off the old man; being renewed in the spirit of their minds; putting on the new man; putting away lying; cessation from stealing; avoidance of corrupt communication; edifying the brethren; grieving not the Holy Spirit; putting away all bitterness, wrath, anger, clamor, evil speaking and malice; and being kind, tenderhearted and forgiving toward one another (Eph. 4:1ff). This is another calling in addition to the call to salvation, for some Christians are blind and do not obey this additional calling (II Pet. 1:9).

The ideas of *calling* and *election* do not always refer to salvation. When God calls or elects, it is a choice that He makes. Paul was *called* to be an apostle (Rom. 1:1; I Cor. 1:1). God has *called* husbands and wives to live in peace (I Cor. 7:15). Obeying the commandments of God in your individual circumstances is a specific *calling* (I Cor. 7:19-24). Brethren have been *called* to practice Christian liberty (Gal. 5:13). Christians are *called* to let the peace of God rule in their hearts (Col. 3:15). Believers are *called* unto holiness (I Thess. 4:7). Saints are *called* to fight the good fight of faith (II Tim. 6:11, 12). Believers are *called* to suffer for evil and railing (I Pet. 3;9). They are *called* to suffer for doing well (I Pet. 2:20, 21). Paul was not pressing to be saved or to be sure that he was saved, but he was pressing for the prize of the *high calling* (Phil. 3:14). Peter is telling his readers that a personal inventory will make them sure of whether or not they are obeying these callings. In II Peter 1:3, the calling under discussion is to virtue and glory.

In the same sense, God has not only elected us to His grace, but He has also elected us unto this vocation of sonship. A synonym for *elected* is the concept of *chosen* (Eph. 1:4; II Thess. 2:13). God has *elected* many things for the believer—and his salvation is only one of them. God *elected* that the Gentiles would hear the gospel through Peter (Acts 15:7). Paul was *elected* to bear the name of Christ before the Gentiles (Acts 9:15; 22:14). The apostles were specially *elected* witnesses (Acts 10:41). God has *elected* foolish things to confound the wise; weak things to confound the mighty and base things and things that are nought to bring to nought the things that are (I Cor. 1:27, 28). Christians are *elected* to be soldiers (II Tim. 2:4). God has *elected* the poor in this world to be rich in faith (Jas. 2:5). God has *elected* those who are called out of darkness to show forth the praises of Him (I Pet. 2:9).

Therefore, it is not one's calling and election to salvation that is made sure by self-examination regarding the items listed in II Pet. 1:5-7. Peter did not doubt the salvation of one who lacked these things (vs. 9). He did not regard the calling and election of such an one to salvation as unsure. Peter's readers have saving faith (vss. 1, 5); they have been given *all things that pertain to life and godliness* (vs. 3); and these things were received *through the knowledge of him who has called* them (vs. 3). The knowledge of God and of Christ is in fact the very sphere where *grace and peace* will *be multiplied* to them (vs. 2). Peter's final word to his readers is an exhortation to *grow in the grace and knowledge of our Lord and Savior Jesus Christ* (3:18). Peter takes for granted that his audience is not only Christian, but is perfectly aware of that fact. Was Peter certain that he was talking to brethren?—

> Dearly beloved, I beseech *you* as strangers and pilgrims, abstain from fleshly lusts, which war against the soul; Having your conversation honest among the Gentiles: that, whereas they speak against you as evildoers, they may by *your* good works, which they shall behold, glorify God in the day of visitation (I Pet. 2:11, 12).

Argument #18: That salvation repentance is a total turning from sin in order to accept the grace of the Savior.[21] We could labor with all of the biblical usages of the term *repentance*, but the reader may have already done this.[22] Repentance [NT *Metanoein*] is a changing of

---

[21] Ibid., *Gospel According To Jesus*, p. 32: "Repentance...Far from being a human work, it is the inevitable result of God's work in a human heart...It is much more than a mere change of mind—it involves a complete change of heart, attitude, interest, and direction. It is a conversion in every sense of the word."

[22] There are three influential books on the market that definitively address the subject of repentance. John F. MacArthur, Jr., *The Gospel According To Jesus* (Grand Rapids: Academie Books, Zondervan Publishing House, 1989). MacArthur identifies *repentance* as personal righteousness yet identifies it solely as an act of God. Zane C. Hodges, *Absolutely Free* (Grand Rapids, Academie Books, Zondervan Publishing House, 1989). Hodges excludes *repentance* from the definition of the saving Gospel of Christ. Charles C. Ryrie, *So Great Salvation: What It Means To Believe In Jesus Christ* (USA, Victor Books, a Division of Scripture Press Publications Inc., 1989). Ryrie holds that *belief, faith* and *repentance* are synonyms in the gospel and do *(Continued on next page)*

the mind. The term, according to its contextual use, may, or may not entail works of personal righteousness. If we wish to define it as a work of righteousness, then works are to be added to faith. But if it is a change of mind about the crucifixion of Christ for our sins and His provision of justification, forgiveness, reconciliation, and sanctification, then it is not works added to faith. If the book of Acts seems to use the terms *faith*, *belief*, and *repentance* interchangeably (as we have already discussed in previous chapters), then we do not have works of personal righteousness being added to faith. If one did not believe in Christ five minutes ago but does so now, he has changed his mind. Salvation repentance is not turning from sin to Christ, but rather a turning to Christ with one's sins. If someone believes in a false gospel, he cannot add Christ to his idol, but must turn his faith from a gospel which cannot save to Him Who can. It is not what one does with his sins, but rather what Christ does with his sins, that saves him.

When a born again Christian falls into sin, he is expected to work at turning from that sin. But this is not a form of works that belongs within the prescribed boundaries of the gospel definition.

A lost person can change his mind about sin and reform from some forms of wickedness, but he will be neither saved nor eternally rewarded for this. He may, however, reap some earthly benefits from living a prudent life.

We do know from Scripture that assurance of salvation is possible, and we also know that no one completely ceases from sin. This brings us to the question of quantification. If salvation repentance entails the work of ceasing from all sin, when does one know that he has ceased enough to be certain of his salvation? The Bible presents absolutely no quantification standards. What sin would assure us that we were never saved in the first place—the first cigarette; the first pack; the first carton; the first crate, or, what if one never quits smoking? When do we quit sinning enough to know that we are saved? No one would know, and assurance of salvation would be impossible.

---

not entail personal works of righteousness in order to lay hold of eternal salvation. It is strongly recommended that the reader obtain and study all three of these books.

Even after we have practiced godliness for extended periods of our lives, what is our guarantee that we will not fall into sin again and suspect that we were never saved in the first place? If we have no such guarantee, then we have no logical basis for assurance even after years of consistent godliness. From such a perspective, the biblical promises that the believer in Christ has eternal life are stripped of their assurance (Jn. 3:16; 5:24; 6:47; Acts 10:43; 16:31; I Jn. 5:13). So, that which would seem to be a "wholehearted willingness" to obey all of Christ's commands would be no grounds for assurance in that many Christians are admonished for not following through with such a commitment. Paul thought it necessary to exhort the Corinthians to perform what they expressed a willingness to do the prior year (II Cor. 8:10, 11).

Therefore, we conclude that the assurance of salvation is not based upon following through with a promise that one will turn permanently from all sin—a promise that no human being has ever kept. Assurance of salvation is to be based solely upon the unconditional promises of God in the finished work of Christ.

Argument #19: If one is truly born again, he will always walk in the light and never in darkness.[23] Except when referring to literal daylight or lamplight, Scripture usually uses the term *light* as a metaphor for truth. The gospel is light, the entire Bible is light, and the teachings of Christ and the apostles are light. The truth of God's word is the illumination of the Holy Spirit. But the Holy Spirit does not irresistibly cause a unified consensus on doctrine within the Body of Christ.

If being born again guarantees walking in the light, and thus walking in the truth at all times, then some very important questions need to be asked. Was Paul assuming that Peter and Barnabas were lost when he said: *but when I saw that they walked not uprightly according to the truth of the gospel...*(Gal. 2:14a)? Was Paul saying that the entirety of the Galatian churches were unregenerate when he said: *I*

---

[23] Ibid., *Faith Works*, p. 167: "Throughout Scripture, light is used as a metaphor for truth—both intellectual and moral truth....To 'walk in the light' means to live in the realm of truth. So all true believers are walking in the light—even when we sin....To trust Jesus Christ is to walk in the light. To walk in the light is to heed the light and live accordingly."

marvel that ye are so soon removed from him that called you into the grace of Christ unto another gospel (Gal. 1:6). Why is it that the one who hates his Christian brother in Christ (I Jn. 2:9) is lying if he says that he is in the light but is instead walking in darkness and is, therefore, walking in blindness (I Jn. 2:11)? Why would Peter state that one who is thus blinded has nontheless been purged from his old sins (II Pet. 1:9)?

Argument #20: The great names of Church history believed in back-loading the Gospel with works.[24] We have cited many authors in this work who have taken a different view of grace than the position we are setting forth. However, in defense of these historic figures, it may be said that there were windows of time in the thinking of several of them in which they understood, and seemingly embraced, the pure grace of Christ solely by faith in His finished work. Let us consider Martin Luther as one example. When the sophists and scholastics argued that the believer's love was a point in the plan of salvation, it was incumbent upon Luther to stress the importance of Christian love without making it a contingency of the gospel. In his lectures on the first four chapters of Galatians, he responded to the scholastics:

> They say that we must believe in Christ and that faith is the foundation of salvation, but they say that this faith does not justify unless it is "formed by love." This is not the truth of the Gospel; it is falsehood and pretence. The true Gospel, however, is this: Works or

---

[24] Ibid., *Gospel According To Jesus*, p. 225: "Virtually all credal statements coming out of the Reformation identified good works as the inevitable expression of saving faith." PP. 223, 224: "The incident that symbolically marked the beginning of the Reformation was Martin Luther's posting of his *Ninety-five Theses* on the door of the Wittenberg Castle Church in 1517. The first four theses show clearly what Luther thought of the necessity of good works: 1. Our Lord and Master Jesus Christ, in saying, 'Repent ye, etc.,' meant the whole life of the faithful to be an act of repentance. 2. This saying cannot be understood of the sacrament of penance (i.e. of confession and absolution) which is administered by the priesthood. 3. Yet he does not mean interior repentance only; nay, interior repentance is void if it does not produce different kinds of mortifications of the flesh. 4. And so penance remains while self-hate remains (i.e. true interior repentance): namely right up to entrance into the kingdom of heaven."

> love are not the ornament or perfection of faith; but faith itself is a gift of God, a work of God in our hearts, which justifies us because it takes hold of Christ as the Savior...Therefore what the scholastics have taught about justifying faith "formed by love" is an empty dream. For the faith that takes hold of Christ, the Son of God and is adorned by Him is the faith that justifies, not a faith that includes love. For if faith is to be sure and firm, it must take hold of nothing but Christ alone.[25]

Luther makes almost the same response to the sophists by not doing away with love and law, but rather placing them outside the boundaries of the saving gospel:

> ...faith in Christ, without the Law or works. The blind sophists do not understand this. Therefore they dream that faith does not justify unless it does the works of love. In this way faith that believes in Christ becomes idle and useless, for it is deprived of the power to justify unless it has been "formed by love." But you set the Law and love aside until another place and time; and you direct your attention to the point at issue here, namely, that Jesus Christ, the Son of God, dies on the cross and bears my sin, the Law, death, the devil, and hell in His body."[26]

Luther came to the place where he found it necessary to be explicit in his view that works cannot be included in the definition of true faith:

> Then What? Is the Law useless for righteousness? Yes, certainly, but does faith alone without works, justify? Yes, certainly. Otherwise you must repudiate Moses, who declares that Abraham is righteous prior to the Law and prior to the works of the Law, not

---

[25] *Luther's Works: Lectures on Galatians Chapters 1-4*, Jaroslav Pelikan, Ed., Walter A Hansen, Associate Ed. (St. Louis: Concordia Publishing House, 1963), Vol. 26, pp. 88, 89.

[26] Ibid., *Luther's Works*, Vol. 26, p. 160.

> because he sacrificed his son, who had not yet been born, and not because he did this or that work, but because he believed God who gave him a promise.
>
> In this passage no mention is made of any preparation for grace, of any faith formed by works, or of any preceding disposition. This, however, is mentioned: that at that time Abraham was in the midst of sins, doubts, and fears, and was exceedingly troubled in spirit.
>
> How, then did he obtain righteousness? In this way: God speaks and Abraham believes what God is saying. Moreover, the Holy Spirit comes as a trustworthy witness and declares that this very believing or this very faith is righteousness or is imputed by God Himself as righteousness and is regarded by Him as such.[27]

Argument # 21: The gospel is to be back-loaded with works because of the fact that *faith* is called a *work* in Jn. 6:28, 29—[28]

> Then said they unto him, What shall we do, that we might work the works of God? Jesus answered and said unto them, This is the work of God, that ye believe on him whom he hath sent.

This is a totally unique application to the term *work*. In this case it cannot mean obedience to the Mosaic Law, pre-Mosaic Law, nor a list of all the commandments of the Great Commission. We can only conclude that the word *work* means that faith is an act on the part of the sinner as a requirement for receiving eternal life. However, it cannot be

---

[27] Ibid., *Luther's Works: Lectures on Genesis Chapters 15-20*, Jeroslav Pelikan, Ed., (St. Louis: Concordia Publishing House, 1961), Vol. 3, pp. 20, 21.

[28] Ibid., *Gospel According To Jesus*, p. 33: "There is a sense in which Jesus calls even the act of believing a work (John 6:29)…"

an act which has saving virtue (Rom. 4:5), though it is a step required of the sinner in order to become born again. Charles Bing explains it coherently with Scripture when he writes:

> Both MacArthur and Mueller use this dialogue between Jesus and some followers to argue that faith is a work. Jesus' answer to those who ask, "What shall we do that we may work the works of God?" is "This is the work of God, that you believe in Him whom He sent." Believing is not here called a work that *God* produces, for the question from the followers is "what shall we do"...Rather, "the work of God" refers to that which God requires of men. This work, however, is not something done as a human merit or a work of the law, which was what the questioners expected to hear as signified by their use of the plural "works." It is only the act of believing that God requires, as indicated by Jesus' answer using the singular "work" (cf. I Jn. 3:23). [29]

They could not be reconciled to God by acts of personal saving virtue. There was only one requirement, or work, that God demands for salvation—to believe.

In the same sense, Paul speaks of the *law of faith* (Rom. 3:27, 28). This is also a unique use of the term *law*. Faith is a law only in the sense that God requires sinners to change their minds about receiving what Christ has completed for them on the cross—which is the meaning of *repent* or *believe* (Acts 17:30). Obedience to this law does not remotely imply obedience to any other law in the Bible.

---

[29] Charles C. Bing, *Lordship Salvation: A Biblical Evaluation and Response* [Th.D. Dissertation: Dallas Theological Seminary], (Burleson, TX: GraceLife Ministries, 1992). This work is definitive reading for those interested in the *lordship salvation* debate. The dissertation can be ordered from GraceLife Ministries, 524 Jayellen Ave., Burleston, TX 76028.

Argument #22: To be a Christian and to be a disciple are exactly the same thing.[30] This means that all of the terms of discipleship in the NT are also the terms of salvation—

> If any *man* come to me, and hate not his father, and mother, and wife, and children, and brethren, and sisters, yea, and his own life also, he cannot be my disciple. And whosoever doth not bear his cross, and come after me, cannot be my disciple (Lk. 14:26, 27).

> So likewise, whosoever he be of you that forsaketh not all that he hath, he cannot be my disciple (vs. 33).

It is said that responding to the discipleship call is to become a Christian and that anything less is simply unbelief. Those who hold this view of the gospel remind us that the Great Commission (Matt. 28:18-20) was to go into all the world and make disciples. But the process of discipleship in this commission required ritual baptism plus learning to observe every command of Jesus Christ. If the writings of the apostles (which are also the commandments of the Lord) are coupled with all the commandments of Christ, we have a total of one hundred and twenty-seven contingencies in the plan of salvation. If this analogy is correct, then salvation is indeed by works of personal righteousness. But if sovereign grace irresistibly causes such obedience apart from any personal effort on the part of the believer, then there would not be such disparities in the degrees of obedience among contemporary Christians nor of saints in the Bible. In such a case, there would be no need for a Judgment Seat of Christ in that God's sovereignty would be accountable to have made all Christians equally obedient.

Argument #23: People will not serve God or contribute to the church if they think that personal righteousness is not necessary

---

[30] Ibid., *Gospel According To Jesus*, p. 196: "The contemporary teaching that separates discipleship from salvation springs from ideas that are foreign to Scripture....Every Christian is a disciple. The Lord's Great Commission was to go into all the world and 'make disciples...teaching them to observe all that I have commanded you'....Disciples are people who believe, those whose faith motivates them to obey all Jesus commanded. The word *disciple* is used consistently as a synonym for believer throughout the book of Acts....Any distinction between the two words is purely artificial."

to salvation. We must stop at this point to say that we are not judging the motives of anyone who back-loads the Gospel with works in the way we have discussed. However, it is easy to meet some who will openly confess their motives. Being overwhelmed by apathetic church members, they find it almost impossible to recruit volunteer workers and staff while at the same time watching the financial contributions moving steadily downward. It is soon discovered that these members will be mobilized by being told that their refusal to serve and give proves that they were never saved in the first place. It is reasoned that if the fear of hell was their best reason to accept Christ, then it will be their best reason to serve Christ as well. The motive in this case is to persuade Christians to obey Christ, which is a noble motive. However, no matter how desperate we are to see Christians come to such a state of commitment to the lordship of Christ, we should never be willing to preach a gospel of works to get them there.

Argument #24: If anyone consciously holds on to any particular sin at conversion, he cannot become born again.[31] This is a return to the question of quantification. Without demanding total compliance to Christ's lordship, it is insisted that if there is a conscious intention to refrain from giving up any particular sin, salvation cannot occur. But the truth is that every time a Christian sins, he is consciously doing so, and is committing an act of rebellion. This is never an act of willingness to obey Christ. Was the Apostle Peter really saved when he said: *not so, Lord* (Acts 10:14), if a truly born again person, by God's sovereign will, cannot say such a thing?

Argument #25: Contradictions are not really contradictory if they exist within our definition of the Gospel.[32] Books which

---

[31] Ibid., *Gospel According To Jesus*, p. 202: "The idea of daily self-denial does not jibe with the contemporary supposition that believing in Jesus is a momentary decision. A true believer is one who signs up for life....It means nothing is knowingly held back, nothing purposely shielded from His lordship, nothing stubbornly kept from His control."

[32] Ibid., *Gospel According To Jesus*, p. 31: "Misunderstanding on that key point is at the heart of the error of those who reject lordship salvation. They assume that because Scripture contrasts faith and works, faith may be devoid of works....They stumble over the twin truths that salvation is a gift, yet it costs everything." P. 140: "Eternal life is indeed a free gift (Rom. 6:23). Salvation cannot be earned with good deeds or purchased with money. It has already been *(Continued on next page)*

mandate the back-loading of the gospel with works of personal righteousness allow contradictions when they insist that salvation is a free gift, yet it costs the believer everything. They say that Jesus paid it all but that the believer pays the ultimate price. These authors say that unless there is a total abandonment of self-will, saving faith is not happening.

In the field of applied logic we call this a contradictory. A syllogism cannot have a combination of *all are* and *some are not*, or a combination of *no are* and *some are*. Not even in a mystical dimension can there be a square circle, a four-sided triangle, or a three-sided square. Theological liberals have long accused Bible believers of excusing alleged contradictions by affirming that an inerrant Bible can have many contradictions but from the perspective of God these are not contradictions after all. But the Bible was inspired to communicate to humans designed by God to think in a linear logical fashion (cf. Rom. 1:18-20). Eternal salvation cannot be without price to the sinner and at the same time personally cost him everything. In college, if a student contradicts himself completely, he will not impress his professor by labeling the contradiction a *further qualification* of his first position. Sound scholarship does not use the term *qualification* so freely.

Argument #26: A carnal Christian cannot exist and is a contradiction in terms.[33] But Paul told the entire Corinthian church

---

bought by Christ, who paid the ransom with His blood. But that does not mean there is no cost in terms of salvation's impact on the sinner's life. This paradox may be difficult but it is nevertheless true: salvation is both free and costly....Thus in a sense we pay the ultimate price for salvation when our sinful self is nailed to the cross. It is a total abandonment of self-will....Nothing less can qualify as saving faith."

[33] Ibid., *Gospel According To Jesus*, p. 97 [footnote 2]: "Paul's words to the Corinthians, 'Are ye not carnal, and walk as men?' (I Cor. 3:3, KJV), were not meant to establish a special class of Christianity. These were not people living in static disobedience; Paul does not suggest that carnality and rebellion were the rule in their lives. In fact, he said of these same people, 'you are not lacking in any gift, awaiting eagerly the revelation of our Lord Jesus Christ, who shall also confirm you to the end, blameless in the day of our Lord Jesus Christ' (1:7, 8). Nevertheless, by having taken their eyes off Christ and created religious celebrities (3:4, 5), they were behaving in a carnal way. Contrast Paul's words about the incestuous man in chapter 5. Paul calls him a 'so-called brother' (v. 11). He doesn't say the man is not a Christian, but *(Continued on next page)*

Attaching Personal Righteousness to the Back-side of the Gospel's Requirements

that they were *carnal* and *not spiritual*, but rather *babies*—yet they were his *brethren* and they were *in Christ* (I Cor. 3:1-3). He spoke of the fornicator in their membership being *delivered to Satan for the destruction of the flesh, that the spirit may be saved in the day of the Lord Jesus* (I Cor. 5:5). Then he instructs the church regarding how to disfellowship itself with certain extreme cases of carnal brethren—

> But now I have written unto you not to keep company, if any man that is called a brother be a fornicator, or covetous, or an idolater, or a railer, or a drunkard, or an extortioner; with such an one, no, not to eat (I Cor. 5:11).

If the incestuous man could not possibly be a brother in Christ and if the nature of saving faith transcends all dispensations, how could Lot have been our brother in justification?—

> And turning the cities of Sodom and Gomorrha into ashes condemned *them* with an overthrow, making *them* an ensample unto those that after should live ungodly; And delivered just Lot, vexed with the filthy conversation of the wicked: (For that righteous man dwelling among them, in seeing and hearing, vexed *his* righteous soul from day to day with *their* unlawful deeds (II Pet. 2:6-8).

Yet Paul thanked God that the Corinthians had *come behind in no gift*—speaking of spiritual gifts (I Cor. 1:4-7). Obviously, spiritual giftedness and spirituality were two separate subjects with Paul. But when Paul told the Corinthians that they *walk as men* (I Cor. 1:3), he was implying that they were walking like unsaved.

In I Cor. 3:15 Paul is describing a saint at the judgment seat of Christ where his works are being tried by fire. After the fire goes out, there is left only the foundation—Jesus Christ—and a pile of ashes—fruitlessness. Carnality was this man's life's story—the same as the life

---

because of the pattern of gross sin, Paul could not affirm him as a brother." Ibid., *Faith Works*, p. 126: "But never in any of his epistles did [Paul] the apostle address two classes of believers....So according to Paul, *all* Christians are spiritual."

of Samson. Yet Paul says that though this carnal *man's work shall be burned, he shall suffer loss: but he himself shall be saved; yet so as by fire.*

When writing to the Romans, Paul assumed that there existed brethren—recipients of God's mercies—who had not sacrificially presented themselves to Christ for service but were instead conformed to this world. He stresses to these brothers in Christ that this is unholy, unacceptable, and unreasonable—

> I beseech you therefore, brethren, by the mercies of God, that ye present your bodies a living sacrifice, holy, acceptable unto God, *which is* your reasonable service. And be not conformed to this world: but be ye transformed by the renewing of your mind, that ye may prove what *is* that good, and acceptable, and perfect, will of God (Rom. 12:1, 2).

It cannot be argued that the flesh does not have a will or that it is not carnal by nature. Actually, to be carnal is to be fleshly. The old man (or old nature) in a Christian still exists and is carnal and fleshly in its mind and will. There was no eradication at salvation, for it is this carnal nature that needs to be mortified by the saint. Paul was speaking to brethren when he said:

> Therefore, brethren, we are debtors, not to the flesh, to live after the flesh. For if ye live after the flesh, ye shall die: but if ye through the Spirit do mortify the deeds of the body, ye shall live (Rom. 8:12, 13).

Argument #27: Nothing less than total yieldedness to the lordship of Christ can qualify as saving faith.[34] However, we can be certain that there were some dimensions in the Corinthian's lives that were not yielded to Christ's lordship. The incestuous brother in I Cor. 5 turned out to be an actual brother. He responded to Paul's prescribed church discipline and the Corinthians were ordered to receive him back into their fellowship (II Cor. 2:6-11). Where does the Bible teach that those who do not respond to church discipline could never have been saved in the first place? The Corinthians who are now *asleep* [dead], obviously did not respond to any discipline—including the Lord's (I Cor. 11:30).

However, some authors say that a believer may turn away almost completely, experiencing more failure than success. But how do we determine when carnality is complete? We cannot!

Argument #28: An individual who rejects the final phase of church discipline is to be regarded as an unregenerate whose salvation is to be sought—[35]

---

[34] Ibid., *Gospel According To Jesus*, p. 33: "Thus salvation cannot be defective in any dimension. As a part of His saving work, God will produce repentance, faith, sanctification, yieldedness, obedience, and ultimately glorification. Since He is not dependent on human effort in producing those elements, an experience that lacks any of them cannot be the saving work of God." PP. 139, 140: "...saving faith retains no privileges. It clings to no cherished sins, no treasured possessions, no secret self-indulgences. It is an unconditional surrender, a willingness to do anything the Lord demands...It is an exchange of all that we are for all that Christ is. And it denotes implicit obedience, full surrender to the lordship of Christ. Nothing less can qualify as saving faith." P. 167: "That demands a spiritual crisis leading to a complete turnaround and ultimately a wholesale transformation. It is the only kind of conversion Scripture recognizes." Ibid., *Faith Works*, p. 61: "But by transforming the heart, grace makes the believer wholly willing to trust and obey." P. 33: "Therefore sinners cannot come to sincere faith apart from a complete change of heart, a turn-around of the mind and affections and will."

[35] Ibid., *Faith Works*, P. 192: "How long can a person continue in sin before we 'conclude that [he or she] was never really saved?' all the way through the discipline process....The Church discipline process our Lord outlined in Matthew 18 is predicated on the doctrine of perseverance. Those who remain hardened in sin only demonstrate their lack of true faith." Ibid., *Gospel According To Jesus* [Revised Edition] pp. 274, 275, On Matt. 18:15-18: *(Continued on next page)*

> Moreover if thy brother shall trespass against thee, go and tell him his fault between thee and him alone: if he shall hear thee, thou hast gained thy brother. But if he will not hear *thee, then* take with thee one or two more, that in the mouth of two or three witnesses every word may be established. And if he shall neglect to hear them, tell *it* unto the church: but if he neglect to hear the church, let him be unto thee as an heathen man and a publican (Matt. 18:15-17).

On the other hand, making unresponsiveness in church discipline a point in the plan of salvation is a dangerous approach, especially in light of the fact that Jesus calls this trespasser a brother. This argument seems to make membership in the visible church essential to salvation because the visible church has no jurisdiction on those who are outside. Look at the passage in Matthew again in light of II Thess. 3:14, 15—

> And if any man obey not our word by this epistle, note that man, and have no company with him, that he may be ashamed. Yet count *him* not as an enemy, but admonish *him* as a brother.

When a church disassociates with a member it has completed the last stage of church discipline. Then why admonish him as a brother if he is not to be considered a Christian?

The Corinthian church was told to complete the last stage of discipline on the incestuous man to the extent that no one was to eat with him (I Cor. 5:7, 11). Yet later Paul told them that one of the devices of Satan would be fulfilled if they did not receive this same man

---

"Notice that the discipline process Jesus outlined is specifically intended to answer the question of whether a person in sin is a true brother or an outsider. 'if he listens to you [if he repents], you have won your brother' (v. 15). But ultimately, 'if he refuses to listen even to the church, let him be to you as a Gentile and a tax-gatherer' (v. 17)—That is, regard him as an unbeliever and pursue him evangelistically....No one who persists in willful, deliberate sin and rebellion against the Lord should be encouraged with any promise of assurance. If you know someone like that who professes faith in Christ, follow the process of Matthew 18 and call that person to repentance. But do not encourage him or her with the promise of security."

back into their fellowship after his repentance (II Cor. 2:6-11). Does anyone ever ask why the church was not told to discipline the fornicating woman in this scenario. If she was not a sister in Christ, it was not the church's business to deal with her—*For what have I to do to judge them also that are without? Do not ye judge them that are within?* (I Cor. 5:12).

Argument #29: Positional and personal/practical sanctification are indivisibly the same.[36] Then why does the author of the Epistle to the Hebrews see the two sanctifications as disconnected? In Heb. 10:10-14 the believer is sanctified *once for all* and is *perfected forever*. But if he forsakes the assembly (vs. 25), he has *trodden under foot the Son of God and hath counted the blood of the covenant, wherewith he was sanctified, an unholy thing, and hath done despite unto the Spirit of Grace* (vs. 29). If this person was ever sanctified positionally, it was *once for all* and *forever*. So, if positional sanctification is *once for all* at conversion and personal/practical sanctification is progressive, how can they be one and the same? They cannot!

If positional and progressive sanctification are one, then why do Christians have to be told to not yield their members *as instruments of unrighteousness unto sin* (Rom. 6:13)? Why would God need to cleanse confessing Christians of *all unrighteousness* if their personal/practical righteousness is the righteousness of God (I Jn. 1:7, 9, 10)? If the imputed righteousness of Christ is perfection by divine decree (II Cor. 5:21) and practical righteousness is short of sinless perfection, how can the two be one and the same righteousness?

Argument #30: There cannot exist a Christian who is fruitless in the eyes of other saints.[37] In the parable of the vineyard

---

[36] Ibid., *Faith Works*, p. 106: "Nowhere in Scripture do we find positional righteousness set against righteous behavior, as if the two realities were innately disconnected...What is no-lordship theology but the teaching that those who have died to sin can indeed live in it? In that regard, no-lordship teaching rests on the same foundation as the doctrine of the 'positional truth' zealot I have just described. It separates justification from sanctification."

[37] Ibid., *Gospel According To Jesus* [Revised Edition], p. 171: "And so the fruitless branches represent counterfeit disciples—people who were never really saved. They do not abide in Christ, the True Vine; they are not truly *(Continued on next page)*

(John 15:1-8) we see unfruitful branches broken off, dried up, gathered up, and cast into fire. This parable is used to argue that fruitlessness results in eternal damnation. But the audience in these eight verses are a group of eleven born again men. Jesus is definitely not guaranteeing them that they will bear fruit, but He does warn everyone of them, except Judas, to abide in Him. Why exhort them to do something that, by God's sovereignty, they cannot fail to do?

The term *abide* does not discuss salvation, but rather fellowship and communion with Jesus Christ. When one ceases to abide in Christ, fruitlessness will result. Jesus is telling the disciples that this could happen to them. Shortly thereafter, it did happen to all eleven of the disciples as they all *forsook Him and fled* (Matt. 26:56). If not abiding is impossible, then it is pointless to warn saints that they must abide. On the other hand, if this parable is describing the terms of salvation, and if the fruitless branches are lost, how could they have ever been living branches in the first place?

Hell is real and is not a parable. But the fire in this story is parabolic. Sometimes the term *fire* metaphorically represents the chastisement of God. The term *fire* can refer to the judgment of God on His own people this side of the grave (Ps. 21:8-10; 79:5; 89:46; 97:2-5; Isa. 5:24, 25; 10:17-19; 29:5-7; Jer. 4:4; 7:20; 15:14; 17:27; 21:12; Amos 1:4, 7, 10, 12, 14). Why must we suppose that the metaphorical use of *fire* in Christ's parable is a reference to eternal damnation? The Apostle Peter uses the term *fire* as a reference to the temporal trials of the born again saint (I Pet. 1:6-7; 4:12).

Some, to support the view of eternal damnation in this parable, will cite Isa. 5:1-7 as a parallel illustration. The Isaiah passage is also a metaphor of a vineyard. However, the passage in Isaiah clearly speaks of God's historical judgment of Israel in the land of Palestine. The Isaiah context is not about everlasting life.

Jesus is teaching that if a believer fails to abide in Christ, he would be broken off from communion with Him. In such a case he should expect to experience the judgment of God as his experience with Christ's fellowship dries up and withers. The next experience of this

---

united with Him by faith....The imagery of burning suggests that these fruitless branches are doomed to hell. Like Judas, they are hopeless apostates."

believer will be to know the fiery chastisement of God. Peter describes this as the state of a born again Christian—

> For if these things be in you, and abound, they make *you that ye shall* neither *be* barren nor unfruitful in the knowledge of our Lord Jesus Christ. But he that lacketh these things is blind, and cannot see afar off, and hath forgotten **that he was purged from his old sins** (II Pet. 1:8, 9). [Emphasis added].

In a literal vine, such broken and withered branches cannot be restored but broken fellowship with Christ can be restored in the prayer and confession of I Jn. 1:7, 9. Remember how the Apostle Peter denied Christ with a curse and yet Jesus had said to him: *and when thou art converted, strengthen thy brethren* (Lk. 22:32). The Laodicean brethren were so broken and withered in their communion with Christ that He wanted to spit them out of His mouth. Yet, He was standing ready to restore them to fellowship—*As many as I love, I rebuke and chasten: be zealous therefore, and repent* (Rev. 3:19). Christ is not portraying Himself in this passage as standing at the heart's door of a lost person, but rather of those in the Laodicean church—*Behold, I stand at the door, and knock: if any man hear my voice, and open the door, I will come in to him, and will sup with him, and he with me* (Rev. 3:20). Here Jesus is expressing the desire to restore broken communion between Himself and the members of the church—*He that hath an ear, let him hear what the Spirit saith unto the churches* (Rev. 3:22).

Argument #31: The NT teaches that those who commit the *works of the flesh* will not go to heaven—

> Now the works of the flesh are manifest, which are *these*; Adultery, fornication, uncleanness, lasciviousness, Idolatry, witchcraft, hatred, variance, emulations, wrath, strife, seditions, heresies, Envyings, murders, drunkenness, revellings, and such like: of the which I tell you before, as I have also told *you* in time past, that they which do such things shall not inherit the kingdom of God (Gal. 5:19-21).

> Know ye not that the unrighteous shall not inherit the kingdom of God? Be not deceived: neither fornicators, nor idolaters, nor adulterers, nor effeminate, nor

abusers of themselves with mankind, Nor thieves, nor covetous, nor drunkards, nor revilers, nor extortioners, shall inherit the kingdom of God (I Cor. 6:9, 10).[38]

For this ye know, that no whoremonger, nor unclean person, nor covetuous man, who is an idolater, hath any inheritance in the kingdom of Christ and of God (Eph. 5:5).

However, going to heaven and the degree of the believer's inheritance upon arrival are two separate subjects in the NT. Eternal life is purchased one hundred percent by the finished work of Christ, but the degree in which one will abundantly enter the kingdom will be an award for the saint's faithfulness during his mortal life. Michael Eaton explains this concept with several important observations.

> Consider Gal. 5:21 and its companion-passages in I Cor. 6:9 and Eph. 5:5. Paul warns: "Those who do such things will not inherit the kingdom of God"...
> Paul includes *thumoi*, outbursts of wrath, yet Calvin confessed shortly before his death that he was prone to impatience and bad temper which, he said, was part of his nature but concerning which he was ashamed [see T. H. L. Parker, *John Calvin* (Lion, 1975), p. 181]. Had he lost his salvation? Paul includes *dichostasiai*, dissensions, and *eritheiai*, rivalries. Yet A. Dillimore entitled a chapter of his biography of George Whitefield "Dissensions and Rivalries in England". [See A. Dallimore, *George Whitefield*, vol.2 (Banner of Truth, 1980), ch. 16]. Were George Whitefield and John Wesley not Christians after all? One remembers also that Luke records a "sharp disagreement (*paraxusmos*) between Paul and Barnabas on one

---

[38] Ibid., *Faith Works*, p. 127: "In those verses the apostle Paul was describing sins of chronic behavior, sins that color one's whole character. A predilection for such sins reflects an unregenerate heart." Ibid., *Gospel According To Jesus*, pp. 215, 216: "Paul's doctrine of justification by faith makes it impossible for people to lay hold of Christ without letting go of sin. Consider these passages: (I Corinthians 6:9-11; Galatians 5:19-21; Ephesians 5:5..."

occasion (Ac. 15:39). Did Paul fall prey to his own warning? Was he in danger of losing—or falsifying—his salvation?

Does it mean that those who are guilty of such things but do not repent do not inherit God's kingdom? Yet do not some Christians remain blind to their weaknesses all their lives? Was not Luther quite blind to the sinfulness of his hostility to fellow reformers? Does not his story indicate that he never did repent of his attitude to Zwingli and others? [See R. H. Bainton, *Here I Stand*, (originally Abingdon, 1950; 1978 rp), pp. 248-251]. Was not Melanchthon nervous even of letting him see Calvin's letter to him because he feared a violent reaction? [See J. Calvin, *Letters*, (Banner of Truth, 1980), p. 71]. Is not the attitude of some Calvinists towards what they think is "antinomian" itself not rather antinomian?[39]

...Surely Calvin lost something at that very point of his life when he lost his temper. Surely the rivalry between Wesley and Whitefield did damage to the kingdom of God and brought blessing to neither of them at that stage of their life...

It is important to distinguish between justification and reward...We should also take seriously the absence from the New Testament of any reference to reversal of justification-regeneration...[40]

---

[39] Eaton makes the following note from J. Gerstner, *A Primer on Justification* (Presbyterian & Reformed, 1983), p. 16: "Gerstner maintains that 'antinomians' (American dispensationalist evangelicals) sing: 'Free from the Law, O blessed condition, / I can sin as I please and still have remission.' But Bliss's hymn reads: 'Free from the Law, O blessed condition, / Jesus hath bled and there is remission' and continues: 'Children of God', O glorious calling, / Surely his grace will keep us from falling.'

[40] Michael Eaton, *No Condemnation: A New Theology of Assurance* (Downers Grove, IL: InterVarsity Press, 1995), pp. 204-206—This book is strongly recommended as definitive reading to anyone interested in the *Lordship Salvation* Debate.

So, I Cor. 6:9, 10 refers to a brother in Christ who forfeits his inheritance within the kingdom of God because of his *works of the flesh.* This is speaking of his conditional inheritance that is contingent upon his personal righteousness. However, he is still a brother in Christ who will enter heaven according to his eternal inheritance of salvation.

But what of verse 11 which says: *And such were some of you: but ye are washed, but ye are sanctified, but ye are justified in the name of the Lord Jesus, and by the Spirit of our God?* Notice the word *you* in verse 11 and compare it with the word *ye* in verse 8—*Nay, ye do wrong, and defraud, and that your brethren.* A fraud and an extortioner are both thieves. Thus, the brother in verse 8 will forfeit his inheritance also, but he is still a brother. Verse 7 describes the utter failure of such a brother in Christ—*Now therefore there is utterly a fault among you, because ye go to law one with another. Why do ye not rather take wrong? why do ye not rather suffer yourselves to be defrauded?*

Again, note the word *you* in verse 11 and the word *fornication* in verse 9 and then compare with the word *you* in I Cor. 5:1—*It is reported commonly that there is fornication among you, and such fornication as is not so much as named among the Gentiles, that one should have his father's wife.* This is a man who is forfeiting his inheritance in heaven, but, if he were to be destroyed by Satan at that moment, would his spirit be saved?—*To deliver such an one unto Satan for the destruction of the flesh, that the spirit may be saved in the day of the Lord Jesus* (I Cor. 5:5). Note the distinction between the fornicators of this world and a fornicator of the brethren. They are to be treated differently because they are different—

> I wrote unto you in an epistle not to company with fornicators: Yet not altogether with the fornicators of this world, or with the covetous, or extortioners, or with idolaters; for then must ye needs go out of the world. But now I have written unto you not to keep company, if any man that is called a brother be a fornicator, or covetous, or an idolater, or a railer, or a drunkard, or an extortioner; with such an one no not to eat. For what have I to do to judge them also that are without? do not ye judge them that are within? But them that are without God judgeth. Therefore put away from among yourselves that wicked person (I Cor. 5:9-13).

So, just as Paul said *such were some of you*, it could be stated just as correctly that *such still are many of you.* Because this is such an important point of contention, let us illustrate our position with an analogy from two separate inheritances for OT Jews.

The inheritance of the Abrahamic Covenant included unconditional promises of possessing the land of Canaan during the millennium and on into eternity (Acts 7:5; Heb. 11:8, 10). This will be a *forever* possession (Ex. 32:13; Gen. 12:1, 7; 13:15; 15:18; 17:7, 8). In Judges 2:1 God promises unconditionally never to break this covenant. Though Israel forsook God and was chastised by Him, He did not utterly forsake them but determined to fulfil the Abrahamic Covenant by grace and mercy (Neh. 9:7, 8, 15-19; cf. vss. 30, 31). In Neh. 9:38 the Israelites made a conditional covenant with God claiming possession of the land contingent on obedience to the Law of Moses. But during the divided monarchy, the Jews were separated into the ten northern tribes of Israel and the two southern tribes of Judah. Ezekiel prophesied a time during the millennium when the two shall be one again and possess the land unconditionally as a gift—and not by conquest (Ez. 37:15-26). This will be the fulfillment of the Abrahamic Covenant promise of an eternal land inheritance for Israel. In Ez. 16 God refers to Israel as an unrepenting harlot (16:35, 58, 59; cf. entire chapter). Yet, even though they had despised the Word of God, He refers again to the unconditional nature of His original covenant (Vs. 60)—*Nevertheless, I will remember my covenant with thee in the days of thy youth, and I will establish unto thee an everlasting covenant.* The future glory of Zion is further described in Isa. 60:21, 22. This is the fulfillment of the promise that Israel will inhabit the land as an inheritance forever. Zechariah also describes the future glory of Zion's possession of the Promised Land (Zech. 8:12). Even the Psalmist mentions the unconditional eternality of the Abrahamic Covenant (Ps. 105:8-10).

But, in a totally different light, the inheritance of the Mosaic Covenant provides for a conditional possession of the land this side of the millennium and eternity. Accordingly, some will inherit more than others (Nu. 26:52-54). Possessing the Mosaic inheritance of the land was contingent on dispossessing the former inhabitants. If Israel failed to do this, God would dispossess them from the land as He intended to dispossess the Canaanites (Nu. 33:50-56). Possessing the Mosaic inheritance was also contingent on obedience to the Mosaic statutes (Deut 4:1, 2). Josh. 13:1 speaks of Israel's failure to take possession of *very much* of the land that had been promised. Judges 2:2-3 records God's refusal to drive the inhabitants of the land out because Israel broke the conditions of the Mosaic Covenant by making leagues with the inhabitants and by not throwing down their altars. David counseled Israel to seek and keep all the commandments of the Lord as a condition for inheriting the land (I Chron. 28:8). Jeremiah calls for repentance and obedience as a condition for dwelling in the land in 610 B.C.—a land which had been promised to the fathers *forever and ever* unconditionally (Jer. 32:3-7). Isaiah asked God to return the Mosaic inheritance which he confessed that Israel deserved to lose (Isa. 63:17, 18).

We must not fail to distinguish between the Abrahamic Covenant's unconditional promises of inheritance and the Mosaic conditional promises of inheritance. The unconditional promises of inheritance to Abraham cannot be disannulled (Gal. 3:15-18), whereas the conditional covenant of Moses can and has been disannulled (Heb. 7:18, 19). Thus, there is the Abrahamic promise to the redeemed of Israel that they will unconditionally inherit the land forever beginning with the millennium, and then there is the Mosaic promise that possession of the promised land this side of the millennium and eternity is contingent upon conquest and national obedience to the Mosaic Covenant.

In like manner, the NT saint has an inheritance which is Christ Himself and eternal life. This is a free gift of grace and mercy and not conditioned in any way upon personal righteousness. But there is also a second, and distinct, inheritance for the saint that is conditioned upon works of righteousness which he has done. This second inheritance is not a gift, but a reward for faithfulness, overcoming and suffering. Christ is the unconditional inheritance of every believer equally because He is their eternal life (I Pet. 1:1-5; I Jn. 1:1-3; Jn. 14:6; Heb. 9:15; Ps. 16:5). Paul illustrates this by describing believers as having sometimes been foolish, disobedient, deceived, lustful, malicious, envious and hateful (Titus 3:3, 4). He then makes it clear that our inheritance is not by *works of righteousness which we have done* but that we are declared justified by the grace and mercy of God. Yet, in verses 8-11 Paul wants Titus constantly to exhort believers to maintain good works in order to avoid heresies which subvert. Thus, being a justified believer by the grace and mercy of God and realizing the importance of maintaining good works are two very important, yet distinct, subjects.

Believers receive the eternal inheritance of salvation and Christ Himself by faith without the addition of any other works of personal righteousness (Rom. 4:5; 3:28). This inheritance is shared equally with all believers (Gal. 3:28; Eph. 1:11, 14; II Tim. 1:9). However, the believer must distinguish between his eternal inheritance of salvation and to what extent he will share in all things that Christ has inherited (Heb. 1:1, 2; Col. 3:24, 25).

Being an heir of God is to be born again, but being a joint-heir with Christ and thus receiving a portion of all that is His inheritance requires, among other things, faithfulness in suffering (Rom. 8:17, 18). For instance, not everyone will reign with Christ to the same degree (Lk. 19:17, 19, 24), but the actual degree will be partially measured by faithfulness in suffering (II Tim. 2:12). Eternal life is one thing, but the crown of life will belong to those who are faithful unto death (Rev. 2:10; cf. I Tim. 3:11; II Tim. 2:2).

Eph. 1:11 speaks of an inheritance that all believers already have, and yet II Pet. 3:9 speaks of an inherited blessing that is contingent upon proper Christian behavior. So, to be a joint-heir with Christ will entitle the suffering saint to share even more in the glory of the Son (I Pet. 4:13; cf. vss. 16, 19).[41]

Joint-heirship with Christ is conditioned upon the believer becoming an overcomer. Of course, when a believer exercises faith in Christ, he does overcome the world in that sense (I Jn. 5:4, 5). Becoming born again is a unique victory over the world. But this does not mean that all Christians are all equally overcomers in their personal day-to-day lives. This is something that the NT nowhere guarantees. Otherwise, why would Paul say to saints: *Be not overcome of evil, but overcome evil with good* (Rom. 12:21) if this could never happen to a believer? Why would Paul tell the brethren of Rome, who had received saving mercy, that not presenting their bodies to God's service was *unholy, unacceptable, unreasonable* and is to be *conformed to this world* (Rom. 12:1, 2)?

---

[41] See also Acts 5:41; 9:16; I Cor. 4:12; 9:12; II Cor. 1:6, 7; Gal. 5:11, 12; Phil. 1:29; 3:8, 10; 4:12; I Thess. 3:4; II Thess. 1:5; I Tim. 4:10; I Pet. 2:19, 20; 3:14, 17; 4:13, 16, 19; Rev. 2:10.

Rev. 2:7 describes the privilege of eating from the tree of life in heaven. But there is no living tree anywhere that can bestow eternal life. Everlasting life is bestowed through the death of Christ in His finished work of salvation. But the right to the *hidden manna* belongs to the believer who is an overcomer (Rev. 2:17; cf. 22:14, 19). Power over the nations will be awarded in proportions (Lk. 19) but the degrees will be contingent upon keeping the works of Christ unto the end as an overcomer (Rev. 2:26). It is the overcoming Christian who will be made a pillar in the Temple of God (Rev. 3:12). It is the overcoming Christian that will reign to the ultimate degree with Christ (Rev. 3:21). And, believers who are overcomers to the greatest extent will share the most in all that Christ has inherited (Rev. 21:7; cf. Heb. 1:1, 2; Ps. 37:18).

Several deductions can be made from the foregoing analogies. First, the believer's eternal inheritance of salvation cannot be diminished (Heb. 1:14). Second, the believer's inheritance, which is not a gift but rather a graded reward, can be diminished through unfaithfulness (II Jn. 8; Col. 2:18; 3:24). Third, a heaven-bound believer can commit the works of the flesh and thus diminish his inheritance when he enters the kingdom of God for eternity (Rom. 6:19; 7:18, 25; 13:14; I Cor. 5:5; 7:28; II Cor. 7:1; Gal. 5:13, 16, 17, 19-21, 26; 6:8; Phil. 3;4; I Pet. 2:11; 4:2; I Jn. 2:15, 16). Fifth, believers are heirs of God equally, but they become joint-heirs with Christ in proportion to their faithfulness, overcoming, and suffering with Christ. Sixth, Jesus Christ is now the appointed heir of all things (Heb. 1:2). If inheriting the kingdom of God means that all Christians shall inherit all that Christ has inherited as joint-heirs with Him, then there can be no degrees of reward and the judgment seat of Christ will be pointless.

So, there is an inheritance which is a gift and an inheritance which is a reward. Even a novice will see this distinction when reading Col. 3:24—*Knowing that of the Lord ye shall receive the reward of the inheritance: for ye serve the Lord Christ.*[42]

---

[42] There are two important works which address the distinction between the conditional and the unconditional inheritance of the Christian: Joseph C. Dillow, *The Reign of the Servant Kings: A Study of Eternal Security and the Final Significance of Man* (Hayesville, NC: Schoettle Publishing Co, 1992) and Zane Hodges, *The Gospel Under Seige* (Dallas, TX: Redencion Viva, 1992).

Some who back-load the gospel with personal obedience in all things seem very confused when they deny that baptism is included in these mandatory acts of submission to the lordship of Christ. When *they of the circumcision* back-loaded the death, burial and resurrection of Christ with circumcision and law, it became another gospel which could not save—

> I marvel that ye are so soon removed from him that called you into the grace of Christ unto another gospel: Which is not another; but there be some that trouble you, and would pervert the gospel of Christ. But though we, or an angel from heaven, preach any other gospel unto you than that which we have preached unto you, let him be accursed. As we said before, so say I now again, If any *man* preach any other gospel unto you than that ye have received, let him be accursed (Gal. 1:6-9).

In the next, and final, chapter of this present work, we will respond to the charge that we are causing division in the true Body of Christ by hesitating to accept works and sacraments as also the gospel of Christ. Are we guilty of *butchering* Christ and His body by being so definitive in the gospel? This charge strikes fear in the hearts of perhaps tens of thousands of Evangelicals world-wide, and entices them to embrace an apostate gospel for the sake of unity.

Chapter Eleven

Does The Baptism Debate Needlessly Divide The *Body Of Christ*?

In the view associated with Cyprian of Carthage (d. 258), there is only one church, the "ark of salvation", and its institutional and spiritual boundaries coincide....

Dictionary Of The Ecumenical Movement, **page 159**

In chapter one of this work we demonstrated what the apostles affirmed: that combining the ritual of circumcision and the law of Moses with the finished work of Christ constitutes another gospel which cannot save. In chapter two we attempted an overview of the purposes and uses of the Mosaic Law and of natural law. We noted that neither law was intended to impart life everlasting. In chapter three we demonstrated that eternal life for any member of Adam's fallen race is by grace through faith, apart from works and ritual, but imparted by the imputed righteousness of God. This has been the plan of redemption agreed upon by the members of the Trinity from before the foundation of the world. In chapter four we affirmed that remission of sins during the ministry of John the Baptist was received by faith in Christ. We demonstrated that the baptisms of John, Jesus and the apostles could not have been a continuation of Essene ritual immersion, nor of an alleged ancient form of Jewish proselyte baptism. We observed that John the Baptist, Jesus Christ, the Apostle Peter and the Apostle Paul all preached the same gospel of remission of sins, and this they did from a topical exposition of the Old Testament. In chapter five we demonstrated that the NT ritual of water baptism did not replace circumcision as the cause of regeneration or as a means of saving grace. Neither ritual has ever been a means of imparting the saving grace of

Christ. In chapter six we discussed an overview of the major arguments in favor of the concept that infant baptism removes original sin, imparts the saving grace of Christ, and places the child into the *body of Christ*. In chapter seven we surveyed the dominance of the baptismal regenerationist position throughout church history. In chapter eight we analyzed many of the subjective arguments that are used to defend baptismal regeneration as well as other theological affirmations. In chapter nine we examined the major proof-texts that are used to objectively demonstrate baptismal regeneration from Scripture. In chapter ten we sought to overturn the major arguments used to support the back-loading of the gospel with personal righteousness in order to obtain, and have assurance of, salvation.

It is regrettable that the position of this present work on the nature of the gospel offends so many in Christendom as if this stance is causing division, contention and disunity in the *Body of Christ*. It is unfortunate that some see this position as literally dissecting the *Body of Christ* by its insistence that there is only one true gospel. It is lamentable that the believer's baptism position sometimes appears to be condemning persons to hell if they do not hold to its view of bapatism and the gospel. On the contrary, no one can know the eternal destiny of anyone who is an advocate an apostate gospel because it is unknowable whether such a person has embraced the true gospel in his earlier life. What can be known, however, is that an apostate gospel does not provide redemption to the one who trusts its promises. In this chapter, we wish to address these concerns and perhaps create comfort as well as caution for those who are still struggling with these issues. Let the reader be assured that most theologians who hold to salvation solely by grace, followed by believer's baptism, expect to meet multitudes of infant-baptized, non-baptized and non-circumcised when they reach eternity. However, some who hold to believer's baptism (present author included) affirm that heaven will be populated uniquely with those who, at some moment in their lives, cast themselves upon the grace and mercy of God alone, apart from ritual and personal righteousness.

Among most NT theologians, the analogy of *Body of Christ* is applied to both the invisible, universal Church and the local church. Yet the student of God's word must clearly distinguish between the two. When the phrase *Body of Christ* describes a functioning ministry designed by God to carry out the Great Commission on earth (Matt. 28:18-20), it is always describing the local church. The NT assumes the presence of division and dissension within the local church. Jesus warned of false prophets which come to the saints in sheep's clothing, but who, in reality, are ravening wolves (Matt. 7:15). Jesus spoke of misguided people who will have prophesied in the name of Jesus, exorcised demons in His name, and performed many wonderful works in His name, yet in reality He never knew them (Matt. 7:22, 23). Paul warned the Ephesian bishops to be vigilantly on guard for the wolves that would enter into the local church, and that even some of the bishops would rise up and cause division in the flock (Acts 20:28-31). When some came to the Ephesian congregation claiming apostolic authority, the church placed them on trial and found them to be liars (Rev. 2:2).

Paul told the Roman church that it was those in the congregation proclaiming extra-apostolic doctrine who were the causes of division and offences—

> Now I beseech you, brethren, mark them which cause divisions and offences contrary to the doctrine which ye have learned; and avoid them (Rom. 16:17).

Today we are told that those who are not open to extra-apostolic doctrines and teachings are blasphemously dissecting the *Body of Christ*, or amputating themselves from the *Body*. Paul severely admonished the Corinthian congregation for being so naïve that they would fall for someone preaching another gospel, another Jesus and offering another spirit:

> For if he that cometh preacheth another Jesus, whom we have not preached, or *if* ye receive another spirit, which ye have not received, or another gospel, which ye have not accepted, ye might well bear with *him* (II Cor. 11:4).

Though division is not the will of God, He permitted heretical divisions in the Corinthian church and made use of them in order to manifest those who were true and faithful to the apostolic teachings—

> For first of all, when ye come together in the church, I hear that there be divisions among you; and I partly believe it. For there must be also heresies among you, that they which are approved may be made manifest among you (I Cor. 11:18, 19).

God has chosen that through the manifestation of such approved workmen He would preserve the true propagation of the gospel—

> Holding fast the faithful word as he hath been taught, that he may be able by sound doctrine both to exhort and to convince the gainsayers. For there are many unruly and vain talkers and deceivers, specially they of the circumcision: Whose mouths must be stopped, who subvert whole houses, teaching things which they ought not, for filthy lucre's sake (Titus 1:9-11).

Jude told the saints that it was their duty to practice contention when the gospel, and the apostolic doctrines, were at stake:

> Beloved, when I gave all diligence to write unto you of the common salvation, it was needful for me to write unto you, and exhort *you* that ye should earnestly contend for the faith which was once delivered unto the saints (Jude 3).

Paul and Barnabas set the example by engaging in great dissension and disputation when the Judaizers from within the Jerusalem church challenged their gospel—

> And certain men which came down from Judaea taught the brethren, *and said*, Except ye be circumcised after the manner of Moses, ye cannot be saved. When therefore Paul and Barnabas had no small dissension and disputation with them, they determined that Paul and Barnabas, and certain other of them, should go up to Jerusalem unto the apostles and elders about this question. (Acts 15: 1, 2).

When the Apostle Peter and Barnabas were intimidated into publicly endorsing the Judaizer's version of gospel, Paul knew that it was not ***The Gospel*** and therefore withstood Peter to the face—

> But when Peter was come to Antioch, I withstood him to the face, because he was to be blamed. For before that certain came from James, he did eat with the Gentiles: but when they were come, he withdrew and separated himself, fearing them which were of the

circumcision. And the other Jews dissembled likewise with him; insomuch that Barnabas also was carried away with their dissimulation. **But when I saw that they walked not uprightly according to the truth of the gospel,** I said unto Peter before *them* all, If thou, being a Jew, livest after the manner of Gentiles, and not as do the Jews, why compellest thou the Gentiles to live as do the Jews? We *who are* Jews by nature, and not sinners of the Gentiles, Knowing that a man is not justified by the works of the law, but by the faith of Jesus Christ, even we have believed in Jesus Christ, that we might be justified by the faith of Christ, and not by the works of the law: for by the works of the law shall no flesh be justified. (Gal. 2:11-16). [Emphsis added]

Paul told the Galatians that another gospel is not the saving gospel:

I marvel that ye are so soon removed from him that called you into the grace of Christ unto another gospel: Which is not another; but there be some that trouble you, and would pervert the gospel of Christ. But though we, or an angel from heaven, preach any other gospel unto you than that which we have preached unto you, let him be accursed. As we said before, so say I now again, If any *man* preach any other gospel unto you than that ye have received, let him be accursed (Gal. 1:6-9).

The founder of the NT church, Jesus Christ, caused much more division than unity during His earthly ministry—

Suppose ye that I am come to give peace on earth? I tell you, Nay; but rather division: For from henceforth there shall be five in one house divided, three against two, and two against three. The father shall be divided against the son, and the son against the father; the mother against the daughter, and the daughter against the mother; the mother in law against her daughter in law, and the daughter in law against her mother in law (Lk. 12:51-53).

> So there was a division among the people because of him (Jn. 7:43).

> Therefore said some of the Pharisees, This man is not of God, because he keepeth not the sabbath day. Others said, How can a man that is a sinner do such miracles? And there was a division among them (Jn. 9:16).

> There was a division therefore again among the Jews for these sayings. And many of them said, He hath a devil, and is mad; why hear ye him? Others said, These are not the words of him that hath a devil. Can a devil open the eyes of the blind (Jn. 10:19-21).

Although God desires to see unity in the visible church on earth (I Cor. 1:10), He knows that it is Satan's mission to infiltrate that church, dilute its gospel and, with his devices, have an advantage over it—*Lest Satan should get an advantage of us: for we are not ignorant of his devices* (II Cor. 2:11). Satan infiltrates churches, not to steel salvation from the saints, but to rob them of a true gospel testimony that would bring light to the lost—

> In whom the god of this world hath blinded the minds of them which believe not, lest the light of the glorious gospel of Christ, who is the image of God, should shine unto them (II Cor. 4:4).

God knows that Satan is an *angel of light* and that he intends to infiltrate the visible church with *ministers of righteousness* who claim apostolic authority and pretend to have moral standards while teaching salvation by personal righteousness—

> For such *are* false apostles, deceitful workers, transforming themselves into the apostles of Christ. And no marvel; for Satan himself is transformed into an angel of light. Therefore *it is* no great thing if his ministers also be transformed as the ministers of righteousness; whose end shall be according to their works (II Cor. 11:13-15).

Does The Baptism Debate Needlessly Divide The Body Of Christ?

In Acts 20:28-31 the Apostle Paul prepared the Ephesian elders to defend the visible church against such an infiltration. This preparation became practical and useful after Paul's departure from their presence—

> Unto the angel of the church of Ephesus write; These things saith he that holdeth the seven stars in his right hand, who walketh in the midst of the seven golden candlesticks; I know thy works, and thy labour, and thy patience, and how thou canst not bear them which are evil: and thou hast tried them which say they are apostles, and are not, and hast found them liars: And hast borne, and hast patience, and for my name's sake hast laboured, and hast not fainted (Rev. 2:1-3).

In *contrast* to the local-visible church, the so-called *mystical universal-invisible Body of Christ* is made up of all believers in the true Gospel of Jesus Christ from the beginning of the church age until the rapture of the saints. For semantical purposes, we prefer to call this entity the *family of God—Of whom the whole family in heaven and earth is named* (Eph. 3:15). The good news is that no human, demonic, nor satanic power can dissect the oneness of that entity. All true Christians of the church age have entered that entity through the baptism of (or *in*) the Holy Spirit—

> For the body is one, and hath many members, and all the members of that one body, being many, are one body: so also is Christ. For by one Spirit are we all baptized into one body, whether we be Jews or Gentiles, whether we be bond or free; and have been all made to drink into one Spirit (I Cor. 12:12, 13).

The goal of a local-visible church should be to translate the oneness of the invisible family into the congregation of the local church. This ideal has never, to our knowledge, been completely accomplished in church history because the local church must exclude from its fellowship some who are not excluded from the universal family—

> I wrote unto you in an epistle not to company with fornicators: Yet not altogether with the fornicators of this world, or with the covetous, or extortioners, or with idolaters; for then must ye needs go out of the

> world. But now I have written unto you not to keep company, if any man that is called a brother be a fornicator, or covetous, or an idolater, or a railer, or a drunkard, or an extortioner; with such an one no not to eat. For what have I to do to judge them also that are without? do not ye judge them that are within? But them that are without God judgeth. Therefore put away from among yourselves that wicked person (I Cor. 5:9-13, see vss. 1-5).

But this ideal of oneness cannot be even properly attempted except through a consensus on the clarity of the saving gospel. Otherwise, we are not speaking of spiritual unity, but of mere uniformity based upon an apostate version of the gospel.

The most powerful prayers ever uttered were from the heart of Jesus Christ Himself. He it was Who petitioned the Father to make a oneness entity of all true believers—

> …Holy Father, keep through thine own name those whom thou hast given me, that they may be one, as we are…That they may be one; as thou, Father, art in me, and I in thee, that they also may be one in us: that the world may believe that thou hast sent me. And the glory which thou gavest me I have given them; that they may be one, even as we are one: I in them, and thou in me, that they may be made perfect in one; and that the world may know that thou hast sent me, and hast loved them, as thou hast loved me. Father, I will that they also, whom thou hast given me, be with me where I am; that they may belold my glory, which thou hast given me: for thou lovedst me before the foundation of the world (Jn. 17:11, 21-23).

In this sense, the departed saints in heaven and the living saints on earth are united into one invisible Body that spans heaven and earth—

> For this cause I bow my knees unto the Father of our Lord Jesus Christ, Of whom the whole family in heaven and earth is named, That he would grant you, according to the riches of his glory, to be strengthened

> with might by his Spirit in the inner man (Eph. 3:14-16).
>
> But God, who is rich in mercy, for his great love wherewith he loved us, even when we were dead in sins, hath quickened us together with Christ, (by grace ye are saved;) And hath raised *us* up together, and made *us* sit together in heavenly *places* in Christ Jesus: That in the ages to come he might shew the exceeding riches of his grace in *his* kindness toward us through Christ Jesus (Eph. 1:4-7).

The universal-invisible *Body of Christ* has one Lord, one faith and one baptism—

> *There is* one body, and one Spirit, even as ye are called in one hope of your calling; One Lord, one faith, one baptism, One God and Father of all, who *is* above all, and through all, and in you all (Eph. 4:4-6).

The one baptism is Spirit baptism, to be distinguished from all forms of ritual baptism. The baptism of the Holy Spirit and the drinking of Christ must be experienced today before water baptism and before the ordinance of the Lord's Table. This present work has been primarily concerned with the distinction between ritual and reality. Although Christian ritual ordinances are sacred, they are only symbols and must not be viewed as imparting the saving grace of Christ. In Acts 10 the Apostle Peter was preaching the Gospel to a household of lost Gentile souls. As he was explaining the plan of salvation (Acts 10:43), his hearers received the baptism of the Holy Spirit into the invisible-universal family—*While Peter yet spoke these words, the Holy Ghost fell on all them which heard the word* (vs. 44). We know that this was Holy Ghost baptism from Peter's description and report of the event to the Jerusalem church:

> And as I began to speak, the Holy Ghost fell on them, as on us at the beginning. Then remembered I the word of the Lord, how that he said, John indeed baptized with water; but ye shall be baptized with the Holy Ghost (Acts 11:15, 16).

It was only after these believers were placed into the invisible-universal *family of Christ* that they were asked to submit to ritual water baptism—

> And they of the circumcision which believed were astonished, as many as came with Peter, because that on the Gentiles also was poured out the gift of the Holy Ghost. For they heard them speak with tongues, and magnify God. Then answered Peter, can any man forbid water, that these should not be baptized, which have received the Holy Ghost as well as we? And he commanded them to be baptized in the name of the Lord (Acts 10:45-48a).

Thus, in the invisible-universal entity during the church age, all have the one baptism of the Spirit, while some have unscriptural ritual baptism, some have scriptural water baptism, and others have no ritual baptism at all.

On the other hand, the local-visible church does not possess God's omniscience and therefore will often admit unregenerate persons into its membership based upon their "professions of faith." Thus, unlike the invisible-universal entity, the local-visible church is comprised of both the saved and the lost.

Just as Spirit baptism is distinguished from ritual baptism in Scripture, the invisible-universal entity of saints must be distinguished from the local-visible church.[1] There are wolves and false professors in many local churches, while there are only truly born again saints in the universal family. The local church is comprised of living mortals

---

[1] There is a school of thought among many godly Baptist brethren which denies the existence of any universal church. They hold that the only Body of Christ in the NT is the local church and refer to the universal/mystical constituency of Christianity as the *family of God*. This position is grounded in their jealously for the Bible doctrine of the local church, and possibly motivated by their reaction to the ecumenical movement's desire to form the universal church into a visible, earthly organization. Most of these these brethren will bear with and work with others who agree with them regarding the nonexistence of a universal/visible church, yet refer to the universal entity as the *Mystical Body of Christ*. These brethren do believe that there is a sense in which all NT saints are invisibly one in Christ. It is this unity to which some refer when speaking of the *universal church* in contrast to the local church.

dwelling on earth while the universal/mystical is mostly comprised of departed saints of centuries past. Being a member of the universal does not make one a member of the local. Even the most devoted ecumenical would concede that ten busloads of Methodists cannot pull into a Presbyterian church parking lot, enter the building, vote in a new board of elders, and call for the pastor to be replaced. Membership in the *universal church* does not give them equal standing in the business of all local churches. The Apostle Paul told the Corinthians to set up judges in the church to arbitrate between brethren rather than appealing to a court of unbelievers in the world (cf. I Cor. 6). He was speaking of a jurisdiction within one local church. A church in Indianapolis cannot set up judges which can order a member of a local church in California to pay reparations to a brother in Indiana. These judges are an alternative to civil law suits between brethren within the same local-visible church.

Almost on a weekly basis, a new leader will speak for God and proclaim that the Lord has called him to make the *universal church* into one functioning organization on earth, suggesting a single bank account and a unified budget. Such a project will often require a moratorium regarding how the gospel should be precisely defined—of course until this leader announces what the new "true gospel" shall be. It should comfort the grieving saint to know that the Scriptures nowhere call for the universal Church to form a unified organization on earth. Any attempt to facilitate such an idea in past history has usually resulted in religious persecution and/or mass executions.

When the Bible admonishes Christians because of their divisiveness, it is addressing a local church situation—

> Now I beseech you, brethren, by the name of our Lord Jesus Christ, that ye all speak the same thing, and *that* there be no divisions among you; but *that* ye be perfectly joined together in the same mind and in the same judgment. For it hath been declared unto me of you, my brethren, by them *which are of the house* of Chloe, that there are contentions among you. Now this I say, that every one of you saith, I am of Paul; and I of Apollos; and I of Cephas; and I of Christ (I Cor. 10:10-12).

Thus, Paul told the local church at Corinth that there *should be no schism in the body*, but rather an atmosphere of mutual care (I Cor. 12:25). In this context, the apostle was calling the local church a *body of Christ* as distinguished from the *universal church* which cannot be spiritually divided. This local church concept is illustrated by the fact that when one member suffers, all members suffer; and when one member is honored, all members are honored (I Cor. 12:25, 26). If this is a description of the universal church, then it must be affirmed that the departed saints in heaven have been suffering with mortal earthly saints since the Day of Pentecost. In such a case, heaven would not be heaven at all.

This brings us to the heart-rendering subject of the breach between varying religious groups in Christendom today. We are constantly reminded that these divisions are caused by doctrine, and, that if all religions would simply give up their dogmas, there would be nothing left about which to contend. Thus, God would be glorified. At this point, it is beneficial to be brutally honest in our observation of Scripture. In the Bible we find that doctrine (and particularly a purely defined gospel as doctrine) was the essential godly basis for any form of true spiritual unity:

> Only let your conversation be as it becometh the gospel of Christ: that whether I come and see you, or else be absent, I may hear of your affairs, that ye stand fast in one spirit, with one mind striving together for the faith of the gospel (Phil. 1:27).

This kind of unity can never occur when the advocates of different gospels are asked to declare a moratorium on their views of salvation in order to form a world-wide, unified, visible church. God knows that the differences among advocates of salvation by grace, salvation by sacraments, salvation by the Law of Moses, salvation by denominational affiliation, etc. are irreconcilable. This truth should not threaten the peace of a true saint.

Any attempt at unity without a clearly defined gospel of grace as the common denominator will not be a unity of God, but rather a uniformity of man. The words "division" and "contention" are part of God's definition of biblical unity. A local church needs to separate, or divide, from a gospel that cannot save, in order to unite under the gospel of Christ. Again, Paul told the brethren to *mark them which cause*

Does The Baptism Debate Needlessly Divide The Body Of Christ?

divisions and offences contrary to the doctrine which ye have learned; and avoid them (Rom. 16:17). The gospel truth is not only the primary basis of true unity among mortal brethren, it is always a source of contention and division. Paul said: *But we preach Christ, crucified, unto the Jews a stumblingblock, and unto the Greeks foolishness* (I Cor. 1:23). Again, Paul said: *As it is written, Behold, I lay in Sion a stumblingstone and a rock of offence: and whosoever believeth on him shall not be ashamed* (Rom. 9:33). The Apostle Peter said:

> Unto you therefore which believe he is precious: but unto them which be disobedient, the stone which the builders disallowed, the same is made the head of the corner, And a stone of stumbling, and a rock of offence... (I Pet. 2: 7, 8a).

People are often heard to boast that they do not preach doctrine, but rather, they only preach Jesus. The Holy Spirit said that all Scripture is *profitable for doctrine* (II Tim. 3:16). How then can we preach Jesus without preaching Scripture? The Bible describes Jesus as follows: *And they were astonished at his doctrine: for he taught them as one that had authority* (Mk. 1:22). The exclusiveness of the gospel has always caused division—*Jesus saith unto him, I am the way, the truth, and the life: no man cometh unto the Father, but by me* (Jn. 14:6); and—*For other foundation can no man lay than that is laid, which is Jesus Christ* (I Cor. 3:11); and...*for if ye believe not that I am he, ye shall die in your sins* (Jn. 8:24b); and finally, *Neither is there salvation in any other: for there is none other name under heaven given among men, whereby we must be saved* (Acts 4:12).

Paul wanted unity in the Corinthian church, but not one based on generic doctrine, or no doctrine at all—

> Now I beseech you, brethren, by the name of our Lord Jesus Christ, that ye all speak the same thing, and *that* there be no divisions among you; but *that* ye be perfectly joined together in the same mind and in the same judgment (I Cor. 1:10).

This kind of unity can only exist when the oneness of mind is grounded upon the doctrines of Christ and the apostles rather than upon personalities—

> For ye are yet carnal: for whereas there is among you envying, and strife, and divisions, are ye not carnal, and walk as men? For while one saith, I am of Paul; and another, I am of Apollos; are ye not carnal? (I Cor. 3:3, 4)

Not only is division between a true and a false gospel profitable, sometimes division between good brethren can be harnessed by God to multiply His work, as in the case when the missionary team of the Apostle Paul split apart over the issue of John Mark—

> And some days after Paul said unto Barnabas, Let us go again and visit our brethren in every city where we have preached the word of the Lord, *and see* how they do. And Barnabas determined to take with them John, whose surname was Mark. But Paul thought not good to take him with them, who departed from them from Pamphylia, and went not with them to the work. And the contention was so sharp between them, that they departed asunder one from the other: and so Barnabas took Mark, and sailed unto Cyprus; And Paul chose Silas, and departed, being recommended by the brethren unto the grace of God. And he went through Syria and Cilicia, confirming the churches (Acts 15:36-41).

Paul could even rejoice that the gospel was being preached by people who didn't like him at all:

> Some indeed preach Christ even of envy and strife; and some also of good will: The one preach Christ of contention, not sincerely, supposing to add affliction to my bonds: But the other of love, knowing that I am set for the defence of the gospel. What then? notwithstanding, every way, whether in pretence, or in truth, Christ is preached; and I therein do rejoice, yea, and will rejoice (Phil. 1:15-18).

Paul laid down several essential qualifications for biblical eldership, two of which were: to be doctrinally convincing and to be able to contend with the advocates of a false gospel (Titus 1:9-11). At

Does The Baptism Debate Needlessly Divide The Body Of Christ?

Philippi, Paul found it necessary to preach the *Gospel of God with much contention* (II Thess. 2:2b).

Paul commanded the Corinthians to make a separation between believers and unbelievers regarding partnership in the Lord's work—

> Be ye not unequally yoked together with unbelievers: for what fellowship hath righteousness with unrighteousness? and what communion hath light with darkness? (II Cor. 6:14).

Further still, the Apostle commanded separation between actual brethren, when one departed from apostolic tradition, or doctrine—

> Now we command you, brethren, in the name of our Lord Jesus Christ, that ye withdraw yourselves from every brother that walketh disorderly, and not after the tradition which he received of us (II Thess. 3:6).

Even in such a case as this, godly Christians must not regard such a brother as an enemy, but rather, as a victim of the enemy—

> And if any man obey not our word by this epistle, note that man, and have no company with him, that he may be ashamed. Yet count *him* not as an enemy, but admonish *him* as a brother (II Thess. 3:14, 15).

Godly Christians must not be intimidated by the unbiblical charge that such separation is *butchering the Body of Christ*.

When the Bible defines love, there is no surrender of truth. The real love of Christ *rejoices not in iniquity, but rejoiceth in the truth* (I Cor. 13:6). Paul said: *Let love be without dissimulation. Abhor that which is evil; cleave to that which is good* (Rom. 12:9). The godly Christian may never be more hated than he will be at the moment when a so-called *apostle of love* fails to persuade him to exchange the truth of the gospel for a mission to *unify the Body of Christ*.

Saints should take comfort in the fact that no amount of human failure will divide the unity of the invisible-universal family in Christ— *For we being many are one bread, and one body: for we are all partakers of that one bread* (I Cor. 10:17).[2] Paul explained that the purpose of apostolic revelation was, *that the Gentiles should be fellow heirs, and of the same body, and partakers of his promise in Christ by the Gospel* (Eph. 3:6). When the saint comes to the realization that the oneness of the universal body cannot be undone, the peace of God can then rule his heart—*And let the peace of God rule in your hearts, to the which also ye are called in one body, and be ye thankful* (Col. 3:15).

Regarding the transformation of the universal family into one functioning organization on earth, this will be accomplished only by Jesus Christ in the prophetic future. The wise and prudent Christian will know this as he contemplates the words of Paul:

> Having made known unto us the mystery of his will, according to his good pleasure which he hath purposed in himself: That in the dispensation of the fulness of times he might gather together in one all things in Christ, both which are in heaven, and which are on earth; even in him (Eph. 1:9, 10).

Prior to this prophetic event, the so-called *universal church* cannot be united into one functioning body on earth and a Christian should not dedicate his time grieving over the fact that this is not happening.

In many major cities it is a popular trend to organize a community-wide worship and praise meeting where Christ is exalted and magnified. Such meetings usually require that the differences in gospels and doctrines be declared insignificant stumbling-blocks to true worship. God's stamp of approval is declared either through the dynamic music program, or perhaps the demonstration of God's power through miracles. It is declared that God is rejoicing to see such unity in the Body of Christ. Those churches not participating are often referred to as *dissecting* the *Body of Christ*, or as having *amputated* themselves from the "*Body of Christ*." They are called *radical, fringe, bigots, out of the mainstream*, etc., but this charge must be put to a biblical test.

---

[2] The *One Bread* to which Paul was referring was Christ and His salvation for there were many partakers of this One Bread in the Corinthian church who should not have participated at the Lords Table because of unconfessed sin in their lives, and for this cause they were sick or dead for doing so (I Cor. 11:2, 30).

Does The Baptism Debate Needlessly Divide The Body Of Christ?

All of the attributes of God, combined and focused, will not justify and save one sinner from eternal condemnation, apart from the crucifixion of Christ as the only source of redeeming grace. This means that the preaching of the simple gospel of Jesus Christ is the greatest demonstration of God's power that can be displayed on earth today—

> For I am not ashamed of the gospel of Christ: for it is the power of God unto salvation to every one that believeth; to the Jew first, and also to the Greek (Rom. 1:16).

> For the preaching of the cross is to them that perish foolishness; but unto us which are saved it is the power of God (I Cor. 1:18).

> For our gospel came not unto you in word only, but also in power, and in the Holy Ghost, and in much assurance; as ye know what manner of men we were among you for your sake (I Thess. 1:5).

God help any of us if we think that we can call an ecumenical meeting and perform a greater demonstration of God's power than the preaching of the one true gospel of pure grace. If we could fling another milkyway across the other side of the heavens, this would not be a greater demonstration of divine power than the simple preaching of the cross. The cross of Christ was the greatest demonstration of God's love for mankind, and, at the same time, the greatest demonstration of God's hatred for the sin of mankind.

The true purpose of worship is that of glorifying God through exaltation, magnification, service, and praise. There are many forms through which this may be done, but one method is ultimately more effective than all others. Paul said of himself and his companions that God had *made us able ministers of the new covenant* which places emphasis on the clear plan of salvation (II Cor. 3:6). The Apostle explained that the Old Covenant glorified God so much that Moses had to vail his face in order to keep from blinding the people when he brought the Law of Moses to them (II Cor. 3:7, 13). But Paul said that the New Covenant glorifies God much more than the Old (II Cor. 3:9). In fact, the gospel excels the glory of the Old Covenant so much that it is almost as if the Old did not glorify God at all—

> For even that which was made glorious had no glory in this respect, by reason of the glory that excelleth. For if that which is done away *was* glorious, much more that which remaineth *is* glorious. Seeing then that we have such hope, we use great plainness of speech (II Cor. 3:10-12).

This means that if the entire human race joined hands and began to recite words of worship, magnification, exaltation, and glorification to God, they could be totally excelled by one man correctly, clearly, and compassionately pronouncing the gospel of the grace of Christ to a lost soul. God help us if we think that we have discovered a better way to worship and glorify You. God help us if we think that we can lay the truth of the gospel aside in order to unite the *universal Body of Christ* in a *true ecumenical worship service*. Jesus Christ exclaimed:

> But the hour cometh, and now is, when the true worshippers shall worship the Father in spirit and in truth: for the Father seeketh such to worship him. God *is* a Spirit: and they that worship him must worship *him* in spirit and in truth (Jn. 4:23, 24).

Rather than spending time and revenue on projects to organize the *Universal Church* on earth, the saint should leave that subject to prophetic fulfillment and seek to unite with a local assembly that is the most thoroughly bound to the doctrine of Jesus Christ from the Scripture, and not afraid of division resulting from the purity of a clear gospel. The Apostle John said:

> Whosoever transgresseth, and abideth not in the doctrine of Christ, hath not God. He that abideth in the doctrine of Christ, he hath both the Father and the Son. If there come any unto you, and bring not this doctrine, receive him not into *your* house, neither bid him God speed: For he that biddeth him God speed is partaker of his evil deeds (II Jn. 9-11).

John's reference to *doctrine of Christ* means primarily the gospel of Christ. Saints do not have to be in agreement on every doctrine of the NT in order to be in fellowship and communion with one another.

Does The Baptism Debate Needlessly Divide The Body Of Christ?

Taking the good news of God's saving grace to every human being is the task of every believer. If we hear of this being accomplished in another group which is not in partnership with us locally, forbid them not, but follow the example of Christ—

> And John answered and said, Master, we saw one casting out devils in thy name; and we forbad him, because he followeth not with us. And Jesus said unto him, Forbid *him* not: for he that is not against us is for us (Lk. 9:49, 50).

Christ did not seek them out to form a unified organization on earth, but rather rejoiced that they were out there, at least doing part of the job right. We are to thank God for anyone who preaches the gospel of grace correctly and clearly, but we are to seek organic unity with brethren who desire to carry out the entire Great Commission (Matt. 28:18-20).

Though the invisible *family of Christ* is universal, and individual earthly members of that entity have been spiritually gifted for ministry (Eph. 4:7; I Cor. 12:7; I Pet. 4:10), the use of these gifts were to be governed by the local/visible church on earth. But the visible church on earth is the local self-governing church. A visible church in one city cannot have jurisdiction over the order and government of a visible church in another city. If a woman in the Corinthian church had the gift of prophecy, order required that she have her head covered while prophesying (I Cor. 11:5). If a member of the Corinthian church had the gift of tongues, he was not to use it while someone else was speaking in tongues, and then only when an interpreter was present (I Cor. 14:27, 28). These gifts were to be regulated by the local church so that all things would be done *unto edifying* (I Cor. 14: 26b), and *decently and in order* (I Cor. 14:39b). Earl Radmacher notes:

> The word *order* occurs four times in connection with the proper direction and control of church affairs. Twice it is used in relation to the regulation of the service of worship by the church (cf. I Cor. 11:34; 14:40) and twice it is used in connection with the organization of the church (cf. Col. 2:5; Titus 1:5). The Greek term for order is *taxis* from the verb *tasso*. It was primarily a military term which was in common use to express the most precise and exact order. It was

commonly used of "drawing up in rank and file, order or disposition of an army." Again, it was the "battle array, order of battle." This order is to be evidenced in their use of spiritual gifts and in the application of the principles of church government...

The principle of order in the use of the gifts was applied by Paul to the Corinthian Church because of their disorderly use of one of the gifts. He rebuked them for their self-elation because of the possession of special gifts and for the confusion occasioned thereby in the services of the church. He reminds them that "God is not the author of confusion, but of peace, as in all the churches of the saints" (I Cor. 14:33)...

Behind all of these statements one can see the symmetry, beauty, decorum, and orderliness of the body of Christ which is to have its manifestation in local churches, especially with regard to the use of the gifts...[3]

That these gifts are primarily for the edification of saints in the local-visible church (Eph. 4:11, 12) is evident in the fact that earthly saints do not have a ministry of edification to dead and departed saints in heaven, of whom most of the so-called *universal Church* is comprised. Therefore, no one is the bishop, elder or pastor of the uiversal church. The universal church does not have a human government on earth with a capital city and jurisdiction over all local churches in the world.

Church historians will remember when the medieval church attempted to govern world Christendom as a universal-visible body. Pope Gregory VII (1073-1085) issued the *Dictatus Papae* ("Dictate of the Pope") claiming:

> That the Roman pontiff alone can with right be called universal.
> That he alone may use the imperial insignia.

---

[3] Earl D. Radmacher, *The Nature Of The Church* (Portland Oregan: Western Baptist Press, 1972), pp. 348, 349.

That of the pope alone all princes shall kiss the feet.
That it may be permitted to him to depose emperors.
That he himself may be judged by no one.
That he who is not at peace with the Roman Church shall not be considered catholic.
That he may absolve subjects from their fealty to wicked men.[4]

When the mortal-visible church on earth is declared to be the universal church with one baptism, then the baptism of the Spirit and ritual baptism are considered to be the same incident (cf. Acts 10:47). Thus, if the "universal governor" of the visible church on earth could withhold the *sacraments* from a "Christian", he could shut that person out of heaven. In the medieval church, when one was excommunicated and anathematized he was indeed barred from heaven's gates. This is what occurred in the clash with Gregory VII and Henry IV. Gregory excommunicated Henry, deposed him, and absolved his subjects from their oaths of allegiance. Thus, Henry's German nobles revolted and Henry was consigned to eternal hell by the governor of the *"universal church."* In January, 1077 Henry appeared before Gregory at a castle in the Apennines called Canossa. There, he stood barefoot in the snow for three days, begging forgiveness until Gregory said: *We loosed the chain of the anathema and at length received him into the favor and communion and into the lap of the Holy Mother Church.*[5]

If the visible church on earth is the universal *Body of Christ* with a human government, then Gregory VII was correct. But he was incorrect. When order and government is given to Christians on earth, the jurisdiction is within a local church. A spiritually gifted saint does not have a divine right to take the platform of just any church and then order the pastor to stand down. Spiritual gifts are not ordered by a human governor of the universal church, but by the jurisdiction of the local church. God does not today grant individual saints a divine jurisdiction to impose themselves at will upon any local church.

---

[4] Harry J. Carroll, Jr., *et al., The Development of Civilization: A Documentary History of Politics, Society, and Thought*, I (Chicago: Scott, Foresman and Co., 1961), pp. 382-383.

[5] Quoted in J. H. Robinson, *Readings in European History*, I (Boston: Ginn and Co., 1904), p. 144.

Therefore, we must reject the charge made by some that we are placing ourselves outside the universal church, and therefore outside of salvation itself, if we refuse to submit to the ecumenical movement with its generic, pluralistic gospel. The evangelism of John the Baptist, Jesus Christ and the apostles required the turning away from a false gospel in order to embrace the saving gospel. Adding the finished work of Christ to the belief that circumcision and the Mosaic Law will save is not the gospel of Christ. We cannot present a saving gospel by adding Christ to the belief in reincarnation, the five pillars of the faith of Islam, the worship of the gods of the pantheon, etc. One must embrace the grace and mercy of God provided by the finished work of Christ alone—*Looking unto Jesus the author and finisher of our faith* (Heb. 12:2a).

We have purposely avoided a discussion of the debate regarding mode of baptism. Though this is an important issue, we have focused on discerning the gospel of grace, which does not include ritual baptism under any mode. Our baptism is not designed to instruct us to embrace Christ by faith, it is our profession that we have already been instructed and have embraced Christ by faith.

We conclude this chapter with an exhortation to the reader to make certain that he/she has laid aside any hope that personal righteousness, sacraments, church membership, etc. will contribute anything to his/her right to possess eternal life. His/her faith must have at some moment been directed away from that which cannot save to salvation by grace accomplished solely by the finished work of Christ on the cross. This must be understood as a 100 percent free gift. The only thing we contribute is our sin. In fact, we did not even contribute that for it was taken from us by Christ and the penalty of it born by Him on His cross. This gift of forgiveness of sin and eternal life is a standing offer to anyone who will receive it by faith from the Lord. The moment you realize you are morally and spiritually bankrupt before God and say *yes* to His offer of this free gift, you have the promise that it is yours forever (I Jn. 5:13). If this has not happened to you, follow Him by receiving that unspeakable gift at this very moment—

> My sheep hear my voice, and I know them, and they follow me: And I give unto them eternal life; and they shall never perish, neither shall any *man* pluck them out of my hand. My Father, which gave *them* me, is greater than all; and no *man* is able to pluck *them* out of my Father's hand (Jn. 10:27-29).

BIBLIOGRAPHY

BIBLIOGRAPHY

Alexander, Carlyle J., *The Christian Church and Liberty*, London: J. Clarke, 1924.

American State Papers on Religious Freedom, Washington D. C.: Review and Herald Publishing.

Ante-Nicene Fathers, The: The Writings of the Fathers down to A.D. 325, (10 Vols.), The Rev. Alexander Roberts, D.D. And James Donaldson, LL.D., Editors, Revised and Chronologically Arranged, With Brief Prefaces And Occasional Notes, by A. Cleveland Coxe, D.D., Grand Rapids, Michigan: Wm. B. Eerdmans Publishing Company, 1977.

Aprcrypha, King James Version.

Aquinas, St. Thomas, *Of God And His Creatures: An Annotated Translation of the SVMMA Contra Gentiles*, Translated by Joseph Rickaby S.J., Westminister, Maryland: The Carroll Press, 1950.

Aquinas, St. Thomas, *The Summa Theologica*, (Vol. III), Literally translated by Fathers of the English Dominican Province, New York: Benziger Brothers, 1914.

Aramaic Bible, The: The Targums, twelve volumes. Project Director, Martin Mc Namara, M.S.C., Collegeville, Minnesota: The Liturgical Press, 1992, [separate volumes have distinct publication dates].

Bailey, Thomas A. & Kennedy, David M., *The American Pageant: A History of the Republic*, Eighth Edition, Lexington, Massachusetts: D. C. Heath and Company, 1987.

Barth, Karl, *Church Dogmatics: The Doctrine of Reconciliation*, (Vol. IV), Editors: Rev. G. W. Bromiley, Ph.D., D.Litt. and Rev. Prof. T. F. Torrance, D.D., D.Theol., Edinburgh: T. & T. Clark, 1980.

Barth, Karl, *The Christian Life (Fragment): Baptism as the Foundation of the Christian Life* (*Church Dogmatic*, Vol. IV), Edinburgh: T. & T. Clark, 1969.

Bates, M. Searle, *Religious Liberty: An Inquiry*, New York: International Missionary Council, 1945.

Beard, Charles A. and Mary R., *The Rise of American Civilization*, (Vol. I), New York: The Macmillan Co., 1947.

Bible Knowledge Commentary, The: New Testament Edition, John F. Walvoord & Roy B. Zuck, Editors, USA: Victor Books, 1983.

Bing, Charles C., *Lordship Salvation: A Biblical Evaluation and Response* [Th.D. Dissertation: Dallas Theological Seminary], Burleson, TX: GraceLife Ministries, 1992.

Blackstone, William, *Blackstone's Commentaries On The Law*, Edited by Bernard C. Gavit, Dean, Indiana University School of Law, Washington, D. C.: Washington Law Book Co., 1941.

Bruce, F. F., *Second Thoughts on the Dead Sea Scrolls*, Great Britain: Paternoster Press, 1966.

Burrows, Miller, *Burrows on the Dead Sea Scrolls*, (Vol. 2) Grand Rapids, Michigan: Baker Book House, 1978.

Calvin, John, *Institutes of the Christian Religion* (Vol. II) Grand Rapids, Michigan: Wm. B. Eerdmans Publishing Company, 1972.

Cambridge History Of The Bible: From the Beginnings to Jerome, The, (Vol. I), P. R. Ackroyd And C. F. Evens, Editors, Cambridge: Cambridge University Press, 1970.

Carroll, Harry J. Jr., *The Development of Civilization: A Documentary History of Politics, Society, and Thought*, I, Chicago: Scott, Foresman And Co., 1961.

Carson, Alexander, *Baptism: Its Mode and Subjects*, Grand Rapids, Michigan: Kregel Publications.

Chafer, Lewis Sperry, *Systematic Theology*, Dallas, Texas: Dallas Seminary Press, 1964.

Chantry, Walter J., *Today's Gospel—Authentic or Synthetic*, London: The Banner Of Truth Trust, 1972.

Christian, John T., *A History Of Baptists*, (Vol. I), Texarkana, Ark.-Tex.: Bogard Press, 1922.

Cobb, Sanford H., *The rise of Religious Liberty in America*, New York: The Macmillan Co., 1902.

Creeds of Christendom, The: With a History and Critical Notes, (Vol. III *The Evangelical Protestant Creeds*), Philip Schaff, Editor; Revised by David S. Schaff, Grand Rapids, Michigan: Baker Books, 1983.

Creeds of Christendom, The: With a History and Critical Notes, (Vol. I, History of the Creeds; Vol. II, *The Greek and Latin Creeds*), Philip Schaff, Editor; Revised by David S. Schaff, Grand Rapids, Michigan: Baker Books, 1996.

Cross, Frank M., *Library of Ancient Qumran And Modern Biblical Studies*, Garden City, New York: Doubleday & Company, Inc., 1958.

Dictionary Of The Ecumenical Movement, Grand Rapids: WCC Publications, Geneva—William B. Eerdmans Publishing Company, 1991.

Dillow, Joseph C., *The Reign of the Servant Kings: A Study of Eternal Security and the Final Significance of Man*, Hayesville, NC: Schoettle Publishing Co, 1993.

Eaton, Michael, *No Condemnation: A New Theology of Assurance*, Downers Grove, IL: InterVarsity Press, 1995.

Edwards, Johathan, *The Works of Johathan Edwards* (Vol. III), Albany, Or: AGES Software (Version 1.0), 1997.

Encyclopedia Judaica Jerusalem (Vol. 13) Jerusalem, Israel: Keter Publishing House Jerusalem Ltd., 1972.

Encyclopedia Judaica Jerusalem, Jerusalem, Israel: Keter Publishing House Jerusalem Ltd., 1971.

Encyclopedia of Judaism, The, Geoffrey Wigoder, Editor-In-Chief, New York: Collier Macmillan Publishers, 1989.

Encyclopedia of Religion and Ethics, Ed., James Hastings (Vol. 2), New York: Charles Scribner's Sons.

Errett, Isaac, *Our Position*, Cincinnati, Ohio: The Standard Publishing Company.

Ferrar, Frederic W., *History of Interpretation*, Grand Rapids, Michigan: Baker Book House, 1979.

Ferrar, Frederic W., D.D., F.R.S., *The Life and Work of St. Paul*, London: Cassell & Company, Limited, 1884.

Friesen, Gary, *Decision Making and the Will of God*, Portland: Multnomah Publications, 1980.

Fundamentals For Today, The, Charles L. Feinberg, Editor, Grand Rapids, Michigan: Kregel Publications, 1964.

Geisler, Norman L. and Nix, William E., *A General Introduction to the Bible*, Chicago: Moody Press, 1968.

Gerstner, J., *A Primer on Justification*, New Jersey: Presbyterian & Reformed, 1983.

Gill, John, D. D., *Exposition: The New Testament* (Vol. 2), London: William Hill Collingridge, 1852.

Graetz, Heinrich Hirsch, *History of the Jews*, Vol. II: *From the Reign of Hyrcanus (135 B.C.E.) to the Completion of the Babylonian Talmud (500 C.E)*, Philadelphia: Jewish Publication Society of America, 1893.

Harper, R. F., T*he Code of Hammurabi*, Chicago: University of Chicago Press, 1904.

Hodge, Charles, *Systematic Theology* (Vol. III), Grand Rapids, Michigan: Wm. B. Eerdmans Publishing Company, 1977.

Hodges, Zane C., *Absolutely Free*, Grand Rapids, Academie Books, Zondervan Publishing House, 1989.

Hodges, Zane, *The Gospel Under Seige*, Dallas, TX: Redencion Viva, 1992.

Holy Bible King James Version.

Horton, Michael S., *Beyond Culture Wars: Is America a Mission Field or Battlefield?*, Chicago: Moody Press, 1994.

Horton, Michael, *In The Face Of God*, Dallas: Word Publishing, 1996.

Interpreter's Dictionary of the Bible, The, (Vol. 1), New York: Abingdon Press, 1962.

Jamieson, Fausset & Brown, *Commentary On The Whole Bible*, Grand Rapids, Michigan: Zondervan Publishing House, 1961.

Jewish Proselytism at the Time of Christian Origins: Chimera or Reality, in Journal for the Study of the New Testament, Francis Watson, Editor, Sheffield, England: Sheffield Accademic Press, 62, 1996.

Josephus, Complete Works, (*Antiquities*, Books XIII, XX), William Whiston: translator, Grand Rapids, Michigan: Kregel Publications, 1966.

Klausner, Joseph, *Jesus of Nazareth: His Life, Times, and Teaching*, Boston: Beacon Press, 1964.

Kramer, S. N., *From the Tablets of Sumer*, Indian Hills, Colorado: The Falcon's Wing Press, 1956.

Lasor, William Sanford, *Discovering What Jewish Miqvoat Can Tell Us About Christian Baptism*, Biblical Archaeological Review, January/February, 1987.

Learsi, Rufus, *Israel: A History of the Jewish People*, Cleaveland: World Publishing Company, 1949.

Living Bible, The: Paraphrased, Wheaton, Illinois: Tyndale House Publishers , 1971.

Luther, Martin, *A Commentary on St. Paul's Epistle to the Galatians: Based on Lectures Delivered at the University of Wittenberg in the Year 1531 and First Published in 1535*, London: James Clarke & Co. LTD., 1956.

Luther's Works: Church and Ministry II, (Vol. 40), Conrad Beregendoff, Editor; Helmut T Lehmann, General Editor, Philadelphia: Muhlenberg Press, 1958.

Luther's Works: Church and ministry III, (Vol. 41) Eric W. Gritsch, Editor; Helmut T. Lehmann, General Editor, Philadelphia: Fortress Press, 1966.

Luther's Works: Lectures on Genesis, (Vol. 3), Jeroslav Pelikan, Ed., St. Louis: Concordia Publishing House, 1961.

Luther's Works: Table Talk, (Vol. 54),Theodore G. Tappert, Editor/Translator; Helmut T. Lehmann, General Editor, Philadelphia: Fortress Press, 1967.

Luther's Works: Word And Sacrament, IV, (Vol. 38), Martin E. Lehmann, Editor; Helmut T. Lehmann, General Editor, Philadelphia: Fortress Press, 1971.

MacArthur, John F., *Faith Works: The Gospel According to the Apostles*, Dallas: Word Publishing, 1993.

MacArthur, John F., *The Gospel According to Jesus*, Grand Rapids: Zondervan Publishing House, 1989.

Maimonides, Code of: Book Ten, the Book of Cleanness, transl., Herbert Danby, New Haven: Yale University Press, 1954.

Massachusetts *Body of liberties* (December 10, 1641, Sections 58, 59, 94) in Richard L. Perry, *Sources Of Our Liberties*, Chicago: American Bar Foundation, 1959.

McBrien, Richard P., *Catholicism* [Study Edition], Minneapolis, MN: Winston Press, Inc., 1981.

Moore, George Foot, *Judaism in the First Centuries of the Christian Era: The Age of the Tannaim*, (Vol. 1), Cambridge: Harvard University Press, 1927.

Morris, Henry M., *Defenders Study Bible: King James Version*, Grand Rapids, Michigan: Word Publishing, 1995.

Myers, Gustavus, *History of Bigotry in the United States*, New York: Random House, 1943.

New Dictionary Of Theology, Sinclair B. Ferguson, David F. Wright, Editors; J. I. Packer, Conculting Editor, Downers Grove, Illinois: InterVarsity Press, 1988.

New Standard Jewish Encyclopedia, The, New York-Oxford: Facts On File, 1992.

Nicene And Post-Nicene Fathers Of The Christian Church, A Select Library Of The, (First Series, 14 Vols), Philip Schaff, D.D., LL.D., Editor, Grand Rapids, Michigan: Wm. B. Eerdmans Publishing Company, 1974.

Nicene And Post-Nicene Fathers Of The Christian Church, A Select Library Of, (Second Series, 14 Vols.), Philip Schaff, D.D., And Henry Wace, D. D., Editors, Translated Into English With Prolegomena and Explanatory Notes, Grand Rapids, Michigan, Wm. B. Eerdmans Publishing Company, 1979.

Our Sunday Visitor's Catholic Encyclopedia, Rev. Peter M. J. Stravinskas, Ph.D., S.T.L., Editor, Huntington, Indiana: Our Sunday Visitor Publishing Division, Inc., 1991.

Oxford Dictionary of the Jewish Religion, The, R. J. Zwi Werblowsky and Geofrey Wigodor, Editors New York: Oxford University Press, 1997.

Packer, J. I., *Concise Theology: A Guide to Historic Christian Beliefs*, Wheaton, Illinois: Tyndale House Publishers, Inc., 1993.

Packer, J. I., *Growing in Christ*, Wheaton, Illinois: Crossway Books, 1994.

Packer, J. I., *I Want to Be a Christian*, Wheaton, Illinois: Tyndale House Publishers, Inc., 1977.

Pentecost, J. Dwight, *Thy Kingdom Come: Tracing God's Kingdom Program And Covenant Promises Throughout History,* Grand Rapids Michigan: Kregel Publications, 1995.

Pfeffer, Leo, *Church, State, and Freedom*, Boston: The Beacon Press, 1953.

Philo, The Works of: Complete And Updated; Translated by C.C. Younge, Peabody, Massachusetts: Hendrickson Publishers, 1993.

Polishook, Irwin H., *Roger Williams, John Cotton and Religious Freedom: A Controversy in New and Old England*, Englewood Cliffs, New Jersy: Prentice-Hall, Inc., 1967.

Potter, Dr. Charles F., *Did Jesus Write This Book?*, Greenwich, Conn.: Fawcett Publications, Inc., 1967.

Potter, The Rev. Dr. Charles Francis, *The Lost Years of Jesus Revealed*, Greenwich, Conn.: Fawcett Publications, 1966.

Pseudepigrapha, The Old Testament: Expansions of the "Old Testament" and Legends, Wisdom and Philosophical Literature, Prayers, Psalms, and Odes, Fragments of Lost Judeo-Hellenistic Works, James H. Charlesworth, Editor, (Vol. 2, Book of Jubilees), Garden City, New York: Doubleday & Company, Inc., 1985.

Radmacher, Earl D., *The Nature Of The Church*, Portland, Oregan: Western Baptist Press, 1972.

Robinson, J. H., *Readings In European History*, I, Boston: Ginn And Co., 1904.

Ryrie, Charles C., *Basic Theology: A Popular Systematic Guide To Understanding Biblical Truth*, USA: Victor Books, 1987.

Ryrie, Charles C., *So Great Salvation: What It Means To Believe In Jesus Christ*, USA: Victor Books, a Division of Scripture Press Publications Inc., 1989.

Schaff, Philip, *Companion to the Greek Testament and the English Version*, Revised Edition, New York: Harper Brothers, 1883.

Schaff, Philip, *History of the Christian Church* (Vols. III & VIII), Grand Rapids, Michigan: Wm. B. Eerdmans Publishing Company, 1972.

Schaff-Herzog Encyclopedia of Religious Knowledge, The New, (Vol. VI), Samuel Macauley Jackson, D. D., LL. D., Editor in Chief, Grand Rapids, Michigan: Baker Book House, 1950.

Schonfield, Dr. Hugh J., *The Passover Plot: A New Interpretation of the Life and Death of Jesus*, New York: Bantam Books, 1967.

Schurer, Emil, D.D., M.A., *A History of the Jewish People in the Time of Jesus Christ*, (First Division, Vol I.)Translated by Rev. John Macpherson, M.A., U.S.A.: Hendrickson Publishers, Inc., 1998.

Schurer, Emil, D.D., M.A., *A History of the Jewish People in the Times of Jesus Christ*, (Division II, Vol. 2), Edinburgh: T & T Clark, 1901.

Shulman, Albert M., *Gateway to Judaism: An Encyclopedic Guide to the Doctrines, Ceremonies, Customs, Languages, and Community Life of the Jews*, (Vols. I, II.) South Brunswick: Thomas Yoseloff, 1971.

Sproul, R. C., *Willing to Believe: The Controversy Over Free Will*, Grand Rapids: Baker Books, 1997.

Sproul, R.C., *Now That's A Good Question*, Wheaton, Illinois: Tyndale House Publishers, 1996.

Stokes, Anson Phelps, *Church and State in the United States*, New York: Harper and Brothers, 1950.

Strong, Agustus Hopkins, *Systematic Theology*, (Three Volumes in One), Valley Forge, Pa.: The Judson Press, 1969.

Sweet, William Warren, *Religion in Colonial America*, New York: Charles Scribner's Sons, 1941.

Theissen, Henry Clarence, *Introductory Lectures In Systematic Theology*, Grand Rapids, Michigan: Wm. B. Eerdmans Publishing Company, 1971.

Twersky, Isadore, *Introduction to the Code of Maimonides (Mishneh Torah)*, New Haven: Yale University Press, 1980.

Vatican II, The Documents of, Walter M. Abbott, S.J. and Joseph Gallagher, Editors, New York: Guild Press, 1966.

Wace, Henry and Bucheim, C. A., *Luther's primary works*, Philadelphia: Lutheran Publication Society, 1885.

Warfield, Benjamin, *The Works of Benjamin Warfield:* And *Studies in Theology*, (Vol. IX), Grand Rapids, Michigan: Baker Book House, 1932.

Warfield, Benjamin, *The Works of: Studies In Tertullian And Augustine* (Vol. IV), Grand Rapids, Michigan: Baker Book House, 1981.

Wellum, Stephen J., *The Compromised Church*, John H. Armstrong, Editor, Wheaton, Illinois: Crossway Books, 1998.

Wesley, Works of, [*Sermons*, Vol. III, Third Edition, Complete And Unabridged], Grand Rapids, Michigan: Baker Book House, 1984.

Wesley, Works of, [*Sermons*, Vol. V Complete And Unabridged], Peabody, Massachusetts: Hendrickson Publishers, Inc., 1994.

Wesley, Works of, [*Sermons*, Vol. VI], Grand Rapids, Michigan: Baker Book House, 1978.

Wesley, Works of, [*Addresses and Essays*, Vol. VIII], Grand Rapids, Michigan: Baker Book House, 1978.

Wilmington, Dr. H. L., *Wilmington's Guide to the Bible,* Wheaton, Illinois: Tyndale House Publishers, Inc., 1984.

Wilson, Edmund, *The Scrolls from the Dead Sea*, New York: Oxford University Press, 1955.

Zdrodowski, Rev. Francis J., M.A., S.T.L., *The Concept of Heresy According to Cardinal Hosius: A Dissertation Submitted to the Faculty of the School of Sacred Theology of the Catholic University of America in Partial Fulfillment of the Requirements for the Degree of Doctor of Sacred Theology*, Washington, D. C.: The Catholic University of America Press, 1947.

INDEX OF SCRIPTURE REFERENCES

A
Acts 10:36, 37, 407
Acts 10:43, 105, 437
Acts 10:43, 44, 241, 491
Acts 16:14, 15, 232
Acts 19:4, 406
Acts 2:38, 410, 411
Acts 22:14-16, 199, 200
Acts 8:15, 16, 403

C
Col. 1:9, 385
Col. 2:11, 12, 175
Col. 2:11-14, 434
Colossians 2:11, 12, 174

E
Eph. 1:9, 10, 498
Eph. 4:1, 394
Eph. 5:25, 26, 417, 418, 419
Eph. 5:26, 207

G
Gal. 3:27, 415, 416, 417
Gal. 3:8, 72

I
I Cor. 1:14-18, 203
I Cor. 2:14, 386
I Cor. 7:14, 237
I Jn. 2:20, 377
I Jn. 5:13, 504
I Pet. 3:18-22, 424, 425, 426
II Chron. 6:8, 9, 389
II Pet. 2:6-9, 74
II Sam. 12, 235
II Timothy 2:2, 346
Isa. 30:20, 21, 383

J
James 4:13-16, 380
Jn. 10:27-29, 504
Jn. 14:26, 343
Jn. 6:28, 29, 462
John 3:5, 334, 335, 336, 337

M
Mk. 16:16, 401, 403, 404
Mt. 18:10, 217
Mtt. 19:14, 218
Mtt. 28:19, 223

P
Prov. 3:5, 387
Ps. 119:105, 380
Ps. 2:8, 388

R
Rom. 11:16, 236
Rom. 12:2, 384
Rom. 6:5, 435
Rom. 8:16, 373
Romans 8:14, 382
Titus 3:5, 422, 423, 424

INDEX OF SUBJECTS

Aathanasius, 231
Abel, 66
Abraham, 69-79, 154
Abrahamic covenant, 56, 161
The Acts Of Xanthippe And Polyxena, 287
Adam and Eve, 65
Agrippa, 109
Albigenses, 224
allegorization, 120
Ambrose, 259, 291
Anabaptists, 178, 243, 270, 316
analogy, 370
anathema, 252, 318
Anglican Church, 320
anointing, 390
Anonymous Bishop, 279
Anonymous Treatise On Re-baptism, 280
anti-kalakhists, 126
antinomian, 450
antitupon, 425
Apocryphal writings, 114
Apostles' Creed, 263
apostolic tradition, 341
application, 396
Aquinas, Thomas, 224, 314
Archelaus, 352
Arles, council of, 274
Augsburg, Peace of, 226
Augustine, 223, 259, 294, 315, 367

Balthasar Hubmaier, 214
baptism of repentance, 140
baptism of the Holy Spirit, 206
Baptists, 182, 210, 320, 330
Baptizo, 184
Barnabas, Epistle of, 121, 266
Basil, 123
belief, 278, 400
believer's baptism, 176, 191, 209, 216, 217, 219, 230, 243, 245, 253

Blackstone, William, Sir, 230
Body of Christ, 484
Book of Jubilees, 152
Book of Traditions, 117
burden of the Lord, 395

call of Abraham, 155, 235
call to the ministry, 391
Calvin, 176, 226, 304, 317
Calvin, John, 104, 174, 231, 261, 474
Campbell, Alexander, 329
Campbell, Thomas, 329
canon, 341
Cardinal Hosius Stanislos, 261
carnal Christian, 466
Carson, Alexander, 192
Carthage, Seventh Council of, 257
Cathari, 274
ceremonial law, 33
cheap grace, 453
Chrysostom, John, 258, 291
church discipline, 469
Church of England, 227
Churches of Christ, 330
circumcision, 1-30, 70, 149-170, 186-207, 216, 220, 233
circumcisional regeneration, 150
circumstantial guidance, 392
Clarke, John, 320
Clement of Alexandria, 59, 255, 267, 339
Clement of Rome, 343
coherence, 366, 400
combination of criteria, 363
consensus, 364
Constitutions Of The Holy Apostles, 288
contention, 494
contradictions, 371, 465
covenant of circumcision, 150, 161, 235
covenant of grace, 167

covenant of redemption, 61
Crandall, John, 320
Creed in Ignatius, 264
Cromwell, Oliver, 227
Cyprian, 123, 167, 210, 257, 269, 351

Daniel, 97
David, 92, 93, 94, 95, 96, 97, 98, 99, 100, 101, 364
Davidic Covenant, 454
Dead Sea Scrolls, 127
Decian persecution, 273
Dionysius bishop of Alexandria, 286
Disciples of Christ, 330
disciples of John the Baptist, 244, 405
discipleship, 464
disobedience, 446
dispensation of John, 144
dispensationalism, 110
division, 487
divisiveness, 493
doctrine, 495
Dutch Reformed Church, 230
dynamis, 340

easy believism, 453
edification, 502
Edwards, Johnathan, 221
efficacious grace, 442
eis, 413
election, 449, 455
Emperor Constantine, 259
Emperor Theodosius, 259
Enoch, 67
Enos, 66
Essene, 127
Essene baptism, 134
Ethiopian Eunuch, 143
Eusebius of Caesarea, 289
excommunication, 275
exousia, 340

faithfulness, 443

false prophets, 485
family of God, 489
feeling, 360
Felix, 108
filth of the flesh, 424
flesh, 445
free-grace preachers, 453
fruits of the Spirit, 358
Fundamentalism, 330

gifts of the Spirit, 358
gospel of circumcision, 314
Governor Endecott, 321
Gregory of Nazainzen, 290
Gregory of Nyssa, 290
Gregory the Great, 292

halakhic interpretations, 126
Hammurabi, code of, 39
Hebrew Text, 354
Henry IV, 503
Henry VIII, 227
Hermas, 267
Hierarchy of Authority, 119, 126
Hillell, 117
Hippolytus, 135
Hittite code, 40
holiness, 444
Holmes, Obadiah, 320
Holy Spirit convictions, 376, 395
Horton, Michael S., 186
Huguenots, 227
Hutchinson, Ann, 229

Ignatius, 265, 344
illumination, 267, 355, 380
independent Christian churches, 330
infant baptism, 209, 211-213, 215-217, 219-260
inheritance of salvation, 479
inheritance of the Abrahamic Covenant, 477
inheritance of the Mosaic Covenant, 477

inheriting the kingdom of God, 480
instinct, 364
interpretation, 354
interpreting signs., 392
intuition, 361
Irenaeus, 167, 268, 344
irresistible grace, 447
Isaac, 74, 76
Isaiah, 98

Jerome, 123, 259, 293
Jerusalem Council, 14
Jerusalem, Council of, 409
Jesus Only Pentecostal movement, 209
Job, 77
John the Baptist, 65, 105-118, 120-123, 125-128, 130, 131, 133-135, 137-141, 143, 145, 146, 148, 196, 215, 254
John's baptism, 112-118, 120-123, 125- 128, 130, 131, 133-135, 137-141, 143, 145, 146, 148, 431
joint-heirship with Christ, 479
Joseph and Mary, 99
Josephus, 114, 131, 134
Joshua, 91
Judah Hakkadosh, 117
judicial law, 35
Judith, 114
Justinian Code, 40

Karaites, 126
kerygma, 349, 352
King Agrippa, 248

Laodicea, Synod of, 293
lapsi, 274
Law of Moses, 8-30
The Law of the Twelve Tables, 40
leading of the Spirit, 373
lordship of Christ, 469
Lot, 74
Louis XIV, 227

Luther, 225, 234, 239, 244, 316, 475
Luther, Martin, 177, 208, 213, 444, 460
Lydia, 232

Maccabees, I, 151
Maccabees, II, 6:10, 151
Maimonides, Code of, 119
Marcion, 351
Martyr, Justin, 8, 122, 175, 266
Massachusetts *Body of liberties*, 227
means of grace, 191, 327
Melanchthon, 225
Melchizedek, 75
Methodius, 287
Mishna, 114
Mishnah, 121
mode of baptism, 504
moral law, 33
mortify the flesh, 451
Mosaic Law, 31-57
Moses, 79-92
Muncer, Thomas of Mulhausen, 367
mystical universal-invisible Body of Christ, 489

Nantes, Edict of, 227
Napoleonic code, 40
natural law, 39
Nazianzen, Gregory, 123
New Covenant, 45
Nicea, Council of, 259
Nicene Creed, 266
Nicodemus, 335
Noah, 67, 425
Novation, 273
Novationists, 252, 274
obedience, 452
Old Testament Pseudepigrapha, 152
Origen, 122, 218, 240
orthodoxy, 348

Packer, J. I., 182, 189, 242, 397, 402
peace of the Spirit, 388
Pelagian Controversy, 299
Pelagiunism, 219
perfect love, 449
perfect will of God, 384
persecution of Hadrian, 152
Peter, Bishop of Alexandria, 285
Philip, 111
Philo, 139
Philo the Jew, 114
Polycarp, 265, 346
Pope Gregory VII, 502
Pope Innocent III, 224
positional sanctification, 417
post-apostolic church, 342
power of the Spirit, 359
Pragmatism, 366
progressive sanctification, 418, 471
proselyte baptism, 113
Psuedo-Clementine literature, 257
Psuedo-Clementine Literature, 289
Puritans, 229, 320

Quakers, 229, 320

Rabbi Juda Hakkadosh, 153
Rabbi Judah the Prince, 124
Rabbi Judah, the Patriarch, 165
Rabbi Nathan, 153
Rahab the harlot, 91
reasoning in a circle, 371
rebaptism, 242, 261, 270
regeneration, 307
repentance, 457
Restoration movement, 209, 336
reward of the inheritance, 480
Rock of his salvation, 84
rod of God's wrath, 88

Septuagint, 7, 354
Simeon of Jerusalem, 99
sinful habit, 450
sinless perfection, 323, 471
Sole authority, 348
Solomon, 96
sovereign grace, 446
Spanish Inquisition, 224
spiritual circumcision, 54
Sproul, R. C., 176, 439
Strong, Augustus H., Dr., 179
Stuyvesant, Peter, 230
suffering servant, 139

talismanic view, 339
Talmud, 119, 124
targums, 116
Teacher of Righteousness, 127, 138
The Teaching of the Twelve Apostles, 257
temporary lapses, 453
Tertullian, 123, 145, 212, 255, 265, 268, 350
they of the circumcision, 9, 50, 119, 170, 332, 365, 439
Torah, 2
total depravity, 440
Trent, Council of, 251, 261, 314, 318

unfruitful branches, 472
Ur-Nammu, code of, 39

variant readings, 354
Victorinus, 145
visible church, 488

walking in the light, 459
Warfield, Benjamin, 178, 295
Wesley, John, 321, 474
Westphalia, Peace of, 226
Whitefield, George, 474
Williams, Roger, 228, 320
witness of the Spirit, 373
works of the flesh, 473
worship, 499
Zacharias, 65, 106
Zechariah, 96, 101
Zwingli, 183, 316, 475

DATE DUE